DATE DUB		
Nov 20'72		
~~May 18'73~~		
Mar 24'75		
GAYLORD M-2		PRINTED IN U.S.A.

LESTER THONSSEN, Ph.D., University of Iowa, is Professor of Speech at Metropolitan State College of Colorado. He taught for many years at the City College of New York. Dr. Thonssen has served as President of the Speech Association of America and as Editor of *Speech Monographs*. He has been Associate Editor of the *Quarterly Journal of Speech* and Advisory Editor of *The Speech Teacher*, and is currently Editor of *Representative American Speeches*.

A. CRAIG BAIRD, Litt.D., Wabash College, is Distinguished Visiting Professor of Speech at Southern Illinois University, and also Professor Emeritus of Speech at the University of Iowa. He has served as President of the Speech Association of America and is the author of numerous books, including *Rhetoric—A Philosophical Inquiry*, published by The Ronald Press Company.

WALDO W. BRADEN, Ph.D., University of Iowa, is Professor of Speech at Louisiana State University. He has served as President of the Speech Association of America and is currently Editor of *The Speech Teacher*. Dr. Braden is the author or co-author of a number of books on public speaking.

SPEECH CRITICISM

LESTER THONSSEN
METROPOLITAN STATE COLLEGE OF COLORADO

A. CRAIG BAIRD
UNIVERSITY OF IOWA

WALDO W. BRADEN
LOUISIANA STATE UNIVERSITY

SECOND EDITION

THE RONALD PRESS COMPANY • NEW YORK

Library of Congress Catalog Card Number: 70–123054
PRINTED IN THE UNITED STATES OF AMERICA

A wise scepticism is the first attribute of a good critic.

JAMES RUSSELL LOWELL

Preface

More than twenty-two years have passed since the publication of the first edition of *Speech Criticism*. During this interval, many of the developments we urgently wished for have materialized: the number of courses in rhetorical appraisal has increased substantially; a spirited interest in the criticism of speeches as an intellectual enterprise has flourished; the number of critical estimates of speakers and public address prepared by scholars in and out of speech departments has multiplied dramatically; and the search for improved methodologies and critical apparata has brought fresh insights and points of view to bear upon the artistry of rhetorical creation and assessment.

This is all to the good. While we make no pretense of influencing this rather remarkable development, we cherish the memory of our early association with the movement, and rejoice in the lively dialogues that have developed recently in scholarly circles on the best ways of shaping a genuinely viable methodology of speech criticism. Responsible difference of opinion in critical inquiry is a wholesomely sure sign that the discipline has reached maturity. Schools of thought should be no more suspect in rhetoric than in literature—where, indeed, they are as common as the rains of early spring.

This revision preserves substantially the point of view developed in the 1948 edition. Now, as then, we believe that, in the world of talk-talk that influences our lives, a commitment and an obligation rest upon the citizenry to appraise intelligently what our leaders say. The nature of our social and political environment imposes upon Everyman the requirement of measured competence in assessing the spoken word. Professional, or at least, well-trained, critics must provide leadership and help in this undertaking.

A well-developed body of theory in public speaking exists. The articulation of critical standards with the theory is the main thrust of this book. The succeeding chapters develop, we trust, a point of view and an operable method for the orderly analysis and evaluation of public address.

We appreciate the generous response which the speech profession has given the original volume during the past two decades. The book has enjoyed wide acceptance throughout the United States in courses in speech criticism, rhetorical theory, and advanced public speaking. And many teachers have favored us through their thoughtful suggestions and counsel for use in subsequent editions.

The reader should understand that we offer no set formula of critical evaluation. What we present, hopefully, is a point of view, or a spring-board—a conception of rhetorical criticism as an intellectual enterprise. Like the poet of history, about which George M. Trevelyan spoke, we invite the rhetorical critic to pursue and fasten upon the fact, and then "let his imagination and art make clear its significance." We simply offer suggestions and statements of theory which are applicable to particular cases and designed to help the critic in relating his rhetorical assessments to the larger pattern of ideas and ideals in oratorical history.

We acknowledge gratefully our debt to the ancient and modern theorists and experimenters, while accepting full accountability for our exposition and application of their findings. With the conviction that intellectual efforts in rhetorical criticism will increasingly reveal the significant role of public address in the historical process, we respectfully offer this introductory treatise.

LESTER THONSSEN
A. CRAIG BAIRD
WALDO W. BRADEN

August, 1970

Acknowledgments

We acknowledge our indebtedness to a host of scholars. Among the many from whose writings we have derived substantial assistance are J. W. H. Atkins, Charles S. Baldwin, Myron F. Brightfield, J. F. D'Alton, Richard C. Jebb, and W. Rhys Roberts. Also, the works in the Loeb Classical Library and other translations have been of inestimable value.

We express thanks to the following for permission to reprint:

APPLETON-CENTURY-CROFTS: W. E. H. Lecky, *A History of England in the Eighteenth Century; Studies in Rhetoric and Public Speaking.*

DONALD C. BRYANT: *Papers in Rhetoric.*

KENNETH BURKE: *The Philosophy of Literary Form, Studies in Symbolic Action,* copyright 1949.

CAMBRIDGE UNIVERSITY PRESS: John E. Sandys, *M. Tulli Ciceronis ad M. Brutum Orator.*

THE CLARENDON PRESS: G. H. Mair, ed., *Arte of Rhetorique* (Thomas Wilson); W. R. Sorley, *Herbert Spencer Lectures,* 2nd series.

COLUMBIA UNIVERSITY PRESS: Bower Aly, *The Rhetoric of Alexander Hamilton,* copyright 1941.

CONSTABLE AND COMPANY and GEORGE M. TREVELYAN: *The Life of John Bright.*

HARPER AND ROW, PUBLISHERS: Sherman Adams, *First Hand Report,* copyright 1961; J. J. Auer, ed., *Antislavery and Disunion, 1858–1861;* Stella Benson, *Pull Devil, Pull Baker;* Dorothy Bishop, "Bryan's Use of Ethical Proof in the 'Cross of Gold' Speech," in *Speech Practices,* copyright 1958 by Waldo W. Braden and Mary Louise Gehring; Philo Buck, *Literary Criticism.*

HARVARD UNIVERSITY PRESS (Loeb Classical Library): J. W. Cohoon, trans., *Dio Chrysostom;* C. R. Haines, trans., *The Correspondence of Marcus Cornelius Fronto;* A. M. Harmon, trans., *Lucian;* R. D. Hicks, trans., *Diogenes Laertius—Lives of Eminent Philosophers;* William Melmoth, trans., *Pliny: Letters;* George Norlin, trans., *Isocrates;* Charles F. Smith, trans., *Thucydides;* W. C. Wright, trans., *Philostratus and Eunapius: The Lives of the Sophists.*

HOUGHTON MIFFLIN COMPANY: Arthur M. Schlesinger, Jr., *A Thousand Days.*

INDIANA UNIVERSITY PRESS: Sidney Kraus, ed., *The Great Debates.*

JOHNS HOPKINS PRESS: *American Journal of Philology.*

LITTLE, BROWN AND COMPANY: W. W. Goodwin, ed., *Plutarch's Miscellanies and Essays.*

LONGMANS, GREEN AND COMPANY: J. F. D'Alton, *Roman Literary Theory and Criticism.*

THE MACMILLAN COMPANY: J. W. H. Atkins, *Literary Criticism in Antiquity* (Cambridge University Press); Charles S. Baldwin, *Ancient Rhetoric and Poetic* and *Medieval Rhetoric and Poetic;* Brand Blanshard, *The Nature of Thought;* S. F. Bonner, *The Literary Treatises of Dionysius of Halicarnassus* (Cambridge University Press); George W. Botsford, *Hellenic History;* J. B. Bury, *The Ancient Greek Historians; Cambridge History of American Literature* (Cambridge University Press); Louis Cazamian, *Criticism in the Making;* F. H. Colson, *M. Fabii Quintiliani Institutionis Oratoriae Liber I* (Cambridge University Press); A. Croiset and M. Croiset, *Abridged History of Greek Literature;* W. A. Edward, trans., *The Suasoriae of Seneca the Elder* (Cambridge University Press); R. C. Jebb, *The Attic Orators;* John Morley, *Life of William Ewart Gladstone;* W. Rhys Roberts, trans., *Dionysius of Halicarnassus on Literary Composition, Longinus on the Sublime,* and *Dionysius of Halicarnassus: The Three Literary Letters* (Cambridge University Press); J. E. C. Welldon, trans., *The Rhetoric of Aristotle* and *The Politics of Aristotle;* C. T. Winchester, *Some Principles of Literary Criticism.*

METHUEN AND COMPANY: John F. Dobson, *The Greek Orators.*

Quarterly Journal of Speech: Several passages.

HENRY REGNERY COMPANY: Richard Weaver, *The Ethics of Rhetoric.*

RUSSELL & RUSSELL: Speech Association of America, *A History and Criticism of American Public Address,* vol. III, ed. by Marie K. Hochmuth Nichols, 1954.

Southern Speech Journal: Selected passages.

Speech Monographs: Selected passages.

WALLACE STEGNER and *The American West:* "On the Writing of History."

Tennessee Historical Quarterly: Gregg Phifer, "Andrew Johnson Delivers His Argument."

THE UNIVERSITY OF CALIFORNIA PRESS: Robert J. Bonner, *Aspects of Athenian Democracy;* Myron F. Brightfield, *The Issue in Literary Criticism;* Frederick J. Teggart, *Theory and Processes of History.*

THE UNIVERSITY OF CHICAGO PRESS: F. I. Carpenter, ed., *The Arte or Crafte of Rhethoryke by Leonard Cox; Ethics; International Journal of Ethics.*

THE UNIVERSITY OF MISSOURI PRESS: Loren D. Reid, ed., *American Public Address.*

THE UNIVERSITY OF PENNSYLVANIA LIBRARY and ALAN F. HERR: *The Elizabethan Sermon.*

UNIVERSITY LIBRARIES, STATE UNIVERSITY OF IOWA: Selected passages from doctoral theses.

Many colleagues have given permission to use passages from their writings. We express our gratitude to Bower Aly, Carroll C. Arnold, J. J. Auer, Fred J. Barton, Leland M. Griffin, Orville Hitchcock, H. Clay Harshbarger, Everett Lee Hunt, Virginia Holland, Wilbur S. Howell, Gregg Phifer, Horace G. Rahskopf, Loren D. Reid, Ota T. Reynolds, John H. Sloan, Hermann G. Stelzner, Karl Wallace, Forest Whan, Herbert A. Wichelns, John F. Wilson, Russel Windes, Jr., Margaret Wood, and W. Hayes Yeager. Walter R. Fisher of the University of Southern California gave us the benefit of his counsel on selected parts of the manuscript.

Contents

Part VI

Reflections on Criticism and Public Address

I

THE NATURE OF
RHETORICAL CRITICISM

1

The Critical Perspective

The art of public speaking has many dimensions. At its core are words through which conceptions are formulated, thereby fashioning a *linguistic* mould. The words shape ideas which, if developed responsibly by a speaker, stamp the discipline as an *intellectual* enterprise. In the expression of thought, man also reveals himself through moods, feelings, predispositions, and attitudes. Thus speech invariably takes on a *psychological* dimension. By extension, these inner promptings acquire *social* meaning since the nature of communicative intent establishes a certain relationship between a speaker and his hearers, between himself and the cultural context which shapes his life. Moreover, public address has a *technical* dimension, as any standard textbook on the subject shows. The art is shaped by a method, by a way of going about the job of preparing a speech. And this immediately suggests an *aesthetic* component, for admittedly some speeches reveal a fuller measure of artistic excellence than others, either through sublimity of thought, felicity of expression, or stylistic elegance. And finally the art of speaking has *ethical* magnitude, for ideas have power to do evil, no less than good.

The complexity of public address is at once the critic's delight and challenge: a delight because it affords wide range for inquiry, and a challenge because its many-faceted nature precludes the arbitrary application of fixed formulas for its assessment. Little wonder that the speech critic, like Argus of Greek mythology, must cast the gaze of a hundred eyes in all directions.

Criticism is an omnibus word. It has many meanings, running the gamut from perceptive appraisal to irresponsible faultfinding. Since it involves matters of taste, it often makes excursions into subjectivity, running from honest predisposition to forthright caprice. Small wonder,

3

then, that criticism itself, to quote W. C. Brownell, "is much criticized—which logically establishes its title." [1]

Although criticism oftentimes has about it an "odour of unsanctity" and neglect, it is an important practice. Of carping objection to what is said and done in public life, there is no shortage; of sentimentalized affirmation and approval, there is no want. But of intelligently critical evaluation and judgment there is not, cannot be, enough.

The criticism of speeches is old; and yet it is new. Plato, Cicero, Quintilian, and a host of other scholars of antiquity engaged in the art. Prior to 1925, however, relatively few students in the modern tradition took time to formulate doctrines of rhetorical evaluation or compose critiques that dealt unmistakably with the assessment of speechmaking. Happily, a lively concern for speech criticism is currently evident, as witnessed by the considerable number of books on the subject and the even more considerable number of critical studies of orators and oratory published in professional journals or separate monographs.

Despite this resurgence of interest in an old art, much of contemporary speech criticism is fragmentary and incidental. The speaking accomplishments of a public figure are often interwoven with the story of his life. This biographical approach, however admirable in its own sphere, usually fails to throw the meaning of a man's speaking efforts into the right focus; the emphasis remains on the sequence of events in the biography, rather than upon the social pattern in which the speaker's thoughts were expressed or upon the responses which the speaker sought to secure from particular audiences. Praiseworthy exceptions to this general rule may be found, however, in such readable contributions as G. M. Trevelyan's *Life of John Bright*, Samuel Rosenman's *Working with Roosevelt*, Bernard Dyer's *Public Career of William Maxwell Evarts*, and Loren D. Reid's *Charles James Fox, A Man for the People*.

In addition to incidental rhetorical criticism in biography, we find scattered speech appraisal in historical surveys and treatises. This is not uniformly satisfactory because the accounts fail to reveal the stature of the men as *speakers*, as persons who exercised leadership largely through their distinctive command of the spoken word. A notable exception to this generalization may be found in the two-volume *American Primer*, edited by Daniel J. Boorstin. This intriguing work underscores indelibly the impact of oratory upon our national life and heritage.

With the steady addition of rhetorical estimates prepared by competent critics, the true measure of our Roosevelts, Websters, Churchills, and Stevensons will unquestionably emerge and, hopefully, be included in the accounts written by professional historians and social theorists.

[1] *Criticism.* New York, 1914, p. 1.

Many contemporary criticisms have sufficient objectivity, discernment, and logical integrity to warrant such inclusion.

Newspapers and periodicals furnish an appreciable amount of speech criticism. The editorial writer and the columnist—neither of whom is necessarily skilled in rhetorical investigation—appraises the important speechmaking of the time. Some of this reviewing contains little more than highly embroidered praise or blame of selected aspects of the speech. On the other hand, certain evaluations are uncommonly good. Speaking of Edward R. Murrow, Elmer Davis once remarked that veteran newspapermen were "mildly scandalized" that such a superb job of reporting could be done by a man who had never "worked on a newspaper in his life." [2] Knowledgeable speech critics often feel the same about the better rhetorical estimates written by commentators Walter Lippmann, James Reston, and Richard Rovere.

But where, it may be asked, does this interest in criticism, however pursued in popular circles, have its origin? The source of any critical inquiry is intellectual curiosity, in the recognition of an unresolved question. Speech criticism is no exception. And since speaking is an importantly practical art, such critical investigation usually derives from a problem in the environment.

The problem arises from two conditions. In the first place, we live in a world of talk. To paraphrase Frederic Harrison, we are witnesses to the "remorseless cataract" of daily speech. Speechmaking is a natural and wholesome consequent of the form of polity under which we live. In deliberation and decision, the democratic way provides for the exchange of views; the oral transmission of ideas is a rightful prerogative of the man who enjoys the estate of free discussion. There is, then, much speechmaking in our everyday world.

But that alone would not necessarily serve as an impulse to critical inquiry, were it not for a second condition in the environment. Abundance of speechmaking becomes a problem because of the necessity of appraising some of the speeches. A semblance of order, a means of determining goodness and badness, a guide to action must be found if the pattern of talk is to be more than an indiscriminate gnarling of points of view. It is at this moment that the role of the critic takes on meaning. Criticism serves to bridge the gap between external stimulus and internal compulsion to belief and action.

Whether the speeches in question were delivered in the age of William Pitt and Charles James Fox, of John Bright and Richard Cobden, or of Franklin D. Roosevelt and Winston Churchill, is of little concern to us here. In the following pages, we shall attempt to point out a

---

[2] Edward R. Murrow, *This Is London.* New York, 1941, p. viii.

course which the critic may follow in arriving at a judgment respecting the character and effectiveness of a speech in any period.

NATURE OF THE MEDIUM

Like other creative workers, the public speaker achieves the end of his art through the resourceful use of reason, memory, imagination, and emotion. In other words, he relies upon the same psychological equipment to realize his purpose as does the sculptor, the painter, or the literary craftsman. There is nothing unique about the mental functioning of the speaker which sets his efforts off sharply from those of skilled individuals in other fields. However, we recognize that the end-products of the speaker's art differ, for example, from those of the novelist or the essayist. The same critical yardstick cannot be applied appropriately and meaningfully both to a novel and to a speech. Some criteria will be similar. For example, when Eliot O'Hara, the well-known watercolorist, urges control and restraint in the amount we should say in a single painting, he reminds us that a similar principle applies in speaking. There, too, we cannot—or at least should not try to—say everything we can conjure up about the subject, lest in our solicitude to express much we end up by expressing precious little. But in the main, either the speech or the novel or the painting—depending upon the character of the critiques—would suffer through common appraisal. This circumstance argues the necessity of looking to the medium in which speech operates before considering the criteria by which a particular speaking performance is evaluated. Consequently, we must first examine the basic nature of the rhetorical art.

Ancient and modern authorities on rhetoric agree that the fundamental purpose of oral discourse is social coordination or control. This implies the use of speech as an instrument of communication, as a tool to convey ideas and feelings from one person to another. Basic to analyses of the theory and practice of rhetoric, this concept postulates *purpose* in all speaking performances. Men use speech, not simply to hear themselves talk, but to achieve certain responses from hearers.

Every situation in which a speaker performs involves, therefore, at least three essential elements: the speaker, the medium of expression, and the recipient of the message. These gross constituents make up the equation of communication. Without any one of them, the process of social control through the instrumentality of rhetoric is destroyed.

The medium through which the communicative function is fulfilled is language. In other words, the coordination and control of social efforts depends upon the use of symbols. Effective in giving formulation and design to oral expression, these symbols are of both audible and visible types. Each of the several sounds of the language is an audible symbol. Each of the many possible movements of the body may have symbolic significance, visually, in the total process of communication. Hence the phonetic and gestural symbols we call language are the external aspects of a highly complex and not too well-known psychological phenomenon, namely, the conception and transference of meaning.

The simple mention of language as the medium of communication, therefore, fails to reveal fully the intricate process of translation which every speaking act involves. Briefly, the process is a two-way affair. The speaker first translates his ideas and feelings into phonetic and gestural symbols. Then, through physical control, he transmits these symbols to the listener, impressing them upon his consciousness as something heard and seen. Immediately the process of retranslation begins, only this time the listener, rather than the speaker, is the active participant. He must now convert the symbols into meaningful, articulated units of thought bearing a faithful resemblance to the original conception of the speaker.

But let us be more specific about the nature of a *speech situation* in which this process of symbolic formulation and translation takes place. In its broadest sense, a speech situation may be regarded as a complex social relationship in which a speaker attempts to secure a particular response from a group of listeners. Except in certain radio and television setups, the situation usually involves face-to-face engagement. What, then, are the distinguishing characteristics of this social pattern in which rhetoric functions?

The speech situation has certain distinctive features, all interrelated:

(1) It admits of unconfined choice as to subject matter. Any subject properly adapted to the specific audience and occasion can be used; it may deal with geometry, music, political science, or any other topic of inquiry. This is another way of saying that rhetoric confines its service to no special class of material; that it is, as Aristotle remarked, the "faculty of discovering all the possible means of persuasion in any subject." Accordingly, speakers use the tools of rhetoric and the speech situation to carry out their communicative ambitions in all subjects.

Although rhetoric may be employed to develop a point on any subject, it is, because of its practical nature, devoted mainly to a small number of considerations. This seeming paradox arises from the fact that the majority of speech situations involve attempts by speakers (a) to establish the justice or injustice, the true or the false, of an action or a condition; (b) to praise or blame someone or something; or (c) to urge that a course of action be or not be followed. Even the last division, dealing with deliberative speaking, is more sharply limited as to the principal matters of discussion than we might surmise. According to Aristotle, and experience leads us to agree, there are five main topics of deliberation: ways and means, war and peace, national defense, imports and exports, and legislation. Hence we see that a speech situation is confined, not as to *possible subject matter*, but as to the *range of effective choice* within the various fields of thought.

(2) All speech settings in which persuasion is active embrace a common element, namely, the imprecise data with which the speaker works. Strictly, rhetoric functions only where uncertainty prevails. If there were no doubt about the wisdom of certain courses of action or about the measures of right and wrong—if decisions could be arrived at with reasonable finality and certainty—there would be no need for an art of persuasion. It would serve no useful purpose. Demonstrations would suffice. Machines could settle the problems; words would be superfluous. But the milieu of social and political life is not of that sort. It subsists on doubt, on the unsure. And persuasion goes to work when man must make decisions on admittedly inadequate, imprecise data.

This circumstance has peculiar—indeed, poignant—relevancy for the speech critic. Many indictments of the art of rhetoric stem from the mistaken belief that a speaker has done his work badly, simply because he has not done it definitively. He is criticized—and along with him, his art—because his words have not produced the ultimate good, the unequivocal answer. Such expectations, based upon the unsophisticated premise that the problems of man can all be settled rationally, are wholly inconsistent with the limitations within which persuasion must operate.

(3) The speech situation is severely controlled by time limitations. Whereas a person may elect to spend a full evening, or a week of evenings, or an entire winter reading a novel, he is obliged to devote his entire attention for a short, continuous period to the hearing of a speech. This circumstance decisively influences the character of oral discourse. The necessity of foreshortening the oral material requires the listener to perceive the import of a subject with maximum speed and minimum detail.

In real life it is, of course, not always so. Some speakers are on uneasy terms with brevity; others never reach a truce with conciseness. But every discriminating speaker knows that the giving of a speech calls for a special kind of contract with hearers. A person who would resent listening to a conversationalist's carrying on for twenty uninterrupted minutes might be willing and even delighted to hear the same man talk for an hour from the platform. But, contrariwise, the same listener might be quite intolerant of a speaker's using ten minutes to say in complex "written" style what could be said in two minutes if the material were adapted to the demands of the oral medium.

(4) The speech situation is always specific in its point of direction. It aims at achieving something. The very nature of any communicative undertaking in which a speaker tries to elicit a response from hearers makes for *purposiveness*. Speaker and listeners come together, not to rejoice in each other's presence, but to realize an end, be it of entertainment, explanation, information, persuasion, or conviction.

(5) Speech situations are of a transitory character. They contain many elements of an evanescent sort, elements that are effective and significant while the speech is being delivered but irretrievably lost once the speaker leaves the platform. Certain subtle reactions of the listeners, adjustments of the speaker to changes in audience behavior, and momentarily pervasive but subsequently irredeemable moods of the occasion are facts which, to some extent at least, disappear with the event.

(6) Speech situations involve direct social interaction among a plurality of persons. Obviously, this statement is subject to some qualification since radio and television speech does not always establish face-to-face engagement. Like all other speaking situations, however, such indirect contact groups are held together by bonds of common language and interest.

Every public speech is an experience in audience adjustment. The speech situation provides give-and-take between speaker and hearer. This interaction, properly achieved, makes for spirited, effective discourse. The speaker stimulates his hearers who in turn respond with visible or audible symbols, or both. To these responses the speaker then makes such adjustments as may be proper and necessary. Thus a speech situation involves circular response, the flow of stimulation running in both directions, from speaker to hearer and from hearer to speaker.

(7) A speech situation embraces a unique attitudinal relationship because the thought, feeling, and purpose of the communicative venture are *directly* controlled by the personal force of the speaker himself. The speaker has full opportunity to create and maintain a certain tone or attitude through the impress of his character and personality. Whereas a writer can only offer *more words* to command attention at a point where words themselves are already discouraging a reader, a speaker can couple words with vocal and bodily action and ethical appeal to keep the theme of his discourse in the field of interest. Thus, he is able to control directly and consequently maintain the proper relation between himself and the audience, and between his subject and the audience.

(8) Finally, and this is essentially a result of the interaction of the foregoing characteristics, a speech situation evokes a distinctive lan-

guage pattern. True, substantially the same words are used in writing as in speaking, just as the same words are used to mould our censure and our praise. But the external facts of time limitation, reciprocal social stimulation, audience adjustment, and personal appeal through the speaker combine to mould the words into a somewhat different configuration. Hence we find that oral and written material dealing with the same unit of thought often differ as to content, idiom, grammatical structure, and arrangement of parts.

Admittedly, the foregoing analysis rests upon an artlessly simple assumption, namely, that there is such a thing as a *written speech*. Although a critic may actually hear the speech (or a recording) that he intends later to assess, in all likelihood he will do most of his work from the printed text. And from then on he is dealing largely with words *written,* rather than *spoken.*

There are many students of public address who will insist that a *written* speech is a contradiction. If it is written, it is not a speech. And if the evaluation derives from a study of the copy, it is not an appraisal of the speaking art. A speech, so these observers say, is not words; it is words *uttered.*

This is a plausible position, and in the most literal sense, irrefutable. A speech—as the living expression of a man on a specific occasion—does in fact evaporate upon conclusion of the event. And no amount of re-playing and re-viewing through electronic wizardry can ever again re-construct exactly what happened. In that sense the speech is over, and what comes down in the form of a text or a recording is but a faded re-minder of what went on.

Without considering it an acceptable answer, we may yet say that the human experience is composed generously of concessions and compromises to conditions over which our puny effort has little or no control. Were we steadfastly to avoid truces with reality, we would doubtless be at odds with ourselves and others in perpetuity. And were we to refuse to engage in intellectual inquiry simply because the ground rules for the pursuit were less than heavenly, we should forever consign the mind and spirit to frustration and inaction. So we accept the speech situation for what it is—an ephemeral occurrence, incapable of complete recon-struction; we accept a written document or a recording of what was said because nothing else remains that is any better. We choose, in short, to live within the framework of rhetorical limitations. Ours may be Hob-son's choice, but we are not the only scholars who have to make them.

CONSTITUENTS OF THE JUDGMENT

A valid judgment of a speech is essentially the same as a valid judg-ment of any other art form. True, it results from a particular training and appreciation on the part of the critic; it relies upon a special set of criteria; and it derives sanction from a body of its own literature. But, qualitatively, it is simply a *good judgment,* and as such contains no elements peculiar to its own field of inquiry. It makes approximately the same demands on the critic, intellectually, as would a comparable pronouncement upon a novel or a personal essay. In the criticism of speeches, as elsewhere, the formulation of a valid judgment results from the orderly fulfillment of certain requirements inherent in the critical process.

There are three principal stages in the critical process: (a) A searching examination of the facts relating to the particular speech. This is primarily a research undertaking, requiring the use of the standard tools of systematic investigation. (b) The formulation of the principles, or criteria, by which the speech is to be appraised. This is largely a theoretical inquiry into the bases of judgment—the fundamentals derived from observation, experience, the accepted works on rhetoric, and from the critic's interpretation of their contents as applied to public address. (c) The critical evaluation of the data. The speech is appraised in the light of the findings from the foregoing to determine the measure of merit assignable to the performance.

Passing judgment on a speech is a complex job. As in other, comparable areas, the rhetorical judgment derives its substance from both the object of criticism—in this case, the speech—and from data and interpretations lying outside it. Through an evaluation, we hope the better to know and appreciate a speech by checking it, if you will, against a standard applicable to the art. By means of analysis and synthesis, the critic hopes to determine the effect, immediate and/or long range, upon the particular audience and society. The word "effect," or "response," is significant. It supports a central reason for rhetorical criticism. Since speaking is a purposive venture, and since a speaker seeks to communicate a particular set of ideas and feelings to a specific audience, it must follow that the rhetorical critic is concerned with the methods used by a speaker to achieve the response consistent with his purpose. In his germinal essay "The Literary Criticism of Oratory," Herbert A. Wichelns comments on the differences between literary and rhetorical criticism, and observes that the point of view of the latter is "patently single." "It is not concerned," he remarks, "with permanence nor yet with beauty. It is concerned with effect." [3] In general, we share this view. But we must be mindful that an orator, seeking a certain response, employs an art and craft—rhetoric—to reach his objective. Accordingly, we cannot, and should not, overlook technical and artistic excellence and other contributing measures of effectiveness in passing judgment on the ultimate quality of an oration.

[3] *Studies in Rhetoric and Public Speaking.* New York, 1925, p. 209.

What are the constituents of the judgment by which the effect and contributory technical merits of a speech are determined?

Speeches occur in social settings. Consequently, their interpretation and criticism must stem from a knowledge of the forces and conditions operative in the social situation at the particular time. In the broadest sense, therefore, the constituents of the rhetorical judgment are without limit as to number and scope; everything that impinges upon the environment plays a part in shaping a speech, and therefore in determining the criticism of it. In short, a rhetorical judgment embraces all the knowledge in the critic's possession; it draws upon his total resources.

But critics, however discerning, cannot embrace a study of the universe, of the total pattern of learning, in the evaluation of a speech. They must rely chiefly upon assumptions, hypotheses, and fixed points of reference derived from *principal* areas of inquiry; and then they must examine available and germane facts in the light of these conceptions. In addition to the purely rhetorical element, the essential constituents of the judgment of a speech derive from philosophy, history, logic, and ethics.

The simple concept of criticism suggests a philosophical approach. A given event—in this case, a speech—is surveyed as a functional unity. Systematically, the critic proposes to look at the larger question of social reality as it relates to a speech—or, more accurately, as the speech relates to it—and to investigate not only the means by which the address was accomplished, but also the ends and purposes which it was intended to serve. In short, the critical process presupposes a search for the larger, the comprehensive view of a problem. The critic is engaged in an exploratory venture; he seeks to make an ordered whole of events having an infinity of interrelationships. Philosophically, therefore, he must concern himself with the factors of causation in the social medium. Criticism deals not alone with the facts of a special subject, but with those of the related subjects as well. It formulates from these many data a principle of explanation having "universal" significance.

The philosophical constituent of rhetorical criticism also is evident when we reflect on the nature of the medium in which oral communication functions. A speech is the product of a complex of social events in which human beings and their problems are equated—at least, attempts are made to equate them—with their environment. The purposive character of public speaking tends, therefore, to make a speech more than a superficial happening, more than the mere expression of an individual's fancy. Instead, it makes it a conditioning factor in both individual and collective behavior. The realization of a particular purpose in a speech may actually affect the structure of men's thoughts and actions, and, consequently, may influence the destiny of a community, a nation, a society. The critic of speeches must, accordingly, recognize the patent fact that communication takes place in a social sphere—that it relates men to their environment; he must also acknowledge as a hypothesis that the communicative intent of a speaker may have *consequential* influence upon the behavior of listeners. These two philosophic considerations are essential elements of any critic's judgment of a public speech.

Finally, the criticism of a speech implies philosophic judgment in that it requires candid recognition of personal attitudes toward certain materials. The critic should hold to the facts as he finds them, and the responsible critic will. But in order to have what James Truslow Adams once called a "delicate intuition" in interweaving the data of history with fidelity to the scientist's love of truth, the critic of speeches must acknowledge his possible prejudices, predispositions, and weaknesses. The rhetorical judgment, therefore, must contain such insight as may be necessary to preserve reasonable objectivity in the evaluation.

A derivative of this line of thinking is the obvious conclusion that the rhetorical judgment contains psychological and literary constitutents. The former is apparent from the fact that the analyst is deeply concerned with such determining factors of speech effectiveness as intellectual and emotional behavior of listeners, personality manifestations, social incentives, attitudes, suggestion, crowd behavior, propaganda techniques, leadership phenomena, and related matters. That the rhetorical judgment contains a literary component, also, is evident. Even though the critic looks upon speechmaking as a practical art, he uses many of the tools and bases many of his conclusions upon the principles of literary craftsmanship. This is true not only in the assessment of a speaker's style, but also in other divisions of the rhetorical art.

In many respects the most important constituent of the rhetorical judgment is historical. It is a truism that speeches are meaningful only when examined in the social settings of which they are a part. Yet that important fact must be emphasized because it constitutes the core of any satisfactory method of rhetorical analysis. Any event, and a speech is a social event, must be examined in perspective; it must be viewed from afar as well as from the nearest point of vantage, if its full significance is to be understood. "The trouble with so many of our critics," commented an editorial writer in *The Saturday Review of Literature*, "is that they know no history." The critic of oratory is no less subject to such a charge than is the critic of literature. Both must regard the present as the logical result of the past; both must have the inclination and the leisure "to turn from the exciting incidents of the hour to the no less portentous events of bygone times," if they are to appreciate and understand the complex forces with which the problem of criticism deals.

The fact that "the past consists of events that have finished happening," as R. G. Collingwood once remarked, is not to be interpreted as meaning that it is dead, and of no consequence.

Whether or not the historian and critic can be united in the same person has been a matter of considerable discussion. Louis Cazamian, commenting on the circumstance that they are "complementary and indispensable to each other," believes they are rarely combined in the same person. According to him, "their efforts will never be entirely reconciled, because they are not on the same plane." [4] In any case, the critic of oratory must have a historical sense as well as skill in historical research if his job is to be done responsibly and comprehensively.

Each public speech is a study in social forces, complex in the extreme. The historical element in the criticism of such a speech includes not only facts which pass under the narrow heading of the data of history, but also related materials from politics, economics, religion, sociology, literature, and law. The Lincoln-Douglas debates, for example, can scarcely be appraised satisfactorily if no account is taken of forces other than the immediate historical details prevailing at the time of each particular speech. There were many other facts—social, economic, and political—which helped to shape the debates and gave them significance; but the discovery of those items of information necessitates a study of forces not immediately discernible in a bare historical account relating only the names and character of the participants, the dates, the number of hearers present, and the length of the speeches. Consequently, the critic of speaking must delve deeply into the past if he is to understand the present. Criticism based upon such research will help establish the "corrective balance" to which Donald C. Bryant refers when he observes that it has been "the fault of the history of literature and oratory, to let the study of figures obscure or blot out the study of forces and social movements." [5]

The rhetorical judgment, then, contains historical constituents because it requires the reconstruction of setting. The critic must, in effect, put on the garment of the past if he would understand fully the forces that shaped a speaker's thinking, the circumstances that prompted a particular speech, and the conditions that modified or determined the outcome of the address. He must, to use the words of George E. Woodberry, conduct all those studies "which assist in the representation of the past, and amplify and clarify historical knowledge."

The critic of oratory will never be able to find all of the historical data relevant to a particular speech. This should not necessarily in-

[4] *Criticism in the Making.* New York, 1929, p. 34.

[5] "Some Problems of Scope and Method in Rhetorical Scholarship." *Quarterly Journal of Speech,* 23:187–188 (April, 1937).

validate his judgment. The facts of an event are "as innumerable as the grains of sand on a stretch of beach." But by connecting known facts, a critic can reconstruct an occasion or incident with sufficient completeness to make valid judgment possible. That some gaps in the information will be present is almost inevitable. But, to quote Myron F. Brightfield, they "are openly confessed and are allowed to remain as genuine elements of the situation, qualifying all judgments drawn therefrom." [6]

We mentioned above that the critic must connect the available facts. Here, again, we notice his identity with the historian whose task, according to Brightfield, may be said "to consist of the establishment of successive series of *liaisons*, both of the facts within the incident, and of the incident itself with other incidents and, possibly, with more extensive subjects involving other divisions of human knowledge." To a singular degree, the critic of speeches must articulate the findings from many fields—history, economics, politics, etc.—to show how they affect the outcome of a particular address.

The acquisition of an adequate body of the present knowledge concerning a given speech requires the establishment of certain hypotheses. The critic must decide which facts to use, which to discard as unimportant or irrelevant. This is a difficult job, for ways of testing these hypotheses are not always immediately available to check the accuracy of judgment. But it is a vital part of the critic's work. It makes a difference whether a critic decides that the revival meetings in a particular community are more relevant to the understanding of a certain speech than the current price of cotton fiber. The example may be far-fetched, but the point it illustrates in rhetorical criticism is important. From the available facts surrounding a speech event, the critic must select those which are most significant to achieve a full appreciation and understanding of the communicative effort. This cannot be determined by rule. It is but one of the several indispensable aspects of the historical judgment which contribute to the criticism of oratory.

We have now discussed briefly the philosophical and historical constituents of the rhetorical judgment. The next essential consideration deals with the logical component in the critical process.

William T. Brewster once referred to criticism as "a form of argumentation . . ." In the main, the appraisal of a speech is an assignment in argumentative discourse, involving both deductive and inductive forms. The criteria, even if determined originally through induction, are employed by the critic, in greater or lesser measure, as general truths. From them he proceeds to a particular conclusion, thus completing the deductive process. For example, the statement that the audience deter-

[6] *The Issue in Literary Criticism.* Berkeley, 1932, p. 11.

mines in large part the end and object of a speech is a general principle
—one of the fundamental hypotheses—in the light of which a particular
speech is evaluated. On the other hand, much of the work of the critic
falls under the inductive method. Search is made for facts relating to a
speech; the social, political, and economic forces having a presumed bearing upon the address are examined; causal relations among the many
items of information are established. And so from a body of particular
data the critic draws a general conclusion covering the speech as a
complete unit.

The importance of the logical element in rhetorical judgment is further
revealed when we remember that historical data figure prominently in
the criticism. Historical thinking is, as has been indicated before, se-
lective. In making use of the data of history, the rhetorical critic must,
therefore, deal continually with causal explanations. As a temporary
historian, to quote E. A. Burtt, he is "trying to find the cause of an
event which never happens twice and whose totality . . . transcends
scientific law and method." [7] But the critic not only selects certain facts
as causally significant, to the exclusion of others; he also deals with
documents and sources the trustworthiness of which is anything but
uniform and the completeness of which is often open to question. He
must continually refute the oft-quoted remark that "history is something
that never happened, written by a man who wasn't there." Consequently, he must test his evidence and determine its degree of validity.

So the question of "whether there is any other sanction than personality for critical opinion" must be referred to the critic himself. Is he
prepared and disposed to subject his data to the tests of verification? To
what extent is he willing to look upon his critical function through the
eyes of the logician, as well as of the philosopher and of the historian?

The valid judgment of a speech results in large part from the ability
of the critic's materials to withstand the usual tests of logic. Accordingly, the critic must test the basic assumptions of his inquiry, assess the
evidence which serves as the raw material of his proof, check the deductive principles of his argumentation, and appraise the inductions
arising from his use of specific examples, causal relations, and analogies.
Here in abundant measure is the source of the logical element in the
criticism of oratory. Here is the avenue of approach to the critical
method "external to the vagaries of a temperament . . ."

Whether or not criticism embraces moral tenets and sanctions is argu-
able. We believe it does, and that ethical considerations are rightful
components of the art of speech appraisal. If indeed a critic tries, among
other things, to find out how effectively a speaker used his resources and

[7] *Principles and Problems of Right Thinking.* New York, 1928, p. 500.

ingenuity in getting a response, and to what extent he succeeded, it would seem relevant to inquire whether the end he sought was ethically defensible. A shrewd demagogue or tyrant whose message brutalized the conscience of sensitive men would scarcely deserve our praise, even though his technical command of rhetoric induced a response fully consistent with his purpose.

With the development and refinement of techniques, experimental studies into the processes of persuasion will doubtless have increasing impact upon rhetorical theory and practice. This in turn will influence the critical assessment of oratory. Research on audience response to a variety of oral appeals, on the influence of personality in changing opinions, on the process of human motivation, on the perception of communicative symbols, on the positioning of arguments for maximum effect—these are but a few of the areas which the social scientists are exploring, and from which data applicable to criticism are likely to issue.

Although set in a reasonably conventional context, the foregoing remarks suggest to the critic the desirability of keeping the channels of communication open to all of the contributing arts and sciences. While we believe that a textbook on rhetorical criticism must outline a methodology that is sufficiently precise and consistent to be useful, we believe additionally that critics must be sensitively flexible to ideas and trends that continuously shape and re-shape our patterns of thought and culture. No one can, for example, anticipate with full accuracy the force of the technological revolution upon our cultural experience. Today we believe that the substance of a speech is its all-important ingredient. Who can deny Marshall McLuhan's thesis that in the immediate future, or for that matter now, the nature of the media by which the communication is effected will exercise greater influence than the contents of the message in shaping our society?

SOURCES OF CERTAIN CANONS OF CRITICISM

The critic of speeches, like the critic of plays and novels, always faces the problem of steering an intelligent course between two extremes. He must avoid adoption of a procrustean system into which all speeches are forced according to rule; and, on the other hand, he must not rely solely upon his own judgment, unsupported by outside authority, to determine the worth of a speaking effort.

The canons of rhetorical criticism must of necessity be relative. "Holding the critic's opinions to be obligatory upon other readers," remarks Gertrude Buck, "is very like 'fiat money'—easy to issue but sometimes harder to realize upon." [8] Speeches are highly variable social events; no

[8] *The Social Criticism of Literature.* New Haven, 1916, p. 50.

two are exactly alike. Consequently, the same critical yardstick cannot be applied to all speeches, as the discussion of the standards of judgment in Part V of this book will indicate.

Without suggesting that the dicta of Aristotle be regarded as the unalterable conditions of oratorical achievement, we may nevertheless look upon certain Aristotelian conceptions as safe points of departure in criticism. The canons of rhetorical criticism derive from a classical concept. Rhetoric, to quote Aristotle, is "the faculty of discovering all the possible means of persuasion in any subject." In other words, rhetoric is an instrument by which a speaker can, through the apt use of certain "lines of argument," make an adjustment to a situation composed of himself, his audience, his subject, and the occasion. The impact of these four forces in a social setting gives rise to a certain effect or outcome, the understanding of which concerns the critic. Consequently, to know and evaluate the outcome of a speech necessitates knowing as much as can be determined about each of the constituents of the speech situation. So canons of oratorical criticism cannot properly be divorced from considerations relating to speaker, audience, subject, and occasion. These are indispensable to critical inquiry.

Another concept in Aristotle's *Rhetoric* serves as a determinant of the canons of judgment. Aristotle believed, and practically all writers since his time have concurred, that the audience determines the speech's end and object. In other words, the important aspect of the speech situation is the speaker-audience relationship. Implicit in this idea is the very core of a theory of rhetoric. It embraces the doctrine of speech as communication, purposiveness in discourse, social interaction, and realization of an end or effect consistent with intention. Here, surely, is another concept which the critic of speeches must take into account when determining his canons of judgment.

RELATION OF CRITICISM TO THEORY AND PRACTICE

Practice, theory, and criticism are, in the broadest sense, indivisible elements of an art. Each influences the other, with the result that all are modified by the circular action.

The effect of these three elements on each other follows a certain chronology. Undoubtedly there was speechmaking—practice—before there was an *art* of speaking. But once an art is systematized, the theory serves as the basis for further practical application. Subsequently, both practice and theory are modified by critical inquiry. In fact, new formulations of theory may even result from this interaction. This is a natural circumstance, occasioned by the fact that the theoretical principles are often inconsistent with or in open violation of the natural and easy practice of the art; criticism then serves to readjust the theory to the practice. Thus a study of the fundamental tenets of rhetorical criticism is also an investigation into the theoretical and practical aspects of public speaking.

GENERAL MEANING OF CRITICISM

Rhetorical criticism is a humanistic enterprise. It is concerned with analysis of the free choices men make in adapting the spoken word to practical problems. Its subject matter is man—the complex of ideas and feelings he expresses orally while seeking a purposeful objective.

Rhetorical criticism contains both a process or method and a judgment. It involves, first, a process by which unsupported individual preference moves toward rationally determined choice. This results from a composite of judgments, not only in rhetoric, but in related fields—particularly history, philosophy, logic, linguistics, ethics, psychology, and aesthetics. In the second place, rhetorical criticism declares a conviction. It seeks an answer to the question: To what extent, and through what resources of rhetorical craftsmanship, did the speaker achieve the end— immediate or delayed—which he sought? By applying appropriate standards which derive from the interaction of subject, speaker, audience, and occasion, the critic assesses the effect of speeches upon particular audiences and, finally, upon society.

TYPES OF CRITICISM

As previously indicated, the bases of judgment in rhetoric are not absolute. Consequently, varying types of criticism may enjoy measures of acceptance at different times. This may not be unwholesome, for, as Gertrude Buck observes, "Each type of criticism, arising to supplement the inadequacies of previous types, has enriched our conception of the critical process." If this is true in literature, it should be no less true in rhetoric.

In his essay, "The Literary Criticism of Oratory," Wichelns examines three types of criticism which modern writers employ in dealing with public speakers. The first is largely biographical, dealing with the general conduct and character of the man rather than with his speaking activities. The second provides a judgment by balancing the biographical and literary points of interest with the work of the speaker. The third concentrates on the oratorical productions rather than on straight biographical details. Each of these types contributes to an understanding of oratory; none of them can be wholly effective unless the critic approaches his problem with an appreciation of rhetoric and a lively conception of its function in the social structure.

Our classification of the types of criticism is drawn in large part from the literary craftsman, but is adapted to the problems and needs of the field of speech. Not all of these types are consistent with the definition set forth in the preceding section, but they are currently employed and therefore deserve notice.

Classified according to type, the criticism of speeches falls under four main heads, all of which overlap to a certain extent. These types are the impressionistic, analytic, synthetic, and judicial.

The impressionistic criticism of speeches, least systematic and scientific of all, simply records a judgment based upon personal preference and predisposition. It is, indeed, criticism by "idle exclamation." The critic likes or dislikes a certain speech, not necessarily because it conforms or fails to conform to traditional criteria nor because it achieved or failed to achieve the end for which it was intended, but because he entertained a particular attitude toward the speaker, or the subject, or the purpose of the talk. Subjectivity characterizes the appraisal. It should be noted, of course, that in many cases the judgments may be valid; however, such results might almost be considered accidental, for analytical and methodical examination of the facts has not made them so. Such criticism is at the mercy of whim and temperament.

On the other hand, such appraisal should not be dismissed with cavalier indifference. At the basic level, all criticism contains impressionistic responses, and the person who says "A speech is good if I like to listen to it" is voicing a judgment of some merit. Simply to express such an opinion without critical comment is insufficient, but to begin with it is not necessarily blameworthy.

The second type may be called analytic, despite the fact that, in a larger sense, all criticism is analytical. In this approach the critic makes a methodical examination of all available facts relating to the speech itself. He effects, by "an exact anatomy," an exhaustive structural analysis of the text. This may take the form of word counts, classifications of arguments, ratios of exposition to argumentation or of description to narration, surveys of sentences according to length and structure, listings of figurative elements, itemizations of pronoun usage, and many other classificatory arrangements. The objective of such criticism is not a revelation of the nature of a speech in its social setting, but an understanding of the speech in its own right. Thus analytic criticism is devoted to the collection of facts relating to the speech alone; there is little evaluation.

Synthetic criticism is the third general type. Here, as in the analytic, the critic collects an abundance of facts; but he goes further. He gathers the data which deal not with the speech alone but with the other elements in the total situation, with the speaker, the audience, and the occasion. His principal aim is to collect and arrange these facts so that a faithful reconstruction of the original situation can be achieved. As far as he goes, the critic employing the synthetic method may conduct an effective piece of work. He falls short of the ideal in criticism, however, if he fails to interpret his results.

The last type of criticism may be called the judicial. It combines the aims of analytic and synthetic inquiry with the all-important element of evaluation and interpretation of results. Thus it reconstructs a speech situation with fidelity to fact; it examines this situation carefully in the light of the interaction of speaker, audience, subject, and occasion; it interprets the data with an eye to determining the *effect* of the speech; it formulates a judgment in the light of the philosophical-historical-literary-logical-ethical constituents of the inquiry; and it appraises the entire event by assigning it comparative rank in the total enterprise of speaking. The material of this book is directed largely toward the development of criticism of this type.

QUALIFICATIONS OF THE CRITIC

"The fact that there is no royal road to achievement in any branch of human knowledge," Brightfield remarks, "is a most fortunate and necessary circumstance." Fortunate, perhaps, in the sense that the aspirations of the human intellect are never in want of challenges; necessary, no doubt, in that the loftiest of attainments never quite solve the perplexing problems in the realm of thought. It is with recognition of these limitations that we begin our discussion of the essentials of critical inquiry. This treatment cannot and should not prescribe a fixed formula for success in the criticism of speeches; it can, however, point to a few personal characteristics which should increase the critic's likelihood of achieving acceptable competence in this field.

It is a painful but nonetheless important truth that the faults of criticism are the faults of critics. In commenting on this problem in its relation to literature, John M. Robertson once said "the snares of criticism . . . may be classed as those set up by defect of real knowledge, defect of aesthetic percipience, defect of logical discipline, and defect of judicial sense or scruple; and it is hard to say which is the more serious." [9] Paraphrase this remark as we please, the conclusion remains that a critic must possess certain accomplishments if he is to carry out his function with propriety and effectiveness. We shall list a few of the qualifications.

(1) The rhetorical critic must have an appreciation of oratory—an

[9] "On Criticism." *The New Criterion*, 4:254 (April, 1926).

effective knowledge of what he is judging. He must be sensitive to the appeal of the spoken word and possessed of a sense of imagination. This sensitivity must be more than perfunctory respect for a few great orations of the past; it must embrace a regard for the influence of oral communication, from the lips of the less important figures as well as from those of acknowledged renown, in the shaping and controlling of man's destiny. In short, the critic of oratory must have what Gertrude Buck once called "an intelligent hospitality of mind" for the spoken word.

(2) An intelligent familiarity with the background of rhetoric is essential to the critic. He must be able to interpret contemporary theory with reference to its antecedents in more remote times. This does not mean, to paraphrase Chesterfield, that he must look upon the moderns with contempt and upon the ancients with idolatry. It simply suggests that, since the present is the logical result of the past, the critic must be sufficiently familiar with what has preceded to understand what he is dealing with now. Such a knowledge of the past gives him added perspective, enables his critical faculty to operate within the framework of his subject, and affords a measure of traditional sanction for his interpretations and judgments.

(3) An inquiring state of mind is essential to the rhetorical critic. Since a large part of the critic's job is of an investigative nature, he must possess a lively respect both for the facts themselves and for the method of research through which the data are accumulated. A certain spirit of inquiry, a sense of satisfaction growing out of the pursuit of causes and effects—these are indispensable.

Furthermore, the critic must be temperamentally disposed to withhold judgment until the area of investigative study has been examined thoroughly. As Richard G. Moulton once remarked, "The mind cannot commence its work of assaying and judging until it has concluded its work of investigating and interpreting . . ."

(4) A dispassionate, objective attitude toward the object of investigation is a further qualification without which the critic works at a disadvantage. Obviously, the critic should derive personal satisfaction from hearing and reading speeches; but his critical inquiries should be characterized by a certain impersonality of treatment, a detachment, which enables him to view facts and arrive at judgments with a minimum of emotional predisposition. He must try to do what Wendell Phillips claimed most men were incapable of, namely, view facts with the eyes instead of the prejudices.

The objectivity of which we are speaking is the product of a certain universality of mind. Possessed of it, the critic can project himself into other periods of time; he can examine and evaluate the works of the past as well as of the present, without operating under the influence or within the framework of contemporary prejudices.

The substance of these qualifications may be resolved to simple terms: The rhetorical critic must be an intelligent man, well-versed in his subject. The tools of his craft are appreciation, knowledge, imagination, intellectual curiosity, investigative skill, a sense of emotional detachment, and good judgment.

FUNCTIONS OF CRITICISM

It may be well to indicate at the outset what the function of rhetorical criticism is *not*. The necessity of approaching the problem negatively arises from the unhappy circumstance that the word "criticism" has, in popular usage, been buffeted about with reckless abandon.

The intelligent criticism of speeches is not a form of censorship. It is not the critic's job to impose checks on ideas and attitudes, even if he were able, simply because they are incompatible with his way of thinking, or because they are contrary to the *status quo*. It does not fall within the province of the critic to discourage the utterance of so-called "rebellious" material, or to dismiss a speech of the past as inconsequential or unworthy of analysis because it was considered "inflammatory" or "reactionary." Perhaps a given speech was "inflammatory." But it is the critic's job to determine that fact in the light of exhaustive investigation of the social situation and the consequences; it is not his prerogative to pre-judge the case or to dismiss the utterance on the ground that it failed to conform to the established political, economic, and social *mores*. The accomplished rhetorical critic appraises the oratory of all men, regardless of their ideological commitments, with the same objective detachment and with the same criteria. Upon careful examination, the critic may find that the ideas of one or more of them are logically untenable; he may find any number of departures from sound rhetorical practice in a given speech; he may find that the speech failed to achieve the end which the speaker set for it. These matters the critic may reveal, interpret, and appraise. A valid judgment, however disapproving, may still be a good criticism.

What, then, is the province of his service? Generally speaking, rhetorical criticism serves four major functions.

(1) It helps to clarify and define the theoretical basis of public address. It does so without proposing to teach the speaker how to manage his art. The didactic element in criticism is not of first importance; undoubtedly interested students could master the principles of speaking more efficiently and rapidly through a study of textbooks devoted to the

subject than through an examination of a comparable body of critical literature. However, criticism helps to reveal the operation of theory in practice, thus clarifying its meaning and perhaps in some instances even formulating new theory.

(2) Rhetorical criticism helps to set up a standard of excellence. Naturally, speech situations are highly variable; each one produces a unique interaction of speaker, audience, subject, and occasion. Fortunately, critical inquiry does not establish dogmatic principles by which all addresses must be appraised. Instead, it provides insight into methods of evaluation which help to free the critic from the rule of whim, thus affording a certain corrective for unfounded and hasty judgment.

(3) Rhetorical criticism helps to interpret the function of oral communication in society. It serves as an effective link between the theory of public address and the outside world. Devoted importantly as it is to a determination of the *effect* or outcome of a speech, it reveals the nature of the process by which a communicative intent finally implements, or fails to implement, social action. A study of theory alone cannot reveal the complete process since it is concerned largely with methodology. But criticism traces the major steps in oral communication straight through to the *effect*, immediate or delayed, of the spoken discourse upon society.

(4) As a field of scholarly inquiry, rhetorical criticism indicates the limits of present knowledge in the field of public speaking. It points out the areas in which valid judgments cannot now be made, either because of an insufficiency of evidence or because of an inability to establish substantially the causal relations among ascertainable facts, especially with respect to the effectiveness of speeches in the past.

SPEECH AS A USEFUL ART

Since the earliest formulations of a theory of speaking, rhetoric has been regarded generally as a useful art. It is largely an instrument of social control. However, some oratory—even though only a fractional part of the total output—seems to go quite beyond the province of sheer utility. It takes on aesthetic characteristics and, in some instances, becomes an object of beauty, permanence, and penetrating insight into human experience. In short, it approaches a fine art. Furthermore, some of our oratorical judgments—as in the case of Burke's speech "On Conciliation"—derive to a considerable extent from aesthetic as well as from practical considerations. While holding to the thesis that speech is a useful art, we must yet allow that there may be a point in rhetorical craftsmanship at which oratory as an instrument of power (utility) meets oratory as a manifestation of aesthetic creation (beauty).

THE ULTIMATE GOAL OF CRITICISM

The rhetorical critic operates within a system or hierarchy of values. The nature of his work requires it. He must make judgments based upon interpretative analyses; he must arrive at certain conclusions despite the fact that a totality of information cannot be secured. But the careful critic bases his value judgments upon reliable data, meticulously tested and checked. In other words, he strives for responsibility of statement.

The rhetorical critic operates largely in the realm of practical affairs. The substance with which he deals is the public speech. The principal end which he seeks to interpret is the result or effect of the utterance. His judgments derive, therefore, from practical, not ideal, considerations. He functions at all times within the realm of the probable. Although, as Brightfield remarks, man's ambitions sometimes may "outrun the existing circumstances in which they are placed," the rhetorical critic is constantly dealing with conditions falling within the limits set by the particular speech situation. That is to say, the goals which serious speakers set for their addresses are usually attainable, though obviously not always attained. And so the critic of oratory, working within the framework of this probability, never deals with the element of make-believe; unlike the literary critic, he does not regard a work as having satisfied the conditions of his art if it goes beyond the limits set by the environment. Accordingly, in his final judgments, the rhetorical critic does not pronounce a "counsel of unattainable perfection." He deals with things as they are, or, in the light of the best available information, as they seem to have been.

This does not mean that the critic of speeches deals only in mundane considerations. On the contrary, he is guided by lofty aspiration since the ultimate goal of his efforts is the realization of truth. Robertson once said of the literary critic that if he "attains to what is new, it is well; if he but attains to what is true, it is still well." So it is with the rhetorical critic. It is indeed well if he gets at and makes known the truth about the speeches with which he deals.

SUMMARY

Rhetorical criticism is a logical extension of the theory and practice of public speaking. Accordingly, an understanding of its principles requires a familiarity with the nature of the medium in which speech operates; it requires a full recognition of the fact that the basic function of speech, as carried out through the use of symbols, is communication. The communicative activity with which the rhetorical critic is concerned takes place in a speech situation which is characterized by: (1) relative free-dom in the use of subject matter; (2) imprecision of data; (3) limitation as to time; (4) specificity of purpose; (5) transitoriness; (6) direct social interaction; (7) personal relationships growing out of the presence of a speaker, and (8) peculiarities of idiom, structure, content, and arrange-ment.

The criticism of oratory involves three stages: the examination of the facts, the formulation of criteria, and the application of the standards to the facts for purposes of general evaluation. The essential constituents of the rhetorical judgment derive mainly from the fields of philosophy, linguistics, ethics, history, and logic. The source of the basic canon of rhetorical criticism is found in the formula: A speech is the result of an interaction of speaker, subject, audience, and occasion. The end toward which the critic's efforts are directed is largely the determination of the *effect* of the speech.

The principal types of criticism are the impressionistic, analytic, syn-thetic, and judicial. It is to the latter type that the major part of the discussion in this book will be directed.

The able critic will have (1) an appreciation of oratory, (2) a fa-miliarity with rhetorical theory and practice, (3) intellectual curiosity, (4) sensitive imagination, and (5) an objective attitude toward his accumulated data.

The ultimate goal of the critic's efforts is the attainment of truth re-garding a particular speech event. The specific functions of his art are (1) to clarify the theory of speaking, (2) to help formulate a standard of excellence, (3) to interpret the influence of oral communication in society, and (4) to indicate the present limits of knowledge in the field of speaking.

Thus we see that the criticism of speeches is a complex undertaking. It draws upon many fields of knowledge, requires much original research, and imposes heavy demands upon reasoning and judgment. In short, it offers a stern but inviting challenge to the serious student of public address.

EXERCISES

1. Define the following terms: oratory, eloquence, rhetoric, public address, and public speaking.
2. What is rhetorical criticism? How do the following writers differ with the point of view expressed in this chapter: Edwin Black, Marie Hochmuth Nichols, Wayland M. Parrish, Anthony Hillbruner, Ernest Bormann, L. H. Mouat, Robert Cathcart. (Their works are listed in the Readings.)
3. What is the purpose of rhetorical criticism? Consult several of the readings.

4. By what yardstick or standard should a critic judge a speech?
5. How does rhetorical criticism differ from literary and dramatic criticism? (See Bormann article.)
6. Is rhetorical criticism as presented in Chapter 1 different from the criticism which the teacher gives in the classroom? For several views of classroom criticism, see "Symposium: Evaluation in the Public Speaking Courses," *The Speech Teacher*, 16:150–164 (March, 1967).
7. For subsequent use in this course, collect specimens of speech criticism found in newspapers and periodicals. Find several reports of the same speech. Compare the accounts, noting similarities and differences.
8. Rhetoric is commonly considered a useful art. How does the circumstance of usefulness make its criticism differ from that of a fine art?
9. Comment on the relation between rhetorical criticism and such fields as ethics, psychology, and politics.
10. To what extent should the literary considerations of permanence and beauty enter into the judgment of a speech?
11. How does the historical method differ from the critical method?
12. What are several points of view from which to pursue criticism? Compare the *effectiveness* point of view and the *artistic* point of view. (See McBurney and Wrage, *The Art of Good Speech*, pp. 21–32.)
13. Comment on John Quincy Adams' definition of rhetorical criticism as "the art of appreciating the real merits of a public speaker."
14. Do you agree with those who say, in effect, that when a speech (as spoken) is converted to cold print in the morning paper or in an anthology, it ceases to be a speech? Explore the implications of your answer. Compare your reflections with this remark by Lord Justice Birkett: "Most speeches when recalled, are without the fire and the glow with which they were invested by the speaker's presence; the dramatic setting has gone; and the emotions of the moment have vanished irrevocably."
15. John Ruskin believed that you could read the character of a nation in its art. From your knowledge of public address, comment on the relevancy of Ruskin's comment to contemporary American speechmaking.
16. Of the important American speeches that you have read, which one would you have liked most to give, and why? Look upon this project as a preliminary exercise in speech criticism. Consult your past experience and observation and reflection in deciding *why* you would select that speech.
17. Do you anticipate that this remark by Samuel Eliot Morison will be equally applicable to the speech critic? "The historian should have frequent recourse to the book of life. The richer his personal experience, the wider his human contacts, the more likely he is to effect a living contact with his audience." Do you believe it is also relevant for the speaker himself?
18. Read Sylvia Angus' " 'It's Pretty, but Is It Art?' " (*Saturday Review*, September 2, 1967, pp. 14–15). Can a speech be brought under the cover of her definition of art?
19. For an extensive summary of quantitative research in rhetoric and public address during the past fifty years, see Wayne N. Thompson, *Quantitative Research in Public Address and Communication* (New York, Random House, 1967). Examine Chapter 3 particularly with the view of assessing the contributions of descriptive and experimental research to a newer conception of rhetorical theory.

READINGS

BOWER ALY. "The Criticism of Oratory." In *The Rhetoric of Alexander Hamilton.* New York, Columbia University Press, 1941. Pp. 25–32.
———. "A Rhetorical Theory for a History of Public Speaking in the United States." In *Papers in Rhetoric.* Edited by DONALD C. BRYANT. St. Louis, privately printed, 1940. Pp. 34–38.
CARROLL C. ARNOLD. "Oral Rhetoric, Rhetoric and Literature." *Philosophy and Rhetoric,* 1:191–210 (Fall, 1968).
A. CRAIG BAIRD. *Rhetoric: A Philosophical Inquiry.* New York, The Ronald Press Company, 1965.
BARNET BASKERVILLE. "The Critical Method in Speech." *Central States Speech Journal,* 4:1–5 (July, 1953).
ERNEST G. BORMANN. "Rhetorical and Dramatic Criticism." In *Theory and Research in the Communicative Arts.* New York, Holt, Rinehart and Winston, Inc., 1965. Pp. 225–250.
EDWIN BLACK. *Rhetorical Criticism: A Study in Method.* New York, The Macmillan Co., 1965.
J. BRONOWSKI. "The Reach of Imagination." *The American Scholar,* 36:193–201 (Spring, 1967).
DONALD C. BRYANT. "Some Problems of Scope and Method in Rhetorical Scholarship." *Quarterly Journal of Speech,* 23:182–189 (April, 1937).
ROBERT CATHCART. *Post Communication: Criticism and Evaluation.* Indianapolis, Bobbs-Merrill Co., Inc., 1966.
ALBERT J. CROFT. "The Functions of Rhetorical Criticism." *Quarterly Journal of Speech,* 42:283–91 (October, 1956).
THEODORE M. GREENE. *The Arts and the Art of Criticism.* Princeton, Princeton University Press, 1940.
RICHARD B. GREGG. "The Study of Rhetorical Criticism." In *The Communicative Arts and Sciences of Speech.* Edited by KEITH BROOKS. Columbus, Ohio, Charles E. Merrill Books, Inc., 1967. Pp. 35–48.
KENNETH G. HANCE. "The Historical-Critical Type of Research: A Re-examination." *Central States Speech Journal,* 13:165–170 (Spring, 1962).
HAROLD F. HARDING. "The College Student as a Critic." *Vital Speeches of the Day,* 18:733–736 (September 15, 1952).
ANTHONY HILLBRUNER. *Critical Dimensions: The Art of Public Address Criticism.* New York, Random House, 1966.
MARIE KATHRYN HOCHMUTH. "The Criticism of Rhetoric." In *A History and Criticism of American Public Address,* vol. III. Edited by MARIE KATHRYN HOCHMUTH. New York, Russell & Russell, 1955. Pp. 1–23.
HOYT H. HUDSON. "Rhetoric and Poetry." *Quarterly Journal of Speech Education,* 10:143–154 (April, 1924).
EVERETT LEE HUNT. "Rhetoric and Literary Criticism." *Quarterly Journal of Speech,* 21:564–568 (November, 1935).
———. "Rhetoric as a Humane Study." *Quarterly Journal of Speech,* 41:114–117 (April, 1955).
IRVING J. LEE. "Four Ways of Looking at a Speech." *Quarterly Journal of Speech,* 28:148–155 (April, 1942).
MARTIN MALONEY. "Some New Directions in Rhetorical Criticism." *Central States Speech Journal,* 4:1–5 (March, 1953).
JAMES H. MCBURNEY and ERNEST J. WRAGE. *The Art of Good Speech.* New York, Prentice-Hall, Inc., 1953. Ch. II, pp. 21–32.
L. H. MOUAT. "An Approach to Rhetorical Criticism." In *The Rhetorical Idiom.* Edited by DONALD C. BRYANT. Ithaca, New York, Cornell University Press, 1957. Pp. 161–177.
MARIE HOCHMUTH NICHOLS. *Rhetoric and Criticism.* Baton Rouge, Louisiana State

University Press, 1963. Ch. V, "Theory and Practice of Rhetorical Criticism," pp. 65–78.

THOMAS R. NILSON. *Essays on Rhetorical Criticism.* New York, Random House, 1968.

WAYLAND MAXFIELD PARRISH. "The Study of Speeches." In *American Speeches.* Edited by WAYLAND MAXFIELD PARRISH and MARIE HOCHMUTH. New York, Longmans, Green & Co., 1954. Pp. 1–20.

LOREN D. REID. *Charles James Fox, A Man for the People.* Columbia, University of Missouri Press, 1969.

JOSEPH SCHWARTZ and JOHN A. RYCENGA, eds. *The Province of Rhetoric.* New York, The Ronald Press Company, 1965.

MALCOLM O. SILLARS. "Rhetoric as Act." *Quarterly Journal of Speech,* 50:277–284 (October, 1964).

KARL R. WALLACE. *Understanding Discourse: The Speech Act and Rhetorical Action.* Baton Rouge, Louisiana University Press, 1970.

HERBERT A. WICHELNS. "The Literary Criticism of Oratory." In *Studies in Rhetoric and Public Speaking in Honor of James A. Winans.* New York, Century Co., 1925. Pp. 181–216.

II

THE DEVELOPMENT
OF RHETORICAL THEORY

2

Foundations of the
Art of Speaking

THE VALUE OF TRADITION

The art of rhetoric is old, very old. Its roots reach deep into the past, into an antiquity which is one with poetry, ethics, politics, and law. By indissoluble ties it is linked with remote times and distant places. Indeed, its tradition wears the proverbial snowy beard.[1]

It is satisfying to know that rhetoric derives from an extensive literature. This written tradition provides an unbroken record of intellectual probing into the operation of an ancient art. It helps to give continuity to our efforts. We are mindful of the labors of our predecessors in the field; we realize, as Barrett Wendell once said of the great figures in literature,

. . . that the names and the works which have survived have done so largely because, though each originally came to light in historical conditions as distinct as those which surround us now, each has proved, when its original surroundings have faded, to appeal for one reason or another to generations widely different from that which it chanced to address in the flesh.[2]

The force of tradition unites the great names and works in a common core of theory, thus linking "generation to generation in the realm of mind, so that, in Pascal's figure, we may regard the whole procession of the ages as one man always living and always learning."[3]

By paying respect to our tradition, by acknowledging the "long se-

[1] Cf. Quintilian. *Institutes of Oratory.* II, 15, for scattered references to early work in the art.
[2] *The Traditions of European Literature.* New York, 1920, p. 2.
[3] W. R. Sorley. *Herbert Spencer Lectures,* 2nd ser. Oxford, 1930, p. 11.

quence of humanized culture" and judgment in the contributions to the art of rhetoric, we do not necessarily commit ourselves to a static conception of the subject. It is possible to appreciate the dignity and worth of a tradition without binding ourselves to the authority of the past. The acceptance of tradition does not imply unthinking obedience to standards based "upon the faults of eminent men." Tradition is not the final criterion of certitude. It is a beacon, however, which helps to light the way to a fuller understanding of the nature of speechcraft.

The alliance of tradition and criticism is a fortunate one. Without the latter, errors and ill-formed conceptions might be perpetuated through custom. Criticism, however, as an active force constantly subjects tradition to the searching analysis that should naturally accompany the enlargement of understanding and appreciation. Criticism tends to keep tradition in step with time, and in line with newly formed truth. As W. R. Sorley says, it protects the individual from the harmful aspects of tradition, "so that the truth and social values that have been handed down from the past may continue to be the inspiration of each man.

> He only earns his freedom, owns existence,
> Who every day must conquer her anew.[4]

The following chapters present briefly the nature of the tradition upon which the art of rhetoric rests; they review the contributions of men whose thoughts helped to form and sustain the theoretical framework of the subject. In short, they represent a pageant of abiding ideas on speechcraft. These are the ideas that form the substructure of the art. They contribute substantially to a true prolegomenon for the criticism of speeches.

HOMERIC EXPRESSION

In a sermon against long extempore prayers, Robert South once remarked that "the reason of things lies in a little compass." He insisted upon the necessity of gathering "the general natures of things out of a heap of numberless particulars," thus making large units of material "portable to the memory." We take heart from such an observation; we are reminded that, although the sources available on the history of rhetorical theory are almost beyond number, all need not be reviewed to afford a true representation of the stream of ideas in this field of knowledge. More important for our purpose than an exhaustive summary of the contributions of all rhetoricians from earliest times to the present, is the perception of common elements in the progression of ideas. Once revealed, those elements will throw light upon the unity of the theory of speaking.

As indicated in the preceding chapter, the practice, theory, and criti-

[4] *Ibid.*, p. 24.

cism of public address are closely interrelated. Each is the function and derivative of the others. Hence, before we have trustworthy records of a theory of speaking, we have testimony of the approved *practice* of competent orators. Perhaps the latter presupposes the existence, in oral or written tradition, of some notion of the former, but our reference at this point should be to authenticated records. George Campbell remarked that "speakers existed before grammarians, and reasoners before logicians, so, doubtless, there were orators before there were rhetoricians, and poets before critics. The first impulse towards the attainment of every art is from nature." [5]

Accordingly, the earliest history of rhetorical theory derives from a study of the social organization which made persuasive speaking, as John F. Dobson points out, one of the first necessities of a society. As soon as "men were organized on terms of equality for corporate action, there must have been occasions when opinions might differ as to the best course to be pursued . . ." Under such circumstances, discussion developed, and that side prevailed "which could state its views most convincingly . . ." [6]

Ancient Greek society developed a rich tradition of oral literature. And the early oratory, as George Kennedy speculates,[7] doubtless drew upon the techniques associated with oral poetry. The Greeks were indeed the first to accord oratorical expression a place of distinction among the cultivated arts. Dobson remarks that with the Greeks "oratory was instinctive"; skill in speaking was no less highly prized "than valour in battle . . ." We would therefore expect speech to have some sort of representation in their early literature. The epic poems of Homer fulfill this expectation.

As epic poems, the *Iliad* and the *Odyssey* depend largely upon narration. However, the characters in the poems are always in the forefront, and they command attention through the speeches they deliver. Alfred Croiset remarks that these speeches, and particularly the ones in the *Iliad*, "form an element of the poem almost as important as the narrations and descriptions." The speeches help to portray character, especially as they reveal the thought and feeling of the orators who deliver addresses of a deliberative sort before the assembly, or of exhortation to renewed effort on the battlefield, or of simple supplication to a single person. Thus, Achilles and Nestor—to mention only two—assume great literary stature through their oratorical presentations. The "specimens of their persuasive speaking in the poems," says J. P. Mahaffy, "show how keenly the rhapsodists and their audiences appreciated this high quality."

The Homeric epics reveal an elementary art of rhetoric. The speeches

[5] *The Philosophy of Rhetoric.* New ed. New York, 1851, p. 19.
[6] *The Greek Orators.* London, 1919, p. 1.
[7] *The Art of Persuasion in Greece.* Princeton, New Jersey, 1963, p. 5.

uttered by the several characters in the *Iliad*, for example, are not without artistic design calculated to secure certain responses. Croiset observes that the characters "well know what words to begin with, and they know how to make men listen—how to win their attention." Indeed, "they set forth their arguments in the order that seems best and in the form most appropriate to gain acceptance from those whom they address. If they have definite conclusions, they formulate them and sum them up in striking terms. All this is the work of reflection, method, and experience." No less an authority than Quintilian remarked that Homer provided "a model and an origin for every species of eloquence." He indicated that Homer's epics displayed ably the arts of legal pleading and deliberation, established and applied "the laws of oratorical exordia," stated the facts of cases with admirable perspicuity, employed stylistic expressions with consummate skill, and developed faultless perorations. Relative to the last point, Quintilian inquired: "What peroration of a speech will ever be thought equal to the entreaties of Priam beseeching Achilles for the body of his son?" Richard C. Jebb believes no oratory of the ancient world approaches "so nearly as the Homeric to the modern ideal."

However significant the rhetoric in the *Iliad* and the *Odyssey* may be, it must not be considered mature and developed. In fact, George Kennedy believes that many of the Homeric speeches, like the discourses in Herodotus, are more nearly conversations than instances of formal oratory. The rhetorical system is patently elementary, embryonic; it results in an oratory which is simply part of the larger literary device of the epic. The speeches are weak in argumentation, a point which Croiset makes with telling emphasis when he shows that they seldom develop reasons, seldom, if ever, anticipate objections, and usually overdraw the pathetic element.

Through the addresses of the principal characters, however, the *Iliad* furnishes one of the first semi-organized fragments of speech theory. Dating about 1000 years before the Christian era, deriving from Homer's genius and the collective inventions of a succession of poets, depicting a life that was a "mingling of the traditional and the ideal with contemporary facts," and expressing ethical and religious motives without open preachment of doctrine, these epics open the way to a fuller understanding of the art of speaking.

THE INFLUENCE OF ATHENIAN DEMOCRACY

The form of government in ancient Greece encouraged public speaking. Men were permitted to voice their opinions and to share in the making of political decisions. The popular Assembly at Athens during the fifth century B.C. included virtually every male citizen "with the leisure and inclination to attend." This Assembly deliberated on questions suggested by the Committee of Five Hundred, which in turn often acted on the recommendations of a prominent statesman, and the Athenian courts offered citizens an opportunity to participate in the administration of justice. Under these conditions a respect for the spoken word developed which is unequalled by any other people at any time. Liberty of expression "the Nurse of all Arts and Sciences," to quote John Lawson, became "in a particular manner the Parent of Eloquence. . . ."

Democratization of the courts during Pericles' time enabled nearly any Athenian citizen over 30 years of age to act as a juror in the courts. Juries were large; "pleaders addressed the jurors as citizens and democrats, and in truth the courts were the stronghold of popular government." George W. Botsford observes that these large gatherings of Athenian citizens "made possible the development of a judicial oratory of universal and eternal literary value." Further, the courts were juries without a judge. Every man was his own pleader; consequently, each case provided a natural stimulus to effective oratorical presentation.

It is of more than passing interest that in this democracy in which free discussion enjoyed a unique position, responsibility of public statement was urgently requested and properly safeguarded. As Robert J. Bonner observes, in Athens "an orator suspected of not giving the best advice to the people could be impeached in the assembly." [8] Callistratus was so impeached, and Demosthenes spoke of a threat by Aeschines to impeach him. Furthermore, Bonner reports that the Athenian system "provided still another means of depriving unworthy citizens of the right to speak in the assembly. It was known as a scrutiny . . . of orators." Evidently, if "one of the regular speakers in the assembly was suspected of certain dishonorable acts, he could be prosecuted, not for the offense, but for continuing to speak in the assembly after committing the offense. The penalty was disqualification." These provisions bespeak a tempered regard for responsibility of utterance and suggest the truly democratic character of the Athenian system.

The man under whom Athens reached this summit of achievement was Pericles, a statesman of unusual vision and an orator on whose lips, according to Cicero, the "graces of persuasion" so dwelt that even when he contradicted the favorites of the people his words "became popular and agreeable to all men . . ." Like Themistocles, Pericles was an orator-patriot whose "deep reflection on and clear perception of what was needful for Athens" gave to his speeches a profound power and solidity. Plato also comments on Pericles' "loftiness of thought and perfect mastery over every subject."

[8] Robert J. Bonner, *Aspects of Athenian Democracy.* Berkeley, 1933, p. 80.

Regrettably, we have no texts of Pericles' speeches. Despite that fact, he is regarded as the first recorded Greek orator. In his history of the war between the Athenians and the Peloponnesians, Thucydides introduces—as was the practice in early Greek historiography—many speeches into his account of the conflict. Among them are several addresses by Pericles, including the celebrated "Funeral Oration" delivered in 431 B.C. on the occasion of the ceremony for the men who fell in the first year of the war.

Whether or not the speeches in Thucydides represent substantially what the characters said in real life is a question beyond the province of this discussion. It is perhaps sufficient to observe that many scholars believe that they do, although the artistic form in which they are cast is manifestly Thucydides'. Like the interpreter who makes a simultaneous translation of a speech delivered in a world assembly, Thucydides may also be charged on occasion with reporting what he thought the speaker should have said in order to be effective. K. O. Müller remarks that the speeches contain "a sum of the motives and causes which led to the principal transactions" and hence summarize "much that was really spoken on various occasions"; [9] A. W. Gomme introduces evidence to show that Thucydides made a sincere effort to find out what words were spoken in the original settings; [10] and Harold N. Fowler asserts that the speeches were more than inventions introduced for the sole purpose of imparting vigor to the story.[11]

In the early part of the narrative, Thucydides himself remarks:

As to the speeches of particular persons either at the commencement or at the prosecution of the war, whether such as I heard myself or such as were repeated to me by others, I will not pretend to recite them in all their exactness. It . . . [has] been my method to consider principally what might be pertinently said upon every occasion to the points in debate, and to keep as near as possible to what would pass for genuine by universal consent.[12]

Both for what they tell about Periclean eloquence and what they reveal about the speechmaking of other individuals, Thucydides' narratives offer valuable material to the student of rhetorical theory. The speeches in the history reveal artistry in conception, appreciation of rhetorical forms, and full understanding of the different types of oratory. Among the representative speeches which reveal Thucydides' mastery of speech reporting and writing are the deliberative addresses before the assembly at which the Corcyraeans and Corinthians pleaded their

9 K. O. Müller. A History of the Literature of Ancient Greece. Translated by J. W. Donaldson. 1858. II, 128.

10 Essays in Greek History and Literature. Oxford, 1937, p. 185.

11 A History of Ancient Greek Literature. Rev. ed. New York, 1923, p. 282.

12 A History of the Peloponnesian War. Translated from Greek of Thucydides by William Smith. Philadelphia, 1836. I, 8.

causes, Archidamus' speech before the generals and chief officers of the various states, and Nicias' speech to his depressed men during the dark hours of the campaign.

Three of Pericles' speeches dominate the narrative. In the first, he addressed the Athenians shortly after the Lacedaemonians had made a final request for the restoration of the Hellenes' independence. The assembly had been called at Athens to consider this issue. There was considerable discussion, with some members favoring war and others suggesting that Athens yield to the demand. Pericles began his patriotic discourse by saying:

I firmly persevere, Athenians, in the same opinion that I have ever avowed —to make no concessions to the Lacedaemonians—though at the same time sensible that men never execute a war with that warmth of spirit through which they are impelled to undertake it, but sink in their ardour as difficulties increase. . . . Their allegations against us they are determined to support by arms, and not by evidence; and here they come no longer to remonstrate but actually to give us law. . . . I exhort you therefore to form a resolution, either timely to make your submission before you begin to suffer; or, if we shall determine for war, which to me . . . [seems] most expedient, without regarding the pretext of it, be it important or be it trifling, to refuse ever the least concession, nor to render the tenure of what we now possess precarious and uncertain.

He then went on to show that the Athenians were in a better position to win the war; the Lacedaemonians were poor, unused to waging great wars, and divided in race. "For in truth," he declared, "I am more afraid of our own indiscretions than the schemes of the enemy." He concluded by saying:

It was thus that our fathers withstood the Medes, and rushing to arms with resources far inferior to ours, nay abandoning all their substance, by resolution more than fortune, by courage more than real strength, beat back the Barbarian, and advanced this state to its present summit of grandeur. From them we ought not to degenerate, but by every effort within our ability avenge it on our foes, and deliver it down to posterity, unblemished and unimpaired.[13]

Compton Mackenzie doubts that this speech does justice to Pericles' effort, although it unquestionably reveals "the lucid policy and clearly defined strategy at the back of it."

In the "Funeral Oration," Pericles pronounced a eulogy upon the causes of Athenian greatness. Fervidly patriotic and proudly jealous of Athenian grandeur, this speech, in the opinion of Botsford, is "one of the most precious documents in the history of civilization."

Finally, mention should be made of Pericles' speech to the Assembly after the second Peloponnesian invasion and after Attica had been rav-

[13] *Ibid.,* I, 47–50.

aged by conquest and plague. In this address, important alike for the technique devised by Thucydides and the statesmanlike resolution displayed by the orator, Pericles tries to bolster the spirit and ardor of the Athenians. His speech closes with words which, in substance, have been the frequent resort of orators through the ages: ". . . They whose minds are least sensitive to calamity, and whose hands are most quick to meet it, are the greatest men and the greatest communities." [14]

THE EARLY SICILIAN RHETORICIANS

The speechmaking of Pericles and Themistocles grew out of practical problems. There were wars to be waged, men to be inspired, and civic affairs to be administered. Spoken discourse served to bring people together; once together, it helped to consolidate their hopes, ambitions, and desires. An art or system of rhetoric, or speechcraft, was a natural outgrowth of the realization that men could govern themselves through persuasive talk. Hence, rhetorical handbooks made an appearance.

The development of the first "system" of rhetoric is traditionally attributed to Corax and to his pupil, Tisias, both Sicilian Greeks. Quintilian refers to them as the "most ancient composers of rules on the art," with the possible exception of the earliest poets and of Empedocles. Cicero also observes that before Corax and Tisias "no one spoke by prescribed method, conformably to rules of art, though many discoursed very sensibly . . ."

The circumstances surrounding the "birth" of rhetoric in Sicily were chiefly political and legal. Perhaps the temperament of the people contributed, however, to the formulation of rhetorical theory, for Cicero remarks that the Sicilians were "very quick and acute, and had a natural turn for disputation." Following the expulsion of Thrasydaeus by the Agrigentines about 472 B.C. and of Thrasybulus by the Syracusans about 466 B.C., when the reign of Gelon, Hieron, and Thrasybulus ended, the "establishment of a democratical constitution and the requirements of the new order of things gave rise to a special demand for instruction in oratory." [15] Because of the change in the form of government, many people returning from exile demanded restitution of property previously confiscated by the tyrants. Accordingly, "rights that under the stress of despotism had, in the case of Syracuse, remained dormant for some twenty years, would be revived; lands that had been arbitrarily assigned to the favourites of the court would be claimed, by the original owners

---

[14] *The History of the Peloponnesian War.* Translated by Richard Crawley. London, 1876, p. 140.

[15] John Edwin Sandys. *M. Tulli Ciceronis ad M. Brutum Orator.* Rev. ed. Cambridge, 1885, p. iv.

or their representatives; rival suitors would present themselves to contest the succession to the property in dispute, and intricate cases would thus require to be disentangled by the newly constituted courts of law." [16] Jebb indicates that if a disinterested person were to survey this condition, he would see that the affected "people must be assisted to deal with an array of complex facts; they must be taught method." Furthermore, he would see that "they must be assisted to dispense with documentary or circumstantial evidence; they must be given hints on the best mode of arguing from general probabilities." [17] Evidently Corax observed what was going on in the courts; meditated over it; and eventually formulated his ideas on the proceedings into a systematic plan. The result was an "art of rhetoric" particularly adapted to forensic speaking, but also usable in deliberative and ceremonial address. Jebb has pronounced the work "the earliest theoretical Greek book, not merely on Rhetoric, but in any branch of art."

Nothing that Corax and Tisias wrote is extant. But the account of the "birth" of rhetoric is plausible. Following most wars or political upheavals, property rights become scrambled. And speakers skilled in the use of persuasive techniques, notably in the establishment of *probable* claims, must come to the aid of litigants, if some measure of rough justice is to be realized.

Corax's system of rhetoric [18] had three distinctive features, each of which contributed materially to the modern conception of speech theory: (1) It defined rhetoric as an art of persuasion, thus making it a practical art designed to elicit responses from hearers—responses consistent with the speaker's purpose. (2) Arrangement of materials received the first formal consideration. Speeches of persuasion were divided into five parts: a proem or opening, narration, argument, subsidiary remarks, and peroration. (3) Corax showed how *probability* applied to rhetorical invention. He demonstrated that it could be used in either of two ways. For example, "if a physically weak man is accused of an assault, he is to ask, 'Is it probable that *I* should have attacked *him?*' If a strong man is accused, he is to ask, 'Is it probable that I should have committed an assault in a case where there was sure to be a presumption against me?'" Aristotle refers specifically to Corax's *Art of Rhetoric* when he takes up the role of probability in spurious syllogisms, observing that this sort of argument shows what is meant "by making the worse argument seem the better." Bromley Smith believes

16 *Ibid.*
17 R. C. Jebb. *The Attic Orators.* London, 1893. I, cxvii.
18 Cf. the modern parallel to Sicilian demands in Hiram Motherwell's article "Hunger, Hatred, and Post-War Europe," *Harper's Magazine,* December, 1942, pp. 33–34.

Aristotle misinterpreted Corax's idea. It is certain, however, that in developing the doctrine of probability, Corax contributed an important idea to rhetorical theory: the principle that "likelihood of truth must always be present in order to be convincing."[19]

The name of Tisias is associated with Corax in this early work on rhetoric. In his independent treatise on the subject, Tisias continued the inquiry initiated by his teacher, especially on the theme of probability. Plato satirically refers to Tisias as one who "found out that probabilities were more to be valued than truths, and who by force of words made small things appear great, and great things small, and new things old, and the contrary new, and who discovered a concise method of speaking and an infinite prolixity on all subjects."[20]

Bonner reminds us that with the development of rhetoric in Sicily, about the middle of the fifth century B.C., oratory became a democratic tool. "Eloquence ceased to be a gift of the favored few; it became an art that could be taught."

INFLUENCE OF THE SOPHISTS AND THE RHETORS

The development of a strong Attic prose resulted largely from the "movement of ideas" known as rhetoric and sophistry. Croiset maintains that Corax, Tisias, and the Greek Sophists gave a practical and clever turn to oral expression, and that the writing of speeches followed as a natural consequence. Nascent rhetoric's "influence would probably have been small, if it had not met, at this very moment, with nascent sophistry, which took possession of it and increased its power for action tenfold." Jebb also speaks of the interacting influence of rhetoric and sophistry upon the development of Attic oratory. He speaks of these as ideas from the "East" and the "West," the former being the "Practical Culture of Ionia," and the latter, the "Rhetoric of Sicily." The Ionian contributors, including Protagoras, Prodicus, Thrasymachus, and Hippias—properly called Sophists—were most directly concerned in their teaching with dialectic, grammar, and even literary criticism; the Sicilian contributors, especially Corax and Tisias and, in a qualified sense, Gorgias, were more deeply engrossed in Rhetoric.

Jebb believes these men were really Rhetors, rather than Sophists. Gorgias' place in this classification is less clear because he represented an intermediate position, "differing from the Eastern Sophists in laying more stress on expression than on management of argument, and from

[19] Bromley Smith. "Corax and Probability." *Quarterly Journal of Speech Education*, 7:38 (February, 1921).

[20] *Phaedrus.* Trans. by Henry Cary. In *Works of Plato*. London, 1854. I, 345–346.

the Sicilian Rhetoricians in cultivating this faculty empirically, not theoretically."

It should be noted that some scholars have seen dangers in the Sophist point of view, citing its "indifference to truth, its aversion to all patient, sincere research, its great fondness for the jingle of words, its anxiety for persuasion rather than knowledge, its attachment to appearance . . ." Others, including George Grote and Henry Sidgwick, have contested the view that the Sophists were charlatans who taught an "art of fallacious discourse," regarding them instead as a profession without any "agreement as to doctrines." [21] Obviously, the word Sophist was indeterminate in meaning. Wilmer Wright points out that the name had been applied formerly "not only to orators whose surpassing eloquence won them a brilliant reputation, but also to philosophers who expounded their theories with ease and fluency." [22] Whether the Sophist position was good or bad matters little in this discussion; what is important is that the Sophists and Rhetors contributed to the art of discourse. In this, even the critics of the Sophists agree.

Protagoras and the Development of Debate

Protagoras, who flourished between 481 and 411 B.C., was the earliest of the Sophists. None of his writings is extant and so his style can be judged only through a study of Plato's dialogue. He was presumably the first to charge a fee for lectures, a practice which, in the words of Wilmer Wright, "is not to be despised, since the pursuits on which we spend money we prize more than those for which no money is charged."

Protagoras contributed to the development of forensic speaking through the use of commonplaces as bases for affirmative and negative argumentation, inventing "themes on which his pupils were to argue the *pros* and *cons*." This led Bromley Smith to call him the "father of debate." While such rhetorical dialectic as Protagoras developed makes possible the charge that its purpose was to enable the user "to get the better of an opponent in any sort of debate," reliable commentary confirms the judgment that the Sophist intended it otherwise. Theodor Gomperz observes that Protagoras

. . . was evidently unpractised in the interchange of question and answer which was founded by Zeno, and developed by Socrates, . . . His own favourite dialectic was obviously of a more rhetorical kind. He did not try to confuse his antagonist nor to goad him to contradiction by the method of

[21] Henry Sidgwick, *Lectures on the Philosophy of Kant and Other Philosophical Lectures and Essays.* London, 1905, p. 325.

[22] Philostratus and Eunapius: *The Lives of the Sophists.* Translated by Wilmer C. Wright. The Loeb Classical Library, 1922, p. 13.

curt interrogation. The chief weapon in his armoury was that of long speeches delivered successively to refute one another.[23]

Protagoras also was responsible for introducing grammar into the curriculum. He constantly stressed the importance of an eloquence based upon correct thinking and speaking. In this sense, he tried to articulate ethics, dialectic, and rhetoric into a common philosophical inquiry. He believed that through eloquence man could govern both himself and others, and hence become virtuous.

The Gorgian Influence on Style

Jebb comments on the difficulty of estimating Gorgias' contributions to rhetorical theory; "he was an inventor whose originality it is hard for us to realize, but an artist whose faults are to us peculiarly glaring." However, his place in the rhetorical continuum is assured. As Bromley Smith indicates, Corax laid the substructure of rhetoric, resting it upon orderly arrangement and persuasion by probability. Protagoras brought out the importance of debate, showing that every question has two sides, and that truth is a matter for each individual to decide. Then came Gorgias, gifted with the ability to weave words into artistic form, to create a style in prose. As "one of the founders of the art of Greek prose," Gorgias made a sound contribution to speechcraft, even though Plato's revelations of him in the dialogue bearing the same name might make us suspicious of the Sophists' craft.

Gorgias embraced a culture which, according to Jebb, "was founded neither upon Dialectic nor upon a systematic Rhetoric. Its basis was Oratory considered as a faculty to be developed empirically." Instead of devoting his attention to rhetorical invention, he concentrated his efforts on a study of language, for which he presumably had a brilliant gift.

In 427 B.C. Gorgias came to Athens from Sicily at the head of a Leontinian embassy to secure aid in the struggle against Syracuse. Evidently, the great teacher of rhetoric astounded the Athenians by his elegant language. Although the Greeks had always liked parallelism and other literary flourishes, Gorgias, "by his exaggerated use of these figures and his deliberate adoption for prose of effects that had been held to be the property of poetry . . . set a fashion that was never quite discarded in Greek prose, though it was often condemned as frigid and precious."

In addition to his use of rhythmical movements in prose, Gorgias set an example, as Philostratus observed, "with his virile and energetic style, his daring and unusual expressions, his inspired impressiveness,

23 Theodor Gomperz. *Greek Thinkers*. Trans. by Laurie Magnus. London, 1920. I, 465.

and his use of the grand style for great themes"; also "with his habit of breaking off his clauses and making sudden transitions, by which a speech gains in sweetness and sublimity; and he also clothed his style with poetic words for the sake of ornament and dignity."[24] Gorgias' name is associated chiefly with panegyric oratory, although even here his writing has been condemned for its "emptiness" of thought. "He very properly directed Attic prose into the path of nobility, precision, and oratorical harmony; but he could not follow along the path, because he had only the appearance of the force necessary—had nothing serious to say."

Despite Gorgias' desire to be what Croiset called a "virtuoso in discourse," some critics offer reasonable extenuation for the Sophist's excesses. Gomperz suggests that in times of great reforms in style, artificiality often creeps in—not only true in Gorgias' time, but during the Renaissance as well. He attributes this to two causes:

> The first is the natural desire at the beginning of a great literary epoch to strike out new modes of expression, the novelty of which is at first taken as the measure of their value. The second is the streaming and unbridled vitality of an age in which the young blood leaps with a wayward pulse, and the mind's activity is in excess of the matter at its disposal.[25]

On the other hand, Jebb maintains that if a style "is new and forcible, extravagances will not hinder it from being received with immense applause on its first appearance. Then it is imitated until its originality is forgotten and its defects brought into relief." Since "Gorgias was the founder of artistic prose . . . his faults are the more excusable because they were extravagant."

Minor Contributors

Prodicus, one of the so-called teachers of "an encyclopaedic culture," offers, according to Jebb, one point of contact with early rhetoric, namely, "his effort to discriminate words which express slight modifications of the same idea . . ." This influence asserted itself in the oratory of Antiphon. Bromley Smith remarks that the writers on philosophy refer to Prodicus only incidentally as the "sire of synonymy." But, adds Smith, it "is doubtful whether he himself would have posed as a philosopher, for he seemed rather to be a teacher of speech who employed in his lessons ethical illustrations and philosophical reasonings for the purpose of training his pupils to become good homekeepers and good citizens."

Hippias of Elis probably dealt with grammar and prosody in his

[24] Philostratus. *The Lives of the Sophists*, p. 31.
[25] *Op. cit.*, I, 479–480.

teaching, but his main contribution to rhetorical theory centers about his promotion of the canon of memory. Tradition has it that Simonides discovered the memory, but undoubtedly Hippias was the first man who "considered the training of the memory as essential discipline in the education of an orator." [26]

Thrasymachus of Chalcedon gave, in the opinion of Jebb, "a new turn to the progress of Attic prose." He made his contribution in the realm of style, founding a form of expression known as the "middle" style which was intermediate "between the Gorgian, or poetical, and the colloquial." Presumably, he was also skilled at representing the pathetic elements of discourse, as his utterances in Plato's *Republic* demonstrate. According to Jebb, Thrasymachus is noteworthy for two reasons:

> In respect to rhythm and to his 'conception' of a middle style, he may be considered as the forerunner of Isocrates. In respect to his development of the terse period, to his training in the forensic Rhetoric, and to the practical bent of his work, he is the pioneer of Lysias and of those orators, whether forensic or deliberative, who are in contrast with Gorgians and Isocratics.[27]

EARLY MASTERS OF EXPRESSION

Canon of the Attic Orators

The Canon of the Ten Attic Orators is essentially a critical yardstick. It reflects the attempt by several critics to set up a standard of excellence in oratory, and to provide distinguished models to justify the criteria.

The exact origin of the Canon is difficult to determine. Its emergence is associated, however, with the issue of Asianism vs. Atticism, and the attempt by zealous Atticists to establish their models of oratorical excellence as approved standards of artistic prose. The question of Asianism vs. Atticism is succinctly expressed by Jebb in these words:

> This controversy involved principles by which every artistic creation must be judged; but, as it then came forward, it referred to the standard of merit in prose literature, and, first of all, in oratory. Are the true models those Attic writers of the fifth and fourth centuries, from Thucydides to Demosthenes, whose most general characteristics are, the subordination of the form to the thought, and the avoidance of such faults as come from a misuse of ornament? Or have these been surpassed in brilliancy, in freshness of fancy, in effective force, by those writers, belonging sometimes to the schools or cities of Asia Minor, sometimes to Athens itself or to Sicily, but collectively called 'Asiatics,' who flourished between Demosthenes and Cicero? [28]

[26] Bromley Smith. "Hippias and a Lost Canon of Rhetoric." *Quarterly Journal of Speech Education*, 12:138 (June, 1926).

[27] *Op. cit.*, II, 426.

[28] *Ibid.*, I, lxi–lxii.

This, briefly, was the issue. But what of the names associated with the authorship of the Canon? Evidently Caecilius of Calacte, then living in Rome, was the first man to mention the Decade. His work, now lost, on the *Style of the Ten Orators* dealt with the prose distinctions of Antiphon, Isocrates, Lysias, Andocides, Deinarchus, Isaeus, Lycurgus, Hyperides, Aeschines, and Demosthenes. Interestingly enough, Dionysius of Halicarnassus, a friend and devotee of the same Atticist convictions as Caecilius, also at that time a resident at Rome, paid no heed to the Decade; and his own critical work listed only Hyperides, Lysias, Aeschines, Isocrates, Isaeus, and Demosthenes. Jebb believes that Dionysius knew of the Canon "but disregarded it, because it was not a help, but a hindrance, to the purpose with which he studied the Attic orators." In any event, Jebb asserts that "from the first century A.D. onwards the decade is established." Charles S. Baldwin comments on the tendency if not the "preoccupation" among ancient critics (also found among moderns) to effect "criticism by labels," as the classification of "ten canonical Attic orators" suggests.[29]

Contributions of the Attic Orators

How, specifically, do the early Greek orators contribute to our understanding of rhetorical theory? Largely in the sense of developing a truly conscious art of speech. As Jebb remarks:

The least gifted people, in the earliest stage of intellectual or political growth, will always or usually have the idea, however rude, of a natural oratory. But oratory first begins to have a history, of which the development can be traced, when two conditions have been fulfilled. First, that oratory should be conceived, no longer subjectively, but objectively also, and from having been a mere faculty, should have become an art. Secondly, that an oration should have been written in accordance with the theory of that art. The history of Greek oratory begins with Gorgias. The history of Attic oratory, properly so called, begins with Antiphon.[30]

The distinction between Athenian and Greek oratory, it should be added, is of some importance. In 353 B.C., Isocrates referred to this difference when defending his theory of culture:

You must not forget that our city is regarded as the established teacher of all who can speak or teach others to speak. And naturally so, since men see that our city offers the greatest prizes to those who possess this faculty, —provides the most numerous and most various schools for those who, having resolved to enter the real contests, desire a preparatory discipline,—and, further, afford to all men that experience which is the main secret of success

[29] Charles Sears Baldwin. *Ancient Rhetoric and Poetic.* New York, 1924, pp. 227–228.
[30] Jebb. *Op. cit.,* I, cvi.

in speaking. Besides, men hold that the general diffusion and the happy temperament of Attic speech, the Attic flexibility of intelligence and taste for letters, contribute not a little to literary culture; and hence they not unjustly deem that all masters of expression are disciples of Athens. See, then, lest it be folly indeed to cast a slur on this name which you have among the Greeks . . . that unjust judgment will be nothing else than your open condemnation of yourselves. You will have done as the Lacedaemonians would do if they introduced a penalty for attention to military exercises, or the Thessalians, if they instituted proceedings at law against men who seek to make themselves good riders.[31]

The Attic orators—and especially Antiphon, Andocides, Isocrates, Lysias, and Isaeus—were responsible for moulding, according to rules of art, a high type of literary prose; they were pioneers in refining techniques for use in forensic speaking. Most of these men were professional speech writers, and unusually successful ones. Lysias, for example, had a wide variety of people as his clients. He was highly skilled in adapting his speeches to the demands of the causes, occasions, and characters for whom they were intended. As Jebb observes, he was "a discoverer when he perceived that a purveyor of words for others, if he would serve his customers in the best way, must give the words the air of being their own."

The Attic orators established, or at least provided, patterns of style in oratory. Antiphon became a lively representative of the austere, dignified style of expression, which Dionysius described as follows:

It wishes its separate words to be planted firmly and to have strong positions, so that each word may be seen conspicuously; it wishes its several clauses to be well divided from each other by sensible pauses. It is willing to admit frequently rough and direct clashings of sounds, meeting like the bases of stones in loose wallwork, which have not been squared or smoothed to fit each other, but which show a certain negligence and absence of forethought. It loves, as a rule, to prolong itself by large words of portly breadth. Compression by short syllables is a thing which it shuns when not absolutely driven to it.

As regards separate words, these are the objects of its pursuit and craving. In whole clauses it shows these tendencies no less strongly; especially it chooses the most dignified and majestic rhythms. It does not wish the clauses to be like each other in length of structure, or enslaved to a severe syntax, but noble, simple, free. It wishes them to bear the stamp of nature rather than that of art, and to stir feeling rather than to reflect character. It does not usually aim at composing periods as a compact framework for its thought; but, if it should ever drift undesignedly into the periodic style, it desires to set on this the mark of spontaneity and plainness. It does not employ, in order to round a sentence, supplementary words which do not help the sense; it does not care that the march of its phrase should have stage-glitter or an artificial smoothness; nor that the clauses should be separately adapted to the length of the speaker's breath. No indeed. Of all such industry it is inno-

[31] *Ibid.*, I, cxxx–cxxxi.

cent. . . . It is fanciful in imagery, sparing of copulas, anything but florid; it is haughty, straightforward, disdainful of prettiness, with its antique air and its negligence for its beauty.[32]

Antiphon's style was somewhat too stately for forensic oratory and so other orators attempted to find a more flexible mode of expression.

In addition to contributing ideas on audience adjustment, Lysias became the representative of the plain style of oratory, according to the traditional division of grand, plain, and middle modes of expression. "The grand style aims constantly at rising above the common idiom; it seeks ornament of every kind, and rejects nothing as too artificial if it is striking. The plain style may, like the first, employ the utmost efforts of art, but the art is concealed; and, instead of avoiding it, imitates the language of ordinary life."

Jebb holds that Andocides' value is largely historical, although his power of graphic description was noteworthy. Isocrates is by far the most important figure of the group. We shall discuss his contributions in some detail later.

Isaeus represents "the final period of transition" from forensic to deliberative address. While trying, in his preparation of speeches for others in the law court, to hold more or less closely to the Lysian "plainness," he found that an oratory of "technical mastery" had developed in full force. According to Jebb, Isaeus vacillated between the two methods and hence became

. . . an able compromise—the first advocate who was at once morally persuasive and logically powerful, without either entrancing by the grace of his ethical charm or constraining by the imperious brilliancy of his art; one from whom Demosthenes learned the best technical lessons that Antiphon or Thucydides could teach, in a form, at once strict and animated, serviceable under conditions which they had not known . . .[33]

Isaeus thus bridges the gap in style and method between forensic speaking and the deliberative oratory which achieved such striking distinction at the hands of Deinarchus, Lycurgus, Hyperides, Aeschines, and, most illustriously, Demosthenes.

Relation of Deliberative to Forensic Speaking

Deliberative oratory in Greece, according to Jebb, did not enjoy an artistic development comparable with and independent of forensic speaking. On the contrary, the great deliberative speakers "are found to owe their several excellences as artists to models taken from the other two departments, to a Thucydides or an Isocrates, to a Lysias or an

[32] *Ibid.*, I, 22–23.
[33] *Ibid.*, II, 311.

Isaeus." Jebb gives three reasons to explain this unexpected circumstance. First, the Greeks were disposed to connect their practice of an art with a theory. It is believed that the earliest rules "could be applied with more precision and more effect in a speech for the law courts than in a speech for the ecclesia," a circumstance resulting from the fact that in forensic speaking the subject is fully and accurately known by the speaker beforehand. Furthermore, "the utmost clearness of division is imperative, and is obtainable by a uniform method; and the problem is, how best to use all the resources of persuasion in a limited space of time." And it is to be recalled that the earliest formulation of rhetorical theory dealt primarily with arrangement and probabilities.

Another possible reason derived from the Greek view that "the citizen was at once general and statesman. So long as this identity lasted, the men at the head of the State neither had leisure for the laborious training necessary to eminence in artistic oratory, nor felt its attainment to be of paramount importance."

Lastly, with the exception of the issues involved in the crises over Philip of Macedon and the restoration of Athens to leadership in the Naval League, there were no "moments favourable to a great political eloquence."

Lycurgus, Hyperides, Demosthenes, and less importantly, Deinarchus and Aeschines were the representatives of what Jebb calls a mature civil eloquence. Their fervid patriotism, practiced skill in speaking, and facility in applying artistic principles of rhetoric to speechmaking stamp them as the most finished performers of the period. They "continued, combined and perfected," to use Jebb's words, the best aspects of forensic speaking.

The Lysian tradition, which Isaeus had striven to ally with the frank strength of technical mastery, is joined by Hyperides to the Isocratic. The Isocratic manner is united, in Lycurgus, to that of the long-neglected school of Antiphon. That same archaic style, studied in a greater master, Thucydides, reaches, in Demosthenes, a final harmony with both the Lysian and the Isocratic; while Aeschines, the clever and diligent amateur, shows, by his failures, how much patient science was needed to bring a faultless music out of all the tones which had now made themselves clear in Attic speech. But, among these various elements, one is dominant. The Isocratic style has become the basis of the rest. That style, in its essential characteristics of rhythm and period, passed into the prose of Cicero; modern prose has been modelled on the Roman; and thus, in forming the literary rhetoric of Attica, Isocrates founded that of all literatures.[34]

Note may also be made that the deliberative orators were reluctant to publish their speeches. Overtones of such fears have resounded to modern times. Many speakers still feel that verbatim reporting and

[34] *Ibid.*, II, 433–434.

recording inhibit them from engaging in full and free expression, and subject them to improper charges and criticism.

UNION OF ORATORY AND CITIZENSHIP: ISOCRATES

"Then behold Isocrates arose, from whose school, as from the Trojan horse, none but real heroes proceeded . . ." This declaration by Cicero is no literary exaggeration, for few men in the history of rhetoric exercised such a pervasive influence over so many people for so many years as did Isocrates. In his comparison of the teachings of Aristotle and Isocrates, such an authority as Jebb clearly gives the advantage to the latter, not on the ground that Aristotle had an inferior grasp of the basic principles, but because Isocrates "was greatly superior in the practical department of teaching," as the host of orators and writers showing the imprint of his influence demonstrates. Jebb goes so far as to say, and George Norlin supports him, that as far as prose style is concerned the Isocratic pattern became the basis of all others.[35] Müller agrees that without Isocrates' "reconstruction of the style of Attic oratory," there could not have been a Demosthenes or a Cicero.

This man whom Cicero called the "father of eloquence" lived almost a hundred years—a century, as Norlin says, "of extraordinary vicissitudes and disenchantments." He was born in 436 B.C. and died in 338 B.C. Throughout that period he entertained a fixed devotion to Athens and to Hellenism "as a way of life." He was under the literary influence of Gorgias and probably had some personal association with him during later years. Although influences of this sort are difficult to trace, Norlin believes that Isocrates owed to Gorgias' teaching and example "the idea which he later made peculiarly his own, namely, that the highest oratory should concern itself with broad, pan-Hellenic themes, and that the style of oratory should be as artistic as that of poetry and afford the same degree of pleasure." Isocrates avoided, however, the "Gorgian excesses of style." He did not rely for effect upon striking words and phrases, but, instead, subordinated "the individual words and clauses to a larger unity." Furthermore, he exercised greater care in preparing the transitions and other parts of his discourses, severely subordinating them "to the design of an organic whole." Thus Jebb and Norlin agree that Isocrates made the artificially constructed Gorgian style artistic.

Unable to participate in Athenian life because of a weak voice, Isocrates spent about ten years writing forensic speeches for the law courts. In later life, however, he virtually renounced this phase of his oratorical activity.

[35] *Ibid.*, II, 434. See also George Norlin, trans., *Isocrates*. The Loeb Classical Library, 1928. I, xvi.

It is through his work as an educator and political thinker that his fame became established. About 392 B.C., he opened what Cicero calls the house which "stood open to all Greece as the *school* of eloquence." From the beginning he was successful; his pupils and others whom he influenced indirectly through his teachings and writings gave testimony to his skill in instruction. Unlike most teachers, he became surprisingly wealthy, although he apparently gave instruction to Athenian pupils free of charge and exacted fees only from foreigners.

Isocrates called his written works "orations" but they qualify as orations only in form and atmosphere. Isocrates never delivered a speech, and few of his discourses were written for delivery. Among his writings, six are definitely political: the *Panegyricus,* the *Philip,* the *Plataicus,* the *Peace,* the *Archidamus,* and the *Areopagiticus.* Two other works are largely educational in character: *Against the Sophists* and the *Antidosis.* Isocrates' theory of culture derives largely from these two contributions. In them he sets forth, as Jebb views them, the "manifesto" and "apologia," respectively, of his professional life. In *Against the Sophists,* he decries those "sophists" who teach Eristic—"a debased form of Dialectic, which consisted of disputation for disputation's sake in the field of ethics"; he condemns the teachers of rhetoric who ascribe too much importance to mere techniques; and he berates those writers who deal almost exclusively with the least elevated branch of rhetoric, namely, the forensic.

The *Antidosis* was prepared near the close of his life. To understand it fully, we must consider briefly the meaning of the title. Norlin tells us that the

. . . wealthier citizens of Athens were required by law to bear the expense of public services known as 'liturgies.' One of these was the 'trierarchy'— that of fitting out a ship of war. Anyone allotted to such a duty might challenge another to accept the alternative of either undertaking this burden in his stead or of exchanging property with him. Such a challenge was called an 'antidosis.' If the challenged party objected, the issue was adjudicated by a court.[36]

Evidently, Isocrates had just faced such a trial. In the *Antidosis* he adopts a factitious charge against his teachings and then presents the defense. The form of the production is, accordingly, similar to the Socratic *Apology.*

On the negative side, the *Antidosis* is, according to Norlin,

. . . a sharp attack upon the Athenian populace for confusing him with the other sophists . . . and it is . . . a criticism . . . of the narrowness or the impracticableness of the teaching of his rivals and of their failure to appreciate at its full value the broad and useful culture for which he himself

[36] Norlin. *Op. cit.,* II, 181.

stood. On its positive side, it is a definition of the culture or 'philosophy' which Isocrates professed.[37]

In the *Panegyricus*, Isocrates declares:

. . . if it were possible to present the same subject matter in one form and in no other, one might have reason to think it gratuitous to weary one's hearers by speaking again in the same manner as his predecessors; but since oratory is of such a nature that it is possible to discourse on the same subject matter in many different ways,—to represent the great as lowly or invest the little with grandeur, to recount the things of old in a new manner or set forth events of recent date in an old fashion—it follows that one must not shun the subjects upon which others have spoken before, but must try to speak better than they.[38]

And that is precisely what he attempted to do. As J. W. H. Atkins remarks, "It is in the new direction, the fresh impulse he gave to the study of rhetoric, that the influence of Isocrates in criticism is perhaps most clearly seen." Unlike the Sophists who were mainly concerned with forensic speaking, Isocrates formulated a new "cultural study" in which "fitting expression was sought for elevated themes, and the art of speaking or writing on large political topics was inculcated as a practical training for the active duties of a citizen." In fact, his "philosophy" was, as Jebb says, "the Art of speaking and of writing on large political subjects, considered as a preparation for advising or acting in political affairs." He proposed, in short, to link oratorical ability and statesmanship.

In Isocrates' theory of culture, speech is recognized as an indispensable skill. In the *Nicocles or the Cyprians*, he says:

. . . for if they [critics of eloquence] are really hostile to eloquence because there are men who do wrong and speak falsehood, they ought to disparage as well all other good things; for there will be found also among men who possess these [wealth and strength and courage] some who do wrong and use these advantages to the injury of many. Nevertheless, it is not fair to decry strength because there are persons who assault people whom they encounter, nor to traduce courage because there are those who slay men wantonly, nor in general to transfer to things the depravity of men, but rather to put the blame on the men themselves who misuse the good things, and who, by the very powers which help their fellow-countrymen, endeavour to do them harm.[39]

Later in the same statement, he pronounces what Werner Jaeger [40] has labeled "the hymn to speech":

[37] *Ibid.*, II, 182.
[38] *Ibid.*, I, 123–125.
[39] *Ibid.*, I, 79.
[40] *Paideia: The Ideals of Greek Culture.* Translated by Gilbert Highet. New York, 1944. III, 89.

For in the other powers which we possess we are in no respect superior to other living creatures; nay, we are inferior to many in swiftness and in strength and in other resources; but, because there has been implanted in us the power to persuade each other and to make clear to each other whatever we desire, not only have we escaped the life of wild beasts, but we have come together and founded cities and made laws and invented arts; and, generally speaking, there is no institution devised by man which the power of speech has not helped us to establish. For this it is which has laid down laws concerning things just and unjust, and things base and honorable; and if it were not for these ordinances we should not be able to live with one another. It is by this also that we confute the bad and extol the good. Through this we educate the ignorant and appraise the wise; for the power to speak well is taken as the surest index of a sound understanding, and discourse which is true and lawful and just is the outward image of a good and faithful soul. With this faculty we both contend against others on matters which are open to dispute and seek light for ourselves on things which are unknown; for the same arguments which we use in persuading others when we speak in public, we employ also when we deliberate in our own thoughts . . .[41]

Not only did Isocrates postulate a high function for speech; he also recognized the importance of the trinity of nature, art, and practice. "I do hold," he observed,

that people can become better and worthier if they conceive an ambition to speak well. . . . [And] if they are to excel in oratory or in managing affairs or in any line of work, they must, first of all, have a natural aptitude for that which they have elected to do; secondly, they must submit to training and master the knowledge of their particular subject. . . . and finally, they must become versed and practised in the use and application of their arts . . .

Accordingly, we agree with Jebb that it was Isocrates' intention to be practical—to avoid "barren subtleties."

A note of high ethical resolve is sounded in the Isocratic system. "I, myself," he indicates, "welcome all forms of discourses which are capable of benefitting us even in a small degree; however, I regard those as the best and most worthy of a king, and most appropriate to me, which give directions on good morals and good government . . ." In the *Antidosis*, he states that

. . . the man who wishes to persuade people will not be negligent as to the matter of character . . . for who does not know that words carry greater conviction when spoken by men of good repute than when spoken by men who live under a cloud, and that the argument which is made by a man's life is of more weight than that which is furnished by words. Therefore, the stronger a man's desire to persuade his hearers, the more zealously will he strive to be honourable and to have the esteem of his fellow-citizens.[42]

[41] Norlin. *Op. cit.*, I, 79–81.
[42] *Ibid.*, II, 239.

In short, he would direct his instruction to the training of "men who take advantage of the good and not the evil things of life."

Isocrates was also one of the first rhetoricians to enunciate the doctrine of propriety in speech, as this passage from *Against the Sophists* reveals:

For what has been said by one speaker is not equally useful for the speaker who comes after him; on the contrary, he is accounted most skilled in this art who speaks in a manner worthy of his subject and yet is able to discover in it topics which are nowise the same as those used by others. But the greatest proof of the difference between these two arts is that oratory is good only if it has the qualities of fitness for the occasion, propriety of style, and originality of treatment, while in the case of letters there is no such need whatsoever.[43]

Next to his refinement of an effective prose style, the most important aspect of his theory of culture dealt with the type of subject matter recommended for orators. Isocrates insisted upon the use of broad, noble themes—"discourses, not for private disputes, but which deal with the world of Hellas, with affairs of State, and are appropriate to be delivered at the Pan-Hellenic assemblies—discourses which . . . are more akin to works composed in rhythm and set to music than to the speeches which are made in court." He remarks that when

. . . anyone elects to speak or write discourses which are worthy of praise and honour, it is not conceivable that he will support causes which are unjust or petty or devoted to private quarrels, and not rather those which are great and honourable, devoted to the welfare of man and our common good. . . . In the second place, he will select from all the actions of men which bear upon his subject those examples which are the most illustrious and the most edifying. . . . It follows, then, that the power to speak well and think right will reward the man who approaches the art of discourse with the love of wisdom and love of honour.[44]

This aspect of the Isocratic conception affected not only rhetoric, but history as well. By stressing the idea of Greek unity, he altered the historical point of view, which previously had emphasized such sectional matters as the histories of particular states. Isocrates exercised this influence chiefly through two of his admirers and students, Ephorus and Theopompus, who, according to Cicero, "applied themselves to history by the persuasion of their master . . and never attended to pleading at all."

An interesting note on the Isocratic method of teaching relates to the saying of Isocrates, as told by Cicero,

. . . that he used to apply the spur to Ephorus, but to put the rein on Theopompus; for the one, who overleaped all bounds in the boldness of his

[43] *Ibid.*, II, 171.
[44] *Ibid.*, II, 337–339.

expressions, he restrained; the other, who hesitated and was bashful, as it were, he stimulated: nor did he produce in them any resemblances to each other, but gave to the one such an addition, and retrenched from the other so much superfluity, as to form in both that excellence of which the natural genius of each was susceptible.[45]

These, then, are some of the things for which Isocrates stood and which he taught. Although admittedly not a man of genius, he made significant contributions toward the establishment of a literary rhetoric designed to improve both the individual and the state. "In his school," Jebb concludes, "he did a service peculiarly valuable to that age by raising the tone and widening the circle of the popular education, by bringing high aims and large sympathies into the preparation for active life, and by making good citizens of many who perhaps would not have aspired to become philosophers."

PLATO'S INQUIRY INTO RHETORIC

Cicero relates an anecdote concerning the poet Antimachus who, when rehearsing a long selection before a special audience, was deserted by all except Plato. Undiscouraged, the poet cried out: *"I shall proceed notwithstanding; for Plato alone is of more consequence to me than many thousands."* [46] The remark, adds Cicero, "was very just."

Plato's reputation in contemporary thinking equals the high esteem accorded him by Antimachus. However, Plato's attitudes toward a technique of speechcraft present a seeming paradox; while satirizing and condemning the art as it appeared to him during his age, he also contributed to its development so materially as to lead such an eminent scholar as W. H. Thompson to call Aristotle's epochal *Rhetoric* in effect an expanded *Phaedrus.*

Plato and Isocrates were contemporaries. The one was, as Jebb points out, the great speculative thinker and seeker after truth; the other, "the great popular educator." "On the one side stands the true philosopher; on the other, the graceless anti-Plato who is continually insisting that his political rhetoric is philosophy." [47] Despite their differences, they probably were not in open hostility.

It was plain that Plato could not follow the doctrines of Isocrates, of the rhetoricians generally, and of the Sophists—particularly Gorgias, Protagoras, Hippias, and Prodicus. "The art of rhetoric," says Everett Hunt, "offered to the Athenian of the fifth century B.C. a method of higher education and, beyond that, a way of life. Plato attacked both.

[45] *De Oratore.* III, 9.
[46] *Brutus.* LI.
[47] *Op. cit.*, II, 36.

He gave rhetoric a conspicuous place in his dialogues because it represented in Athenian life that which he most disliked." [48] His reasons for disliking it no doubt were numerous. He evidently opposed the Sophists' practice of charging fees, and he opposed whatever part rhetoric had in influencing public opinion in Athenian life. As Hunt says, he "despised mere opinion almost as much as he did the public"—for even right opinion, in Plato's judgment, "fell far short of philosophic knowledge." He opposed a form of government not controlled by philosopher-kings, and, consequently, any government in which rhetoric was employed by merchants and others not possessed of "true wisdom" to decide questions of public policy; he opposed any discipline which, like rhetoric, attempted to get at true virtue by something short of true knowledge; and he opposed rhetoric for its very practical nature—for attempting to train citizens to function in a governmental system which was too faulty, so he thought, to warrant preservation. In short, Plato's indictment of rhetoric is incidental to his condemnation of the civilization he knew.

We are principally concerned with two of Plato's writings, the *Gorgias* and the *Phaedrus*. Like his other works, they are in dialogue form, with Socrates serving as the key spokesman and reflecting Plato's ideas with greatest fidelity. That the dialogue form makes the ready systematization of his point of view difficult is no doubt true. In the opinion of Alfred Weber and Ralph Barton Perry, however, Plato employs this form precisely because he has no finished system. The dialogue might be considered an unsuitable method of exposition if it concealed the philosopher's thoughts. But it hides nothing; form and content are here the same, and the dialogues of Plato present his philosophy in its psychological development.[49] The dialogue is an intriguing literary form. As Orville Prescott once remarked,[50] it permits the presentation of conflicting views "with the sole purpose of circling some important subject" and provoking independent thought. This note on the dialogue is of passing concern since a goodly number of rhetoricians, including Cicero, Tacitus, Alcuin, and Fénelon, employed the same method.

The *Gorgias*

The participants in the *Gorgias* are Callicles, Chaerephon, Socrates, Polus, and Gorgias. Despite the fact that the dialogue bears his name, Gorgias does not play an important part; he seems, instead, to be "the destined victim of the philosopher's dialectical prowess." In the strictest

[48] Everett Lee Hunt. "Plato and Aristotle on Rhetoric and Rhetoricians." *Studies in Rhetoric and Public Speaking.* New York, 1925, p. 3.
[49] Alfred Weber and Ralph Barton Perry. *History of Philosophy.* New York, 1925, p. 55.
[50] *The New York Times*, March 20, 1964.

sense, the *Gorgias* is more than a critical treatise on rhetoric; it also aims "to discuss the ethical principles which conduce to political well-being." [51] However, in his indictment of the Sophists' teachings Plato brings out an important distinction, as he sees it, between true and false rhetoric. Expressing high admiration for the dialogue, Cicero believed it revealed Plato as an "eminent orator" while he was in the very act of ridiculing orators.

In the *Gorgias*, Plato attacks the Gorgian kind of rhetoric as a way of life, in contrast with philosophy. He doubts that rhetoric is an art since it does not have its roots in universal principles. It deals in words, as do many other arts, and has no specific field of its own. Socrates inquires wherein rhetoric has its peculiar efficiency as contrasted, for example, with arithmetic:

> Just as if anyone should ask me respecting any of the arts which I but now mentioned: Socrates, what is the arithmetical art? I should say to him, as you did just now, That it is one of the arts that have their efficiency in words. And if he should further ask me, In reference to what? I should answer, In reference to the knowledge of even and odd, how many there may be of each. But if again he should ask me, What do you mean by the art of computation? I should answer, that this also is one of those arts whose whole efficiency consists in words. And if he should further ask me, In reference to what? I should answer, as they do who draw up motions in the assemblies of the people, That in other respects computation is the same as arithmetic, for it has reference to the same object, that is to say, the even and the odd; but it differs in this respect, that computation considers what relation even and odd have to themselves and to each other in regard to quantity.[52]

Later in the discourse, Socrates remarks:

> It appears to me . . . to be a certain study, that does not belong to art, but to a soul that is sagacious and manly, and naturally powerful in its intercourse with men. The sum of it I call flattery. Of this study there appears to me to be many other divisions, and one of them is that of cookery; which, indeed, appears to be an art, but, as I maintain, is not an art, but skill and practice. I also call rhetoric a division of this, and personal decoration, and sophistry, these four divisions relating to four particulars. If, therefore, Polus wishes to enquire, let him enquire, for he has not yet heard what division of flattery I assert rhetoric to be. . . .
>
> For rhetoric, in my opinion, is a semblance of a division of the political art. . . .
>
> . . . I wish to tell you, after the manner of geometricians, . . . that what personal decoration is to gymnastics, that is cookery to medicine: or rather thus, that what personal decoration is to gymnastics, that is sophistry to legislation, and that what cookery is to medicine, that is rhetoric to justice.

[51] W. H. Thompson. *The Gorgias of Plato*. London, 1871, pp. i–ii.
[52] *Gorgias*. Translated by Henry Cary. In *Works of Plato*. London, 1854. I, Secs. 12–13.

Plato also doubts that rhetoric can be an actual good to a person. Rhetoricians presumably attempt through words to achieve the good, but they lack insight and wisdom. Consequently, the supposed power of rhetoric goes for nought. Returning to the dialogue between Socrates and Callicles, we note:

Socr. Do the rhetoricians appear to you always to speak with a view to what is best, aiming at this, that the citizens may be made as good as possible by their discourses? or do they, too, endeavour to gratify the citizens, and neglecting the public interest for the sake of their own private advantage, do they treat the people as children, trying only to gratify them, without being in the least concerned whether they shall become better or worse by these means?

Cal. This is not a simple question that you ask me. For there are some who, looking to the interest of the citizens, say what they do; but others are such as you describe.

Socr. That is enough. For, if this also is twofold, one part of it will be flattery, and a base popular speaking, but the other will be honourable, namely, that which endeavours to make the souls of the citizens as good as possible, and strives to speak what is best, whether it be pleasant or unpleasant to the hearers. But you have never yet seen this kind of rhetoric.

Furthermore, the use of rhetoric in forensic situations is open to suspicion, as the conversation between Socrates and Polus suggests:

Socr. . . . Polus, what is the great utility of rhetoric? For, from what has been now agreed on, every one ought especially to beware of acting unjustly, for that, *if he does so act,* he will sustain great evil. Is it not so?

Pol. Certainly.

Socr. And if a man has committed injustice, either himself, or any one else for whom he has regard, he ought of his own accord to betake himself thither, where as soon as possible he will be punished, to a judge as to a physician, taking every pains lest the disease of injustice becoming inveterate should render the soul corrupt and incurable; or what must we say, Polus, if our former admissions are to stand? Do not these things necessarily harmonize with the former in this, but in no other way?

Pol. For what else can we say, Socrates?

Socr. For the purpose, then, of excusing injustice, our own, or that of our parents, or friends, or children, or country, when it acts unjustly, rhetoric is of no use to us at all, Polus, unless on the contrary, any one supposes that he ought especially to accuse himself, and afterwards his relatives, and any other of his friends, who may have acted unjustly, and not conceal the crime, but bring it to light, in order that he may be punished, and restored to health; moreover, that he should compel both himself and the others to lay aside fear, and with eyes shut, and in a manly way, deliver himself up, as to a physician, to be cut and cauterised, pursuing the good and the beautiful, without paying any regard to what is painful; if he has committed a wrong worthy of stripes, delivering himself up to be beaten, if of bonds, to be bound, if of a fine, to pay it, if of exile, to be banished, if of death, to die, being himself the first accuser of himself, and others his relatives, not sparing either himself or them, but employing rhetoric for this very purpose, that, the crimes being exposed, they may be freed from the greatest of evils, injustice. Shall we say thus, Polus, or not?

Pol. These things appear to me, Socrates, to be absurd; but it must be admitted, they accord with what was before said.

Socr. Must not, therefore, either our former conclusions be done away with, or these results necessarily follow?

Pol. Yes; such is the case.

Socr. Contrariwise, if it is requisite to do ill to any one, whether to an enemy, or any other person, provided only that he is not himself injured by his enemy; for this is to be guarded against; but if an enemy injures another, we should endeavour by all possible means, both by actions and words, that he may not be punished, nor brought before a judge: but, if he is brought before him, we should contrive so that our enemy may escape, and not suffer punishment: and if he has robbed us of a great quantity of gold, that he should not restore it, but should retain it and spend it on himself and his associates unjustly and impiously; and if he has committed an injustice worthy of death, we should contrive that he may not die, if possible never, but that he may be immortal in depravity, or if this cannot be, that he may live in this state for as long a period as possible. For such purposes, Polus, rhetoric appears to me to be useful, since to him who does not intend to act unjustly, its utility does not appear to me to be great, if indeed it is of any utility at all . . .

The *Phaedrus*

The *Phaedrus* has been described by Thompson as "a dramatized treatise on Rhetoric." Like the *Gorgias,* it ridicules the earlier and contemporary rhetoricians; it differs from it in its partial development of a "new and philosophical rhetoric," based partly on dialectic and partly on psychology.

Socrates and Phaedrus are the only participants in this dialogue. The treatment of rhetoric develops from a comparison of three speeches, one of which is represented as the product of Lysias, and the other two, the work of Socrates.

The Platonic conception of rhetoric presented in the *Phaedrus* is based upon the all-important dictum, issuing from Plato's belief that Lysias' speeches were lacking in logical resource, that good speaking derives from a speaker who knows "the truth of the subject on which he is about to speak."

In Hunt's orderly analysis of Plato's "ideal system of rhetoric," this point receives special attention. Hunt remarks, however, that the above principle "cannot be interpreted as an injunction to speak the truth at all times. It is rather to *know* the truth in order (a) to be persuasive by presenting to the audience something which at least resembles truth, and (b) to avoid being oneself deceived by probabilities. In order to know the truth, the rhetorician must be a philosopher." A second canon, as classified by Hunt, is that the "rhetorician must define his terms, and see clearly what subjects are debatable and what are not. He must also be able to classify particulars under a general head, or to break up universals into particulars." [53] In short, he must be a logician. As Socrates remarks in the *Phaedrus*:

The art, then, of arguing on both sides has not only to do with courts of justice and popular assemblies, but as it seems, it must be one and the same art, if it is an art, with respect to all subjects of discourse, by which a man is able to make all things appear similar to each other so far as they are capable of being made [to] appear so, and to drag them to light, when another attempts to make them appear similar and conceals his attempt.[54]

An acceptable rhetoric must also contain principles dealing with the arrangement of materials. ". . . Every speech," said Socrates, "ought to be put together like a living creature, with a body of its own, so as to be neither without head, nor without feet, but to have both a middle and extremities, described proportionately to each other and to the whole."

The next feature of the Platonic scheme requires that the rhetorician know the nature of the soul, that he be conversant with psychological data. After setting in order "the different kinds of speech and of soul, and the different manners in which these are affected, he will go through the several causes, adapting each to each, and teaching what kind of soul is necessarily persuaded, and what not persuaded, by particular kinds of speech, and for what reason." Socrates adds a note on this and the following consideration:

Since the power of speech is that of leading the soul, it is necessary that he who means to be an orator should know how many kinds of soul there are: but they are so many, and of such and such kinds; whence some men are of this character and some of that character. These then being thus divided, there are again so many kinds of speech, each of a certain character. Now men of such a character are for this particular reason easily persuaded by certain speeches, and persons of a different character are for these reasons with difficulty persuaded. It is necessary, therefore, that he, after having sufficiently understood all this, when he afterwards perceives these very things taking place in actions, and being done, should be able to follow them rapidly by perception, otherwise he will know nothing more than the very things which he formerly heard from his preceptor. But when he is sufficiently competent to say, what kind of person is persuaded by what kind of speeches, and is able, when he sees him before him, to point out to himself that this is the person and this the nature for which those speeches were formerly made now actually present before me, and to which these particular speeches are to be addressed, in order to persuade him to these particular things,—when he has acquired all this, and has learnt moreover the proper seasons for speaking and being silent, and again has made himself master of the seasonable

[53] *Op. cit.*, p. 37.
[54] Plato. *Phaedrus*, 97.

and unseasonable occasions for brevity, plaintiveness, and vehemence, and all the other several kinds of speech which he has learnt, then his art will be beautifully and perfectly accomplished, but not before. But whoever is deficient in any of these particulars, either in speaking, or teaching, or writing, and yet asserts that he speaks by art, is overcome by the person who will not be persuaded.[55]

In the fifth place, the rhetorician must, says Hunt in interpreting Plato, know the "instruments" through which the soul is influenced. These instruments are style and delivery.

"The art of writing will not be highly regarded," Hunt comments on the sixth point in his summary of Plato's scheme of rhetoric, "nor will continuous and uninterrupted discourse be regarded as equal to cross examination as a means of instruction." Evidently this is "Plato's way of saying that any method of attempting to persuade multitudes must suffer from the very fact that it is a multitude which is addressed, and that the best of rhetoric is unequal to philosophic discussion."[56]

Lastly, the "rhetorician will have such a high moral purpose in all his work that he will ever be chiefly concerned about saying that which is 'acceptable to God.'" Therefore, rhetoric "is not an instrument for the determination of scientific truth, nor for mere persuasion regardless of the cause; it is an instrument for making the will of God prevail. The perfect rhetorician, as a philosopher, knows the will of God."

Near the close of the dialogue, Phaedrus asks Socrates to repeat the requisites for artful preparation of speeches. Socrates' brief summary serves as the capstone to this section of our study:

Before a man knows the truth of each subject on which he speaks or writes, and is able to define the whole of a thing, and when he has defined it again knows how to divide it into species until he comes to the indivisible; and in like manner, having distinguished the nature of the soul, and having found out what kind of speech is adapted to the nature of each, he so disposes and adorns his speech, applying to a soul of varied powers speeches that are various and all-harmonious, and simple ones to a simple soul, before this is done, he will not be able to manage speech with art, as far as it might be done, either for the purpose of teaching or persuading. . . .[57]

ARISTOTLE'S INVESTIGATION OF RHETORIC

General Nature of the *Rhetoric*

Aristotle (384–322 B.C.) is perhaps the most highly esteemed figure in ancient rhetoric. His *Poetics* and *Rhetoric* compose an analytically thorough treatment of the two phases of writing and speaking which

[55] *Ibid.*, pp. 125–126.
[56] *Op. cit.*, pp. 37–38.
[57] *Phaedrus.* 141.

deal respectively with the "art of imaginative appeal" and the "art of daily communication, especially of public address." The *Rhetoric* is generally considered the most important single work in the literature of speechcraft.

Philosophical in its point of view and treatment, the *Rhetoric* nevertheless came late—too late, some would say—in the history of the subject. As contrasted with the school of Isocrates which produced many great orators, the school of Aristotle "in which Rhetoric was both scientifically and assiduously taught" produced but one orator of note, Demetrius Phalereus. This peculiar condition resulted not from a difference in mastery of principles, for Aristotle was clearly the superior in his understanding of the nature of speech. "Aristotle's philosophy of Rhetoric proved comparatively barren, not at all because Rhetoric is incapable of profiting materially by such treatment, but because such treatment can be made fruitful only by laborious attention to the practical side of the discipline." Jebb is not here referring to Aristotle's conception of rhetoric as a useful, practical art; rather, he is suggesting that Isocrates had the advantage because he taught by exercises, using his own writings as models. All in all, Jebb concludes that if Aristotle's *Rhetoric* had "been composed a century earlier, it would have been inestimable to oratory. As it was, the right thing was done too late." [58]

Cicero refers to this difference in the teaching methods of Isocrates and Aristotle, adding that when the latter "saw Isocrates grow remarkable for the number and quality of his scholars . . . [Aristotle] changed on a sudden almost his whole system of teaching. . . ." Thereafter he evidently "adorned and illustrated all philosophical learning, and associated the knowledge of things with practice in speaking." [59]

There is a legend that Aristotle's *Rhetoric* grew out of a feud between Isocrates and himself. However, Atkins is confident that if such a feud existed, it must have been forgotten with Isocrates' death, for Aristotle relies to some extent upon Isocratic doctrine. If an antagonism had existed, Aristotle probably would not have relied upon the teachings of his foe. It is to be remembered that he virtually ignored Demosthenes, doubtless for political reasons.

In many respects the *Rhetoric* accepts, elaborates, and systematizes doctrines set forth in the *Phaedrus*. Aristotle adopted the typically Platonic principles that the contemporary writers were treating rhetoric in an "unscientific" manner, that rhetoric was closely related to dialectic, and that the orator should be conversant with the laws of human nature as they affected the responses of hearers.

Despite Aristotle's evident reliance upon many of Plato's ideas, the

[58] Jebb. *Op. cit.*, II, 433.
[59] *De Oratore.* III, xxxv.

Rhetoric reveals, to use Hunt's expression, "certain philosophical and temperamental divergences from Plato." Hunt ventures the generalization that "Plato sought to reform life, while Aristotle was more interested in reorganizing theory about life. For this reason Aristotle's *Rhetoric* is largely detached from both morality and pedagogy. It is neither a manual of rules nor a collection of injunctions. It is an unmoral and scientific analysis of the means of persuasion." [60]

In Baldwin's opinion, the *Rhetoric*, though short, reveals the "full reach" of Aristotle's intelligence. The treatise is in three books, or sections. According to Baldwin's classification Book I deals with the necessities and opportunities of the speaker; Book II, with the audience; and Book III, with the speech itself. George Kennedy [61] says Books I and II deal with invention; Book III, with style and arrangement. Either division is tenable and useful.

It is of interest to indicate, in a preliminary way, that the *Rhetoric* emphasizes deliberative speaking more than the other types. Heretofore the writers on rhetoric had confined their treatments largely to courtroom oratory. Aristotle explained this by saying that forensic oratory offered more inducements to deal in "nonessentials," such as appeals to the feelings of the judges. Furthermore, said he, political oratory "admits less of malicious sophistry than judicial pleading, [and] is more widely interesting. . . ." [62] That his predecessors had stressed forensic oratory and that courtroom speaking as an art had matured somewhat earlier, were manifestly true. Aristotle's explanation of the cause, however, is open to doubt. Jebb's reasons, as set forth on pages 49–51, seem more plausible.

Book I

Book I opens with a definition: "Rhetoric is the counterpart of Dialectic." It may be described "as a faculty of discovering all the possible means of persuasion in any subject." [63] In other words, it enables a person to find suitable material for achieving persuasion in *any* field of inquiry, for, unlike geometry and certain other disciplines, Rhetoric does not have a subject matter of its own. But, as Baldwin interpolates, it does have subject matter "in every given case." "No less than logic, it is a means of bringing out truth, of making people see what is true and fitting."

The tool which the speaker finds best adapted to effecting persuasion

[60] *Op. cit.*, p. 44.

[61] *Op. cit.*, pp. 87, 103.

[62] *Aristotle's Treatise on Rhetoric*. Translated by Theodore Buckley. London, 1883, p. 6.

[63] *Rhetoric*. Translated by J. E. C. Welldon. London, 1886, pp. 1, 10. (Unless otherwise indicated, subsequent references in this chapter are to the Welldon edition.)

on public questions is the enthymeme, or approximate syllogism. Through its use in rhetoric (1) truth and justice may be guarded against falsehood and wrong; (2) discussion may be conducted where absolute proof through scientific argument is impossible of attainment; (3) both sides of a question may be surveyed; and (4) the self may be defended.

Aristotle draws a distinction between artistic and inartistic, or intrinsic and extrinsic, proofs:

> By 'inartistic' proofs I mean all such as are not provided by our own skill but existed before and independently, e.g. witnesses, tortures, contracts and the like; by 'artistic', such as admit of being constructed systematically and by our own skill; in fine, the former we have only to apply and the latter we have to invent.[64]

As Baldwin indicates, this is "a division of the springs of composition, the sources of effectiveness, into those that lie outside and those that lie inside of utterance, or presentation."

The components of artistic proof—or, as they are more popularly known, the modes of persuasion—constitute the basic pattern for much of the contemporary work in rhetorical criticism. According to Aristotle, the instrumentalities of rhetoric through which proof can be achieved are of three types:

> The instrument of proof is the moral character, when the delivery of the speech is such as to produce an impression of the speaker's credibility; for we yield a more complete and ready credence to persons of high character not only ordinarily and in a general way, but in such matters as do not admit of absolute certainty but necessarily leave room for difference of opinion, without any qualification whatever. (It is requisite however that this result should itself be attained by means of the speech and not of any antecedent conception of the speaker's character.) . . . Secondly, proof may be conveyed through the audience, when it is worked up by the speech to an emotional state. For there is a wide difference in our manner of pronouncing decisions, according as we feel pleasure or pain, affection or hatred; and indeed *the power of working upon the emotions* is, as we assert, the one end or object to which our present professors of the rhetorical art endeavour to direct their studies. . . . Lastly, the instrument of proof is the speech itself, when we have proved a truth or an apparent truth from such means of persuasion as are appropriate to a particular subject.[65]

Aristotle recognizes the importance of the audience in the total speech situation. "For a speech is composed of three elements, viz. the speaker, the subject of the speech, and the persons addressed; and the end *or object* of the speech is determined by the last, viz. by the audience." Since the audience is so essential to an understanding of a speech,

[64] *Rhetoric*, p. 10.
[65] *Rhetoric*, pp. 10–12.

Aristotle classifies the types of speeches according to the kinds of audiences to which they are given.

Audiences are necessarily either critics or judges; and if the latter, they may be judges of things lying either in the past or in the future. A member of the Public Assembly may be taken as an instance of a judge of the future, a member of the Courts of Law as an instance of a judge of the past; while one who judges merely of the ability *displayed in a speech* is the critic. It follows that there must necessarily be three kinds of rhetorical speeches, the deliberative, the forensic and the epideictic.

The remainder of Book I is devoted to an analysis of the topics, or common subjects, such as virtue, happiness, and the like, relating to deliberative, forensic, and epideictic fields. The *topics,* according to Aristotle, were the proper subjects of dialectical and rhetorical syllogisms, *i.e.,*

. . . such as are equally suitable to questions of justice, physics or politics, and to many questions of many different kinds. Such is e.g. the topic of 'the more or less,' or *of degree,* which will serve equally well to construct a syllogism or enthymeme about justice, physics or anything else, although these are subjects differing in kind. Special topics on the other hand are such as spring from the propositions appropriate to a particular species or class of subjects. Thus there are propositions in physics from which it is impossible to form an enthymeme or syllogism upon ethics, ethical propositions again from which it is impossible to form an enthymeme or syllogism upon physics, and so on through the whole range of subjects.

Book II

Whereas Book I dealt with "rhetoric as conceived," Book II of Aristotle's work is devoted to "rhetoric as received." The first part of Book II presents an analysis of the emotions, a study of the division and characteristics of people according as they are young, middle-aged, and old, and a survey of the traits usually observed in people of social preeminence, wealth, power, and good fortune. In this section, says Baldwin, "Aristotle is attempting neither an analysis of mental operations nor a science of human nature, but such a practical classification as may inculcate the habit of adaptation to the feelings of an audience."

Aristotle's approach to the study of audience behavior can best be understood through an examination of his analysis of a typical emotion. Regarding envy, for example, he says:

Nor is it difficult to see what are the occasions and objects of envy and the conditions under which we feel envious, envy being defined as a species of pain felt at conspicuous prosperity on the part of persons like ourselves in respect of such goods as have been already described, and this not with any view to our own personal advantage but solely because they are prosperous.
For people will be envious, if there are or if they think there are persons like themselves, like, I mean, in race, family, age, habit of mind, reputation

or possessions. Or if they only just fall short of having everything *which men can desire;* hence the envious disposition of persons who are engaged in important affairs or who are highly prosperous, as they fancy all the world is robbing them of their due. Or again if they have a permanent reputation for something, and especially for wisdom or happiness. Ambitious persons too are more liable to envy than the unambitious. Pretenders to wisdom are envious, as being ambitious of the credit of wisdom; and in general persons who are eager for reputation in a particular subject are envious in regard to it. Lastly, mean-minded persons are envious; for everything appears important to them. As regards the occasions of envy, the goods which provoke it have been already stated; for all achievements or possessions of which we covet the reputation or are ambitious, all things which arouse in us a longing for reputation, as well as all the various gifts of Fortune are practically without exception natural objects of envy, and of these such especially as we ourselves either desire or imagine we have a right to possess, or as by their acquisition confer a slight superiority or inferiority.

It is clear too who are the natural objects of envy, as they are implied in the statement which has just been made; they are persons who are near to us in time, place, age or reputation. Hence the saying,

'For to be kin is to be envious.'

We are envious too of people whom we are ambitious of rivalling, i.e. of such people as have been mentioned, but not of those who lived many ages ago or who are yet unborn or dead or at the ends of the world. Nor again, where there are people to whom we think we are far inferior or far superior, whether we depend upon our own opinion only or upon that of the world at large, have we the same feeling of rivalry in regard to them and in cases like theirs. But as this rivalry extends to those who are our antagonists in any competition or in love and indeed to all who aspire to the same things as ourselves, these will necessarily be the principal objects of envy; whence the proverb 'Two of a trade never agree.'

Again, we are envious of people who have attained a rapid success, if we have succeeded with difficulty or have not succeeded at all. Or of people whose possession of a thing or whose success is a reproach to us, such people again being near and similar to ourselves; for as it is evidently our own fault that we fail to obtain the good *which they obtain,* it is the annoyance of this fact which produces in us the feeling of envy. Or again of people who either naturally or by acquisition possess anything which naturally belonged to us or had been acquired by us; this is the reason why seniors are envious of their juniors. Lastly, people who have spent a large sum upon a particular thing are envious of those who have spent little upon it *with an equal result.*

We see now clearly the occasions upon which envious people experience a feeling of pleasure, the persons whose cases give rise to such a feeling and the conditions under which people experience it; for, whatever be the conditions the absence of which produces pain *at certain things,* their presence will produce pleasure at the opposite things. Hence if the audience has been brought to an envious condition of mind and the persons on whose behalf a claim to compassion or to good of any kind is advanced are such as have been described, *i.e. proper objects of envy,* it is evident that they will not meet with compassion at the hands of those who are masters of the position.[66]

[66] *Rhetoric,* pp. 158–161.

Since Aristotle condemned previous writers for giving too much attention to emotional proof, saying it was a "mere accessory," it may seem paradoxical that he then devoted such a large part of his own book to the same topic. Surely he did discuss at length the ways of producing impressions upon listeners through appeals to sympathy, indignation, and the like. E. M. Cope explains and justifies Aristotle's position. He points to the necessity of using emotional proof in order to meet the inclinations of certain hearers; but more importantly, he shows that its use is "scientific," provided it is regarded as *one of the three modes of proof* which form the art of rhetoric in the strict sense. Emotional proof may, however, be used unscientifically "by the introduction of considerations *ab extra* or beside the real point, arguments *ad hominem* and *ad captandum,* such as *direct* appeals to the feelings, impassioned and exaggerated language . . . or even, as was often done, the actual production of the widow and orphans or friends of a deceased person to excite compassion and blind the judges to the real merits of the case." [67] Cope concludes, therefore, that to some extent

. . . the study and analysis of human motives, passions, and feelings belong to rhetoric, and are indeed an essential part of it; and the rules derived from it may be applied *through the speech* to excite certain emotions in the audience: this may however be carried a great deal too far: and the fault that Aristotle finds with the Arts of preceding Rhetoricians on this point is that they confined themselves to this indirect mode of proving their case, and neglected the more regular and scientific mode of proof by logical enthymeme.[68]

In the remaining sections of Book II, Aristotle continues his analysis of the common topics previously mentioned, considering them largely from the point of view of their availability and of their effect on listeners. The following analysis will suggest the importance of the topics in Aristotle's scheme:

If there are two opposites, and the existence or production of one of them is possible, so presumably is the existence or production of the other. For instance, if a human being can be cured, he can also fall ill, inasmuch as the potentiality of opposites, *qua* opposites, is identical. Again, if there are two similar things, and one of them is possible, so is the other. Or if the more difficult of two things is possible, so is the easier. Or if the production of a thing in an excellent and noble form is possible, its production generally is possible, as the making of a fine house is harder than the making of a house. Again, if the beginning of a thing is possible, so is the completion of it, as no impossibility ever comes or begins to come into being; the commensurability e.g. of the diagonal of a square with its side cannot begin to come, nor ever does come, into being. Or if the completion of a thing is possible, so is its beginning; for whatever comes into being originates from a beginning. Or

[67] E. M. Cope. *An Introduction to Aristotle's Rhetoric.* London, 1867, p. 5.
[68] *Ibid.,* p. 6.

if the posterior in essence or in generation is capable of coming into being, so is the prior; thus if a man can come into being, so can a boy, the boy being prior in generation, and if a boy can come into being, so can a man, the man being *essentially* a beginning. Again, the objects of natural love or desire are possible, as in general nobody is enamoured or desirous of impossibilities. Again, the existence of any science or art implies the possibility of the existence or production of the objects with which it deals. The same is true of anything, if the origin of its production depends upon things which we can influence by force or persuasion, i.e. upon persons whose superiors or masters or friends we are. Again, if the parts of a thing are possible, so is the whole, and if the whole is possible, so in general are the parts; thus if it is possible to produce an instep, toe-cap and body of a shoe, it is possible also to produce shoes, and if it is possible to produce shoes, it is possible also to produce an instep, toe-cap and body. Again, the possibility of producing the genus as a whole implies the possibility of producing the species, and *vice versa;* the possibility e.g. of producing a vessel implies the possibility of producing a trireme, and the possibility of producing a trireme implies the possibility of producing a vessel. And of two things which are naturally interdependent if one is possible, so is the other; if double e.g. is possible, so is half, and if half, so is double. Again, if a thing can be produced without art and preparation, it can *a fortiori* be produced by means of art and careful pains; whence the lines of Agathon

> 'Of some must art be mother, some accrues
> To us of fortune or necessity.'

Lastly, if a thing is possible to inferior, weaker and less intelligent people, it is possible *a fortiori* to their opposites, . . .

On the subject of the impossible, it is evident that *the orator* has a stock *of topics* ready to hand in the opposites of those which have been mentioned.

The fact of a thing having occurred or not in the past is to be examined by the light of the following considerations. In the first place, if that which is less likely to have occurred has occurred, it would appear that that which is more likely has also occurred. Or if that which is usually subsequent has occurred, *it may be argued* that that which is usually antecedent has occurred, as e.g., if a person has forgotten something, that he had once learnt it. Or if a person had at once the power and the will to do a certain act, *it may be argued that* he has done it; for everybody acts, when he has the power to do what he wishes, as there is then no impediment to his action. The same is true, if he had the wish and there was no external obstacle, or if he had the power and was in an angry mood, or if he had the power and with it the desire; for it is a general rule that people, when they are eager to do a thing, actually do it, as soon as they have the power, if they are bad people from the lack of self-control, and if they are good, because the objects of their desire are honourable. Again, if it was a person's intention to do a thing, *it may be argued that he did it,* as there is always a probability that the intention was carried out. Or if all the natural preliminaries or means to a thing have occurred, *it may be argued that the thing itself occurred,* as e.g., if it lightened that it thundered too, and if a thing was attempted, that it was done. Similarly, if the natural sequel or end of anything has occurred, *it may be argued that* the preliminaries and means to it have occurred also, as e.g., if it thundered, that it lightened, and if a thing was done, that it was attempted. In all these cases the rule is sometimes one of necessity, and sometimes one of only general validity.

Arguments against the occurrence of an event in the past may evidently be derived from the topics opposite to these.

As to arguments in regard to the future, it is clear *that they may be derived* from the same sources. *It may be argued* that a thing will be done, if there is both the power and the wish to do it or if there is desire, anger and calculation combined with power. Accordingly it will be done, if one has an immediate impulse or an intention to do it; for what is intended is generally more likely to happen than what is not; or if it has been preceded by all its former natural antecedents; if e.g. the sky is clouded, there is a probability of rain. Finally, if the means to an end have happened, there is a probability of the end itself happening; thus the foundation of a house implies the house itself.

The topic of the greatness and smallness of things, in themselves and in comparison with each other and of great and small things generally, is evident from the remarks we have already made. . . . Hence as in each of the three kinds of Rhetoric the end proposed is good, whether expediency, honour or justice, it is evident that these must be the means of supplying the materials of amplification in each case. It is idle to look for anything more than this in regard to abstract greatness and superiority, particular facts being more important than general truths to the purpose *which we have now in hand.*[69]

Aristotle said there were two forms of proof common to the three types of oratory, namely, the example and the enthymeme.

It is proper in default of enthymemes to make use of examples as logical proofs, these being the natural means of producing conviction, but otherwise to make use of them as testimonies by way of a supplement to our enthymemes. For if we put them first, they resemble an induction, and induction is something inappropriate to Rhetoric unless in exceptional cases; but if we put them last, they resemble testimonies, and testimony is invariably persuasive. And from this it follows that, if we put them first, it is necessary to employ a considerable number of them, but if last, a single one is sufficient, as even a single credible witness is of service.[70]

Enthymemes are of two species: the demonstrative "which prove that a thing is or is not so," and the refutative, the difference between them being "the same as between a refutation and a syllogism in dialectics. The demonstrative enthymeme consists in drawing conclusions from admitted propositions, the refutative in drawing conclusions which are inconsistent *with the conclusions of one's adversary."*

The materials of enthymemes, said Aristotle, are probabilities, examples, demonstrations, and signs.

They are probabilities, when the conclusion is derived from such facts as either are or are supposed to be generally true; examples, when it is reached by induction from an analogy of one or several instances, the universal rule

---

[69] *Rhetoric*, pp. 176–180.
[70] *Ibid.*, p. 184.

being first ascertained and the particulars afterwards inferred from it; demonstrations, when it depends upon a rule which is necessary and absolute; signs, when upon general or particular statements which may be either true or false.

Among the topics of enthymemes are the following:

(1) One topic of demonstrative enthymemes may be derived from a consideration of opposites. *If we take any two things, of which one is said to be predicable of the other*, we have to consider whether the opposite of the one is predicable of the opposite of the other, upsetting *the original proposition*, if it is not predicable, and confirming *the original proposition*, if it is, as, e.g., arguing that self-restraint is expedient on the ground that licentiousness is injurious.

(2) A second topic is derived from the inflexions of the same stem, as that which is or is not predicable of one is or is not predicable of another. Thus *we may argue* that justice is not always good; else the word "justly" would always have a good sense, whereas to be justly put to death is the reverse of desirable.

(3) There is another arising from relative terms. *It may be argued that,* if 'honourably' and 'justly' are terms which are predicable of the action of the agent, they are predicable also of the suffering of the patient, and that if they are predicable of the command, they are predicable of its execution.

(4) Another topic is the argument from degree. Thus *it may be argued that,* if the Gods themselves are not omniscient, much less are men, meaning that if a condition is not realized, where it would be more natural, it will evidently not be realized, where it would be less so.

(5) There is another topic depending upon a consideration of the time. Thus Iphicrates in defending himself against Harmodius said, "Suppose that before the action I had demanded the statue in case of doing it, you would have granted it; now that the action has been done, will you refuse it? Do not then make a promise in anticipation, and defraud me of it, when you have received the benefit."

(6) Another topic consists in applying to our adversary's case anything that he has said about ourselves.

(7) There is another topic arising from definition, as, e.g., the *argument* that the supernatural must be either God or the work of God; but anybody who believes in the existence of a work of God necessarily believes also in the existence of Gods.

(8) Another topic springs from the various senses of a word. . . .

(9) Another [arises] from division, as, e.g., if there are three possible causes of a crime, and while two of these are out of the question, the third is not alleged even by the prosecution.

(10) Another topic depends upon induction. . . .

(11) There is another topic derivable from a judgment already pronounced upon the same or similar or an opposite question, especially if it is the judgment of all men and all times, or, failing that, of a large majority or of all or nearly all the wise or good or again of the judges themselves or of those whose authority they admit or whose judgment admits of no contradiction. . . .

(12) Another topic consists in *taking separately* the parts *of a subject, in considering* e.g. . . . what sort of motion the soul is, as it must be this or that.

(13) Also, as it happens in the great majority of cases that the same thing has consequences partly good and partly bad, another topic consists in using

the attendant circumstances as means of exhortation or dissuasion, accusation, or defence, eulogy or censure.

(14) There is another topic when in reference to two opposite things it is necessary to employ exhortation or dissuasion and to apply to both the method already described, the difference being that, whereas in the last case it was any two things, it is here two opposites that are contrasted.

(15) Again, as there is a difference between the objects which people praise in public and in secrecy, and, while they make a show of lauding justice and honour above everything else, they prefer expediency in their hearts, another topic consists in trying to use *an adversary's premises, whichever mode of sentiment he adopts,* to infer the opposite *of his conclusion;* for there is no topic of paradoxes so entirely effective as this.

(16) Another topic is derived from analogy of results. Iphicrates, for instance, resisted an effort to impose a public burden upon his son because of his size, although he was under the legal age, by saying, "If you reckon tall boys men, you will have to vote short men boys."

(17) Another topic consists in arguing identity of cause from identity of effect.

(18) There is another topic depending upon the fact that people do not always make the same choice at a later as at an earlier time, but often reverse it.

(19) Another topic consists in treating the conceivable as the actual reason of a thing existing or having come into existence, as in the supposition that a person would make a present in order to inflict the pain of taking it away.

(20) There is another topic common to forensic and deliberative oratory, viz. to consider the inducements and discouragements and the motives of acting or abstaining from action; for these are the conditions, the presence or the absence of which renders action desirable or the reverse.

(21) There is yet another topic in the case of things which are supposed to happen but are difficult to believe.

(22) Another topic, which is proper to refutation, consists in examining whether there is any contradiction in the series of dates, actions or words. . . .

(23) Another topic, where there is or appears to be a prejudice against particular persons or things, is to state the explanation of the circumstance which is unaccountable, as there is always something which accounts for the appearance.

(24) Another topic consists in arguing from the presence or absence of the cause the existence or non-existence of the effect; for cause and effect go always hand in hand, and there is nothing which has not a cause.

(25) Another topic is to consider whether it was or is possible to take a better course than that which the person either recommends or takes or has taken in action; for if this course has not been taken, it is evident that he has not done the deed, as nobody voluntarily and intentionally chooses what is bad.

(26) Again, if an intended action is inconsistent with some action already performed, there is another topic which consists in viewing them side by side.

(27) Another topic is to discover a ground of accusation or defence in any mistake that has been made.

(28) [And, finally] another topic is derivable from a play on names. . . .[71]

[71] *Ibid., passim,* 194–211.

Refutative argument may be carried to successful completion through the use of counter-syllogism or through the introduction of an objection.

It is clear that the counter-syllogisms may be constructed out of the same topics as the syllogisms of which we have spoken; for it is the common opinions of the world which form the materials of syllogisms, and opinions are often contradictory. Objections on the other hand . . . may be adduced in four different ways, viz., either from the enthymeme of your adversary himself, or from analogy, or from antithesis, or from a previous decision.

Thus Aristotle devotes a large part of Book II to the logical mode of persuasion. At the same time he urges the speaker to analyze carefully the audience for which the arguments are intended.

It should be borne in mind that, whereas Plato "held that the rhetorician must know the Truth, because probability was engendered by a likeness to Truth," Aristotle made probability the essential substructure of his rhetorical system. The topics mentioned in Books I and II were statements designed chiefly to bring to mind quickly the several arguments usable for either side of a case. They constituted, in Hunt's estimation, a "sort of rhetorician's first aid. They were to assist him in producing immediately, and perhaps without any special knowledge of the subject, a plausible argument upon either side of a debatable proposition."

Aristotle's substitution of the enthymeme for the formal syllogism, and the example for the induction—made necessary by the failure of audiences to follow close reasoning—was additional evidence, according to Hunt, that Aristotle recognized the "merely contingent and probable nature of rhetoric." "The enthymeme was a rhetorical syllogism; that is, a syllogism drawn, not from universal principles belonging to a particular science, but from probabilities in the sphere of human affairs."

Book III

In Book III—which Kennedy feels gives "something of the impression of an afterthought"—Aristotle deals first with delivery, linking it in a general way with style. The concept receives only brief examination. He indicates somewhat apologetically that delivery is not properly considered an elevated topic of inquiry.

Still as the entire study of Rhetoric has regard to appearance, it is necessary to pay due attention to declamation, not that it is right to do so but because it is inevitable. Strict justice, indeed, if applicable to Rhetoric, would confine itself to seeking such a delivery as would cause neither pain nor pleasure. For the right condition is that the battle should be fought out on the facts of the case alone; and therefore everything outside the *direct* proof

72 *Op. cit.*, p. 103.

is *really* superfluous; although extraneous matters are highly effective, . . . owing to the depraved character of the audience.[73]

The art of delivery, as Aristotle sees it, "consists in understanding (1) the proper use of the voice for the expression of the several emotions, *i.e.*, when it should be loud or low or intermediate, (2) the proper use of the accents, *i.e.*, when the tone should be acute or grave or intermediate, and (3) the rhythms suitable to each emotion." Although some perceive in Aristotle's treatment a certain philosophic contempt for delivery, Baldwin doubts that such an impression can be confirmed.

Style should be characterized by perspicuity, purity, dignity, and propriety. Aristotle analyzes each of these elements. As for the stylistic structure, it should be "neither metrical nor wholly unrhythmical. If it is the former, it lacks persuasiveness from its appearance of artificiality, and at the same time diverts the minds of the audience from the subject by fixing their attention upon the return of the similar cadence. . . ."

With an eye to adapting style, in the broad sense, to the demands of oratory, Aristotle remarks:

> The style of political oratory is precisely similar to scene-painting. For the greater the crowd, the more distant is the view: hence it is that in both a finished style appears superfluous and unsuccessful. The forensic style on the other hand is more finished, especially when addressed to a single judge; for he is least subject to rhetorical influences, as he can take a more comprehensive view of what is germane to the case or alien to it and, as there is no actual contest, is not prejudiced in his judgment. Accordingly it is not the same orators who succeed in all the different styles of Rhetoric; but, where there is most opportunity for declamation, there is the least possibility of finish. And this is the case where voice, and especially where a loud voice, is required.
>
> The epideictic style is best suited to literary purposes, as its proper function is to be read; and next to it the forensic style.[74]

Book III closes with a brief analysis of oratorical structure. "A speech has two parts. It is necessary first to state the case and then to prove it." These are the so-called "indispensable" parts, but if more are added, Aristotle indicates, "they must not exceed four, viz. exordium, exposition, proof and peroration." As for the functions of the exordium, they correspond to those of the prologue in poetry and prepare the way for what is to follow. The peroration has four objects: "to inspire the audience with a favourable opinion of yourself and an unfavourable one of your adversary, to amplify or depreciate the subject, to excite the emotions of the audience and to recall the facts to their memory."

[73] *Rhetoric,* p. 226.
[74] *Rhetoric,* p. 273.

Philosophical Significance

We have presented this summary because Aristotle's *Rhetoric* is the true pioneer in the field, the one upon which practically all subsequent treatises rely to a considerable extent. It is for us the first orderly, systematic attempt to set down the principles of the art of public speaking. The *Rhetoric* provides a philosophically sound *rationale* of the subject. It embraces a philosophy of discourse relatively free from pedantry and deeply rooted in the basic tenets of the speaking art. Its peculiar distinction, apart from the body of principles which it classifies, derives from four fundamental postulates upon which the work rests:

The first of Aristotle's basic postulates deals with the nature of rhetoric. He assumed that it was a useful art, operating in the social medium for the purpose of *doing* something. He conceived of the art in purely functional terms. This is in keeping with Aristotle's general point of view, confirming John MacCunn's interpretation that "He who would win the harper's skill must win it by harping; he who would write, by writing; he who would heal the sick, by healing them. In these, as indeed in all the arts, *faculty is begotten of function,* and definite proclivity comes of determinate acts." [75] As it relates to the subject of our discussion, rhetoric enables a person (1) to maintain truth against falsehood; (2) to advance discussion where definitive proofs are impossible of attainment; (3) to expose irregularities in argument as well as see both sides of a controversy; and (4) to defend himself with reason as well as with physical strength. In other words, speech is an instrument of social adaptation.

The postulate that rhetoric is a useful social tool has an important implication. A rhetoric of simple display, of hollow ostentation, is definitely foreign to this concept. There is no glorification of form to the neglect of substance. Speaking is not declamatory utterance divorced of social consequences. It is, instead, a practical skill serving as a direct link between the individual and his immediate social environment on the one hand and the larger political pattern of the state on the other. Logically, such a position argues for a close relation between the speaking art and the allied fields of social inquiry. The Aristotelian system provides for precisely such an interrelation.

Aristotle also held that rhetoric could be taught. In making this assumption, he believed, first, that rhetoric was composed of a body of material yielding to systematic treatment, and second, that it was possible through practice to develop speaking skills. He observed that all

[75] "The Ethical Doctrine of Aristotle." *International Journal of Ethics,* 16:301 (April, 1906).

men use speech "either at random or through practice and from acquired habit." Since both ways were possible, the subject could be handled systematically, thus permitting an inquiry into "the reason why some speakers succeed through practice and others spontaneously. . . ." Taking a body of more or less unrelated facts, Aristotle moulded it into a system the essential pattern of which may be found in practically every contribution worthy of the name published since that time.

The *Rhetoric* presents unmistakable evidence of Aristotle's inquiring mind. Everywhere we perceive the attempt to determine the causes of things. Aristotle realized that some speakers got favorable responses while others did not. He recognized the necessity of systematizing the discoverable principles in order that they might be applied to practice. While Plato had, in a very general way, shown *how* the rhetorician could do certain things, Aristotle gave orderly direction to the principles and observations relevant to the art. According to W. Rhys Roberts, no one has, either before or since, "enriched the subject with so great a store of acute observations on the workings of the ordinary mind and heart." [76]

Charles Woolbert used to say that there is only one rule in public speaking and that is that there are no rules. While Aristotle referred to the systematic principles of rhetoric and to the means and methods of succeeding in speech, he, too, doubted the advisability of setting up formal rules. His emphasis upon the variable nature of the speaker, subject, and audience is adequate evidence to reveal this point of view. He did not conceive of the speaking art as a stereotyped system. He saw in it an instrument for making many and diverse adjustments to a multitude of social conditions.

Aristotle was convinced that the random performances of speakers could be improved through the study and application of orderly principles. In this he was reflecting the spirit of Greek education. Thomas Davidson tells us that "to the realization of their ideal in any individual the Greeks conceived three conditions to be necessary, (1) a noble nature, (2) persistent exercise or training in right action, (3) careful instruction. If any one of these was lacking, the highest result could not be attained." [77] The primary function of imposing habit or exercise upon original nature and finally crowning it with instruction was twofold: first, "to make action free, by making it rational," and second, "to make possible an advance to original action."

Aristotle's "unmistakable emphasis upon habituation" needs no discussion. Whether he was concerned with the formation of moral character or the refinement of a technique in speaking, he was alike convinced, especially during the later years of his teaching, that there was no sub-

[76] "Aristotle on Public Speaking." *Fortnightly Review,* 122; 204 (August 1, 1924).
[77] *Aristotle and Ancient Educational Ideals.* New York, 1902, p. 9.

stitute for exercise or practice. In fact, there are responsible authorities who believe that the value of exercise was "far better understood by the ancients than by the moderns."

The importance of Aristotle's assumption that rhetorical refinements result from practice can scarcely be overemphasized. Modern pedagogical method rests squarely upon that base. Like our contemporaries, Aristotle saw certain shortcomings in the original nature of many speakers. And as John MacCunn has said, "it is precisely the shortcomings of nature that are the educator's opportunity. Here, as elsewhere, art must remedy the imperfections of nature. . . ." [78] By demonstrating that rhetoric was a teachable art, Aristotle established a tenet upon which all subsequent systems of speech instruction depend and from which present training derives much of its just claim to dignity in the scheme of learning.

The two foregoing postulates refer chiefly to the purpose and the scope of rhetoric. The third basic assumption involves both purpose and method. Aristotle believed that a sound projection of rhetorical theory was based upon the doctrine of the Mean. This concept reveals the true value of practice and instruction in speech by providing a standard of artistic excellence. The Greek mind sought *proportion* in all human manifestations. Aristotle urged an avoidance of both excess and deficiency. Although not stated as plainly as in the *Nicomachean Ethics,* the doctrine of the Mean permeates the *Rhetoric* and gives it an artistic as well as a practical point of view. Concretely stated, the doctrine asserts itself in the speech proper; the quality of an address is directly related to its quantitative proportions. Certain quantitative relations must exist if a product partaking of perfection is to develop. In the words of W. D. Ross, "there is a right amount of each, a right time, a right manner, right objects for each." [79] What these right amounts are, will depend upon the speaker and the social circumstances.

Aristotle states the doctrine of the Mean when he says:

. . . now people tell us, ridiculously enough, that the narration should be rapid. And yet I would say, as did one to a baker, who inquired 'whether he should knead his bread hard or soft,'—'What,' said he, 'is it then impossible to knead it properly?' And so here [in rhetoric a mean is to be observed]. For one should not narrate at too great length, just as he should not make too long an exordium, nor state his proofs [too fully]. For neither in this case does propriety consist either in rapidity or conciseness, but in a mean betwixt both: and this is the stating just so much as will make the matter clear. . . . [80]

[78] MacCunn. *Op. cit.,* p. 300. (Cf. note 75.)
[79] *Aristotle.* London, 1923, p. 195.
[80] *Rhetoric.* Translated by Theodore Buckley. London, 1883, pp. 258–259.

This standard, however difficult to define because of the varying conditions in different speech situations, makes balance, proportion, and freedom from extremes the ideals toward which practice and instruction should lead. In a general sense, the current practice of adapting speech programs to the individual needs and capacities of students is essentially a corollary of Aristotle's Relative Mean. This Mean, with relation to ourselves, said Aristotle,

. . . is neither too much nor too little for us. But this is not one and the same to all; as, for example, if ten is too many, and two too few, six is taken for the absolute mean, for it exceeds two as much as it is exceeded by ten. But this is the mean according to arithmetical proportion. But the relative mean is not to be taken in this manner; for it does not follow, that if ten pounds are too much for any person to eat, and two pounds too little, the training-master will prescribe six pounds; for perhaps this is too much or too little for the person who is to eat it. For it is too little for Milo, but too much for one just commencing gymnastics; and the case is similar in running and wrestling. Thus, then, every person who has knowledge shuns the excess and the defect, but seeks for the mean, and chooses it; not the absolute mean, but the relative one.[81]

Speech teachers point out today that much of their instruction applies with reference to *particular cases*. Too much and too little are purely relative considerations. Hence our modern instruction rests upon what in reality amounts to a doctrine of the Mean.

The last assumption or postulate of the Aristotelian system deals with the function of rhetoric in the body politic. While any set of rhetorical principles may be open to the charge of being partly inconsistent with the best interests of an enlightened state because unprincipled speakers will always be able to use legitimate techniques in an irregular way, Aristotle came as near giving a true ethic of discourse as any writer, including Isocrates.

Aristotle assumed that the logical mode of persuasion was the only true constituent of the art of rhetoric. In his system the appeal to reason or rational conduct receives primary emphasis. Being a discerning analyst, however, he knew the elements of rhetorical effectiveness. So it is quite natural that the so-called "accessories"—the emotional proofs— are given reasonable prominence in the *Rhetoric*. The inescapable conclusion, however, is that, by and large, Aristotle was concerned with giving effectiveness to truth.

This conclusion agrees with Aristotle's conception of the social order in which the speaker performed. He believed that man was a social being with definite relations to the political community. Hence his idea of the field of Politics was fairly comprehensive. "Politics" was virtually

81 *The Nichomachean Ethics of Aristotle*. Translated by R. W. Browne. London, 1850. II, vi, 4–5 (pp. 43–44).

an omnibus term, embracing Economics and, as its groundwork, Ethics. The ideal community was a society held together by moral and rational principles. Moral virtue in the individual was indispensable to the establishment of reasonable institutions in the body politic.

Aristotle's basic philosophy did not tolerate compromise with the moral integrity and design of the speaker. Perhaps when Aristotle enters upon his analysis of arguments, he becomes at times more concerned, as Everett Hunt suggests, with "rhetorical effectiveness" than with "moral justifiability." That is the point, however, at which we encounter what may be the internal contradiction of any ethics of discourse. If rhetoric is concerned with securing responses, however enlightened in purpose, it is evident that techniques and devices capable equally of honorable and evil use will receive systematic treatment. Certain of the "accessories" will creep in. The truth, if that word may be used, must sometimes be made more palatable; and an increase in palatability may mean a decrease in rigidly rational content. Aristotle recognized this fact fully when he discussed delivery. It is right, he said, "that the contest be carried on by means of the facts themselves. . . ." But a defect in the art of rhetoric and in the hearers made such a condition impossible. Rhetoric aimed at ends different from those of geometry, for example, and it often dealt with individuals whose intellectual accomplishments were limited. Consequently, emotional flourishes were sometimes necessary. This does not mean that Aristotle either condoned or recommended the use of guile and suspiciously crafty artifice in speaking situations. It would seem that a fair reading of the *Rhetoric* reveals no significant departures from the high moral principles enunciated in the *Nicomachean Ethics*.

That the man who follows Aristotle's suggestions regarding the speaking art will be shrewd and perhaps artfully adroit in manipulating rhetorical instruments, is certainly true; that he will be culpably crafty, cannot be fully demonstrated. The Aristotelian position is clearly revealed in the sixth book of the *Ethics*. Aristotle refers to the faculty of cleverness "the nature of which is to be able to do, and to attain, those things which conduce to the aim proposed." He then goes on to say that "if . . . the aim be good, the cleverness is praiseworthy; but if it be bad, it becomes craft." [82] In other words, the Aristotelian thesis postulates that "cleverness and character must *strike alliance*." [83]

It would seem, therefore, that Aristotle's emphasis upon logical proof as the essential mode of persuasion, together with his insistence upon the prudent use of the instruments by means of which ends are attained, constitutes the basis of an acceptable standard for a twentieth century

[82] *Ethics,* VI, xii, 8 (p. 173).
[83] MacCunn. *Op. cit.,* p. 298; cf. *Ethics,* VI, xii, 10.

philosophy of rhetoric. Aristotle's principal contribution lies not alone in his development of rhetorical details, important as they are, but also in his broad, philosophic conception of the place of rhetoric in the scheme of learning. His *Rhetoric* continues to impress students as a succinct, timelessly relevant treatise. It represents a dignified and intellectually respectable statement of the place of Speech in the field of knowledge.

SUMMARY

The tradition of rhetoric is rich in names and deeds of distinguished men from the earliest period of recorded history. A part of that tradition rests upon oral testimony communicated from generation to generation by people who cherished the dignity and the value of an art of rhetoric. But, in the main, the sources of the subject are fairly specific, traceable in writing, and open to investigative study. Many valuable writings, regrettably, are not extant; others have unquestionably suffered from what Samuel Johnson once called the "pest of speech"—frequency of translation. These shortcomings notwithstanding, we can view the history of the subject over the span of centuries and observe the signal contributions that have illuminated the way for speakers and critics. Only with this historical perspective can we hope to understand and appreciate the theory upon which the art of speaking rests today, and from which the critic gets both his point of view and his methodology.

Long before there was a system of speechcraft, there were speakers. Ideas had to be communicated, either for reasons of practical necessity or of primitive artistic desire. The first systematic art of speaking dates from the period when Corax devised his scheme to meet the needs of the dispossessed people who returned to Sicily to reclaim their lands following the expulsion of the tyrants. The Sophists and the Rhetors of ancient Greece, the great orators of the Attic canon, and the writings of Isocrates on a newer conception of rhetoric—all contributed to the refinement of the art and to the development of an effective prose style.

In Plato we find one of the most acute critics of rhetorical theory, as well as one of the most brilliant contributors to the art. In his ideal system—never as completely developed as we should like, but still sufficiently clear to make the way easier for later theorists—he postulates the quest for truth and familiarity with the souls of men as cardinal features of an enlightened speechcraft. The influence of these tenets upon subsequent contributions was incalculably large.

With Aristotle's *Rhetoric*, the subject of speechmaking achieved genuine maturity and dignity. In three short books, Aristotle stated the principles of the art with a succinctness and accuracy which even today elicit the unqualified respect of scholars everywhere. The *Rhetoric* is the most literate and forthright analysis of the art of speaking in print. Knowing it, one knows much of what was written on the subject after Aristotle's time, and is in a favored position to appraise the theory and criticism of public address to this very hour.

EXERCISES

1. Distinguish among the following terms: rhetoric, poetics, dialectic, and philosophy.
2. Distinguish among the following: rhetorician, sophist, Attic orator, and philosopher.
3. Compare and contrast the English term "orator" with the Latin term *orator* and the Greek word *rhetor*. Also find several definitions of the word *rhetoric*. What is the relationship of rhetoric to oratory? Contrast the classical meaning of the term rhetoric with modern meaning. (See definition in the *Columbia Encyclopedia* or *Encylopaedia Britannica*.)
4. Review the evidence for the assertion that "Ancient oratory was a fine art."
5. Study carefully Pericles' "Funeral Oration." What does this speech tell us about Athenian life and aspirations? The speech is found in Houston Peterson's *A Treasury of the World's Great Speeches* (New York, 1954).
6. Prepare an oral report on the contribution of one of the sophists of the fourth and fifth century B.C.
7. Prepare an oral report on the influence on Athenian life of one of the following: Socrates, Plato, Isocrates, and Aristotle. The class may wish to organize a symposium in which each figure is analyzed.
8. Prepare a class symposium on the subject: "Socrates Deserved His Fate" or "Athens Was on Trial—Not Socrates."
9. Explain the relation of deliberative to forensic and epideictic oratory in the history of Greek public address.
10. Compare and contrast Demosthenes' and Aeschines' speeches "On the Crown."
11. Compare Plato's *Phaedrus* and Aristotle's *Rhetoric* as to (*a*) relationship of rhetoric to truth, (*b*) relationship of rhetoric to dialectic, and (*c*) relationship of rhetoric to philosophy.
12. To what extent can the rhetorician be regarded as representative of the culture of his time? To what extent was Isocrates successful in establishing that concept?
13. Prepare a paper on the concept of the "golden mean."
14. Discuss the relation of history to rhetoric. Assess the reflections of the principal contributors to rhetorical theory apropos of this theme.
15. Comment on this statement by Jebb: "The broadest characteristic of modern oratory, as compared with ancient, is the predominance of a sustained appeal to the understanding."
16. Comment on Lord Brougham's observation: "There is hardly one of the political or forensic orations of the Greeks that might not be delivered in similar circumstances before our senate or tribunals."
17. Do you believe that a union of statesmanship and oratory, as envisaged by Isocrates, is possible in the modern world? As a background reading,

examine John F. Kennedy's "Education of an American Politician," delivered on February 19, 1957, and reprinted in the *Congressional Record*, February 21, 1957.

18. Oratorical literature contains some great speeches of self-vindication: Demosthenes' "On the Crown," Plato's "Apology," and Isocrates' "Antidosis," among them. Compare one of these statements with a modern counterpart such as those given in recent years by David Lilienthal, Richard Nixon, Douglas MacArthur, to mention but a few.

19. Against the background of this chapter, comment on Bower Aly's "Rhetoric: Its Natural Enemies," *The Speech Teacher*, 17:1–10 (January, 1968).

READINGS

J. W. H. ATKINS. *Literary Criticism in Antiquity: A Sketch of Its Development*, vol. I, *Greek*. Gloucester, Massachusetts, Peter Smith, 1961.

CHARLES SEARS BALDWIN. *Ancient Rhetoric and Poetic*. New York, The Macmillan Co., 1924.

GORDON E. BIGELOW. "Distinguishing Rhetoric from Poetic Discourse." *Southern Speech Journal*, 19:83–97 (December, 1953).

EDWIN BLACK. "Plato's View of Rhetoric." *Quarterly Journal of Speech*, 44:361–374 (December, 1958).

J. RICHARD CHASE. "The Classical Conception of Epideictic." *Quarterly Journal of Speech*, 46:293–300 (October, 1961).

DONALD LEMEN CLARK. *Rhetoric in Greco-Roman Education*. New York, Columbia University Press, 1957. Ch. II, "What the Ancients Meant by Rhetoric."

LANE COOPER. "The Rhetoric of Aristotle." *Quarterly Journal of Speech*, 21:10–19 (February, 1935).

———, trans. *The Rhetoric of Aristotle*. New York, Appleton-Century-Crofts, Inc., 1932. (This edition is admirably adapted to the needs of speech students.)

EDWARD P. J. CORBETT. *Classical Rhetoric for the Modern Student*. New York, Oxford University Press, 1965.

LAWRENCE J. FLYNN. "Aristotle: Art and Faculty of Rhetoric." *Southern Speech Journal*, 21:244–254 (Summer, 1956).

———. "The Aristotelian Basis for the Ethics of Speaking." *Speech Teacher*, 6:179–187 (September, 1957).

GEORGE GROTE. *A History of Greece*. New edition, 10 volumes. London, John Murray, 1888. Vol. VII, chs. 47–48 (see discussion of Sophists).

MOSES HADAS. *Old Wine, New Bottles*. New York, Simon and Schuster, Inc., 1962.

EDITH HAMILTON. *The Greek Way*. New York, New American Library, 1958.

———. "The Lessons of the Past." In *Adventures of the Mind*. Edited by RICHARD THRUELSEN and JOHN KOBLER. New York, Vintage Books, 1959. Pp. 76–87.

LEWIS M. HAMMOND. "Rhetoric and Dialectic." In *Eastern Public Speaking Conference: 1940*. Edited by HAROLD F. HARDING. New York, The H. W. Wilson Co., 1940. Pp. 173–182.

D. A. G. HINKS. "Tisias and Corax and the Invention of Rhetoric." *The Classical Quarterly*, 34:59–69 (April, 1940).

EVERETT LEE HUNT. "Plato and Aristotle on Rhetoric and Rhetoricians." In *Studies in Rhetoric and Public Speaking*. New York, Century Co., 1925. Pp. 3–60.

HOYT H. HUDSON. "The Tradition of Our Subject." *Quarterly Journal of Speech*, 17: 320–329 (June, 1931).

WERNER JAEGER. *Paideia*. GILBERT HIGHET, trans. Vol. III. New York, Oxford University Press, 1944. "The Rhetoric of Isocrates and Its Cultural Ideal," pp. 46–70; "Isocrates Defends His Paideia," pp. 132–155; "Plato's Phaedrus: Philosophy and Rhetoric," pp. 182–196.

RICHARD JEBB. "The Age of Pericles." In *The Greek Genius and Its Influence*. Edited by LANE COOPER. New Haven, Yale University Press, 1917. Pp. 63–76.

————. *The Attic Orators*. London, Macmillan & Co., 1893. Two volumes.

GEORGE KENNEDY. *The Art of Persuasion in Greece*. Princeton, Princeton University Press, 1963.

H. I. MARROU. *A History of Education in Antiquity*. Translated by GEORGE LAMB. New York, Sheed and Ward, 1956. Parts I and II.

PRENTICE A. MEADOR, JR. "The Classical Epicheireme: A Re-examination." *Western Speech*, 30:151–155 (Summer, 1966).

JOHN D. MONTGOMERY. *The State Versus Socrates: A Case Study in Civic Freedom*. Boston, Beacon Press, 1954.

"Rhetoric." *Encyclopaedia Britannica* (1969). Vol. 19.

LAWRENCE W. ROSENFIELD. "Rhetorical Criticism and An Aristotelian Notion of Process." *Speech Monographs*, 33:1–16 (March, 1966).

PAUL SHOREY. "What Teachers of Speech May Learn from the Theory and Practice of the Greeks." *Quarterly Journal of Speech Education*, 8:105–131 (April, 1922).

GEORGE A. SIMCOX and WILLIAM H. SIMCOX. *The Orations of Demosthenes and Aechines on the Crown*. Oxford, Clarendon Press, 1872. (Material on the life of Demosthenes, the oration, the text, nature of the evidence, etc.)

BROMLEY SMITH. "Thrasymachus: A Pioneer Rhetorician." *Quarterly Journal of Speech Education*, 13:278–291 (June, 1927).

————. "Corax and Probability." *Quarterly Journal of Speech Education*, 7:13–42 (February, 1921).

————. "Theodorus of Byzantium: Word-Smith." *Quarterly Journal of Speech*, 14: 71–81 (February, 1928).

————. "The Father of Debate: Protagoras of Abdera." *Quarterly Journal of Speech Education*, 4:196–215 (March, 1918).

————. "Gorgias: A Study of Oratorical Style." *Quarterly Journal of Speech Education*, 7:335–359 (November, 1921).

————. "Hippias and a Lost Canon of Rhetoric." *Quarterly Journal of Speech Education*, 12:129–145 (June, 1926).

————. "Prodicus of Ceos: The Sire of Synonymy." *Quarterly Journal of Speech Education*, 6:51–68 (April, 1920).

A. E. TAYLOR. *Plato: The Man and His Work*. New York, Dial Press, Inc., 1936. Pp. 103–129, 229–319.

LESTER THONSSEN. "A Functional Interpretation of Aristotle's *Rhetoric*." *Quarterly Journal of Speech*, 16:297–310 (June, 1930).

Thucydides. CHARLES F. SMITH, trans. New York, G. P. Putnam's Sons, 1928. "The Funeral Oration," Book II, sections xxxv–xlvi, pp. 319–341.

RUSSELL H. WAGNER. "The Rhetorical Theory of Isocrates." *Quarterly Journal of Speech Education*, 8:323–337 (November, 1922).

RICHARD M. WEAVER. "The *Phaedrus* and the Nature of Rhetoric." In *The Ethics of Rhetoric*. Chicago, Henry Regnery Co., 1953. Pp. 3–26.

ALFRED E. ZIMMERN. *The Greek Commonwealth*, 3d ed. rev. Oxford, Clarendon Press, 1922. "Notes on the Ideal of Citizenship," ch. 8, pp. 198–209.

3

Extensions of
Basic Principles

INTERRELATION OF GREEK AND ROMAN THINKING

The Greeks gave us the basic principles of rhetoric. But the Romans and Graeco-Romans were highly skilled students whose penchant for organization and refinement of traditional lore asserted itself in their treatment of speechcraft. They may not have added much that was new, but they elaborated upon the old tenets and placed them in sharper focus. Furthermore, the practical turn of the Roman mind insured the likelihood of certain departures from the philosophical point of view regarding rhetoric, to a more purely pragmatic, pedagogical development. This is most clearly shown in the treatises of Cicero, the orator speaking on his art, and in the writings of Quintilian, the teacher discoursing on methods of instruction.

Despite certain differences in emphasis and point of view between early Greek and Graeco-Roman writings on rhetoric, the latter quite naturally and uninterruptedly grows out of and blends with the former, so that the tradition of the subject is sustained in unbroken continuity. The following sections show how the basic postulates of Greek inquiry served as the substructure of Roman thinking.

THE AD HERENNIUM

Neither the exact title nor the author of the work we call *Rhetorica ad Herennium* [1] is known. Perhaps written during the first century B.C.—

[1] *Ad C. Herennium.* Translated by Harry Caplan. Cambridge, Massachusetts, 1954, p. vii.

86 B.C. has been mentioned as the possible date—it provides a severely methodical analysis of the art of public speaking, mirroring the teaching practices of the time and emphasizing the value of declamatory exercises. Harry Caplan, whose admirable translation and introductory notes on *Rhetorica ad Herennium* appeared in 1954, remarks that the author of the treatise "gives us a Greek art in Latin dress, combining a Roman spirit with Greek doctrine." According to Atkins, it is "the first work of real significance belonging to the first century B.C. . . ." [2]

The authorship of the work has been an object of much inquiry. For many years it was attributed to Cicero, doubtless mistakenly. In a loose way, Cornificius, to whose work Quintilian refers several times in the *Institutes*, is linked to the *ad Herennium*. But, as Harry Caplan indicates, Cornificius' dates do not agree with those of the *ad Herennium*'s author, as deduced from other evidence.

The *ad Herennium* is in four books.

Book I deals with the kinds of oratory and the parts of rhetoric. Demonstrative, deliberative, and judicial oratory represent the types of causes that a speaker may consider. In order to carry out his assignment, an orator must deal with five aspects or parts of rhetoric: *inventio, dispositio, elocutio, memoria,* and *pronuntiatio.* Each of these five parts can be acquired by an orator through art, imitation, and practice.

An orator's invention is revealed in six sections of an address: *exordium, narratio, divisio, confirmatio, confutatio,* and *conclusio.*

Three kinds of causes, or *constitutio causae,* are mentioned: those of fact (*coniecturalis*), interpretation (*legitima*), and right or wrong (*iuridicialis*). Under the heading of the *status,* or *state,* these concepts are discussed in a later section.

Book II treats of invention as it relates to forensic oratory; Book III, as it relates to deliberative and demonstrative speaking. *Dispositio, memoria,* and *pronuntiatio* receive special consideration.

The last book of the *ad Herennium* is devoted to *elocutio,* or style, and takes up about half of the entire treatise. A. S. Wilkins remarks that this section is of interest, not only because it is the first work on the subject in Latin, but also because it provides an abundance and excellence of illustration.

The author lists three kinds of style—*gravis, mediocris,* and *attenuata.* The general requirements of the speaker's language are elegance, or word choice; composition, or the union of words; and dignity, or adornment. To further the realization of the last requisite, the *ad Herennium* provides a long list of figures (*verborum exornatio* and *sententiarum exornatio*).

[2] J. W. H. Atkins. *Literary Criticism in Antiquity.* London, 1934. II, 16.

THE CLASSICAL DIVISIONS OF RHETORIC

The parts or canons of rhetoric set forth in the *ad Herennium* represent the broad divisions of the whole subject; in many respects, they constitute the basic pattern of all theoretical and critical investigations into the art and practice of speaking.

According to the classical tradition, all rhetoric is divided into five parts: invention, disposition, elocution, memory, and delivery. This five-fold division is fairly standard in the major works after Aristotle until the eighteenth century. Minor changes in the meaning of the terms are developed in various treatises, but the pattern remains the same until the time of George Campbell, when *memory* practically drops out of the analysis.

These parts have distinctive functions. They are not only the concepts with which an orator must deal and which he must master in order to deliver an effective speech; they are also the aspects of the delivered oration which the critic, viewing the finished speech as a creative product, examines and evaluates.

The exact origin of the fivefold plan is in doubt. The first division of speech materials was probably into substance and form; next, into invention and arrangement.

The Inventive Aspect

Invention involves the attempt on the part of the orator, as Cicero says, "to find out what he should say. . . ." It is an investigative undertaking, embracing a survey and forecast of the subject and a search for the arguments suitable to the given rhetorical effort. As Baldwin remarks in his commentary, it refers to "investigation, analysis, and grasp of the subject matter." [3] Thus certain writers—Aristotle among them—give more attention to invention than to the other parts of rhetoric. This is done on the ground, and perhaps properly, that the content is the most important part of a speech.

Without proposing to categorize the constituents of rhetorical theory, we may say in general that the concept of invention includes the entire investigative undertaking, the idea of the *status*, and the modes of persuasion—logical, emotional, and ethical—in all of their complex interrelations.

Disposition of Materials

Disposition covers the concept of arrangement, of orderly planning and movement of the whole idea, and the proportioning of the parts of

[3] Charles Sears Baldwin. *Ancient Rhetoric and Poetic.* New York, 1924, p. 43.

a speech. Although the treatment of it differs within a narrow range among the several treatises, the general meaning is twofold: the appreciation of a plan for the speech as a whole, and the development of the specific parts of the speech, such as the exordium, narration, proof, peroration, and whatever other divisions the authors specify. Baldwin is correct in saying that what is noticeably missing, not only in Aristotle's treatment of disposition, but in the other works of the classical tradition as well, "is some definite inculcation of consecutiveness."

In some treatises, ancient and modern, invention and disposition are treated under a common head—the assumption being that the orderly arrangement of the materials constitutes an essential part of the inventive process.

The Stylistic Feature

The third part of rhetoric was originally called *elocutio,* and it referred specifically to style. It embraced the concept of expression in language, resulting, basically, from the choice of words and their arrangement or composition. Among the ancient rhetoricians, the study of words and composition led to an analysis of the distinguishing marks of the kinds of style. The several kinds of style were systematically analyzed. Thus, in the *ad Herennium,* for example, we find detailed treatment of the plain or simple, the middle or moderate, and the grand style. Caplan says Book IV offers "the oldest extant division of the kinds of style into three, and the oldest extant formal study of figures." [4] In the *Orator,* Cicero also described and analyzed in some detail the three major styles mentioned above.

The Memory in Rhetoric

According to Caplan, the *ad Herennium* furnishes the oldest extant discussion of memory. In it, two kinds of memory are discussed: the artificial, consisting of backgrounds and images, which can be improved by training; and the natural or inborn, which also yields to discipline.

Memoria, as the fourth part of rhetoric, does not receive systematic treatment in Aristotle's *Rhetoric.* Cicero and Quintilian deal with it in fair detail. When we come to the major works of the eighteenth century, however, we note that the canon has virtually been dropped. In contemporary texts it usually receives incidental treatment. Recent exceptions include Lionel Crocker's *Public Speaking for College Students,* in which a full chapter is given to "The Memory in Speech," and Horace Rahskopf's *Basic Speech Improvement* contains a chapter on "The Speaker's Memory."

[4] *Op. cit.,* p. xx.

In the older sense, memory was a fairly comprehensive concept, embracing the speaker's endowment for memorial recall, the method of discipline for its improvement, and, of course, the demonstrated mastery of material for subsequent development in discourse. "Why should I remark," asks Cicero,

> . . . how excellent a thing it is to retain the instructions which you have received with the cause, and the opinion which you have formed upon it? to keep all your thoughts upon it fixed in your mind, all your arrangement of language marked out there? to listen to him from whom you receive any information, or to him to whom you have to reply, with such power of retention, that they seem not to have poured their discourse into your ears, but to have engraven it on your mental tablet? [5]

That Cicero regarded memory as an important part of the orator's equipment is further revealed in his criticism of the eminent speakers. He censures Curio for his "extremely treacherous" memory, saying

> . . . after he had divided his subject into three general heads, he would sometimes, in the course of speaking, either add a fourth, or omit the third. In a capital trial, in which I had pleaded for Titinia, the daughter of Cotta, when he attempted to reply to me in defense of Servius Naevius, he suddenly forgot every thing he intended to say, and attributed it to the pretended witchcraft and magic artifices of Titinia.[6]

In commenting on Hippias' contribution to rhetoric, and on the subsequent disappearance of the canon of memory, Bromley Smith says:

> With the passing of the years . . . the notion that the memory of orators can be trained by systematic devices has almost disappeared. Memory itself remains and is highly esteemed, yet it has lost its ancient importance. Long ago Plato foresaw this when he remarked that the invention of writing by the Egyptian God, Theuth, caused learners to trust external written characters rather than themselves. That he was right may be judged from the number of speakers who read their addresses. Hippias, however, belonged to the old school; he believed he could train the memories of the future statesmen. His labors must have had a measure of success, sufficient indeed to encourage others. Since his days thousands have followed his idea, like a will-o'-the-wisp, through the bogs of discipline. At last sinking below their depth, they have disappeared, leaving only a few bubbles to remind the world that Memory, 'the warder of the mind,' was once a canon of rhetoric.[7]

Delivery

The last part of rhetoric—*pronuntiatio*—is the art of delivery. Its constituent elements are vocal utterance and bodily action. From Aristotle

---

[5] *De Oratore.* Translated by J. S. Watson. Philadelphia, 1897. II, lxxxvii.
[6] *Brutus.* LX.
[7] "Hippias and a Lost Canon of Rhetoric." *Quarterly Journal of Speech Education,* 12:144 (June, 1926).

to the present day all systematic treatises on rhetoric have given some space to this canon.

A GREAT ORATOR'S CONCEPTION OF HIS ART: CICERO

A Functional Approach to Speechmaking

"The Romans," said W. S. Teuffel, "were naturally well qualified for oratory by their acute intellect, their love of order and their Italian vivacity, tempered with Roman gravity." [8] They were practical people; so it is natural that their works on speaking should emphasize the functional aspects of the art. Cicero represented this practical inclination at its best. "The most eminent orator of Roman civilization, he wrote more than any other orator has ever written on rhetoric; and historically he has been more than any other an ideal and model." [9]

While discussing the efforts of the philosophers—Aristotle and Theophrastus included—as writers on rhetoric, Cicero inquires whether it would not be advantageous to consider the art of speaking from the point of view of the practicing orator *and* the philosopher. Surely the orator would be able to "set forth with full power and attraction" those same topics of virtue, equity, laws, and the like, with something more than the "tame and bloodless phraseology" of the philosophers. Accordingly, Cicero would interest himself in the development of an orator so "accomplished and complete" that he would be able to "speak on all subjects with variety and copiousness."

Cicero tried, as his works show, to restore rhetoric to something of its earlier scope and vitality. As Atkins indicates,[10] he was "protesting against the narrowing of the province" of the speaking art, hoping to restore rhetoric as a "system of general culture" which would train men to write and speak competently on all possible subjects. In this effort Cicero was influenced and guided by the doctrines of Isocrates whom he regarded as the "father of eloquence."

Cicero was an eclectic. With the possible exception of the *Brutus*, the contents of all his works originate in the contributions of his predecessors and contemporaries. However, he embellished the old, often saying it so much better that it took on a character of finality.

The Substance of the De Oratore

De Oratore is Cicero's most important book on rhetorical theory. Like many treatises of its kind, it is in dialogue form, with the celebrated

---

[8] *Teuffel's History of Roman Literature.* Translated by George C. W. Warr. London, 1891. I, 64.
[9] Baldwin. *Op. cit.*, p. 37.
[10] Atkins. *Op. cit.*, II, 23.

orators Crassus and Antonius playing the major roles; and Scaevola, Catulus, Cotta, Sulpicius, Caesar, and Rufus serving in a minor way as interlocutors.

In Book I Crassus comments on the qualifications of the Ideal Orator, while in Book III he develops the Ciceronian conception of oratorical style. Antonius, serving as the protagonist in Book II, discourses on invention and disposition. Incidental remarks on humor are also introduced by Caesar.

Book I

In the first book we find, reminiscent of Isocrates and Aristotle, a development of the theme that to be successful the orator must conform to high and exacting qualifications. He must be a man of great learning.

A knowledge of a vast number of things is necessary, without which volubility of words is empty and ridiculous; speech itself is to be formed, not merely by choice, but by careful construction of words; and all the emotions of the mind, which nature has given to man, must be intimately known; for all the force and art of speaking must be employed in allaying or exciting the feelings of those who listen. To this must be added a certain portion of grace and wit, learning worthy of a well-bred man, and quickness and brevity in replying as well as attacking, accompanied with a refined decorum and urbanity. Besides, the whole of antiquity and a multitude of examples is to be kept in the memory; nor is the knowledge of laws in general, or of the civil law in particular, to be neglected. And why need I add any remarks on delivery itself, which is to be ordered by action of body, by gesture, by look, and by modulation and variation of the voice, the great power of which, alone and in itself, the comparatively trivial art of actors and the stage proves, on which though all bestow their utmost labor to form their look, voice, and gesture, who knows not how few there are, and have ever been, to whom we can attend with patience? What can I say of that repository for all things, the memory, which, unless it be the keeper of the matter and words that are the fruits of thought and invention, all the talents of the orator, we see, though they be of the highest degree of excellence, will be of no avail? Let us then cease to wonder what is the cause of the scarcity of good speakers, since eloquence results from all those qualifications. . . .[11]

Then Cicero sets forth the oft-quoted remark that the "proper concern of an orator, . . . is language of power and elegance accommodated to the feelings and understandings of mankind."

We note that Cicero, through his mouthpiece, Crassus, insists upon the orator's having virtually universal knowledge and skill. In the dialogue, Antonius holds that somewhat less learning is necessary, although he, too, urges broad familiarity with the field of knowledge. But he insists upon a more *intensive* training leading to the acquisition of oratorical

[11] *De Oratore.* I, v.

excellence. Antonius would develop the orator's natural talents and capacities for oratory, even if his intellectual control over the field of learning were somewhat more moderate than Crassus believed essential. Baldwin feels that, in a sense, both Crassus and Antonius are right. "Normally rhetoric is both extensive and intensive, both a comprehensive study of life and a specific art, even as the means of persuasion are both extrinsic and intrinsic." [12]

The core of the controversy posed by Crassus and Antonius deals of course with the respective claims of rhetoric and philosophy to superiority in the educational system, or at least to the prevailing practices of the time. And the arguments of the philosophers—Critolaus, Charmadas, and Carneades, for example—echo in hypnotic refrain to this hour. They are surely as old as Plato and as young as today's occasional detractor of rhetorical practices. Is rhetoric in fact an art? Can its principles be systematized and taught? Does not the orator frequently speak without knowledge? How do you account for the fact that many accomplished speakers are untrained in rhetoric? Is oratorical practice moral? Is it a discipline overladen with rules and dreary technicalities? Perhaps Cicero would not have protested some of these objections. Moreover, perhaps the philosophers themselves did not take all of them seriously. At any rate, Cicero's conception of the ideal orator seems praiseworthy. He makes him a broadly trained, wise, and skillful practitioner of the art of persuasion.

In Book I, Crassus also delineates the five parts of rhetoric:

If, therefore, any one desires to define and comprehend the whole and peculiar power of an orator, that man, in my opinion, will be an orator, worthy of so great a name, who whatever subject comes before him, and requires rhetorical elucidation, can speak on it judiciously, in set form, elegantly, and from memory, and with a certain dignity of action.[13]

However, the principal reference at this point is to *invention*.

Book II

The second book treats mainly of invention and disposition, and with particular emphasis, of course, upon these concepts in their relation to forensic oratory. Care is taken to point out that the orator's painstaking investigation of the facts is indispensable to inventive skill. The accomplished orator will conduct research before taking the platform, will "take one time for premeditation, and another for speaking."

Though not original, Cicero's treatment of the *status*—determination

[12] *Op. cit.*, p. 46.
[13] *De Oratore.* I, xv.

of the character and issues of the case—is important to the study of rhetorical theory. He remarks:

> There are in all, therefore, three sorts of matters, which may possibly fall under doubt and discussion; what is now done, what has been done, or what is to be done; what the nature of a thing is, or how it should be designated; for as to the question which some Greeks add, whether a thing be rightly done, it is wholly included in the inquiry, what the nature of the thing is.[14]

These are frequently called states of conjecture, definition, and quality, respectively. Cicero remarks that these considerations apply to all types of oratory in which dispute centers—forensic, deliberative, and panegyric.

The objects of discourse are said to be: "That we prove what we maintain to be true; that we conciliate those who hear; that we produce in their minds whatever feeling our cause may require." The whole business of speaking, Cicero allows, rests upon these things for success in persuasion.

Cicero's treatment of pathetic and ethical proof adds little, if anything, that is new. He indicates that "mankind makes far more determinations through hatred, or love, or desire, or anger, or grief, or joy, or hope, or fear, or error, or some other affection of mind, than from regard to truth, or any settled maxim, or principle of right, or judicial form, or adherence to the laws." He therefore comments on the way to make audience analyses, to move people to various emotional states, and to make the speaker's character aid in the persuasive undertaking.

Cicero's treatment of arrangement is conventional. He indicates that two methods may be observed: "one, which the nature of causes dictates; the other, which is suggested by the orator's judgment and prudence." The plan of organization he then describes is more detailed than Aristotle's, the difference resulting largely, however, from the fact that he is making an adjustment to forensic speaking.

Memory, as a distinct part of rhetoric, receives attention in Book II. Cicero opens his discourse by recalling the traditional incident which presumably prompted Simonides to "invent" the art of memory:

> For they relate, that when Simonides was at Crannon in Thessaly, at an entertainment given by Scopas, a man of rank and fortune, and had recited a poem which he had composed in his praise, in which, for the sake of embellishment, after the manner of the poets, there were many particulars introduced concerning Castor and Pollux, Scopas told Simonides, with extraordinary meanness, that he would pay him half the sum which he had agreed to give for the poem, and that he might ask the remainder, if he thought proper, from his Tyndaridae, to whom he had given an equal share of praise. A short time after, they say that a message was brought in to Simonides, to desire him to go out, as two youths were waiting at the gate who earnestly

14 *Ibid.*, II, xxvi.

wished him to come forth to them; when he arose, went forth, and found nobody. In the meantime the apartment in which Scopas was feasting fell down, and he himself, and his company, were overwhelmed and buried in the ruins; and when their friends were desirous to inter their remains, but could not possibly distinguish one from another, so much crushed were the bodies, Simonides is said, from his recollection of the place in which each had sat, to have given satisfactory directions for their interment. Admonished by this occurrence, he is reported to have discovered, that it is chiefly order that gives distinctness to memory; and that by those, therefore, who would improve this part of the understanding, certain places must be fixed upon, and that of the things which they desire to keep in memory, symbols must be conceived in the mind, and ranged, as it were, in those places; thus the order of places would preserve the order of things, and the symbols of the things would denote the things themselves; so that we should use the places as waxen tablets, and the symbols as letters.[15]

Cicero observes that those things "are the most strongly fixed in our minds, which are communicated to them, and imprinted upon them, by the senses . . ." And for the orator, the "memory of things is the proper business . . ." "This we may be enabled to impress on ourselves by the creation of imaginary figures, aptly arranged, to represent particular heads, so that we may recollect thoughts by images, and their order by place."

Book III

In addition to restating the theme on the union of rhetoric and philosophy, the last book of De Oratore considers style and delivery.

The section on style deals chiefly with word choice, composition, and the various ornaments of speech. Cicero's point of view is stated clearly in this passage:

A speech, then, is to be made becoming in its kind, with a sort of complexion and substance of its own; for that it be weighty, agreeable, savoring of erudition and liberal knowledge, worthy of admiration, polished, having feeling and passion in it, as far as is required, are qualities not confined to particular members, but are apparent in the whole body; but that it be, as it were, strewed with flowers of language and thought, is a property which ought not to be equally diffused throughout the whole speech, but at such intervals, that, as in the arrangement of ornaments, there may be certain remarkable and luminous objects disposed here and there.[16]

Baldwin looks upon Cicero's twenty chapters on style as a "brilliant instance of what the ancients meant by amplification. Logically they do little more than iterate the truism that style is inseparable from substance; but actually they make the truism live." [17]

[15] Ibid., II, lxxxvi.
[16] Ibid., III, xxv.
[17] Op. cit., p. 55.

Finally, Book III of the *De Oratore* sets forth a general theory of delivery, that phase of oratory which Cicero said had "the sole and supreme power." Without effective delivery, "a speaker of the highest mental capacity can be held in no esteem, while one of moderate abilities, with this qualification, may surpass even those of the highest talent." Cicero comments on the use of gestures and bodily action, and on the necessity of varying the tones in vocal expression.

It may be said that, while constructing the pattern for the Ideal Orator, Cicero kept constantly in mind the practical requirements of one who proposed to play "the part of a true Roman citizen in the conflicts of the assembly and the law courts."

The *Orator* and a Conception of Style

Cicero's *Orator* is less comprehensive than the *De Oratore,* being devoted almost wholly to style. John E. Sandys says the purpose of it was to "meet the wishes of Brutus" and "to win over Brutus to his own side in the controversy with the Atticists. . . ." Another purpose, surely, was "to delineate the ideal orator." And it is evident that "the living image of his own oratorical greatness forms the foundation on which he builds his ideal fabric. His own speeches supply him with examples of every variety of oratorical excellence. . . ." [18] Baldwin remarks, apropos of the *Orator,* that few men "writing on style have shown in their own styles so much precision and charm."

The Doctrine of the Three Styles

In the *Orator,* which Sandys says belongs to the "aesthetics of oratory," Cicero classifies and describes the three kinds of style: the plain, the moderate, and the grand. These types arise from the orator's attempt to prove, to please, and to move; and the skilled orator should be able to do all three.

Regarding the plain style, Cicero says:

. . . we must give a sketch of the man whom some consider the only orator of the Attic style.

He is a gentle, moderate man, imitating the usual customs, differing from those who are not eloquent in fact rather than in any of his opinions. Therefore those who are his hearers, even though they themselves have no skill in speaking, still feel confident that they could speak in that manner. For the subtlety of his address appears easy of imitation to a person who ventures on an opinion, but nothing is less easy when he comes to try it; for although it is not a style of any extraordinary vigour, still it has some juice, so that even though it is not endowed with the most extreme power, it is still . . . in per-

[18] John Edwin Sandys. *M. Tulli Ciceronis ad M. Brutum Orator.* Cambridge, 1885, pp. lviii, lxiv.

fect health. First of all, then, let us release it from the fetters of rhythm. For there is, as you know, a certain rhythm to be observed by an orator, proceeding on a regular system; but though it must be attended to in another kind of oratory, it must be entirely abandoned in this. This must be a sort of easy style, and yet not utterly without rules, so that it may seem to range at freedom, not to wander about licentiously. He should also guard against appearing to cement his words together; for the hiatus formed by a concourse of open vowels has something soft about it, and indicates a not unpleasing negligence, as if the speaker were anxious more about the matter than the manner of his speech. But as to other points, he must take care, specially as he is allowed more licence in these two,—I mean the rounding of his periods, and the combination of his words; for those narrow and minute details are not to be dealt with carelessly. . . .

The language will be pure and Latin; it will be arranged plainly and clearly, and great care will be taken to see what is becoming. . . .

There will be a moderate use of what I may call oratorical furniture; for there is to a certain degree what I may call our furniture, consisting of ornaments partly of things and partly of words. . . .

He will have besides this, action, not tragic, nor suited to the stage, but he will move his body in a moderate degree, trusting a great deal to his countenance; not in such a way as people call making faces, but in a manner sufficient to show in a gentlemanlike manner in what sense he means what he is saying to be understood.

Now in this kind of speech sallies of wit are admissible, and they carry perhaps only too much weight in an oration. Of them there are two kinds, —facetiousness and raillery,—and the orator will employ both; but he will use the one in relating anything neatly, and the other in darting ridicule on his adversaries.[19]

As for the moderate style, it is

. . . more fertile, and somewhat more forcible than this simple style of which we have been speaking; but nevertheless tamer than the highest class of oratory . . . In this kind there is but little vigour, but there is the greatest possible quantity of sweetness; for it is fuller than the plain style, but more plain than that other which is highly ornamented and copious.

Every kind of ornament in speaking is suitable to this style; and in this kind of oratory there is a great deal of sweetness. It is a style in which many men among the Greeks have been eminent; but Demetrius Phalereus, in my opinion, has surpassed all the rest; and while his oratory proceeds in calm and tranquil flow, it receives brilliancy from numerous metaphors and borrowed expressions, like stars. . . .

The same kind of oratory (I am speaking of the moderate and temperate kind) admits of all sorts of figures of expressions, and of many also of ideas. Discussions of wide application and extensive learning are explained in it, and common topics are treated without any impetuosity. In a word, orators of this class usually come from the schools of philosophers, and unless the more vigorous orator, whom I am going to speak of presently, is at hand to be compared with them, the one whom I am now describing will be approved of.[20]

[19] *Orator.* From *The Orations of Marcus Tullius Cicero.* Translated by C. D. Yonge. London, 1852. IV, 403–407, *passim.*
[20] *Ibid.,* IV, 407–409, *passim.*

The orator who uses the grand style

. . . is the sublime, copious, dignified, ornate speaker, in whom there is the greatest amount of grace. For he it is, out of admiration for whose ornamented style and copiousness of language nations have allowed eloquence to obtain so much influence in states; but it was only this eloquence, which is borne along in an impetuous course, and with a mighty noise, which all men looked up to, and admired, and had no idea that they themselves could possibly attain to. It belongs to this eloquence to deal with men's minds, and to influence them in every imaginable way. This is the style which sometimes forces its way into and sometimes steals into the senses; which implants new opinions in men, and eradicates others which have been long established. But there is a vast difference between this kind of orator and the preceding ones. A man who has laboured at the subtle and acute style, in order to speak cunningly and cleverly, and who has had no higher aim, if he has entirely attained his object, is a great orator, if not a very great one; he is far from standing on slippery ground, and if he once gets a firm footing, is in no danger of falling. But the middle kind of orator, whom I have called moderate and temperate, if he has only arranged all his own forces to his satisfaction, will have no fear of any doubtful or uncertain chances of oratory; and even if at any time he should not be completely successful, which may often be the case, still he will be in no great danger, for he cannot fall far. But this orator of ours, whom we consider the first of orators, dignified, vehement, and earnest, if this is the only thing for which he appears born, or if this is the only kind of oratory to which he applies himself, and if he does not combine his copiousness of diction with those other two kinds of oratory, is very much to be despised. For the one who speaks simply, inasmuch as he speaks with shrewdness and sense, is a wise man; the one who employs the middle style is agreeable; but this most copious speaker, if he is nothing else, appears scarcely in his senses. For a man who can say nothing with calmness, nothing with gentleness; who seems ignorant of all arrangement and definition and distinctness, and regardless of wit, especially when some of his causes require to be treated in that manner entirely, and others in a great degree; if he does not prepare the ears of his hearers before he begins to work up the case in an inflammatory style, he seems like a madman among people in their senses, or like a drunken man among sober men.[21]

Baldwin believes that the philosophy of such a classification, whatever its origin, "has been vicious as pedagogy." "Historically, the trail of the three styles has been baneful. For inculcating style perhaps the least fruitful means is classification." [22]

One of Aristotle's pupils, Theophrastus, is sometimes credited with formulating the threefold classification of style. In Latin literature, the *ad Herennium* furnishes the first statement of the doctrine. That Aristotle recognized a distinction among types of literary expression is evident from several of his remarks in the *Rhetoric*. In the third book, he

---

[21] *Ibid.*, IV, 409–410.
[22] *Op. cit.*, pp. 56–57.

remarks that "to each kind of rhetoric is adapted a peculiar style," and goes on to show how written and oral style differ in that the former is more "precise" while the latter "partakes more of declamation." Furthermore, he implies throughout that the different types of speaking—deliberative, forensic, and epideictic—call for different styles. However, he does not classify the styles according to the divisions which we have just discussed. Later theorists, it may be added, sometimes added a fourth kind. Philodemus evidently conceived of a fourfold classification; and Demetrius added the "forcible" type to the original three.

The doctrine of the three styles permeates the literature of rhetoric, either through open statement or implication. "In the sphere of oratory," J. F. D'Alton remarks,

> . . . the division became important, when it was adapted to the theory of the 'officia oratoris,' according to which it was the orator's duty to instruct, delight, and move his audience. The Plain style, with its predominant qualities of clearness and logical subtlety, was best suited to the purposes of instruction. When the Middle style became identified with the 'genus floridum,' with its characteristics of smoothness and charm, it was naturally assigned the task of giving pleasure to, or winning over an audience. The orator, however, could point to his greatest achievements as effected through the medium of the Grand style, which was calculated to play at will upon the feelings of an assembly. Cicero and Quintilian considered this style to be supreme, just as they considered that to stir the emotions was the highest function of the orator.[23]

The necessary qualities of a good style, as Cicero interpreted Theophrastus' teaching, were correctness, clearness, appropriateness, and ornament. Cicero did not, however, ascribe ornamentation to the Plain style, that being reserved in part for the Middle, and wholly for the Grand. Accordingly, we note that the so-called "virtues," or essential qualities, were not necessarily applied to all styles; instead, they were often assigned to particular styles for which they seemed uniquely suitable.

Treatment of Rhythm

Cicero's theory of oratorical rhythm derives largely from Gorgias and Isocrates. Commenting on the nature of his doctrine, he says:

> Let oratory then be, . . . mingled and regulated with regard to rhythm; not prosaic, nor on the other hand sacrificed wholly to rhythm; composed chiefly of the paeon, . . . with many of the other feet which he passes over intermingled with it.
> But what feet ought to be mingled with others, like purple, must be now explained; and we must also show to what kind of speech each sort of foot and rhythm is the best adapted. For the iambic is most frequent in those

[23] J. F. D'Alton. *Roman Literary Theory and Criticism*. London, 1931, pp. 74–75.

orations which are composed in a humble and lowly style; but the paeon is suited to a more dignified style; and the dactyl to both. Therefore, in a varied and long-continued speech these feet should be mingled together and combined. And in this way the fact of the orator aiming at pleasing the senses, and the careful attempt to round off the speech, will be the less visible, and they will at all times be less apparent if we employ dignified expressions and sentiments. For the hearers observe these two things, and think them agreeable: (I mean, expressions and sentiments.) And while they listen to them with admiring minds, the rhythm escapes their notice; and even if it were wholly wanting they would still be delighted with those other things. . . .

Accordingly, if the question is raised as to what is the rhythm of an oration, it is every sort of rhythm; but one sort is better and more suitable than another. If the question is, what is the place of this rhythm? it is in every portion of the words. If you ask where it has arisen; it has arisen from the pleasure of the ears. If the principle is sought on which the words are to be arranged; that will be explained in another place, because that relates to practice, . . . If the question is, when; always: if, in what place, it consists in the entire connexion of the words. If we are asked, What is the circumstance which causes pleasure? we reply, that it is the same as in verse; the method of which is determined by art; but the ears themselves define it by their own silent sensations, without any reference to principles of art.[24]

The observations on the preceding pages suggest that, all in all, the *Orator* is to be regarded as one of Cicero's important works. It is, in the opinion of Torsten Petersson, "Cicero's final statement not only of his oratorical idea but also of what he conceived himself to have attained." [25]

Other Rhetorical Treatises

Among Cicero's other rhetorical works, excluding the *Brutus* and *On the Best Style of Orators* which may more appropriately engage our attention later, are *On Topics*, *A Dialogue Concerning Oratorical Partitions*, and *On Rhetorical Invention*.

On Topics is largely an abstract of Aristotle's treatment of the same subject. Cicero defines a topic as "the seat of an argument, and . . . an argument is a reason which causes men to believe a thing which would otherwise be doubtful." [26] The sources and types of topics receive a fairly full measure of analysis.

A Dialogue Concerning Oratorical Partitions includes a brief and superficial discussion between Cicero and his son on the elements of the speaking situation—orator, speech, and subject—and on the parts of an oration—opening, narration, confirmation, and peroration.

On Rhetorical Invention, written when Cicero was about twenty-one

---

24 *Orator.* IV, 442–445, *passim.*
25 Torsten Petersson. *Cicero: A Biography.* Berkeley, 1919, p. 442.
26 *On Topics.* In *The Orations of Marcus Tullius Cicero.* Translated by C. D. Yonge. London, 1919. IV, 460.

years of age, demonstrates the truth of a remark found in the same work: "of those who are worthy of fame or recollection, there is no one who appears either to have said nothing well, or everything admirably." [27] Indeed, this is no consummate statement of the art of rhetoric, although it does reveal Cicero's early enthusiasm for oratory and, in a juvenile sort of way, his early mastery of many of its details. Only two of the four books remain. In later years, Cicero himself renounced the whole work as being "scarcely worthy of my present standing in life." His treatment of what Wilbur S. Howell calls the "Positions of Argument" is, however, important to rhetorical theory. Says Howell:

Both in *De Inventione* and the *Rhetorica ad Herennium*, analysis and synthesis are specific procedures designed on the one hand to yield, and on the other to employ, arguments and appeals which meet the severest tests of relevance and coherence. Each book is important to us because it gives expression to a precise intellectual method contrived to render purposeful the speaker's search for the natural divisions and the underlying unity of his speech.[28]

Cicero's contributions, in general, are less concise than Aristotle's *Rhetoric;* they are given more fully to the encouragement in the orator of copiousness in language; but they are developed more consistently from the point of view of the orator himself.

PEDAGOGICAL INQUIRY INTO RHETORIC: QUINTILIAN

". . . The premier teacher of imperial rhetoric and the greatest Latin authority upon education"—that is J. Wight Duff's [29] estimate of Quintilian who, about A.D. 95, brought out the truly monumental *Institutes of Oratory,* or the Teaching of Rhetoric. Like Cicero, Quintilian was erudite in an eclectic sort of way; in the *Institutes* he reveals a remarkably wide familiarity with and deep appreciation of the Greek and Latin writers. Living during the so-called Silver Age of Latin life, about A.D. 14 to 138, when, as Duff indicates, the "main clue to the literary qualities is to be found in education, and particularly in rhetorical education," Quintilian preserved much of the classical tradition and integrity of rhetoric. He did this at a time when rhetoric was no longer a powerful instrument in public affairs; when it was no longer a severe discipline, devoid of exhibitionism, for training the average man for active citizenship.

[27] *On Rhetorical Invention.* In *ibid.,* IV, 309.
[28] Wilbur S. Howell. "The Positions of Argument: An Historical Examination." In *Papers in Rhetoric.* Edited by Donald C. Bryant. St. Louis, 1940, p. 9.
[29] J. Wight Duff. *A Literary History of Rome in the Silver Age.* New York, 1927, p. 387.

Point of View of the *Institutes*

On the side of rhetorical theory, there is relatively little in the *Institutes* of an original character. Because most of what Quintilian sets down on the side of systematic rhetoric has been said before, we shall confine our summary to those aspects of the *Institutes* which enlarge the conception of theoretical speechcraft; and we shall omit most of the pedagogical details which, though interesting and significant, are not germane to this inquiry.

Quintilian sets out to form the Perfect Orator who, in his words, "cannot exist unless as a good man." The orator conforming to his standards is, therefore, the good man speaking well.

> Since an orator, then, is a good man, and a good man cannot be conceived to exist without virtuous inclinations, and virtue, though it receives certain impulses from nature, requires notwithstanding to be brought to maturity by instruction, the orator must above all things study *morality*, and must obtain a thorough knowledge of all that is just and honourable, without which no one can either be a good man or an able speaker.[30]

Quintilian's conception of the orator as a good man tends to refute the charge of insincerity against the *Institutes* voiced by a critic who called it a treatise on "Lying as a Fine Art for Those Fully Conscious of Their Own Rectitude."[31] However, students of rhetoric often point out, not without reason, that some of the practices mentioned in the *Institutes* scarcely conform to the lofty standard of the *good* man.

The formation of this perfect orator is not to be left to the philosophers; instead, the orator shall receive the necessary "excellence of mind" through rhetorical education. "I cannot admit," Quintilian observes, "that the principles of moral and honourable conduct are . . . to be left to the philosophers. . . ." Further in the discourse, he remarks:

> As to the objection which some make, that it is the business of *philosophy* to discourse of what is good, useful, and just, it makes nothing against me; for when they say a philosopher, they mean a good man; and why then should I be surprised that an orator, whom I consider also to be a good man, should discourse upon the same subjects? especially when I have shown, . . . that philosophers have taken possession of this province because it was abandoned by the orators, a province which had always belonged to oratory, so that the philosophers are rather trespassing upon our ground.[32]

Hence, he voices what Colson calls "the age-long antithesis between rhetoric and philosophy." Colson also indicates that

[30] *Institutes of Oratory.* Translated by J. S. Watson. London, 1856. XXII, ii, 1.
[31] F. H. Colson. *M. Fabii Quintiliani Institutionis Oratoriae Liber I.* Cambridge, 1924, p. xxviii.
[32] *Institutes.* II, xxi, 12–13.

Quintilian's view of the superiority of the 'rhetor' to the philosopher is clearly reflected in two events of the time. The first of these is the endowment of rhetoric by Vespasian. The other is the expulsion of the philosophers from Rome about A.D. 94. The latter, whatever its other causes may have been, was certainly from one point of view a triumph for Quintilian's educational views.[33]

Use of Rules

While Quintilian respected rules in rhetoric, he did not allow them to interfere with the common-sense principles of speech preparation. He advocated a flexibility of usage, observing that "one great quality in an orator is discretion, because he must turn his thoughts in various directions, according to the different bearings of his subject." A forensic orator, for instance, should, in his pleadings, "keep two things in view, *what is becoming,* and *what is expedient;* but it is frequently *expedient,* and sometimes *becoming,* to make some deviations from the regular and settled order. . . ." Quintilian says "rhetoric woud be a very easy and small matter, if it could be included in one short body of rules; but rules must generally be altered to suit the nature of each individual case, the time, the occasion, and necessity itself. . . ."

A Conception of the *Status*

The plan of the *Institutes* is based upon Quintilian's acceptance of the fivefold division of the art of rhetoric: invention, disposition, elocution, memory, and delivery; of the threefold classification of the types of oratory: deliberative, forensic, and panegyric; and of the threefold analysis of the speaker's object or purpose: to inform, to move, and to please.

A feature of Quintilian's treatment of invention which differs in scope and detail from that of many of his predecessors is that of the *status,* or *state of a cause.* The *status,* or the location of a center of argument, finds formal embodiment in the *ad Herennium* and in Cicero's *On Invention.* The elaboration of this concept is among the most important contributions of the Latin writers to rhetorical theory. By elevating the study of invention, and by providing the speaker with methods by which to find, evaluate, and use his ideas on a given case, this doctrine exercised a profound influence upon subsequent theory and practice in public speaking and debating.

Status is a perplexing concept. In his edition of the *ad Herennium,* Caplan translates the term *constitutio,* or *status,* as *issue,* and defines it as "the conjoining of two conflicting statements, thus forming the centre

[33] *Op. cit.,* p. xxiv–xxv.

of the argument and determining the character of the case. . . ."[34] The author of *ad Herennium* dealt with three kinds of issues: conjectural, legal, and juridical. Commenting on *constitutio*, as the Romans interpreted the Greek *stasis*, Otto A. L. Dieter observes that the former "is a synthesis, a conjunction, co-stasis, or 'standing together' of specific statements, or declarations, between which there is an interval of conflict, or disagreement."[35]

After examining the views adopted by previous writers on the subject, Quintilian thinks it best "to regard that as the *state of the cause* which is the strongest point in it, and on which the whole matter chiefly turns."[36] "Status," Baldwin comments, "meaning the essential character of the case as it appeared to preliminary survey of all the material and all the bearings, had come to denote a uniform system of determining that essential character by leading questions."[37] Through the medium of the status, therefore, the investigator or orator was able to find out what the body of material in the case meant.

Quintilian discusses two general states—the legal and the ratiocinatory. The former has many species, "as laws are numerous, and have various forms." The latter includes the status of conjecture or fact, the status of definition, and the status of quality.

These general states are, then, of two kinds: those depending upon legality, and those depending upon reasoning. The ratiocinatory states are simpler since they consist "merely in the contemplation of the nature of things. . . ." Briefly, they deal with these possible points in a case: whether a thing is—a matter of fact; what it is—a matter of definition; and of what species it is—a matter of quality. Thus, a case in the courtroom might center about the status of conjecture: Brown was either guilty or innocent of the charge of murder. Or, a case might deal with the status of definition: Brown killed a man but it was in self-defense, and hence was not murder. Or the status might concern quality: "Horatius committed a crime, for he killed his sister; he committed no crime, for he had a right to kill her who mourned at the death of an enemy."

Style Treated Conventionally

Quintilian recommends that the greatest possible care be given to expression,

. . . provided we bear in mind that nothing is to be done for the sake of words, as words themselves were invented for the sake of things, and as those words are the most to be commended which express our thoughts best,

[34] *Op. cit.,* p. 32n.
[35] "Stasis." *Speech Monographs,* 17:35–39 (November, 1950).
[36] *Institutes.* III, vi, 21.
[37] *Op. cit.,* p. 74.

and produce the impression which we desire on the minds of the judges. Such words undoubtedly must make a speech both worthy of admiration and productive of pleasure; but not of that kind of *admiration* with which we wonder at monsters; or of that kind of *pleasure* which is attended with unnatural gratification, but such as is compatible with true merit and worth.[38]

Then follows a long and reasonably conventional discussion of style. The classifications and definitions of the figures and tropes are more systematically handled, however, than in any previous contribution.

Attitude Toward Delivery

It is of interest to note Quintilian's defense of "extempore" speaking:

But the richest fruit of all our study, and the most ample recompense for the extent of our labour, is *the faculty of speaking extempore;* and he who has not succeeded in acquiring it, will do well, in my opinion, to renounce the occupations of the forum, and devote his solitary talent of writing to some other employment; for it is scarcely consistent with the character of a man of honour to make a public profession of service to others which may fail in the most pressing emergencies, since it is of no more use than to point out a harbour to a vessel, to which it cannot approach unless it be borne along by the gentlest breezes. There arise indeed innumerable occasions where it is absolutely necessary to speak on the instant, as well before magistrates, as on trials that are brought on before the appointed time; and if any of these shall occur, I do not say to any one of our innocent fellow citizens, but to any of our own friends and relatives, is an advocate to stand dumb, and, while they are begging for a voice to save them, and are likely to be undone if succor be not instantly afforded them, is he to ask time for retirement and silent study, till his speech be formed and committed to memory, and his voice and lungs be put in tune? [39]

Practically, this manner of speaking requires a techique differing from the ordinary mode of address.

Yet if any chance shall give rise to such a sudden necessity for speaking extempore, we shall have need to exert our mind with more than its usual activity; we must fix our whole attention on our matter, and relax, for the time, something of our care about words, if we find it impossible to attend to both. A slower pronunciation, too, and a mode of speaking with suspense and doubt, as it were, gives time for consideration; yet we must manage so that we may seem to deliberate and not to hesitate.[40]

Final Estimate

Colson has pronounced the *Institutes* "one of the most remarkable and interesting products of Roman common sense." At all points in the twelve books we are impressed by the sanity of the author in refusing

[38] *Institutes.* VIII, introd., 32–33.
[39] *Ibid.,* X, vii, 1–2.
[40] *Ibid.,* X, vii, 22.

to be bound by inflexible rules, and by his insistence upon shaping his doctrine to the varying demands of different speech situations. Eclectic as the treatment is, the contents take on new color and vitality at Quintilian's hands because he weaves his teaching experience and wise counsel into the fabric of the old theory.

EXCESSES IN THEORY AND PRACTICE

Tendencies of the Sophistic

After Aristotle, oratory declined in Greece. Whereas in the better days of Greek achievement the virtues of moderation and balance had been distinguishing marks of creative effort, now the tendencies toward excess and affectation became apparent. This unhappy circumstance asserted itself in Hellenistic prose, and particularly in oratory. About 250 B.C., Hegesias of Magnesia became the leader of the "Asiatic" school of thought. In violation of Aristotelian and Isocratean standards, this school produced an artificial style which, in the words of Atkins, "depended for its effects on epigrams, strained metaphors, false antitheses, over-elaborate rhythms, and the like." This style, which Atkins claims was "a breakdown of earlier traditions, rather than a fusion of the Asiatic and Hellenic geniuses," exercised considerable influence throughout the third and second centuries B.C. A certain reaction to the degradation of Greek oratory was provided by the rhetorical system of Hermagoras of Temnos who recaptured some of the spirit of his distinguished predecessors and who won the praise of Quintilian for his admirable treatise on the art of rhetoric.

During the second century A.D., there was evidence of a new interest in rhetoric, although the note of artificiality was present. Greek literature was receiving some patronage at the hand of Hadrian; exigencies of law courts in the Roman Empire were creating a certain need for forensic speaking; the great Roman writers and teachers of rhetoric were active; and many of the Rhetors came to Athens. Some of the Greek rhetoricians travelled from place to place, declaiming in the temples and elsewhere. Among these men were Dio Chrysostom and Hermogenes, the latter being the author of rhetorical works on issues, invention, and the forms and preparation of orations. Baldwin sees in Hermogenes' effort a typical pattern of the work of the period. "There some of the most characteristic habits of form in sophistic oratory are seen as prolongations of school exercises." [41]

During the second, third, and fourth centuries A.D., a type of rhetoric prevailed which is generally referred to as the "second sophistic." While

[41] Charles Sears Baldwin. *Medieval Rhetoric and Poetic.* New York, 1928, p. 23.

the term is applied chiefly to Greek activity, it is equally applicable to the Latin. The distinguishing mark of the era is the separation of speaking from the affairs of the everyday world, with the consequent emphasis upon themes dealing with the past, or with pure fiction. Accordingly, style came to be cultivated for its own sake, a sad circumstance in the field of oral persuasion. As Baldwin remarks, "Sophistic is the historic demonstration of what oratory becomes when it is removed from urgency of subject matter."

Seeking some inspiration for public occasions, it revives over and over again a dead past. Thus becoming conventionalized in method, it turns from cogency of movement to the cultivation of style. Cogency presupposes a message. It is intellectual ordering for persuasion, the means toward making men believe and act. Style, no longer controlled by such urgencies of subject, tends toward decoration and virtuosity.[42]

In Dio's discourse *On Training for Public Speaking*, we find him saying that statesmen should have training and practice in speechmaking.

For it is true that this will prove of very great help toward making him beloved and influential and esteemed instead of being looked down upon. For when men are afraid, what does more to inspire them than the spoken word? And when they wax insolent and uplifted in spirit, what more effectively brings them down and chastens them? What has greater influence in keeping them from indulging their desires? Whose admonitions do they endure more meekly than the man's whose speech delights them? [43]

During his early years Dio was evidently committed to the sophistic culture. However, he abandoned that interest in later life.

Dio refers to the great orators, mentioning particularly Demosthenes "for the vigour of his style, the impressiveness of thought, and the copiousness of his vocabulary, qualities in which he surpasses all other orators." He also comments on the work of Lysias, Hyperides, Aeschines, and Lycurgus. Furthermore, he suggests that the prospective speaker not remain unacquainted with the modern orators, adding

For the powers they display can be more useful to us because, when we read them, our judgment is not fettered and enslaved, as it is when we approach the ancients. For when we find that we are able to criticize what has been said, we are most encouraged to attempt the same thing ourselves, and we find more pleasure in comparing ourselves with others when we are convinced that in the comparison we should be found to be not inferior to them, with the chance, occasionally, of being even superior.[44]

In addition to Dio and Hermogenes, this period produced such men as Pollux, Apollonius, and Herode Atticus. Most of these orators and

---

[42] *Ibid.*, p. 7.
[43] *Dio Chrysostom.* Translated by J. W. Cohoon. Cambridge, Massachusetts, 1939, pp. 213–215.
[44] *Ibid.*, p. 225.

rhetoricians were subsequently considered in a semi-critical manner by Philostratus in his *Lives of the Sophists.*

Roman rhetorical history afforded examples of high and low points of development. With the downfall of the Republic, however, oratory declined. This decline was well under way by Quintilian's time. He tried to revive the spirit of Ciceronianism while protesting the false tastes that were taking hold of the age.

The Era of Declamations

Shortly before as well as after the time Quintilian wrote the *Institutes,* the tendency was to elaborate more and more upon the rules of rhetoric. Many manuals of the art were published and scores of teachers taught the subject, for, in the larger sense, the entire educational plan centered about rhetoric. One of the exercises that enjoyed a fabulously widespread vogue was declamation. Quintilian conjectures that Demetrius Phalereus invented the declamation on fictitious subjects. Originally a school exercise, it soon became little more than a showpiece permitting display and exhibitionism.

Quintilian approved of the declamation, as he understood it, but not as it was practiced about him. He admitted that the "practice has so degenerated through the fault of the teachers, that the license and ignorance of declaimers have been among the chief causes that have corrupted eloquence." But "of that which is good by nature we may surely make a good use." [45] So he recommended its use *as an exercise* having "a very close resemblance to reality," even though admitting that the current practice was out of gear with his intentions. As Baldwin remarks:

> Instead of training youth to lead in public policy and to secure justice for individuals, *declamatio* had become an end in itself, the rhetor's own kind of oratory. As an exhibition of skill it was his easiest means of winning pupils, and of holding them by letting them exhibit themselves. The inherent vice of artificiality, which Quintilian admits by implication, he nevertheless assigns entirely to perverted educational practise. He would recall *declamatio* from invention to actuality, and from display to exercise.[46]

Why was the declamation so popular? The answer probably can be traced in part to the changed political conditions. The Republic was dead and the power of Augustus was established. Assemblies were both infrequent and perfunctory, for their decisions could be altered at any moment "by the Emperor's personal intervention." Pleading in the courts was restricted, and the causes were not of the type that evoked

---

[45] *Institutes.* II, x, 3.
[46] *Ancient Rhetoric and Poetic,* p. 71.

great oratory. There was no longer free outlet in public life for oratorical activity. Consequently, other fields for such endeavor were sought.

One might surmise that under these conditions the interest in oratory would wane. But it did not. According to William A. Edward, the explanation was complex, but it involved certain known elements:

A decline in the number of successful teachers, a falling-off in interest and in the number of students, a closing down of the schools would have caused no surprise: but it took some time, and Augustus's crafty dissimulation helped this, for the changed conditions to be appreciated. Parents and pupils did not realise all at once that the old prizes were no longer open to success, or that, if open in name, they were empty in substance, and gave only pomp and not the reality of power. By the time the facts of the case were too patent to be ignored the schools were firmly established and had created an interest of their own. The young people of the day had to have their natural and national liking for the beauty of the spoken word satisfied. The declamation as a work of literary art had become an end in itself.[47]

Since the study of expression was virtually the higher education of the period, the declamation offered a convenient instrument to further the instruction. And as time went on, it became a hollow, sterile showpiece, divorced from reality and serving only one purpose fully—that of providing students with a vehicle of display. The mere declaiming became an all-sufficient end in itself.

The Stricture of Petronius

Petronius' *Satyricon* (meaning, really, a "miscellany," and probably prepared during the middle of the first century A.D.) voices a sharp protest against the rhetoric of the day, declaring that the Asianist influences had destroyed the restraint and dignity of classical Greek and early Roman style. Petronius decried the use of the declamation and inveighed against its false ornamentation.

Commenting on the turgidity of the declaimer, or "tub-thumper," Petronius said: ". . . the net result of all these high-flown themes and the empty thunder of their platitudes is that, when the pupils make their *début* in the courts, they feel themselves translated into a foreign world." [48] He placed the responsibility for the decay of oratory squarely upon the Asian school whose teachers provided their students with a diet of "sticky rhetorical lollypops," or "honeyed little balls of words." Oratory had degenerated into "inflated, extravagant word-spinning," completely removed from the world of reality.

[47] *The Suasoriae of Seneca the Elder.* Translated and edited by William A. Edward. London, 1928, pp. xviii–xix.
[48] *Petronius: The Satyricon.* Translated by J. M. Mitchell. London, n.d., p. 1.

But the onus of the condition was perhaps not attributable to the teachers alone. In the early part of his work, Petronius remarks through one of the participants in the story that "the professors provide this stupid jargon because they find that in a madhouse they too must be mad." Consequently, "the professor of elocution is in the same position as a fisherman: if he doesn't bait his hook with the particular dainty which he knows will make the little fishes bite, he will hang about on the rock without any hope of sport."

Seneca

In the *Controversiae* and the *Suasoriae* of Seneca—probably written toward the close of the first half of the century—we find an anthology, as it were, of declamations delivered by celebrated rhetors. The *Controversiae* were fictitious speeches on assumed forensic cases; the *Suasoriae*, fictitious deliberative speeches on historical subjects, designed principally for younger students. In other words, unreal cases were set up, and the students spoke to the point of the themes announced in the exercises. Seneca also provides comparative studies of the cases prepared by different declaimers. Baldwin indicates that Seneca divides the declamations by "a threefold critical classification"—the *sententiae*, implying the high points in leading interpretations; the *divisio*, or analysis of the case; and *colores*, or the imaginative development.[49] Baldwin finds these units "a poor substitute for the five traditional parts of rhetoric," and concludes: "*Elocutio*, thus left to itself, tended inevitably toward an art of display. The history of rhetoric has no more striking proof that style, when cultivated in artificial isolation, goes bad."

Other Contributors to a Rhetoric of Display

Valerius Maximus, in his *Facta et Dicta Memorabilia*, probably written between A.D. 30 and 40, devoted nine books to various subjects that an orator might wish to discuss. This was an adaptation to the demands of the prevailing rhetorical system. By making his collection of anecdotes and subjects accessible, Valerius Maximus provided, to use Duff's expression, "a serviceable *vade mecum* for speakers or teachers."

The name of Fronto should be included in any consideration of declamations. Not only did he make the writing of controversial themes a part of his scheme of instruction, but he also formulated a partial theory of rhetoric. Fronto, who was born about A.D. 100, assigned *con-*

[49] *Ancient Rhetoric and Poetic*, p. 97.

troversiae to Marcus Aurelius in addition to offering sundry advice on public speaking.

"With me," said Fronto in a letter to Lollianus Avitus, "eloquence holds the most honoured place. . . ." And in a letter to Caesar:

Herein lies that supreme excellence of an orator, and one not easily attainable, that he should please his hearers without any great sacrifice of right eloquence, and should let his blandishments, meant to tickle the ears of the people, be coloured indeed, but not along with any great or wholesale sacrifice of dignity: rather that in its composition and fabric there should be a lapse into a certain softness but no wantonness of thought.[50]

Philosophy, he remarked, "will tell you what to say, Eloquence how to say it. . . ." Eloquence is sovereign: "It inspires fear, wins love, is a spur to effort, puts shame to silence, exhorts to virtue, exposes vices, urges, soothes, teaches, consoles."

The eloquence Fronto talked about, however, consisted almost wholly of stylistic flourishes. Quoting Nepos, he said: "*The supremest eloquence is to speak of sublime things in the grand style, of homely things in simple language. . . .*" His chief interest was in words. In a letter to Augustus, he said "the distinction between a first-rate orator and ordinary ones [is] that the others are readily content with good words, while the first-rate orator is not content with words merely good if better are to be obtained." After an orator's words have been examined,

. . . then from the whole word-population, so to speak, just as in war, when a legion has to be enrolled, we not only collect the volunteers but also search out the skulkers of military age so when there is need of word-reinforcements, we must not only make use of the voluntary recruits that offer themselves, but fetch out the skulkers and hunt them up for service.[51]

He also commented frequently on the importance of similes, on the necessity of the orator's mastering them, and on the wisdom of returning to the words of the older Latin authors—Ennius, Plautus, Naevius, and Lucretius, among them.

Fronto's contribution to rhetorical theory is minor, although he was evidently held in high esteem during his time. In searching for simplicity of style he merely accentuated certain artificialities which were already menacing the language. His was an appeal for the use of archaic words and obsolete expressions. D'Alton remarks, "whatever we may think of Fronto's theories, his attempt to reanimate Latin prose will at least rank as an interesting experiment." [52]

[50] *The Correspondence of Marcus Cornelius Fronto*. Edited and translated by by C. R. Haines. Cambridge, Massachusetts, 1919. I, 121.

[51] *Ibid.*, II, 53–55.

[52] *Op. cit.*, p. 320.

Appraisal of the Declamation

A final estimate of the place of the declamation in the rhetorical scheme cannot safely be ventured. However, the view of Edward is temperate and wise:

> As scholarship becomes ignorant and uncritical, as men of genius become rarer, as the world settles into barbarism, it is little wonder that these exercises become more arid, more wearisome, more sterile, and lose all merit until the very name of rhetoric becomes a term of reproach. But this is no more true of the declamation than of all other literary forms. We no longer regard it as a form of fictitious literature worth cultivating. It may be doubted whether we should not do better to cultivate a little more our sense of beauty and propriety in public speaking. If we have the best of matter for eloquent expression it is to be regretted that we do not devote more pains to finding the best expression for our matter. At any rate we should not disparage so much as we have done and still do, these declamations that in Seneca's time were cultivated by the best intellects of the day with an enthusiasm almost too great for pastime.[53]

And Baldwin says:

> Besides Aristotle's conception of rhetoric as the art of giving effectiveness to truth there had persisted the conception of it as the art of giving effectiveness to the speaker. Though the two conceptions are not mutually exclusive, the dominance of the one or of the other tends either to give rhetoric those manifold relations and that constant answer to reality which mark its great ancient achievements, or on the other hand to narrow it toward virtuosity and display. The large pedagogy of Quintilian is animated by the Aristotelian conception. The other conception, brilliant in Gorgias and his life, had already animated not only the *declamatores* at Rome, but that larger 'second sophistic' which became pervasively the rhetoric of the imperial centuries, in Greek and in Latin, throughout the Roman world. Ancient rhetoric offers the historic example, then, of a divergence that has remained typical.[54]

Tacitus Evaluates Oratory

Just as Quintilian saw a real danger in the undisciplined use of the declamation, so Tacitus, in his *Dialogue Concerning Oratory*, written about A.D. 80, and hence before the *Institutes*, considered the declamation a destructive influence in Roman culture. The *Dialogue* deals chiefly with the decadence of oratory; but it may also be a sort of farewell to public speaking and an explanation of the author's desertion of rhetoric in favor of his endorsement of history. Four eminent men participate in the dialogue: Maternus, the poet, who assumes the role of the idealist; Aper, the advocate, who gives the discussion a practical

---

[53] *Suasoriae of Seneca the Elder,* p. xxxvi.
[54] *Ancient Rhetoric and Poetic,* pp. 100–1.

turn; Secundus, the historian, who reveals the quiet, refined character; and Messala, the Roman of high birth, who champions the past.

In his analysis of the decline of oratory. Tacitus alleges that the true causes are: "The dissipation of our young men, the inattention of parents, the ignorance of those who pretend to give instruction, and the total neglect of ancient discipline." [55] He claims further that eloquence "has lost her field of glory," that the great theatres of speechcraft—the assemblies and courtrooms—are no longer open to the orators; or, if open, are no longer "kept alive by fresh materials." In other words, changed political and social conditions brought about the decline of oratory.

But, surely, the instruction now offered the youth was largely at fault, Tacitus alleged. No longer did the orator follow a discipline such as made Cicero and Demosthenes celebrated.

To form that illustrious character, it was not thought necessary to declaim in the schools of rhetoricians, or to make a vain parade in fictitious controversies, which were not only void of all reality, but even of a shadow of probability. Our ancestors pursued a different plan: they stored their minds with just ideas of moral good and evil; with the rules of right and wrong, and the fair and foul in human transactions. These on every controverted point are the orator's province. In courts of law, just and unjust undergo his discussion; in political debate, between what is expedient and honourable, it is his to draw the line; and those questions are so blended in their nature, that they enter into every cause. On such important topics, who can hope to bring variety of matter, and to dignify that matter with style and sentiment, if he has not, beforehand, enlarged his mind with the knowledge of human nature? with the laws of moral obligation? the deformity of vice, the beauty of virtue, and other points which do not immediately belong to the theory of ethics? [56]

Here, then, we have another indictment—not expressed as clearly and directly as others, but nevertheless an indictment—of speaking which glorified *elocutio* to the neglect of the other parts of rhetoric.

Lucian Satirizes Oratory

The most satirical indictment of the second sophistic period and of its teachings came from Lucian, himself a former devotee of sophistic culture. In his essay entitled *A Professor of Public Speaking*, directed, in the opinion of some scholars, at the lexicographer Pollux—and hence written after A.D. 179—Lucian satirizes the meretricious methods of acquiring quickly a full measure of skill in speaking. At this time, many speakers felt the need for a short cut to oratorical skill, and it is that idea which Lucian attacks.

[55] *The Works of Cornelius Tacitus.* Translated by Arthur Murphy. London, 1813. II, 421.
[56] *Ibid.,* II, 423–424.

The essay opens with a promise: "Do not be daunted, however, and do not be dismayed at the greatness of your expectations, thinking to undergo untold labours before you achieve them. I shall not conduct you by a rough road, or a steep and sweaty one, so that you will turn back halfway out of weariness." He indicates that there are two roads leading to Lady Rhetoric. ". . . One of them is but a path, narrow, briery, and rough, promising great thirstiness and sweat. . . ." "The other . . . is level, flowery, and well-watered. . . ."[57]

At the starting point of the two roads, the lover of Rhetoric will be approached by a man who is the guide to the rough road.

In exhorting you to follow him, he will point out the footprints of Demosthenes and of Plato. . . . Then he will tell you to imitate those ancient worthies, and will set you fusty models for your speeches. . . . And he will say that hard work, scant sleep, abstention from wine . . . are . . . indispensable.[58]

On the other road, the lover of Rhetoric will find many people, and among them will be a handsome man acting as the guide. "If, then, you go to him and put yourself in his hands, you will at once, without effort, become an orator, the observed of all, and, as he himself calls it, king of the platform, driving the horses of eloquence four-in-hand."

Through the medium of the handsome guide, Lucian states the qualifications of the prospective speaker:

Bring with you, then, as the principal thing, ignorance; secondly, recklessness, and thereto effrontery and shamelessness. Modesty, respectability, self-restraint, and blushes may be left at home, for they are useless and somewhat of a hindrance to the matter in hand. But you need also a very loud voice, a shameless singing delivery, and a gait like mine. . . . Let your clothing be gaily-coloured. . . . Have also many attendants, and always a book in hand.[59]

As for rules,

First of all, you must pay especial attention to outward appearance, and to the graceful set of your cloak. Then cull from some source or other fifteen, or anyhow not more than twenty, Attic words, drill yourself carefully in them, and have them ready at the tip of your tongue. . . . Whenever you speak, sprinkle in some of them as a relish. Never mind if the rest is inconsistent with them, unrelated, and discordant. Only let your purple stripe be handsome and bright, even if your cloak is but a blanket of the thickest sort. Hunt up obscure, unfamiliar words, rarely used by the ancients. . . . As for reading the classics, don't you do it—either that twaddling Isocrates or that uncouth Demosthenes or that tiresome Plato. No, read the speeches of

[57] *Lucian.* Translated by A. M. Harmon. Cambridge, Massachusetts, 1925. IV, 137, 143.
[58] *Ibid.*, IV, 145–147.
[59] *Ibid.*, IV, 155.

the men who lived only a little before our own time, and these pieces that they call 'exercises,' in order to secure from them a supply of provisions which you can use up as occasion arises. . . .[60]

Furthermore, "When you really must speak, and those present suggest themes and texts for your discussion, carp at all the hard ones and make light of them as not fit . . . for a real man."

Rhetorical disposition comes in for comment: "Take no pains at all that the first thing, just because it really is first, shall be said at the appropriate time, and the second directly after it, and the third after that, but say first whatever occurs to you first. . . ."

Finally, the prospective speaker should remember that "extemporary readiness goes a long way with the crowd to absolve your mistakes and procure you admiration; so see to it that you never write anything out or appear in public with a prepared speech, for that is sure to show you up."

These quotations throw only incidental light upon the development of rhetorical theory. But they reflect the attitude of a critic toward the speaking practices of his day, and, accordingly, establish at least a partial standard of excellence in critical inquiry for that period.

CRITICAL INVESTIGATIONS INTO STYLE

The Work of Dionysius

Written sometime between 20 and 10 B.C., Dionysius' *On Literary Composition* deals largely with word order, and provides today's student with a lucid analysis of style from the classical point of view.

In practically all speaking, says Dionysius,

. . . two things must have unremitting attention: the ideas and the words. In the former case, the sphere of subject matter is chiefly concerned; in the latter, that of expression; and all who aim at becoming good speakers give equally earnest attention to both these aspects of discourse.[61]

George Ammon's analysis of Dionysius' complete rhetorical system is recast by Baldwin, showing the division indicated in the passage above. It reveals that Dionysius placed invention and disposition under the head of "subject matter" and then devoted the rest of his scheme to style.

The major divisions of Dionysius' works cover the nature of composition, the aims and means of attaining skill in writing, the varieties of composition, and the poetical element in prose as well as the prose elements in poetry. Composition is defined as "a certain arrangement

[60] *Ibid.*, IV, 155–159.
[61] *Dionysius of Halicarnassus on Literary Composition.* Edited with translation by W. Rhys Roberts. London, 1910, p. 67.

of the parts of speech, or elements of diction. . . ." The processes involved in the art are, first,

> . . . that of observing the combinations which are naturally adapted to produce a beautiful and agreeable united effect; the second is that of perceiving how to improve the harmonious appearance of the whole by fashioning properly the several parts which we intend to fit together; the third is that of perceiving what is required in the way of modification of the material—I mean abridgment, expansion and transformation—and of carrying out such changes in a manner appropriate to the end in view.[62]

Those who compose verse and prose should aim at charm and beauty.

> Among the sources of charm and beauty in style there are . . . four which are paramount and essential,—melody, rhythm, variety, and the appropriateness demanded by these three. Under 'charm' I class freshness, grace, euphony, sweetness, persuasiveness, and all similar qualities; and under 'beauty' grandeur, impressiveness, solemnity, dignity, mellowness, and the like.[63]

Dionysius then describes the three modes of composition. The austere style

> . . . requires that the words should be like columns firmly planted and placed in strong positions, so that each word should be seen on every side, and that the parts should be at appreciable distances from one another, being separated by perceptible intervals. It does not in the least shrink from using frequently harsh sound-clashings which jar on the ear; like blocks of building stone that are laid together unworked, blocks that are not square and smooth, but preserve their natural roughness and irregularity. It is prone for the most part to expansion by means of great spacious words. In its clauses it pursues not only these objects but also impressive and stately rhythms, and tries to make its clauses not parallel in structure or sound, nor slaves to a rigid sequence, but noble, brilliant, free. It wishes them to suggest nature rather than art, and to stir emotion rather than to reflect character.[64]

Antiphon's speech illustrates this mode of expression.

The smooth composition

> . . . does not intend that each word should be seen on every side, nor that all its parts should stand on broad, firm bases, nor that the time intervals between them should be long; nor in general is this slow and deliberate movement congenial to it. It demands free movement in its diction; it requires words to come sweeping along one on top of another, each supported by that which follows. . . . It tries . . . to give, as far as possible, the effect of one continuous utterance. . . . It requires that all its words shall be melodious, smooth, soft as a maiden's face; and it shrinks from harsh, clashing syllables, and carefully avoids everything rash and hazardous.[65]

62 *Ibid.*, p. 105.
63 *Ibid.*, p. 121.
64 *Ibid.*, pp. 211–213.
65 *Ibid.*, p. 235.

As to figures, it employs "for the most part those which are dainty and alluring, and contain much that is seductive and fanciful." Isocrates achieved eminence through the use of this style of composition.

The harmoniously blended or intermediate composition is essentially a union of the other two types. It is a golden mean of expression, best cultivated by Demosthenes. Thus he assigns to Demosthenes "the palm for oratorical mastery." In him, Dionysius finds a "standard alike for choice of words and for beauty in their arrangement."

Longinus' Analysis of Artistic Sublimity

A second work which considers oratory from the point of view of literary craftsmanship is *On the Sublime,* associated with the name of Longinus but probably not the product of his hand. Although the date of preparation is also in doubt, it is believed that the work was completed in the first century A.D.

Devoted solely to style, or to the heightening of effect, *On the Sublime* links poetical and rhetorical effort in a fairly close union. It shows at least that they are interdependent. Intellectual and emotional capacities are essential in the orator, as in the poet, if the resulting style is to have imaginative and rhythmic properties. The author indicates that there are five sources

. . . from which the Sublimity of eloquence most copiously flows: presupposing as a groundwork common to all these five, a certain power of elocution without which they are nothing. The first and most effectual of these is, a successful boldness in regard to the sentiments. . . . The second is, vehement and enthusiastic passion. These two are, for the most part, natural constituents of Sublimity: the others are chiefly the result of art. The third is, a suitable combination of figures, which are of two kinds: those relating to the sentiment (or Metaphors) and those belonging to the language (or tropes). Next (and in the fourth place) is majesty of expression, which again may be divided into a judicious selection of words, and a diction sufficiently elaborate, and elevated by Tropes. The fifth constituent of Sublimity, which includes all those that precede it, is a dignified and elevated composition.[66]

Later, a distinction is drawn between sublimity and amplification:

Sublimity . . . consists in elevation, and Amplification in quantity: so that the former is frequently found in a single thought, whereas the latter requires enumeration and circumstantiality. Amplification . . . is the completing of a sentence with all its parts and members; which gives a powerful conception of the subject under discussion, by causing the mind to dwell upon it.[67]

[66] *Longinus on the Sublime.* Translated by William T. Spurdens. London, 1836. VIII.

[67] *Ibid.,* XIII.

Near the close of the essay, the author indicates, however, that few orators ever attain the heights of sublimity, chiefly because they are too engrossed in the material things of life. Men become petty and ignoble through their devotion to money, pleasures, and associated evils. Here, then, we find a treatise in which motive, moral idealism, dominates the scene.

The short section on imagery points to a truth not so clearly stated in previous works:

> Every mental conception communicable by language, whencesoever derived, is known in common discourse by the term *imagery:* but, in a more peculiar sense it is used when, through an enthusiastic feeling, you seem to see what you describe, and to place it before the eyes of your hearers. You must, however, have remarked that there is a difference between the imagery of the orator, and that of the poet: the object of the latter being surprise, and that of the former, elucidation; although they both seek to produce emotion. . . .
> The imagery of the poet will allow . . . of an excess of fiction quite surpassing credibility: but that of the orator is always the more beautiful, in proportion to its appearance of feasibility and truth.[68]

On the Sublime contributes certain tenets to a philosophy of rhetoric, chiefly through the relation that it establishes between rhetorical theory and moral standards. More than that, it gives us a measure of insight into the constituents of artistic creation in literary expression. As Baldwin remarks in his summary of the treatise:

> Aristotle's theory of rhetoric determines its function. Cicero dignifies even its conventional tasks as training for leadership. Quintilian surveys it as a comprehensive pedagogy. Dionysius analyzes its art. But the great unknown moves us to share the art ourselves.[69]

SUMMARY

Based largely upon the work of Aristotle, the contributions discussed in this chapter elaborate upon the early Greek tenets. They give them more clear-cut form, establish more detailed classifications, and initiate certain departures respecting the philosophical substructure of the art. But, in the main, they do not go appreciably beyond the line previously established by the Greeks.

The division of rhetoric into five constituent parts—invention, disposition, elocution, memory, and delivery—is firmly grounded in the treatises of this period. Serving as the basis of the *ad Herennium*, it also formed the framework of the theoretical inquiries of Cicero and Quintilian. Although present in the treatises of the Greeks, it did not serve quite so mechanically to separate the features of the systems they developed. The tradition of the five parts of speaking, however, has been persistent

[68] *Ibid.,* XV.
[69] *Ancient Rhetoric and Poetic,* p. 131.

and influential; even to this day, with some modifications, it serves to divide the essential aspects of the art, both in theory and in criticism.

With the division of the subject into its component parts, theorists with certain preferences and interests came soon to develop treatises dealing almost solely with individual aspects of the art. Thus Dionysius and Longinus contributed to the subject through their works on style. Although these contributions did not present balanced accounts of rhetoric as a whole, they afforded additional insight into the sphere of artistic creation. In this way, they helped later writers to provide comprehensive analyses of the speaking art.

The great names of this period are, of course, Cicero and Quintilian. The former left the most complete set of works on rhetorical theory and criticism ever assembled by one man. Writing as an orator of consummate ability, he set forth, in terms more copious than necessary perhaps, a virtual prolegomenon to the whole art of speaking. Quintilian, on the other hand, spoke as a teacher intent upon preserving the good in rhetorical education during a period when the excesses of exhibitionism and declamatory show were threatening not only this art, but the whole system of culture. His *Institutes* represent the most comprehensive contribution in print on the training of public speakers.

The pedagogical device most frequently associated with the immoderate and affected aspects of rhetoric during the decline of oratory was the declamation. Through its injudicious use, artificiality flourished in speech training, and so eclipsed the true function of speaking as an instrument of communication. Rhetoric became divorced from the social reality in which it normally and properly functions.

EXERCISES

1. Compare and contrast the points of view held by Aristotle, Cicero, and Quintilian on the following concepts: (a) function of orator; (b) ends of oratory; (c) qualifications of the speakers; (d) invention; (e) arrangement; (f) memory; (g) delivery.
2. Investigate the relationship between Cicero's concepts of the *doctus orator* and the modern view of liberal arts. (See Gwynn, *Roman Education from Cicero to Quintilian*, ch. 6).
3. To what extent and in what ways, specifically, do you believe that Cicero's and Quintilian's treatises devote attention to what we would now label "tricks of oratory"?
4. On the bases of what you find in Cicero's *De Inventione* and in the *Rhetorica ad Herennium*, write a paper on the nature of speech education during the time of Cicero's youth.
5. What similarities would you note between Edmund Burke's "Impeachment of Warren Hastings" and Cicero's "Prosecution of Verres"?
6. Through a study of typical orations by Cicero, compare and contrast his practice with his theory.
7. What is the full significance of Cicero's statement: "For the proper con-

cern of an orator . . . is language of power and elegance accommodated to the feelings and understandings of mankind"?

8. Compare and contrast the treatments of refutation in Cicero and Quintilian.

9. In the light of present-day pedagogical practices, evaluate Quintilian's suggestions concerning (a) the reading of history and speeches, (b) the writing of compositions, and (c) the practice of declamation.

10. Appraise Quintilian's concept of the "perfect" orator. Include a discussion of the orator as a civic leader and as a "good" man.

11. Contrast the treatment of character and style in F. L. Lucas' *Style* (ch. 2) with the corresponding material in Quintilian's *Institutes*.

12. Investigate the merits of *imitation* as a method of teaching. How was it used in Roman education?

13. Investigate the merits of *declamatio* as a means of training orators. For the pros and cons see Donald Lemen Clark, *Rhetoric in Greco-Roman Education* (see Readings, Chapter 2), and Harry Caplan, "The Decay of Eloquence at Rome in the First Century." In *Studies in Speech and Drama in Honor of Alexander M. Drummond*. Ithaca, 1944.

READINGS

J. W. H. ATKINS. *Literary Criticism in Antiquity: A Sketch of Its Development: Graeco-Roman*. Vol. II. Gloucester, Massachusetts, Peter Smith, 1961.

GASTON BOISSIER. "The Schools of Declamation at Rome." In *Tacitus and Other Roman Studies*. Translated by W. G. HUTCHINSON. London, Archibald Constable, 1906. Pp. 163–194.

HARRY CAPLAN. "The Decay of Eloquence at Rome in the First Century." In *Studies in Speech and Drama in Honor of Alexander M. Drummond*. Ithaca, New York, Cornell University Press, 1944. Pp. 295–325.

HARRY CAPLAN, trans. *Ad C. Herennium de ratione dicendi*. Cambridge, Harvard University Press, 1954. (Especially see Introduction.)

DONALD LEMEN CLARK. *Rhetoric in Greco-Roman Education*. New York, Columbia University Press, 1957. (See the last four chapters.)

––––––. "Some Values of Roman *Declamatio*." *Quarterly Journal of Speech*, 35: 280–283 (October, 1949).

M. L. CLARKE. *Rhetoric at Rome*. London, Cohen and West, 1953.

F. R. COWELL. *Cicero and the Roman Republic*. Baltimore, Penguin Books, 1964.

OTTO A. L. DIETER. "Stasis." *Speech Monographs*, 17:345–369 (November, 1950).

AUBREY GWYNN. *Roman Education from Cicero to Quintilian*. Oxford, Oxford University Press, 1926. (Also issued in paperback by Teachers College Press.)

EDITH HAMILTON. *The Roman Way*. New York, New American Library, 1957.

HAROLD F. HARDING. "Quintilian's Witnesses." *Speech Monographs*, 1:1–20 (1934).

LEE S. HULTZÉN. "Status in Deliberative Analysis." In *The Rhetorical Idiom*, edited by DONALD C. BRYANT. Ithaca, New York, Cornell University Press, 1958. Pp. 97–123.

H. I. MARROU. *A History of Education in Antiquity*. Translated by GEORGE LAMB. New York, Sheed and Ward, 1956. Part III, Classical Education and Rome.

RAYMOND E. NADEAU. "The *Progymnasmata* of Aphthonius in Translation." *Speech Monographs*, 19:264–285 (November, 1952).

WILLIAM M. SMAIL. *Quintilian on Education*. New York, Teachers College Press, 1938. (Consult Introduction for summary of Quintilian's theory and practice.)

WILLIAM M. SATTLER. "Some Platonic Influences in the Rhetorical Works of Cicero." *Quarterly Journal of Speech*, 35:164–169 (April, 1949).

LESTER THONSSEN, comp. *Selected Readings in Rhetoric and Public Speaking*. New York, The H. W. Wilson Co., 1942.

4

Contributions of the
Modern Theorists

THE TRANSITION PERIOD

A host of contributors sustained the rhetorical tradition during the period between the second sophistic and about the fifteenth century. Since preaching was the "characteristic form of oratory" during much of this middle period, it is understandable that some of the contributors should deal importantly with that aspect of speech doctrine. And of course the school books, especially in their treatments of the trivium and quadrivium, also helped to keep the heritage of rhetoric intact.

Among the names that appear often in the surveys of medieval rhetoric are Martianus Capella, whose *Marriage of Philology* and *Mercury* (c. 430) contained a division of studies in which rhetoric figured rather prominently, with all of the five parts of the classical division receiving attention; Cassiodorus, whose *Institutiones* (c. 570) helped to sustain the tradition of the seven arts, although rhetoric was not treated comprehensively; Isidore, whose *Etymologiae or Origines* (seventh century) contained summaries of all the seven arts; the Venerable Bede whose considerations of metre and rhythm had wide favor during the eighth century; and Alcuin, whose *Rhetoric of Alcuin and Charlemagne* (c. 794) represented a fairly substantial restatement of Cicero's *De Inventione* and Julius Victor's *Ars Rhetorica*.

CHRISTIAN PREACHING AND RHETORIC

A major contributor to medieval rhetoric was St. Augustine (A.D. 340–430) who, in *On Christian Doctrine*, applied a strict Ciceronian conception to the theory of preaching, as indeed did other writers in Latin, such as Cassiodorus, Capella, and Isidore of Seville. In some respects, this treatise resembles Quintilian's *Institutes of Oratory*. Although it is not so comprehensive, it has a similar pedagogical flavor. It is intended as a teaching device, supplying both a point of view toward Christian preaching and a small body of general principles for practical use. Augustine's work has historical significance in that it restored rhetoric to the high estate of the best Ciceronian tradition. It ignored sophistic—to the advantage of the cause of rhetoric—and reestablished the pursuit of Truth as the guiding principle of public speaking.

Books I, II, and III of *On Christian Doctrine* were probably written about 397; Book IV, about 426. Book IV deals most directly with rhetorical theory.

Augustine justifies his role as an instructor by saying: "He who reads to an audience pronounces aloud the words he sees before him: he who teaches reading, does it that others may be able to read for themselves. Each, however, communicates to others what he has learnt himself. Just so, the man who explains to an audience the passages of Scripture he understands is like one who reads aloud the words before him. On the other hand, the man who lays down rules for interpretation is like one who teaches reading, that is, shows others how to read for themselves." [1] The interpretation of Scripture depends, according to Augustine, upon "the mode of ascertaining the proper meaning, and the mode of making known the meaning when it is ascertained."

To discover the meaning of Scripture, the preacher must attend both to *things* and *signs*. The former includes things to be *enjoyed*—the triune God; those to be *used*; and those to be *used* and *enjoyed*. *Signs* are symbols—words, for instance. Augustine discusses at some length the possibilities of obscurity arising from words. He urges the careful use of logical reasoning and definition to keep meanings straight. In short, he asks the preacher to employ logic as a tool of expression. Furthermore, he begs the preacher to curb ambiguities arising from faulty observation of punctuation and from incorrect pronunciation. Words must be appreciated in context; tropes must be fully understood; figurative expressions must not be interpreted literally, or literal expressions figuratively.

Once the meaning is ascertained, it must be made known. This requires expression. And that calls for an elucidation of rhetorical principles. Although Augustine's treatise is not intended as a textbook (he specifically instructs Christian preachers to turn elsewhere for such a

[1] *On Christian Doctrine*. Translated by J. F. Shaw. In *The Works of Aurelius Augustine, Bishop of Hippo*. Edited by the Rev. Marcus Dods. Edinburgh, 1873. IX, 5.

body of rules) *On Christian Doctrine* turns out to be a modified manual of instructions.

Like many of his predecessors, Augustine tries to assess the relative value of rules in rhetoric. Rules, he believes, are helpful, provided they are used judiciously. In any event, they must be learned quickly and at an early age. This is but a confirmation of Roman doctrine, especially as set forth by Cicero and Quintilian.

Augustine enters an admonition on the use of rhetoric and dialectic for the determination of Scriptural meaning:

But the art previously spoken of, which deals with inferences, and definitions, and divisions, is of the greatest assistance in the discovery of the meaning, provided only that men do not fall into the error of supposing that when they have learnt these things they have learnt the true secret of a happy life. Still, it sometimes happens that men find less difficulty in attaining the object for the sake of which these sciences are learnt, than in going through the very intricate and thorny discipline of such rules. It is just as if a man wishing to give rules for walking should warn you not to lift the hinder foot before you set down the front one, and then should describe minutely the way you ought to move the hinges of the joints and knees. For what he says is true, and one cannot walk in any other way; but men find it easier to walk by executing these movements than to attend to them while they are going through them, or to understand when they are told about them. . . . And in the same way a clever man often sees that an inference is unsound more quickly than he apprehends the rules for it.[2]

Indeed, "men of quick intellect and glowing temperament find it easier to become eloquent by reading and listening to eloquent speakers than by following rules of eloquence." Furthermore, "I think there are scarcely any who can do both things—that is, speak well, and, in order to do this, think of the rules of speaking while they are speaking." The speeches of eloquent men do not necessarily demonstrate the close observance of rules. "For it is because they are eloquent that they exemplify these rules; it is not that they use them in order to be eloquent."

Insistence upon Truth as the over-all objective of speaking is a cardinal tenet of Augustine's treatise. This is a significant point for it represents a negation of the spurious goals of decadent rhetoric and sophistic. The rules of rhetoric are true, says Augustine, despite the evil use to which they may be put. "There are also rules for a more copious kind of argument, which is called eloquence, and these rules are not the less true that they can be used for persuading men of what is false; but as they can be used to enforce the truth as well, it is not the faculty itself that is to be blamed, but the perversity of those who put it to a bad use."

In all cases, wisdom is to be honored above eloquence. "To speak

[2] *Ibid.*, pp. 72–73.

eloquently, then, and wisely as well, is just to express truths which it is expedient to teach in fit and proper words,—words which in the subdued style are adequate, in the temperate, elegant, and in the majestic, forcible." Consequently, "the man who cannot speak both eloquently and wisely should speak wisely without eloquence, rather than eloquently without wisdom." Indeed, "men who teach lies are the more pitiable if they happen to be eloquent in speech."

All expression should be perspicuous. ". . . the best mode is that which secures that he who hears shall hear the truth, and that what he hears he shall understand." In addition, the expression should display, as far as possible, the merits of beauty and persuasivenes. This is true regardless of whether the style is subdued, temperate, or majestic. In any event, the diction must be appropriate to the subject matter; adapted to the occasion; and sufficiently varied to avoid monotony. Augustine appraises certain passages from Ambrose and Cyprian to illustrate the types of style; and he affirms the value, especially for the young preacher, of imitating the practices of great Christian preachers. Thus he returns to his basic contention that rules, however lucid and however useful to the young student, may be less valuable for the preachers intent upon a great Christian mission than the reading and hearing of truly eloquent models.

Augustine uses the three Ciceronian ends of discourse—to teach, to delight, and to move—as the basis of his instruction. Of these ends, teaching, he believes, is the most essential. It depends on *what* is said, whereas the other two rely on the *way* it is said. However, this analysis does not preclude the use of emotional detail. On the contrary, Augustine recognizes the necessity of moving hearers to action:

> The eloquent divine, then, when he is urging a practical truth, must not only teach so as to give instruction, and please so as to keep up the attention, but he must also sway the mind so as to subdue the will. For if a man be not moved by the force of truth, though it is demonstrated to his own confession, and clothed in beauty of style, nothing remains but to subdue him by the power of eloquence.[3]

On Christian Doctrine is important for setting a high ideal of Truth before the Christian preacher; for avoiding the excesses and obvious falsities of sophistical rhetoric; and for revitalizing the best in Ciceronian doctrine.

In a recent study, James J. Murphy points up the importance of Rabanus Maurus' (776–856) *De institutione clericorum* (A.D. 819) in the history of rhetoric. Like Augustine, Rabanus dealt in one part of his treatise with the functions of the preacher, or more specifically, the priest. But Murphy refers to a significant difference between the treat-

[3] *Ibid.*, p. 141.

ments by the two men. Whereas Augustine used Cicero as the exemplar and Ciceronian counsel as the approved word, Rabanus drew upon several sources, including Cicero, Augustine, and himself. Rabanus "is the first of many medieval writers to make a pragmatic choice of only those ideas which are useful to him without swallowing the whole system which gave birth to the ideas." [4]

Rabanus was a pupil of Alcuin (c. 735–804), whose *Rhetoric of Alcuin and Charlemagne* (c. 794) represented a rather slavish adherence to Cicero's *De Inventione* and Julius Victor's *Ars Rhetorica* (fourth century A.D.). Wilbur S. Howell's notes and translation of Alcuin reveal the emphasis which the work placed on invention, and particularly on the concept of argumentative positions or issues. [5]

Although Alcuin stressed invention, he shaped his work about the five-part scheme associated with the Ciceronian rhetoric. Many years would elapse before Cicero would again assert his full influence. Howell says the next significant appearance is noted in the thirteenth century in *Poetria Nova* by Geoffrey of Vinsauf. [6] In the seventeenth century, however, the Ciceronian pattern had a rebirth in such works as Thomas Vicars' *Manductio ad Artem Rhetoricam* (1621) and Thomas Farnaby's *Index Rhetoricus* (1625).

Howell's commentary on Alcuin contains a perceptive analysis of the differences between rhetoric and dialectic as competing philosophies of education. [7] The dichotomy has critical significance. If rational analysis—strictly, invention and arrangement—is assigned to the province of dialectic, and only style and delivery (and possibly memory) are regarded as legitimate concerns of rhetoric, the social role of the rhetorician is obviously restricted and the assessment of his efforts is correspondingly changed. The Platonic view, which had considerable acceptance during the middle centuries, did subordinate the position of rhetoric to a concern with stylistic expression. The contrasting view, essentially Aristotelian, holds that dialectic and rhetoric, though related, are independent arts, each with its own system. Accordingly, the broad conception of rhetoric includes the full sweep of the five traditional parts of rhetoric.

But the restricted view of rhetoric has had pervasive—and, we believe, an unhealthy—influence on the subject and its general acceptance. It has, for one thing, tended to fragment learning experiences that should be interrelated, if not unitary; and it has divorced, at least in the public

[4] *Western Speech*, Spring, 1967, p. 91.
[5] *The Rhetoric of Alcuin and Charlemagne.* Translated by Wilbur S. Howell. Princeton, New Jersey, 1941, pp. 3–64.
[6] "English Backgrounds of Rhetoric." In *A History of Speech Education in America.* Edited by Karl R. Wallace. New York, 1954, p. 8.
[7] *Op. cit.,* pp. 45–58.

mind, the substance of discourse (search, investigation, facts, analysis, the rational development of thought) from the merely outward expression and ornamentation of ideas. Ramean rhetoric (as deduced from the *Dialectica* of Peter Ramus [1555] and the enlargement of the scheme by his associate, Omer Talon [Talaeus] in *Rhetorica* [1584]) reveals this circumstance. The trivium (grammar, dialectic, and rhetoric) is sharply confined; each discipline operates exclusively within the designated area, and in such a pedagogical scheme rhetoric is likely to suffer since much of its legitimate work will have been usurped by the other two subjects. When invention and arrangement are removed from the rhetorical armory, the art is enfeebled.

JOHN OF SALISBURY

Just as Aristotle's *Rhetoric* was in part a protest against the teachers and manuals that gave disproportionate emphasis to emotional proof, so John's *Metalogicon* was partially a dissent from the view of one Cornificius who had questioned the value of the liberal studies. The *Metalogicon*, probably prepared about 1159, presents a defence of logic, rhetoric, and grammar. More particularly, it is a discourse on the functions of words. Rhetoric, *per se,* does not receive extensive formal treatment; instead, much of the detail relating to composition is articulated with the analysis of *dialectic.*

John's contribution derives largely from his defence of eloquence as a positive good, subordinate only to virtue and wisdom. Despite the claims of the "Cornificians," he holds that eloquence can be learned—that natural aptitude can be defined by theory and practice.

John reveals a thorough familiarity with Aristotle's works on logic. In fact, the *Metalogicon* becomes in substantial part a summary and analysis of the *Organon.* John was not acquainted with Aristotle's *Rhetoric;* but he knew and drew freely upon Quintilian's *Institutes of Oratory.*

The *Metalogicon* is a fairly vigorous plea for Truth as the end of discourse. It becomes a sort of intellectual prospectus for the attainment of a literary education. The learner begins with grammar—the base of the trivium; proceeds to poetry, which is related to grammatical inquiry; moves on to logic and rhetoric; then to the mathematical studies comprising the quadrivium; next to Natural Philosophy; and, finally, to the pursuit of Moral Philosophy—the capstone of orderly study.

THE FIRST RHETORIC IN THE ENGLISH LANGUAGE: COX

The first reasonably complete rhetoric in the English language, Leonard Cox's *Arte or Crafte of Rhethoryke,* helps to sustain the continuity of thinking in the province of oral expression between classical antiquity and the Renaissance. During the sixteenth century in England, says Frederic I. Carpenter, the theory of prose clung "to the traditions of oratory and the classifications and precepts of ancient rhetoric, as modified and interpreted by Medieval and Renaissance thought." [8] The sixteenth century treatises on rhetoric performed a useful service by suggesting an "ordered utterance" and by setting forth a theory of prose. Cox's was the first in the field, coming out before 1530. His was not, however, the first rhetoric printed in England. A Latin treatise, *Nova Rhetorica*, by Traversagni was issued by the Caxton Press about 1479.

Cox's chief service, according to Carpenter, "was that of a translator and commentator."

[He] served as an intermediary in the transmission to England of the Renaissance and Humanistic influence and literature. He had a reputation of his own among European scholars and men of the new learning, and he helped to carry their work into England. And so the questions of rhetoric and of literary form which deeply concerned all the men of the new learning came to concern Cox also, and to their elucidation . . . he devoted a large share of his attention.[9]

A practical aim guided Cox in his preparation of the *Rhethoryke*. With the spread of education, the establishment of new schools, and the growing recognition of form and style in prose, he sensed the need for a book on rhetoric in English. His book, accordingly, is "little concerned with the theory of rhetoric." "His aim is to tell very plainly the manner of putting together of orations of the several kinds then recognized by the rhetoricians." And he illustrates his points by citing examples. "The whole method is that of the Ciceronians and the Renaissance educators simplified and put in the vernacular."

The Plan of Cox's Book

Cox's *Rhethoryke*, a slim volume, deals almost exclusively with invention and disposition as they relate to the preparation of logical, demonstrative, and judicial speeches. Ethical and pathetic proof do not receive systematic treatment. For those of his readers who wished further instruction, Cox recommended a study of the treatises by Hermogenes, Cicero, or Trapesuntius.

Cox discusses the essentials of the art of rhetoric in these words:

Whosomeuer desyreth to be a good oratour or to dyspute and commune of any maner thynge/hym behoueth to haue foure thynges. The fyrste is called Inuencyon, for he muste fyrste of al imagyne or inuent in his mynde

[8] Leonard Cox. *The Arte or Crafte of Rhethoryke*. Edited by Frederic Ives Carpenter. Chicago, 1899, p. 7.
[9] *Ibid.*, p. 29.

what he shall saye. The ii. is named iudgement/for he muste haue wyt to discerne and iudge whether tho thinges that he hathe founde in his mynde be conuenient to the purpose or nat/for often tymes yf a man lake thys propriete he may as well tell that that is agaynste hym/as with hym/as experience doth dayly shew. The iii. is dysposycyon wherby he maye knowe howe to ordre and set euery thynge in his due place. Leste thoughe his inuencyon and iudgement be neuer so goode he maye happen to be counted as the commune prouerbe sayeth To put the carte afore the horse. The iiii. & is such thynges laste as (sic) he hathe Inuentid and by iudgement knowen apte to his purpose when they ar set in theyr ordre so to speke them that it maye be pleasant and delectable to the audience.[10]

Cox's *Rhethoryke* is largely an adaptation of other works, and particularly of the 1521 edition of the *Institutiones Rhetoricae* of Melanchthon, the humanist educator and religious reformer of Germany. A comparison of Melanchthon's section on invention with Cox's *Rhethoryke,* both of which appear in the Carpenter edition, reveals a remarkably close textual correspondence. Melanchthon, in turn, relied chiefly upon Hermogenes, Trapesuntius, Cicero, and Quintilian. Cox does not, however, refer to Quintilian.

Carpenter believes that Cox's book "served its turn with its own generation, but any direct influence from it on later English rhetorical writers can scarcely be traced." Although not a significant figure in the establishment of an artistic English prose style, which was then in the making, Cox did, through his straightforward presentation, afford a precept if not a model for subsequent writers.

THE RESTATEMENT OF CLASSICAL DOCTRINES

Thomas Wilson's *Arte of Rhetorique,* issued in 1553 and published eight times during the following thirty years, offers for the first time in the English Renaissance a comprehensive treatment of the main divisions of rhetorical theory in the true Ciceronian tradition. Wilson reassembled the many observations and principles derived from ancient and medieval treatises and put them into an acceptable English prose pattern. He relied heavily upon the *ad Herennium,* Cicero, and Quintilian for the theoretical pattern of the art.

According to Russell Wagner, "Wilson's is the first rhetoric since Quintilian's to give a full and unified treatment of the best of the classical doctrines and to make them really useful in the world of practical affairs." [11]

Cox had devoted his efforts chiefly to invention and partially to dis-

---

[10] *Ibid.,* p. 43.
[11] Russell H. Wagner. "Thomas Wilson's Contributions to Rhetoric." In *Papers in Rhetoric.* Edited by Donald C. Bryant. St. Louis, 1940, p. 2.

position; Richard Sherry, in the *Treatise of Schemes and Tropes* (1550) and in the *Figures of Grammar and Rhetoric* (1555), had concentrated on elocution or style; but Wilson embraced *all* five traditional parts of rhetoric in his work, and thus gave the first rounded account of classical doctrine in the English language.

Wilson's Contribution

The main features of Wilson's *Rhetorique* are duplicates of the classical pattern, with such modifications as a sixteenth-century adaptation necessitated. His book treats of invention, disposition, elocution, memory, and delivery; considers demonstrative, deliberative, and judicial oratory; sets up teaching, delighting, and persuading as the ends of oratory; examines the following as the parts of an oration: entrance or beginning, narration, proposition, division or several parting of things, confirmation, confutation, and conclusion; describes and illustrates the conjectural, legal, and judicial states, or issues; and, through it all, avoids setting up a stereotyped pattern of theoretical detail. For, as Wilson said:

Rules were therefore giuen, and by muche obseruation gathered together, that those whiche could not see Arte hid in an other mannes dooynges, shold yet see the rules open all in an order set together: and thereby iudge the rather of their dooynges, and by earnest imitation, seeke to resemble suche their inuention.[12]

This observation was followed by the pithy remark: "And I knowe that rules were made first by wisemen, and not wisemen made by rules."

Wagner believes that one of Wilson's specific contributions is his conception of rhetoric as the art of *oral* discourse. Although the *Rhetorique* opens with the definition that "Rhetorique is an Arte to set forthe by vtterance of woordes"—and the reference here is probably to written and oral discourse—the word "orator," as Wagner points out, appears immediately and continuously thereafter. Wagner asserts that the "orators" Wilson had in mind were the lawyers and the preachers. "Rhetoric, then, though it ministers to the needs of writers, is to Wilson, as to the Greeks, the art of the speaker; and so it has remained, consistently in British thought, less so in American."

Another doctrine which distinguishes the Wilsonian treatment of rhetoric concerns the orator's need of getting and holding the attention of his hearers. On the second page of his book, Wilson remarks: ". . . an Orator must labour to tell his tale, that the hearers maie well know what he meaneth, and vnderstand hym wholie, the whiche he shall with ease doe, if he vtter his mynde in plaine woordes, such as are vsuallie receiwed, and tell it orderly, without goyng about the

[12] Thomas Wilson. *Arte of Rhetorike.* London, 1580 (1567 ed.), p. 162.

busshe." Again, the orator must "chere his geastes and to make them take pleasure, with hearing of thinges wittely devised, and pleasauntly set foorth." Furthermore, "such quicknesse of witte must be shewed, and such pleasaunt sawes so well applied, that the eares may finde much delite, whereof I will speake largely, when I shall intreate of moving laughter." [13]

Wilson's detailed analysis of amplification also relates to the problem of getting and holding attention. According to Wagner, Wilson makes

> . . . getting and holding attention the essential principle of effective oral discourse, and, with emotional proof, into which it rapidly fuses, the grand principle of persuasion. This concept and emphasis, differing from that of all his predecessors, is, of course, largely conditioned by the peculiar needs of the times. And whether right or wrong, whether Wilson has been directly influential or not, the principle persists in rhetorical theory today.[14]

Some 40 pages of Wilson's book are devoted to Amplification. Although this figure receives attention in Quintilian's *Institutes*, it gets its first comprehensive analysis at Wilson's hand. "Amplification," he says, "is a figure in *Rhetorique*, whiche consisteth moste in augmentyng, and diminishyng of any matter, and that diuers waies." [15] The kinds and methods of achieving amplification are numerous. Among the important ones are:

> The first kinde of amplification is, when by changyng a worde, in augmentyng we vse a greater, but in diminishyng, we vse a less. . . .
>
> Now in all these kindes, where woordes are amplified thei seeme muche greater, if by correction the sentence be vtterde, and greater wordes compared with them, for whom thei are vtterde. In the which kinde of speeche, we shall seeme as though we went vp by staiers, not onely to the toppe of a thyng, but also aboue the toppe. . . .
>
> There is an othere kinde of Amplification, when vnto the hiest there is added somethyng higher then it is. . . .
>
> Sometyme we amplifie by comparyng, and take our ground vpon the weakest and leaste, the whiche if thei seeme greate, then must that needes appeare greate, which we would amplifie and increase. . . .
>
> By contraries sette together, thynges oftentymes appeare greater. . . .
>
> There is also a notable kinde of amplification, when we would extenuate and make lesse great faultes, whiche before wee did largely increase: to the ende that other faultes might seeme the greatest abou all other. . . .
>
> There is a kinde of amplifying, whiche in speaking of twoo that fought together, we praise hym muche that hadde the worse, because we would the other to haue more praise.
>
> From the straightnesse of a thyng. Eloquence must nedes be a wonderfull thyng, when so fewe haue attained it. Likewise, notable aduentures doen by

13 Edition of 1567. London, 1909, pp. 2–4.
14 *Op. cit.*, p. 5.
15 Edition of 1567, p. 123.

a fewe, are more praise worthie, then such as haue been doen by a greate nomber. . . .

Vehemincie of wordes, full often helpe the matter forwards when more is gathered by cogitation, then if the thyng had bene spoken in plaine woordes. . . .

We encrease our cause, by heapyng of woordes and sentences together couchyng many reasons into one corner, whiche before were scatterde abroade, to the intent that our talke might appere more vehement. . . .

It is an excellent kinde of amplifiyng, when things encreased, and thynges diminished, are bothe sette together, that the one maie the rather beautifie the other. . . .

Likewise, contraries beyng rehearsed, and euill immediately vttered after the good, make muche for encrease.[16]

Related to the theme of amplification and attention, and discussed under the head of the former, is the subject of the Passions. While Wilson did not consider ethical persuasion, he looked upon emotional proof generally as an important aspect of rhetorical theory. He defined the Passions in these terms:

Because the beauty of amplifiyng, standeth moste in apte mouyng of affections: It is nedefull to speake somewhat in this behalfe, that the better it maie be knowen what thei are, and howe it maie bee vsed. Affections therefore (called Passions) are none other thyng, but a stirryng or forcyng of the mynde, either to desire, or els to deteste and lothe any thynge, more vehemently then by nature we are commonly wont to doe. We desire those thynges, we loue theim, like theim earnestly, that appere in our iudgement to be Godly: we hate and abhorre those thynges that seme naught, vngodly, or harmefull vnto vs. Neither onely are we moued with those things, whiche we thinke either hurtfull, or profitable for our selues, but also wee reioyse, wee sorie, or wee pittie an other mannes happe.[17]

In moving the affections

. . . and stirring the judges to be greeved, the waight of the matter must be set forth, as though they sawe it plaine before their eyes, the report must be such, and the offence made so hainous, that the like hath not bene seen heretofore, and all the circumstaunce must thus be heaped together: The naughtinesse of his nature that did the dede, the cruell ordering, the wicked dealing, and malicious handling, the tyme, the place, the maner of his doing, and the wickednesse of his will to have done more. The man that sustained the wrong, how little he deserved, how well hee was esteemed among his neighbours, how small cause he gave him, how great lack men have of him. Now, if this be not reformed, no good man shall live saufe, the wicked will overflow all the world, and best it were for saufeguard to be nought also, and so take part with them, for no good man shall go quiet for them if there be not speedie redresse found and this fault punished to the example of all other.[18]

[16] *Ibid.*, pp. 123–132.
[17] *Ibid.*, p. 132.
[18] Mair edition. London, 1909, p. 131.

Then follow analyses of pity, laughter, pleasant behavior, and other emotional states.

Carpenter holds that the chief interest of Wilson's *Rhetorique* "is in his discussion of English style and diction," a view generally accepted today. Elocution, said Wilson, reveals invention through words, commending the matter of discourse with such beauty that reason seems clothed in purple. The essential parts of elocution are plainness, aptness, composition, and exornation.

Among all other lessons this should first be learned, that we neuer affect any straunge ynkehorne termes, but to speake as is commonly receiued: neither seking to be ouer fine, nor yet liuyng ouercareless, vsing our speeche as moste men doe, and ordering our wittes as the fewest haue doen. . . .

Such are thought apt wordes, that properly agree vnto that thyng whiche thei signifie, and plainly expresse the Nature of the same. . . .

Composition . . . is an apte iouynyng together of woordes in suche order, that neither the eare shall espie any gerre, nor yet any man shalbe dulled with ouerlong drawyng out of a sentence, nor yet muche confounded with minglyng of clauses suche as are needeless, beyng heaped together without reason, and vsed without number. . . .

Exornation, is a gorgious beautifiyng of the tongue with borrowed wordes, and change of sentence or speeche with muche varieties.[19]

On the negative side, Wilson speaks of some of the faults of composition, observing:

For by such meanes the hearers will be forced to forget full ofte, what was sayd first, before the sentence bee halfe ended: or els be blinded with confounding of many things together. Some againe will be so short, and in such wise curtail their sentences, that they had neede to make a commentary immediately of their meaning, or else the most that heare them shalbe forced to keepe counsaill.

Some will speake Oracles, that a man can not tell which way to take them, some will be so fine and so poeticall withall, that to their seeming there shall not stande one haire a misse, and yet every body else shall thinke them meeter for a Ladies chamber, then for an earnest matter in an open assemblie.

Some will rove so much and bable so farre without order, that a man would thinke they had a greate love to heare them selves speake.

Some repeate one worde so often, that if such wordes could be eaten, and chopt in so oft as they are uttered out, they would choke the widest throte in England. . . . Some use overmuch repetition of some one letter, as pitifull povertie for a penie, but puffed presumption passeth not a point, pampering his panch with pestilent pleasure, procuring his passeport to poste it to hell pit, there to bee punished with paines perpetuall. Some will so set their words, they must be faine to gape after every word spoken, ending one word with a vowell, and beginning the next with an other, which undoubtedly maketh the talke to seem most unpleasaunt. . . . Some end their sentences all alike, making their talke rather to appeare rimed Meeter, then to seeme

19 Edition of 1567, pp. 164–172, *passim*.

plaine speeche, the which as it much deliteth being measurably used, so it much offendeth when no meane is regarded. . . .

Some will tell one thing twentie times, nowe in, nowe out, and when a man would thinke they had almost ended, they are ready to beginne againe as fresh as ever they were. . . . Some are so homely in all their doings, and so grosse for their invention, that they use altogether one maner of trade, and seeke no varietie to eschue tediousnesse.

Some burden their talke with needlesse copie, and will seeme plentifull when they should be short. An other is so curious and so fine of his tongue, that he can not tell in all the world what to speake. Every sentence seemeth common, and every worde generally used, is thought to be foolish in his wise iudgement. Some use so many interpositions . . . that they make their sayings as darke as hell.[20]

Wagner concludes that

Here we have, in embryonic form, a statement of those broad and pervasive qualities of style with which we have become so familiar—unity, coherence, and emphasis,—with clearness and brevity added for good measure. This may be the first statement of the principles of composition, in English, as we today conceive them.[21]

There is reason to believe, then, that Wilson's *Rhetorique* is the most important treatise on public speaking produced by sixteenth-century England. In Wagner's words:

In re-uniting, selecting and adapting the classical principles of public address, Wilson restored the body and, to some extent, reformed the concepts of rhetorical theory. In recalling rhetoric from the museum to the marketplace, he not only re-established the ancient conception of rhetoric as the art of the speaker, but, because of his own self-imposed purpose of adapting old doctrines to new times and new needs, he effected far reaching changes which have greatly influenced the theories of public address we hold today.[22]

BACON REVITALIZES CLASSICAL DOCTRINES

Emphasis upon Logical Proof

Called by one of his biographers [23] a man of "monstrous self-confidence," Francis Bacon left his mark on seventeenth-century rhetorical theory by revitalizing in part the classical doctrines of Greece and Rome. Furthermore, he gave rhetoric a fairly prominent place in his "total enterprise of learning." Deserving most consideration here, however, are his distinct contributions to the concept of speech invention.

Rhetoric, in Bacon's way of thinking, is the application of reason to

[20] Mair edition, pp. 166–167.
[21] *Op. cit.*, p. 7.
[22] *Ibid.*
[23] Edwin A. Abbott. *Francis Bacon.* London, 1885, p. xviii.

imagination "for the better moving of the will." Thus the persuasive power of rhetoric acts as an intermediary; it establishes a compact, or a confederacy, between the pictorial representations of the imagination and the impulse to action residing in the will. Affirming the value of ornamentation and imaginative coloring in address, Bacon nevertheless believes that sound reasoning, the "logical integrity of ideas, is the *sine qua non* of rhetorical discourse." Although the "affections themselves carry ever an appetite to good," they "beholdeth merely the present" while reason "beholdeth the future and sum of time." [24]

In line with his interest in logical proof, Bacon concerns himself with the analysis of invention. He doubts that invention of speech or argument is really invention, however, because "to invent is to discover that we know not, and not to recover or resummon that which we already know." Consequently, "the use of this invention is no other but, out of the knowledge whereof our mind is already possessed, to draw forth or call before us that which may be pertinent to the purpose which we take into our consideration." On last analysis, then, invention "is readiness and present use of our knowledge, and not addition or amplification thereof."

Two courses may be followed in procuring this use of knowledge. The first is Preparation, which consists essentially of diligence rather than "of any artificial erudition." Demosthenes, for example, "had ready framed a number of prefaces for orations and speeches" in order that he might be prepared to enter upon and have ready access to causes. The second part or course of invention is Suggestion, which assigns or directs us "to certain marks or places, which may excite our mind to return and produce such knowledge as it hath formerly collected, to the end we may make use thereof."

Aids to Invention

Consistent with his belief that effective invention required ready access to "certain marks or places" of argument, and in recognition of the shortcomings of the ancient writers in this particular, Bacon brought forth the *Antitheta, Formulae, Apophthegmes,* and *Colours of Good and Evil.*

The *Antitheta* were designed to furnish the speaker with a store of arguments for and against certain contentions. Their function was to serve as substructures for argument. Typical examples of the *antitheta* are the following:

[24] *The Works of Francis Bacon.* New edition. Edited by Basil Montagu. London, 1825. II, 209, 211.

For the letter of the law:
> Interpretation which recedes from the letter is not interpretation, but divination;
> When the judge recedes from the letter, he becomes a legislator.

For the intention of the law:
> We must gather from all the words taken together the sense in which each is to be interpreted.[25]

The *Formulae,* said Bacon,

> . . . are but decent and apt passages or conveyances of speech, which may serve indifferently for differing subjects; as of preface, conclusion, digression, transition, excusation, etc. For as in buildings, there is great pleasure and use in the well casting of the staircases, entries, doors, windows, and the like; so in speech, the conveyances and passages are of special ornament and effect.[26]

The following is a typical *formula:*

> A conclusion in a deliberative:
> So may we redeem the faults passed, and prevent the inconveniences future.

Apophthegmes are "pointed speeches" or little "salt pits" from which "you may extract salt out of, and sprinkle it where you will." They may be used in continued speech, or recited by themselves. Bacon's collection included items from previous writers, together with some prepared by himself. Typical of the *apophthegmes* are these two:

> (1) Many men, especially such as affect gravity, have a manner after other men's speech to shake their heads. Sir Lionel Cranfield would say, 'It was as men shake a bottle to see if there were any wit in their head or no?'
> (2) One of the Seven was wont to say; 'That laws were like cobwebs; where the small flies were caught, and the great brake through.' [27]

The *Colours of Good and Evil* were sophisms, with their refutations. The following example illustrates the use of this device in the invention of speech materials:

> That which keeps a matter safe and entire is good; but what is destitute and unprovided of retreat is bad: for whereas all ability of acting is good, not to be able to withdraw one's self is a kind of impotency.
> Hereof Aesop framed the fable of the two frogs that consulted together in the time of drought, when many plashes that they had repaired to, were dry. What was to be done, and the one propounded to go down into a deep well, because it was like the water would not fail there; but the other an-

---

[25] *Advancement of Learning.* XVIII, 8.
[26] *Ibid.,* XVIII, 9.
[27] *Apophthegmes,* Nos. 21 and 181.

swered, yea, but if it do fail, how shall we get up again. And the reason is, that human actions are so uncertain and subject to perils, as seemeth the best course which hath most passages out of it. Appertaining to this persuasion, the forms are, you shall engage yourself, on the other side, 'tantum quantum.' Vales, 'sumes ex fortuna,' etc. You shall keep the matter in your own hand. The reprehension of it is, that proceeding and resolving in all actions is necessary. For as he saith well, not to resolve, is to resolve, and many times it breeds as many necessities, and engageth as far in some other sort, as to resolve. So it is but the covetous—man's disease translated into power; for the covetous man will enjoy nothing, because he will have his full store and possibility to enjoy the more; so by this reason, a man should execute nothing, because he should be still indifferent, and at liberty to execute any thing. Besides necessity and this same 'jacta est alea', hath many times an advantage, because it awaketh the powers of the mind, and strengthened endeavour, 'caeteris paret necessitate certe superiores istes.' [28]

Doctrine of Audience Adaptation

Bacon also contributed to rhetorical theory through his observation that the materials of speech should be adapted to the particular audience. While this idea was as old as the earliest rhetoricians, it nevertheless received renewed emphasis in Bacon's works. It appears also, he remarked, that logic differs from Rhetoric,

. . . not only as the fist from the palm, the one close the other at large; but much more in this, that logic handleth reason exact and in truth, and rhetoric handleth it as it is planted in popular opinions and manners. And, therefore, Aristotle doth wisely place rhetoric as between logic on the one side, and moral or civil knowledge on the other, as participating of both; for the proofs and demonstrations of logic are toward all men indifferent and the same; but the proofs and persuasions of Rhetoric ought to differ according to the auditors. . . . Which application, in perfection of idea, ought to extend so far, that if a man should speak to them all respectively and several ways: though this politic part of eloquence in private speech it is easy for the greatest orators to want. . . . [29]

THE INFLUENCE OF STYLISTIC RHETORIC

Emphasis on Ornament

Unquestionably, the treatises that contributed most to the development and refinement of practical and critical standards of speechcraft were those offering a balanced account of all the essential parts of the subject, namely, invention, disposition, elocution, memory, and delivery. Certain movements in the history of rhetorical theory—and in educational trends generally—did, however, give rise to books on speaking

[28] *Works of Francis Bacon.* I, 231 f.
[29] *Ibid.,* II, 212.

which stressed one of the aspects of the subject to the neglect of the others.

Elocutio, for instance, commanded a position of supremacy in several treatises. While their authors were not unmindful of the role of the other phases of rhetorical inquiry, they looked upon stylistic embellishment as of first importance. In 1550 Richard Sherry brought out his *Treatise of Schemes and Tropes*, followed in 1555 by his *Figures of Grammar and Rhetoric*. These works plainly presuppose the doctrine that rhetoric is significantly style. Substantially the same view prevailed in other works of the latter half of the sixteenth century, including Henry Peacham's *Garden of Eloquence*, George Puttenham's *Arte of English Poesie*, and Butler's *Rhetoricae libri duo*. A cursory examination of Warren Taylor's dictionary of *Tudor Figures of Rhetoric* will suggest the elaborate extent to which the study of *elocutio* went during this period. Taylor's list of figures, incidentally, is drawn from the works mentioned above, and from Angel Day's *The English Secretary*, Dudley Fenner's *The Artes of Logike and Rhetorike*, Abraham Fraunce's *The Arcadian Rhetorike*, John Hoskins' *Directions for Speech and Style*, and Richard Rainolde's *The Foundacion of Rhetorike*. (Fenner's and Fraunce's works were largely translations or adaptations of Ramus and Talaeus.)

Thomas Gibbons and John Stirling are the most important eighteenth-century figures to devote their treatises exclusively to the devices of stylistic ornamentation, the former in the *Rhetoric*, and the latter in the *System of Rhetoric*.

The Work of Thomas Gibbons

Gibbons' *System of Rhetoric* is a good example of the stylistic approach. In the introduction, Gibbons acknowledges reliance upon classical writers, particularly Aristotle, Cicero, Dionysius, Hermogenes, and Tiberius Rhetor. The book contains numerous quotations from the ancients and the moderns to illustrate the embellishments.

Gibbons opens his treatise by distinguishing between a trope and a figure:

A Trope is a change of a word or sentence from one sense into another, which its very etymology imports; whereas it is the nature of a Figure not to change the sense of words, but to illustrate, enliven, ennoble, or in some manner or another embellish our discourses: and so far, and so far only, as the words are changed into a different meaning from that which they originally signify, the Orator is obliged to the Tropes, and not to the Figures of Rhetoric.[30]

[30] Thomas Gibbons. *Rhetoric*. London, 1767, p. 3.

His plan, then, is to classify, define, and illustrate the principal tropes and figures. This is carried out with meticulous regard for details, and with an abundance of examples. It is of interest to observe, however, that Gibbons recognized the danger resulting from inept use of the ornaments of rhetoric. With regard to the tropes, he said:

As Tropes infuse a dignity into our language, and shed a lustre over our expressions, when they are well-chosen and applied; so, on the other hand, when they are mean in themselves, when they are thrown out without judgment, or are in any other respect defective and faulty, they render our discourses mean and contemptible, or in some way or another miserably sink their value.[31]

He showed how tropes might render a style barren, provided they were excessive in number, too extravagant, too mean, too harsh, too affected, or lacking in delicacy.

Tropes may be sown too thick, or disgust by being injudiciously and profusely clustered. . . .

. . . an injudicious multitude of Tropes, instead of enlightening and enlivening, in which consists their great service, cloud and obscure, and it may be sometimes even what I might call *strangle* our meaning, and therefore they ought to be discreetly used, and rather sparingly sprinkled, than superfluously lavished upon our discourses. . . .

Tropes may be blamable for being too extravagant, and beyond the just allowances of nature and reason, and even of the indulgence that may be granted to the most bold and fiery genius. . . .

Tropes may become faulty by being too mean and low. As Tropes should not swell into a vain and wild extravagance, so neither should they shrivel into a minute and contemptible littleness. . . .

We should guard against all far-fetched and obscure Tropes. Let the materials out of which our Tropes are formed lie within the reach of every person's understanding, if possible, and not cost the learned pains to investigate their propriety, and leave the unlearned only a company of hard unintelligible words on which to ruminate, when they should gain from our discourses clear and profitable ideas. . . .

Another fault of Tropes consists in their being harsh and unsuitable to what they would represent. There ought to be care taken that there be an agreement or analogy between the Trope and the proper word for which it stands. . . .

We should guard against every Trope that may appear in the least degree finical and fantastical. Our Tropes should be bold and manly, free and natural, without being stiffened by affectation, or subtilised by a puerile and trifling fancy. . . .

Let us avoid all filthy and impure Tropes. We should take heed that no Tropes we make use of, either as to sound or sense, convey any idea that will not be agreeable to a chaste mind, or make any trespass upon delicacy.[32]

[31] *Ibid.*, pp. 3–4.
[32] *Ibid.*, pp. 4–17, *passim.*

The same warning was coupled to the treatment of figures.

Let our discourses be founded upon reason, and let us establish everything we advance with solid and convincing arguments. We are first to labour to enlighten the understanding, and inform the judgment, and then introduce our *Figures* to affect and engage the passions, and thereby secure a complete triumph over our audience. . . .

Let us be sparing in the use of *Figures*. We should not needlessly multiply them, and seem in our discourses overwrought, and . . . encumbered with *Figures*. . . .

Let not our *Figures* be too much adorned and refined into too nice an exactness. The less art the better.[33]

Emphasis on Delivery

A second movement of ideas in rhetoric that influenced the teaching of the subject and the development of the theory was the one that placed the principal, and in some instances the exclusive, emphasis upon the fifth canon of rhetoric, namely, delivery. As early as 1617 Robert Robinson had brought out his *Art of Pronynciation*, a work devoted to delivery proper. And in 1644 John Bulwer issued his major treatise *Chirologia . . . and Chironomia*, in which the action phase of delivery received exclusive consideration. This detailed work represents a highly systematized classification of the many gestures that a speaker may use to convey various shades of meaning. Even more, it is a sort of rationale of the whole subject of gesture, containing notes on the historical antecedents of action in literature and on the use to which action can be put generally. As Bulwer stated, both reason and the judgments of the ancients confirm the "gestures of the Hand to be things of great moment, & the very Palme and Crown of Eloquence. . . ."

Chirologia contains 64 descriptive analyses of the gestures of the hand and, under the subdivision of *Dactylogia*, 25 additional analyses of the gestures of the fingers. *Chironomia*, which is subjoined to *Chirologia*, contains 49 canons of the gestures of the hand; and under the subhead of *Indigitatio*, appear 30 additional canons of the gestures of the fingers.

Another manifestation of interest in delivery as an important canon of rhetoric resulted from the criticisms levelled against the contemporary orators by such eighteenth-century writers as Addison, Swift, and Chesterfield. "It is certain," wrote Addison, "that proper gestures and exertions of the voice cannot be too much studied by a public orator. They are a kind of comment on what he utters; and enforce everything he says with weak hearers, better than the strongest arguments he can make

[33] *Ibid.*, pp. 122–124, *passim.*

use of." [34] And Swift, in his *Letter to a Young Clergyman,* imposes a stricture on the reading of sermons, asserting that it destroys the effectiveness of the preacher. Chesterfield's *Letters to His Son* reveal clearly his interest in good enunciation and his belief that delivery is of great moment to the speaker. "A certain degree of good sense and knowledge," he wrote, "is requisite . . . but beyond that, the purity of diction, the elegancy of style, the harmony of periods, a pleasing elocution, and a graceful action, are the things which a public speaker should attend to the most. . . ."

Elocutionary Movement

By far the most influential individuals in this movement which gave to delivery a position of prominence were the so-called "elocutionists," including, among others, Thomas Sheridan, James Burgh, Joshua Steele, and John Walker. These men are best known as teachers, although their theorizing about methods of instruction resulted in certain positive contributions to the art of rhetoric.

Although Thomas Sheridan and John Walker are often mentioned as representative of two schools of thought within the elocutionary movement, the differences between them are probably not as great as alleged. Sheridan advocated the so-called natural manner in delivery. He was opposed to devices and techniques that interfered in any way with the spontaneous, conversational expression of the speaker. In his *Lectures on Elocution* (1763), he deplores the general deficiency of skill in reading and speaking, offering the following observation as a clue to the condition he criticizes:

> When we reflect that the end of public speaking is persuasion . . . ; and that in order to persuade others to the belief of any point, it must first appear, that the person who attempts it is firmly persuaded of the truth of it himself; how can we suppose it possible that he should effect this, unless he delivers himself in the manner which is always used by persons who speak in earnest? How shall his words pass for the words of truth, when they bear not its stamp? [35]

The "just" delivery which Sheridan sought

> . . . consists in a distinct articulation of words, pronounced in proper tones, suitably varied to the sense, and the emotions of the mind; with due observation of accent; of emphasis, in its several gradations; of rests or pauses of the voice, in proper places and well-measured degrees of time; and the whole accompanied with expressive looks, and significant gesture. [36]

---

[34] Joseph Addison. "On Public Speaking."
[35] Thomas Sheridan. *Lectures on Elocution.* London, 1781, p. 6.
[36] *Ibid.,* p. 12.

In partial opposition to this view was the doctrine set forth by John Walker in the *Elements of Elocution* (1781) and other books. Walker was fond of rules; accordingly, he devised an elocutionary scheme in which they appear with almost unbelievable frequency.

In the introduction to his *Elements of Elocution,* Walker staes:

Elocution, in the modern sense of the word, seems to signify that pronunciation which is given to words when they are arranged into sentences and form discourse.

Pronunciation, in its largest sense, may signify the utterance of words, either taken separately, or in connection with each other; but the pronunciation of words, connected into a sentence, seems very properly specified by elocution.

Elocution, therefore, according to this definition of it, may have elements or principles distinct from those of pronunciation in its most limited sense; and we may consider the elements of elocution, not as these principles which constitute the utterance of single words, but as those which form the just enunciation of words in dependence on each other for sense: at this point the present work commences. The delivery of words formed into sentences, and these sentences formed into discourse, is the object of it; and as reading is a correct and beautiful picture of speaking; speaking, it is presumed, cannot be more successfully taught, than by referring us to such rules as instruct us in the art of reading.[37]

After setting forth his theory of rhetorical punctuation, Walker establishes the rules for the pauses, inflections, modulations, accent, and emphases. These rules are also applied to the delivery of many types of sentences and passages.

In 1775 Joshua Steele brought out *Prosodia Rationalis,* an elaborate attempt at devising a notational scheme to record vocal variations in speech. He hoped to be able to plot the melodic and rhythmic patterns of speech, much as music does for song.

A similarly ambitious undertaking, *Chironomia* by Gilbert Austin, came out in 1806. An Irish clergyman and teacher, Austin felt that the fifth part of rhetoric—*pronuntiatio* or *actio*—was seriously neglected by British orators. However skillful they were in developing well-reasoned speeches, they did less than well because their delivery was dull. Moreover, Austin brooded over what was then patent, namely, that there was no way of preserving the spoken eloquence of any speaker or actor. So, drawing upon the wisdom of the classical rhetoricians, ancient and modern orators, and his own very considerable experience, he shaped a theory of delivery, embracing both voice and action, which continues to enjoy respect. His analysis of action—of countenance and gesture—is doubtless the most extensive in the literature of rhetoric, with the possible exception of John Bulwer's work of the same title, which Austin does not mention, indeed, may not have seen. Austin's notational system for

[37] John Walker. *Elements of Elocution,* 3d ed. London, 1806, p. 1.

explaining gestures and preserving patterns of delivery is properly illustrated in his text. Among the many authors whose manuals showed dependence upon Austin's analysis of voice and action are Jonathan Barber, Increase Cooke, C. P. Bronson, Merritt Caldwell, Albert M. Bacon, and Joseph A. Mosher.

FORERUNNER OF CONTEMPORARY THEORY: CAMPBELL

James McCosh once remarked that "the Scottish Metaphysicians following Shaftesbury were fond of speculating about beauty and taste, and that all the Scottish thinkers at this time were anxious to acquire an elegant style." [38] Like the other men to whom McCosh refers—Adam Smith, Lord Kames, and Hugh Blair, among them—George Campbell published his speculations. His was a formal treatise on *The Philosophy of Rhetoric* (1776), a book that exercised a salutary influence on the teaching of public speaking. The style in which Campbell clothed his ideas is itself worthy of notice, although he modestly allowed that since his effort was didactical and addressed only to the understanding, "the style in general admits no higher qualities than purity and perspicuity."

Campbell's treatment of rhetoric is not essentially didactic; rather, it is an inquiry into the relation between rhetoric and human nature, consonant with the author's conception of a theory of mind. According to Lloyd F. Bitzer,[39] in his perceptive introduction to the recently reprinted edition in the Landmarks in Rhetoric and Public Address series, Campbell's theory of rhetoric is subsumable under three propositions: "1. The vivacity or liveliness of ideas is the quality primarily responsible for attention and belief. . . . 2. Of the kinds of perceptions, sensations are typically most vivid, ideas of memory are less vivid, and ideas of imagination are least vivid. . . . 3. There is an attraction or association among . . . the ideas of the mind."

The Ends of Oratory

There is reason to believe that Campbell's greatest contribution to rhetorical theory is set forth in the first chapter of his book, in which he comments on the *ends* or objects of discourse and enlarges the classical doctrine that the primary aim of rhetoric is persuasion. "In speaking," says Campbell,

. . . there is always some end proposed, or some effect which the speaker intends to produce in the hearer. The word *eloquence*, in its greatest latitude, denotes 'that art or talent by which the discourse is adapted to its end.'

[38] James McCosh. *The Scottish Philosophy*. New York, 1875, p. 241.
[39] *The Philosophy of Rhetoric by George Campbell*. Edited by Lloyd F. Bitzer. Carbondale, Illinois, 1963, pp. xxv–xxvi.

All the ends of speaking are reducible to four; every speech being intended to enlighten the understanding, to please the imagination, to move the passions, or to influence the will.

Any one discourse admits only one of these ends as the principal. Nevertheless, in discoursing on a subject, many things may be introduced which are more immediately and apparently directed to some of the other ends of speaking, and not to that which is the chief intent of the whole. But then these other and immediate ends are in effect but means, and must be regarded conducive to that which is the primary intention. Accordingly, the propriety or impropriety of the introduction of such secondary ends will always be inferred from their subserviency or want of subserviency to that end which is, in respect of them, the ultimate. For example, a discourse addressed to the understanding, and calculated to illustrate or evince some point purely speculative, may borrow aid from the imagination, and admit metaphor and comparison, but not the bolder and more striking figures, as that called vision or fiction, prosopopoeia, and the like, which are not so much intended to elucidate a subject as to excite admiration. Still less will it admit an address as to the passions, which, as it never fails to disturb the operation of the intellectual faculty, must be regarded by every intelligent hearer as foreign at least, if not insidious. It is obvious that either of these, far from being subservient to the main design, would distract the attention from it.[40]

Campbell goes on to show that the only form of address in which assistance from the fancy is inappropriate is mathematical demonstration.

As this doth not, like moral reasoning, admit degrees of evidence, its perfection in point of eloquence, if so uncommon an application of the term may be allowed, consists in perspicuity. Perspicuity here results entirely from propriety and simplicity of diction, and from accuracy of method, where the mind is regularly, step by step, conducted forward in the same track, the attention no way diverted, nothing left to be supplied, no one unnecessary word or idea introduced. On the contrary, an harangue framed for affecting the hearts or influencing the resolves of an assembly, needs greatly the assistance both of intellect and of imagination.

In general, it may be asserted that each preceding species, in the order above exhibited, is preparatory to the subsequent; that each subsequent species is founded on the preceding; and that thus they ascend in a regular progression. Knowledge, the object of the intellect, furnisheth materials for the fancy; the fancy culls, compounds, and by her mimic art, disposes these materials so as to affect the passions; the passions are the natural spurs to volition or action, and so need only to be rightly directed. This connexion and dependency will better appear from the following observations.

When a speaker addresses himself to the understanding, he proposes the *instruction* of his hearers, and that, either by explaining some doctrine unknown, or not distinctly comprehended by them, or by proving some position disbelieved or doubted by them. In other words, he proposes either to dispel ignorance or to vanquish error. In the one, his aim is their *information;* in the other, their *conviction.* Accordingly, the predominant quality of

[40] George Campbell. *The Philosophy of Rhetoric.* New edition. New York, 1851, pp. 23–24.

the former is *perspicuity;* of the latter, *argument.* By that we are made to know, by this to believe.[41]

These passages bring out the ideas essential to an understanding of speech ends. At the same time they throw some light on the distinction between appeals to the understanding and appeals to the feelings. Campbell's concept of speech ends, so William P. Sandford believes,

> . . . with its inevitable corollary that the means by which the orator shall accomplish his purpose must differ according to the nature of the effect desired, and that whatever material is introduced into the speech must be judged according to its 'subserviency or want of subserviency to that end' strikes the keynote of modern theories of speech composition.[42]

Campbell's analysis of the speech situation, while deriving surely from the work of his predecessors, is nevertheless a succinct statement directly usable by the critic of oratory. He lists, as the basis for his consideration of forensic, deliberative, and pulpit speaking, the following components or particulars: "the speaker, the hearer or persons addressed, the subject, the occasion, and the end in view, or the effect intended to be produced by the discourse. . . ." In terms similar to those used today, Campbell names the elements which figure in the interaction of a speech situation.

The Modes of Proof

The three traditional modes of persuasion—logical, emotional, and ethical—receive systematic treatment.

Campbell opens his discussion of logical proof by showing the relation of logic to eloquence:

> The sole and ultimate end of logic is the eviction of truth; one important end of eloquence, though, as appears from the first chapter neither the sole, nor always the ultimate, is the conviction of the hearers. Pure logic regards only the subject, which is examined solely for the sake of information. Truth, as such, is the proper aim of the examiner. Eloquence not only considers the subject, but also the speaker and the hearers, and both the subject and the speaker for the sake of the hearers, or, rather, for the sake of the effect intended to be produced in them.[43]

Logical proof is of two classes: intuitive evidence and deductive evidence. The former includes "everything whose evidence results from the simple contemplation of the ideas or perceptions which form the proposition under consideration, and requires not the intervention of any third ideas as a medium of proof." Accordingly, this division includes "the truths of pure intellection, of consciousness, and of common sense." On

---

41 *Ibid.*, pp. 24–27.
42 William P. Sandford. *English Theories of Public Address, 1530–1828.* Columbus, 1931, p. 146.
43 *Op. cit.*, pp. 54–55.

the other hand, "rational or deductive evidence is derived from one or other of these two sources: from the invariable properties or relations of general ideas; or from the actual, though perhaps variable connexions, subsisting among things. The former we call demonstrative; the latter moral." Moral reasoning includes experience, analogy, and testimony. Campbell believes that the "proper province of rhetoric is the second, or moral evidence; for to the second belong all decisions concerning fact, and things without us."

Induction, rather than syllogistic reasoning, meets more fully the demands of the rhetoric Campbell envisages. Agreeing with Locke "that the syllogistic art, with its figures and moods, serves more to display the ingenuity of the inventor, and to exercise the address and fluency of the learner, than to assist the diligent inquirer in his researches after truth," Campbell gives four reasons why the syllogism "bears the manifest indications of an artful and ostentatious parade of learning, calculated for giving the appearance of great profundity to what, in fact, is very shallow." To begin with, "this method of arguing has not the least affinity to moral reasoning, the procedure in the one being the very reverse of that employed in the other." Secondly, "though this manner of arguing has more of the nature of scientific reasoning than of moral, it has, nevertheless, not been thought worthy of being adopted by mathematicians as a proper method of demonstrating their theorems." Next, "in the ordinary application of this art to matters with which we can be made acquainted only by experience, it can be of little or no utility." Finally, "the proper province of the syllogistical science is rather the adjustment of our language, in expressing ourselves on subjects previously known, than the acquisition of knowledge in things themselves."

To emotional proof Campbell gives a treatment that is not fundamentally new, but is more fully conceived in the light of psychological data, and especially of the so-called "faculties" of the mind. He considers hearers from two points of view, "as men in general, and as such men in particular."

In order to evince the truth considered by itself, conclusive arguments alone are requisite; but in order to convince me by these arguments, it is moreover requisite that they be understood, that they be attended to, that they be remembered by me; and, in order to persuade me by them to any particular action or conduct, it is farther requisite that, by interesting me in the subject, they may, as it were, be felt. It is not, therefore, the understanding alone that is here concerned. If the orator would prove successful, it is necessary that he engage in his service all these different powers of the mind, the imagination, the memory, and the passions. These are not the supplanters of reason, or even rivals in her sway; they are her handmaids, they are liable to be seduced by sophistry in the garb of reason, and sometimes are made ignorantly to lend their aid in the introduction of falsehood.

But their service is not on this account to be dispensed with; there is even a necessity of employing it founded in our nature.[44]

Campbell therefore analyzes hearers as endowed with understanding, imagination, memory, and passions.

Developing seven circumstances which are instrumental in operating on the passions, Campbell gives a novel turn to this phase of emotional proof.

The first is *probability,* which is now considered only as an expedient for enlivening passion. Here again there is commonly scope for argument. Probability results from evidence, and begets belief. Belief invigorates our ideas. Belief raised to the highest becomes certainty. . . .

The second circumstance is *plausibility,* a thing totally distinct from the former, as having an effect upon the mind quite independent of faith or probability. It ariseth chiefly from the consistency of the narration, from its being what is commonly called natural and feasible. . . .

The third circumstance I took notice of was *importance,* the appearance of which always tends, by fixing attention more closely, to add brightness and strength to the ideas. . . .

An action may derive importance from its own nature, from those concerned in it as acting or suffering, or from its consequences. It derives importance from its own nature if it be stupendous in its kind, if the result of what is uncommonly great, whether good or bad, passion or invention, virtue or vice, or what in respect of generosity is godlike, what in respect of atrocity is diabolical; it derives importance from those concerned in it when the actors or the sufferers are considerable, on account either of their dignity or of their number, or of both; it derives importance from its consequences when these are remarkable in regard to their greatness, their multitude, their extent, and that either as to the many and distant places affected by them, or as to the future and remote periods to which they may reach, or as to both. . . .

[Fourth], as to *proximity of time,* every one knows that any melancholy incident is the more affecting that it is recent. Hence it is become common with story-tellers, that they may make a deeper impression on their hearers, to introduce remarks like these: that the tale which they relate is not old, that it happened but lately, or in their own time, or that they are yet living who had a part in it or were witnesses of it. Proximity of time regards not only the past, but the future. An event that will probably soon happen hath greater influence upon us than what will probably happen a long time hence. . . .

Local *connexion,* the fifth . . . , hath a more powerful effect than proximity of time. . . .

Who is not more curious to know the notable transactions which have happened in his own country from the earliest antiquity, than to be acquainted with those which have happened in the remotest regions of the globe, during the century wherein he lives? It must be owned, however, that the former circumstance is more frequently aided by that of personal relation than the latter. Connexion of place not only includes vicinage, but every other local relation, such as being in a province under the same govern-

[44] *Ibid.,* p. 94.

ment with us, in a state that is in alliance with us, in a country well known to us, and the like. . . .

Still greater is the power of *relation* to the persons concerned, which was the sixth circumstance mentioned, as this tie is more direct than that which attacheth us to the scene of action. It is the persons, not the place, that are the immediate objects of the passions love or hatred, pity or anger, envy or contempt. . . .

Some have generally greater influence than others; some, again, have greater influence with one person, others with another. They are consanguinity, affinity, friendship, acquaintance, being fellow-citizens, countrymen, of the same surname, language, religion, occupation, and innumerable others. . . .

But of all the connexive circumstances, the most powerful is *interest*, which is the last. . . .

The reason is, a person present with us, whom we see and hear, and who, by words, and looks, and gestures, gives the liveliest signs of his feelings, has the surest and most immediate claim upon our sympathy. We become infected with his passions. We are hurried along by them, and not allowed leisure to distinguish between his relation and our relation, his interest and our interest.[45]

Campbell's treatment of ethical proof centers chiefly about sympathy as the "main engine by which the orator operates on the passions." Whatever weakens sympathy of the hearers toward the speaker militates against the likelihood of his achieving the end consistent with his purpose. Such loss in sympathy may result from (a) a low opinion of the speaker's intellectual abilities, (b) a bad opinion of his moral character, and (c) violent party spirit.

Language in Rhetoric

Books II and III of *The Philosophy of Rhetoric* deal with style.

Eloquence hath always been considered, and very justly, as having a particular connexion with language. It is the intention of eloquence to convey our sentiments into the minds of others, in order to produce a certain effect upon them. Language is the only vehicle by which this conveyance can be made. The art of speaking, then, is not less necessary to the orator than the art of thinking. Without the latter, the former could not have existed; without the former, the latter would be ineffective.[46]

Holding that a sound theory of style requires that the words used be reputable, national, and in present use, he goes on to discuss the canons of good usage. Finally, he treats, and in some detail, the qualities of perspicuity and vivacity as elements of true rhetorical significance. The other elements of importance are purity, elegance, animation, and music.

---

[45] *Ibid.*, pp. 103–112, *passim.*
[46] *Ibid.*, p. 162.

The Merit of Campbell's Book

The Philosophy of Rhetoric accomplished in part what its author said no moderns had done before, namely, the making of certain improvements on the rules laid down by the Greeks and the Romans. It went even further, by providing a treatise which helped to establish a standard of criticism for public speeches. In Campbell's words, "the artist and the critic are reciprocally subservient and the particular province of each is greatly improved by the assistance of the other."

The over-all dimension of Campbell's contribution to rhetorical theory and criticism is considerable. In the conclusion to his intensive analysis of Campbell's theory of public speaking as derived from a study of the *Philosophy of Rhetoric* and the *Lectures on Systematic Theology and Pulpit Eloquence,* C. W. Edney [47] lists the following distinctive features: (1) Campbell's classification of speech ends in terms of audience response; (2) his conception of audience analysis; (3) his classification of the sources of evidence; and (4) his emphasis upon the use of words to bring out exact meanings.

WHATELY'S CONTRIBUTION TO ARGUMENTATIVE COMPOSITION

The Kinds of Argument

In the introduction to his *Rhetoric,* published in 1828, Richard Whately indicates that in his time the province of rhetoric comprehended two extremes: some looked upon it as "composition in Prose" while others confined it to "Persuasive Speaking." So, he adds, "I propose . . . to adopt a middle course between these two extreme points; and to treat of 'Argumentative Composition,' *generally,* and *exclusively;* considering Rhetoric . . . as an offshoot from Logic." [48] The result is a vigorous restatement of classical doctrine, with particular application to practical matters in oral discourse, and with the major emphasis upon logical proof.

Remarking that the numerous and involved classifications of argument have "contributed so much to lessen the interest and the utility of systems of Rhetoric," Whately proposes to simplify and regularize those divisions. He sets up two principal classes: first, such arguments "as might have been employed—not *as* arguments, but—to *account for* the fact or principle maintained, supposing its truth granted: secondly, such as could *not* be so employed." The former class includes the arguments from

[47] C. W. Edney. *George Campbell's Theory of Public Address.* Ph.D. thesis. University of Iowa, 1946.
[48] Richard Whately. *Elements of Rhetoric.* New edition. Boston, 1861, p. 21.

probability, such as cause to effect and effect to cause. The latter is of two general types: (a) arguments from sign, including testimony, concurrent circumstance, oaths, negative probabilities, and the like; and (b) arguments from example, including induction, experience and analogy.

The Burden of Proof

Closely related to the analysis of argument is Whately's discussion of presumption and the burden of proof.

It is a point of great importance to decide in each case, at the outset, in your own mind, and clearly to point out to the hearer, as occasion may serve, on which side the *Presumption* lies, and to which belongs the (onus probandi) *Burden of Proof*. For though it may often be expedient to bring forward more proofs than can be fairly *demanded* of you, it is always desirable, when this is the case, that it should be *known*, and that the strength of the cause should be estimated accordingly.

According to the most correct use of the term, a 'Presumption' in favor of any supposition, means, not . . . a preponderance of probability in its favor, but, such a *preoccupation* of the ground, as implies that it must stand good till some sufficient reason is adduced against it; in short, that the *Burden of proof* lies on the side of him who would dispute it.[49]

Whately goes on to say that a normal measure of common sense

. . . will enable any one to perceive, and to show, on which side the Presumption lies, when once his attention is called to this question; though, for want of attention, it is often overlooked: and on the determination of this question the whole character of a discussion will often very much depend. A body of troops may be perfectly adequate to the defence of a fortress against any attack that may be made on it; and yet, if, ignorant of the advantage they possess, they sally forth into the open field to encounter the enemy, they may suffer a repulse. At any rate, even if strong enough to act on the offensive, they ought still to keep possession of their fortress. In like manner, if you have the 'Presumption' on your side, and can but *refute* all the arguments brought against you, you have, for the present at least, gained a victory: but if you abandon this position, by suffering this Presumption to be forgotten, which is in fact *leaving out one of, perhaps, your strongest arguments,* you may appear to be making a feeble attack, instead of a triumphant defence.[50]

As a tentative guide in such a search, Whately offers several suggestions:

There is a Presumption in favor of every *existing* institution. Many of these . . . may be susceptible of alteration for the better; but still the 'Burden of Proof' lies with him who proposes an alteration; simply, on the ground that since a change is not a good in itself, he who demands a change should

49 *Ibid.,* p. 139.
50 *Ibid.,* p. 140.

show cause for it. No one is *called on* . . . to defend an existing institution, till some argument is adduced against it; and that argument ought in fairness to prove, not merely an actual inconvenience, but the possibility of a change for the better. . . .

There is a 'Presumption' against anything *paradoxical, i.e.* contrary to the prevailing opinion: it may be true; but the Burden of proof lies with him who maintains it; since men are not to be expected to abandon the prevailing belief till some reason is shown. . . .

A Presumption evidently admits of various degrees of strength, from the very faintest, up to a complete and confident acquiescence.

The person, Body, or book, in favor of whose decisions there is a certain Presumption, is said to have, so far, 'Authority'; in the strict sense of the word. And a recognition of this kind of Authority,—an *habitual* Presumption in favor of such a one's decisions or opinions,—is usually called 'Deference.' . . .

Those who are habitually wanting in Deference towards such as we think entitled to it, are usually called 'arrogant;' the word being used as distinguished from self-*conceited, proud, vain,* and other kindred words. Such persons may be described as having an habitual and exclusive 'self-deference.' . . .

With some persons, . . . Authority seems to act according to the law of Gravitation; inversely as the squares of the *distances.* They are inclined to be of the opinion of the person who is *nearest.* Personal *Affection,* again, in many minds, generates Deference. They form a habit of first, *wishing,* secondly, *hoping,* and thirdly, *believing* a person to be in the right, whom they would be *sorry* to think mistaken. . . .

. . . though . . . questions of *fact* and of *opinion,* ought to be decided on very different grounds, yet, with many persons, a statement of facts is very little attended to when coming from one for whose judgment (though they do not deliberately doubt his veracity) they have little or no Deference. . . .

It is to be observed, that a Presumption may be *rebutted* by an opposite Presumption, so as to shift the Burden of proof to the other side. . . .

Again, there is . . . a presumption . . . in respect of each question, in favor of the judgment of the most eminent men in the department it pertains to;—of eminent physicians, *e.g.* in respect of medical questions, . . .

But there is a counter-presumption, arising from the circumstance that men eminent in any department are likely to regard with jealousy any one who professes to bring to light something unknown to themselves; especially if it promise to *supersede,* if established, much of what they have been accustomed to learn, and teach, and practise.[51]

Whately recognizes a difference between the understanding and the will of the individual, and to this extent he accepts the dichotomy of persuasion and conviction in rhetorical appeal. He also senses the fact that the two processes are interrelated:

The *Conviction* of the understanding . . . is an essential *part* of Persuasion; and will generally need to be effected by the Arguments of the Writer or Speaker. For in order that the Will may be influenced, two things are requisite; *viz.* 1. that the proposed *Object* should appear desirable; and

51 *Ibid.,* pp. 141–157, *passim.*

2. that the *Means* suggested should be proved to be conducive to the attainment of that object; and this last, evidently must depend on a process of Reasoning. . . .

Persuasion, therefore, depends on first, *Argument,* (to prove the expediency of the Means proposed,) and secondly, what is usually called *Exhortation,* i.e. the excitement of men to adopt those Means, by representing the end as sufficiently desirable.[52]

Advocacy of the Natural Manner

A final distinguishing feature of Whately's *Rhetoric* is his stricture upon the elocutionary methods of delivery, and his recommendation of the Natural Manner.

As Douglas Ehninger [53] indicates in his introduction to the reprint in the Landmarks in Rhetoric and Public Address series, *The Elements of Rhetoric* bears an ecclesiastical stamp, for Whately was a churchman. And his interest in oral reading was not idly speculative; it was directed toward "improving the delivery of the church service." Apropos of the artificial systems of the elocutionists, he remarks that his objection to their emphasis upon *delivery* is not a recommendation for *general inattention* to that aspect of rhetoric.

But it is evident that if any one wishes to *assume the Speaker* as far as possible, *i.e.,* to deliver a written composition with some degree of the manner and effect of one that is extemporaneous, he will have a considerable difficulty to surmount: since though this may be called, in a certain sense, the Natural Manner, it is far from being what he will naturally, *i.e., spontaneously,* fall into. It is by no means natural for any one to *read* as if he were *not* reading, but speaking. And again, even when any one is reading what he does not wish to deliver as his own composition, . . . it is evident that this may be done better or worse, in infinite degrees; and that though . . . a studied attention to the sounds uttered, at the time of uttering them, leads to an affected and offensive delivery, yet, on the other hand, an utterly careless reader cannot be a good one.[54]

The practical rule which Whately adopts, then, is

. . . not only to pay no studied attention to the Voice, but studiously to *withdraw* the thoughts from it, and to dwell as intently as possible on the Sense, trusting to nature to suggest spontaneously the proper emphases and tones.[55]

The orator who follows these suggestions will not attain perfection immediately, but

[52] *Ibid.,* pp. 209–210, *passim.*
[53] *Elements of Rhetoric by Richard Whately.* Edited by Douglas Ehninger. Carbondale, Illinois, 1963, p. x.
[54] *Elements of Rhetoric.* Boston, 1861, p. 398.
[55] *Ibid.,* p. 404.

. . . he may be assured that, while he steadily adheres to this plan, he is in the right road to it; instead of becoming,—as on the other plan,—more and more artificial, the longer he studies. And every advance he makes will produce a proportional effect: it will give him more and more of that hold on the attention, the understanding, and the feelings of the audience, which no studied modulation can ever attain. Others indeed may be more successful in escaping censure, and insuring admiration; but he will far more surpass them, in respect of the proper object of the Orator, which is, *to carry his point*.[56]

Final Appraisal

Perhaps there is little in Whately's book that is distinctly new. Wayland M. Parrish feels that its chief claim to originality "must consist . . . in his novelty of illustration and of arrangement." But the *Rhetoric* has a good Aristotelian flavor. It contains new and refreshing classifications of old facts; and it introduces some material—particularly on presumption and the burden of proof—which students of argumentative discourse have found helpful. Among the other distinctive features of the rhetorical scheme, according to Orville L. Pence,[57] are (1) Whately's clarification of the concepts of *sign, example,* and *probability* in logical proof; (2) his analysis of fallacies, and particularly those rising from ambiguity; (3) his differentiation of analogy and example; and (4) his inquiry into the calculation of probability as affording sufficient reasons for action.

RECENT CONTRIBUTIONS

A host of scholars, both in Speech and in other divisions of knowledge, have contributed richly to the field of rhetoric and public speaking since Whately's time. It is plainly impossible to record a full list of the contributors. High on the list, of course, would be the names of John F. Genung, Everett Lee Hunt, Hoyt Hudson, Herbert A. Wichelns, Charles Henry Woolbert, Wilbur S. Howell, Harry Caplan, and Donald L. Clark. Many have refined certain of the techniques and theoretical details previously set forth by the classical rhetoricians; some have conducted experimental research into problems having a direct bearing upon our conception of public address; and still others have attempted to articulate the classical and the scientific data into more realistic systems of instruction. All of these varied inquiries have helped to sustain and further the field of Speech.

We might single out a specific development which has exercised a profound influence on the theory and teaching of public speaking in America.

---

56 *Ibid.*, pp. 442–443.
57 Orville L. Pence. *The Concept and Function of Logical Proof in the Rhetorical System of Richard Whately.* Ph.D. thesis. University of Iowa, 1946.

Relying upon the data of each other's fields, the rhetorician and the psychologist have pooled some of their resources and, accordingly, have enlarged the conception of the speaker-audience relationship. A respected name in this development is that of James A. Winans who, in 1915, published the textbook *Public Speaking* in which a substantially new theory of persuasion was announced. Basing his treatment largely upon the psychological concepts of William James, Winans developed a theory of public address in which *attention* became the focal principle. Persuasion, he said, is a process through which hearers are induced to give attention to the ideas set forth by a speaker. On this premise he established a system which explored the psychological ramifications of the intellectual and emotional processes operative in the act of communicating thought and feeling to an audience. Said Lee S. Hultzén at a commemorative meeting of the Speech Association of America in 1957: "It is Winans' claim to something like greatness that he carried the principle of attention through the whole business of public speaking." [58]

Although a considerable body of new psychological data has been amassed since 1915 (and especially on the dynamic forces of motives, interests, and desires as they affect the reception of logical propositions), Winans' *Public Speaking* still remains the greatest contribution to rhetorical theory since George Campbell's *Philosophy of Rhetoric*.

SUMMARY

The three hundred year period between the appearance of the first rhetoric in the English language and the contributions of Richard Whately produced significant adaptation of rhetorical theory to modern conditions. Beginning with Cox and carrying through the mid-nineteenth century, the scholars of the period took the cardinal principles of speechcraft derived from antiquity, gave them current expression, refined some of their outmoded features, added such new ones as would accommodate the art to the new day, and thus established the pattern for much of the theoretical substructure in present day textbooks on speech composition and debate.

Regrettably, in this relatively short chapter, many treatises deserving notice have been omitted, including, to name but one, Hugh Blair's *Lectures on Rhetoric and Belles Lettres,* a near encyclopedic restatement of much that is best in Cicero and Quintilian. We shall, however, refer later to Blair's contributions as a critic.

Cox, Wilson, Campbell, Bacon, and Whately helped to revitalize the classical tradition in rhetoric. Furthermore, they demonstrated that tradition is not inimical to change; that to be guided by it is not necessarily

[58] *Published Papers,* p. 23.

to impede cultural growth. Campbell and Whately, especially, showed how competent writers can use the wisdom of the past in reformulating the principles of an art for the new day. They used the basic rhetorical principles of the ancients as springboards for dealing with the realities of their age.

EXERCISES

1. What were the Seven Liberal Arts? What significance did Rhetoric have in this curricular program?
2. Compare and contrast Thomas Wilson's *Arte of Rhetorique* with John F. Genung's *Practical Elements of Rhetoric* (Boston, Ginn and Co., 1886) with reference to (a) the treatment of the five traditional parts of rhetoric; (b) the principal types of public speech; (c) the ends of speaking; (d) the several parts of a speech; (e) the forms and methods of proof; and (f) the principles of audience adaptation.
3. Investigate the forces in England responsible for the development of elocution.
4. Compare and contrast the theories of Thomas Sheridan and John Walker on elocution. Indicate how the principles set forth by these writers are reflected in modern textbooks on the fundamentals of speech.
5. Investigate the popularity of Campbell, Blair, and Whately in American colleges of the nineteenth century.
6. What is the significance of belletristic analysis in the writings of Blair? What influence did this emphasis have on American rhetoric?
7. Douglas Ehninger has argued that Campbell, Blair, and Whately marked a departure from classicism and moved in new and essentially non-classical directions (see Douglas Ehninger, "Campbell, Blair, and Whately: Old Friends in a New Light," *Western Speech*, 19:263–269 [October, 1955], and "Campbell, Blair and Whately Revisited." *Southern Speech Journal*, 28:169–182 [Spring, 1963]. What evidence do you find to support or refute this thesis?
8. Ehninger says that Campbell, Blair, and Whately "wrote with the problems of the Christian preacher constantly in mind" (see "Campbell, Blair, and Whately Revisited," *Southern Speech Journal*, 28:175 [Spring, 1963]). What evidence of this trend do you find? You may wish to concentrate on only one figure.
9. From time to time the need for the sermon in church service is questioned. Comment on this view. As a background reading, examine Arthur J. Bronstein's "In Defense of Sermons," in *Essays in Honor of Walter Plaut* (New York, 1964), pp. 16–23.
10. Apply the tests of readability and applicability to this inquiry: Do you find Aristotle's *Rhetoric* more or less readable and usable for possible classroom adoption than either Wilson or Campbell or Whately?
11. Appraise the contributions of certain modern teachers to the development of a theory of rhetoric. Include estimates of the contributions of James A. Winans, Charles H. Woolbert, George P. Baker, and William Norwood Brigance.
12. Examine James J. Murphy's "Cicero's Rhetoric in the Middle Ages," *Quarterly Journal of Speech*, 53:334–341 (December, 1967).

READINGS

J. JEFFERY AUER and JERALD L. BANNINGA. "The Genesis of John Quincy Adams' *Lectures on Rhetoric and Oratory.*" *Quarterly Journal of Speech,* 49:119–132 (April, 1963).

GILBERT AUSTIN. *Chironomia.* MARY MARGARET ROBB and LESTER THONSSEN, eds. Carbondale, Illinois, Southern Illinois University Press, 1966. (See Editors' Introduction, pp. ix–xxix.)

KARL R. WALLACE. *Francis Bacon on the Nature of Man.* Urbana, University of Illinois Press, 1967.

WALLACE A. BACON. "The Elocutionary Career of Thomas Sheridan (1719–1788)." *Speech Monographs,* 31:1–53 (March, 1964).

HUGH BLAIR. *Lectures on Rhetoric and Belles Lettres.* Edited by HAROLD F. HARD-ING. Carbondale, Illinois, Southern Illinois University, 1965. (See Editor's Introduction in Vol. I, pp. vii–xxxv.)

BERT E. BRADLEY, JR. "The *Inventio* of John Ward." *Speech Monographs,* 26:56–63 (March, 1959).

———. "John Ward's Concept of *Dispositio.*" *Speech Monographs,* 24:258–263 (November, 1957).

WAYNE E. BROCKRIEDE. "Bentham's Philosophy of Rhetoric." *Speech Monographs,* 23:235–246 (August, 1956).

GEORGE CAMPBELL. *The Philosophy of Rhetoric.* Edited by LLOYD F. BITZER. Carbondale, Illinois, Southern Illinois University Press, 1963. (See Editor's Introduction, pp. ix–xxxvii.)

EDWARD T. CHANNING. *Lectures Read to the Seniors in Harvard College.* Edited by DOROTHY I. ANDERSON and WALDO W. BRADEN. Carbondale, Southern Illinois University Press, 1968.

DONALD LEMEN CLARK. "Rhetoric and Literature of the English Middle Ages." *Quarterly Journal of Speech,* 45:19–28 (February, 1959).

JAMES W. CLEARY. "John Bulwer: Renaissance Communicationist." *Quarterly Journal of Speech,* 45:391–398 (December, 1959).

LIONEL CROCKER. "The Break with Elocution—The Origins of James A. Winans' *Public Speaking.*" *Today's Speech,* 6:23–26 (April, 1958).

———. "The Evolution of Public Speaking." *Southern Speech Journal,* 8:4–8 (September, 1942). (Also reprinted in *Readings in Rhetoric,* edited by Crocker and Carmack. Springfield, Illinois, Charles C. Thomas, 1965, pp. 549–555.)

WILLIAM G. CRANE. *Wit and Rhetoric in the Renaissance.* New York, Columbia University Press, 1937. ("Rhetoric in the Schools of the Sixteenth Century," pp. 57–79; "English Rhetorics of the Sixteenth Century," pp. 97–112.)

ERNST ROBERT CURTIUS. *European Literature and the Latin Middle Ages.* Translated by WILLARD R. TRASK. New York, Pantheon Books, Inc., 1953. Ch. IV, "Rhetoric" and ch. VIII, "Poetry and Rhetoric."

THOMAS DE QUINCEY. *Selected Essays on Rhetoric.* Edited by FREDERICK BURWICK. Carbondale, Illinois, Southern Illinois University Press, 1967.

CLARENCE W. EDNEY. "Campbell's Lectures on Pulpit Eloquence." *Speech Monographs,* 19:1–10 (March, 1952).

———. "English Sources of Rhetorical Theory in Nineteenth-Century America." In *A History of Speech Education in America: Background Studies,* edited by KARL R. WALLACE. New York, Appleton-Century-Crofts, 1954. Pp. 80–104.

———. "George Campbell's Theory of Logical Truth." *Speech Monographs,* 15:19–32 (1948).

DOUGLAS EHNINGER. "Campbell, Blair, and Whately: Old Friends in a New Light." *Western Speech,* 19:263–269 (October, 1955).

———. "Dominant Trends in English Rhetorical Thought, 1750–1800." *Southern Speech Journal,* 18:3–12 (September, 1952).

———. "George Campbell and the Revolution in Inventional Theory." *Southern Speech Journal*, 15:270–276 (May, 1950).

———. "John Ward and His Rhetoric." *Speech Monographs*, 18:1–16 (March, 1951).

DOUGLAS EHNINGER and JAMES GOLDEN. "The Intrinsic Sources of Blair's Popularity." *Southern Speech Journal*, 21:12–30 (Fall, 1955).

JAMES GOLDEN and DOUGLAS EHNINGER. "The Extrinsic Sources of Blair's Popularity." *Southern Speech Journal*, 22:16–32 (Fall, 1956).

GILES WILKESON GRAY. "Some Teachers and the Transition to Twentieth-Century Speech Education." In *A History of Speech Education in America: Background Studies*. Edited by KARL R. WALLACE. New York, Appleton-Century-Crofts, Inc., 1954. Pp. 422–446.

———. "What Was Elocution?" *Quarterly Journal of Speech*, 46:1–7 (February, 1960).

WARREN GUTHRIE. "The Elocution Movement in England." *Speech Monographs*, 18:17–30 (March, 1951).

FREDERICK W. HABERMAN. "De Quincey's Theory of Rhetoric." In *Eastern Public Speaking Conference: 1940*. Edited by HAROLD F. HARDING. New York, H. W. Wilson Co., 1940. Pp. 191–203.

———. "English Sources of American Elocution." In *A History of Speech Education in America: Background Studies*. Edited by KARL R. WALLACE. New York, Appleton-Century-Crofts, Inc., 1954. Pp. 105–125.

DONALD E. HARGIS. "James Burgh and *The Art of Speaking*." *Speech Monographs*, 24:275–284 (November, 1957).

WILBUR SAMUEL HOWELL. "Classical and European Traditions of Rhetoric and Speech Training." *Southern Speech Journal*, 23:73–78 (Winter, 1957).

———. "English Backgrounds of Rhetoric." In *A History of Speech Education in America: Background Studies*. Edited by KARL R. WALLACE. New York, Appleton-Century-Crofts, Inc., 1954. Pp. 1–47.

———. *Fénelon's Dialogues on Eloquence*. Princeton, Princeton University Press, 1951.

———. *Logic and Rhetoric in England, 1500–1700*. Princeton, Princeton University Press, 1956.

———. "Ramus and English Rhetoric." *Quarterly Journal of Speech*, 37:299–310 (October, 1951).

———. *The Rhetoric of Alcuin and Charlemagne*. Princeton, Princeton University Press, 1941.

———. "Sources of the Elocutionary Movement in England: 1700–1748." *Quarterly Journal of Speech*, 45:1–18 (February, 1959).

HOYT H. HUDSON. "Jewel's Oration Against Rhetoric: A Translation." *Quarterly Journal of Speech*, 14:374–392 (June, 1928).

———. "*Compendium Rhetorices* by Erasmus: A Translation." In *Studies in Speech and Drama in Honor of Alexander M. Drummond*. Ithaca, New York, Cornell University Press, 1944. Pp. 326–340.

LEE S. HULTZÉN. "Charles Butler on Memory." *Speech Monographs*, 6:44–65 (1939).

RICHARD MCKEON. "Rhetoric in the Middle Ages." *Speculum*, 17:1–32 (January, 1942).

JAMES J. MURPHY. "Aristotle's *Rhetoric* in the Middle Ages." *Quarterly Journal of Speech*, 52:109–115 (April, 1966).

———. "The Earliest Teaching of Rhetoric at Oxford." *Speech Monographs*, 27:345–347 (November, 1960).

———. "The Medieval Arts of Discourse: An Introductory Bibliography." *Speech Monographs*, 29:71–78 (June, 1962).

———. "Saint Augustine and the Christianization of Rhetoric." *Western Speech*, 22:24–29 (Winter, 1958).

RAY NADEAU. "Delivery in Ancient Times: Homer to Quintilian." *Quarterly Journal of Speech*, 50:53–60 (February, 1964).

———. "Thomas Farnaby: Schoolmaster and Rhetorician of the English Renaissance." *Quarterly Journal of Speech*, 36:340–344 (October, 1950).

WALTER J. ONG. *Ramus Method, and the Decay of Dialogue*. Cambridge, Harvard University Press, 1958.

WAYLAND M. PARRISH. "Whately and His Rhetoric." *Quarterly Journal of Speech*, 15:58–79 (February, 1929).

———. "Elocution: A Definition and a Challenge." *Quarterly Journal of Speech*, 43:1–11 (February, 1957).

WILSON B. PAUL. "John Witherspoon's Theory and Practice of Public Speaking." *Speech Monographs*, 16:272–289 (September, 1949).

JOSEPH PRIESTLEY. *A Course of Lectures on Oratory and Criticism*. Edited by VINCENT M. BEVILACQUA and RICHARD MURPHY. Carbondale, Illinois, Southern Illinois University Press, 1965. (See Editors' Introduction, pp. ix–liii.)

RONALD F. REID. "The Bolyston Professorship of Rhetoric and Oratory, 1806–1904: A Case Study in Changing Concepts of Rhetoric and Pedagogy." *Quarterly Journal of Speech*, 45:239–257 (October, 1959).

———. "Research Notes: John Ward's Influence in America: Joseph McKean and the Boylston Lectures on Rhetoric and Oratory." *Speech Monographs*, 27:340–344 (November, 1960).

PAUL E. RIED. "Joseph McKean: The Second Boylston Professor of Rhetoric and Oratory." *Quarterly Journal of Speech*, 46:419–424 (December, 1960).

———. "The Boylston Chair of Rhetoric and Oratory." *Western Speech Journal*, 24:83–88 (Spring, 1960).

MARY MARGARET ROBB. "The Elocutionary Movement and Its Chief Figures." In *A History of Speech Education in America: Background Studies*. Edited by KARL R. WALLACE. New York, Appleton-Century-Crofts, Inc., 1954. Pp. 178–202.

———. "Ebenezer Porter, Early American Teacher." *Western Speech*, 13:9–14 (May, 1949).

WILLIAM P. SANDFORD. "English Rhetoric Reverts to Classicism." *Quarterly Journal of Speech*, 15:503–525 (November, 1929).

———. *English Theories of Public Address, 1530–1828*. Columbus, Ohio, H. L. Hedrick, 1938.

DANIEL E. VANDRAEGEN. "Thomas Sheridan and the Natural School." *Speech Monographs*, 20:58–64 (March, 1953).

RUSSELL H. WAGNER. "Thomas Wilson's *Arte of Rhetorique*." *Speech Monographs*, 27:1–32 (March, 1960).

———. "Wilson and His Sources." *Quarterly Journal of Speech*, 15:525–537 (November, 1929).

———. "Thomas Wilson's Contributions to Rhetoric." In *Papers in Rhetoric*. Edited by DONALD C. BRYANT. St. Louis, privately printed, 1940. Pp. 1–7.

CLEMENT C. J. WEBB. *John of Salisbury*. London, Methuen & Co., 1932. "John's Metalogicon and Entheticus," pp. 75–101.

KARL R. WALLACE. "Aspects of Modern Rhetoric in Francis Bacon." *Quarterly Journal of Speech*, 42:398–406 (December, 1956).

———. "Rhetorical Exercises in Tudor Education." *Quarterly Journal of Speech*, 22:28–51 (February, 1936).

———. "Early English Rhetoricians on the Structure of Rhetorical Prose." In *Papers in Rhetoric*. Edited by DONALD C. BRYANT. Pp. 18–26.

———. *Francis Bacon on Communication and Rhetoric*. Chapel Hill, University of North Carolina Press, 1943.

RICHARD WHATELY. *Elements of Rhetoric*. Edited by DOUGLAS EHNINGER. Carbondale, Illinois, Southern Illinois University Press, 1963. (See Editor's Introduction, pp. ix–xxx.)

James A. Winans. "Whately on Elocution." *Quarterly Journal of Speech,* 31:1–8 (February, 1945).

———. *Public Speaking.* New York, Century Co., 1915. (Chapters on Attention, Emotion, and Persuasion.)

W. Ross Winterowd. *Rhetoric: A Synthesis.* New York, Holt, Rinehart and Winston, Inc., 1968.

III

THE METHODS
OF THE CRITICS

5

The Critics of Antiquity

Establishment of a Point of View

We have already referred to the manifest interrelation of theory, practice, and criticism. Nearly all writers on rhetorical theory are, in a very real if not a formal sense, critics of speaking. The distinction between theory and criticism is, then, hard to draw, and even the most modest attempt to review the work of the critics of orators will become fabulously detailed unless certain common-sense differentia are established.

It is necessary, therefore, that we distinguish between the critics of *oratory as a subject,* and the critics of *orators per se;* likewise, that we discriminate between the critics who appraise a *general class* or *group of orators,* and those who evaluate *particular members of the class.*

Plato's Analysis of Rhetoric

Plato was one of the most discerning critics of oratory. His appraisal is, however, more directly concerned with rhetoric as a field of inquiry than it is with the particular excellences or defects of the speakers. Indeed, Plato directs his indictment against the Sophists and the orators, but behind these attacks is the studied attempt to show the inherent weaknesses of the current system of rhetoric which trains people for active participation in public life. Because the art of rhetoric admits of separations from truth, often employs questionable techniques in order to achieve persuasion, and hence exercises an unwholesome influence upon the social group, Plato dislikes it; he evaluates it, and finds it wanting, at least in the form which it assumed during his time.

Although it is impossible to determine the absolute beginnings of criticism in any field, many significant doctrines of critical inquiry into rhetoric can be traced back to Plato. Like many of the early Greeks, he liked to philosophize; and in the recently invented art of rhetoric he found opportunity to apply his intellectual skills. The result was the stricture against a rhetoric which concerned itself with "nonessentials," and the subsequent development of his own Ideal Theory which emphasized the importance of subject matter; recognized the need of natural endowment, knowledge of art, and practice; stressed the desirability of order and arrangement of materials; and insisted upon the speaker's having a thorough knowledge of emotional behavior. In postulating an ideal theory of rhetoric, Plato went far toward establishing critical standards for the art.

It should be noted, of course, that Plato also evaluated the work of individual orators. Thus, in the *Phaedrus*, he offers a critical analysis of Lysias' speaking; in the *Protagoras*, he virtually "parodies" the work of Protagoras and Hippias; in the speech of Pausanias, in the *Symposium*, he criticizes the "unmeaning tricks of rhythm and the neglect of ordered thought then fashionable"; and so on through a long list of examples. However, these individual evaluations are subordinate, both in purpose and in value, to the broad critical investigation of rhetoric as an art. And since rhetoric in antiquity embraced practically all prose literature, we find in Plato's work the first solid contribution to a philosophy of expression. By urging adherence to the *essentials* of the rhetorical art, he placed criticism "on an exalted plane." [1]

Aristotle's Point of View

Aristotle's contribution to the theory of public address also results from a critical indictment of what he called a false system of rhetoric. Atkins believes that with the *Poetics* and the *Rhetoric* "we have reached one of the supreme moments in critical history." In the early part of the *Rhetoric*, Aristotle expresses his opposition to those writers and systems which stress the "mere accessories"—the appeals to the emotions—and consequently neglect the logical proofs which are the "true constituents" of the art. He also criticizes previous writers for devoting all their attention to forensic oratory, despite the fact that political speaking "admits less of malicious sophistry than judicial pleading." Then follows his development of a theory of rhetoric which outlines the practical details of speechcraft and also sets forth a fairly complete rationale of the subject.

[1] J. W. H. Atkins. *Literary Criticism in Antiquity*. London, 1934. I, 66.

Methodologies of the Critics

Both the Platonic and Aristotelian treatises provide partial yardsticks for the critical evaluation of oratory. The consideration of these works in previous chapters illustrates the nature of the contributions. The display of theoretical detail also reveals the essential aspects of the critiques which the authors establish, at least indirectly, for appraising individual speeches. It is to be noted, however, that neither the *Phaedrus* nor the *Rhetoric* was intended as a treatise on the criticism of speeches, and whatever such use we make of them today is purely incidental and extra-functional to their original design.

In this chapter we shall summarize briefly the methodology employed by a selected group of critics who not only had a philosophy of rhetoric, but also were patently interested in appraising the activities of certain orators; we will consider writers who, directly concerned with the criticism of speeches or speakers, offered at least partially systematic plans for carrying out their purpose. We shall also make incidental reference to a few individuals whose contributions to a critique of speechcraft are not specifically covered in preceding chapters.

The controlling *rationale* for the chapter is twofold: (1) We shall reveal the method which the critic used in the evaluation of speeches; and (2) we shall attempt to isolate the *principle*, or determining point of view, which guided each critic in his evaluative undertaking.

A Necessary Condition of Criticism

J. E. Spingarn once observed that the purpose of criticism was chiefly the interpretation of finished productions, and that the intellectual processes involved in the effort were vitally akin "to those which first produced the works themselves. . . ."[2] Both creation and criticism presuppose, therefore, a certain degree of cultural progress which permits the free use of the imagination and the intellect.

But critical inquiry needs more than a measure of cultural attainment. It requires, for full expression, what D'Alton calls "a certain advance in self-consciousness." There must be an acknowledgment, a recognition, of the place that the novel or the speech or the play occupies in the continuum of artistic endeavor, and an awareness of the critic's relation to the particular work. Whereas the orator, for example, might fashion an effective speech through his natural instinct for expression, coupled with his awareness of the social significance of the words, the critic, if he were to rely upon the same resources, would doubtless fail to get beyond the boundaries imposed by those limitations, unless he also had

[2] "Origins of Modern Criticism." *Modern Philology*, 1:1 (April, 1904).

a growing consciousness of the philosophy or the *why* of the activity to govern and direct his intellectual efforts.

Correlative to the presupposition that a stage of self-consciousness is a necessary condition of critical inquiry is the all-important necessity of a *standard of comparison*. Evaluative judgments derive their substance from comparisons; and finished criticism results from the reasoned application of a certain production to the criteria of a model or standard of reference. Thus competent criticism of Cicero's oratory is facilitated because the Demosthenean model is available for comparison. Contemporary political oratory yields more easily to intelligent appraisal because the eighteenth century produced a model philosophic speaker in the person of Edmund Burke.

THE ATTICIST-ASIANIST CONTROVERSY

Cicero's distinction as a rhetorical critic derives in large part from his controversy with the men who set up an ideal in Attic oratory and who charged him with Asiatic tendencies. "Asianism" in rhetoric meant all that was florid, luxuriant, even bombastic; Atticism implied tempered restraint and decorum in expression. The declamations on fictitious themes, discussed previously, may well be considered the extremes in Asiatic quality. Cicero did not, of course, live to witness the most pronounced artificialities of declamatory utterance, but he was thoroughly conversant with the Asiatic characteristics. D'Alton asserts that it is one of Cicero's "great merits as a critic that, before he could witness Asianism in its most perverted form, he was able to put his finger on many of its corrupt tendencies." [3]

Pivotal Position of Style

The quarrel between the Atticists and the Asianists was largely over matters of style. D'Alton looks upon Atticism as "a movement towards the Ancients," characterized by an attempt to set up the great orators of the past as models of effective prose. On the other hand, Asianism was "more indicative of the modern tendencies in Rhetoric," with its consequent attachment to the living speech and its possible defects.

The true source of Asianism is difficult to trace. Certain aspects of it, however, may go back to the earliest Sophists with whom Plato quarreled because of their stylistic extravagances. The Gorgian influence, with its appeal to rhythmical effect and figurative embellishment, was particu-

[3] J. F. D'Alton. *Roman Literary Theory and Criticism.* London, 1931, p. 214. (Our analysis of the Atticist controversy and of Cicero's critical theory draws heavily upon the conclusions of J. F. D'Alton.)

larly pervasive. But the greatest excesses in style—those which made the term Asianism offensive to the purists—came with the decline of oratory, the loss of political liberty, and the subsequent declamatory practice divorced from the realities of the everyday world.

Among the Roman orators who favored a revival of the true Attic standards in prose style were Calvus and Calidius, both of whom were active in forensic pleadings about 60 B.C. These men, as the mouthpieces of the Neo-Atticist movement, were staunch advocates of the Plain style. They favored a style characterized by simplicity, restraint, purity, correctness, and clearness. Cicero praises Calvus for his nicety of language and for his good taste, but believes that his exacting concern for refinement of style "suffered all the force and spirit of it to evaporate." Quintilian also remarks on the circumstance of Calvus' imposing such severe criticism upon himself as to diminish his natural force as a speaker. As for Calidius, Cicero commended his precision and nicety of expression, but, as in the case of Calvus, believed that the meticulous regard for Attic simplicity and correctness militated against his oratorical effectiveness. That Calidius was able to *instruct* and to *please* his hearers, Cicero did not doubt. But that he would be able to carry out the third phase of an orator's business, namely, *to move the passions*, Cicero contested. "He had no force, no exertion," Cicero alleged, "and as a result, had no influence over the feelings of his hearers." [4]

Cicero's Place in the Controversy

Cicero's *De Oratore* does not reveal clearly the presence of the Atticist-Asianist controversy. In all probability, the issues did not enter open dispute until after its publication. However, D'Alton believes "it is more than probable that the treatise was accepted as a challenge by those whose ideal of style differed from that of Cicero, and who felt themselves aggrieved by his exaltation of a style which some of them at least would regard as extravagant and bombastic." D'Alton quotes H. Heck as saying that, upon the publication of the *De Oratore*, Calvus stigmatized the Ciceronian ideal as Asianist. But D'Alton thinks that "Cicero's critics directed their attack quite as much against his practice as against his theory." "At any rate," he continues, "they took up the position that the Plain Style characterized by elegance, restraint, and purity of diction, was the genuine Attic style, and that they alone were the true representatives of the Attic tradition." [5]

In the *De Oratore*, Cicero announces the functions of the orator, saying they are to inform, to conciliate, and to move the listeners. He also

[4] *Brutus.* Translated by E. Jones. LXXX.
[5] *Op. cit.*, pp. 225–226.

comments on the kind of style peculiarly suited to each of these functions. Thus the Grand and the Plain styles are contrasted, the distinctions centering sometimes about changes in delivery and, at other times, about matters of composition and diction. There can be no doubt, however, that Cicero evinces in the *De Oratore* a preference for the Grand style. In fact, the Plain and the Middle styles receive treatment that is far short of systematic; whereas the emphasis upon a rich, impassioned, and moving style immediately attracts notice. Cicero appeals for copiousness in expression, for, as he saw it, "the proper concern of an orator . . . is language of power and elegance accommodated to the feelings and understandings of mankind." [6]

The *De Oratore* does not, however, contain severe strictures on the Plain style. Surely Cicero expresses a preference for the Grand, but he speaks temperately of the shortcomings of the other types. He praises the Stoic conception of style for its subtlety and acuity, but affirms that it is not well adapted to oratory on great issues before assembled multitudes. Furthermore, he praises the "extremely keen and subtle species of oratory" practiced by Cotta who was, as D'Alton remarks, a true "Atticist in pre-Atticist days at Rome." And Cicero admits that different orators achieve eminence in their own ways, without imitating anyone or any standard of excellence. A pointed observation is made by Cicero in the *Brutus* when he remarks that there are two classes of *good* orators,

> . . . of which the former are distinguished by the simple neatness and brevity of their language, and the latter by their copious dignity and elevation; but although the preference must always be given to that which is great and striking; yet, in speakers of real merit, whatever is most perfect of the kind is justly entitled to our commendation. It must, however, be observed, that the close and simple orator should be careful not to sink into a dryness and poverty of expression; while, on the other hand, the copious and more stately speaker should be equally on his guard against a swelling and empty parade of words.[7]

The works of Cicero in which evidence of the quarrel with the Atticists is most pronounced are the *Orator, Brutus,* and *On the Best Style of the Orators.* In these works, Cicero is not only defending a thesis; he is also defending his personal reputation. Having for some time been the great leader and virtual model of oratorical excellence, he resented the move to establish other men as the true representatives of the best style in speaking. The Atticists announced their preference for the Plain style; accordingly, they regarded Lysias as their model.

Cicero was not disposed to contest Lysias' claim to eminence. In fact,

---

[6] *De Oratore.* Ed. by J. S. Watson. I, xii.
[7] *Brutus.* LV.

in the early part of the *Brutus,* he remarks that one might almost call Lysias a "complete orator." But, said Cicero, the Atticists were not sufficiently severe in their critical judgment when they set up Attic orators as models while at the same time holding that the Plain style was almost synonymous with Attic oratory.

But which of them does he mean to fix upon? for they are not all of the same cast. Who, for instance, could be more unlike each other than Demosthenes and Lysias? or than Demosthenes and Hyperides? Or who more different from either of them than Aeschines? Which of them, then, do you propose to imitate? If only *one,* this will be a tacit implication that none of the rest were true masters of Atticism; if *all,* how can you possibly succeed, when their characters are so opposite? Let me farther ask you, whether Demetrius Phalereus spoke in the Attic style? In my opinion, his orations have the very taste of Athens. But he is certainly more florid than either Hyperides or Lysias; partly from the natural turn of his genius, and partly by choice.[8]

Thus Cicero shows that Atticism may mean any one of several things, it being a notorious fact that even Hegesias, a thoroughgoing Asianist, claimed that he followed Attic models and "was so vain of his own taste for Atticism that he considered his predecessors, who were really masters of it, as mere rustics in comparison with himself."

Cicero would not have disapproved of Thucydides as a model of Plain style, provided one were interested in "composing histories instead of pleading causes."

For Thucydides was both an exact and a stately historian; but he never intended to write models for conducting a judicial process. I will even go so far as to add, that I have often commended the speeches which he has inserted in his history in great numbers; though I must frankly own that I neither *could* imitate them if I *would,* nor *would* if I *could.* . . .[9]

In another work, Cicero voices the same sentiment, affirming that Thucydides has no real connection with the orator since "it is one thing to unfold the actions of men in a narration, and quite a different one to accuse and get rid of an accusation by arguing." [10]

To Demosthenes, Cicero grants unconditional recognition as the complete, or supreme orator.

No keen, no artful turns could have been contrived for the pleadings he has left behind him, which he did not readily discover; nothing could have been expressed with greater nicety, or more clearly and poignantly, than it has been already expressed by him; and nothing greater, nothing more rapid

[8] *Ibid.,* LXXXII.
[9] *Ibid.*
[10] *On The Best Style of Orators.* Translated by C. D. Yonge. In *The Orations of Marcus Tullius Cicero.* London, 1919. IV, 531.

and forcible, nothing adorned with a nobler elevation, either of language or sentiment, can be conceived, than what is to be found in his orations.[11]

Cicero attempts to show that Demosthenes was always his model; that the imitation of his excellences was the goal toward which he directed his efforts and his wishes. Thus Cicero tries to harmonize his avowed preference for the Grand style with the Demosthenean idea of Attic simplicity.

This attempted reconciliation is not completely consistent with the generally accepted view that the complete orator, or the ideal model, should be a master of all three styles. Cicero believed, however, that only an impassioned and rich style of oratory could move multitudes to action. Not that he condoned Asianist tendencies of an extreme sort. He condemned the defects present in the orators of the Asian school; and he listed certain faults which Attic speakers should avoid, among them "a dry and lifeless manner." Perhaps a specious note is found in Cicero's defense of his position, for in his early speeches he yielded to some of the Asian excesses which he subsequently condemned.

Cicero's position in the Atticist controversy is, therefore, not completely unequivocal. D'Alton's interpretation of a passage in the Brutus furnishes a valuable hint of Cicero's view. According to D'Alton, Cicero looked upon Asianism as "an excess of the Grand style. Just as the orator of the Plain style had to beware of becoming bald and jejune (a tendency marked among the Atticists, according to Cicero), so the orator of the Grand style had to guard against passing into tasteless bombast."[12] Despite his respect for the Grand style, Cicero recognized the folly of using it when the minds of the hearers were not properly prepared for it.

For the man who can say nothing with calmness, nothing with gentleness; who seems ignorant of all arrangement and definition and distinctness, and regardless of wit, especially when some of his causes required to be treated in that manner entirely, and others in a great degree; if he does not prepare the ears of his hearers before he begins to work up the case in an inflammatory style, he seems like a madman among people in their senses, or like a drunken man among sober men.[13]

In D'Alton's opinion, this "distinction between the Grand style and the excesses to which it might easily lead, is a point of cardinal importance."

Cicero's controversy with the Atticists included critical appraisals of compositional elements and rhythm, as well as of the general features of the kinds of style. The advocates of the Plain style, naturally, were suspicious of rhythmical qualities in prose; they looked upon them as contributing little or nothing to clearness and correctness of speech.

[11] Brutus. IX.
[12] Op. cit., p. 240.
[13] Orator. In The Orations of Marcus Tullius Cicero, Yonge translation. IV, 410.

Furthermore, rhythmic qualities, openly sought by the speaker, tended to create a certain measure of artificiality; they nurtured a symmetry in form and structure which was removed from the natural expression of plain speech.

In the *Orator*, Cicero discusses rhythm at considerable length, treating its nature, causes, and fields of effective operation. He insists that the prose movement should be pleasing to the ear, this quality resulting largely from the use of symmetrical clauses and the traditional feet employed in poetry. Although Cicero defends vigorously the use of rhythm in speech, he is anxious to assure his readers that oratory chiefly for rhythmical effect is pointless. Those elements which please the ear should not command the attention, to the exclusion of subject matter. Likewise, the orator should be mindful that spontaneity in rhythmic effect is indispensable. Impressiveness of prose movement should be indissolubly linked with impressiveness of sentiment, thought, and language.

All in all, Cicero's defense of rhythm and his announcement of its limitations amount to a defense of his own style of speaking, of his own practice over a long period of years. The Atticists, in their advocacy of the Plain style, were levelling their criticism as much against Cicero's performances as against his critical theory. Cicero's replies served, therefore, both to set up a standard of criticism for oratory and to offer a veiled apology and vindication of his own practice.

THE VERSATILE GENIUS OF CICERO

Cicero's most important critical works are the *Orator* and the *Brutus*. The purpose of the first was to present a view of the Ideal Orator; it was as Torsten Petersson remarks, "Cicero's final statement not only of his oratorical ideal but also of what he conceived himself to have attained." [14] In one sense, it contained substantially the same content as the *De Oratore*, but the expression of it was fundamentally different. Evidently Cicero tried, though with not too much expectation of success, to win Brutus over to his position in the quarrel with the Atticists. Through the medium of the *Orator*, in which he delineated the character of the ideal speaker, he revealed himself as the master of oratorical excellence, worthy of imitation and support. Since Brutus did not approve of emotional oratory, it seems reasonable to believe that Cicero's argument in the *Orator* failed to draw him away from his Atticist sympathies. It should be borne in mind, however, as G. L. Hendrickson says, that it was "an outgrowth and product of dissenting criticism." Since the *Orator* is, by its nature, critical rather than didactic—there being a

[14] Torsten Petersson. *Cicero: A Biography.* Berkeley, Calif., 1919, p. 442.

positive minimum of precept in it—it seems likely that this work, which Sandys called an "aesthetics of oratory," was intended both as a justification of Cicero's style and as a criticism of those who dissented from his theory of rhetoric.

The Brutus

The *Brutus* is the first comprehensive history and criticism of orators and oratory. Written, as was the *Orator,* about 46 B.C., it is Cicero's most original treatise. Devoted almost exclusively to historical exposition and criticism, it contains a didactic note; it involves a veiled attempt to influence Brutus by showing how certain orators had failed to achieve distinction. In the *Brutus,* Cicero directs his argument against the style of oratory which the Atticists encouraged, and of which Calvus was the most distinguished advocate. "Under the appearance of historical objectivity," says Hendrickson; "Cicero seeks to effect an inductive proof in vindication of his own position, showing by appeal to history that the type of emotional discursive oratory which he himself represented had always been the more admired and effective." [15]

Cicero was eager to reveal in the *Brutus,* as he had in the *De Oratore,* that the attainment of great skill in eloquence was a difficult task, and that few men ever achieved the heights of effectiveness. Whether it was attained by art, nature, or practice, eloquence, he affirmed, "is the most difficult of all attainments. . . ." When in the course of the dialogue, Atticus reminds Cicero that he is discussing some men who were really the "dregs of oratory," Cicero replies: "I wish it to be noticed, that after recounting all who ever ventured to speak in public, we find but few (very few indeed!) whose names are worth recording, and not many who had even the repute of being orators." [16] Without imputing evil design to him, it can be appreciated that the job of making his own oratorical mastery shine forth in a brighter light was made easier by commenting on the arduousness of the assignment, and by contrasting his accomplishments with the shortcomings of many other orators, some relatively insignificant.

In the *Brutus,* we find a fairly large number of short critical appraisals of Greek and Roman speakers with some reputation for eloquence, from earliest times to Cicero's own day. Naturally, however, the treatment of the Greeks is short in Cicero's work. But the fact that he drew upon them for comparative study is important in the development of criticism. It is freely accepted that a critic has a great advantage if he can compare the products of two languages. Without this comparison, George Saints-

---

[15] G. L. Hendrickson. "Cicero's Correspondence with Brutus and Calvus on Oratorical Style." *American Journal of Philology,* 47:251. (1926).
[16] *Brutus.* LXIX.

bury once remarked, "not merely is the diagnosis of qualities mostly guesswork, but even the discovery of them becomes extremely difficult." [17] Cicero took advantage of this opportunity as fully as the available materials would permit.

Method in Cicero's Criticism

Cicero's use of the historical method in the *Brutus* is particularly noteworthy. Taking oratory as his theme, he traces the development of speaking achievement from early times to his own period. More than that, he shows that a principle of growth or improvement operates to heighten the effectiveness of orators as the years go by, until finally, perhaps in Cicero's own person, we find the realization of consummate, if not perfect, skill. A principle of progress is thus enunciated; and the history of the orators, as Cicero presents it, reveals its operation and movement toward a mature manner of oral expression.

The dictum upon which Cicero's historical investigation rests derives from a discussion of sculpture and painting. Commenting on the fact that artistic expression in those fields did not spring into fullest glory at one time—but, instead, developed and improved through a process of orderly refinement—Cicero concludes that the same is true in other arts, including oratory. There "is not one of them," according to his key remark, "which was invented and carried to perfection at the same time." This principle suggests two important things: First, it postulates the doctrine of gradual development in the realization of the highest oratorical skill, both in the individual and in the oratory of a nation; and second, it establishes the concept of continuity in oratorical literature—the conviction that, as Atkins suggests, orations "are not isolated phenomena, but products related to one another. . . ."

Precisely what the criteria of progress in oratory are, Cicero does not express clearly. An interpretation of the text suggests, however, that he was thinking of the orator's growing facility in emotional expression, of his attainments in learning and rhetorical skill, of his development of an effective prose style, and of his power to move audiences, as well as to instruct and please.

The Ciceronian conception of historical method in criticism includes another tenet which serves the critic of oratory well. In the *Orator*, Cicero remarks that the "prudence of the hearers has always been the regulator of the eloquence of the orators. For all men who wish to be approved of, regard the inclination of these men who are their hearers,

---

[17] George Saintsbury. *A History of Criticism and Literary Taste in Europe.* Edinburgh, n.d. I, 355.

and form and adapt themselves entirely to their opinions and wishes."
He continues:

> . . . in Caria and Phrygia and Mysia, which are nations of no very great
> refinement or eloquence, men have adopted a sort of fat and coarse kind of
> oratory, as best suited to their ears, which their neighbours the Rhodians,
> though separated from them by only a narrow sea, have never approved of;
> and the Greeks still less; and which the Athenians have utterly rejected; for
> they have at all times had a discerning and accurate judgment, so as to be
> unable to tolerate anything which was not pure and elegant. And as the
> orator was bound to comply with their doctrine on the subject, he never dared
> to make use of any unusual or ill-sounding expression.[18]

In other words, Cicero regarded men as moulded by the age in which
they lived; that they were shaped by their environment, and, as far as
oratory was concerned, were to be judged by the criteria or standards of
their period. Thus Cicero recognizes a certain relativity in standards
based upon the varying conditions of the environment and culture in
which orators participate. "Considering the time in which he lived," says
Cicero of Quintus Pompeius, he was "no contemptible orator." Admitting that Cato's language had an "antiquated air" and that some of
his expressions were "harsh and inelegant," Cicero asks us to remember
that "this was the language of the time. . . ." ". . . only change and
modernize it, which it was not in his [Cato's] power to do; add the improvements of number and cadence, give an easier turn to his sentences,
and regulate the structure and connection of his words, and you will find
no one who can claim the preference to Cato." [19] This indicates Cicero's
recognition that the standards of criticism must fit the standards of oratorical achievement at a given period in history. Needless to say, this is
a significant contribution to a philosophy of critical analysis.

Bases of Cicero's Oratorical Appraisals

We have observed that Cicero used the historical method in preparing
the studies in the *Brutus*. How, specifically, did he apply the method to
the several orators?

The basis of Cicero's work derives from the more or less conventional
divisions and classifications of rhetoric. Thus, in the first place, he appraises speakers according as they conform to his formula for success in
the art. To what extent do the speakers evince natural endowment,
thorough familiarity with the rules of the art, and seasoned practice in
the use of the theory? The trinity of nature, art, and practice serves as a
tool for the determination of essential strength or weakness. The following quotation from Cicero's analysis of Scaurus' oratory indicates the way

[18] *Orator.* p. 388.
[19] *Brutus.* XVII.

in which the critic used the prerequisites for oratorical success as guides to evaluation:

It will not be amiss to give a short account of Scaurus and Rutilius; neither of whom, indeed, had the reputation of being a first-rate orator, though each of them pleaded a number of causes. But some deserving men, who were not remarkable for their genius, may be justly commended for their industry; not that the persons I am speaking of were really destitute of genius, but only of that particular kind of it which distinguishes the orator. For it is of little consequence to discover what is *proper* to be said, unless you are able to express it in a free and agreeable manner; and even that will be insufficient, if not recommended by the voice, the look, and the gesture. It is needless to add, that much depends upon *art;* for though, even without this, it is possible, by the mere force of nature, to say many striking things; yet, as they will after all be nothing more than so many lucky hits, we shall not be able to repeat them at our pleasure. The style of Scaurus, who was a very sensible and an honest man, was remarkably grave, and commanded the respect to the hearer; so that, when he was speaking for his client, you would rather have thought he was giving evidence in his favor than pleading his cause. This manner of speaking, however, though but indifferently adapted to the bar, was very much so to a calm debate in the senate, of which Scaurus was then esteemed the father; for it not only bespoke his prudence, but, what was still a more important recommendation, his credibility. This advantage, which it is not easy to acquire by art, he derived entirely from nature; though you know that even *here* we have some precepts to assist us.[20]

Another way in which Cicero appraised the orators was through the use of the ends of oratory. In the *De Oratore,* he remarks that persuasion consists of three processes: instructing, conciliating, and moving the listeners. The first duty requires "mildness of address"; the second, "penetration"; and the third, "energy." Cicero believed, it will be recalled, that the great orator was one who could move listeners to action. Consequently, Cicero could not follow the Atticists in their unconditional advocacy of the Plain style.

In comparing the respective skills of Crassus and Scaevola, Cicero turns to the oratorical functions for his guide. Speaking of the trial of Manius Curius, he says:

. . . no man could explain and define, or discuss a point of equity, with a more copious facility than Crassus, as sufficiently appeared upon many other occasions, but particularly in the cause of Manius Curius, which was tried before the centumviri. For he urged a great variety of arguments in the defense of right and equity, against the literal *jubet* of the law; and supported them by such a numerous series of precedents, that he overpowered Quintus Scaevola . . . though the case before them was only a matter of legal right. But the cause was so ably managed by the two advocates, who were nearly of an age, and both of consular rank, that while each endeavored

[20] *Ibid.,* XXIX.

to interpret the law in favor of his client, Crassus was universally allowed to be the best lawyer among the orators, and Scaevola to be the most eloquent civilian of the age; for the latter could not only discover with the nicest precision what was agreeable to law and equity, but had likewise a conciseness and propriety of expression which was admirably adapted to his purpose. In short, he had such a wonderful vein of oratory in commenting, explaining, and discussing, that I never beheld his equal; though in amplifying, embellishing, and refuting, he was rather to be dreaded as a formidable critic, than admired as an eloquent speaker.[21]

Another instance of the use of the ends of speaking as the yardstick of critical measurement is found in Cicero's analysis of Calidius' oratory.

Nothing could be so easy as the turn and compass of his periods; nothing so ductile; nothing more pliable and obsequious to his will; so that he had a greater command of words than any orator whatever. In short, the flow of his language was so pure and limpid that nothing could be clearer, and so free that it was never clogged or obstructed. Every word was exactly in the place where it should be, and disposed . . . with as much nicety as in a curious piece of mosaic work. We may add, that he had not a single expression which was either harsh, unnatural, abject, or far-fetched; and yet he was so far from confining himself to the plain and ordinary mode of speaking, that he abounded greatly in the metaphor—but such metaphors as did not appear to usurp a post that belonged to another, but only to occupy their own. These delicacies were displayed, not in a loose and effeminate style, but in such a one as was strictly *numerous,* without either appearing to be so, or running on with a dull uniformity of sound. He was likewise master of the various ornaments of language and thought which the Greeks call *figures,* whereby he enlivened and embellished his style as with so many forensic decorations. We may add that he readily discovered, upon all occasions, what was the real point of debate, and where the stress of the argument lay; and that his method of ranging his ideas was extremely artful, his action gentlemanly, and his whole manner very engaging and very sensible. In short, if to speak agreeably is the chief merit of an orator, you will find no one who was better qualified than Calidius.

But as we have observed a little before that it is the business of an orator to instruct, to please, and *to move the passions,* he was, indeed, perfectly master of the first two; for no one could better elucidate his subject, or charm the attention of his audience. But as to the third qualification, the moving and alarming the passions, which is of much greater efficacy than the former, he was wholly destitute of it. He had no force, no exertion; either by his own choice, and from an opinion that those who had a loftier turn of expression, and a more warm and spirited action, were little better than mad men; or because it was contrary to his natural temper and habitual practice; or, lastly, because it was beyond the strength of his abilities. If, indeed, it is a useless quality, his want of it was a real excellence; but if otherwise, it was certainly a defect. I particularly remember, that when he prosecuted Quintus Gallius for an attempt to poison him, and pretended that he had the plainest proofs of it, and could produce many letters, witnesses, information, and other evidences to put the truth of his charge beyond a doubt, interspersing

21 *Brutus.* XXXIX.

many sensible and ingenious remarks on the nature of the crime—I remember, I say, that when it came to my turn to reply to him, after urging every argument which the case itself suggested, I insisted upon it as a material circumstance in favor of my client that the prosecutor, while he charged him with the design against his life, and assured us that he had the most indubitable proofs of it then in his hands, related his story with as much ease, and as much calmness and indifference, as if nothing had happened. 'Would it have been possible,' said I (addressing myself to Calidius), 'that you should speak with this air of unconcern, unless the charge was purely an invention of your own? And, above all, that you, whose eloquence has often vindicated the wrongs of other people with so much spirit, should speak so coolly of a crime which threatened your life? Where was that expression of resentment which is so natural to the injured? Where that ardor, that eagerness, which extorts the most pathetic language even from men of the dullest capacities? There was no visible disorder in your mind, no emotion in your looks and gesture, no smiting of the thigh or the forehead, nor even a single stamp of the foot. You were, therefore, so far from interesting our feelings in your favor, that we could scarcely keep our eyes open while you were relating the dangers you had so narrowly escaped.' . . . 'But is it possible to doubt,' cried Brutus, 'whether this was a sensible quality or a defect? For as the greatest merit of an orator is to be able to inflame the passions, and give them such a bias as shall best answer his purpose, he who is destitute of this must certainly be deficient in the most capital part of his profession.' 'I am of the same opinion,' said I. . . .[22]

In Cicero's treatises we find full recognition of the five parts of rhetoric. This traditional classification serves also as a framework about which to assemble his critical comments on the orators. Thus, when Cicero appraises Antonius' speaking, he deals specifically with invention—Antonius' comprehension of "everything which could be of service to his cause"; with disposition—"as a skillful general posts the cavalry, the infantry, and the light troops, where each of them can act to most advantage, so Antonius drew up his arguments in those parts of his discourses, where they were likely to have the best effect"; with the "quick and retentive memory"; with elocution—his "language, indeed, was not so refined as to pass for the standard of elegance; for which reason he was thought to be rather a careless speaker; and yet, on the other hand, it was neither vulgar nor incorrect, but of that solid and judicious turn which constitutes the real merit of an orator as to the choice of his words"; and finally, with his delivery, which had a peculiar excellence, both as to voice and to gesture. These excerpts reveal the fidelity with which Cicero adhered to the conventional rhetorical pattern in many of his criticisms. Unvaried adherence to this method would, of course, result in a measure of artificiality. To avoid the plainly stereotyped formula, Cicero sometimes rearranged the parts, considering style or memory before invention. This variation is observable in the criticism of

[22] *Ibid.*, LXXIX–LXXXI.

Caius Piso, where he commented first on his style, later on his invention. Proficiency in all five parts of oratory was deemed indispensable to the accomplished speaker. In fact, a full knowledge of the art of speaking (as embraced in invention, disposition, elocution, memory, and delivery) might even partially compensate for cultural deficiency. Thus Cicero observes that several able orators, including Sulpicius and Antonius, were not well versed in the poets or in law, but those defects were minimized because they had an elaborate knowledge of rhetoric. Furthermore, certain orators excelled in one part of rhetoric, some in others. Antonius, though skilled in all parts, was uncommonly able in delivery; Curio, though weak in invention and disposition, was possessed of a "brilliant and ready flow of expression." However, Curio had both a bad memory and a faulty pronunciation.

Like many of his fellow rhetoricians, Cicero adhered to the threefold classification of deliberative, forensic, and ceremonial oratory. He had a particular fondness for courtroom speaking; accordingly, he devoted considerable attention to it. To deliberative speaking, however, he assigned a fair measure of importance; but ceremonial oratory, divorced as it was from practical affairs, received little systematic treatment.

As might be expected of the critic who remained ever close to his theory, Cicero used the types of oratory as an extension of his methodology in criticism. Thus some men were appraised as forensic speakers, others as deliberative speakers. Scaurus' manner of speaking, for instance, is commended for its appropriate adaptation to "debate in the senate." "It not only bespoke his prudence, but, what was a still more important recommendation, his credibility." Numidicus and Silanus are mentioned as being skilled in deliberative speaking. These examples, among many others, suggest the use to which Cicero put his classificatory talents in evaluating the orators.

In the preceding sections we observed that, for Cicero, rhetoric was more than a single art or discipline. It was an all-embracing subject which eventually became an elaborate theory of culture. Like Isocrates, whom he followed in much of his thinking, Cicero conceived of the Ideal Orator as a man of full and ripened wisdom, conversant with the liberal arts, and disciplined in the ways of practical life.

Interestingly enough, Cicero made the cultural achievements of orators a basic indicator of his critical evaluation. Anxious to restore rhetoric to its former position when it had both scope and vitality, he examined the attainments of Roman orators with an eye to improving the taste of his countrymen and with the hope of giving rhetoric unquestioned status as a general theory of culture.

Cicero commends Lepidus for his apparent knowledge of the Grecian masters. Carbo is praised for his application to studies. Caius Sulpicius

Gallus was "better acquainted with the Grecian literature than all the rest of the nobility, and to his reputation as a graceful orator, he added the highest accomplishments in every other respect." And Marcus Piso "derived all his talents from his erudition; for he was much better versed in Grecian literature than any of his predecessors." Cicero's regard for Crassus, whom he makes the protagonist of his views in the *De Oratore*, results in large part from the latter's command of the field of learning, his acknowledged versatility, if not genius. Thus we note that Cicero's critical judgments were developed in part from a recognition of cultural attainment in the speakers. An Ideal Orator, possessed of a knowledge and understanding rarely found in human beings, always stood near by, serving as the standard of excellence in speaking achievement.

The Fundamental Standard of Achievement

The standard of excellence which Cicero sets up for judging the orator is plainly his own oratorical accomplishment and his own theory of speechmaking. In the *De Oratore*, he presented the requirements of the Ideal Orator; in the *Brutus*, he appraised the orators in the light of those essentials; and in the *Orator*, he presented the composite view of the finished orator, with the point of reference always toward himself and his speeches.

Thus it is, as Petersson observes, that the criticisms in the *Brutus* are made from two points of view: an absolute standard, i.e., the contents of the *De Oratore*, and a relative standard, i.e., the orator's own time and culture.[23] The absolute character of the criterion is revealed by a remark that Cicero makes in *The Best Style of the Orators:*

I do not divide the orator as to class. . . . For I am seeking a perfect one. And of perfection there is only one kind; and those who fall short of it do not differ in kind.[24]

He goes on to say that the differences among orators are ones of degree, not kind, but he is seeking that "perfection which combines every kind of excellence."

Cicero most assuredly believed that he approached or even reached that perfection. As Sandys remarks: "the living image of his [Cicero's] own oratorical greatness forms the foundation on which he builds his ideal fabric. His own speeches supply him with examples of every variety of oratorical excellence." [25] Although he feigned modesty when referring to his own experience, he nevertheless made it clear at every

[23] *Op. cit.*, p. 436.
[24] *The Best Style of the Orators.* p. 527.
[25] John E. Sandys. *M. Tulli Ciceronis ad M. Brutum Orator.* London, 1885, p. lxiv.

turn that he was himself the criterion by which others were to be judged.

There is a further, and perhaps more fundamental, basis of judgment, however, that stamps Cicero's rhetorical criticism as intelligent, discerning, and relatively free from pedantry. Cicero does not appraise the effectiveness of oratory on the ground of simple adherence to formulated rules of speaking. Interested as he was in theory, he did not permit that predilection to obscure the fact that oratory, to be successful, must affect the individuals to whom it is addressed. Conformity to rules is important only to the extent that it makes possible the acquisition of responses sought by the speaker. Hence, Cicero makes the impression on the public, and on the social group generally, the test of appeal. The effect of the oratory upon people becomes a determining point of judgment; oratory, therefore, requires adaptation to listeners, and its effectiveness is dependent upon the skill with which this adaptation is made. As Cicero remarks, an abstruse poem

> . . . only requires the approbation of the judicious few, but a discourse intended for the people should be perfectly suited to their taste. If Demosthenes, therefore, after being deserted by the rest of his audience, had even Plato left to hear him, and no one else, I will answer for it, he could not have uttered another syllable. Nor could you yourself, my Brutus, if the whole assembly were to leave you, as it once did Curio.[26]

Whereupon Brutus, offering a commentary in the dialogue, replies:

> To open my whole mind to you, I must confess that even in such causes as fall under the cognizance of a few select judges, and not of the people at large, if I were to be deserted by the casual crowd who came to hear the trial, I should not be able to proceed.[27]

Cicero then brings out the cardinal principle to which he gives heed in his criticism:

> The case, then, is plainly this, . . . as a flute, which will not return its proper sound when it is applied to the lips, would be laid aside by the musician as useless, so the ears of the people are the instrument upon which an orator is to play; and if these refuse to admit the breath he bestows upon them, or if the hearer, like a restive horse, will not obey the spur, the speaker must cease to exert himself any farther.[28]

Commenting on the likelihood of receiving uniform judgments of orators both from the common man and the expert critic, Cicero observes:

> . . . I had rather my *sentiments* on the qualifications of an orator should please you and Brutus, than all the world besides; but as to my *eloquence*, I should wish *this* to please everyone. For he who speaks in such a manner as to please the people, must inevitably receive the approbation of the

[26] *Brutus.* LI.
[27] *Ibid.*
[28] *Ibid.*

learned. As to the truth and propriety of what I hear, I am indeed to judge of this for myself, as well as I am able; but the general merit of an orator must and will be decided by the effects which his eloquence produces. For . . . there are three things which an orator should be able to effect; viz., to *inform* his hearers, to *please* them, and to *move their passions*. By what qualities in the speaker each of these effects may be produced, or by what deficiencies they are either lost, or but imperfectly performed, is an inquiry which none but an artist can resolve; but whether an audience is really so affected by an orator as shall best answer his purpose, must be left to their own feelings, and the decision of the public. The learned therefore, and the people at large, have never disagreed about who was a good orator, and who was otherwise.[29]

It is, Cicero maintains, "the invariable prerogative of an accomplished orator to be reckoned such in the opinion of the people."

The question might arise, then, as to what advantage, if any, the trained critic has over the hearer who is not conversant with the art of rhetoric. Cicero replies that the advantage is considerable and important, "if it is, indeed, a matter of any consequence to be able to discover by what means that which is the true and real end of speaking is either obtained or lost." The skilled critic

. . . has likewise this additional superiority, that when two or more orators, as has frequently happened, have shared the applauses of the public, he can judge, on a careful observation of the principal merits of each, what is the most perfect character of eloquence, since whatever does not meet the approbation of the people must be equally condemned by the more intelligent hearer. For as it is easily understood by the sound of a harp, whether the strings are skillfully touched; so it may likewise be discovered from the manner in which the passions of an audience are affected, how far the speaker is able to command them. A man, therefore, who is a real connoisseur in the art, can sometimes, by a single glance, as he passes through the forum, and without stopping to listen attentively to what is said, form a tolerable judgment of the ability of the speaker. When he observes any of the bench yawning, or speaking to the person who is next to him, or looking carelessly about him, or sending to inquire the time of day, or teasing the quaestor to dismiss the court, he concludes very naturally that the cause upon trial is not pleaded by an orator who understands how to apply the powers of language to the passions of the judges, as a skillful musician applies his fingers to the harp. On the other hand, if, as he passes by, he beholds the judges looking attentively before them, as if they were either receiving some material information, or visibly approved what they had already heard; if he sees them listening to the voice of the pleader with a kind of ecstasy, like a fond bird to some melodious tune; and, above all, if he discovers in their looks any strong indications of pity, abhorrence, or any other emotion of the mind; though he should not be near enough to hear a single word, he immediately discovers that the cause is managed by a real orator, who is either performing, or has already played his part to good purpose.[30]

[29] *Ibid.*, XLIX.
[30] *Ibid.*, LIV.

Cicero's Contributions

An over-all examination of Cicero's critical work strikes a note of considerable authority. Undoubtedly, his critical estimates would have been more significant if he had made fuller use of the speeches for which the orators were distinguished. This is, indeed, a defect as judged in terms of contemporary evaluation. Likewise, Cicero places what may seem to us a disproportionately heavy emphasis upon delivery as a determinant of success in oratory. Furthermore, no one could claim that Cicero's criticism is characterized by a dispassionate regard for merit, regardless of the school of thought to which the orator was committed. The *Brutus* and the *Orator* both reveal the presence of polemic, of controversy over the Atticist movement; and to that extent both works are intended to show the superiority of the Ciceronian conception of style. Finally, it is obvious that some of Cicero's critical estimates are superficial and others somewhat uninspired in that they fail to reveal the character, the living spirit, of the particular speakers. Even these possible shortcomings, however, do not dim the genius of this man whom Duff called "the supreme index of his age." [31]

Cicero knew the theory of rhetoric, and he was a seasoned practitioner of the art. His criticism reveals the sweep of his intelligence and the acuity of his observation. Taken as a group, the *De Oratore*, the *Brutus,* and the *Orator* establish a *rationale* of rhetorical criticism which is at once discerning and ingenious. Cicero's work was not the product of accident. Essaying, especially in the *Brutus*, to present a systematic history of orators, he employed a designed method which revealed complete mastery over the technical details of rhetorical theory, and full understanding of the influence of history upon the development and refinement of artistic endeavor. He had constantly before him a point of view regarding the function of oratory, a method of effecting critical analysis, a criterion of judgment, and a test for measuring the effectiveness of speeches. If he failed to become the distinguished critic for which his abilities so eminently fitted him, it was not because he was confused as to method or objective. He knew what to do. But, unfortunately, his quarrel with the Atticists impelled an enthusiasm for both open and veiled rebuttal which frequently distorted the critical focus so essential to the judge of orators and oratory.

THE LOST WORKS OF CAECILIUS

J. D. Denniston says that one fact about Greek literary criticism which immediately attracts attention is the important position held by

---

[31] J. Wight Duff. *A Literary History of Rome from the Origins to the Close of the Golden Age.* New York, 1928, p. 351.

the prose writers, and especially the orators. It is not surprising, therefore, that much of the extant criticism "originates in the effort to purify oratorical style by bringing it back to Attic principles." [32] Caecilius of Calacte and Dionysius of Halicarnassus, the two principal literary critics of Greece and Rome during the time of Augustus, confirm this observation.

Caecilius was a Sicilian rhetorician whose works, regrettably, have not survived. He evidently wrote a treatise on rhetoric and another on figures of speech; to both of these works Quintilian refers frequently in the *Institutes*. Caecilius and Dionysius met at Rome, and there, "united by friendship, by community of labours and by zeal for the Atticist revival," they became the leading exponents of the Attic prose style.[33] Baldwin refers to an interpolation of F. Nassal that the similarity of critical treatment by Dionysius and Cicero argues for a common source, and that this source is probably Caecilius.[34]

The lost work in which we are most interested was entitled *On the Style of the Ten Orators,* and included analyses of Antiphon, Andocides, Lysias, Isocrates, Isaeus, Lycurgus, Aeschines, Hyperides, Demosthenes, and Deinarchus. According to Jebb, Caecilius was one of the earliest writers to be familiar with the canon of the ten orators.

Caecilius was concerned principally with the purification of literary taste, the movement comprehensively known as Atticism. With Longinus, he perceived that what the age needed was not further analysis of rhetoric, but a "better aesthetic criticism" of it. He saw in the florid tendencies of the Asiatic school a *virtual extinction* of the great artistic spirit which had animated true Attic eloquence. In this respect both Caecilius and Dionysius differ from Cicero, for, as Jebb remarks, Cicero "conceives Atticism as an unbroken tradition, which was merely adulterated and debased by those influences which are called Asiatic." [35]

From the fragmentary data on Caecilius' works it is known that he used the comparative method in critical analysis. He compared Demosthenes with Aeschines, and also with Cicero. Furthermore, one of his works dealt with the differences between the Attic and the Asiatic style. Although he favored Lysias as a model, Caecilius criticized him "on the ground that he was less skillful in the arrangement of arguments than in invention." [36]

Regarding the critical work of Caecilius and Dionysius, W. Rhys Roberts says:

---

[32] J. D. Denniston. *Greek Literary Criticism.* London, 1924, p. xxxii.
[33] R. C. Jebb. *The Attic Orators.* London, 1893. I, lxii.
[34] Charles Sears Baldwin. *Ancient Rhetoric and Poetic.* New York, 1924, p. 105.
[35] Jebb. *Op. cit.,* II, 453.
[36] W. Rhys Roberts. "Caecilius of Calacte." *American Journal of Philology,* 18: 307, 1897.

They were true men of letters, not mere masters of technic. Their view of literary criticism was not mechanical, but aesthetic. They had something of the wide outlook and sympathy possessed by the best Roman writers, such as Cicero, for whom the adoption of a pure Attic standard has a living, and not simply an antiquarian interest.[37]

THE CRITICAL WORKS OF DIONYSIUS

The revival of Atticism, as Jebb observes, did not mean the same thing for Rome as for Greece. "Rome was only developing her artistic literature: Greece had seen hers pass through maturity to decay." Hence, the revival gave "Rome true canons for living work. It gave Greece, not this, but the only thing now possible, a standard for the appreciation of the past." Cicero was the representative of the revival for Rome, while Dionysius, "the greatest critic of the ancient world who was not a philosopher," was the representative for both Greece and Rome.[38]

Associated with Caecilius, Dionysius recommended as models the best Attic orators. Strongly influenced by Isocrates, he believed that rhetoric was subordinate to the broader concept of citizenship, although in his critical analyses he gives little heed to historical details and concentrates chiefly on stylistic considerations.

Dionysius' estimates of the Attic orators constitute, in the opinion of Atkins, "the most considerable body of literary appreciations that has come down from antiquity."[39] These studies were intended to establish a standard for Greek prose, "applicable alike to oratory and to every other branch of composition."

Dionysius projected critical judgments of six orators, grouping them into two distinct classes: Lysias, Isocrates, and Isaeus are the "inventors"; Demosthenes, Hyperides, and Aeschines are the "perfecters" of conceptions developed in the history of Attic prose. The studies of the inventors are extant; only the first part of the treatise on Demosthenes has come down to us to represent Dionysius' treatment of the perfecters. It is regrettable that the second part of the criticism of Demosthenes is not preserved. It dealt with the orator's control over subject matter, and might have eased the emphasis which, in the other studies, tends so fully toward stylistic matters.

The pattern of Dionysius' criticisms is a trifle mechanical. It follows, in the main, a set of formulae, tends toward a liberal use of classifications, and frequently becomes openly pedantic. Each account of an orator contains a limited amount of biographical details, notes on the orator's

[37] *Ibid.*, p. 312.
[38] *Op. cit.*, II, 451.
[39] Atkins, *op. cit.*, II, 104–105.

style and subject matter, comparative estimates of other masters of prose, and selected quotations from the orator which reveal the critic's bases of judgment.

The *De Lysia*, conforming to the above pattern, provides an exacting scrutiny of the orator's style. Dionysius applies his "system of virtues" as developed in the *De Imitatione:* purity, accuracy, lucidity, brevity, compactness, vividness, character portrayal, appropriateness, and persuasiveness. Each virtue is examined carefully in the light of the Lysian material. S. F. Bonner summarizes by saying that Dionysius, in dealing with the virtues of style, treats the subject from the point of view of inventive power, the selection of arguments, and arrangement; and in selecting his specimen of Lysian style, he follows the "tradition which divided oratory into forensic, deliberative, and epideictic." [40] Finally, Dionysius considers Lysias' powers as revealed in the parts of a speech: proem, narrative, proof, and epilogue.

De Isocrate is similar in design and critical method to *De Lysia*, except that the comparison of Isocrates with Lysias provides additional detail. There is some reason to believe, however, that pure rhetorical theory influences this essay more than it did *De Lysia*. Evidence for this is found in the fact that Dionysius disapproves of Isocrates' style on at least three counts: (a) it is not effective from the point of view of the *hearer;* (b) it lacks the power to inflame and stir the feelings; and (c) it is overloaded in places with figurative expressions. These elements are important in indicating the methodological approach of the critic to the problem of rhetorical effectiveness.

In the *De Isaeo*, there is no departure from the critical pattern set forth in Dionysius' other works. In it, as Bonner says, Dionysius' aim was to offer advice, "for purposes of imitation, on the standard models."

Perhaps the most important work in the list of studies by Dionysius is *De admiranda vi dicendi in Demosthene*, in which the method of the rhetorician is used freely. In this essay, he makes reference to the three styles—plain, middle, and grand—and then sets up the true model of excellence in prose, namely, Demosthenes.

As examples of the grand style, Dionysius turns to Gorgias and Thucydides; of the middle, to Thrasymachus; and of the plain, to Lysias. The style of Thucydides, he says,

. . . has power to shock the mind, the style of Lysias to gratify it; the one can rally and brace it, the other relax and soothe it; the one can work upon the emotions, the other inspire tranquil sentiment. Moreover, it is a characteristic of Thucydides' style to insist and drive the point home, of Lysias' to mislead and to conceal the facts. Innovation and venturesomeness

[40] S. F. Bonner. *The Literary Treatises of Dionysius of Halicarnassus.* London, 1939. Pp. 45–46.

are inseparable from the historian's character, as are cautiousness and avoidance of risk from the orator's.[41]

Demosthenes is then established as the "all-sufficient model," as the one who combined the virtues and avoided the defects of the various styles. Here we find a true standard of excellence, a model to guide both critic and creative artist in his search for a satisfactory prose form. In order to bring out the superiority of Demosthenes' style, Dionysius compares him with Thucydides, and finds that "Thucydides uses this method [the grand style] of obtaining distinction so unsparingly as to become obscure, whereas Demosthenes always aims at the golden mean and, as a result, does not violate the essential principles of perspicuity and propriety." As for the comparison with Lysias, Dionysius finds some points of similarity. But Demosthenes revealed more vigor in his proof; consequently, he was more effective.

According to Dionysius, Isocrates is definitely inferior to Demosthenes.

Who would refuse to acknowledge the complete superiority of this style to that of Isocrates? Demosthenes has expressed the subject-matter with greater nobility and magnificence, has clothed the ideas with a finer style, and brought them out in a more concise, compact, and finished fashion; he has shown greater power and a sturdier strength, and avoided those frigid, childish figures in which the other indulges to excess; but it is in movement, action, emotional effect, that he is completely and absolutely superior.

Furthermore,

. . . when I read a speech of Isocrates, I become serious in spirit, and experience great mental calm, like those who listen to the pipes during libations or to Dorian or enharmonic melodies. But when I take up one of Demosthenes' speeches, I am entranced and borne hither and thither, experiencing one emotion after another, distrust, anxiety, fear, contempt, hatred, pity, benevolence, anger, envy, every emotion in fact that is wont to dominate the human mind. I seem to be no whit different from those who perform rites of initiation. . . . If then we, who are so far removed in time, and are not concerned about the issue, are thus swayed and mastered, and borne whithersoever the speech carries us, how must the Athenians and the Greeks in general have felt when their living interests were at stake, and when the orator himself, at the height of his fame, revealed his own personal experience and laid bare the inmost feelings of his soul?[42]

These and other comparisons establish Dionysius' reasons for assigning to Demosthenes "the palm for oratorical mastery." The achievements of Demosthenes, Dionysius makes clear in his critical inquiries, result from painstaking efforts to attain perfection. "Dionysius more than once reminds us," says Roberts, "of the oft-forgotten truth that the excellence of the ancient authors was the result of ingenious and elabo-

41 *Ibid.*, p. 63.
42 *Ibid.*, pp. 65–66.

rate art." [43] The Demosthenean speeches, which were like the finest poems and lyrics, did not spring into finished form without the most meticulous observance by the speaker of the details and rules of the rhetorical art. And it was proper that the speaker attend faithfully to those details.

For it appears to me far more reasonable for a man who is composing public speeches, eternal memorials of his own powers, to attend even to the slightest details, than it is for the disciples of painters and workers in relief, who display the dexterity and industry of their hands in a perishable medium, to expend the finished resources of their art on veins and down and bloom and similar minutiae.[44]

The essays of Dionysius have an unmistakable rhetorical outlook, despite the fact that they do not draw fully upon the historical materials relevant to the orator's speechmaking. To the extent that they indicate the point of view of oratory, and employ the comparative method, they are significant in the development of rhetorical criticism. In his almost passionate endeavor to delineate stylistic details, however, Dionysius divorced style from subject matter, and vitiated partially the integrity of the critical effort. As Jebb remarks, "Dionysius tends to rest the criticism of oratory too much on literary grounds." [45]

THE CRITICAL STANDARDS OF LONGINUS

The great critics of antiquity provide much that the present-day student searches for in his effort to understand rhetorical theory. The considered judgments of these critics serve as the bridge between yesterday and today, for "in art, as in life, it is the part of wisdom to let the ages instruct the years." [46]

In the preceding chapters we mentioned the contribution made by the author of *On the Sublime* to rhetorical theory. Now we shall return briefly to this work to determine its relationship to criticism. Longinus, or whoever the author may have been, made three contributions, not necessarily original, which helped to establish a critique of oratory.

Standard of Excellence

In the first place, the author established a fixed standard of excellence in oratory. Since he adopted a view favoring the return to Greek classical art, he naturally turned to Demosthenes for his model. Under Demosthenes' approach, oratorical imagery becomes effective, fusing

[43] Roberts edition, p. 46.
[44] *Ibid.*, p. 267.
[45] *Op. cit.*, II, 301.
[46] Atkins, *op. cit.*, II, 354.

"vehemence and passion into spoken words" and following trains of reasoning while at the same time indulging flights of imagination.[47] And when the author inquires into the value of interrogations, he turns again to passages from Demosthenes which show that if they had not been handled by a master, they "would have been altogether weaker." As in other matters, in the use of metaphors Demosthenes is established as the standard.

Comparative Analyses

A second feature giving *On the Sublime* critical value is its use of the comparative method of appraisal. In comparing Cicero with Demosthenes, the author remarks:

> . . . the latter is characterized by sublimity which is for the most part rugged, Cicero by profusion. Our orator, owing to the fact that in his vehemence,—aye, and in his speed, power, and intensity,—he can as it were consume by fire and carry away all before him, may be compared to a thunderbolt or flash of lightning. Cicero, on the other hand, it seems to me, after the manner of a wide-spread conflagration, rolls on with all-devouring flames, having within him an ample and abiding store of fire, distributed now at this point now at that, and fed by an unceasing succession. This, however, you will be better able to decide; but the great opportunity of Demosthenes' high-pitched elevation comes where intense utterance and vehement passion are in question, and in passages in which the audience is to be utterly enthralled. The profusion of Cicero is in place where the hearer must be flooded with words; for it is appropriate to the treatment of commonplaces, and to perorations for the most part and digressions, and to all descriptive and declamatory passages, and to writings on history and natural science, and to many other departments of literature.

Likewise, we may turn to the comparative estimate of Demosthenes and Hyperides:

> If successful writing were to be estimated by number of merits and not by the true criterion, thus judged Hyperides would be altogether superior to Demosthenes. For he has a greater number of accents than Demosthenes and a greater number of excellences, and like the pentathlete he falls just below the top in every branch. In all the contests he has to resign the first place to his rivals, while he maintains that place against all ordinary persons.
> Now Hyperides not only imitates all the strong points of Demosthenes with the exception of his composition, but he has embraced in a singular degree the excellences and graces of Lysias as well. For he talks with simplicity, where it is required, and does not adopt like Demosthenes one unvarying tone in all his utterances. He possesses the gift of characterisation in a sweet and pleasant form and with a touch of piquancy. There are innumerable signs of wit in him—the most polished raillery, high-bred ease, supple skill in the

[47] *Longinus On the Sublime*. Translated by W. Rhys Roberts. In *Aristotle's Poetics and Longinus On the Sublime*. Edited by Charles Sears Baldwin. New York, 1930, p. 87.

contests of irony, jests not tasteless or rude after the well-known Attic manner, but naturally suggested by the subject, clever ridicule, much comic power, biting satire with well-directed fun, and what may be termed an inimitable charm investing the whole. He is excellently fitted by nature to excite pity; in narrating a fable he is facile, and with his pliant spirit he is also most easily turned towards a digression . . . ; while he has treated his Funeral Oration in the epideictic vein with probably unequalled success. Demosthenes, on the other hand, is not an apt delineator of character, he is not facile, he is anything but pliant or epideictic, he is comparatively lacking in the entire list of excellences just given. Where he forces himself to be jocular and pleasant, he does not excite laughter, but rather becomes the subject of it, and when he wishes to approach the region of charm, he is all the farther removed from it. If he had attempted to write the short speech about Phryne or about Athenogenes, he would have all the more commended Hyperides to our regard. The good points of the latter, however, many though they be, are wanting in elevation; they are the staid utterances of a sober-hearted man and leave the hearer unmoved, no one feeling terror when he reads Hyperides. But Demosthenes draws, as from a store, excellences allied to the highest sublimity and perfected to the utmost, the tone of lofty speech, living passions, copiousness, readiness, speed (where it is legitimate), and that power and vehemence of his which forbid approach. Having, I say, absorbed bodily within himself these mighty gifts which we may deem heaven-sent . . . , he thus with the noble qualities which are his own routs all comers even where the qualities he does not possess are concerned, and over-powers with thunder and with lightning the orators of every age. One could sooner face with unflinching eyes a descending thunderbolt than meet with steady gaze his bursts of passion in their swift succession.[48]

A minor comparison of Plato with Lysias brings out essentially the same method, and reminds us that the author of *On the Sublime* sought the attainment of a certain ideality in the sublime utterance.

Tests of Excellence

Finally, *On the Sublime* provides an interesting doctrine which tends to negate Macaulay's contention that Longinus "gives us eloquent sentences, but no principles." The dictum is laid down that *the sublime* and *imitation* of great masters are not incompatible. When we are "elaborating anything which requires lofty expression and elevated conception," we should think of three possible tests: (1) How would Homer "have said this very thing, or how would it have been raised to the sublime by Plato or Demosthenes or by the historian Thucydides"? "If the image of those men were presented to us, our ardor would be inflamed and our path illumined." (2) "What sort of hearing would Homer, had he been present, or Demosthenes have given to this or that when said by me, or how would they have been affected by the other?"

[48] *Ibid.*, pp. 111–113.

(3) "In what spirit will each succeeding age listen to me who have written thus?"

TACITUS ON ORATORY

The meaning of the *Dialogue Concerning Oratory*, written about A.D. 80, is not always perfectly clear. Varying points of view are expressed by the several participants, and it is often difficult to determine which one represents Tacitus' convictions. In fact, it is not improbable that the dialogue reflects a conflict of belief in the author's mind.

Relativity in Critical Standards

The critical note of greatest importance in the *Dialogue* grows out of some remarks Maternus makes near the end of the treatise. Commenting on the fact that there is no stability in human affairs, Maternus says:

We find that the discourse of men always conforms to the temper of the times. Among savage nations language is never copious. A few words serve the purpose of barbarians, and those are always uncouth and harsh, without the artifice of connection; short, abrupt, and nervous. In a state of polished society, where a single ruler sways the sceptre, the powers of the mind take a softer tone, and language grows more refined. But affectation follows, and precision gives way to delicacy. The just and natural expression is no longer the fashion. Living in ease and luxury, men look for elegance, and hope by novelty to give a grace to adulation. In other nations, where the first principles of the civil union are maintained in vigour; where the people live under the government of laws, and not the will of man; where the spirit of liberty pervades all ranks and orders of the state; where every individual holds himself bound, at the hazard of his life, to defend the constitution framed by his ancestors; where, without being guilty of an impious crime, no man dares to violate the rights of the whole community; in such a state, the national eloquence will be prompt, bold, and animated. Should internal dissensions shake the public peace, or foreign enemies threaten to invade the land, Eloquence comes forth arrayed in terror; she wields her thunder, and commands all hearts. It is true, that upon those occasions men of ambition endeavour, for their own purposes, to spread the flame of sedition; while the good and virtuous combine their force to quell the turbulent, and repel the menaces of a foreign enemy. Liberty gains new strength by the conflict, and the true patriot has the glory of serving his country, distinguished by his valour in the field, and in debate no less terrible by his eloquence.

In furtherance of this thesis, Maternus continues:

The subject, beyond all doubt, lifts the mind above itself; it gives vigour to sentiment, and energy to expression. Let the topic be a paltry theft, a dry form of pleading, or a petty misdemeanor: will not the orator feel himself cramped and chilled by the meanness of the question? Give him a cause of magnitude, such as bribery in the election of magistrates, a charge for plundering the allies of Rome, or the murder of Roman citizens, how different then his emotions! how sublime each sentiment! what dignity of language! The effect, it must be admitted, springs from the disasters of society. It is true, that form of government, in which no such evils occur, must, beyond all question, be allowed to be the best; but since, in the course of human affairs, sudden convulsions must happen, my position is, that they produced, at Rome, that flame of eloquence which at this hour is so admired. The mind of the orator grows and expands with his subject. Without ample materials no splendid oration was ever yet produced.[49]

Thus Tacitus enunciates the doctrine that standards of style are relative, and that each speaker and each age must work out its own literary salvation. In expounding the variability of standards, Tacitus acknowledges that historical events and tendencies influence speechmaking and that a full understanding of oratory derives from intelligent insight into the age in which it flourished. Atkins says that in Tacitus' hands criticism, "for the first time, ceases to be dogmatic and scholastic in kind; a return is made to the dialectical methods of Plato, so that literature is now approached, not with the object of laying down absolute rules, but in order to inquire, to understand, and thus to explain." [50]

STYLISTIC APPROACH TO CRITICISM: DEMETRIUS

Both the date and authorship of the work called *On Style* are in doubt. Modern scholars seem to believe, however, that the treatise was not written, as was sometimes claimed, by Demetrius Phalereus; rather, it has been suggested that it might have been prepared by Demetrius of Tarsus, a contemporary of Plutarch. Thus it probably originated sometime during the first century A.D.

As the title indicates, *On Style* is devoted exclusively to the *elocutio* of classical rhetoric, and its chief purpose is to set forth the principles of prose style, rather than to comment on the decline of the art of expression.

The principal sections of Demetrius' work deal with four kinds of style: the plain, the stately, the polished, and the powerful. Demetrius discusses these types with respect to word choice, arrangement of words, and the subject matter appropriate to each. Certain of the excesses or vices to which each is liable are pointed out.

The stately, or elevated, style requires "idea, expression, and suitable composition." [51] Figures of speech and thought, such as metaphors, hyperboles, word coinages, and the like, receive brief treatment. Through the discussion runs an important theme, namely, that subject matter moulds style, and that style, to be effective, must always preserve pro-

[49] Tacitus, *A Dialogue Concerning Oratory*. In *The Works of Cornelius Tacitus.* Edited by Arthur Murphy. London, 1813. II, 436–439.

[50] Atkins, *op. cit.*, II, 195–196.

[51] *Demetrius on Style*. Translated by T. A. Moxon. In *Aristotle's Poetics: Demetrius on Style*. Everyman's Library. New York, p. 210.

priety. Accordingly, "style must be appropriate to its subject—a modest style to a modest subject, and a grand style to a grand subject."

The polished style—also referred to as the elegant style—possesses "grace and brightness." It is characterized by rhythmical flow and figurative expressions.

The plain style is appropriate to ordinary oral expression. Demetrius alludes to its persuasiveness, adding that its characteristic qualities are clearness and simplicity. "If it is lacking in either of these it fails to persuade. We must aim at a diction which is neither overladen nor ponderous if we wish to persuade; a diction, too, with a steady rhythm and no suggestion of metre." Commenting further, Demetrius remarks:

> Theophrastus adds that every detail must not be described at length, but some points must be left to the intelligence and elaboration of the hearer. When he thinks of the points which you have omitted, he becomes not only a hearer, but a witness and a very partial witness, too. He thinks that he is clever, thanks to your action in giving him an opportunity to use his intelligence. To press home every detail, as though your hearer were a fool, seems like casting a slur on his intelligence.[52]

The last kind of style mentioned by Demetrius is the powerful, or, as Roberts calls it, the forcible. Not completely dissimilar from the stately type, it is characterized by vigorous diction and the liberal use of figures. The proper arrangement of words also conduces to power. Thus he recommends placing the strongest thought at the end; "whatever is buried in the middle of the sentence loses its power." D'Alton believes that the characteristics of the powerful style "were probably in the main derived from a study of the oratory of Demosthenes, whose dominant quality was considered to be his vehemence."

Although it is doubtful whether classifications of style have ever been particularly useful or illuminating, Demetrius' treatment is not without merit. As Atkins observes, "it may fairly be described as forming a part of that first-century movement which had for its object the establishment of classical standards in literature." Concerned chiefly with "the niceties of Greek prose," Demetrius "was instrumental in directing men's attention anew to the models of earlier Greece, by holding up for their imitation the standards of classical art."[53]

THE RELATION OF PHILOSOPHY TO RHETORIC

Points of View of the Masters

We have observed in previous sections that many rhetoricians, as well as their critics, were deeply interested in the relation of rhetoric to phi-

---

52 *Ibid.*
53 *Op. cit.*, II, 208–209.

losophy. Plato's strictures against the Sophists dealt largely with that theme; Isocrates attempted to join the two fields in his theory of culture; Aristotle, granting rhetoric dignified status, nevertheless joined Plato in calling rhetoric a counterpart of dialectic, and in articulating it with ethics. This controversy over the relative merit and position of philosophy and rhetoric persisted for many years, and eventually became closely associated with the history of education. This developed from the respective claims of the two areas of learning for control over the education of youth.

It has often been said that any intellectually eager man with a broad field of interest will eventually turn to philosophy. Cicero was actively concerned with effecting a union of rhetoric and philosophy, embracing all in a comprehensive culture. Philosophy would be the handmaid of rhetoric; and an end would be put to what Cicero called the "absurd, useless, and reprehensible" division that divorced the "tongue from the heart" and forced acceptance of the belief that "one class of persons should teach us to think, and another to speak, rightly." [54] The controversy over this point led to the establishment of divergent schools of thought.

The Peripatetic school was founded by Aristotle. It emphasized the importance of Dialectic and, since it provided for intensive training in handling both sides of a question, gained Cicero's favor. D'Alton believes, however, that Theophrastus "did much to make the Peripatetic school acceptable in the eyes of Cicero, who was indebted to him for many features in his theory of style." Cicero's own attachment to the Peripatetics is indicated in this remark:

If, however, we must be indebted for every thing to the philosophers, the Peripatetic discipline is, in my mind, much the most proper to form our language. For which reason, my Brutus, I the more approve your choice, in attaching yourself to a sect (I mean the philosophers of the old Academy) in whose system a just and accurate way of reasoning is enlivened by a perpetual sweetness and fluency of expression; but even the delicate and flowing style of the Peripatetics and Academics is not sufficient to complete an orator; nor yet can he be complete without it.[55]

Cicero often speaks of the Academics and the Peripatetics in one breath, and considers them the best adapted to the training of the speaker. The Platonic school was once headed by Xenocrates, although as the New Academy its origin stemmed from Arcesilas. Carneades was its best representative. [56]

Cicero has a good deal to say about Stoicism in its relation to the

[54] *De Oratore.* III, xvii.
[55] *Brutus.* XXXI.
[56] *De Oratore.* III, xvii–xviii.

training of speakers. Remarking that the Cynics, afterwards the Stoics, sprung from Antisthenes' "patience and endurance recommended in the discourses of Socrates," he indicates that the Stoics "declared eloquence to be virtue and wisdom." D'Alton ventures the opinion that Cato's well-known description of the orator as "a good man speaking well" probably is of Stoic origin. But Cicero dismisses the teachings of the Stoics for two reasons:

. . . there are two peculiarities in their doctrine, which are quite unsuitable to that orator whom we are forming; one, that they pronounce all who are not wise, to be slaves, robbers, enemies, and madmen, and yet do not admit that any person is wise (but it would be very absurd to trust the interests of an assembly of the people, or of the senate, or any other body of men, to one to whom none of those present would appear to be in their senses, none to be citizens, none to be freemen); the other, that they have a manner of speaking which is perhaps subtle, and certainly acute, but for an orator, dry, strange, unsuited to the ear of the populace, obscure, barren, jejune, and altogether of that species which a speaker cannot use to a multitude.[57]

In the *Brutus*, Cicero remarks that the language of the Stoics "is too close and contracted to suit the ears of common people." Among the orators of the Stoic school were Q. Mucius Scaevola and Aelius Tubero, both of whom are evaluated in the *Brutus*. Naturally, Cicero found the elaborate analysis, the rigid adherence to dialectical systems, the failure to employ emotional proof, and the insistence of the Stoics upon plain, unadorned language, unsuited to his conception of oratory.

The Stoics' fear that departure from the plain facts would endanger truth finds its counterpart many years later in John Locke's remark in the *Essay Concerning Human Understanding:*

. . . we must allow that all the art of rhetoric, besides order and clearness, all the artificial and figurative application of words eloquence hath invented, are for nothing else but to insinuate wrong ideas, move the passions, and thereby mislead the judgment; and so indeed are perfect cheats; and therefore, however laudable or allowable oratory may render them in harangues and popular addresses, they are certainly, in all discourses that pretend to inform or instruct, wholly to be avoided; and, where truth and knowledge are concerned, cannot but be thought a great fault either of the languages or persons that make use of them.[58]

Incidentally, Lord Bolingbroke did not consider Locke's comments on figurative style an indictment of the use of figures. Rather, it was a condemnation of the *abuse* of them.

False eloquence there is, no doubt, and fraudulent eloquence too. Figurative style often causes one, and is often employed by the other; but there

[57] *Ibid.*
[58] John Locke. *An Essay Concerning Human Understanding.* London, p. 411.

is false and fraudulent reasoning too without eloquence: and we may find as much trifling and fallacy in some of the most dry didactic writings, as can be shown in those of poets and orators.

Naturally, then,

Rhetoric may be a powerful instrument of deceit and error, and so may logic too. Both of them are impertinent when they are reduced into arts, and are cultivated and followed as such. But if rhetoric were banished out of the world, and logic with it, eloquence and reason would still remain . . . We may disaffect eloquence as much as we please, or nature may have saved us this trouble by refusing us the talent, but we must cease to speak if we lay figurative speech wholly aside. Figures are so necessary in the communication, at least, of our thoughts, that they are wove into the very constitution of language. . . .[59]

But let us return from our digression. The Stoics, we repeat, were interested in a simple treatment of the facts, and Cicero was committed to the copious style of oratory in which feeling and rhetorical floursh figured importantly.

The last school of thought to which we shall allude is the Epicurean. Founded by Epicurus, this school looked upon science as the servant of life and considered theory important only as it related to practice. The over-all aim of philosophy was to provide men with tranquillity and peace of mind. In general, the Epicureans rejected rhetoric as useless. Perhaps the only branch of the subject which at least one of the disciples of the school, Philodemus, would recognize as a fit field of inquiry was the epideictic. The reason for admitting epideictic oratory to fuller status was that its rules could be systematized, a condition not possible in other branches of speaking which depended upon the ability of speakers to gain popular favor.

The Position of Philodemus

In the *Rhetoric* of Philodemus (first century B.C.), fragments of which have come down to us, we find some of the reasons why Cicero considered the Epicurean point of view unsuited to his conception of oratorical training. It should always be borne in mind, too, that in the *De Oratore* Cicero was not so much concerned with finding out which philosophy was nearest to truth, but rather, which was "the best suited to the orator."

Philodemus supports the claim that sophistic rhetoric is an art. In fact, he devotes considerable space to matters of definition, trying to determine what an "art" is and what "rhetoric" is. He finally decides that an art is a

. . . state or condition resulting from the observation of certain common and elementary principles, which apply to the majority of cases, accomplish-

[59] *The Works of Lord Bolingbroke.* Philadelphia, 1841. III, 129–130.

ing such a result as cannot be attained by one who has not studied it, and doing this regularly and certainly and not by conjecture.[60]

In the controversy over the relative merits of philosophy and rhetoric, the former is easily the victor. Rhetoric, so Philodemus announces, deals in probabilities and guesses; philosophy, in logic. Rhetoric offers no safeguards as to its use, and so unwise men can employ it craftily; philosophy is in itself a positive good which makes men happy in their state. As Philodemus puts it:

We do not claim that rhetoric is bad in itself, even if it furnishes weapons for wicked men, but it does not indicate what use is to be made of the power it gives, so as to fit in with our principles of justice and honor. Rhetoricians are like pilots, who have a good training but may be bad men.[61]

The devices of the rhetorician are therefore suspect. "For it is well said that the juryman is not affected by any form of speech as much as by the just and prudent actions of the uneducated, and in trials they fear being misled by the rhetor."

Philodemus berates Aristotle for stepping down from philosophy to rhetoric, and extols Isocrates for stepping up from rhetoric to philosophy. Since rhetoric is associated with an active life in the world of affairs— and that is where rhetors do harm—it is better to turn to philosophy, by which men get away from mundane transactions. "Philosophy shows us how to find and use everything necessary for a happy life."

Unwilling to recommend imitation of the ancients, Philodemus looks to everyday language as the best style of expression. "Much of delivery," he remarks, "is the natural and unconscious bodily expression of the emotions." And the "formal instruction in delivery is a product of recent foolishness. . . ."

Here, briefly, were some of the philosophical doctrines which influenced the course and style of oratory. They were the sects, as Cicero called them, that presumably had something to offer toward the training of a speaker. Cicero appraised them all in his *De Oratore* and the *Brutus*.

PLINY'S THOUGHTS ON ORATORY AND ORATORS

"I honour and revere all who discover any talent for oratory," said Pliny the Younger in a letter to Restitutus, "for the Muse of Eloquence is a coy and haughty dame, who scorns to reside with those who despise her." [62] The frequent references to oratory in Pliny's letters attest to his own interest in the art, as does the fact that he himself attended lectures

---

[60] *The Rhetoric of Philodemus.* Translated by Harry M. Hubbell. In *Connecticut Academy of Arts and Sciences*, 23, September, 1920, p. 276.

[61] *Ibid.*, pp. 307–308.

[62] *Pliny: Letters.* Translated by William Melmoth. Rev. by W. M. L. Hutchinson. Loeb Classical Library. 1915. Book VI, 17.

by Quintilian and Nicetes, a point which he reveals in his letter to Fundamus.

Pliny did not commit himself openly in the controversy over the ancients and the moderns. He tried, in the main, to steer a middle course, as his letter to Caninus suggests: "Though I acknowledge myself an admirer of the ancients, yet I am very far from despising . . . the genius of the moderns. . . ." He seems, however, to get his principal inspiration from the older models. In a letter to Voconius Romanus, he indicates specifically that in his own speaking he tried to emulate Cicero, "and am by no means contented with taking my example from modern eloquence." And in a communication to Maximus, he intimates that contemporary eloquence is ruined and extinct, except for certain "unmanly" elocutions. Again, in a letter to Arrianus, he says that, in a certain composition presented for criticism, he tried to imitate Demosthenes and Calvus "who is lately become mine" [model for imitation]. He admits that his imitation is confined to *manner*, since only a choice few have been able to catch their "sublime spirit."

Pliny's own style tended toward the elevated or the grand manner of expression. In a letter to Voconius Romanus, he expresses the opinion, however, that the lofty and elevated style should not always be used; for "as shades in a picture best bring out the high lights, so the plain and simple style in writing is as effective as the sublime." It is to be noted that Pliny used several styles to please different groups of hearers, believing that mere variety would have some effect in recommending the work as a whole. But there can be no doubt about Pliny's sympathy for the more dazzling and florid type of speaking, as this passage from a letter to Lupercus shows:

 . . . the true orator should be bold and elevated, and sometimes even flame out and be hurried away with all the warmth and violence of passion, in short, he should frequently soar to great, and even dangerous heights. For precipices are generally near whatever is towering and exalted, whereas the plain affords a safer, but for that reason a more humble and inglorious path; they that run are more likely to stumble than they that creep; but the latter gain no honour by not slipping, while the former fall with glory. It is with eloquence as with some other arts; she is never more pleasing than when she hazards most.[63]

For the actual work at the bar, Pliny urged a style that struck a mean between brevity and reasonable completeness. But, as just mentioned, he favored the majestic in oratory. In a letter to Tacitus, he remarked:

I have frequent debates with a learned and judicious person of my acquaintance, who admires nothing so much in the eloquence of the bar as conciseness. I admit, where the cause will admit of this matter, it ought to

[63] *Ibid.*, IX, 26.

be pursued; but insist, that to omit what is material to be mentioned, or only slightly to touch upon those points which should be repeatedly inculcated, and urged home to the minds of the audience, is, in effect, to betray the cause one has undertaken.[64]

Evidently, he was a bit suspicious of those speeches that "were cut in two by nightfall," while at the same time he insisted upon adequate coverage of a forensic case.

Pliny was interested in the differences between written and spoken style. In the same letter to Tacitus, he remarked:

> But, it is objected, there is a wide difference between a good *spoken* and a good *written* oration. This opinion I acknowledge, has had some favourers; nevertheless I am persuaded . . . that it is possible a speech may be well received by the audience, which has not merit enough to recommend it to the reader; but an oration which is good on paper cannot be bad when delivered; for the oration on paper is, in truth, the original and model of the speech that is to be pronounced. It is for this reason we find in many of the best orations extant numberless extempore figures of rhetoric; and this even where we are sure they were never spoken at all: as for instance in the following passage from the oration against Verres. . . .[65]

It should be noted that in this passage Pliny expresses a regard for the authenticity of texts, allowing that speeches as printed often contain material not used in the oral delivery.

That Pliny was deeply interested in the probable response of the audience is reflected in several of his letters. He believed that the orator "should so adapt himself to his audience as to throw out something to every one of them, that he may receive and approve as his own peculiar thought." As a part of his technique, he urged the method of taking up many points in forensic discourses, saying,

> As in agriculture, it is not my vineyards, or my woods, alone, but my fields also that I cultivate; and as I do not sow those fields with only spelt and winter-wheat, but employ also barley, beans, and the other leguminous plants; so in my pleadings at the bar, I spread at large a variety of matter like so many different seeds, in order to reap from thence whatever may happen to sprout; for the disposition of your jurors is as precarious and as little to be ascertained, as that of soils and seasons.[66]

His defense of this system was clear. "To delight and to persuade requires time," he said, "and a great compass of language; while to leave a *sting* in the minds of his audience is an effect not to be achieved by an orator who slightly pushes, but by him, and him only, who thrusts home and deep." Returning to his conception of elevation in style, he observed "it is not concise and curtailed, it is copious, majestic, and

---

[64] *Ibid.*, I, 19.
[65] *Ibid.*, I, 20.
[66] *Ibid.*

sublime oratory, that with blaze and thunder perturbs and confounds the universe."

Like many other theorists and critics of antiquity, Pliny was interested in the relation between history and oratory. In a letter to Titinius Capito, Pliny commented at length on the relative positions of the two fields, declaring that history "however executed, always pleases, for mankind are naturally inquisitive, and information, however badly presented, has its charm for beings who adore even small talk and anecdote." Oratory and poetry, on the other hand, always require a full measure of eloquence. Asserting that history and oratory possess a number of common features, Pliny remarks

. . . in these very apparent resemblances, there are several contrasts. Both deal in narrative, but each after a different fashion. Oratory must concern itself as a rule with the low and vulgar facts of everyday life; history treats only of what is recondite, splendid, elevated; a dry, forcible, nervous style befits the one, but embellishments, and what one may call *top-knots*, the other. Oratory pleases most when it is vigorous, biting, and vehement. History, when it is diffusive, bland, and even dulcet. Lastly, diction, rhythm, and the structure of the periods, are distinctly different in these two arts.[67]

Perhaps the best specimen of Pliny's rhetorical criticism is found in a letter to Nepos, in which he urges the latter to pay heed to Isaeus.

He possesses the utmost facility and copiousness of expression, and though always extempore his discourses have all the propriety and elegance of the most studied and elaborate composition. He employs the Greek language, or rather the genuine Attic. His prefatory remarks are terse, easy, and harmonious; and, when occasion requires, serious and majestic. He proposes several questions for discussion, gives his audience liberty to call for any they please, and sometimes even to name what side of it he shall take. . . . He handles every point with almost equal readiness; profound ideas occur to him as he proceeds; his language—but how admirable that is. So choice, so refined! . . . He opens his subject with great propriety; his narration is clear; his controversy ingenious, his logic forcible and his rhetoric sublime. In a word, he at once instructs, entertains, and affects you, and each in so high a degree, that you are at a loss to determine in which of those talents he most excels. He abounds in enthymemes and syllogisms; the latter of a formal exactness, not very easy to attain even in writing. His memory is so extraordinary, that he can recollect what he has before spoken extempore, word for word.[68]

Although Pliny's analysis is short, even perfunctory perhaps, it does reveal his grasp of the problems of rhetoric, the estimate showing, among other things, that he knew what to judge in oratory. If he had elaborated upon his materials, a criticism of genuine merit might very well have resulted.

[67] *Ibid.*
[68] *Ibid.*, II, 3.

THE POINT OF VIEW OF THE THEORIST-TEACHER

Quintilian and the Atticist-Asianist Quarrel

Distinguished for his sanity and good judgment on educational matters, Quintilian shunned the open espousal of either extreme in the Atticist-Asianist issues. Avoiding the extremists, he urged the study of both ancient and modern orators. In the early part of the *Institutes*, he remarks:

There are two points in style on which I think that the greatest caution should be used in respect to boys: one is that no master, from being too much an admirer of antiquity, should allow them to harden, as it were, in the reading of the Gracchi, Cato, and other like authors; for they would thus become uncouth and dry; since they cannot, as yet, understand their force of thought, and, content with adopting their style, which, at the time it was written, was doubtless excellent, but is quite unsuitable to our day, they will appear to themselves to resemble those eminent men. The other point, which is the opposite of the former, is, lest, being captivated with the flowers of modern affectation, they should be so seduced by a corrupt kind of pleasure, as to love that luscious manner of writing which is the more agreeable to the minds of youth in proportion as it has more affinity with them.

Later, he indicates that

. . . nature has not condemned us to stupidity, but we ourselves have changed our mode of speaking, and have indulged our fancies more than we ought; and thus the ancients did not excel us so much in genius as in severity of manner. It will be possible, therefore, to select from the moderns many qualities for imitation, but care must be taken that they be not contaminated with other qualities with which they are mixed. Yet that there have been recently, and are now, many writers whom we may imitate entirely, I would not only allow, . . . but even affirm.[69]

Commenting on stylistic ornamentation, Quintilian says

. . . ornaments of style are the very eyes, as it were, of eloquence; but I should not wish eyes to be spread over the whole body; lest other members should be obstructed in their functions; and, if I were compelled to make a choice, I should prefer the rudeness of the ancients to the affectation of the moderns. But a middle course is open between them; as, in our mode of living and dress, a certain elegance may be observed which is free from blame. Let us add, therefore, as far as we can, to the merits of our style; but let it be our first care to avoid faults, lest, while we wish to be better than the ancients, we make ourselves merely unlike them.[70]

These quotations illustrate the scope of Quintilian's sympathies; they show him steering a middle course in the controversy over whether the

[69] *Institutes.* II, v, 21–24.
[70] *Ibid.*, VIII, v, 34.

ancients were to be preferred to the moderns as models for imitations.[71] This does not mean that Quintilian lacked convictions as to the best style of oratory. Despite his tolerance and his recognition of the need for diversity of style to meet varying conditions, he expressed unqualified preferences which threw light upon his conception of the critical function.

There are some forms of eloquence of a rude nature in agreement with the times in which they appeared, but indicating mental power in the speakers; among whom we may number the Laelli, Africani, Catos, and Gracchi; and these we may call the Polygnoti and Callones of oratory. Of the middle kind Lucius Crassus and Quintus Hortensius may be thought the chief representatives. There may be contemplated a vast multitude of orators, all flourishing about the same time. Among them we find the energy of Caesar, the natural talent of Caelius, the subtlety of Calidius, the accuracy of Polio, the dignity of Messala, the austerity of Calvus, the gravity of Brutus, the acuteness of Sulpicius, and the severity of Cassius. Among those, also, whom we have ourselves seen, we recollect the copiousness of Seneca, the force of Julius Africanus, the mature judgment of Domitius Afer, and agreeableness of Crispus, the sonorous pronunciation of Trachalus, and the elegance of Secundus.

Quintilian follows this analysis with a defence of the Ciceronian style:

But in Cicero we have not merely a Euphranor, distinguished by excellence in several particular departments of art, but eminent in every quality that is commended in any orator whatever. Yet the men of his own time presumed to censure him as tumid, Asiatic, redundant, too fond of repetition, indulging in tasteless jests, loose in the structure of his sentences, tripping in his manner, and . . . almost too effeminate in his general style for a man.

Commenting on the Atticist quarrel, he remarks:

But his severest critics were those who desired to be thought imitators of the Attic orators. This band of calumniators, as if they had leagued themselves in a solemn confederacy, attacked Cicero as though he had been quite of another country, neither caring for their customs nor bound by their laws; of which school are our present dry, sapless, and frigid orators.[72]

Quintilian distinguishes between Attic and Asiatic orators by saying the former are regarded as "compressed and energetic" while the latter are "inflated and deficient in force." He also refers to the third type of eloquence, the Rhodian, which was presumably of a middle character. Then he remarks that the

. . . difference in the character of the speakers and their audiences seems to have caused the difference in their styles of oratory; for the people of Attica, being polished and of refined taste, could endure nothing useless or

---

[71] Cf. J. F. D'Alton, *Roman Literary Theory and Criticism*. London, 1931, pp. 266–353.

[72] *Institutes*. XII, x, 10–14.

redundant; while the Asiatics, a people in other respects vain and ostentatious, were puffed up with fondness for a showy kind of eloquence.[73]

Recognizing that there was a wide variety of genius within each category, Quintilian openly announced his belief that "of the three styles, that of the Attics is by far the best." But it must be remembered that he saw some good in all types.

Quintilian's Conception of Style

Despite Quintilian's temperate stand in the quarrel between the Atticists and the Asianists, he nevertheless reveals throughout the *Institutes* his displeasure with the stylistic abuses of his period. His theory of style clearly reveals his advocacy of a return to the speech of ordinary life, elevated and made impressive as the conditions of speaker, subject, and occasion demand. Thus his conception of style centers about the choice of words, the employment of appropriate ornamentation, and the orderly and artistic arrangements of the selected words.

These essentials of style were always to be studied in relation to existing conditions under which the language flourished. This is a significant point in critical theory. Here we have the reminder that the characteristics of a language at a given time determine in some measure the nature of style. In the Twelfth Book, he remarks:

He, therefore, that shall require from the Latin the graces of the Attic tongue, must give it a similar sweetness of tone, and a similar abundance of words. If this be impossible, we must adapt our thoughts to the words which we have, and not clothe extremely delicate matter in phraseology which is too strong, not to say too gross, for it, lest the excellences of both be diminished by the union. The less able our language is to assist us, the more efforts we must make in the production of thought. Sublime and varied conceptions must be brought forth. Every feeling must be excited, and our speech illumined by the splendour of metaphor. We cannot be so plain as the Greeks; let us be more forcible. We are excelled by them in refinement; let us surpass them in weight. Exactness of expression is more surely attained by them; let us go beyond them in fulness. The Greek geniuses, even those of inferior degree, have their proper seaports; let us be impelled, in general, with larger sails, and let stronger breezes swell our canvas; but not so that we may always steer out to the deep sea, for we must sometimes coast along the land. The Greeks can easily pass through our shallows; I shall find a port somewhat, though not much deeper, in which my boat may be in no danger of sinking. For if the Greeks succeed better than we in plainer and simpler subjects, so that we are beaten on such ground . . . [we] must cultivate it as far as we can, and we can, at least, rival the Greeks in the temper and judgment with which we treat our subjects; while grace of style, which we have not among us by nature, must be sought from a foreign source.[74]

[73] *Ibid.*, XII, x, 17.
[74] *Ibid.*, XII, x, 35–38.

Quintilian confidently asserted that whereas Latin eloquence was the equal of Greek eloquence in invention, arrangement, judgment, and related matters, it was patently inferior in *elocution*, especially in beauty of diction and agreeableness of sounds.

He also contended that ordinary speech and true eloquence differed in nature.

> . . . for if it were sufficient for an orator to express his thoughts plainly, he would have nothing to study beyond mere suitableness of words; but since he has to please, to move, and to rouse the minds of his audience to various states of feeling, he must have recourse, for those purposes, to the means which are afforded us by the same nature that supplies us with ordinary speech; just as we are led by nature to invigorate our muscles with exercise, to increase our general strength, and to acquire a healthy complexion.[75]

This naturally suggested the possible distinction between writing and speaking.

> To me it appears that *to speak well* and *to write well* are but the same thing; and that a written oration is nothing else but a record of an oration delivered. Written oratory must accordingly, I think, be susceptible of every species of excellence; I say every species of excellence, not every species of fault, for I know that what is faulty sometimes pleases the ignorant. How, then, will what is written and what is spoken differ? I reply that if I were to address myself to a tribunal composed only of wise men, I would cut off much from the speeches, not only of Cicero, but even of Demosthenes, who is much less verbose; for, in speaking to such an audience, there will be no necessity for exciting the feelings, or for soothing the ear with delight; since Aristotle thinks that in such a case even exordia are superfluous, as wise men will not be moved by them; and to state the subject in proper and significant words, and establish proofs, will be sufficient. But when the people, or some of the people, are before us as judges, and when illiterate persons, and even ploughmen, are to pass sentence, every art which we think likely to conduce to the attainment of the object which we have in view, must be employed; and such arts are to be displayed not only when we speak, but when we write, that we may show how the speech should be spoken. Would Demosthenes have spoken badly in speaking exactly as he wrote, or would Cicero? Or do we know them to have been excellent orators from any other source than from their writings? Did they speak, we may ask, better than they wrote; if better, they ought to have written as they spoke?[76]

Shall the orator, therefore, always speak just as he writes? Quintilian says Yes, but recognizes that it is not always possible to do so. For,

> . . . if the time allowed by the judge prevents him from doing so by its shortness, much that might have been said will be withheld; but the speech, if published, will contain the whole. But what may have been introduced to suit the capacity of the judges, will not be transmitted unaltered to

---

[75] *Ibid.*, XII, x, 43.
[76] *Ibid.*, XII, x, 51–54.

posterity, lest it be thought to be the offspring of his judgment, and not a concession to circumstances.[77]

In passing judgment upon an orator's style, Quintilian reminds us that since many species of eloquence flourish, it is

. . . extremely foolish to inquire which of them an orator should follow, since every species, if it be but of a genuine character, has its use, and all that people commonly call *ways of speaking* falls under the management of the orator; for he will employ every variety of speech so as to suit, not merely a particular cause, but particular parts of any cause. Thus he will not speak in the same strain in defence of a man who is accused of a capital crime, in a suit respecting an inheritance, and in cases of interdicts, sponsions, and loans; he will observe distinctions between the delivery of opinions in the senate, in the assembly of the people, and in private deliberations; he will vary his style greatly in conformity with the difference of persons, occasions, and places; he will adopt different arts for conciliating, even in the same speech; he will not try to excite anger and pity by dwelling on similar topics; he will employ one style to state his case to the judge, and another to move the judge's feelings. The same colour of diction will not be observable in his exordium, his statement of facts, his arguments, his digressions, and his perorations. He will be able to speak gravely, austerely, sharply, strongly, spiritedly, copiously, bitterly, affably, gently, artfully, soothingly, mildly, agreeably, succinctly, politely; he will not be always alike, yet always consistent with himself. Thus he will not only attain that object for which the use of speech was chiefly intended; I mean, that of speaking to the purpose, and with ability sufficient to establish that which he has in view; but he will also obtain applause, not merely from the learned, but even from the common people.[78]

Thus, what the orator strives for should be

. . . *great* without extravagance; *sublime,* without audacity; *energetic,* without rashness; *severe,* without repulsiveness; *grave,* without dulness; *plenteous,* without exuberance; *pleasing,* without meretriciousness; *grand,* without tumidity. Such judgment will be shown with regard to other qualities; and the path in the middle is generally the safest, because error lies on either side.[79]

Certain Postulates of Quintilian's Critical Standard

Like Cicero, for whom he had a deep admiration, Quintilian had a clearly defined conception of the Ideal Orator. His was perhaps more complete than Cicero's. In addition to possessing the characteristics ascribed by Cicero to the perfect speaker, Quintilian's ideal was presumably even more highly qualified as a participant in public life because he had to be a *good* man. Not lacking, to be sure, in the Ciceronian treatments, this attribute was nevertheless discussed at greater length and accorded greater emphasis by Quintilian.

[77] *Ibid.,* XII, x, 55.
[78] *Ibid.,* XII, x, 69, 72.
[79] *Ibid.,* XII, x, 80.

It is probable that Cicero influenced Quintilian in the adoption of the principle of progress in artistic creation. At any rate, Quintilian perceives in the history of oratorical achievement a principle of orderly, gradual growth. His expression of this doctrine, similar in every detail to Cicero's, runs as follows:

For men of the earliest ages did not speak with our exactness and care, nor had any knowledge of *preparing* an audience with an exordium, *enlightening* them with statements of facts, *convincing* them with arguments, and *exciting* them with appeals to their feelings. They were ignorant of all these arts, and not of composition merely; and if we ought to speak in no respect better than they, huts should never have been relinquished for houses, dresses of skins for decent apparel, or mountains and forests for cities. What art too, we may ask, came to perfection at once? What is not improved by culture? Why do we prune our vines? Why do we dig about them? Why do we root our brambles from our fields, when the ground naturally produces them? But, in truth, a thing is most natural, when nature has allowed it to be brought into the best condition.[80]

As a corollary of this observation, Quintilian suggests that "nature has herself appointed that nothing great is to be accomplished quickly, and has ordained that difficulty should precede every work of excellence"; and that "everything great and admirable had some peculiar time at which it was brought to its highest excellence."

Although Quintilian had a point of view regarding the basic assumptions of critical inquiry, he remained unquestionably the *theorist* who was trying to check the decline of oratory in his day. His work as a critic is not systematic; neither is it sufficiently complete to enable us to observe the application of the technique, with which he was competently familiar, for the establishing of standards for exacting appraisal of orators.

Quintilian's Critical Estimates

Scattered criticisms of the orators appear in all of the books of the *Institutes*. In the Tenth Book, however, in which he discusses the improvement of skill in speaking through reading, hearing, and writing, he introduces short critical estimates of a few of the great Greek and Roman speakers, including among others Demosthenes, Lysias, Isocrates, Cicero, Pollio, and Messala.

When he considers Demosthenes, he calls him a most eminent Attic speaker—one who

. . . has been almost the sole model for oratory; such is his energy, so compact in his whole language, so tense, as it were, with nerves, so free from

[80] *Ibid.*, IX, iv, 4–5.

anything superfluous; and such the general character of his eloquence, that we can neither find anything wanting in it, nor anything superfluous.[81]

And he makes a comparative analysis of Cicero and Demosthenes:

But our *orators* may, above all, set the Latin eloquence on an equality with that of Greece; for I would confidently match Cicero against any one of the Greek orators. Nor am I unaware how great an opposition I am raising against myself, especially when it is no part of my design at present to compare him with Demosthenes, for it is not at all necessary, since I think that Demosthenes ought to be read above all other orators, or rather learned by heart. Of their great excellences I consider that most are similar; their method, their order of partition, their manner of preparing the minds of their audience, their mode of proof, and, in a word, everything that depends on invention. In their style of speaking there is some difference; Demosthenes is more compact, Cicero more verbose; Demosthenes argues more closely, Cicero with a wider sweep; Demosthenes always attacks with a sharp-pointed weapon, Cicero often with a weapon both sharp and weighty; from Demosthenes nothing can be taken away, to Cicero nothing can be added; in the one there is more study, in the other more nature. In wit, certainly, and pathos, two stimulants of the mind which have great influence in oratory, we have the advantage. Perhaps the custom of his country did not allow Demosthenes pathetic perorations; but, on the other hand, the different genius of the Latin tongue did not grant to us those beauties which the Attics so much admire. In the epistolary style, indeed, though there are letters written by both, and in that of dialogue, in which Demosthenes wrote nothing, there is no comparison. We must yield the superiority, however, on one point, that Demosthenes lived before Cicero, and made him, in a great measure, the able orator that he was; for Cicero appears to me, after he devoted himself wholly to imitate the Greeks, to have embodied in his style the energy of Demosthenes, the copiousness of Plato, and the sweetness of Isocrates. Nor did he, by zealous effort, attain only what was excellent in each of these, but drew most, or rather all excellences, from himself, by the felicitous exuberance of his immortal genius. He does not, as Pindar says, *collect rain water, but overflows from a living fountain*, having been so endowed at his birth, by the special kindness of Providence, that in him eloquence might make trial of her whole strength. For who can instruct a judge with more exactness, or excite him with more vehemence? What orator had ever so pleasing a manner? The very points which he wrests from you by force, you would think that he gained from you by entreaty; and when he carries away the judge by his impetuosity, he yet does not seem to be hurried along, but imagines that he is following of his own accord. In all that he says, indeed, there is so much authority, that we are ashamed to dissent from him; he does not bring to a cause the mere zeal of an advocate, but the support of a witness or a judge; and, at the same time, all these excellences, a single one of which any other man could scarcely attain with the utmost exertion, flow from him without effort; and that stream of language, than which nothing is more pleasing to the ear, carries with it the appearance of the happiest facility. It was not without justice, therefore, that he was said by his contemporaries *to reign supreme in the courts;* and he has gained such esteem

---

[81] *Ibid.*, X, i, 76.

among his posterity, that Cicero is now less the name of a man than that of eloquence itself. To him, therefore, let us look; let him be kept in view as our great example; and let that student know that he has made some progress to whom Cicero has become an object of admiration.[82]

Quintilian's Place in Rhetorical Criticism

Quintilian undoubtedly achieved a measure of success in urging the return to the best Ciceronian standards in oratory. This was a practical result of his careful teaching. He made an eloquent and sincere attempt to restore the classical ideal in Rome at a time when the tides of excess were flowing against such a movement. His contributions to a sound educational philosophy were numerous. In the strict sense, however, his contributions as a critic are of greater importance to the literary craftsman than to the rhetorician. That is, he did more toward developing critical theory—e.g., the elaborate analysis of style—than in applying the doctrines to the judgment of particular speeches. He is a better critic of *oratory* as a form of culture than of individual *orators*.

THE COMPARATIVE STUDIES OF PLUTARCH

Method in Plutarch's Criticism

Atkins refers to the work of Plutarch (A.D. 48–120) as "another of those cross-currents of doctrine that give to this period its many-sided interest."

In keeping with the plan of his *Lives,* Plutarch presents the parallel accounts of Demosthenes and Cicero and follows them with a comparative study. In the early part of the life of Demosthenes, Plutarch remarks:

> . . . my comparison of their natural dispositions and their characters will be formed upon their actions and their lives as statesmen, and I shall not pretend to criticise their orations one against the other, to show which of the two was the more charming or the more powerful speaker. For there, as Ion says—
> 'We are but like a fish upon dry land';
>
> a proverb which Caecilius perhaps forgot, when he employed his always adventurous talents in so ambitious an attempt as a comparison of Demosthenes and Cicero; and, possibly, if it were a thing obvious and easy for every man to *know himself,* the precept had not passed for an oracle.[83]

Despite the disclaimer of interest in a comparison of speeches, Plutarch uses the technique in appraising the characteristics of the orators.

[82] *Ibid.,* X, i, 105–112.
[83] *Plutarch: The Lives of the Noble Grecians and Romans.* Rev. by Arthur H. Clough. New York. p. 1023.

Thus, in the comparison of Demosthenes and Cicero, following the parallel biographical accounts, Plutarch writes:

But omitting an exact comparison of their respective faculties in speaking, yet thus much seems fit to be said; that Demosthenes, to make himself a master in rhetoric, applied all the faculties he had, natural or acquired, wholly that way that he far surpassed in force and strength of eloquence all his contemporaries in political and judicial speaking, in grandeur and majesty all the panegyrical orators, and in accuracy and science all the logicians and rhetoricians of his day; that Cicero was highly educated, and by his diligent study became a most accomplished general scholar in all these branches, having left behind him numerous philosophical treatises of his own on Academic principles; as, indeed, even in his written speeches, both political and judicial, we see him continually trying to show his learning by the way.

Again, in the same vein, he remarks:

And one may discover the different temper of each of them in their speeches. For Demosthenes's oratory was without all embellishment and jesting, wholly composed for real effect and seriousness; not smelling of the lamp, as Pytheas scoffingly said, but of the temperance, thoughtfulness, austerity, and grave earnestness of his temper. Whereas Cicero's love of mockery often ran him into scurrility; and in his love of laughing away serious arguments in judicial cases by jests and facetious remarks, with a view to the advantage of his clients, he paid too little regard to what was decent. . . .

Later, he observes:

It is necessary, indeed, for a political leader to be an able speaker; but it is an ignoble thing for any man to admire and relish the glory of his own eloquence. And, in this matter, Demosthenes had a more than ordinary gravity and magnificence of mind, accounting his talent in speaking nothing more than a mere accomplishment and matter of practice, the success of which must depend greatly on the good-will and candour of his hearers, and regarding those who pride themselves on such accounts to be men of a low and petty disposition.[84]

Here we find observations that seem to presuppose a method which the author hesitated to use. Whether he willed it or not, Plutarch was comparing speeches, or at least establishing judgments which, if responsible, postulated such comparison.

Criteria in the Moralia

Some of the essays in the *Moralia* shed light upon Plutarch's critical judgment. In "Of Hearing," he discusses the point of view and attitude of the discerning listener, or critic. Commenting on the mistaken notion often held by young men that speaking requires study and attention

---

[84] *Ibid.*

while "hearing cannot be a thing of any difficulty," he announces some general rules apropos of the observation "that Nature has given every man two ears and but one tongue, as a secret intimation that he ought to speak less than he hears."

The listener should bring with him a "modest and unwearied attention" for then "whatever is beneficial in the discourse he makes his own, . . . he more readily discovers what is false or impertinent. . . ." Furthermore,

> . . . envy and detraction and prejudice are in no case good, but always a great impediment to what is so; yet nowhere worse than when they are made the bosom-friends and counsellors of a hearer, because they represent the best things to him as unpleasant and impertinent, and men in such circumstances are pleased with anything rather than what deserves their applause.[85]

The listener must, accordingly, come "to a kind of truce and accommodation with vainglory, and preserve the same evenness and cheerfulness of humor he would bring with him if he were invited to a festival entertainment or the first-fruits' sacrifice, applauding the orator's power when he speaks to the purpose, and where he fails receiving kindly his readiness to communicate what he knows and to persuade others by what is wrought upon himself."

Plutarch holds that careful listening helps the critic to correct his own mistakes, "For there is nothing in the world more easy than to discover the faults of others; but it is done to no effect if we do not make it useful to ourselves in correcting and avoiding the like failures."

The critic should have a discerningly sensitive ear. Decrying the mood of the fool who, according to Heraclitus, "was put in a flutter at every thing he heard," Plutarch urges tempered consideration.

> We ought indeed to use all the candor imaginable in praising the speaker, yet withal as great caution in yielding our assent to what he says; to look upon his expression and action with a favorable construction, but to inspect the usefulness and truth of his doctrine with the nicest and most critical judgment; that speakers may cease to be malicious, and that what they say may do no mischief.[86]

The listener must separate "the trash and trumpery of an oration, that [he] may come at the more fruitful and useful part. . . ." ". . . A well-meaning sincere hearer ought to pass by the flowers of an oration, leaving the gaudy show and theatrical part to entertain dronish Sophists; and, diving into the very mind of the speaker and the sense of his speech, he must draw thence what is necessary for his own service. . . ."

Expressing his dissatisfaction with the schools that emphasize the

---

[85] *Plutarch's Miscellanies and Essays.* Rev. by W. W. Goodwin. Boston, 1898. I, 445.

[86] *Ibid.*, I, 448.

importance of *manner* to the neglect of *matter* in speaking, Plutarch advises the listener not to make his personal pleasure "the only end of hearing"; he should not ask for "perfumes and essences" when "he has need of a poultice and fomentations." "But let him learn to be thankful to him that purges away the darkness and stupidity of his mind, though . . . with an offensive or unpalatable discourse."

> . . . though it lies upon a speaker to take some care that his expression be pleasing and plausible, yet a hearer ought not to make that the first thing he looks after. Afterward, indeed, when he has satisfied his appetite with the substance and has taken breath, he may be allowed the curiosity of examining the style and expression . . . : as men quench their thirst first before they have time to admire the embossing of the bowl. But now such a one as is not intent on the subject-matter, but demands merely that the style shall be plain and pure Attic, is much of his foolish humor who refuses an antidote unless it be mixed in Attic porcelain, or who will not put on a coat in the winter because the cloth is not made of Attic wool. . . .[87]

Plutarch condemns those who "mind nothing but words and jingles, and express themselves extravagantly upon what they think well said, without ever understanding or enquiring if it be useful and necessary, or needless and vain."

The foregoing remarks do not establish Plutarch as a great critic, but they throw light upon the basis of his judgment. They do reveal his studied regard for the contextual matter of discourse, as contrasted with style simply for its own sake.

Plutarch's Oratorical Estimates

Plutarch's interest in oratory was unquestionably genuine. However, his writings on the orators fail to give us much insight into his critical analysis of speechmaking. His *Lives of the Ten Orators* furnishes additional evidence that the purely biographical treatment of speakers seldom results in effective rhetorical criticism, unless the total venture is conceived from the point of view of speechcraft and unless the details of the lives are articulated with that theme.

In the *Lives of the Ten Orators*, Plutarch deals briefly with Antiphon, Andocides, Lysias, Isocrates, Isaeus, Aeschines, Lycurgus, Demosthenes, Hyperides, and Dinarchus. His treatment covers chiefly those details relating to the orator's family background, principal activities in the state, and isolated family lore, often of a personal or gossipy nature. Only now and then does he appraise the speaker's skill. Thus, in the biography of Antiphon, he remarks:

> He is most accurate in his orations, in invention subtle; and he would frequently baffle his adversary at unawares, by a covert sort of pleading; in

[87] *Ibid.*

troublesome and intricate matters he was very judicious and sharp; and as he was a great admirer of ornamental speaking, he would always adapt his orations to both law and reason.[88]

Plutarch reminds us that Isocrates "used to tell his scholars that he taught his art for ten minas; but he would give any man ten thousand, that could teach him to be bold and give him a good utterance." Then follows the discerning observation concerning Isocrates: ". . . being once asked how he, who was not very eloquent himself, could make others so . . . he answered, Just as a whetstone cannot cut, yet it will sharpen knives for that purpose." Andocides' style, Plutarch observes, "is plain and easy, without the least affectation or any thing of a figurative ornament." And Lysias was "very cogent in his persuasions, and was always very brief in what he delivered. . . . His style seems plain and easy, though hardly imitable." [89] Hyperides "never affected much action in his orations to the people, his chief aim being to lay down the matter plainly, and make the case as obvious to the judges as he could." And Dinarchus "imitated Hyperides; or, as some incline to judge, rather Demosthenes, because of that vigor and force to move the affections, and the rhetorical ornaments that are evident in his style." Plutarch announces the classic Demosthenic remark that the first, second, and third parts of rhetoric are *action*.

These excerpts, representing much of Plutarch's critical analysis, reveal the treatments to be disappointing. The individuality of the ten men, as orators, never quite emerges. Plutarch attempts the difficult if not futile task of energizing biographies of orators, while neglecting to consider the orations for which the men were distinguished.

His effort is consistent, however, with his recognition of the place of the orator in public life. Although he was interested in oratory, he did not consider it as important as military and civic accomplishment. In his essay on "Whether the Athenians Were More Warlike or Learned," he indicates specifically that, whereas the writings of the poets are "mere bubbles," the "rhetoricians and orators indeed have something in them that renders them in some measure fit to be compared with great captains." But they come off a second best, it would seem, for greater courage is demanded of the captains. Thus Isocrates could hardly compare with the heroes of Marathon. "How would that man have been affrighted at the clattering of weapons or the routing of a phalanx, who was so afraid of suffering one vowel to clash with another, or to pronounce a sentence where but one syllable was wanting!" Plutarch concludes his essay by comparing Demosthenes and other orators with Mil-

---

[88] *Plutarch's Essays and Miscellanies.* V, 18.
[89] *Ibid.,* V, 25–26.

tiades and Alcibiades, the commanders coming off with the greater renown for their work in defending the honor of the country.

Plutarch formulated no original doctrines in criticism, but offered a body of suggestive observations sufficiently interesting and revealing to insure him a place in the history of critical thought. His writings throw some light upon Alexandrian learning and upon the teachings of such significant figures as Gorgias, Isocrates, and Aristotle.

PHILOSTRATUS APPRAISES DECLAMATORY SPEECH

Proud of the sophistic tradition, anxious "to preserve for all time a picture of the triumphs of his tribe, when sophists were at the height of their glory," [90] Philostratus demonstrates in his *Lives of the Sophists* the type of criticism that naturally derives from an age in which the conception of rhetoric virtually ignores subject matter and glorifies stylistic, declamatory utterance. Born about A.D. 170, Philostratus falls within the period of the second sophistic, and accordingly conceives of rhetoric largely in terms of sophistical performance, or of oratory based upon themes—historical and fictitious.

We must regard the ancient sophistic art as philosophic rhetoric. For it discusses the themes that philosophers treat of, but whereas they, by their method of questioning, set snares for knowledge, and advance step by step as they confirm the minor points of their investigations, but assert that they have still no sure knowledge, the sophist of the old school assumes a knowledge of that whereof he speaks.[91]

The Critical Standards

In the *Lives*, written between 230 and 238, Philostratus praises the sophists for their work in declamation. The teaching and practice of the time followed almost identical patterns. As Charles S. Baldwin remarks, "in method, in composition, there was little difference between a teacher's assignments to his amateur pupils and his own professional orations." [92] Philostratus did not consider *declamatio* solely as an exercise; it was "a form of public speaking on a par with any other."

Passages from the *Lives* will reveal Philostratus' studied regard for style as the end of rhetoric. They will confirm Baldwin's belief that the "constant implication of Philostratus probably echoes the ideal of orator and audience alike: behold a greater speaker."

[90] Wilmer Cave Wright, trans. and ed., *The Lives of the Sophists*. Loeb Classical Library. 1922, p. xii.
[91] *Ibid.*, p. 5.
[92] *Medieval Rhetoric and Poetic*, p. 10.

In his analysis of the oratory of Dio of Prusa, Philostratus concerns himself chiefly with style:

His style has the ring of Demosthenes and Plato, but Dio has besides a peculiar resonance of his own, which enhances theirs as the bridge enhances the tone of musical instruments; and it was combined with a serious and direct simplicity of expression. . . .
Again, in Dio's orations the elements of his own noble character were admirably displayed. For though he very often rebuked licentious cities, he did not show himself acrimonious or ungracious, but like one who restrains an unruly horse, with the bridle rather than the whip; and when he sets out to praise cities that were well governed, he did not seem to extol them, but rather to guide their attention to the fact that they would be ruined if they should change their ways.[93]

Critias receives Philostratus' praise for substantially the same reasons:

As regards the style of his oratory, Critias abounded in brief and sentkentious sayings, and he was most skilful in the use of elevated language, but not of the dithyrambic sort, nor did he have recourse to words borrowed from poetry; but his was the kind of elevated language that is composed of the most appropriate words and is not artificial. I observe, moreover, that he was a master of concise eloquence, and that even when he maintained the tone proper to a speech in defence, he used to make vigorous attacks on his opponents; and that he Atticized, but in moderation, nor did he use outlandish words—for bad taste in Atticizing is truly barbarous—but his Attic words shine through his discourse like the gleams of the sun's rays. Critias also secures a charming effect by passing without connectives from one part of his speech to another. Then, too, Critias strives for the daring and unusual both in thought and expression, yet his eloquence is somewhat lacking in virility, though it is agreeable and smooth, like the breath of the west wind.[94]

In Aeschines' orations, Philostratus remarks, "shines the light of perfect lucidity. . . ." Aeschines "is at once sublime and seductive, energetic and delightful, and in a word his sort of eloquence defies the efforts of those who would imitate it."

Isaeus' style was neither "exuberant nor meagre, but simple and natural and suited to the subject matter. Moreover, a concise form of expression and the summing up of every argument into a brief statement was peculiarly an invention of Isaeus. . . ."

It is deserving of note that subject matter, *per se*, receives practically no attention. The charm of speech and of speaker commands the forefront. Dio of Prusa, we are told, had a persuasive charm that captivated "even men who were not versed in Greek letters." When Favorinus delivered speeches in Rome,

. . . the interest in them was universal, so much so that even those in his audience who did not understand the Greek language shared in the pleas-

[93] *Lives of the Sophists*, pp. 17–19.
[94] *Ibid.*, pp. 49–51.

ure that he gave; for he fascinated even them by the tones of his voice, [which were evidently shrill], by his expressive glance and the rhythm of his speech.[95]

And Aeschines employed an "inspired manner" that invariably won applause. In Lollianus' oratory, there were brilliant passages that suddenly came to an end "like a flash of lightning." Polemo's utterance "was clear and incisive, and there was a fine ringing sound in the tones of his voice." "Polemo's style of eloquence is passionate, combative, and ringing to the echo. . . . The Demosthenic cast of his thought lends it distinction and a gravity which is not dull or inert but brilliant and inspired, as though delivered from the tripod."

Personal charm in a speaker, Philostratus thus held, should be considered an important element in rhetorical effectiveness. Concerning Hermocrates, he said:

In his public declamations Hermocrates was aided in the first place by his great-grandfather's renown, since it is human nature to set a higher value on abilities that have been handed down from father to son. . . . But he was also aided by the beauty of his personal appearance, and he was indeed possessed of great charm and looked like a statue with the bloom of early youth. . . . Moreover his easy flow of words and the striking effects of his voice contributed to his success, and the fact that he could review his themes in the twinkling of an eye, and that what he recited from a manuscript or declaimed was more what one expects from hoary old age than from a mere youth to invent and deliver.[96]

The references to inventive skill are incidental, almost mechanical. For example, Polemo is defended briefly against the charge that he was not skilled in defence; that he was unable to establish sustained arguments but "was forced off the course like a horse for whom the ground is too rough. . . ." And Herodes' disposition of materials elicits this comment:

The structure of his work was suitably restrained, and its strength lay in subtlety rather than in vigour of attack. He was impressive in the plain style, sonorous after the manner of Critias; his ideas were such as would not occur to the mind of another; he had an easy and urbane wit which was not dragged in, but inspired by the subjects themselves; his diction was pleasing and abounded in figures and had grace and beauty; he was skilful in varying his constructions; his tone was not vehement but smooth and steady, and, speaking generally, his type of eloquence is like gold dust shining beneath the waters of a silvery eddying river.[97]

Antiochus, we are told, "handled the emotions more skilfully than any other sophist, for he did not spin out long monodies or abject lamentations, but expressed them in a few words and adorned them with ideas

95 *Ibid.*, p. 29.
96 *Ibid.*, pp. 277–279.
97 *Ibid.*, p. 179.

better than I can describe. . . ." Philostratus remarks that Herodes re-
proached Philagrus of Cilicia for "not trying to win the good-will of
his hearers. . . ." Aristeides' strength is reputed to have been "in the
elaborate cogitation of a theme; for which reason he refrained from
extempore speaking."

Significance of the *Lives*

At best, the *Lives* represents superficial rhetorical criticism True,
the form of the *Lives* is suggestive of sounder critical values, for we find
data on the speakers' early youth, training, activities, personal appearance, style, and related details. Examples from typical speeches illustrate some of the points relative to the speakers' style. Within narrow
ranges, the comparative method of analysis is employed. But the standards of excellence that Philostratus sets up presuppose the all-sufficiency
of style as the measure of speaking. Unless speaking well is accepted
as an absolute standard, which cannot properly be granted, the *Lives*
affords a type of criticism that is unmistakably capricious.

Philostratus presented, however, a body of semicritical estimates consistent with the spirit and temper of his age. An oratory of themes held
sway, and he accepted and defended it. Accordingly, he conceived of
rhetoric as an instrument for giving effectiveness to the speaker, rather
than to the message. Divorced, as Baldwin expresses it, from "the urgencies of matter and motive," rhetoric thus became empty, ostentatious.
Philostratus' criticism is correspondingly deficient. Devoted to the appraisal of exhibitionistic skill, it loses sight of the ideas that normally
constitute the reason for speaking.

THE DOCTRINE OF IMITATION

The literature on rhetoric contains numerous references to imitation
—to its necessity, usefulness, and general role in the training of speakers.
Indirectly, it concerns the critical functions as well, for some of the
greatest orators, in the opinion of the rhetoricians, are imitators. However, they imitated their predecessors with such consummate skill that
the critics accredit the actions as artistic refinements.

Quintilian asserts that "a great portion of art consists in *imitation,*
since, though to invent was first in order of time, and holds the first
place in merit, yet it is of advantage to copy what has been invented
with success." Imitation, in itself, is not enough. "When those who
had no master in any subject, have transmitted so many discoveries to
posterity, shall not the experience which we have in some things assist
us to bring to light others, or shall we have nothing but what we derive

from other men's bounty, as some painters aim at nothing more than to know how to copy a picture by means of compasses and lines?" In short, it "is dishonourable even to rest satisfied with simply equalling what we imitate." [98]

Quintilian believes it proper to imitate the excellences of several orators, rather than one only. "Of all the Greek orators Demosthenes is by far the most excellent; yet others, on some occasions have expressed themselves better; and he himself has expressed many things better on some occasions than on others. But he who deserves to be imitated most, is not therefore the only author to be imitated." [99]

An orator's artistry can never assert itself wholly through simple imitation. Everything "that is the resemblance of something else, must necessarily be inferior to that of which it is a copy, as the shadow of the substance, the portrait to the natural face, and the acting of the player to the real feeling. The same is the case with regard to oratorical composition; for in the originals, which we take for our models, there is nature and real power, while every imitation, on the contrary, is something counterfeit, and seems adapted to an object not its own." So while the student is asked to make "whatever is excellent in each author his own," he also is warned that borrowing must become more than common plagiarism: ". . . he who shall add to these borrowed qualities excellences of his own, so as to supply what is deficient in his models, and to retrench what is redundant, will be the complete orator whom we desire to see; and such an orator ought now surely to be formed, when so many more examples of eloquence exist than fell to the lot of those who have hitherto been considered the best orators; for to them will belong the praise, not only of surpassing those who preceded them, but of instructing those who followed." [100]

Cicero also believed that the student should seek out good models and, equally important, copy the chief excellences rather than the faults. He remarks that the practice of truly great orators bespeaks the value of imitation: Lysias and Critias "retained the vigorous style of Pericles"; Demosthenes, Hyperides, Aeschines, Lycurgus, and Dinarchus, although unlike in their skills, "all engaged in imitating the same kind of material excellence; and as long as the imitation of their manner lasted, so long did that character and system of eloquence prevail." [101]

One of the more extensive modern treatments of imitation is found in John Ward's *System of Oratory*, published in 1759. Ward shares the view of the ancients that imitation means expressing the best in the

[98] *Institutes.* X, ii, 6–7.
[99] *Ibid.*, X, ii, 24.
[100] *Ibid.*, X, ii, 11–28, *passim.*
[101] *De Oratore.* II, xxii–xxiii.

chosen models and striving for advantages "above the original." Consequently, it is consistent with the free exercise "and improvement of our abilities." The true art consists in so diversifying "what we take from others, as, if we can, to improve it, or at least not suffer it to receive any detriment by our alteration." This can be done in four ways: (1) Enlarge a thought or expression taken from another. Cicero observed this principle in his orations against Mark Antony, which evidently were copied in part from the Demosthenean pronouncements against Philip. (2) Abridge or take only a part of what others have said. After the battle of Chaeronea, in which the Athenians were defeated by Philip, Demosthenes delivered a funeral oration upon which Cicero drew subsequently for parts of his fourteenth Philippic. (3) Keep the thought but apply it to a different subject, as Cicero, drawing upon Demosthenes' defense of Ctesiphon, did in parts of his oration for Quinctius. (4) Change the order of thoughts or represent them in a different dress. In his defense of Cluentius, Cicero relied thus upon parts of Demosthenes' oration against Aristogiton. [102]

Many of the best artists, according to Ward, have imitated others. Homer was assisted by writers whose works are no longer extant; Vergil imitated Homer; Terence copied after Menander; Plautus, after Epicharmus; Sulpicius imitated Crassus; and Cicero drew upon the practices of many Greek orators.

It seems, then, that many theorists exercise extreme care in applying the test of originality to oratorical composition. While assigning great importance to original invention, they recognize that the flow of ideas in history is a continuum; and they allow that skilful and improved adaptation of old thoughts and techniques to new conditions may stamp an orator as an accomplished model, rather than as a plagiarist.

SUMMARY

The distinguished theorizers on rhetoric were willing to apply their tenets to the criticism of speeches. They used the principles and precepts which they laid down for others; and in so doing, they demonstrated further that the theory and criticism of speaking are common aspects of an indivisible art.

Hence the earliest theorizers were also critics. Beginning with Plato and continuing through the long line of ancient contributors to rhetoric, we note the studied attempt to hit upon criteria of artistic judgment by which the relative merits of prose forms can be assessed. In this chapter we have seen how patterns of evaluation began to take form; how the

[102] London, 1759, pp. 410 ff.

comparative method soon came into use; how the impact of historical forces upon speechmaking was early recognized as a determinant of rhetorical effectiveness. These critical tenets received their most elaborate embodiment in the efforts of Cicero. Especially in the *Orator* and in the *Brutus* did Cicero establish just claim to distinction as a pioneer in the criticism of speeches, and as the first systematic historian of oratory.

EXERCISES

1. To what extent can the critical standards of the ancients be applied to contemporary speechmaking?
2. Define Asianism; indicate its origins, limitations, tendencies, and alleged defects in contrast to Atticism.
3. Do we have contemporary schools of thought that are roughly analogous to the old Atticist-Asianist division? Justify your answer by presenting illustrative data.
4. Are we justified in applying Cicero's standard of "cultural achievements" of the orators as basic indicators of their merit? Did Cicero's enthusiasm for his own rhetorical tenets vitiate his critical judgments? Are rhetorical critics of today (*e.g.,* the contributors to *History and Criticism of American Public Address*) governed by similar limitations?
5. In the light of Philostratus' assumptions concerning the ends of rhetoric, comment on the place of declamation in present-day school and college education.
6. To what extent does Cicero's method of criticizing the orators conform to the general suggestions set forth in Chapter 1 of this volume?
7. Study the *Brutus* to determine whether or not Cicero used "service to friends" as a subsidiary criterion of oratorical excellence (*e.g.,* his treatment of Caius Caelius, Lucius Gellius, etc.). Give your view.
8. After careful study of Cicero's *Brutus*, write an evaluation of Cicero as a critic.
9. Does Cicero's concept of the complete or perfect orator provide a critical yardstick by which to judge a speaker? How does Cicero use this measure in his *Brutus?*
10. The *New Yorker* magazine (February 4, 1961, pp. 23–24) contained a critical estimate of John F. Kennedy's Inaugural Address. The evaluation was along strictly classical lines. Examine the piece with an eye to determining how successfully the Aristotelian formula can be applied to modern speechmaking.
11. Is it possible to present a criticism of speakers through a criticism of the rhetorical theory of a period? In part, Plato made the attempt. Would such an analysis be at all revealing in the modern scene?

READINGS

J. W. H. ATKINS. "The Critical Beginnings at Rome and the Classical Reaction: Terrence, Lucilius and Cicero" and "The Critical Revival and Theories of Style of Tacitus and Demetrius." In *Literary Criticism in Antiquity*, Vol. II. London, Cambridge University Press, 1934. Pp. 1–46, 175–209.

M. L. CLARKE. *"Non Hominis Nomen, Sed Eloquentiae."* In *Cicero,* T. A. Dorey, ed. New York, Basic Books, Inc., 1965. Pp. 81–107.

E. M. COPE. *An Introduction to Aristotle's Rhetoric.* London, Macmillan & Co., 1867.

G. M. A. GRUBE. *A Greek Critic: Demetrius on Style.* Toronto, University of Toronto Press, 1961. (See the introduction.)

R. C. JEBB. "The Decline and the Revival." In *The Attic Orators from Antiphon to Isaeus,* Vol. II. London, Macmillan & Co., 1893. Pp. 435–457.

EVERETT LEE HUNT. "Rhetoric and Literary Criticism." *Quarterly Journal of Speech,* 21:564–568 (November, 1935).

R. G. M. NISBET. "The Speeches." In *Cicero,* T. A. Dorey, ed. New York, Basic Books, Inc., 1965. Pp. 47–79.

W. RHYS ROBERTS. *Greek Rhetoric and Literary Criticism.* New York, Longmans, Green & Co., 1928.

6

The Critics of the Intermediate Period, 1600-1850

Perhap no one has ever considered himself a professional rhetorical critic. For many years, however, men have sought a system by which speeches might intelligently and responsibly be judged. Often, as in the case of the critics of antiquity, these systems were not deliberately established for the purpose of analyzing talks. Instead, they grew out of the general theorizing which was the business of men who probed the operation of an art. Thus Aristotle's *Rhetoric*—however valuable it may be today as a pattern of critical judgment—surely was not designed originally as a yardstick of criticism. In this chapter we shall examine the theories of a selected group of men, some of whom sought to establish, at least for themselves, formal patterns of critical analysis for public speeches.

RAPIN AND SEVENTEENTH-CENTURY FRENCH ORATORY

The Theoretical Basis of Rapin's Report

René Rapin's essay on eloquence [1] is essentially a report on the state of public speaking during the seventeenth century. Specifically, it is an analysis of the major defects evident in the speakers of the period, together with certain suggestions for the correction of faults. Rapin makes no claim of presenting new contributions to rhetorical theory, although his treatment of pulpit eloquence reveals a fair measure of originality. In the main, he relies upon the masters of antiquity for his theory. In

[1] René Rapin. *Reflexions on Eloquence*. In *The Whole Critical Works of Mon. Rapin*. Translated by Basil Kennet . . . and others. London, 1731. Two volumes.

the preface to the essay, he pays tribute to the "admirable Memoirs from the Rhetorical Instructions of Aristotle, Cicero, and Quintilian whose Works in this kind are so exact, and their Pourtrait of Eloquence so just, and so accomplish'd, as to leave no Room for our Improvements, nor even for our Wishes." Accordingly, Rapin draws upon those contributors, as well as upon Longinus, for the critical standards by which to appraise the speaking of the day. Marginal references to the ancients are sprinkled liberally throughout the first part of the essay.

Reflexions on Eloquence, first printed in 1672, is in three parts: "Reflexions upon the Eloquence of the Times in General," "Reflexions upon the Eloquence of the Bar," and "Reflexions upon the Eloquence of the Pulpit." Of the three divisions, the last receives by far the most detailed treatment.

"Reflexions upon the Eloquence of the Times in General" contains, in a negative way, Rapin's standard of effective speaking. The chief sources of eloquence are said to be two: (1) natural talent for speaking, "without which it is not possible to succeed, and with which it is almost impossible to miscarry," and (2) comprehensive knowledge and a severe application. Then follows a long list of the faults found in the speakers of the period. Each of these defects is said to result from the violation of some principle set forth by Aristotle, Cicero, Quintilian, or Longinus. Most of the speakers, Rapin indicates do not train themselves in composition as they used to do; they pay too little attention to the accurate expression of ideas; they neglect study in pronunciation; they are careless in their use of logic; they do not adapt their styles to the circumstances, and hence fail to get the proper measure of sublimity; they frequently add too much ornamentation to their addresses; they often fail to adhere closely enough to nature; and they sometimes mar the style of their discourses by artificiality and affectation. Furthermore, certain speakers do not have that "just Temperament which ought to be used in mixing Reason with Authority, Comparison and Similitude with Example and Induction"; others amuse only "the Head, without affecting the Heart"; still others fail to arrange and dispose properly the things which they invent. Rapin closes his summary of ills by saying that eloquence must gain admiration, and that it must come from a speaker who is genteel and modest.

In the two subsequent sections of his essay, Rapin relates the foregoing abuses to forensic and pulpit speaking, respectively, and suggests the proper means of avoiding the faults. However, his treatment of forensic eloquence is highly abbreviated, and in general unenlightening.

Rapin deplores the scarcity of good pulpit speakers, especially since Biblical subjects offer unusual opportunities for distinguished effort. He attributes a good share of the failure in this field to the deficiencies of the preachers in learning and study. These shortcomings encourage preachers to copy boldly from one another; "they draw from the Stream, because they are Strangers to the Fountainhead."

Rapin believes that preachers must construct a rhetoric for their own use, since the ancient writers on speechcraft had no idea of the requirements of pulpit speaking.

> For no Man ought to speak of God, and of heavenly Things, without the utmost Dignity of Style, and such *a Voice of great Words* as the Prophet mentions. 'Twould be in vain to seek this Pitch of Eloquence in *Aristotle's* Rhetorick, in the Ideas of *Hermogenes,* or the Institutions of *Quintilian.*[2]

Rapin believes the true standard of preaching "should be taken from the Manner of St. *Peter* and St. *Paul,* in their Sermons to the first Believers."

Rapin's Comparative Analysis of the Great Orators

Rapin's major critical work in rhetoric is "A Comparison of Demosthenes and Cicero," the avowed pupose of which is "no other than to propose to the present Age an accomplished Standard of Eloquence; it being universally agreed, that *Demosthenes* and *Cicero* are the Men who have carried this Art to its utmost Height, and most absolute Perfection." Intent upon establishing a satisfactory criterion of oratorical excellence, Rapin establishes a rule by which comparative estimates can be made. Assuming that the critic has a "competent share of Natural Abilities," a "good stock of sound and solid Sense," a recognition of the effect of time and age on artistic creations, and an uncorrupted judgment "gained and improv'd by being well vers'd in Ancient Writers," Rapin concludes, after a survey of controlling rules for the making of comparisons, that Aristotle's doctrines on the nature of eloquence are the most fundamental and practical of all. So he accepts Aristotle's dictum that the end of oratory is persuasion, and that there are "three Things which have the chief Power to persuade, the Merit of the speaker, the Disposition of those to whom he speaks, and his Manner of Speaking." This Aristotelian formula constitutes the basic pattern of Rapin's critical method.

According to the restatement that Rapin makes of Aristotle's rule, three things are essential in comparative estimates of orators: an examination of their personal merits, a fixation of "the Character of Wit and Sense" in the age in which the speaker lived, and a study of the orator's manner of speaking. If we were to make a rough analysis of Rapin's scheme or method of criticism, it would appear as follows:

[2] *Ibid.,* II, 65.

I. Personal Merit of the Speaker
   A. Abilities
      1. Education
      2. Influence of Parents
      3. Instruction
      4. Reading Activities
   B. Integrity—Sincerity and Honesty
   C. Agreeableness (less important than Ability and Integrity, but still essential)
II. Consideration of the Inclination and Disposition of the Audience
   A. State of Mind of the People Addressed
   B. Temper of the Age
III. Manner of Speaking
   A. Recognition of Natural Inclinations and Their Cultivation
      1. Sprightliness and Vigor
      2. Deep Understanding
      3. Voice, Action, Gestures
      4. Learning and Art
      5. Grace in Doing Things
      6. Sense of Arrangement of Parts; Sense of Proportion
      7. Charm in Delivery
      8. Use of Ornamentation in Speech
   B. Mastery of Subject Matter
   C. Artistic Use of Rhetoric, without Betrayal of the Art
   D. Adaptation of Style to Subject Matter

Using this formula in an almost mechanical way, Rapin appraised the respective merits of the two great models of ancient eloquence. His preference in nearly all departments of judgment inclined toward Cicero, in whose oratory, he believed, there was evidence of more skilful handling of the passions and manners of men. This is in contrast with the conclusion of another French theorist and critic of oratory, Fénelon, whose favorite was Demosthenes. Ignoring some of the minor arguments that Rapin advanced in Cicero's behalf, it is clear that the critic was using the *effect of oratory in influencing people* as the final measure of success. In this respect he was, indeed, applying a canon to which much contemporary criticism adheres. While admitting that Demosthenes' reasoning was closer than Cicero's, Rapin holds that if that man is most eloquent who persuades most, then the Roman was unquestionably the superior. As though he were reluctant to formulate a final judgment, however, Rapin leaves with his readers the query as to whether an appeal to the heart is preferable to an appeal to the mind.

Rapin's method of analysis, it will be observed, was quite comprehensive. If used intensively, and with adequate reliance upon the speeches themselves as well as upon the outcome, it would undoubtedly result in exacting criticism. As used by Rapin, it was only moderately successful, for he neglected to rely adequately upon the speeches for which the orators were distinguished. Despite this shortcoming, he did formulate the most systematic and clearly defined method for criticizing speeches since the time of Cicero. His method is formal and almost stereotyped, but it reveals an intelligent recognition of the nature of rhetorical analysis.

PROSE WRITERS APPRAISE ENGLISH DELIVERY

Incidental rhetorical criticism appeared in the works of certain eighteenth-century prose writers, including Swift, Addison, and Lord Chesterfield. Their chief point of interest is delivery, however, so we do not find here a comprehensive inquiry deserving detailed notice.

Swift's Analysis

In his "Letter to a Young Clergyman," Jonathan Swift revealed his displeasure with preachers who read their sermons. He frankly admitted "taking some little offence" at this practice, saying there was a difference between reading and speaking which the clergy often overlooked. Futhermore, he remarked,

> . . . you will observe some clergymen with their heads held down from the beginning to the end within an inch of the cushion to read what is hardly legible: which beside the untoward manner, hinders them from making the best advantage of their voice: others again have a trick of popping up and down every moment from their paper to the audience, like an idle school boy on a repetition day.[3]

Addison's Dissent

In a similar vein, Joseph Addison protested the oratorical customs of his countrymen. He believed that the British speakers of his time should either "lay aside all kinds of gesture (which seems to be very suitable to the genius of our nation,) or at least to make use of such only as are graceful and expressive." Criticizing the English preachers, debaters, and courtroom speakers for their failure to make proper use of action and gestures, Addison remarks:

> It is certain that proper gestures and vehement exertions of the voice cannot be too much studied by a public orator. They are a kind of comment

[3] Jonathan Swift. *Works.* Edited by T. Sheridan. London, 1803. VIII, 14–15.

to what he utters, and enforce everything he says, with weak hearers, better than the strongest arguments he can make use of. They keep the audience awake, and fix their attention to what is delivered to them, at the same time that they show the speaker is in earnest, and affected himself with what he so passionately recommends to others.

Later, he comments:

We are told that the great Latin orator very much impaired his health . . . by the vehemence of action, with which he used to deliver himself. The Greek orator was likewise so very famous for this particular in rhetoric, that one of his antagonists, whom he had banished from Athens, reading over the oration which had procured his banishment, and seeing his friends admire it, could not forbear asking them, if they were so much affected by the bare reading of it, how much more they would have been alarmed, had they heard him actually throwing out such a storm of eloquence?

How cold and dead a figure, in comparison of these two great men, does an orator often make at the British bar, holding up his head with the most insipid serenity, and stroking the sides of a long wig that reaches down to his middle! The truth of it is, there is often nothing more ridiculous than the gestures of most of our English speakers: you see some of them running their hands into their pockets as far as ever they can thrust them, and others looking with great attention on a piece of paper that has nothing written on it; you may see many a smart rhetorician turning his hat in his hands, moulding it into several different cocks, examining sometimes the lining of it, and sometimes the button, during the whole course of his harangue.[4]

Chesterfield Joins in the Criticism

Further evidence to suggest that delivery and style were important features by which oratory was appraised during this period comes from the *Letters* of Chesterfield to his son. Although the Earl of Chesterfield looked upon Cicero and Demosthenes as good models, and urged his son to study them, he directed most of his advice to the necessity of acquring an agreeable delivery and manner of expression. In a letter written in 1748, he admonishes his son for rapidity of utterance, adding, "An agreeable and distinct manner of speaking adds greatly to the matter; and I have known many a very good speech unregarded, upon account of the disagreeable manner in which it has been delivered, and many an indifferent one applauded, from the contrary reason."[5]

Two months later, Chesterfield urged his son to strive for good enunciation, asking as he had on previous occasions that the boy note the stress Cicero and Quintilian "lay upon the gracefulness of it." "Had Roscius spoken *quick, thick,* and *ungracefully,*" Chesterfield says,

I will answer for it, that Cicero would not have thought him worth the oration which he made in his favor. Words were given us to communicate

---

[4] *The Works of Joseph Addison.* New York, 1850. II, 132–133.
[5] *Letters to His Son,* by the Earl of Chesterfield. Washington, 1901. I, 66.

our ideas by: and there must be something inconceivably absurd in uttering them, in such a manner as that either people cannot understand them, or will not desire to understand them.[6]

Closely associated with accuracy and care in enunciating sounds, a "graceful manner of presenting yourself"—"a genteel carriage"—was also essential to effective oral address.

The style of utterance should be cultivated, for "the very first principle of an orator is to speak his own language . . . with the utmost purity and elegance." Purity and elegance, he affirmed, cover many faults in speakers and writers. "For my own part, I confess . . . that if a speaker should ungracefully mutter or stammer out to me the sense of an angel, deformed by barbarism and solecisms, or larded with vulgarisms, he should never speak to me a second time, if I could help it." And, he added, "Gain the heart, or you gain nothing; the eyes and the ears are the only roads to the heart. Merit and knowledge will not gain hearts, though they will secure them when gained." "Engage the eyes by your address, air, and motions; soothe the ears by the elegance and harmony of your diction; the heart will certainly follow. . . ."

In his letter of December 5, 1749, Chesterfield appraised the deliberative speaking then current in England Believing that the nature of the British constitution made eloquence more useful than in any European country, he indicated that a

. . . certain degree of good sense and knowledge is requisite for that, as well as for everything else; but beyond that, the purity of diction, the elegance of style, the harmony of periods, a pleasing elocution, and a graceful action, are the things which a public speaker should attend to the most; because his audience certainly does, and understands them the best. . . .[7]

Examples from oratorical history sustain the judgment. Thus, according to Chesterfield, Lord Chancellor Cowper derived his strength from the "purity and elegance of his style," not from his reasoning, which was frequently weak. Lord Townshend, who excelled in argument but was inelegant in diction, invariably failed to please his hearers. The Duke of Argyll, "though the weakest reasoner, was the most pleasing speaker I ever knew in my life."

Chesterfield advises his son, therefore, to mind his diction and delivery, for they are the important elements in speaking. The complete orator about whom Cicero talks—the man of great learning—is to be regarded as an ideal, virtually impossible of attainment. Accordingly, Chesterfield holds him to be the most complete orator "who speaks the best upon that subject which occurs; whose happy choice of words,

[6] *Ibid.*, I, 83.
[7] *Ibid.*, I, 253.

whose lively imagination, whose elocution and action adorn and grace his matter, at the same time that they excite the attention and engage the passions of his audience."

On repeated occasions Chesterfield gave this advice to his son. Always the characteristic admonition seemed to be: "Most people have ears, but few have judgment; tickle those ears, and depend upon it, you will catch their judgments, such as they are." Surely this was a cynical, unenlightened conception of the role of oratory in public life. But it was indicative of a trend which subsequently gave rise to the elocutionary movement in rhetorical theory.

BLAIR'S PROLEGOMENON TO CRITICISM

The Basis of Critical Inquiry

In the first lecture of his treatise, published in 1783, Hugh Blair makes it evident that his undertaking is of an omnibus nature. He is writing a book to appeal to three distinct groups: those whose inclination tends toward a study of composition; those who are interested in public speaking; and, finally, those who "may wish only to improve their taste with respect to writing and discourse, and to acquire principles which will enable them to judge for themselves in that part of literature called the Belles Lettres." [8] Clearly, Blair is concerned with rhetorical criticism; he directs his remarks to the critics, as well as to the students of composition and oratory. "To them," he says, referring to the critics,

. . . rhetoric is not so much a practical art as a speculative science; and the same instructions which assist others in composing will assist them in discerning and relishing the beauties of composition. Whatever enables genius to execute will, will enable taste to criticize justly.[9]

The criticism with which Blair proposed to deal, however, avoided the "frigid application of certain technical terms, by means of which persons are taught to cavil and censure in a learned manner." Instead, he projected a prolegomenon to criticism, as it were, which derived from "good sense and refined taste."

According to Blair, the first topic of inquiry into critical and creative activity is Taste. This he defines as the "power of receiving pleasure from the beauties of nature and of art." The source of taste rests basically upon "a certain natural and instinctive sensitivity to beauty," but *reason* assists and enlarges the operation of the internal feeling of sense. All men have, in some degree, a sense of taste, but the range varies

---

[8] Hugh Blair. *Lectures on Rhetoric and Belles Lettres.* London, n.d., p. 3.
[9] *Ibid.,* p. 5.

widely. Generally, in "the powers and pleasures of taste, there is a more remarkable inequality among men, than is usually found, in point of common sense, reason, and judgment." However, frequent exercise and "curious attention to its proper objects must greatly heighten its power." Blair indicates that devotion of attention "to the most approved models, study of the best authors, comparisons of lower and higher degrees of the same beauties, operate towards the refinement of Taste." This would suggest the validity of Blair's claim that enlarged understanding—the exercise of reason generally—improves taste.

When richly improved, the characters of taste are in Blair's judgment reducible to two, namely *delicacy* and *correctness*. The former "respects principally the perfection of that natural sensibility on which Taste is founded." Delicacy of taste presupposes that the person "feels strongly and feels accurately." Anyone possessing this character is able to see "distinctions and differences where others see none; the most latent beauty does not escape him, and he is sensible of the smallest blemish." Correctness, on the other hand, results from the application of understanding to the faculty of taste.

A man of correct Taste is one who is never imposed on by counterfeit beauties; who carries always in his mind that standard of good sense which he employs in judging of every thing. He estimates with propriety the comparative merit of the several beauties which he meets with in any work of genius; refers them to their proper classes; assigns the principles, as far as they can be traced, whence their power of pleasing flows; and is pleased himself precisely in that degree in which he ought, and no more.[10]

This presupposes, however, the existence of a criterion, of a standard to which critics may appeal in distinguishing between good and bad artistic endeavor. Recognizing that there must be a standard or else all taste will be equally good, Blair indicates that diversity does not necessarily imply corruption. "The Tastes of men may differ very considerably as to their object, and yet none of them be wrong." Hence, it

. . . is not in matters of Taste, as in questions of mere reason, where there is but one conclusion that can be true, and all the rest erroneous. Truth, which is the object of reason, is one; Beauty, which is the object of Taste, is manifold. Taste, therefore, admits of latitude and diversity of objects, in sufficient consistency with goodness or justness of Taste.[11]

The standard to which Blair appeals when there is opposition of taste is clear. A standard, properly conceived, "signifies that which is of such undoubted authority as to be the test of other things of the same kind." Admitting that nature herself is a partial standard, Blair shows that it is not adequate. So he appeals to the taste of *men in general*. "That which

10 *Ibid.*
11 *Ibid.*, p. 16.

men concur the most in admiring must be held to be beautiful. His Taste must be esteemed just and true, which coincides with the general sentiments of men." Thus he acknowledges the "sense of mankind" as the ultimate basis of judgment. As supplements to the "approbation of the majority," Blair mentions the reason and the sound judgment of the critic. Just as reason and judgment apply in the study of science and philosophy, so they figure in the determination of merit in the arts.

> He who admires or censures any work of genius, is always ready, if his Taste be in any degree improved, to assign some reasons for his decision. He appeals to principles, and points out the grounds on which he proceeds. Taste is a sort of compound power, in which the light of the understanding always mingles, more or less, with the feelings of sentiments.[12]

Blair openly announces his criterion, then, and assures us that the doctrine of universal testimony is valid only if the men involved live in situations which are conducive "to the proper exertions of Taste." The doctrine deals largely with the "sentiments of mankind in polished and flourishing nations; when arts are cultivated and manners refined; when works of genius are subjected to free discussion, and Taste, is improved by Science and Philosophy." Time itself becomes the determiner of value; posterity is sure to discern faults where authority or prejudice may, in one age, have afforded temporary repute. In short, "Time overthrows the illusions of opinion, but establishes the decisions of nature."

This is the substructure of Blair's critical system. Criticism for him is the application of taste and good sense to the various artistic productions. The rules by which this critical function is carried out are not derived from abstract reasoning; on the contrary, they grow wholly out of experience—out of the "observations of such beauties as have come nearest to the standard" previously discussed.

As might be expected, Blair devotes a large section of the *Lectures* to style. He treats first the constituents of effective expression, namely words, perspicuity, precision, sentence development, harmony, and figurative forms; and secondly he appraises the style of various writers in the several fields of literary production. His conception of style derives chiefly from Quintilian and Cicero, to whom he turns frequently for precept and illustration.

Estimates of Orators

In Lectures XXV through XXX, we find Blair's most direct efforts at rhetorical criticism. Postulating as his definition of Eloquence, "the art of Speaking in such a manner as to attain the end for which we speak," he gives a short history of Grecian and Roman oratory, in which he

12 *Ibid.,* p. 18.

evaluates chiefly the style of the major speakers. Thus Isocrates' style is pronounced "swelling and full"; that of Lysias, "pure and Attic in the highest degree." Using Demosthenes and Cicero as his model speakers, Blair crowds out most of the other public figures in order that the truly great may receive proper attention. Demosthenes is praised for the "strength and vehemence" of his style. His orations are strongly animated,

> . . . and full of the impetuosity and fire of public spirit. They proceed in a continued train of inductions, consequences, and demonstrations, founded on sound reason. The figures which he uses, are never sought after; but always rise from the subject. He employs them sparingly indeed; for splendour and ornament are not the distinction of this orator's composition. It is an energy of thought peculiar to himself, which forms his character, and sets him above all others. He appears to attend much more to things than to words. We forget the orator, and think of the business. He warms the mind, and impels to action. He has no parade and ostentation; no methods of insinuation; no laboured introductions; but is like a man full of his subject, who, after preparing his audience by a sentence or two for hearing plain truths, enters directly on business.

Demosthenes uses a style which is

> . . . strong and concise, though sometimes, it must not be dissembled, harsh, and abrupt. His words are very expressive; his arrangement is firm and manly; and though far from being unmusical, yet it seems difficult to find in him that studied, but concealed number and rhythmus, which some of the ancient critics are fond of attributing to him. Negligent of these lesser graces, one would rather conceive him to have aimed at that Sublime which lies in sentiment.[13]

As contrasted with Aeschines, Demosthenes appears to real advantage. Aeschines "makes much less impression on the mind," whereas Demosthenes "is a torrent, that nothing can resist. He bears down his antagonist with violence; he draws his character in the strongest colours. . . ."

Cicero, "whose name alone suggests every thing that is splendid in Oratory," knew "the power and force of words" better than any other man.

> He rolls them along with the greatest beauty and pomp: and, in the structure of his sentences, is curious and exact to the highest degree. He is always full and flowing, never abrupt. He is a great amplifier of every subject; magnificent, and in his sentiments highly moral. His manner is on the whole diffuse, yet it is often happily varied, and suited to the subject.

But he had certain defects. These shortcomings resulted from his making "too visible a parade of Eloquence." On some occasions,

> . . . he is showy rather than solid; and diffuse, where he ought to have been pressing. His sentences are, at all times, round and sonorous; they can-

---

[13] *Ibid.*, pp. 288–289.

not be accused of monotony, for they possess variety of cadence; but, from too great a study of magnificence, he is sometimes deficient in strength. On all occasions, where there is the least room for it, he is full of himself. His great actions, and the real services which he had performed to his country, apologize for this in part; ancient manners, too, imposed fewer restraints from the side of decorum; but, even after these allowances [are] made, Cicero's ostentation of himself cannot be wholly palliated; and his orations, indeed all his works, leave on our minds the impression of a good man, but withal, of a vain man.

Blair then compares the oratory of Demosthenes and Cicero:

The character of Demosthenes is vigour and austerity; that of Cicero is gentleness and insinuation. In the one, you find more manliness; in the other more ornament. The one is more harsh, but more spirited and cogent; the other more agreeable, but withal, looser and weaker.[14]

Blair speculates that the differences in style may result from the types of audiences they addressed. He doubts, however, that that will provide the complete explanation.

Perhaps we shall come nearer the truth, by observing, that to unite all the qualities, without the least exception, that form a perfect orator, and to excel equally in each of those qualities is not to be expected from the limited powers of human genius. The highest degree of strength is, I suspect, never found united with the highest degree of smoothness and ornament; equal attentions to both are incompatible; and the genius that carries ornament to its utmost length, is not of such a kind, as can excel as much in vigour. For there plainly lies the characteristical difference between these two celebrated orators.[15]

On last analysis, Blair gives the palm for greater excellence to Demosthenes. His explanation is both interesting and revealing:

I am of opinion, that were the state in danger, or some great national interest at stake, which drew the serious attention of the public, an oration in the spirit and strain of Demosthenes would have more weight, and produce greater effects, than one in the Ciceronian manner. Were Demosthenes's Philippics spoken in a British assembly, in a similar conjuncture of affairs, they would convince and persuade at this day. The rapid style, the vehement reasoning, the disdain, anger, boldness, freedom, which perpetually animate them, would render their success infallible over any modern assembly. I question whether the same can be said of Cicero's orations; whose eloquence, however beautiful, and however well suited to the Roman taste, yet borders oftener on declamation, and is more remote from the manner in which we now expect to hear real business and causes of importance treated.[16]

In this judgment Blair agrees with the thesis developed by David Hume in the "Essay upon Eloquence." Hume, in his attempt to determine why modern oratory was inferior to that of the ancients, pointed

14 *Ibid.*, pp. 292–294.
15 *Ibid.*
16 *Ibid.*, pp. 294–295.

to the "elevated conceptions"—the vehemence of thought, expression, and action—which so signally stamped the efforts of a Demosthenes. Commenting on the moderns' satisfaction with mediocrity, Hume urged a return to the study of true models of sublime eloquence. And, he added, "of all human productions the orations of Demosthenes present to us the models which approach the nearest to perfection." [17]

Structure of Blair's Critical Method

Blair's critical investigations reveal a clearly defined method which, though mechanical, is nevertheless systematic and useful. He offers a descriptive analysis of the three kinds of speaking, and illustrates each type by quoting selected passages from a great orator who engaged actively in that field. He recognizes that certain rules apply in common to deliberative, judicial, and demonstrative speaking; at the same time, he wishes to consider the characteristics of spirit and manner peculiar to each type.

Deliberative Speaking

Since, in Blair's judgment, the eloquence of popular assemblies throws much light upon other types, he opens by indicating that the object of deliberative speaking is, "or always ought to be, Persuasion. There must be some end proposed, some point, most commonly of public utility or good, in favour of which we seek to determine the hearers." [18] Accordingly, the principal constituent of such speaking is *material* that will convince the audience.

Let it be their first study, in addressing any popular assembly, to be previously master of the business on which they are to speak; to be well provided with matter and argument, and to rest upon these the chief stress. This will always give to their discourse an air of manliness and strength, which is a powerful instrument of persuasion. Ornament, if they have genius for it, will follow of course; at any rate it demands only their secondary study. . . . 'To your expression be attentive, but about your matter be solicitous,' is an advice of Quinctilian, which cannot be too often recollected by all who study oratory.[19]

Furthermore, the deliberative speaker must himself be persuaded of whatever he proposes to his hearers. "Seldom or never will a man be eloquent, but when he is in earnest, and uttering his own sentiments." Of course, the speaker will provide as much time as possible for assembling his thoughts and sentiments, although deliberative speaking—

[17] David Hume. *Essays and Treatises on Several Subjects.* Edinburgh, 1817. II, 99.
[18] Blair. *Op. cit.*, p. 203.
[19] *Ibid.*, p. 304.

and particularly debate—does not always permit such preliminary investigation. "The arguments must be suited to the course which the debate takes; and as no man can exactly foresee this, one who trusts to a set speech composed in his closet, will, on many occasions, be thrown out of the ground which he had taken."

The style and expression of deliberative speaking should be animated and elevated.

The very aspect of a large assembly, engaged in some debate of moment, and attentive to the discourse of one man, is sufficient to inspire that man with such elevation and warmth, as both give rise to strong impressions, and give them propriety. Passion easily rises in a great assembly, where the movements are communicated by mutual sympathy between the Orator and the Audience. Those bold figures, of which I treated formerly as the native language of passion, have then their proper place. That ardour of Speech, that vehemence and glow of Sentiment, which arise from a mind animated and inspired by some great and public object, form the peculiar characteristics of Popular Eloquence, in its highest degree of perfection.[20]

The delivery before such groups should be firm and "determined."

An arrogant and overbearing manner is indeed always disagreeable; and the least appearance of it ought to be shunned: but there is a certain decisive tone, which may be assumed even by a modest man, who is thoroughly persuaded of the sentiments he utters; and which is best calculated for making a general impression. A feeble and hesitating manner bespeaks always some distrust of a man's own opinion; which is by no means, a favourable circumstance for his inducing others to embrace it.[21]

Having examined some of the special characteristics of deliberative speaking, Blair exemplifies the species by quoting passages from Demosthenes' *Philippics* and *Olynthiacs*. Because of the lack of commentary on the passages, the attempt at criticism is somewhat abortive. The preliminary establishment of the criterion tends, however, to give some significance to the effort.

Forensic Speaking

Following the same method in the next section of his criticism, Blair shows that judicial oratory differs in its object from the deliberative type.

In Popular Assemblies, the great object is persuasion; the Orator aims at determining the hearers to some choice or conduct, as good, fit, or useful. For accomplishing this end, it is incumbent on him to apply himself to all the principles of action in our nature; to the passions and to the heart, as well as to the understanding. But, at the Bar, conviction is the great object. There, it is not the Speaker's business to persuade the Judges to what is good

[20] *Ibid.*, p. 307.
[21] *Ibid.*, pp. 310–311.

or useful, but to show them what is just and true; and, of course, it is chiefly, or solely, to the understanding that his Eloquence is addressed. This is a characteristical difference which ought ever to be kept in view.

Furthermore, the audience situation is unique.

Speakers at the Bar address themselves to one, or to a few Judges, and these, too, persons generally of age, gravity, and authority of character. There they have not those advantages which a mixed and numerous Assembly affords for employing all the arts of Speech, even supposing their subject to admit them. Passion does not rise so easily; the Speaker is heard more coolly; he is watched over more severely; and would expose himself to ridicule, by attempting that high vehement tone, which is only proper in speaking to a multitude.[22]

The nature of the subject matter also differs in judicial pleading. The deliberative speaker has a wide range of action.

He is seldom confined to any precise rule; he can fetch his topics from a great variety of quarters; and employ every illustration which his fancy or imagination suggests. But, at the Bar, the field of speaking is limited to precise law and statute. Imagination is not allowed to take its scope. The Advocate has always lying before him the line, the square, and the compass. These, it is his principal business to be continually applying to the subjects under debate.[23]

Eloquence of the Bar

. . . is of the calm and temperate kind, and connected with close reasoning. Sometimes a little play may be allowed to the Imagination, in order to enliven a dry subject, and to give relief, to the fatigue of attention; but this liberty must be taken with a sparing hand. For a Florid Style, and a sparkling manner, never fail to make the speaker be heard with a jealous ear by the judge. They detract from his weight, and always produce a suspicion of his failing in soundness and strength of argument. It is purity and neatness of expression which is chiefly to be studied: a Style perspicuous and proper, which shall not be needlessly overcharged with the pedantry of law terms, and where, at the same time, no affectation shall appear of avoiding these, when they are suitable and necessary.[24]

Hence, the speaker should eschew verbosity and cultivate distinctness.

Unlike his attempt to exemplify deliberative discourse by quoting passages from Demosthenes, Blair gives a detailed analysis of Cicero's *Pro Cluentio* to illustrate the characteristics of judicial oratory. He reconstructs partially the historical setting of the case; reviews the narrative details of the action; analyzes the parts of the oration; reviews and appraises the argument and reasoning; and introduces occasional quotation

---

[22] *Ibid.*, pp. 318–319.
[23] *Ibid.*, p. 319.
[24] *Ibid.*, p. 322.

to support the critical findings. This represents a serious attempt to find the orator's method of procedure and to evaluate the force and conduct of the arguments used in the case.

Pulpit Speaking

The last type of speaking Blair examines is that of the pulpit. This type of eloquence has certain advantages over other kinds, a few of which he enumerates:

> The dignity and importance of its subjects must be acknowledged superior to any other. They are such as ought to interest every one, and can be brought home to every man's heart; and such as admit, at the same time, both the highest embellishments in describing, and the greatest vehemence and warmth in enforcing them. The Preacher has also great advantages in treating his subjects. He speaks not to one or a few Judges, but to a large Assembly. He is secure from all interruption. He is obliged to no replies, or extemporaneous efforts. He chooses his theme at leisure; and comes to the public with all the assistance which the most accurate premeditation can give him.

The preacher should entertain a just view of the end of his speaking. This end is "to persuade men to become good."

> Every Sermon therefore, should be a persuasive oration; not but that the Preacher is to instruct and to teach, to reason and to argue. All persuasion . . . is to be founded on conviction. The understanding must always be applied to in the first place, in order to make a lasting impression on the heart; and he who would work on men's passions or influence their practice, without first giving them just principles, and enlightening their minds, is no better than a mere declaimer. He may raise transient emotions, or kindle a passing ardour; but can produce no solid or lasting effect. At the same time, it must be remembered, that the Preacher's instructions are to be of the practical kind; and that persuasion must always be his ultimate object. It is not to discuss some abstruse point, that he ascends the Pulpit. It is not to illustrate some metaphysical truth, or to inform men of something which they never heard before; but it is to make them better men; it is to give them at once, clear views, and persuasive impressions of religious truth. The Eloquence of the Pulpit, then, must be Popular Eloquence. One of the first qualities of preaching is to be popular; not in the sense of accommodation to the humours and prejudices of the people . . . , but in the true sense of the word, calculated to make impression on the people; to strike and seize their hearts. I scruple not therefore to assert, that the abstract and philosophical manner of preaching, however it may have sometimes been admired, is formed upon a very faulty idea, and deviates widely from the just plan of Pulpit Eloquence. Rational, indeed, a Preacher ought always to be; he must give his audience clear ideas on every subject, and entertain them with sense, not with sound; but to be an accurate Reasoner will be small praise, if he be not a persuasive speaker also.[25]

25 *Ibid.,* pp. 333–336.

It is clear that Blair expected the preacher to be a good man, as well as a persuasive talker, in order to impart gravity and warmth to his discourses.

Perspicuity is the first requirement of the preacher's style.

As discourses spoken there are calculated for the instruction of all sorts of hearers, plainness and simplicity should reign in them. All unusual, swollen, or high-sounding words, should be avoided; especially all words that are merely poetical, or merely philosophical. Young Preachers are apt to be caught with the glare of these; and in young Composers the error may be excusable; but they may be assured that it is an error, and proceeds from their not having yet acquired a correct Taste. Dignity of expression, indeed, the Pulpit requires in a high degree; nothing that is mean or grovelling, no low or vulgar phrases, ought on any account to be admitted. But this dignity is perfectly consistent with simplicity. The words employed may be all plain words, easily understood, and in common use; and yet the Style may be abundantly dignified, and, at the same time, very lively and animated. For a lively and animated Style is extremely suited to the Pulpit. The earnestness which a Preacher ought to feel, and the grandeur and importance of his subjects, justify and often require warm and glowing expressions. He not only may employ metaphors and comparisons, but, on proper occasions, may apostrophise the saint or the sinner; may personify inanimate objects, break out into bold exclamations, and, in general, has the command of the most passionate figures of Speech.

Blair did not favor the reading of sermons.

No discourse, which is designed to be persuasive, can have the same force when read, as when spoken. The common people all feel this, and their prejudice against this practice is not without foundation in nature. What is gained hereby in point of correctness, is not equal, I apprehend, to what is lost in point of persuasion and force. They, whose memories are not able to retain the whole of a Discourse, might aid themselves considerably by short notes lying before them, which would allow them to preserve, in a great measure, the freedom and ease of one who speaks.[26]

Lecture XXX is devoted exclusively to a critical examination of a sermon entitled "Praise and Thanksgiving" by Bishop Atterbury who, in Blair's opinion, "is deservedly accounted one of our most eloquent writers of sermons." This selection unquestionably is the best critical estimate in Blair's *Lectures*. It amounts to a paragraph by paragraph analysis of the virtues and defects, both of style and matter, in the sermon. The interpolations and commentaries reveal Blair not only as a discriminating analyst of the characteristics of pulpit speaking; they also throw some light upon his sense of word value, his appreciation of religious themes, and his fine discernment of stylistic excellence.

[26] *Ibid.*, pp. 341–343.

Final Estimate

Not concerned with the biographical approach to rhetorical criticism, Blair recognized that sound criticism should rest upon criteria to which various disinterested scholars could appeal. He had the insight to perceive that the social setting—the audience situation generally—had much to do with exact assignment of merit and defect. His liberal use and interpretation of passages from the orators' speeches is an important feature of the work. In spite of his formal adherence to a semifixed pattern as determined by the kinds of oratory under evaluative scrutiny, he contributed richly, especially in the field of style, to critical doctrines of public address.

BARRON'S STYLISTIC APPROACH TO CRITICISM

In his *Lectures on Belles Lettres and Logic,* published in 1806 and originally delivered at the University of St. Andrews, William Barron sets aside a small amount of space for the criticism of orators. Like many writers before and since his time, he turns to Cicero for the standard of excellence. As might be expected from his general approach to oratory, his estimation of speakers derives in large part from stylistic considerations. In terms of contemporary standards, however, his appraisals are not particularly penetrating, chiefly, perhaps, because they lack essential articulation with a speaker-audience situation.

Cicero, Barron remarks, possesses every characteristic of the accomplished orator, although he is not equally great in each department.

He never fails to seize the view of a cause most favourable to the purpose he wishes to support, and displays great art in removing prepossessions, and conciliating the favour of his hearers. His information is pertinent and satisfactory; his illustrations are ingenious, beautiful, and learned; his arguments are solid and convincing. Though he always addresses first the understanding, yet he does not stop there. He often assails the imagination and the passions with vigour and success. Bold metaphors, vivid interrogations, striking antitheses, passionate apostrophes and exclamations are his instruments on such occasions. Sometimes he rises to the Demosthenic fire and thunder, he gets entire command of his hearers, and pours along with a vehemence irresistible. His expression is perspicuous, and in general harmonious. Many of his periods present the most beautiful construction of members, which grow one above another in sound and importance, and exhibit much variety in their length, melody, and arrangement.

Cicero's oratorical virtues, however, are mixed with disfiguring faults.

He is often diffuse in his illustrations, and profuse of his arguments, without resting his cause only upon the best. His orations are sometimes extended to a length that tires the reader, and we cannot easily conceive that the patience of his hearers should not have been exhausted. He is too fond of gay ornaments, which approach the florid style. Many of his periods are long and involved, devoid of much cadence or harmony, and they are often enfeebled with redundant words.[27]

Barron believes that Cicero's most censurable defect is his vanity. "Wonderful is the artifice he displays in introducing his own praise . . ."

Mindful of the value of the comparative method in assessing oratorical skill, Barron closes his analysis by matching the relative accomplishments of Cicero and Demosthenes.

[Demosthenes] totally disappears, and the reader attends to nothing but the argument; the latter [Cicero] is always in the fore-ground of the picture and one of the principal objects in the eye of the spectator. The former seems to speak the language of nature only, the latter never fails to mix a portion of that of art. Demosthenes indulges no argument, nor illustration, not even word which is not necessary to communicate the sense. Cicero is superabundant in all these respects. The leading characteristics of the former are gravity, solidity, vehemence; of the latter, vivacity, solidity, dignity.[28]

LORD MANSFIELD'S FRAGMENTARY CRITICISM

Regarded by John Lord Campbell as the first Scotchman ever to gain distinction "in the profession of the law in England," Lord Mansfield was singularly adept at investing his legal cases with logical acuity and literary dignity. It was a common saying that his *statement* of a case was worth the *argument* of any other man. Campbell remarks that Mansfield's presentation "seemed to suggest trains of thinking rather than to draw conclusions; and so skilfully did he conceal his art, that the hearers thought they formed their opinion in consequence of the workings of their own minds, when in truth it was the effect of the most refined dialectics." [29]

Although Mansfield's distinction derives from his conduct as a lawyer, he made a minor contribution to criticism. During his early years he prepared a critical analysis of Demosthenes in Latin, and a fragment of the essay has been preserved. His comparison of the technique of Cicero and Demosthenes is perhaps the most interesting part of the appraisal:

Cicero having convinced the understanding of the judges before whom he pleads, they, after deliberation, pronounce in his favour the sentence which they think just; the eloquence displayed by him, however, being so brilliant, that we conceive there is nothing which would not be conceded to it. Demosthenes does not *ask*—he *seizes*—by an energy almost divine, he wrests from the hands of the judges the sentence which he desires. Being captivated

---

[27] Barron. *Lectures on Belles Lettres and Logic.* London, 1806. I, 478–479.
[28] *Ibid.,* I, 479–480.
[29] *The Lives of the Chief Justices of England.* London, 1849. II, 562.

by the witching art of Cicero as by the song of the Sirens, they are better pleased to go astray with him than to decide righteously with others. Such authority does Demosthenes carry along with him, that his hearers are ashamed to differ from him, and, when struck by the lightning of his eloquence, they do not seem to be carried away by the art of the orator, but believe themselves to obey a natural impulse, and to yield to the dictates of right reason.[30]

ROLLIN'S STANDARD COMPARISON

The two orators most frequently compared in critical analyses are, of course, Demosthenes and Cicero. Furthermore, they represent the models or standards of excellence by which much of ancient and modern eloquence is assessed.

Charles Rollin's criticism of the Greek and Roman masters affords little, if anything, that is new on the side of methodology. However, his process of appraisal serves to remind us that Cicero's standards of judgment exercised a powerful influence upon the ways of the critics. Rollin seeks the measure of the orators largely by determining their skill in the several kinds of public address—a standard to which Cicero appealed frequently in the *Brutus*. Asserting that both Demosthenes and Cicero excelled in all "as every one must do who is truly eloquent," Rollin continues: "They know how to vary their style as their subjects varied; sometimes simple and subtile in causes of small consequence, in narrations and proofs; and, at others, adorned and embellished, when there was a necessity of pleasing; sometimes elevated and sublime, when the dignity of the subject required it." [31]

Thus Rollin holds to a relative standard. Affirming that orators, quite different in style and character, may yet be "equally perfect," he says Cicero knew the "high merit of Demosthenes' eloquence" but doubted whether his (Cicero's) audiences always wanted such austerity and exactness. Consequently, Cicero "believed it necessary to indulge something to the ears and to the delicacy of his auditors, who required more elegance and graces in orations."

HAZLITT CONTRASTS WRITING AND SPEAKING

Observations on Discourse

William Hazlitt's easay "On the Difference between Writing and Speaking" is a highly acid statement which warrants notice because of

[30] *Ibid.*, II, 324n.
[31] *The Method of Teaching and Studying the Belles Lettres,* 7th ed. London, 1779. II, 223–224.

the cogency of some of its logic and because of the applicability of certain of its tenets to great orators.

Hazlitt opens his discourse by announcing that he will illustrate the difference between writing and speaking "by familiar examples, rather than by analytical reasonings. The philosopher of old was not unwise, who defined motion by getting up and walking."

An essential distinction between writing and speaking concerns the time factor. "The chief requisite for the one . . . appears to be quickness and facility of perception—for the other, patience of soul, and a power increasing with the difficulties it has to master." [32] Thus, in speaking, "less is required of you, if you only do it at once, with grace and spirit: in writing, you stipulate for all that you are capable of, but you have the choice of your own time and subject." And there is a further difference:

Besides habit, and greater or less facility, there is also a certain reach of capacity, a certain depth or shallowness, grossness or refinement of intellect, which marks out the distinction between those whose chief ambition is to shine by producing an immediate effect, or who are thrown back, by a natural bias, on the severer researches of thought and study.

Referring to the popular speaker, Hazlitt comments on the function of the audience:

[He] is like a vulgar actor off the stage—take away his cue, and he has nothing to say for himself. Or he is so accustomed to the intoxication of popular applause, that without that stimulus he has no motive or power of exertion left—neither imagination, understanding, liveliness, common sense, words nor ideas—he is fairly cleared out; and in the intervals of sober reason, is the dullest and most imbecile of all mortals.

Hazlitt doubts that a speaker can move beyond commonplaces. If he does, he loses his hearers.

An orator can hardly get beyond *common-places:* if he does, he gets beyond his hearers. The most successful speakers, even in the House of Commons, have not been the best scholars or the finest writers. . . . Those speeches that in general told best at the time, are not now readable. What were the materials of which they were chiefly composed? An imposing detail of passing events, a formal display of official documents, an appeal to established maxims, an echo of popular clamor, some worn-out metaphor newly vamped-up,—some hackneyed argument used for the hundredth, nay thousandth time, to fall in with the interests, the passions, or prejudices of listening and devoted admirers;—some truth or falsehood, repeated as the Shibboleth of party time out of mind, which gathers strength from sympathy as it spreads, because it is understood or assented to by the million, and finds,

[32] William Hazlitt, *Table Talk.* In *The Miscellaneous Works of William Hazlitt.* Philadelphia, 1848. II, 170.

in the increased action of the minds of numbers, the weight and force of an instinct.[33]

The commonplace, he holds, "is enshrined in its own unquestioned evidence, and constitutes its own immortal basis." Accordingly, it operates mechanically, "and opens an instantaneous and infallible communication between the hearer and speaker."

Ways of the Orators

Edmund Burke "did not often shock the prejudices of the House: he endeavoured to *account for them,* to 'lay the flattering unction' of philosophy 'to their souls.' They could not endure him." The reason Burke emptied the House was that he uttered thoughts requiring time for consideration, of which there was too little. If one reads, one may take his time; but, "in hearing we are . . . in the company of fools; and time presses." Referring to the British government, Hazlitt added: "If we were to wait until Noble Lords and Honorable Gentlemen were inspired with a relish for abstruse thinking, and a taste for the loftier flights of fancy, the business of this great nation would shortly be at a stand." "The impression of anything delivered in a large assembly," Hazlitt continued,

. . . must be comparatively null and void, unless you not only understand and feel its value yourself, but are conscious that it is felt and understood by the meanest capacity present. Till that is the case, the speaker is in your power, not you in his. The eloquence that is effectual and irresistible must stir the inert mass of prejudice, and pierce the opaquest shadows of ignorance.[34]

Unlike Burke whose oratory was "too recondite for his hearers," Chatham was a great debater. "He vanquished because he could not yield." He held fast to strong points in an argument.

He himself evidently had a strong possession of his subject, a thorough conviction, an intense interest; and this communicated itself from his *manner,* from the tones of his voice, from his commanding attitudes, and eager gestures, instinctively and unavoidably to his hearers. . . . He did not wheedle, or palliate, or circumvent, or make a studied appeal to the reason or the passions—he *dictated* his opinions to the House of Commons.

Both Pitt and Fox were speakers, not authors.

There is no thought in them [their speeches] that implies a habit of deep and refined reflection . . . ; there is no knowledge that does not lie within the reach of obvious and mechanical search; and as to the powers

[33] *Ibid.*
[34] *Ibid.*

of language, the chief miracle is, that a source of words so apt, forcible, and well-arranged, so copious and unfailing, should have been found constantly open to express their ideas without any previous preparation.

Exceedingly critical of the House of Commons, Hazlitt comments on the repetition of material in speech after speech.

Read over the collections of old Debates, twenty, forty, eighty, a hundred years ago; they are the same, *mutatis mutandis,* as those of yesterday. . . . You wonder to see how little has been added; you grieve that so little has been lost. . . . You must serve an apprenticeship to a want of originality, to a suspension of thought and feeling. . . . A man of simplicity and independence of mind cannot easily reconcile himself to all this formality and mummery. . . .[35]

In short, Hazlitt believes the "greatest test of courage" one can conceive "is to speak truth in the House of Commons."

DE QUINCEY ARTICULATES INVENTION AND STYLE

Basis of De Quincey's Conception

Thomas De Quincey is not always lucid in his analyses of the rhetorical process; neither is he completely consistent in his interpretations, unless his readers engage in an inordinate amount of analysis to set the seeming contradictions right. But he is provocative, and in a way that furthers critical investigation.

His chief contributions to a study of the theory and criticism of speaking are found in the "Rhetoric," a review of Richard Whately's book of the same title; in the essay called "Style"; and in other studies in which he examines the literature of the ancient Greeks.

De Quincey's most astute rhetorical conception is his formula for the presentation of ideas. In a peculiarly happy way, he brings the processes of rhetorical invention and style together in an indivisible unity. *Matter* and *manner* are thus blended. Ideas are not mechanically clothed with language; being inner manifestations of inventive skill, they still must be embodied in words that reflect accurately the existing mental concept. Says De Quincey:

Ponderable facts and external realities are intelligible in almost any language: they are self-explained and self-sustained. But the more closely any exercise of mind is connected with what is internal and individual in the sensibilities, that is, with what is philosophically termed *subjective*, precisely in that degree, and the more subtly, does the style of the embodying

[35] *Ibid.,* II, 178–180.

of the thoughts cease to be a mere separable ornament, and in fact the more does the manner . . . become confluent with the matter.[36]

He then refers to the Wordsworthian dictum that "it is in the highest degree unphilosophic to call language or diction 'the *dress* of thoughts.' . . . He would call it 'the *incarnation* of thoughts.'" Commenting further on this idea, De Quincey observes:

> . . . if language were merely a dress, then you could separate the two: you could lay the thoughts on the left hand, the language on the right. But, generally speaking, you can no more deal thus with poetic thoughts, than you can with soul and body. The union is too subtle; the intertexture too ineffable, each co-existing not merely *with* the other, but each *in* and *through* the other. An image, for instance, a single word, often enters into a thought as a constituent part. In short, the two elements are not united as a body with a separable dress, but as a mysterious incarnation. And thus, in what proportion the thoughts are subjective, in that same proportion does their very essence become identical with the expression, and the style become confluent with the matter.[37]

De Quincey recognizes the variable elements in style—the elements that change with the purpose of the speaker and the character of the audience. "That is good rhetoric for the hustings which is bad for a book." Likewise, in the senate, "and for the same reason in a newspaper, it is a virtue to reiterate your meaning: tautology becomes a merit: variation of the words, with a substantial identity of the sense and dilution of the truth, is oftentimes a necessity." [38]

Written discourse has an advantage over oral in permitting a return to a passage upon which subsequent sense depends. Thus the time factor enters again. Both the speaker and the hearer profit by keeping important propositions "before the eye a good deal longer than the chastity of taste or the austerity of logic would tolerate in a book."

> Time must be given for the intellect to eddy about a truth, and to appropriate its bearings. There is a sort of previous lubrication, such as the boa-constrictor applies to any subject of digestion, which is requisite to familiarize the mind with a startling or a complex novelty. And this is obtained for the intellect by varying the modes of presenting it,—now putting it directly before the eye, now obliquely, now in an abstract shape, now in the concrete; all which being the proper technical discipline for dealing with such cases, ought no longer to be viewed as a licentious mode of style, but as the just

[36] Thomas De Quincey. *Historical and Critical Essays.* Boston, 1871. II, 183. (See *Selected Essays on Rhetoric by Thomas De Quincey.* Carbondale, Illinois, 1967.) Edited by Frederick Burwick, the edition contains reprintings of the major essays, together with a penetrating introductory analysis and critique of De Quincey as a rhetorician.

[37] *Ibid.,* II, 183–184.

[38] *Ibid.,* II, 69.

style in respect to those licentious circumstances. And the true art for such popular display is to contrive the best forms for appearing to say something new, when in reality you are but echoing yourself; to break up massy chords into running variations; and to mask, by slight differences in the manner, a virtual identity in the substance.[39]

Application of the Doctrine to Oratory

It is interesting to see how De Quincey applies this doctrine of style to the critical estimate of Burke, "the supreme writer of his century, the man of the largest and finest understanding." Declaring his displeasure with the critics who talked about Burke's "fancy," De Quincey says:

Fancy in your throats, ye miserable twaddlers! as if Edmund Burke were the man to play with his fancy, for the purpose of separable ornament. He was a man of fancy in no other sense than as Lord Bacon was so, and Jeremy Taylor, and as all large and discursive thinkers are and must be: that is to say, the fancy which he had in common with all mankind, and very probably in no eminent degree, in him was urged into unusual activity under the necessities of his capacious understanding.

Then follows more of his remarkable prescription for rhetorical skill:

His great and peculiar distinction was that he viewed all objects of the understanding under more relations than other men, and under more complex relations. According to the multiplicity of these relations, a man is said to have a *large* understanding; according to their subtilty, a *fine* one; and in an angelic understanding, all things would appear to be related to all. Now, to apprehend and detect more relations, or to pursue them steadily, is a process absolutely impossible without the intervention of physical analogies. To say, therefore, that a man is a great thinker, or a fine thinker, is but another expression for saying that he has a *schematizing* (or, to use a plainer but less accurate expression, a figurative) understanding. In that sense, and for that purpose, Burke is figurative. . . .

But De Quincey chides Burke's critics by adding:

. . . understood as he has been understood by the long-eared race of his critics, not as thinking in and by his figures, but as deliberately laying them on by way of enamel or after-ornament,—not as *incarnating*, but simply as *dressing* his thoughts in imagery,—so understood, he is not the Burke of reality, but a poor fictitious Burke, modelled after the poverty of conception which belongs to his critics.[40]

Recapitulation of the Doctrine

Hoyt Hudson gives a clear summary of the foregoing considerations when he remarks:

[39] *Ibid.*, II, 70.
[40] *De Quincey's Literary Criticism.* "Rhetoric." Edited by H. Darbishire. London, 1909, pp. 67–68.

De Quincey teaches that the rhetorical process, the process of *presenting an idea attractively,* whether as a display of power, in play, in poetic exuberance, or for a persuasive purpose, involves an inner and an outer activity. The inner activity we may call rhetorical invention; the outer, rhetorical style. The first is a mode of thinking about one's subject, turning the subject over in one's mind, and viewing it in as many relations as possible. The second is the incarnation in speech of the thoughts (or of a selection from the thoughts) engendered by the preceding mental activity. No one has shown so well the organic union of these two.[41]

BROUGHAM APPRAISES ANCIENT ORATORY

Reappearance of Ancients vs. Moderns Controversy

One of the several persistent themes in the history of rhetorical criticism is the controversy over the relative merits of the ancients and the moderns. Indeed, nearly every competent theorist and critic has referred to this dualism, either as it relates to the choice of models for imitation or as it concerns the establishment of standards of excellence in criticism.

In the literature on rhetoric and oratory, however, there is probably no more studied and sincere effort to establish the claims of the ancients to superiority than is found in Henry Brougham's *Dissertation on the Eloquence of the Ancients.* Steeped in classical learning himself, and jealously proud of the heritage of antiquity, Brougham tried in a closely reasoned analysis to demonstrate the "immeasurable superiority" of the Greeks and the Romans, and especially the former, over the modern orators.

In his Inaugural Address, Brougham made his preference for the Greeks clearly evident when he said:

. . . were we to rest satisfied with studying the Roman, we should only be imitating the imperfect copy, instead of the pure original—like him who should endeavour to catch a glimpse of some beauty by her reflection in a glass, that weakened her tints, if it did not distort her features.[42]

And, he added, "if a further reason is required for giving the preference to the Greek orators, we may find it in the greater diversity and importance of the subjects upon which their speeches were delivered."

The central theme of Brougham's argument is that the Athenian audiences were careful critics of oratory, and that the orators accordingly made every possible effort to meet the wishes of the hearers. The audi-

[41] Hoyt H. Hudson. "De Quincey on Rhetoric and Public Speaking." In *Studies in Rhetoric and Public Speaking in Honor of James Albert Winans.* New York, 1925, pp. 141–142.

[42] *The Works of Henry Lord Brougham.* "Rhetorical and Literary Dissertations and Addresses." London, 1856. VII, 121–122.

ence had what Brougham called a "delicate sense of rhetorical excellence." "No fact in history," he remarked, "is more unquestionable than the union of the two capacities in the Athenian audience,—their exquisite discrimination and high relish of rhetorical beauties, with their susceptibility of the strongest emotions which the orator could desire to excite." The Athenian audience assembled for two purposes: (1) to consider practical matters, and (2) "to enjoy a critical repast." [43] As Brougham observes:

> . . . the orators of Greece and Rome regarded their art as one of eminent display, considered it their province to please as well as to move their audience, and addressed the assembly, not only as hearers who were to be convinced or persuaded, but as critics also who were to judge of rhetorical merit . . . [This] is clear from numberless considerations, some of which must here be adverted to, in order to show that Ancient Oratory held a place among the Fine Arts properly so called, and was, like them, an appeal to the taste, ending in the mere pleasure of contemplation, as well as an appeal to the reason or the passions, leading to practical consequences, and having action for its result. An attention to this subject will explain many things in the structure of ancient orations, which would otherwise be with difficulty apprehended.[44]

Internal Evidence: Ancient Oratory as Fine Art

Brougham considers the evidence which in his opinion supports the theses set forth in the preceding quotation. Turning to internal evidence, he mentions, first, "the exquisite finish and perfect polish of their [Greek orators'] composition." Furthermore, it is evident

> that the exquisite structure of the sentences, the balanced period, the apt and perfect antithesis, the neat and epigrammatic turn, the finished collocation, all indicate an extreme elaboration, and could hardly have been the suggestion of the moment, because the choice of the earlier expressions is often regulated by those which occur subsequently.

And the well-chosen figures

> . . . with which the ancient speeches are interspersed, and the highly skilful disposition of their materials, do not perhaps furnish more decisive proofs than the diction. But the exemplary temperance with which topics are used, and the conciseness with which ideas of the most important kind are expressed, and images portrayed, certainly can hardly be the effect of any experience or practical skill.

Further evidence develops from the fact that passages

> . . . are very frequently to be found in one oration, sometimes word for word the same with those contained in another by the same speaker, some-

---

[43] *Ibid.*, VII, 193–194. Review of French ed. of Demosthenes and Aeschines.
[44] *Ibid.*, VII, 5. On "Eloquence of Ancients."

times varying in certain particulars, and apparently varying because subsequent reflection, perhaps aided by the criticism of others, or by the effects observed to be produced on the audience, had suggested the change, as an improvement upon the earlier composition.

Since the orators often used the same figures in different situations, it follows that they

. . . had other objects in view than the mere furtherance of the matter actually in hand, and that those passages were repeated, rather because they had been found successful in striking and delighting the audience when first pronounced, and were therefore likely to please in the repetition, than because they conduced materially to carry conviction to their minds, and gain their concurrence to a practical proposition.[45]

And unlike the modern orators, including the illustrious Chatham, the ancient Greeks made sure that *all* parts of their orations, rather than selected "brilliant passages," were "elaborated with extreme art."

Brougham summarizes the internal evidence of his argument by remarking:

The examination . . . is not more so than was necessary to show the extreme care of composition which guided the workmanship of the Greek orators; to prove that they delivered their orations as finished productions, with the view of satisfying a critical audience; and to illustrate the position, that the audience flocked to hear them, as well for the pleasure of the treat thus afforded to their refined taste, as for the more useful purpose of hearing state affairs practically discussed.[46]

External Evidence

Brougham introduces several subordinate theses to reveal the external evidence favoring the ancients. In the first place, the

. . . number of speeches written, published, and preserved, and which yet never were spoken, is among the most remarkable of these proofs. Nothing can more strikingly illustrate the difference between Ancient and Modern Rhetoric. With us, a speech written at all before delivery, is regarded as something anomalous, and almost ridiculous; because, the proofs of preparation being inconsistent with the inspiration of the moment and the feelings under which the orator is always supposed to speak, we naturally enough feel that it should be carefully concealed from the eye of the audience, and that their being admitted as it were behind the scenes, at once dispels the illusion so necessary to be kept up. But a speech, written and published, which never was spoken at all, is with us at once given over to extreme ridicule; and a speech intended to have been spoken is a kind of by-word for something laughable in itself. . . .[47]

45 *Ibid.*, VII, 6–9.
46 *Ibid.*, VII, 31.
47 *Ibid.*

Furthermore, the presence of many Prooemia, or introductions, which were apparently never used, suggests that great care was taken to develop compositional graces and artistic skills. The testimony of historians and other writers indicates "how vast the pains were, and how various, and how unremitting," which the orators took in elaborating their speeches. Indeed, the accounts reaching us of the "training and study which the ancient orators went through previous to venturing upon the formidable scene of rhetorical display, and even after they had begun their career of eloquence, afford additional proofs of the extreme care bestowed upon their art."

Finally, the "exquisite taste of the Athenian audience both proved their delight in the pleasures of the Forum, or Ecclesia, so to speak, and showed how well they were trained to a nice discernment of oratorical merit."

Further Differentia: Ancient vs. Modern Oratory

These, then, are the bodies of evidence and the reasons accounting for the superiority of the ancients, and revealing, particularly, the taste and critical judgment of the Athenian audience. Brougham appends a further comment, however, which we should examine. Admitting that the ancient orations do not compare favorably with the modern ones from the point of view of substance, he says:

Any merely critical remarks in a modern speech are hardly permitted. It is not a charge which can now-a-days be made against an adversary either at the Bar or in debate, that he has made a bad speech, that his eloquence is defective, that his figures are out of keeping, his tones inharmonious, or his manner awkward. Yet these are topics of ordinary recrimination and abuse between Demosthenes and Aeschines. To have argued inconclusively, to counsel badly, to act corruptly, or feebly, or inconsistently, are the charges to which the combatants in the more close and business-like battles of our Senate must confine themselves. With us it is no matter of attack that an adversary's tropes are in bad taste, or his manners inelegant, or his voice unmusical. So we may perceive the exquisite care taken by the ancient orators to strike and to please their audience, in the attention paid by them to the rhythm or numbers of their periods.[48]

Demosthenes, the Model

The great model of ancient oratory, the one who was at the head "of all the mighty masters of speech," was Demosthenes. Brougham does not try to establish Demosthenes as a close reasoner; instead, he points to him as a craftsman of words and sentences. Unquestionably, the Greek orator could have excelled in the use of argument, but that would

[48] *Ibid.*, VII, 43.

not have pleased his audience; and Demosthenes was a master of the art of adapting discourse to listeners. "What was wanted," Brougham says of the Athenian audience, to move, to rouse, and also to please them,

> . . . was a copious stream of plain intelligible observations upon their interests—appeals to their feelings—recollections of their past, and especially their present history—expositions of the evils to be apprehended from inaction and impolicy of any sort—vindications of the orator's own conduct, upon grounds simple and uncontested—contrasts to show the inconsistency of those who differed from him, or refused to follow his advice—invectives, galling and unmeasured, against all his adversaries abroad and at home. By urging these topics in rapid succession, in the purest language, with a harmony never broken, save where the sense and the ear required a discord, he [Demosthenes] could move and could master the minds of the people, make their enemy quake upon his barbaric throne, and please the exquisite taste of the 'fierce democratie' whom he was chiding and controlling.[49]

Preference for Stylistic Matters

Brougham regarded the stylistic features of discourse with strong favor. In the final paragraph of his essay on the ancients, and particularly where he is appraising the greatness of Demosthenes, he leaves the impression that the proper effect of eloquence is to move and to please, but not necessarily to secure the effect through argument. "The two," he says, referring to argument and compositional excellence, "may be well combined, but they differ specifically from each other." Previously, he had shown that modern assemblies were "eminently places of business" where men did not come to have "their fancy charmed with choice figures." In the light of his unqualified preference for the ancient models, the combination of these remarks tends to show that style was a major concern. An observation from Brougham's review of a French edition of Demosthenes and Aeschines sums up the whole matter concisely. Discussing Demosthenes' skill, Brougham says:

> Let any reader who has been accustomed to hear debates in Parliament, note what passages have struck him most in those works, and he will find that they are the sort of things which have the most instantaneous success in modern speeches; which produce the most sudden and thrilling sensations; and finding in every bosom an echo, occasion the loudest expressions of assent. Now, some speakers may create admiration by careful composition alone, or without sallies; but they do not find their way as the old Greek did to our hearts. Others may find their way thither without the just care of composition; but he united both powers, and concealed, for the time at least, the labour by which the combination was effected. Can we marvel that his success was prodigious—and that it was equally complete with hearers whom he was to move, and with critics whom he was to please?[50]

[49] *Ibid.*, VII, 58.
[50] *Ibid.*, VII, 195.

Brougham had a profound repect for emotional proofs that were competently presented through graceful composition.

MACAULAY'S PHILOSOPHY OF RHETORIC

An examination of Thomas Babington Macaulay's writings on oratory and orators shows a rather clearly formulated theory of public address, as well as a point of view regarding the role of the critic in national life. It is doubtful whether Macaulay contributed directly to rhetorical criticism with respect to method, but his rationale of oratorical judgment has philosophical significance.

The Critic's Knowledge of the Social Milieu

Like many other critics of eloquence, Macaulay was concerned with the relation between oratory and statesmanship. In his judgment, however, consummate skill in the one field did not necessarily imply great distinction in the other. "Themistocles or Pericles would have been no match for Demosthenes in the assembly, or for Iphicrates in the field. But surely they were incomparably better fitted than either for the direction of affairs." [51] And in his review of the life of William Pitt, Macaulay declares:

Parliamentary government is government by speaking. In such a government, the power of speaking is the most highly prized of all the qualities which a politician can possess; and that power may exist, in the highest degree, without judgment, without fortitude, without skill in reading the characters of men or the signs of the times, without any knowledge of the principles of legislation or of political economy, and without any skill in diplomacy or in the administration of war. Nay, it may well happen that those very intellectual qualities which give a peculiar charm to the speeches of a public man may be incompatible with the qualities which would fit him to meet a pressing emergency with promptitude and firmness. It was thus with Charles Townshend. It was thus with Windham. It was a privilege to listen to those accomplished and ingenious orators. But in a perilous crisis they would have been found far inferior in all the qualities of rulers to such a man as Oliver Cromwell, who talked nonsense, or as William the Silent, who did not talk at all. [52]

The job of the critic is, then, to pass judgment upon the orators in the light of the social circumstances in which they lived. On this point, Macaulay is specific. He believes that oratory is a venture in adaptation, and that criticism must operate within the province of that adaptive function. Speeches, he goes on to say,

[51] *The Complete Works of Thomas Babington Macaulay.* New York, 1900. VI, 53. University ed.
[52] *The Works of Lord Macaulay.* Edinburgh ed. New York, 1897. VII, 378.

. . . must be read with the temper of those to whom they are addressed, or they must necessarily appear to offend against the laws of taste and reason. . . . This is perpetually forgotten by those who criticise oratory. Because they are reading at leisure, pausing at every line, reconsidering every argument, they forget that the hearers were hurried from point to point too rapidly to detect the fallacies through which they were conducted; that they had no time to disentangle sophisms, or to notice slight inaccuracies of expression; that elaborate excellence, either of reasoning or of language, would have been absolutely thrown away.[53]

Macaulay points to the analogy of a sister art, observing that "these connoisseurs examine a panorama through a microscope, and quarrel with a scene-painter because he does not give to his work the exquisite touch of Gerard Dow." In short, the critic will have to divest himself of the modern's "feelings and acquirements" if he is to appreciate the speeches of the past, and especially of antiquity. Emphasizing the necessity of knowing the audience situations, Macaulay indicates that seeming defects in certain Greek orations may actually have been virtues. Consequently, if we acknowledge that assumption, we may find that

. . . the frequent violation of those excellent rules of evidence by which our courts of law are regulated, the introduction of extraneous matter . . . , the assertions, without proof, the passionate entreaties, the furious invectives, are really proofs of the prudence and address of the speakers.[54]

It is surely time, Macaulay concluded, "that ancient literature should be examined in a different manner, without pedantical prepossessions, but with a just allowance, at the same time, for the difference of circumstances and manners."

Place of Oratory in Society

Not only did Macaulay insist upon the critic's understanding the social situation in which an orator performed; he was also convinced that the critic should have a sound point of view relative to the function of oratory. With a mildly satirical touch, he remarks:

Propositions which are advanced in discourse generally result from a partial view of the question, and cannot be kept under examination long enough to be corrected. Men of great conversational powers almost universally practice a sort of lively sophistry and exaggeration, which deceives, for the moment, both themselves and their auditors.

Later, he suggests that the

. . . very circumstances which retarded the growth of science were peculiarly favorable to the cultivation of eloquence. From the early habit of

---

[53] *Complete Works.* I, 49.
[54] *Ibid.*, VI, 50.

taking a share in animated discussion the intelligent student would derive that readiness of resource, that copiousness of language, and that knowledge of the temper and understanding of an audience, which are far more valuable to an orator than the greatest logical powers.[55]

Thus we are led to believe that the rational appeal may not be as important in speaking as is commonly believed. Whether or not we accept the doctrine, Macaulay evidently considered it true. He contended that oratory had to be estimated according to principles that differed from those used in other artistic productions. "The object of oratory alone is not truth," he remarked, "but persuasion. . . ." And then he uttered the oft-quoted statement: "A speaker who exhausts the whole philosophy of a question, who displays every grace of style, yet produces no effect on his audience, may be a great essayist, a great statesman, a great master of composition; but he is not an orator."

Tools of the Critic

These comments make it clear that Macaulay looked upon rhetoric as a useful tool; that he conceived the function of oratory to be peculiarly practical, confined to eliciting responses from hearers.

The critic who evaluates these practical efforts must, indeed, be intelligent and discerning, but he need not necessarily have the status of an expert. Commenting on a remark made by Eugene of Savoy, Macaulay observes

. . . the greatest generals have commonly been those who have been at once raised to command, and introduced to the great operations of war, without being employed in the petty calculations and manoeuvres which employ the time of an inferior officer. In literature the principle is equally sound. The great tactics of criticism will, in general, be best understood by those who have not had much practice in drilling syllables and particles.[56]

The important requisite was that the critic be able to appreciate the circumstances and manners of the age whose men he proposed to appraise.

The Standards of Judgment

Macaulay holds up a specific standard of judgment for the critic. In his essay "On the Athenian Orators," he surely infers, even if he does not openly express the belief, that certain speakers of antiquity furnish effective models of public address. He has a deep respect for good models, saying it is not "by turning over libraries, but by repeatedly perusing and intently contemplating a few great models, that the mind

[55] *Ibid.*, I, 48–49.
[56] *Ibid.*, I, 44.

is best disciplined." Severity should characterize the pattern of imitation; thoroughness should stamp the study habits and practice work of aspiring orators.

Rumford, it is said, proposed to the Elector of Bavaria a scheme for feeding his soldiers at a much cheaper rate than formerly. His plan was simply to compel them to masticate their food thoroughly. A small quantity, thus eaten, would, according to that famous projector, afford more sustenance than a large meal hastily devoured. I do not know how Rumford's proposition was received; but to the mind, I believe, it will be found more nutritious to digest a page than to devour a library.[57]

Reverting to his analogy of oratory and warfare, Macaulay remarked:

There is indeed a remarkable coincidence between the progress of the art of war, and that of the art of oratory, among the Greeks. They both advanced to perfection by contemporaneous steps, and from similar causes. The early speakers, like the early warriors of Greece, were merely a militia. It was found that in both employments practise and discipline gave superiority.[58]

As the great model in eloquence, Demosthenes stands at the head of the list. In the *History*, Macaulay announces that there are speeches, "some speeches of Demosthenes particularly, in which it would be impossible to alter a word without altering it for the worse."

Macaulay's Critiques

Macaulay's critical estimates of orators are found chiefly in his reviews and essays. Included among the entries are studies of Chatham, Hastings, Holland, Barère, Mackintosh, and Pitt. In none of these criticisms, however, does he assume the full role of the rhetorical critic; instead he makes the studies largely biographical-historical, with a sufficiently full measure of material on the oratorical activities of the men to reveal his theory of public speaking.

The most distinctive feature of the criticisms, from the point of view of rhetorical evaluation, is the emphasis Macaulay places upon the early speech training, practice, and capacities of the orators. In his reviews of Chatham and Pitt the Younger, particularly, this professed interest in accounting for the speakers' subsequent proficiency in oratory is patently evident. In the study of Pitt the Younger, Macaulay comments frequently on Pitt's early education, his familiarity with classical literature, his study of the ancient orators, and his early study of parliamentary debates. "His education," Macaulay allows, "was well adapted to form a great parliamentary speaker." Later, he remarks:

[57] *Ibid.*, I, 47.
[58] *Ibid.*, VI, 49.

There is . . . abundant evidence that nature had bestowed on Pitt the talents of a great orator; and those talents had been developed in a very peculiar manner, first by his education, and secondly by the high official position to which he rose early, and in which he passed the greater part of his public life.[59]

It should be observed that a considerable body of contemporary research in rhetoric and oratory derives from suggestions offered by Macaulay in his critical reviews. Many theses have been prepared recently which trace the factors accounting for the oratorical abilities of certain speakers. These studies sustain a tradition that traces back, in part at least, to the essays of Macaulay.

SUMMARY

The intermediate period to 1850 produced relatively few major contributions to the art of rhetorical criticism.

Macaulay offered some suggestions as to the method of tracing factors responsible for the development of oratorical skills in individuals, and he was sensibly conscious of the need for understanding the social conditions out of which speeches developed. In general, however, he remained a theorist whose reflections dealt chiefly with the place of oratory in public life, rather than with the critical standards by which such oratory was appraised.

De Quincey and Hazlitt were primarily concerned with stylistic matters, although the latter evaluated the role of the speaker in a democratic society. Brougham revived the persistent theme of the ancients versus the moderns in oratorical achievement. Swift, Addison, and Chesterfield furnished incidental criticism, but chiefly of delivery.

Although Rapin and Blair used critical methods characterized by a certain inflexibility and formality, they are by all odds the most important contributors of this period. Both evinced an intelligent insight into the variables of public address; both had a sound theoretical knowledge of the speech art; and both proceeded methodically in their criticism, working with criteria which, however rigidly employed, gave unmistakable order to their efforts.

EXERCISES

1. Apply the Rapin formula to the criticism of a recent speaker.
2. Prepare a report on Fénelon as a critic of rhetorical theory and of French public speakers.
3. Prepare a report on Samuel Johnson as a critic of rhetorical theory and practice.

[59] *Works of Lord Macaulay.* Edinburgh ed. VII, 380.

4. Trace the influence of contemporary psychology, logic, and philosophy on the rhetorical principles and critical tenets of Blair.

5. Construct a tabular analysis of Blair's scheme or method of criticism, structurally similar to that of Rapin's method as outlined in this chapter.

6. Evaluate Hazlitt's observations on the differences between written and oral style by reference to experimental, normative, and other evidence from later studies. Indicate lines of further investigation of oral and written style.

7. Criticize in detail Brougham's argument that ancient oratory has "immeasurable superiority" over that of the moderns.

8. Make a study of Macaulay as a critic of orators. In your analysis refer to his critical opinions in the essays on "William Pitt," "Sir James Macintosh," "William Pitt, Earl of Chatham," "Warren Hastings," and "On the Athenian Orators."

9. Examine the *Historical and the Posthumous Memoirs of Sir Nathaniel William Wraxall,* ed. by H. B. Wheatley (New York, Scribner and Welford, 1884, 5 vols.) to determine his attitude toward orators and oratory.

10. Compare the methods and results of the critical evaluations of Daniel Webster by Edwin P. Whipple (*Reviews and Essays*, I, 172–207) and Wilbur S. Howell and Hoyt H. Hudson (*History and Criticism of American Public Address,* edited by W. N. Brigance [New York: Russell & Russell, 1943], II, 665–733).

READINGS

J. W. H. ATKINS. *English Literary Criticism: The Medieval Phase.* New York, The Macmillan Co., 1943. "Early Grammarians: Bede and Alcuin," pp. 36–58.

CHARLES SEARS BALDWIN. *Renaissance Literary Theory and Practice.* New York, Columbia University Press, 1939. Ch. III, "Imitation of Prose Forms," "Ciceronianism Rhetorics," pp. 39–53).

VINCENT M. BEVILACQUA. "Lord Kames's Theory of Rhetoric." *Speech Monographs,* 30:309–327 (November, 1963).

———. "Philosophical Assumptions Underlying Hugh Blair's *Lectures on Rhetoric and Belles Lettres.*" *Western Speech,* 31:150–164 (Summer, 1967).

———. "Rhetoric and Human Nature in Kames's *Elements of Criticism.*" *Quarterly Journal of Speech,* 43:46–60 (February, 1962).

HENRY BROUGHAM. *Rhetorical Theories and Literary Dissertations and Addresses.* London, R. Griffin & Co., 1856.

DONALD C. BRYANT. "Burke's Opinion of Orators." *Quarterly Journal of Speech,* 20:241–254 (April, 1934).

JOHN LORD CAMPBELL. *The Lives of the Chief Justices of England,* Vol. II. London, John Murray, 1849. (Lord Mansfield—pp. 302–584.)

HERMAN COHEN. "Hugh Blair's Theory of Taste." *Quarterly Journal of Speech,* 44:265–274 (October, 1958).

JAMES L. GOLDEN. "Hugh Blair: Minister of St. Giles." *Quarterly Journal of Speech,* 38:155–160 (April, 1952).

HAROLD F. HARDING. "The Listener on Eloquence: 1750–1800." In *Studies in Speech and Drama in Honor of Alexander M. Drummond.* Ithaca, New York, Cornell University Press, 1944. Pp. 341–353.

WILBUR SAMUEL HOWELL. "Oratory and Poetry in Fénelon's Literary Theory." *Quarterly Journal of Speech,* 37:1–10 (February, 1951).

———. "De Quincey on Science, Rhetoric, and Poetry." *Speech Monographs,* 13:1–13 (1946).

HOYT H. HUDSON. "De Quincey on Rhetoric and Public Speaking." In *Studies in Rhetoric and Public Speaking in Honor of James A. Winans.* New York, Century Co., 1925. Pp. 133–151.

RAY E. KEESEY. "Lawson's *Lectures Concerning Oratory.*" *Speech Monographs,* 20: 49–57 (March, 1953).

THOMAS BABINGTON MACAULAY. "On the Athenian Orators." In *The Complete Works of Thomas B. Macaulay,* Vol. VI. New York, Sully and Kleintech, 1900. Pp. 40–56.

DWAIN E. MOORE. "John Morley: Critic of Public Address." *Quarterly Journal of Speech,* 44:161–165 (April, 1958).

RAY NADEAU. "Talaeus Versus Farnaby on Style." *Speech Monographs,* 21:59–63 (March, 1954).

7

The Modern Critics

The most ambitious attempts at rhetorical criticism, excepting only Cicero's *Brutus*, are products of the past hundred and twenty-five years. In this period, the criticism of speeches has become a more dignified and intellectually challenging art because the subject matter of speech has again become a highly respected curricular discipline in our schools and colleges. It would seem, therefore, that the criticism of rhetoric ebbs and flows with the tides of academic acceptance. It is subject, moreover, to the influence of fads and fashions in thinking, just as are literary criticism and the related arts. In short, it reflects the spirit of the age and the character of its educational philosophy. The past century, it seems clear, has favored the revival of rhetoric. Sharpening of critical faculties in this field, accordingly, is an objective eagerly sought and already in process of realization.

THE MASTER OF THE NINETEENTH CENTURY: GOODRICH

Goodrich's Theoretical Bases

No name in the history of rhetorical criticism has been more favorably received during the recent revival of interest than that of Chauncey Goodrich, Professor of Rhetoric at Yale from 1817 to 1839. For many years Goodrich taught rhetoric to sophomores at Yale and also conducted a combined section in rhetorical theory and criticism for seniors, the latter course including an intensive study of the Demosthenean orations and the masterpieces of English public address. In addition to these duties, he spent considerable time in lexicographical work, revising and editing Webster's *Dictionary*. In 1852, he publishd *Select British Eloquence*. Although he planned at a later time to bring out a comparable volume on American oratory, the pressure of other duties prevented his finishing the project.

Goodrich was both a theorist and a critic of oratory. Some of the notes recently discovered by John Hoshor, and now in the possession of the Yale University Library, throw considerable light upon Goodrich's conception of public speaking. His theory of address stems directly from the classical pattern, with audience adaptation as its crowning feature. The essential components of his scheme are the traditional types of proof: the logical mode in which *probability,* rather than *exact truth,* is the necessary element; the emotional mode through which the accomplished speaker gains access to the hearer's reason; and ethical persuasion through which a man's character is revealed to the audience. Since an orator's character may be bad and his cause good, Goodrich affirms that whereas virtue is an unquestioned aid to eloquence, it is not a positive essential. This point of view, though subject to certain qualifications, is not without merit. It is perhaps more realistic than that which insists a man cannot be regarded as a real orator unless he is virtuous.

Goodrich's Critical Method

We should note that Goodrich approaches the theory of oratory through the criticism of it. Thus he quotes at the beginning of his *Select British Eloquence* a remark of Hume's to the effect that " 'he who would teach eloquence must do it chiefly by example.' " Goodrich then observes that this remark struck him forcibly; and

. . . in entering on the office of Professor of Rhetoric in Yale College . . . , [I] took Demosthenes' Oration for the Crown as a text-book in the Senior Class. . . . [My object] was not only to awaken in the minds of the class that love of genuine eloquence which is the surest pledge of success, but to aid them in catching the spirit of the authors read, and, by analyzing passages selected for the purpose, to initiate the pupil in those higher principles which . . . have always guided the great masters of the art, till he should learn the *unwritten* rules of oratory, which operate by a kind of instinct upon the mind, and are far more important than any that are found in the books.[1]

Select British Eloquence was the product of that teaching method, articulated with the study of the English orators. Fortunately for the method he adopted, Goodrich chose to include most of the orations in their entirety. His reason was plain and defensible. "The object is to have each of them studied as a complete system of thought." He then continues:

Detached passages of extraordinary force and beauty may be useful as exercises in elocution; but, if dwelt upon exclusively as models of style, they

[1] *Select British Eloquence.* New York, 1853. Preface, iii.

are sure to vitiate the taste. It is like taking all one's nutriment from highly seasoned food and stimulating drinks.[2]

What Goodrich calls "the aids afforded for the study of these speeches" represent the method he employs in making his critical estimates. These "aids" include (1) a "memoir of each orator, designed to show his early training in eloquence, the leading events of his public life, the peculiar cast of his genius, and the distinctive characteristics of his oratory"; (2) a historical introduction to each speech, "explaining minutely the circumstances of the case, the state of parties, and the exact point at issue"; (3) an analysis of the longer speeches "in side-notes, giving the divisions and subdivisions of thought"; (4) a body of explanatory notes covering the more minute facts; (5) critical notes "as specimens of the kind of analysis which the author has been accustomed to apply to the several parts of an oration"; (6) translations of passages quoted from foreign languages; and (7) a concluding statement "of the way in which the question was decided, with occasional remarks upon its merits or the results produced by the decision."

Goodrich's Studies of the Orators

Goodrich deals with twenty orators, if we include the Letters of Junius, ranging from Sir John Eliot, who was born in the latter part of the sixteenth century, to Lord Brougham, who was still alive when *Select British Eloquence* was written. The larger part of the treatise deals, however, with the key figures of the eighteenth century, including Chatham, Mansfield, Burke, Fox, Pitt, and Erskine.

An examination of Goodrich's estimate of Burke will serve to illustrate the type of appraisal which characterizes *Select British Eloquence*. In an extended passage of some thirty-five pages—the equivalent of about one hundred ordinary octavo pages in Pica type—Goodrich develops the biographical-historical setting for a careful study of Burke's speeches. In no other treatise prior to 1850 is there such an ambitiously detailed account of the social forces which give to oratorical criticism its essential substructure. Scattered throughout the historical section appear hints and collateral critiques of Burke as a speaker, as a literary figure, and as a political philosopher. All of these preliminary guides to an understanding of the orator are supplemented later by specific information concerning each of the occasions or settings of the speeches chosen for criticism, as well as by marginal notes on the texts of the speeches.

Let us consider the final estimate of Burke as an orator. In it we observe a fine expression of Goodrich's method of evaluation.

[2] *Ibid.*

As an orator he derived little or no advantage from his personal qualifications. He was tall, but not robust; his gait and gesture were awkward; his countenance, though intellectual, was destitute of softness, and rarely relaxed into a smile; and as he always wore spectacles, his eye gave him no command over an audience. 'His enunciation,' says Wraxall, 'was vehement and rapid; and his Irish accent, which was as strong as if he had never quitted the banks of the Shannon, diminished to the ear the effect of his eloquence on the mind.'

The variety and extent of his powers in debate was greater than that of any other orator in ancient or modern times. No one ever poured forth such a flood of thought—so many original combinations of inventive genius; so much knowledge of man and the working of political systems; so many just remarks on the relation of government to the manners, the spirit, and even the prejudices of a people; so many wise maxims as to a change in constitutions and laws; so many beautiful effusions of lofty and generous sentiment; such exuberant stores of illustration, ornament, and apt allusion; all intermingled with the liveliest sallies of wit or the boldest flights of a sublime imagination. In actual debate, as a contemporary informs us, he passed more rapidly from one exercise of his powers to another, than in his printed productions. During the same evening, sometimes in the space of a few moments, he would be pathetic and humorous, acrimonious and conciliating, now giving vent to his indignant feelings in lofty declamation, and again, almost in the same breath, convulsing his audience by the most laughable exhibitions of ridicule or burlesque. In respect to the versatility of Mr. Burke as an orator, Dr. Parr says, 'Who among men of eloquence and learning was ever more profoundly versed in every branch of science? Who is there that can transfer so happily the results of laborious research to the most familiar and popular topics? Who is there that possesses so extensive yet so accurate an acquaintance with every transaction recent or remote? Who is there that can deviate from his subject for the purposes of delight with such engaging ease, and insensibly conduct his hearers or readers from the severity of reasoning to the festivity of wit? Who is there that can melt them, if the occasion requires, with such resistless power to grief or pity? Who is there that combines the charm of inimitable grace and urbanity with such magnificent and boundless expansion?'

A prominent feature in the character of Mr. Burke, which prepared him for this wide exercise of his powers, was *intellectual independence*. He leaned on no other man's understanding, however great. In the true sense of the term, he never borrowed an idea or an image. Like food in a healthy system, every thing from without was perfectly assimilated; it entered by a new combination into the very structure of his thoughts, as when the blood, freshly formed, goes out to the extremities under the strong pulsations of the heart. On most subjects, at the present day, this is all we can expect of *originality;* the thoughts and feelings which a man expresses must be *truly his own.*

In the structure of his mind he had a strong resemblance to Bacon, nor was he greatly his inferior in the leading attributes of his intellect. In imagination he went far beyond him. He united more perfectly than any other man the discordant qualities of the philosopher and the poet, and this union was equally the source of some of his greatest excellences and faults as an orator.

The first thing that strikes us in a survey of his understanding is its remarkable *comprehensiveness*. He had an amplitude of mind, a power and compass of intellectual vision, beyond that of most men that ever lived. He looked on a subject like a man standing upon an eminence, taking a large and rounded view of it on every side, contemplating each of its parts under a vast variety of relations, and those relations often extremely complex or remote. To this wide grasp of original thought he added every variety of information gathered from abroad. There was no subject on which he had not read, no system relating to the interests of man as a social being which he had not thoroughly explored. All these treasures of acquired knowledge he brought home to amplify and adorn the products of his own genius, as the ancient Romans collected every thing that was beautiful in the spoils of conquered nations, to give new splendour to the seat of empire.

To this largeness of view he added a surprising *subtlety of intellect*. So quick and delicate were his perceptions that he saw his way clearly through the most complicated relations, following out the finest thread of thought without once letting go his hold, or becoming lost or perplexed in the intricacies of the subject. This subtlety, however, did not usually take the form of mere logical acuteness in the detection of fallacies. He was not remarkable for his dexterity as a disputant. He loved rather to build up than to pull down; he dwelt not so much on the differences of things, as on some hidden agreement between them when apparently most dissimilar. The association of *resemblance* was one of the most active principles of his nature. While it filled his mind with all the imagery of the poet, it gave an impulse and direction to his reasoning as a philosopher. It led him, as his favorite employment, to trace out analogies, correspondencies, or contrasts . . ; thus filling up his originally comprehensive mind with a beautiful series of associated thoughts, showing often the identity of things which appeared the most unlike, and binding together in one system what might seem the most unconnected or contradictory phenomena. To this he added another principle of association, still more characteristic of the philosopher, that of *cause and effect*. 'Why?' 'Whence?' 'By what means?' 'For what end?' 'With what results?' these questions from childhood were continually pressing upon his mind. To answer them in respect to *man* in all his multiplied relations as the creature of society, to trace out the working of political institutions, to establish the principles of wise legislation, to lay open the sources of national security and advancement, was the great object of his life; and he here found the widest scope for that extraordinary subtlety of intellect of which we are now speaking. In these two principles of association, we see the origin of Mr. Burke's inexhaustible richness of thought. We see, also, how it was that in his mode of viewing a subject there was never any thing ordinary or commonplace. If the topic was a trite one, the manner of presenting it was peculiarly his own. As in the kaleidoscope, the same object takes a thousand new shapes and colors under a change of light, so in his mind the most hackneyed theme was transformed and illuminated by the radiance of his genius, or placed in new relations which gave it all the freshness of original thought. . . .

Then follow equally incisive analyses of Burke's power of generalization, the principles governing his social and political convictions, his rhetorical methods, skill in reasoning, use of imagery, and the character of his language.

In conclusion, we may say, without paradox, since oratory is only one branch of the quality we are now considering, that while Mr. Burke was inferior as an orator to Lord Chatham and Mr. Fox, he has been surpassed by no one in the richness and splendor of his eloquence; and that he has left us something greater and better than all eloquence in his countless lessons of moral and civil wisdom.[3]

Use of the Comparative Method

In common with many of the better critics of oratory, Goodrich relied upon comparisons or contrasts to delineate the characteristic style and method of certain speakers. Two passages will illustrate the use to which he put this method. The first is from his analysis of Charles James Fox:

Sir James Mackintosh has remarked that 'Fox was the most Demosthenean speaker since Demosthenes,' while Lord Brougham says, in commenting on this passage, 'There never was a greater mistake than the fancying a close resemblance between his eloquence and that of Demosthenes.' When two such men differ on a point like this, we may safely say that both are in the right and in the wrong. As to certain qualities, Fox was the very reverse of the great Athenian; as to others, they had much in common. In whatever relates to the forms of oratory—symmetry, dignity, grace, the working up of thought and language to their most perfect expression—Mr. Fox was not only inferior to Demosthenes, but wholly unlike him, having no rhetoric and no ideality; while, at the same time, in the structure of his understanding, the modes of its operation, the soul and spirit which breathes throughout his eloquence, there was a striking resemblance. This will appear as we dwell for a moment on his leading peculiarities.

(1.) He had a luminous simplicity, which gave his speeches the most absolute unity of impression, however irregular might be their arrangement. No man ever kept the great points of his case more steadily and vividly before the minds of his audience.

(2.) He took everything in the concrete. If he discussed principles, it was always in direct connection with the subject before him. Usually, however, he did not even discuss a subject—he grappled with an antagonist. Nothing gives such life and interest to a speech, or so delights an audience, as a direct contest of man with man.

(3.) He struck instantly at the heart of his subject. He was eager to meet his opponent at once on the real points at issue; and the moment of his greatest power was when he stated the argument against himself, with more force than his adversary or any other man could give it, and then seized it with the hand of a giant, tore it in pieces, and trampled it under foot.

(4.) His mode of enforcing a subject on the minds of his audience was to come back again and again to the strong points of his case. Mr. Pitt *amplified* when he wished to impress, Mr. Fox *repeated*. Demosthenes also repeated, but he had more adroitness in varying the mode of doing it.

(5.) He had rarely any preconceived method or arrangement of his thoughts. This was one of his greatest faults, in which he differed most from the Athenian artist. If it had not been for the unity of impression and feeling mentioned above, his strength would have been wasted in disconnected efforts.

[3] *Ibid.*

(6.) Reasoning was his forte and his passion. But he was not a regular reasoner. In his eagerness to press forward, he threw away everything he could part with, and compacted the rest into a single mass. Facts, principles, analogies, were all wrought together like the strands of a cable, and intermingled with wit, ridicule, or impassioned feeling. His arguments were usually personal in their nature, *ad hominem*, &c., and were brought home to his antagonist with stinging severity and force.

(7.) He abounded in *hits*—those abrupt and startling turns of thought which rouse an audience, and give them more delight than the loftiest strains of eloquence.

(8.) He was equally distinguished for his *side* blows, for keen and pungent remarks flashed out upon his antagonist in passing, as he pressed on with his argument.

(9.) He was often dramatic, personating the character of his opponents or others, and carrying on a dialogue between them, which added greatly to the liveliness and force of his oratory.

(10.) He had astonishing dexterity in evading difficulties, and turning to his own advantage every thing that occurred in debate.

In nearly all these qualities he had a close resemblance to Demosthenes.[4]

The second passage is not original with Goodrich. He quotes a contemporary of Lord Brougham and George Canning to show how the qualities of the two orators are the more clearly revealed through juxtaposition of their characteristics:

'Canning was airy, open, and prepossessing; Brougham seemed stern, hard, lowering, and almost repulsive. Canning's features were handsome, and his eye, though deeply ensconced under his eyebrows, was full of sparkle and gayety; the features of Brougham were harsh in the extreme: while his forehead shot up to a great elevation, his chin was long and square; his mouth, nose, and eyes seemed huddled together in the center of his face, the eyes absolutely lost amid folds and corrugations; and while he sat listening, they seemed to retire inward or to be veiled by a filmy curtain, which not only concealed the appalling glare which shot from them when he was aroused, but rendered his mind and his purpose a sealed book to the keenest scrutiny of man. Canning's passions appeared upon the open champaign of his face, drawn up in ready array, and moved to and fro at every turn of his own oration and every retort in that of his antagonist. Those of Brougham remained within, as in a citadel which no artillery could batter and no mine blow up; and even when he was putting forth all the power of his eloquence, when every ear was tingling at what he said, and while the immediate object of his invective was writhing in helpless and indescribable agony, his visage retained its cold and brassy hue; and he triumphed over the passions of other men by seeming to be without passion himself. When Canning rose to speak, he elevated his countenance, and seemed to look round for applause as a thing dear to his feelings; while Brougham stood coiled and concentrated, reckless of all but the power that was within himself.

'From Canning there was expected the glitter of wit and the glow of spirit—something showy and elegant; Brougham stood up as a being whose

[4] *Ibid.*, pp. 460–461.

powers and intentions were all a mystery—whose aim and effect no living man could divine. You bent forward to catch the first sentence of the one, and felt human nature elevated in the specimen before you; you crouched and shrunk back from the other, and dreams of ruin and annihilation darted across your mind. The one seemed to dwell among men, to join in their joys, and to live upon their praise; the other appeared a son of the desert, who had deigned to visit the human race merely to make it tremble at his strength.

'The style of their eloquence and the structure of their orations were just as different. Canning arranged his words like one who could play skillfully upon that sweetest of all instruments, the human voice; Brougham proceeded like a master of every power of reasoning and the understanding. The modes and allusions of the one were always quadrable by the classical formulae; those of the other could be squared only by the higher analysis of the mind; and they soared, and ran, and pealed, and swelled on and on, till a single sentence was often a complete oration within itself; but still, so clear was the logic, and so close the connection, that every member carried the weight of all that went before, and opened the way for all that was to follow after. The style of Canning was like the convex mirror, which scatters every ray of light that falls upon it, and shines and sparkles in whatever position it is viewed; that of Brougham was like the concave speculum, scattering no indiscriminate radiance, but having its light concentrated into one intense and tremendous focus. Canning marched forward in a straight and clear track; every paragraph was perfect in itself, and every coruscation of wit and of genius was brilliant and delightful; it was all felt, and it was felt all at once: Brougham twined round and round in a spiral, sweeping the contents of a vast circumference before him, and uniting and pouring them onward to the main point of attack.[5]

Postscript on Goodrich's Method

Goodrich's analyses of the several orators are not of equal merit. The studies of Fox and Burke are no doubt the best. But in all of them there is a sense of direction, a point of view that keeps the audience and the age clearly in focus. Unlike many of his predecessors, Goodrich prepared his critiques with an eye to capturing the rhetorical, rather than the strictly literary, mood. His method was adapted to the realization of that end. Goodrich was an uncommonly successful critic of public address.

JEBB EVALUATES THE ATTIC ORATORS

Method of Analysis

For more than fifty years the name of Richard C. Jebb has been closely associated in the minds of rhetoricians with all that is scholarly

[5] *Ibid.*, pp. 888–889.

and exacting in the study of ancient oratory. Jebb's *Attic Orators* [6] is unquestionably the most readable and penetrating analysis in print of the great ancient figures in oratory.

Originally published in 1876, Jebb's study deals chiefly with the Attic orators before Demosthenes. Thus, instead of covering the complete Attic decade, Jebb offers a systematic and detailed account of Antiphon, Andocides, Lysias, Isocrates, and Isaeus. In a concluding chapter, he includes, however, a section on the "mature civil eloquence" best exemplified in the activities of Lycurgus, Hyperides, Aeschines, and Demosthenes.

The purpose of Jebb's work transcends straight rhetorical criticism. Not content simply with appraising the relative merits of a few orators of antiquity, he proposed to reveal the essential relation between oratorical expression and Greek prose generally. Accordingly, through the lives and works of the great figures, he shows how Greek oratory developed, and in turn how Greek prose was influenced by refinements in that branch of expression. This is an assignment of no mean proportions, requiring as it does a thorough command of the historical, literary, and social facts that contributed to the formation of a style of utterance.

The *Attic Orators* is, then, several projects in one—and all competently handled. It is a history of rhetoric from earliest times to the Rome of Augustus; it is a commentary on the social and political forces that helped to mould the artistic expression of ancient Greece; it is a careful textual study of the speeches of the first five great orators before Demosthenes; and, finally, it is a critical estimate of the stylistic excellences of the Attic orators who were actively responsible for shaping their language into artistic form.

In our previous discussion of the antecedents of contemporary rhetorical theory, we referred frequently to conclusions and judgments derived by Jebb from his painstaking researches. It remains now to examine the methods he employed in his rhetorical criticism.

Jebb says he is not interested in adopting a "uniform scale" for analyzing the orations; instead, he prefers to make the studies "more or less full according to the interest of the subject matter or the nature of its difficulties." In keeping with this dictum, he gives a relatively short analysis of Andocides; but to Isocrates he accords more than half of the second volume of his treatise.

Despite the fact that the spatial distributions of the work vary widely with the orators, Jebb uses a strictly uniform pattern for the divisions of study within each analysis. His studies are divided into three sections, dealing with the life, the style, and the works of each orator. To

[6] *The Attic Orators.* London, 1893. Two volumes.

this scheme he adheres with the single deviation of Isocrates, to whose study he adds a chapter on the celebrated Theory of Culture.

Perhaps more fully than any earlier critic with the exception of Goodrich, Jebb recognized the importance of historical study in making critical estimates of orators. Remarking that an oration from Antiphon or Isocrates "will often be poor food for the mind if it is read alone," he goes on:

> What is necessary to make it profitable is some idea of the world in which it was spoken. These orators who were not conspicuous actors in history must be read, not fragmentarily or in the light of notes which confine themselves to explaining what are termed 'allusions,' but more systematically, and with some general comprehension of the author and the age.[7]

Jebb observes that Brougham, distinguished critic that he was, found Isaeus hard to read. But, counters Jebb, if Brougham

> . . . had considered Isaeus, not as merely a writer on a series of will-cases, but as the oldest and most vivid witness for the working of inchoate testation in a primitive society, and, on the other hand, as the man who, alone, marks a critical phase in the growth of Attic prose, it is conceivable that Brougham should have thought Isaeus worthy of the most attentive perusal.[8]

The analyses Jebb makes of the orators furnish abundant testimony to his conviction that history is an essential constituent of the critical judgment of oratory.

Another distinguishing feature of Jebb's analyses is the way he interlaces critical comment on political and artistic events with biographical details. Indeed, Jebb gives biography considerable prominence in his studies; but, unlike many critics who were similarly convinced of its importance, he confines the biographical elements to a frame of reference in which the literary and rhetorical point of view constantly shines forth. He is interested in the biography of the orator only to the extent that it enlarges the understanding of the character as a user and moulder of prose expression. Thus in his summation of the life of Antiphon, Jebb says:

> It was the power of a subtle and quick mind backed by a thorough command of the new rhetoric. He was masterly in device and in utterance. Fertility of expedient, ingenuity in making points in debate, were the qualities which the oligarchs most needed; and it was in these that the strength of Antiphon lay. In promptness of invention where difficulties were to be met on the instant he probably bore some likeness to Themistocles; but there is no reason for crediting him with that largeness of view, or with any share

---

[7] *Ibid.*, I, xiii.
[8] *Ibid.*

of that wonderful foresight, which made Themistocles a statesman as well as a diplomatist.[9]

Here the emphasis is plainly upon the relation of words to the destiny of states. As Jebb observes:

> Antiphon's first and strongest claim to eminence was his mastery over the weapons now indispensable in the ecclesia and the lawcourts; it was this accomplishment, no less fashionable than useful, which recommended him to the young men of his party whom he had no other pretension to influence. . . . In his person the practical branch of the new culture for the first time takes a distinct place among the qualifications for political rank. The Art of Words had its definite share in bringing in the Four Hundred: it was a curious nemesis when seven years later it was banished from Athens by the Thirty.[10]

Jebb is more deeply concerned with the analysis of the orator's style than are most present-day critics. In this regard, he is, perhaps, less the rhetorical and more the literary critic. However, this emphasis is consistent with the plan of his work. He was tracing the development of Greek prose expression; since oratory was the principal form of utterance at that time, he naturally found it necessary to examine its structure with care, to the end that he might determine its influence upon Attic prose generally.

Jebb's analyses conform to a fairly conventional pattern. He reconstructs briefly the setting of the speech; outlines the logical points developed by the speaker; inspects the evidence used in establishing the case; appraises the arrangement of speech materials; and analyzes the style of the oration as a whole. He relies, therefore, upon the usual divisions of rhetoric for the basic scheme of his critical undertakings.

Selections from Jebb's Criticisms

Short passages from the studies of certain orations will illustrate the procedure. In the summary of Antiphon's speech "On the Murder of Herodes," Jebb remarks:

> In reviewing the whole speech as an argument, the first thing which strikes us is the notable contrast between the line of defence taken here and that traced for a case essentially similar in the model-speeches of the First Tetralogy. There, the defendant employs all his ingenuity in suggesting explanations of the mysterious crime which shall make the hypothesis of his own guilt unnecessary. Here, the defendant pointedly refuses to do anything of the kind. It is enough if he can show that he was not the murderer; it is not his business to show who was or might have been. On this broad, plain ground the defence takes a firm stand. The arguments are presented in a

[9] *Ibid.*, I, 15–16.
[10] *Ibid.*, I, 17.

natural order, as they arise out of the facts narrated, and are drawn out at a length proportionate to their consequence,—by far the greatest stress being laid on the worthlessness of the slave's evidence; in discussing which, indeed, the speaker is not very consistent. One apparent omission is curious. The prisoner incidentally says that he never left the vessel on the night when Herodes went on shore and disappeared; but he does not dwell upon, or attempt to prove, this all-essential *alibi*. If the numerous commonplaces and general sentiments seem to us a source of weakness rather than strength, allowance must be made for the taste and fashion of the time; and every one must recognise the effectiveness of the appeal to divine signs in which the argument finds its rhetorical climax.

As a composition, the speech has great merits. The ethos, indeed, is not artistic; a style so dignified and so sententious is scarcely suitable to a speaker who is constantly apologising for his youth and inexperience. Nor, except in the passage which touches on the ruin of Mytilene, is there even an attempt at pathos. But there is variety and versatility; the opening passage is artistically elaborate, the concluding, impressive in a higher way; while the purely argumentative part of the speech is not encumbered with any stiff dignity, but is clear, simple and sufficiently animated. Altogether the style has less sustained elevation, but shows more flexibility, greater maturity and mastery, than that of the Tetralogies.[11]

In the summary of his criticism of Andocides' speech "On the Mysteries," Jebb reveals other features of his rhetorical judgment:

It is impossible to read the speech On the Mysteries without feeling that, as a whole, it is powerful in spite of some evident defects. The arrangement is best in what we have called the first division . . . , which deals with two distinct groups of facts, those relating to the Mysteries case and those relating to the Hermae case. These facts are stated in an order which is, on the whole, clear and natural, though not free from the parentheses of which Andocides was so fond. . . . Less praise is due to the second part of the speech . . . , devoted to the various enactments which had made the decree of Isotimides obsolete. It is at once full and obscure, giving needless, and withholding necessary, details. The third part . . . is a mere string of topics, unconnected with each other, and but slightly connected with the case. This confused appendix to the real defence is, however, insignificant. It shows the anxiety of Andocides to make the judges understand the rancorous personal feeling of his enemies; an anxiety natural in a man who for sixteen years had been pursued by unproved accusations. The passages about Callias and Agyrrhius probably had a stronger effect upon the court than any conventional appeal to compassion would have produced.

As regards style, the language of the speech is thoroughly unaffected and easy, plain without studied avoidance of ornament, and rising at the right places—as when he speaks of the old victories of freedom . . . , and in the peroration. . . . But the great merit of the composition is its picturesqueness, its variety and life. The scene is the prison . . . and the description of the panic at Athens . . . are perhaps the best passages in this respect. If Andocides had not many rhetorical accomplishments, he certainly had perception of character, and the knack of describing it. Diocleides bargaining

11 *Ibid.*, I, 59–61.

with Euphemus . . .—Charmides exhorting Andocides to save the pris-
oners . . .—Peisander urging that Mantitheus and Aphepsion should be put
on the rack . . .—are well given in a few vivid touches.[12]

Jebb's Regard for Texts

Finally, Jebb's criticism rests upon a deep regard for authenticity of
text. Through appeals to authorities and to research he establishes the
speeches as genuine before concerning himself with their evaluation.
And, once established, parts of the text are quoted freely to illustrate
the points in his critical survey.

Similar Studies

In many particulars, Jebb's studies coincide in methodology and substance with those of other scholars who have studied the orations of
ancient Greece. For instance, J. P. Mahaffy's [13] analysis of Demosthenes'
oratory follows substantially the same line of thinking. John F. Dobson,
in *The Greek Orators*,[14] does about the same thing, and in some respects
does as good a job as Jebb.

Dobson's chapter on Demosthenes merits separate notice. In addition to dealing with the usual features of the orator's biography, the
historical background of the speeches, the logical and emotional contents, the arrangement, and the style, Dobson introduces particularly
acute comments on audience behavior and on the measures of oratorical
effectiveness.

Commenting on the fact that Demosthenes was not completely free
from sophistry, Dobson says:

Like many good orators in good or bad causes he laboured from time to
time to make a weak case appear strong, and in this effort was often absolutely disingenuous. The whole of the de Corona is an attempt to throw the
judges off the scent by leading them on to false trails.

Further on, he remarks:

. . . a study of other speeches results in the discovery of many minor
points in which, accurately gauging the intelligence of his audience, he has
intentionally misled them. Thus, his own knowledge of history was profound; but experience has proved that the knowledge possessed by any audience of the history of its own generation is likely to be sketchy and inaccurate. . . . This gives the politician his opportunity of so grouping or misrepresenting facts as to give a wrong impression.[15]

[12] *Ibid.*, I, 124–125.
[13] *A History of Classical Greek Literature.* New York, 1880. II, 292–353.
[14] London, 1919, pp. 199–267.
[15] *Ibid.*, pp. 250–251.

Despite these assertions, Dobson was nevertheless convinced that Demosthenes was motivated by noble aspirations. "Until the end he had hopes for Greek freedom, freedom for Athens, not based on any unworthy compromise, but dependent on a new birth of the old Athenian spirit."

Dobson's conception of the function of rhetoric is sound. He looks upon the orator as a communicator of ideas, not as an exhibitionist who is anxious to display his skills. Persuasion is acknowledged to be the end of rhetoric. Referring again to Demosthenes' speeches, Dobson says:

A good speech was to him a successful speech, not one which might be admired by critics as a piece of literature. It is only incidental that his speeches have a literary quality which ranks him among the foremost writers of Attic prose; as an orator he was independent of this quality.[16]

In summary we may say that Jebb, as well as Mahaffy, Dobson, and other scholars, contributed to the art of rhetorical criticism by stressing the importance of accurate texts—even though that does not mean the same thing in a study of ancient orators as it does in the analysis of contemporary oratory; by reaffirming the doctrine that speeches can best be studied in the light of the social pattern in which they were originally set; and by articulating (particularly in the studies of antiquity where facts are scattered and often fragmentary) the oratorical efforts with the audience responses in the world of practical action. Although Jebb's studies give too much attention to style to permit us to consider them comprehensively balanced criticisms, they represent mature investigations into the art of expression.

HISTORICAL-BIOGRAPHICAL APPROACHES

History and public address are traditional allies. The early historians wove speeches—fictional or authentic—into their narratives, thereby investing them with a sense of the occasion and capturing a bit of the living drama of the time. The modern historian or biographer knows equally well that what public figures say contributes both to an understanding of the speakers and the flow of events. And the interest of educational institutions in preserving speeches and assorted memorabilia in archives of "oral history" attests to the esteem in which scholars hold the spoken work.

Let us refer briefly to two representative examples illustrating the way in which history and biography have helped to shape the modern conception of rhetorical criticism.

16 *Ibid.*, p. 240.

Lecky's View of Oratory

Among the distinguished historians who had a clear idea of the role of public address in the social process was William Edward Hartpole Lecky (1838–1903). His concern was largely with the relation of speech to statesmanship. In the first volume of his *History of England in the Eighteenth Century*, he remarks:

It is the custom of some writers to decry parliamentary institutions as being simply government by talking, and to assert that when they exist mere rhetorical skill will always be more valued than judgment, knowledge, or character. The exaggeration of such charges may be easily established. It is, no doubt, inevitable that where business is transacted chiefly by debate, the talent of a debater should be highly prized; but it is not true that British Legislatures have shown less skill than ordinary sovereigns in distinguishing solid talent from mere showy accomplishments, or that parliamentary weight has in England been usually proportioned to oratorical power. St. John was a far greater orator than Harley; Pulteney was probably a greater orator than Walpole; Stanley in mere rhetorical skill was undoubtedly the superior of Peel. Godolphin, Pelham, Castlereagh, Liverpool, Melbourne, Althorp, Wellington, Russell, and Palmerston are all examples of men who, either as statesmen or as successful leaders of the House of Commons, have taken a foremost place in English politics without any oratorical brilliancy. Sheridan, Plunket, and Brougham, though orators of almost the highest class, left no deep impression on English public life; the ascendency of Grey and Canning was very transient, and no Opposition since the early Hanoverian period sank so low as that which was guided by Fox. The two Pitts are the only examples before our own generation, of speakers of transcendent power exercising for a considerable time a commanding influence over English politics. It is, I believe, quite true that the amazing eloquence and debating skill of the younger Pitt concealed defects in statesmanship which in a less brilliant orator would have been clearly seen, but it would be a grave error to attribute solely to these gifts the long ascendency which he enjoyed. Much was due to his conspicuous ability in managing the finances and commercial interests of the country; to the well-founded confidence of the nation in the purity, loftiness, and strength of his character; to the discredit which had fallen on his opponents; to the inherited lustre of a great name; to the steady support of the King. The case of his father is less disputable. He was guilty of many faults and of some foibles, but the pinnacle of glory to which he raised his country is surely a sufficient proof that if he was the greatest orator he was also the greatest war minister that England has ever known.[17]

In this statement, he gives to the orators the praise and credit they deserve; but he does not overassess their importance or underestimate their influence.

Lecky evaluates the public address of several key figures of the

[17] W. E. H. Lecky. *A History of England in the Eighteenth Century*. New edition. New York, 1892. I, 422–423.

eighteenth century. His comments on Edmund Burke suggest the method which he used in dealing with other speakers. Of Burke, Lecky said:

. . . no other politician or writer has thrown the light of so penetrating a genius on the nature and working of the British Constitution, has impressed his principles so deeply on both of the great parties in the State, and has left behind him a richer treasure of political wisdom applicable to all countries and to all times.[18]

The appeal is evidently to the reader as well as to the listener, for Lecky remarks that the "time may come when they [Burke's works] will be no longer read. The time will never come in which men would not grow the wiser by reading them." This is like the remark once made by Grattan that Burke's speeches "were far better suited to a patient reader than an impatient hearer."

Lecky follows with the statement that

. . . there is scarcely a perceptible difference between the style of his essays and the style of his published speeches; and if the reader selects from his works the few passages which possess to an eminent degree the flash and movement of spoken rhetoric, he will be quite as likely to find them in the former as in the latter.

His final estimate of Burke's speaking is generous:

He far surpassed every other speaker in the copiousness and correctness of his diction, in the range of knowledge he brought to bear on every subject of debate, in the richness and variety of his imagination, in the gorgeous beauty of his descriptive passages, in the depth of the philosophical reflections and the felicity of the personal sketches which he delighted in scattering over his speeches.[19]

These short quotations cannot capture the spirit of Lecky's complete appraisal. They suggest, however, the rhetorical outlook that characterizes much of his investigation into the activities of the central figures of the century. In addition to such remarks as we have examined, note should be made that Lecky quotes other authorities relative to Burke's oratorical skills; investigates fully the historical factors with which Burke and others had to deal; and probes searchingly into Burke's thinking, basic premises, mental qualities, and personal characteristics. In short, Lecky provides a tolerably complete portrait of an orator.

Contemporary rhetorical critics have taken an occasional leaf from the book of suggestions provided by Lecky's example.

[18] *Ibid.*, III, 382.
[19] *Ibid.*

Trevelyan's Analysis of John Bright's Oratory

No scholar of recent years has been more successful in using rhetorical criticism to enforce biographical portrayal than George M. Trevelyan. In his *Life of John Bright,* Trevelyan keeps oratory and speeches constantly in view; and to an extent uncommon in studies of its type, he reveals the true character of his subject by examining what the man spoke from the public platform. At the beginning of the book, Trevelyan makes clear that he will emphasize speechmaking as the symbol of Bright's activities. Immediately we come upon references to the "bell-like clearness" of Bright's voice, and the "absence of gestures" in his platform performances. Bright is at once considered an orator whose speechmaking much be dealt with if his character is to be revealed. "His oncoming," says Trevelyan, "was as the surge of the full swollen tide, not of the sea in storm; he awed his listeners by the calm of his passion, a terrible steed restrained by a yet stronger hand."

Lest his biography be misinterpreted, Trevelyan explains his liberal use of materials from Bright's speeches:

> It will, perhaps, be remarked by some readers that this work contains more numerous quotations from speeches than is usual in a political biography. If so, there is reason enough. Not only were Bright's speeches his one form of perfect achievement, but they were his one great political weapon. Not by administration or legislation, not by arguing in the Cabinet or sharing in the counsels of the party, but by his public orations as a private citizen he profoundly modified English politics and the relations and balance of English classes. He himself, when consulted as to a biography, used to put the question aside by saying 'My life is in my speeches.' But after two generations have gone by, not even the greatest speeches can be widely read or completely understood, except with the help of historical comment, and of such reproduction of a great personality as the biographer, by aid of private letters and recollections, can all too feebly accomplish.[20]

It should be noted that Trevelyan worked with an abundance of source material. He had the facts on Bright's oratorical achievements. In his possession were notes and clippings of Bright's speeches from 1860 onward, to say nothing of the letters and documents that threw further light upon the addresses. Bright had kept a diary for fifty years; those observations, together with other papers, were at Trevelyan's disposal. Other historians, indeed, have had comparable data with which to construct their biographical studies, but few have used those materials as fully as Trevelyan to bring out the importance of public speaking in the life of a man, and in the destiny of a nation.

[20] George M. Trevelyan. *The Life of John Bright.* Boston, 1913, p. 4.

The biography of Bright is, therefore, a useful study for the rhetorician. Without using the terminology of the present-day critic of speeches and speakers, Trevelyan traces the biographical and historical details against a background of speaking achievement. He comments on the early influences of home, religion, and education that tended to form the speaker; he traces the sources of Bright's ideas and reveals the premises of his thinking; he establishes the background of the many speech occasions; he quotes freely from the speeches to illustrate the man's accomplishments; and, throughout the work, he keeps in view the bearing of oratory upon public affairs. On numerous occasions, he comes back to the thought that Bright helped bring about the repeal of the Corn Laws; that he helped to keep England from casting her lot with the Confederates during the American Civil War; that he figured responsibly in the establishment of the Reform Measures of 1867; and that he assisted materially in disestablishing the Church of England in Ireland. These were concrete accomplishments, realized in large part through Bright's speaking campaigns during a long and active life. Here, indeed, were tangible measures of speech effectiveness.

Trevelyan relies heavily upon comparative analyses to reveal the nature of Bright's oratory. Gladstone and Cobden, particularly, are involved in the comparisons. The following passage illustrates his method:

John Bright had the merits and defects of simplicity, Gladstone of complexity. Gladstone—even in the whirlwind of his own oratory, arms overhead and eyes flashing—was always a debater, meeting his opponent's every argument, instructing his audience, often exciting them over the details of some financial or legislative measure. Bright, on the other hand, for all that he never gave the rein to his passion, never swung his arm and scarcely raised his voice—was first and foremost a preacher of broad principles in their moral and poetic force, a speaker less instructive but even more moving than Gladstone. He has himself described the difference betwen them thus: 'When I speak, I strike across from headland to headland. Mr. Gladstone follows the coastline; and when he comes to a navigable river he is unable to resist the temptation of tracing it to its source.'

Of the two, it is Bright whose speeches can be read with greatest pleasure, though that, perhaps, is no test of oratory. Gladstone's orations suffer in the reading from a quality which make them delightful to hear, their dependence on the skill of the speaker to effect his escape with grammar intact from the maze of parentheses—an operation safely sustained on that magnificent voice and by those dramatic gestures. Bright's voice, too, was a gift of heaven; he had never to shout in order that it might thrill with its music the farthest corner of the largest hall. But he had no gesture except to raise his hand, and that not above the level of his breast. Gladstone was everything at once —actor, missionary, debater, exponent of legislative detail—such an one as never before or since rose to address an audience; Bright excelled in pure oratory in its stricter sense.[21]

21 *Ibid.*, pp. 383–384.

Trevelyan appraises the temper of the age in his effort to provide additional insight into the role of speechmaking in a well-organized state:

In the 'fifties and 'sixties a political meeting was a noticeable event, and wherever a politician of the first rank made a long speech, he was reported and read at full, not merely in excerpts and headlines. Full reports of great speeches were eagerly awaited and read by a political nation that had very little else in the way of politics brought to its door. For the same reason parliamentary debates were better reported and more closely followed than they are in our own time, although the general level of political interest and understanding is higher today, if all ranks of society are taken into account.

This state of things set a premium on careful oratory that would not only move the audience but would read well in the paper next morning and in the pamphlet next month. For all these purposes Bright's art was supreme. He moved his audiences more than Gladstone, though he instructed them less; and yet his speeches formed a body of literature which spread his ideas among students of all classes. Since quality rather than quantity in speaking was then required to make an effective politician, Bright was able to indulge his natural preference for leisurely prepared speeches, which stand the test of literature as well as those of oratory.[22]

Not only does Trevelyan make each chapter of his book a virtual analysis of a nineteenth-century speaker; he also includes a separate chapter on "Bright's Oratory." In it he appraises Bright's delivery; discusses his methods of speech preparation (and includes, incidentally, facsimiles of some of the notes used by Bright); evaluates the style and language of the speaker; mentions Bright's mannerisms in speaking; comments on the general and specific effects of the oratory; and considers Bright's philosophy of utterance, both as determined from the orator's letters and from a study of his speeches over a fifty-year span.

In short, *The Life of John Bright* is a praiseworthy example of biography in which oratory is allowed to function as a major component of the man's claim to distinction. Trevelyan has shown rhetorical critics how letters and speeches, together with the intelligent interweaving of historical narrative and interpretation, can reveal the true stature of an orator.

THE TWENTIETH CENTURY

The Classical Revival

In the nineteen twenties, students of public address discovered a systematic basis for *speech* criticism in rhetorical writings of classical rhetoricians, namely, Plato, Isocrates, Aristotle, Cicero, and Quintilian. They steadily appropriated the wisdom of later writings, including me-

[22] *Ibid.,* p. 277.

dieval tracts, various French and German rhetorics, and of course major English sources: Thomas Wilson, Francis Bacon, John Ward, Jeremy Bentham, John Lawson, George Campbell, Joseph Priestley, Thomas De Quincey, Hugh Blair, and Richard Whately. They further modified their views in light of their study of American major and minor rhetorical critics and theorists of the eighteenth, nineteenth, and twentieth centuries, namely John Witherspoon, John Quincy Adams, Edward T. Channing, Ebenezer Porter, Chauncey Goodrich, John F. Genung, and James A. Winans.

These rhetorical ancestors have all influenced present criticism. This totality of tradition and the later modifications constitute the warp and woof of these twentieth century judgments. The common view of the present authors is that the substantial background of principles derived from Greece, Rome, and later Western civilization must continue to furnish the foundations of mature judgment.[23]

Influential in this renascence of classical theory were Herbert Wichelns, his colleagues, and students of Cornell University. Through their provocative research into classical and English sources, they first pointed the way to the critical methodology that has held sway since 1925. Among the most prolific and perceptive of the Cornell group have been Hoyt H. Hudson, Everett Lee Hunt, Harry Caplan, Harold F. Harding, Russell H. Wagner, Karl R. Wallace, Wilbur Samuel Howell, Wayland Maxfield Parrish, Wilbur E. Gilman, Donald C. Bryant, and Ross Scanlan.[24]

A significant landmark in the classical revival and in developing the

[23] A series of volumes, "Landmarks in Rhetoric and Public Address," was issued by the Southern Illinois University Press (Carbondale and Edwardsville), under Dave Potter, general editor. In each case the editor or editors of each volume evaluated the contribution of the given rhetorician. The publications during the first seven years were: A Craig Baird, ed., *Essays from Select British Eloquence by Chauncey Allen Goodrich*, 1963, pp. xiii–xlxiv; Lloyd F. Bitzer, *The Philosophy of Rhetoric by George Campbell*, 1963, pp. ix–xxxvii; Douglas Ehninger, *Richard Whately's Elements of Rhetoric*, 1963, pp. ix–xxx; Harold F. Harding, *Lectures on Rhetoric and Belles Lettres by Hugh Blair*, 2 vols., 1965, pp. vii–xxxv; Vincent Bevilacqua and Richard Murphy, *A Course of Lectures on Oratory and Criticism by Joseph Priestley*, 1965, pp. lx–lviii; Mary Margaret Robb and Lester Thonssen, *Chironomia, or A Treatise on Rhetorical Delivery, by Gilbert Austin*, 1966, pp. ix–xxix; Frederick Burwick, *Selected Essays on Rhetoric by Thomas De Quincey*, 1967, pp. xi–xlviii; Dorothy Anderson and Waldo W. Braden, *Lectures Read to the Seniors in Harvard College by Edward T. Channing*, 1968, pp. ix–liv.

[24] See *Studies in Speech and Drama in Honor of Alexander M. Drummond*. Ithaca, New York, 1944. Wilbur E. Gilman. *Milton's Rhetoric in Defense of Liberty*. In *The University of Missouri Studies*, XIV (July 1, 1939). Donald C. Bryant, ed., *The Rhetorical Idiom, Essays in Rhetoric, Oratory, Language, and Drama*. Ithaca, New York, 1958; Donald C. Bryant, ed., *Papers in Rhetoric* (privately printed, 1940); Raymond F. Howes, ed., *Historical Studies of Rhetoric and Rhetoricians*. Ithaca, New York, 1961; Karl R. Wallace, *Francis Bacon on Communication and Rhetoric*. Chapel Hill, North Carolina, 1943.

present methodology of speech criticism was the publication in 1925 of Herbert A. Wichelns' essay entitled "The Literary Criticism of Oratory." [25] Donald C. Bryant has declared that this piece "has had a greater and a more continuous influence upon the development of scholarship of rhetoric and public address than any other single work published in this century." [26] After "spying out" how literary historians, critics, essayists, and biographers dealt with speeches, the Cornell scholar rejected the focus of literary criticism upon aesthetic excellence and permanence as a measure of the worth of speeches. He noted that "rhetorical criticism . . . is not concerned with permanence, nor yet with beauty. It is concerned with effect. It regards a speech as a communication to a specific audience, and holds its business to be the analysis and appreciation of the orator's method of imparting his ideas to his hearers" [27] In the following paragraph based upon the classical canons of rhetoric, Wichelns provided an outline to be followed:

Rhetorical criticism is necessarily analytical. The scheme of a rhetorical study includes the element of the speaker's personality as a conditioning factor; it includes also the public character of the man—not what he was, but what he was thought to be. It requires a description of the speaker's audience, and of the leading ideas with which he plied his hearers—his topics, the motives to which he appealed, the nature of the proofs he offered. These will reveal his own judgment of human nature in his audiences, and also his judgment on the questions which he discussed. Attention must be paid, too, to the relation of the surviving texts to what was actually uttered: in case the nature of the changes is known, there may be occasion to consider adaptation to two audiences—that which heard and that which read. Nor can rhetorical criticism omit the speaker's mode of arrangement and his mode of expression, nor his habit of preparation and his manner of delivery from the platform; though the last two are perhaps less significant. 'Style'—in the sense which corresponds to diction and sentence movement—must receive attention, but only as one among various means that secure for the speaker ready access to the minds of his auditors. Finally, the effect of the discourse on its immediate hearers is not to be ignored, either in the testimony of witnesses, nor in the records of events. And throughout such a study one must conceive of the public man as influencing the men of his own times by the power of his discourse.[28]

Significant in the application of the classical and post-classical methodology of speech criticism were early graduate students who worked under A. Craig Baird at the State University of Iowa. Among these first doctoral students were William Norwood Brigance, Orville A. Hitch-

[25] *Studies in Rhetoric and Public Speaking in Honor of James Albert Winans.* New York, 1962, pp. 181–216.
[26] Donald C. Bryant, ed., *The Rhetorical Idiom, Essays in Rhetoric, Oratory, Language, and Drama.* Ithaca, New York, 1958, p. 5.
[27] *Studies in Rhetoric and Public Speaking . . .* , p. 209.
[28] *Ibid.,* pp. 212–213.

cock, Horace G. Rahskopf,[29] Herold Truslow Ross,[30] and Loren D. Reid.[31] Of special note were Brigance's essay entitled "Whither Research,"[32] and a second one by Reid on "The Perils of Rhetorical Criticism."[33] Well grounded in history as well as rhetoric, Brigance expanded the rhetorical frame of reference and urged a combination of historical and critical study of speakers. He observed:

> Oratorical literature is a special form, quite distinct from poetry, essays, drama, and other forms of prose literature with which it is often confused by biographers and literary critics. The tools of rhetoric may indeed be the same as those of literature, but the atmosphere and purpose are different. The literary artist writes with his eye on his subject. He is concerned with permanence and beauty. But the statesman who must dominate a crisis, or the advocate who must mold the mind of a court or jury, has no time to polish plaudits for posterity. He is concerned with deadly and immediate effect. He must seize the hour, strike the iron at white heat, adapt himself to the mind, mood, and temperature of the audience and the occasion. It is impossible ever to read the speech apart from the hopes, fears, prejudices, and passions that beset the hearers at its moment of delivery.[34]

Brigance brought his concepts to fruition as editor of the two-volume *History and Criticism of American Public Address*,[35] published in 1943 under the auspices of the Speech Association of America. This work contains introductory historical details and critical appraisals of twenty-eight men whose influence through speechmaking affected the American scene. It is by far the most ambitious and comprehensive project ever completed in this field, Cicero's *Brutus* and Chauncey Goodrich's *Select British Eloquence*—its nearest competitors—not excepted.

Besides the introductory studies which deal with the historical background of American public address, the two volumes contain critical essays on the speechmaking of representative leaders in religion (Jonathan Edwards, Theodore S. Parker, Henry Ward Beecher, and Phillips Brooks); in reform (Wendell Phillips, Robert G. Ingersoll, Henry W. Grady, and Booker T. Washington); in law (Rufus Choate, Jeremiah S. Black, and William M. Evarts); in general culture (Ralph Waldo

---

[29] "John Quincy Adams' Theory and Practice of Public Speaking." *Archives of Speech*, 1:7–98 (September, 1936).

[30] "The Oratorical Principles and Practice of Beveridge." *Archives of Speech*, 1:99–168 (September, 1936).

[31] *Charles James Fox: A Study of Effectiveness of an Eighteenth Century Parliamentary Speaker.* Iowa City, 1932.

[32] *Quarterly Journal of Speech*, 19:552–561 (November, 1933).

[33] *Quarterly Journal of Speech*, 30:416–422 (December, 1944).

[34] William Norwood Brigance. "Whither Research." *Quarterly Journal of Speech*, 19:552–561 (November, 1933).

[35] New York, McGraw-Hill Book Co., Inc., 1943.

Emerson); in education (Charles W. Eliot and Edwin A. Alderman); in labor (Samuel Gompers); and in statecraft (Patrick Henry, Henry Clay, John C. Calhoun, Daniel Webster, William L. Yancey, Charles Sumner, Stephen A. Douglas, Abraham Lincoln, James G. Blaine, William Jennings Bryan, Albert J. Beveridge, Robert M. La Follette, and Woodrow Wilson).

A variety of approaches to critical inquiry may be found in the *History and Criticism of American Public Address*. Some of the studies deal largely with the developmental history of the particular orators, their methods of speech preparation, their ways of handling audiences, and their successes in the various branches of oratory. Others concentrate more fully upon the traditional topics of rhetoric: the speaker's invention, plan of arrangement, kinds of proof, style, and delivery. Certain contributors limit their studies to specific aspects of the total rhetorical process: to the audiences a speaker dealt with, or to a particular kind of oratory. Throughout the work, however, there is evidence that Aristotelian standards of criticism are not only highly regarded by the scholars in the field, but are also uncommonly useful as general yardsticks of rhetorical evaluation.

Since the publication of the first edition of the present book, numerous essays and books have further amplified the classical approach to speech evaluation. Among the best are Marie Hochmuth Nichols' "The Criticism of Rhetoric," the lead essay in Volume III of *A History and Criticism of American Public Address*,[36] Wayland Maxfield Parrish's essay "The Study of Speeches" found in *American Speeches*,[37] Albert J. Croft's "The Function of Rhetorical Criticism," [38] and Malcolm O. Sillars' "Rhetoric as Act." [39] Also worthy of note are Marie Hochmuth Nichols' *Rhetoric and Criticism*,[40] Robert Cathcart's *Post Communication: Criticism and Evaluation* [41] and Anthony Hillbruner's *Critical Dimensions: The Art of Public Address Criticism*.[42] Significant criticism appeared in *Antislavery and Disunion, 1858–1961, Studies in the Rhetoric of Compromise and Conflict*, edited by J. Jeffery Auer,[43] and in *American Public Address*, edited by Loren Reid.[44]

[36] Marie Hochmuth Nichols, ed. *A History and Criticism of American Public Address.* Vol. III. New York, Longmans, Green & Co., 1955, pp. 1–23.

[37] Wayland Maxfield Parrish and Marie Hochmuth, eds. *American Speeches.* New York, Longmans, Green & Co., 1954.

[38] *Quarterly Journal of Speech*, 42:283–291 (October, 1956).

[39] *Quarterly Journal of Speech*, 50:277–284 (October, 1964).

[40] Baton Rouge, Louisiana, 1963; 151 pp.

[41] Indianapolis, Indiana, 1966; 125 pp.

[42] New York, New York, 1966; 180 pp.

[43] New York, 1933.

[44] Columbia, Missouri, 1961.

Movement and Related Studies

In recent years some students of public address have advocated a shift from the investigation of the individual orator and his speeches to a consideration of the efforts of groups of speakers as they function within a social, political, economic, religious, and intellectual setting.[45] Freed from biographical detail and the time limits imposed by a single career, this type of study explores "the selected acts and atmosphere of public address in order to concentrate upon" a multiplicity of speakers, speeches, audiences and occasions." [46] The genre develops from the basic assumption that the context of speeches, for example, a movement or institution, colors and shapes the ideas and speaking practices of those swept along in the surge. The critic seeks to isolate, describe, analyze, and evaluate "patterns of public discussion, the configuration of discourse, the physiognomy of persuasion," peculiar to (1) a movement, (2) a period, (3) a region, or (4) an institution.

In studying a movement, Leland Griffin, leading proponent, suggests that the critic should analyze

. . . fundamental issues, the successive emergence of argument, appeal, counter-argument and counter-appeal, and the sanctions invoked by rhetoricians of both sides; he will note, by a process of imaginative re-living in the age, by an analysis of consequences, the persuasive techniques which were effective and those which were ineffective; and he will note a time, very likely, when invention runs dry, when both aggressor and defendant rhetoricians tend to repeat their stock of argument and appeal. He will naturally note, during the period of inception, the emergence of a group of aggressor rhetoricians and a group of defendant rhetoricians; and he will note, as the movement progresses, the gradual swelling of their ranks. He will be concerned with the discourse of both writers and speakers; with those who invented and those who echoed, with lecturers, pulpit, political, legislative, academic, and forensic orators, with editors, journalists, novelists, dramatists, and poets. He will also note the development and employment of media of discourse. Assuming the movement selected occurred during the first half of the nineteenth century, for example, he will find the opposing groups using some or all of such channels of propagation as books, pamphlets, broadsides, tracts, almanacs, newspapers, and periodicals, the pulpit, the lecture platform, the political rostrum, the stump, and the stage. He may note the development of organizations designed to facilitate the dissemination of argument, such as the lecture bureau, the committee of correspondence, and the political party. Finally, as he reads, the student will note the in-

[45] Bower Aly. "The History of American Public Address as a Research Field." *Quarterly Journal of Speech,* 29:302–304 (October, 1943). S. Judson Crandell. "The Beginnings of a Methodology for Social Control Studies in Public Address." *Quarterly Journal of Speech,* 33:36–39 (February, 1947). Leland M. Griffin. "The Rhetoric of Historical Movements." *Quarterly Journal of Speech,* 38:184–188 (April, 1952).

[46] Leland M. Griffin. "The Rhetoric of Historical Movements." *Quarterly Journal of Speech,* 38:184–188 (April, 1952).

creasing circulation and the ultimate extent of the appeal; the development of audiences; and as the movement spreads, the geographical and social stratification of these audiences.[47]

Demonstrating his method, Griffin produces two excellent essays: "The Rhetorical Structure of the 'New Left' Movement: Part I"[48] and "The Rhetorical Structure of the Antimasonic Movement."[49] In the latter, he tells us what governs his analysis:

Among these assumptions are the following: (1) that two broad classes of rhetorical movements may be said to exist: *pro* movements, in which the rhetorical attempt is to arouse public opinion to the creation or acceptance of an institution or idea, and *anti* movements, in which the rhetorical attempt is to arouse public opinion to the destruction or rejection of an existing institution or idea; (2) that within each movement two classes of rhetoricians may be distinguished: *aggressor* orators and journalists, who attempt in the *pro* movement to establish and in the *anti* movement to destroy, and *defendant* rhetoricians, who attempt in the *pro* movement to resist reform and in the *anti* movement to defend institutions; and (3) that within each movement at least three phases of development may be noted: a period of *inception*, a period of *rhetorical crisis*, and a period of *consummation*.[50]

Griffin's discussion suggests that the critic who seeks to comprehend the rhetoric of movement has before him an ambitious task in viewing the efforts of multi-performers, their motivations, and their philosophical systems. As Griffin recognizes, the searcher must go beyond speakers and speeches to consider other media as diverse as popular song books and farmers' almanacs.

After considering the aspects which Griffin mentions, what does the critic really learn about speaking and speakers? Perhaps he comprehends the speaker's relationship to other speakers and events and acquires a broad view of a period, a region, or an institution; but in his concentration upon "aggressor rhetoricians" and "defendant rhetoricians," upon organizations and channels, the critic may entangle himself in abstractions, nameless intangibles, and broad theoretical concepts. He may concentrate upon certain limited aspects of invention involving the flow of argument and counter-argument and give little attention to organization, language, and delivery. In his attempt to comprehend the totality of his problem, the critic may overlook or be unable to attend carefully to the individual speaker; consequently he does not make judgments about the *worth* of a speaker or a speech. Both Griffin and S. Judson Crandell indicate that these techniques of analysis draw heavily upon the fields of history, sociology, and social psychology.

[47] *Ibid.*, pp. 186–187.
[48] Leland Griffin. *Quarterly Journal of Speech*, 50:133–135 (February, 1964).
[49] Donald C. Bryant, ed. *The Rhetorical Idiom*. Ithaca, New York, 1958, pp. 145–160.
[50] *Ibid.*, p. 146.

Social and Intellectual History Approach

Closely related to movement studies is the social and intellectual history approach to public address. From this frame of reference the researcher looks at a speech or a series of speeches to discover what is revealed about "cultural strivings and heritage" of a group or period, not what are the characteristics of the speaker. These studies are therefore "idea centered," not "speaker centered." [51] Wrage and Baskerville explain:

Although a speech is primarily expressive of the mind of a speaker, it also is a gauge to the mind of his audience, both listeners and readers. What speakers choose to talk about and what listeners choose to listen to are matters esteemed by both parties. In still other ways a speech bears the impress of an audience, always covertly, often overtly. . . . In short, speeches on critical issues are vibrant with the immediacy of life, with the sense of interaction between speaker and listeners.[52]

The volume *Antislavery and Disunion, 1858–1861, Studies in Rhetoric of Compromise and Conflict,* edited by J. Jeffery Auer,[53] has been declared "the speech profession's most imposing exercise in social and intellectual history." [54] This project, the fourth in the series on public address prepared under the auspices of the Speech Association of America, embraces twenty-three *case studies* concerning "the issue of antislavery and disunion, chronologically organized in the period from September, 1858 to April, 1861." The editor explains the approach as "an intensive, even microscopic, investigation . . . made, *in situ* of an individual 'case'." [55] Each contributor strives to report and analyze every facet of the total speaking situation including the speaker, the historical setting, the specific issues and causes for discussion, the occasion, the physical circumstances, the audience, the speaker, the speech, and its immediate and long range effects. The editor has sought to include *representative* and *significant* occasions which tell us how the "issues of antislavery and disunion so vitally affected the fundamental structure of American society." [56]

The essays fall roughly into two groups. Nine discuss specific occa-

51 Ernest J. Wrage. "Public Address: A Study in Social and Intellectual History." *Quarterly Journal of Speech*, 33:453–454 (December, 1947).

52 Ernest J. Wrage and Barnet Baskerville, eds. *American Forum: Speeches on Historic Issues, 1788–1900.* New York, 1960, pp. iii–ix.

53 New York: Harper and Row, 1963.

54 Wayne C. Minnick. "Review of Antislavery and Disunion, 1858–1861." *Quarterly Journal of Speech*, 49:84–87 (February, 1963).

55 J. Jeffery Auer. *An Introduction to Research in Speech.* New York, 1959, p. 120.

56 J. Jeffery Auer. *Antislavery and Disunion, 1858–1861,* p. vii.

sions: The Brownlow-Pryne Debate, September, 1858; William H. Seward on the "Irrepressible Conflict," October 25, 1858; The Oberlin-Wellington Rescue Case, 1859; Robert Barnwell Rhett's Speech, July 4, 1859; Owen Lovejoy on "The Barbarism of Slavery," April 5, 1860; Ford Douglass' Fourth of July Oration, 1860; Carl Schurz's Republican Jubilation Speech, November 16, 1860; Benjamin Morgan Palmer's Thanksgiving Sermon, 1860; and Lincoln's First Inaugural Address. The remaining fourteen consider speaking campaigns, closely akin to movement or institution studies: Jefferson Davis, Sectional Diplomat, 1858; Controversy Among College Students, 1858–1861; The Lyceum Movement and Sectional Controversy, 1860; Methodist Debates and Union Sentiment on the Border, 1860–1861; The Democratic Convention of 1860; the Republican National Convention of 1860; Springfield Lincoln Rally, 1860; The Campaign for Memphis, 1860; The Annual Meeting of the Pennsylvania Anti-Slavery Society, 1860; The Campaign of Stephen A. Douglas in the South, 1860; The Senate Committee of Thirteen; December 6–13, 1860; The Secession Debate in Georgia; November, 1860–January, 1861; New Governors Speak for War, January, 1861; and The Washington Peace Conference of 1861.

Those who look to speeches as sources of social and intellectual history find kindred ideas expressed in such works as Henry Steele Commager's *The American Mind,* Vernon L. Parrington's *Main Currents in American Thought,* Merle Curti's *The Growth of American Thought,* Ralph H. Gabriel's *The Course of American Democratic Thought,* and Stow Persons' *American Minds.* Their approach may be characterized as follows:

1. They are interested in groups of speakers and collections of speeches.
2. They can pursue their research as well with the printed speech as with the spoken speech.
3. They are as much concerned about the speaking of lesser known speakers and lesser known speeches as they are in the more prominent speakers and famous orations.
4. In method they are oriented more toward the historical than the critical and rhetorical.
5. They take as a goal that of "verifying or revising generalizations offered by other workers in social and intellectual history."

There is no denying, of course, that the study of the ideas of a speech is indeed worthwhile as an avenue to understanding of "man's cultural strivings and heritage," and "that students of public address may contribute in substantial ways to the history of ideas." But we must remember with Loren Reid that "rhetorical criticism is not simply a discussion of the speaker's ideas"; or as Wrage suggests, "the rhetoric of ideas fails to account for all the forces at work." [57]

This approach lacks sufficient dimension for adequate rhetorical criticism, for it does not judge the worth or quality of a speech or a speaker. Dealing at best with only an aspect of invention, the critic does not look into the other interacting elements of the speaking situation including language, delivery, and complexity of adjustment of speakers to the other elements of the speaking situation.

The volume *Oratory in the Old South* (Baton Rouge: Louisiana State University Press, 1970), edited by Waldo W. Braden, the eighth one under the auspices of the Speech Association of America, includes nine case studies: Ralph T. Eubanks, "The Rhetoric of the Nullifiers"; Merrill G. Christophersen, "The Anti-Nullifiers"; Robert C. Gunderson, "The Southern Whigs"; Lindsey Perkins, "The Moderate Democrats, 1830–1860"; Bert Bradley and Jerry Tarver, "John Calhoun's Rhetorical Method in Defense of Slavery"; Owen Peterson, "Speaking in the Southern Commercial Conventions, 1837–1859"; Donald W. Zacharias, "The Know-Nothing Party and the Oratory of Nativism"; H. Hardy Perritt, "The Fire Eaters"; James Golden, "The Southern Unionists, 1850–1860."

Criticism and The New Rhetoric

In his *The Philosophy of Rhetoric*, published in 1936, I. A. Richards announced the coming of a "new rhetoric" to replace the "old rhetoric" that he said expired with Richard Whately. Coming largely from outside the field of speech and communication and interested in widely diverse types of discourse, the proponents of the new rhetoric seek to develop alternatives to classical or traditional rhetoric. In pursing their objectives they have been more active in advancing their theories than they have been in demonstrating how to apply their concepts to the evaluation of speeches. Among this group are Richard M. Weaver, Kenneth Burke, I. A. Richards, Edwin Black, and the General Semanticists.

Richard M. Weaver and the Rhetoric of Values. The most traditional and the most classical of advocates of an alternative frame of reference for traditional rhetoric was Richard M. Weaver, Professor of English of the University of Chicago. He would perhaps have objected to being thought of in any other way than that of a classicist. Weaver, an ardent conservative and devoted Platonic idealist,[58] explained his view of rhetoric as follows:

[57] Wrage. "Public Address: A Study in Social and Intellectual History," p. 456.
[58] Richard L. Johannesen. "Richard Weaver's View of Rhetoric and Criticism." *Southern Speech Journal*, 32:133–145 (Winter, 1966).

Rhetoric seen in the whole conspectus of its functions is an art of emphasis embodying an order of desire. Rhetoric is advisory; it has the office of advising men with reference to an independent order of goods and with reference to their particular situation as it relates to these. The honest rhetorician therefore has two things in mind: a vision of how matters should go ideally and ethically and a consideration of the special circumstances of his auditors. Toward both of these he has a responsibility.[59]

What Weaver points to is a "rhetoric of values," a "rhetoric of commitment," or what Eubanks and Baker call "an axiological rhetoric" by which to evaluate the speaker's purposes and practices. They explain their point of view as follows:

Keyed to master conceptions of the "desirable" in a democratic commonwealth rather than to the merely "desired," this rhetoric would stress the axiological more than the purely psychological, the cultural more than the merely personal, the moral more than the manipulative. Such a rhetoric . . . would vitally involve . . . the pursuit of humane wisdom without which modern man may hardly hope to stay the engines of nihilism. And under the aegis of such a rhetoric, the ancient art itself can be brought closer to the Platonic ideal echoed in one of Socrates' replies to Gorgias—the ideal of a rhetoric whose "propositions are always about justice." [60]

In similar vein Weaver declares "that a man's method of argument is a truer index of his belief than his explicit profession of principles" and "the type of argument a man chooses gives us the profoundest look we get at his principles of integration." How Weaver proposes to judge a speaker is reflected when he emphasizes that "rhetoric confronts us with chances involving values." He continues:

As rhetoric confronts us with choices involving values, the rhetorician is a preacher to us, noble if he tries to direct our passion toward noble ends and base if he uses our passion to confuse and degrade us. Since all utterance influences us in one or the other of these directions, it is important that the direction be the right one, and it is better if this lay preacher is a master of his art.[61]

Where does this view of rhetoric lead the critic? The central task of this kind of rhetorical criticism is to assess "the worth (or intrinsic excellence) of a speech" according to "the degree in which it inclines men and women away from the brutish state toward the civilized ideal of the educated and the free." [62] Drawing strength from Isocrates and Plato, Weaver proposes to judge whether a speaker is "noble" or "base."

[59] Richard M. Weaver. "Language Is Sermonic." In *Dimensions of Rhetorical Scholarship,* edited by Roger I. Nebergall. Norman, Department of Speech, University of Oklahoma, 1963, p. 54.

[60] *Quarterly Journal of Speech,* 48:168 (April, 1962).

[61] "Language Is Sermonic," p. 43.

[62] Virgil L. Baker and Ralph T. Eubanks. *Speech in Personal and Public Affairs.* New York, 1965, p. 90.

He *proposes to consider the speaker's morality.*[63] To reach his conclusions he concentrates upon motives, choice of premises, and kinds of argument.

In pursuit of these goals, Weaver proposes what he calls "a hierarchy of realities" or formal categories. In other words, he suggests a classification or index of argumentative methods by which a speaker "advises" his listeners.

Weaver says that "the highest order of appeal" is argument based upon genus or definition or the nature of things. This type of structure depends upon relations of proposition or premises and hence is close to dialectic in its method and appeal. In his essay entitled "Abraham Lincoln and the Argument from Definition," [64] he shows how the Illinoian argues from fixed premises.

Second in rank in Weaver's hierarchy is argument from relationship or similitude: "analogy, metaphor and figuration." He places this type second because he says "behind every analogy lurks the possibility of a general term or genus." But he observes "the user of analogy is hinting at an essence which cannot at the moment be produced."

Third and fourth on his scale are arguments from cause and effect and those from circumstance or "pure expediency." The latter is "a lower-order source of argument" he says "because it deals in the realm of the phenomenal [that] . . . is easily converted into the sensational. Sensational excitements always run the risk of arousing those excesses which we deplore as sentimentality or brutality." In an essay "Edmund Burke and the Argument from Circumstance," he discusses how the Englishman's "argument was dictated by circumstances." [65] Weaver believes that this type of argument finds its power "through a widely shared human weakness, which turns out on examination to be shortsightedness." At another time he says, "this argument amounts to a surrender of reason."

"Standing apart" from the other types is argument from testimony and authority. Unlike the first four types, which have a relationship to philosophy (dialectic), this last type utilizes "external sources." Weaver observes, "The sound maxim is that an argument based on authority is as good as the authority."

Weaver reveals himself and his criticism in his analysis of Edmund Burke.

The type which provides our access to Burke, is the argument from *circumstance*. The argument from circumstance is, as the name suggests, the nearest of all arguments to purest expediency. This argument merely reads the circumstances—the 'facts standing around'—and accepts them as coercive, or

---

[63] *Ibid.* Also see Johannesen, *op. cit.*, pp. 133–145.
[64] *The Ethics of Rhetoric.* Chicago, 1953, pp. 85–114.
[65] *Ibid.*, pp. 55–84.

allows them to dictate the decision. If one should say, 'The city must be surrendered because the besiegers are so numerous,' one would be arguing not from genus, or similitude, but from a present circumstance. The expression 'In view of the situation, what else are you going to do?' constitutes a sort of proposition-form for this type of argument. Such argument savors of urgency rather than of perspicacity; and it seems to be preferred by those who are easily impressed by existing tangibles. Whereas the argument from consequence attempts a forecast of results, the argument from circumstance attempts only an estimate of current conditions or pressures. By thus making present circumstance the overbearing consideration, it keeps from sight even the nexus of cause and effect. It is the least philosophical of all the sources of argument, since theoretically it stops at the level of perception of fact. . . .

We shall examine him . . . on another major subject to engage his statesmanship, the rebellion of the North American Colonies against Great Britain. By common admission today, Burke's masterpiece of forensic eloquence is the speech moving his resolutions for conciliation with that disaffected part of the Empire, delivered in the House of Commons on March 22, 1775. In admiring the felicities with which this great oration undoubtedly abounds, it is easy to overlook the fact that it is from beginning to end an argument from circumstance. It is not an argument about rights or definitions, as Burke explicitly says at two or three points; it is an argument about policy as dictated by circumstances. Its burden is a plea to conciliate the colonies because they are waxing great. No subtlety of interpretation is required to establish this truth, because we can substantially establish it in the express language of Burke himself.

To see the aspect of this argument, it is useful to begin by looking at the large alternatives which the orator enumerates for Parliament in the exigency. The first of these is to change the spirit of the Colonies by rendering it more submissive. Circumventing the theory of the relationship of ruler and ruled, Burke sets aside this alternative as impractical. He admits that an effort to bring about submission would be 'radical in its principle' (i.e., would have a root in principle); but he sees too many obstacles in geography, ethnology, and other circumstances to warrant the trial.

The second alternative is to prosecute the Colonists as criminal. At this point, the 'magnitude of the object' again enters his equation, and he would distinguish between the indictment of a single individual and the indictment of a whole people as things different in kind. The number and vigor of the Americans constitute an embarrassing circumstance. Therefore his thought issues in the oft-quoted statement 'I do not know the method of drawing up an indictment against a whole people.' This was said, it should be recalled, despite the fact that history is replete with proceedings against rebellious subjects. But Burke had been an agent for the colony of New York; he had studied the geography and history of the Colonies with his usual industry; and we may suppose him to have had a much clearer idea than his colleagues in Parliament of their power to support a conflict.

It is understandable, by this view, that his third alternative should be 'to comply with the American spirit as necessary.' He told his fellow Commoners plainly that his proposal had nothing to do with the legal right of taxation. 'My consideration is narrow, confined, and wholly limited to the policy of the question.' This policy he later characterizes as 'systematic indulgence.' The outcome of this disjunctive argument is then a measure to accommodate a circumstance. The circumstance is that America is a grow-

ing country, of awesome potentiality, whose strength, both actual and im-
minent, makes it advisable for the Mother Country to overlook abstract rights.
In a peroration, the topic of abstract rights is assigned to those 'vulgar and
mechanical politicians,' who are 'not fit to turn a wheel in the machine' of
Empire.

With this conclusion in mind, it will be instructive to see how the orator
prepared the way for his proposal. The entire first part of his discourse may
be described as a depiction of the circumstance which is to be his source of
argument. After a circumspect beginning, in which he calls attention to the
signs of rebellion and derides the notion of 'paper government,' he devotes
a long and brilliant passage to simple characterization of the Colonies and
their inhabitants. The unavoidable effect of this passage is to impress upon
his hearers the size and resources of this portion of the Empire. First he
takes up the rapidly growing population, then the extensive trade, then the
spirit of enterprise, and finally the personal character of the Colonists
themselves. . . .

The long recital is closed with an appeal which may be fitly regarded as
the *locus classicus* of the argument from circumstance. For with this impressive review of the fierce spirit of the colonists before his audience, Burke
declares: 'The question is, not whether the spirit deserves praise or blame,
but—what, in the name of God, shall we do with it?' The question then is
not what is right or wrong, or what accords with our idea of justice or our
scheme of duty; it is, how can we meet this circumstance? 'I am not determining a point of law; I am restoring tranquillity.' The circumstance becomes the cue of the policy. We must remind ourselves that our concern
here is not to pass upon the merits of a particular controversy, but to note
the term which Burke evidently considered most efficacious in moving his
hearers. 'Political reason,' he says, elsewhere, 'is a computing principle.'
Where does political reason in this instance leave him? It leaves him inevitably in the middle, keeping the Colonies, but not as taxable parts of the
Empire, allowing them to pay their own charge by voluntary grants. In
Burke's characteristic view, the theoretic relationship has been altered by
the medium until the thirteen (by his count fourteen) colonies of British
North America are left halfway between colonial and national status. The
position of the Tories meant that either the Colonies would be colonies or
they would terminate their relationship with the Empire. Burke's case was
that by concession to circumstance they could be retained in some form,
and this would be a victory for policy. Philosophers of starker principle,
like Tom Paine, held that a compromise of the Burkean type would have
been unacceptable in the long run even to the Americans, and the subsequent crystallization of American nationality seems to support this view.
But Burke thought he saw a way to preserve an institution by making way
for a large corporeal fact. . . .

In a brilliant passage on the American character, he had observed that
the Americans were in the habit of judging the pressure of a grievance by
the badness of the principle rather than *vice versa*. Burke's own habit, we
now see, was fairly consistently the reverse: he judged the badness of the
principle by the pressure of the grievance; and hence we are compelled to
suppose that he believed politics ought to be decided empirically and not
dialectically. Yet a consequence of this position is that whoever says he is
going to give equal consideration to circumstance and to ideals (or prin-

ciples) almost inevitably finds himself following circumstances while preserving a mere decorous respect for ideals.[66]

As we pointed out earlier, Weaver seeks to judge the speaker in terms of goodness and badness, how he reasons and orders his materials, and how he appeals to his listeners.

Kenneth Burke on Social Cohesion and the Perfect Society. One of the most prolific and the most discussed writers who has been associated with the phrase "the new rhetoric" is Kenneth Burke. Since his first book, *Counter-Statement*, published in 1931, he has stirred sufficient interest to be called "the most perceptive critic now writing in America." Marie Hochmuth Nichols declares him to be "essentially a classicist in his theory of rhetoric." In the introduction to *Rhetoric of Motives*, Burke declares his position by saying that "traditionally, the key term for rhetoric is . . . 'persuasion'." He suggests that his "treatment . . . is decidedly not meant as a substitute for the sound traditional approach . . . but an accessory to the standard lore." [67] Perhaps it is true that Burke's ideas are not "a counterpart of those of Aristotle, [but] a kind of counterpoint." [68]

Although he is a careful student of Aristotle, drawing freely upon the classics, Burke would turn criticism in a different direction from that which is more traditionally oriented. Instead of evaluating a persuasive effort in terms of method and effect, Burke argues somewhat like Weaver that the "ultimate end of the rhetorical critic is to promote social cohesion and to perfect society." [69] and that the central theme should be "peace and union." Daniel Fogarty observes that Burke has "dedicated his work to the fashioning of peace. His theory of rhetoric pervades all his work. It is directed toward the achievement of peace, as the highest end for which he could have been born." [70]

Broad in his view of the function and scope of rhetoric, Burke is interested in the spoken and written language, in poems, plays, novels, and all types of prose, including public address, but he does not make a point of his interest in rhetorical criticism. It is mainly through efforts of Marie Hochmuth Nichols and Virginia Holland, that his theories have been called to the attention of speech critics.

Seeing criticism as comprehensive and going beyond conventional patterns, he recommends a "dramatistic" division involving five elements:

---

[66] *Ibid.*, pp. 57, 62–65, 73.

[67] New York, 1963, p. x.

[68] Virginia Holland. *Counterpoint: Kenneth Burke and Aristotle's Theories of Rhetoric.* New York, 1959, p. 108.

[69] L. Virginia Holland. "Kenneth Burke's Dramatistic Approach in Speech Criticism." *Quarterly Journal of Speech*, 41:352 (December, 1955).

[70] Daniel Fogarty. *Roots of a New Rhetoric.* New York, 1959, pp. 56–57.

the act, the scene, the agent, the agency, and the purpose. Holland explains that this pentadic plan encompasses "five interrelated motivational or causal points of view."

The pentad considers the *Act* (that is, it names *what* took place in thought or deed), the *Scene* (the background of the Act, the situation in which it occurred), the *Agent* (the actor, or kind of person who performed the act), the *Agency* (what means or instruments he used), and the *Purpose* (motive or cause which lay behind a given act). In this pentadic approach man is an actor who *purposively acts* through certain *means* (symbolical or linguistic methods as well as physical), and he carries out his action against the backdrop of the historical *scene*—the time and place in which he lives.

If we were to use this dramatistic method in speech criticism, for example, we would ask ourselves, "What did the speech say (act)? Who was the speaker (actor)? What means, or symbolical linguistic devices did he use to accomplish his purpose (agency)? What was the speaker trying to accomplish through his speech (purpose)? What was the background or situation within which the speech was generated and given (scene)? [71]

Burke's terminology is difficult and at times abstruse and even confusing. In explaining his views of rhetoric and criticism, Burke uses three key terms: consubstantiality, identification, and strategies. By the first term, appropriated from Christian theology, he implies the state of being united in one common substance. Burke says, "A doctrine of *consubstantiality*, either explicit or implicit, may be necessary to any way of life. For substance, in the old philosophies, was an *act*; and a way of life is an *acting together*; and in acting together, men have common sensations, concepts, images, ideas, attitudes that make them *consubstantial*." [72]

The second term, *identification*, refers to the process by which the speaker (actor) attempts to achieve togetherness or consubstantiality. He says, "Two persons may be identified in terms of some principle they share in common, an 'identification' that does not deny their distinctness." The concept is not unlike what is sometimes called rapport or common ground. In other words speaker and listeners share "common sensations, concepts, images, ideas, and attitudes." He explains that pure identification implies agreement and unity between two persons or within the group and that the speaker should eliminate or overcome division and conflict through aligning his interests with those of his listeners.

Burke affirms the significance of *identification* as a key concept because men are at odds with one another, or because there is 'division.' 'Identification is compensatory to division. If men were not apart from one another, there would be no need for the rhetorician to proclaim their unity. If men were wholly and truly of one substance, absolute communication would be

---

[71] Holland. "Kenneth Burke's Dramatistic Approach . . . ," p. 353.
[72] Kenneth Burke. *A Rhetoric of Motives*. New York, 1953, p. 21.

of man's very essence.' 'In pure identification there would be no strife. Likewise, there would be no strife in absolute separateness, since opponents can join battle only through a mediatory ground that makes their communication possible, thus providing the first condition necessary for their interchange of blows. But put identification and division ambiguously together . . . and you have the characteristic invitation to rhetoric. Here is a major reason why rhetoric, according to Aristotle, 'proves opposites.' [73]

The third term, *strategies,* suggests the plan or method that the speaker (actor) follows to achieve his ends. It is in this phase that the Burkeian critic finds his principal task, studying "what took place in thought and deed" (the speech). Centermost in this type of analysis and interpretation is a scrutiny of symbolical or linguistic devices and language patterns. The critic asks how and what speaker's symbols reflect upon his thought patterns and purposes and even his ethics.

An example of what has been recognized as "the successful application" of Burkeian analysis of strategies is Virginia Holland's discussion of Wendell Phillips' "Murder of Lovejoy" address. We quote a brief excerpt:

The rhetorical critic is now confronted with the first problem: *How did the speaker say it,* in order to accomplish his objectives? Abandoning the traditional approach for a moment, the critic may apply Burke's technique and ask the question, *"What were Phillips' strategies?"*
The accurate naming of the strategies obviously depends upon a careful analysis of the speaker's language pattern to determine what words most realistically *name* the associative grouping of ideas which the speaker makes in his language . . .
The opening lines of the Lovejoy speech supply an example:
"We have met for the freest discussion of these resolutions, and the events which gave rise to them. I hope I shall be permitted to express my surprise at the sentiments of the last speaker,—surprise not only at such sentiments from such a man, but at the applause they have received within these walls. A comparison has been drawn between the events of the Revolution and the tragedy at Alton. We have heard it asserted here, in Faneuil Hall, that Great Britain had a right to tax the Colonies, and we have heard the mob at Alton, the drunken murderers of Lovejoy, compared to those patriot fathers who threw the tea overboard! Fellow citizens, is this Faneuil Hall doctrine?"
What are the words *doing* in his passage? In substance Phillips has said to the audience, 'You have heard a man who should know better expressing sentiments contradicting your ideas of justice and freedom. You have just heard him draw an ignoble comparison between the acts of your patriotic fathers and a mob of murderers, and you have accepted these base sentiments in Faneuil Hall, the Cradle of Liberty!' Is Phillips ridiculing the audience? admonishing it? rebuking it? What word names what the associated ideas in this paragraph are doing? Phillips is doing more than ridiculing or belittling the audience; he is not admonishing or warning it. He is sharply and

[73] Marie Hochmuth. "Kenneth Burke and the 'New Rhetoric'." *Quarterly Journal of Speech,* 38:137 (April, 1952), 137.

sternly reproving it for accepting the words of Austin. Consequently, the word which most nearly approximates the ideas culminating in the cry, 'is this Faneuil Hall doctrine,' is the word *rebuke*. Phillips' attitude of indignation may be said then to be activated in the strategy of rebuking. . . .

Continuing with strategies vindicating the acts of our forefathers and heaping absurdities on Austin, Phillips follows with emotional, patriotic words which may be comprehended within the *strategy of flagwaving*. He says:

"Sir, when I heard the gentleman lay down principles which place the murderers of Alton side by side with Otis and Hancock, with Quincy and Adams, I thought those pictured lips (pointing to the portraits in the hall) would have broken into voice to rebuke the recreant American,—the slanderer of the dead."

Then, vehemently denouncing Austin, Phillips uses the *strategy of invective:*

"The gentleman said that he should sink into insignificance if he dared to gainsay the principles of these resolutions. Sir, for the sentiments he has uttered, on soil consecrated by the prayers of Puritans and the blood of patriots, the earth should have yawned and swallowed him up." Defiantly refusing to take back these words when the audience roars its protest, Phillips swings into the second issue: were the Illinois rioters patriotically engaged in helping Missouri uphold her slave laws? He makes short work of Austin's assertion that they were, using the *strategy of absurdity* which is climaxed in the comparison:

"The Czar might as well claim to control the deliberation of Faneuil Hall, as the laws of Missouri demand reverence, or the shadow of obedience, from an inhabitant of Illinois."

Giving his attention to the third issue: did the northern agitator, Lovejoy, act presumptuously and imprudently and deserve to die for his interference, Phillips denies these charges with the *strategy of vindication*. This over-all strategy of reciting vindicating facts which set the audience straight and show that Lovejoy was not imprudent or presumptuous is shot through with numerous *strategies of invective, flagwaving, and prayer*. The last is illustrated by such a statement as:

"Shades of Hugh Peters and John Cotton, save us from such pulpits. . . ."
. . . . speech as a whole? Do the strategies add up to an overall, master strategy which would *name* Phillips' action in general? Phillips has rebuked the audience, pointed out absurdities in Austin's contentions, ridiculed his claims, vindicated Lovejoy's actions, prayed the country be saved from the encroachments upon liberty which Austin has favored, and waved the flag. Might not all these strategies be comprehended within the *name* exhortation? Phillips' master strategy, or overall style, then, may be designated as *exhortation*.[74]

Burke's analysis of Hitler's *Mein Kampf* is usually considered as representative of how he applies his concepts.[75] In opening his essay, he

---

[74] Virginia Holland. "Rhetorical Criticism: A Burkeian Method," *Quarterly Journal of Speech*, 39:446–448 (December, 1953).

[75] Kenneth Burke. "The Rhetoric of Hitler's 'Battle'." In *The Philosophy of Literary Form, Studies in Symbolic Action*. Baton Rouge, Louisiana, 1949, pp. 191–220. We are indebted to Professor Marie Hochmuth Nichols for calling this essay to our attention.

announces that his goal is to "try also to discover what kind of 'medicine' this medicine-man has concocted, that we may know, with greater accuracy, exactly what to guard against, if we are to forestall the concocting of similar medicine in America."

In this statement, Burke declares in favor of exhortation, a warning "to guard against" other medicine men. What follows is a description and analysis of Hitler's strategies—his "snakeoil"—to control the German people. Conversant with sociology, religion, psychology, and psychoanalysis as well as rhetoric, Burke points out how Hitler selected Munich as "a mecca" from which to launch his movement, focussed the hate of the Germans upon "international Jews" as "a common enemy" and a scapegoat, and took advantage of "sexual symbolism," characterizing "Germany in dispersion" as the "dehorned Siegfried" and suggesting that the masses were "feminine," eager for the leadership of a "dominating male" who would woo them away from the seducing rival—the villainous Jew. He traces how Hitler perfected his organization, silenced his opposition, used sales campaigns to promote politics like "soap," and intensified his persuasion by endless repetition, motive appeals to security and national pride and, of course, identification.

The flavor of Burke's criticism of *Mein Kampf* is strongly evident in his closing paragraphs:

As for the basic Nazi trick: the "curative" unification by a fictitious devil-function, gradually made convincing by the sloganizing repetitiousness of standard advertising techniques—the opposition must be as unweary in the attack upon it. . . .

Above all, I believe, we must make it apparent that Hitler appeals by relying upon a bastardization of fundamentally religious patterns of thought . . . And it is the corruptors of religion who are a major menace to the world today, in giving the profound patterns of religious thought a crude and sinister distortion.

Our job, then, our anti-Hitler battle, is to find all available ways of making the Hitlerite distortions of religion apparent, in order that politicians of his kind in America be unable to perform a similar swindle. The desire for unity is genuine and admirable. The desire for national unity, in the present state of the world, is genuine and admirable. But this unity, if attained on a deceptive basis, by emotional trickeries that shifts our criticism from the accurate locus of our trouble, is not unity at all. For, even if we are among those who happen to be "Aryans," we solve no problems even for ourselves by such solutions, since the factors pressing toward calamity remain. Thus, in Germany, after all the upheaval, we see nothing beyond a drive for ever more and more upheaval, precisely because the "new way of life" was no new way, but the dismally oldest way of sheer deception—hence, after all the 'change,' the factors driving toward unrest are left intact, and even strengthened. True, the Germans had the resentment of a lost war to increase their susceptibility to Hitler's rhetoric. But in a wider sense, it has repeatedly been observed, the whole world lost the War—and the accumulating ills of the capitalist order were but accelerated in their movements toward confusion. Hence, here too there are the resentments that go with frustration of men's ability to work and earn. At that point a certain kind of industrial or financial monopolist may, annoyed by the contrary voices of our parliament, wish for the momentary peace of one voice, amplified by social organizations, with all the others not merely quieted, but given the quietus. So he might, under Nazi promptings, be tempted to back a group of gangsters who, on becoming the political rulers of the state, would protect him against the necessary demands of the workers. His gangsters, then, would be his insurance against his workers. But who would be his insurance against his gangsters? [76]

Nichols summarizes Burke's application of his five-pronged approach to *Mein Kampf* as follows:

ACT—Bastardization of religious thought.
  AGENT—Hitler.
AGENCY—Unity identifications, such as "one voice," Reich, Munich, Army, German democracy, race, nation, Aryan heroism, etc. vs. Disunity identifications, such as images, ideas, etc., of parliamentary wrangle of the Habsburgs, Babel of opinion, Jewish cunning, together with spiritualization and materialization techniques.
PURPOSE—Unification of the German People.
  SCENE—Discordant elements in a culture weakened progressively by capitalistic materialism. [77]

The last paragraph of his analysis suggests that Kenneth Burke seeks a goal comparable to what Weaver recommended. He has described Hitler's "snake oil" to warn Americans to beware of others who employ similar magic. It is evident that Burke's analysis and views of rhetoric go "far beyond conventional pattern." Instead of confining his attention to measuring rhetorical method and speaker effectiveness, he describes, analyzes, and evaluates primarily *inventio* in order to bring about reform. He apparently agrees with Weaver that rhetoric is "sermonic." Objectivity is not his concern; he is more interested in exhortation.

In summary, Burke suggests that the speaker must gain control over his theme and its details, over the structure and thought as well as the emotional-imaginative appeals and proofs in order to minimize conflicts and cultivate areas of mutual satisfaction. In many respects Burke's process of establishing identification is markedly similar to the humanistic goals of classical rhetoric; but it also shares objectives similar to those of Weaver.

I. A. Richards. Literary critic, student of language, and teacher, I. A. Richards has written several significant works on rhetoric and communication, namely, *The Meaning of Meaning* (with C. K. Ogden), *The*

---

[76] *Ibid.*, pp. 200–221.
[77] Hochmuth. "Burkeian Criticism," p. 94.

Philosophy of Rhetoric (1936), and *The Principles of Literary Criticism* (1934). As an advocate of the "new rhetoric" he declares his chief concern to be "how words work in discourse," and "a study of misunderstanding and its remedies." [78] With Burke, he shares the desire to give rhetoric a wider scope, to make it more inclusive. But unlike Burke, he expresses openly his hostility for ancient rhetoric, particularly as it relates to persuasion. He believes that "persuasion is only one among the aims of discourse. It poaches on the others—especially on that of *exposition,* which is concerned to state a view, not to persuade people to agree or to do anything more than examine it."

Nichols observes that "Richards roundly condemns most of the theory and the practices of the past. 'From *Gorgias* onwards too much in the literature of rhetoric has been sales-talk and selling sales-talk; and for very good reasons we are more interested today in defensives against than in aids to eloquent persuasion.' " [79]

He has declared his method of inquiry to be "Platonic and dialectical rather than Aristotelian and organizational." Fogarty also finds "three additional differences" which characterize Richards' point of view. "(1) He uses the findings of modern biology and psychology to help him explain the functions of rhetorical language. (2) He regards metaphor as a central aspect of rhetoric. (3) He deals with rhetoric not only as speech but as part of the communication process, whether a person is speaking, listening, writing, or reading to achieve efficient comprehension." [80]

It is difficult to determine how Richards would evaluate a speech. He does not tell us and his most astute interpreters fail to go much beyond what he says. He does of course emphasize his interest in what ministers to understanding and how "to prevent misunderstanding" or as he says "how much and in how many ways . . . good communication [may] differ from bad" (*The Philosophy of Rhetoric,* p. 3). In pursuing what she figuratively refers to as "Alpine climbing," Nichols attempts to clarify Richards' position as follows:

He has argued that the function of rhetoric is to 'give insight into the different modes of speech and their exchanges and disguises.' Its chief concern is with such things as 'statement, full and explicit, or condensed (by abstractions, ambiguity or implication, the hint, the aposiopesis); statement literal or direct, and indirect (by metaphor, simile, comparison, parallel, etc.); suasion, open (from appeal to cajolery) or concealed (either as mere statement or as mere ornament) and so on.' [*Interpretation of Teaching,* pp. 14–15]. Rhet-

---

[78] I. A. Richards. *The Philosophy of Rhetoric.* New York, London, 1936, pp. 3–5.
[79] Marie Hochmuth Nichols. *Rhetoric and Criticism.* Baton Rouge, Louisiana, 1963, p. 97. Quotation from Richards, *Speculative Instruments,* p. 166.
[80] Fogarty, *op. cit.,* p. 97.

oric should be concerned with 'the fundamental laws of the use of language, not just a set of dodges . . .' [*Philosophy*, p. 7].[81]

The "new rhetoric" of Richards concerns "the differentiation of referential and emotive language function in order to produce understanding or to explain misunderstanding in any type of discourse. . . . It is concerned with the smallest structure units of discourse and not with the large scale ordonnance of arguments." [82]

One wonders whether Hermann G. Stelzner's essay on "'War Message,' December 8, 1941: An Approach to Language" [83] is not what Richards advocates as rhetorical criticism. Although Stelzner also shows that he has been markedly influenced by Kenneth Burke, in this essay the critic declares that "his posture . . . is microcosmic." He attempts to assess "the configuration of its language. . . . Interest centers on the order, movement, meaning, and interrelations of the language: the object is to discover not only what goes on but how it goes on. The aim is full discourse." What follows is a line-by-line, word-by-word explication of the speech. The flavor of the criticism can be sensed in this passage:

That a sense of and a sensitivity of history operates can be seen by testing alternatives: *Yesterday, a day which will live in infamy*. . . . Here the appositive is omitted, a possibility because it was unlikely that any member of the immediate audience would have been unaware of the date. History, however, catalogues dates, not yesterday or days; the date is supplied. Omitting the appositive also makes necessary the revision of 'a date which' to 'a day which'; the former is somewhat more precise and sustains better the historical overtones of the initial announcement. Thus, the first twelve words of Roosevelt's address join past and future; the present is represented by speaker and audience. And the immediate present—unsettled, disrupted, and anxiety-provoking—is somewhat stabilized by the past-future continuum which provides a sense of continuity. In the speaker's judgmental aside, the future renders a verdict on present activities which favors us; implicatively the future is on 'our side.' . . .
Time remains, central to the development. 'The United States was at peace'—past, 'still in conversation'—present, 'looking toward the maintenance'—future. The actors in the drama are polarized. Responding to a Japanese 'solicitation,' we were still concerned with tomorrow, even as they were not. The formal, diplomatic language symbolizes a mask behind which duplicity is hidden. The duplicity, one dimension of a key term, 'infamous' is woven into the texture of the address. For example, the close relationship of 'yesterday' to the repeated 'deliberately' intensifies and supports the duplicity or infamy.

[81] Nichols. *Rhetoric and Criticism*, p. 100.

[82] Marie Hochmuth Nichols. "I. A. Richards and the 'New Rhetoric'." *Quarterly Journal of Speech*, 44:10–11 (February, 1958).

[83] Hermann G. Stelzner. "'War Message,' December 8, 1941: An Approach to Language." *Speech Monographs*, 33:419–437 (November, 1966).

'Indeed,' injecting emphasis and force, begins the recitation and colors the neutrality of formal, diplomatic language. Not *yet, still, but* nor *however* would have functioned as well to introduce the formal, but false, overtures of the Japanese. 'Indeed' imprints a reaction of the individual 'I' on the yet-to-be-stated particulars. Moreover, 'indeed' gains force and support from the earlier 'yesterday,' 'infamy,' 'deliberately,' 'at peace,' 'still in conversation,' and 'maintenance of peace.' Following the expletive, the speaker says 'one hour after' not merely *after*. 'One hour after' makes time concrete, supports the emotional dimensions of 'indeed,' and forecasts the brazen, formal action of the Japanese Ambassador and the duplicity behind his formality. Also supporting duplicity is a subdued temporal pattern: after Japanese air squadrons attacked—past, the Ambassador delivers his reply—present, concerning *future* relationships.

'Japanese air squadrons' were the instruments of attack. The phrase might have been rendered: *after the Japanese air force or after Japanese air forces*. These alternatives parallel better the first reference to the Japanese military; but therein lies a weakness. The modified repetition provides some variety. More important is the matter of image. *Air force* and *air forces* denote and connote mass, a large quantity which blankets a sky. Such a mass moves, but in droning and lumbering fashion. 'Air squadrons' is a sharper, definable form of the force, as an image in the mind's eye. The image is of small groups, of well-defined patterns in the total mass, of tightly knit units sweeping in and out over the target.

'Air squadrons' is quantitative, definitive, and repetitive. To the extent that squadrons are patterns, the image presents formal patterns inflicting damage. Formal patterns are the enemy: of the past—'one hour after' as well as the near present—'The Japanese Ambassador . . . delivered.' The formality of pattern connoted by 'Japanese air squadrons' is also explicitly denoted of the Ambassador's act; he delivers a 'formal reply' which is contrasted to a slightly less formal 'American message.' Had the description been of an *American note*, it would have been overly informal. Slightly more formal and rigid than 'our Secretary of State' is 'the Japanese Ambassador.' If there is in these lines a heightened sense of the 'formal' and if formality marks the enemy, all formality becomes symbolic—a mask—for duplicity and infamy. The closed, distant, difficult-to-read 'formal' opposes the somewhat easier-to-read, open 'informality.' Such suggestion is consistent with the Western, especially American, stereotype of the Orient and Oriental, *circa* 1941. Duplicity masked by formality is thus further intensified. On first glance the construction of line 11 appears anticlimactic. 'War' is more encompassing and potentially more dangerous than 'armed attack.' However, 'war' connotes a formal, open declaration of conflict. The Japanese dispensed with that formality, favoring 'armed attack,' an action outside the conventions of diplomacy. . . .[84]

Like the General Semanticists, Richards is most concerned with communication—words, and meaning, with levels of abstraction, and the mingling of referential and emotive qualities. He objects to limiting rhetoric to persuasion, and he sees no point in giving consideration to anything but the canon of *elocutio*—how words work in discourse. He shares the concern of Weaver and Burke to reform the world. Unfor-

---

84 *Ibid.*, pp. 424, 425–426.

tunately, we must judge him only on his theorizing; he has not applied his theories specifically to evaluating the speech.

Edwin Black. One of the recent advocates of different orientation for rhetorical criticism is Edwin Black of the University of Wisconsin. In his book *Rhetorical Criticism* (1965) [85] he has analyzed what he calls neo-Aristotelian criticism, as exemplified in fifteen selected essays found in the three volumes of *A History and Criticism of American Public Address* and as developed by Wichelns, Thonssen and Baird, Parrish, and Nichols. He argues that these traditionally oriented critics and theorists have been handicapped because they have relied too much on Aristotle and have been too literal in interpreting the ancient seer. Like Weaver, Burke, and Richards, Black also hopes to broaden the purview of rhetoric. Hence he finds several faults with those whom he classifies as neo-Aristotelians. First, he argues that "rhetorical discourse" should not be limited to the spoken word or orations; it should include essays, dialogues, and perhaps almost all prose. Second, he suggests that it is untenable to confine judgment to immediate effects. Third, he feels that the so-called neo-Aristotelians have excluded, or have been unable to cope with, non-rational discourse and that discourse which is not persuasive in intent. In the course of his presentation he inserts critical comments: on John Jay Chapman's Coatesville Address, which is perhaps more an essay than a speech; on the Platonic dialogues; and on John Henry Newman's *Apologia pro Vita Sua*, which was a pamphlet answering an attack of Charles Kingsley.

As an answer to neo-Aristotelianism, Black proposes what he says is not "a system of rhetorical criticism but at best, an orientation to it" or "an alternative frame of reference." Instead of evaluating a single speech in terms of the response that it elicits, he proposes to focus upon the process of a given genre. The critic is to place each type along a hypothetical scale extending from didacticism to brainwashing. To locate a genre, the critic is to consider what Black calls "a rhetorical transaction" which involves a synthesis of "strategies [characteristics of a discourse], rhetorical situations [extra linguistic influences], and audience effects [response to strategies]." He explains that "since these three elements are intimately related and interact, a scale of one will perforce involve the other two." The goal of the critic is to explain; not evaluate, the interacting process. Although he does not make clear the final value of this approach, he seems to imply that each new instance of a given genre considered may be better understood through compari-

[85] Edwin Black. *Rhetorical Criticism: A Study in Method.* New York, The Macmillan Co., 1965.

son with the prevailing pattern. Black then illustrates his method by presenting an analysis of two types: exhortation and argumentation.

In his terminology and point of view, Black suggests that he shares many points of view with Kenneth Burke and other recent writers. But as he admits, he is a part of classical tradition; his "alternative frame of reference" seems to complement traditional criticism more than to serve as mutually exclusive methodology.

Criticism Through the Semantic Approach

During recent years, increasing attention has been devoted by critics and teachers to the problem of semantic analysis. Guided by the investigations of Alfred Korzybski, C. K. Ogden, I. A. Richards, and others, critics have approached the task of speech appraisal by asking: "What does this speech mean? Am I taking the speaker's words to mean what he intends them to convey?" Unlike the student who emphasizes primarily the literary values of the speech, the semanticist tries to find out whether the language reflects with fidelity the meaning that the speaker hopes to transmit. This is a challenging venture, requiring not only a thorough familiarity with the way language works, but also an unusual ability to interpret the meaning of words in context.

The critic whose interest is largely semantic will be on guard to detect ambiguities arising from the metaphorical use of language, from generalities growing out of statements that embrace broad areas of inquiry, and from such abstractions as "mankind," whose referents are indeterminate, if not indeterminable.

In his discussion of the semanticist's way of looking at a speech, Irving J. Lee lists a few of the procedures used by the critic in determining the meaning of discourse. Among the more important methods of fixing these areas of reference are: (1) the investigation of "the key terms in their setting and context as the ground of meaning"; (2) the analysis of metaphorical usage into what Richards calls its tenor and vehicle; (3) the listing of "modes of definition which were used in the speech and those which may be applied in further clarification and explanation"; (4) the attachment of "observed entities" to the abstractions or "fictions" in language; (5) the making of paraphrases, in the restricted vocabulary of Basic English, of the original materials used in the speech.[86]

In his *Language in Thought and Action*, S. I. Hayakawa stresses the

[86] Irving J. Lee. "Four Ways of Looking at a Speech." *Quarterly Journal of Speech*, 28:151 (April, 1942).

interdisciplinary elements of language as function and language as thought, and the goal of semantics as cooperation vs. conflict.

Semantics is the study of human interaction through communication. Communication leads sometimes to cooperation and sometimes to conflict. The basic ethical assumption of semantics, analogous to the medical assumption that health is preferable to illness, is that cooperation is preferable to conflict. This assumption, implicit in *Language in Action*, was made explicit as a central and unifying theme in *Language in Thought and Action*, an expansion of the earlier work, published in 1949. It remains the central theme of the present revised edition.

Insight into human symbolic behavior and into human interaction through symbolic mechanisms comes from all sorts of disciplines: not only from linguistics, philosophy, psychology, and cultural anthropology, but from attitude research and public opinion study, from new techniques in psychotherapy, from physiology and neurology, from mathematical biology and cybernetics. How are all these separate insights to be brought together and synthesized? This is a task which I cannot claim to have performed here, but I have examined the problem long enough to believe that it cannot be done without some set of broad and informing principles such as is to be found in the General Semantics of Korzybski.[87]

In the appendix to his popular book entitled *The Tyranny of Words*, Stuart Chase provides several examples of prose material which, when subjected to semantic analysis, fall a trifle short of being meaningful. As the criteria for evaluation, Chase suggests that the critic translate the passages into sense, keeping constantly in mind such points as clarifying high-order abstractions, the position and accessibility of referents, and the simple inquiry: "Does the speaker appear to know what he is saying?" [88]

In his *Power of Words*, Chase would do more than to correct the distortions of vocabulary, syntax, and other semantic problems. He would deal with the deeper implications of communication.

This study is not an attempt to remake good, human talk; it is an argument for a somewhat greater proportion of talk devoted to human survival. If we had to begin at the beginning it would be harder. Fortunately, as I have tried to show, a series of disciplines in communication have been clearing the way. Men of good will, I believe, should help with the clearing, for it may well mark the road along which the company must now go.

Perhaps the next great revolution, following the industrial, will be the revolution in communication.[89]

And Chase adds that his study "is a small contribution to that end."

[87] S. I. Hayakawa. *Language in Thought and Action*. London, George Allen and Unwin, Ltd., 2d ed., 1965. Preface, ix, x.

[88] Stuart Chase. *The Tyranny of Words*. Harcourt, Brace & Co., New York, 1938, p. 363.

[89] Stuart Chase. *The Power of Words*. Harcourt Brace & Co., New York, 1954, p. 292.

That the development of critical technique in semantic analysis will continue to contribute to the fuller understanding and more penetrating appraisal of speeches is generally acknowledged. But that it provides something distinctly new, something which has not heretofore been operative in the work of the critic, is open to serious question. Surely, previous investigations into the logical and emotional proof of speeches have dealt with the problems of meaning, of definition, and of contextual implication. Like the semanticists, the rhetoricians have been concerned with the vagaries of language and with the necessity of remarks making sense.

A FINAL OBSERVATION

How shall we view speech criticism? We are now in a position to draw some conclusions about these new approaches to public address.

First, the alternative frames of reference have sought to broaden criticism to include more than public address. Some seek to view all prose. Others would extend their range even into the sphere of the poetic to consider poetry and drama. This emphasis, of course, is not new; it has troubled rhetorical scholars since the seventeenth century and even before. In the eighteenth century Lord Kames and Hugh Blair argued in this same vein. During the nineteenth century Edward T. Channing and later Boylston Professors at Harvard University continued this trend. In 1925, Wichelns reversed the trend and directed our attention back to classically oriented speech criticism.

Second, in spite of differences in direction, many of the reformers have started with, and have depended heavily upon, classical sources. In some cases their ideas are little more than modifications of classical and post-classical theory. In many ways, they would redirect and extend rhetoric but they would not deny its ancient heritage. This observation is certainly true for the most part of Weaver, Burke, and Black. In direct contrast, Richards and the General Semanticists find pernicious the classical influence. In fact, the General Semanticists want to be known as non-Aristotelians because they feel that many of our problems arise from our dependence upon or misinterpretation of the ancient seer.

Third, the new critics have drawn freely from history, psychology, sociology, and literary criticism. They are wont to turn to allied disciplines for what they call new and provocative. At times they seem to lean more toward being historians, sociologists, psychologists, and even preachers than they do toward being speech critics.

Fourth, in addition to pursuing different methods, they seek goals different from traditionally oriented critics who seek to measure what they call artistic excellence. Weaver and the axiologists would develop the rhetorical criticism of commitment. Burke would promote identification and move human behavior toward peace and union, hoping to warn his readers against "the medicine man" and his "snake oil." Richards wants to show how misunderstanding results from language; Korzybski and his disciples seek to eliminate miscommunication and hence stimulate cooperation and rationality. Wrage and Griffin strive to correct or expand intellectual history.

Fifth, these diverse points of view have not produced in any case a sufficient body of published critical material to permit judgment on the basis of performance. They have theorized, but they have not applied their theories to any sizable amount of public address nor have they outlined a system or method in detail to be followed by others. In some cases the most stimulating insights into their theories and their application to public address have come from interpreters like Nichols, Holland, Johannesen and Eubanks. Hence, conclusions about the desirability of following any of these systems must wait until we have a greater body of critical material to judge them by.

The central objective of *speech* criticism should be the *speech* as it is used as a method of social control. Since the time of the ancient Greeks, rhetoric has concerned itself with *method,* that is, with how a speaker communicates with listeners, or in Donald Bryant's words, "the function of adjusting ideas to people and of people to ideas." There is much truth in G. W. Gray's observation that a "speech consists not of language and delivery but of delivered language." The confrontation between speaker and listener involves a dimension not found on the printed page and not found in other types of discourse.

Aristotle observed long ago that when one attempts to build up rhetoric "not as a faculty, but as an exact science," he will "inadvertently destroy its nature." The new critics often tread on or near this shaky ground. The classical canons of rhetoric still provide a feasible structure for understanding and evaluating a speech in progress.

EXERCISES

1. Prepare a paper on "Chauncey Goodrich as a Critic of the Oratory of Richard B. Sheridan" (or "of Thomas Erskine").
2. Prepare a paper on one of the following: (*a*) Albert J. Beveridge as a critic of Lincoln; (*b*) Claude M. Fuess as a critic of Webster; (*c*) V. L. Parrington as a critic of speakers.
3. Analyze the procedures for the criticism of oral discourse suggested by S. I. Hayakawa in his *Language in Thought and Action,* 2d ed. (New York, Harcourt, Brace and World, Inc., 1964).
4. Investigate the influence of John Dewey on the speech philosophy of teachers of public speaking.

5. Prepare a critique of an article in a recent number of the *Quarterly Journal of Speech* or *Speech Monographs* dealing with the criticism of a speaker or of the theory of public speaking.

6. Compare and contrast the critical method of Cicero with that of Goodrich; of Jebb; of Brigance (in his study of Jeremiah S. Black in the *History and Criticism of American Public Address,* ed. by William N. Brigance [New York: Russell & Russell, 1943], I, 459–482).

7. Comment on this remark by William Barron (*Lectures on Belles Lettres and Logic,* I, 452): "The best unpremeditated spoken language would make an indifferent figure when subjected to the eye of a nice reader."

8. Appraise the critical method employed by G. H. Francis in his essays on "Mr. Bright," "Lord Palmerston," and "Mr. Roebuck" in *Orators of the Age* (New York, Harper & Bros., 1847).

9. Prepare a comparative analysis of two contemporary speakers. Does the method of comparison and contrast enable you to delineate the speakers' characteristics more sharply than would be possible in an individual appraisal? Specify.

10. Compare and contrast the following appraisals of Jonathan Edwards: (1) in Charles Angoff's *Literary History of the American People* (New York, Knopf, 1931), I, 289–310; in (2) *History and Criticism of American Public Address,* ed. by William N. Brigance (New York, Russell & Russell, 1943), I, 213–235; and in (3) V. L. Parrington's *Main Currents in American Thought* (New York, Harcourt, Brace, 1927), I, 148–163.

11. In many critical estimates, attempts are made to trace the influence of certain persons or their writings upon great orators. For a perceptive analysis and refutation of an alleged influence, see William L. Finkel's 'Robert Ingersoll's Oratory and Walt Whitman's Poetry" (*Speech Monographs,* 16:41–56, August, 1949).

12. For some delightful observations on the methods and speaking accomplishments of certain English advocates, see Lord Birkett's *Six Great Advocates* (London, 1961). Assess Lord Birkett's conception of the role of the advocate in public life (pp. 97–110).

13. Examine Sir Isaiah Berlin's "Mr. Churchill" (*Atlantic,* 184:35–44, September, 1949). Do you find in this analysis that use is made of the critical yardstick to which we have referred in this book?

14. How would you differentiate between a review of a speech and a criticism of it? Are reviewing and reporting of speeches substantially the same? Cf. "News of Speeches and Meetings" in Mitchell V. Charnley's *Reporting,* 2nd ed. (New York, Holt, Rinehart and Winston, 1966).

15. Compare and contrast the approach in Edwin Black's rhetorical estimate of John Jay Chapman's "Coatesville Address" (*Rhetorical Criticism* [New York: The Macmillan Co., 1965], pp. 78–90) with any comparable study in the conventional manner in the *History and Criticism of American Public Address,* edited by William N. Brigance (New York: Russell & Russell, 1943).

16. Assess Carl Sandburg's skill in rhetorical criticism as revealed in his *Abraham Lincoln: The War Years* (New York: Harcourt Brace & Co., 1939) II, 452–477 and IV, 85–96.

17. Compare the approaches and methods used in two studies of Harry

Emerson Fosdick: Robert D. Clark's "Harry Emerson Fosdick" in *A History and Criticism of American Public Address*, III, pp. 411–458, and Roy C. McCall's "Harry Emerson Fosdick: A Study in Sources of Effectiveness" in *American Public Address*, edited by Loren Reid (Columbia: University of Missouri Press, 1961), pp. 59–71.

18. Examine Wilbur S. Howell's "John Locke and the New Rhetoric," (*Quarterly Journal of Speech*, 53:319–333 (December, 1967), with the view of determining Locke's place in the newer conceptions of rhetoric.

19. Examine the symposium on "The Influence of John Dewey upon Speech," *Western Speech*, 32:114–149 (Spring, 1968). In addition to an introductory statement by Robley Rhine, the symposium contains papers on "John Dewey and Rhetorical Theory" by Don M. Burks; "John Dewey and Speech Education" by Gladys L. Borchers; and "John Dewey and Discussion" by R. Victor Harnack.

READINGS

Bower Aly. "The History of American Public Address as a Research Field." *Quarterly Journal of Speech*, 29:308–314 (October, 1943).

Dorothy I. Anderson. "Edward T. Channing's Definition of Rhetoric." *Speech Monographs*, 14:18–92 (1947).

———. "Edward T. Channing's Teaching of Rhetoric." *Speech Monographs*, 16: 69–81 (August, 1949).

J. J. Auer. *The Rhetoric of Our Times*. New York, Appleton-Century-Crofts, 1969.

Carroll C. Arnold. "Goodrich Revisited." *Quarterly Journal of Speech*, 48:13–14 (February, 1962).

———. "Invention in the Parliamentary Speaking of Benjamin Disraeli, 1842–1852." *Speech Monographs*, 14:66–80 (1947).

———. "Rhetoric in America Since 1900." In *Re-establishing the Speech Profession*. Edited by Robert T. Oliver and Marvin G. Bauer. Speech Association of the Eastern States, 1959. Pp. 3–8.

J. Jeffery Auer, ed. *Antislavery and Disunion, 1858–1861: Studies in the Rhetoric of Compromise and Conflict*. New York, Harper and Row, 1963.

Jerald L. Banninga. "John Quincy Adams as a Contemporary Critic." *Central States Speech Journal*, 16:173–178 (August, 1965).

Barnet Baskerville. "The Dramatic Criticism of Oratory." *Quarterly Journal of Speech*, 45:39–45 (February, 1959).

———. "Emerson as a Critic of Oratory." *Southern Speech Journal*, 18:150–162 (March, 1953).

———. "Principal Themes of Nineteenth-Century Critics of Oratory." *Speech Monographs*, 19:11–26 (March, 1952).

———. "Selected Writings on the Criticism of Public Address." *Western Speech*, 21:110–118 (Spring, 1957).

———. "Some American Critics of Public Address, 1850–1900." *Speech Monographs*, 17:1–23 (March, 1950).

William A. Behl. "Theodore Roosevelt's Principles of Invention." *Speech Monographs*, 14:93–110 (1947).

Haig A. Bosmajian. "Rhetoric of Martin Luther King's Letter from Birmingham Jail." *The Midwest Quarterly*, 8:127–143 (Winter, 1967).

Edward Boyle. *Biographical Essays, 1790–1890*. London, Oxford University Press, 1936. "The Oratory of Victor Hugo," pp. 74–99.

Waldo W. Braden, ed. *Oratory in the Old South*. Baton Rouge, Louisiana State University Press, 1970.

William Norwood Brigance, ed. *History and Criticism of American Public Address*. New York, Russell & Russell, 1943. (Study the following specimens of contemporary rhetorical criticism: Wilbur S. Howell and Hoyt H. Hudson,

"Daniel Webster," vol. II, pp. 665–733; BRIGANCE, "Jeremiah S. Black," vol. I, pp. 459–482; KARL R. WALLACE, "Booker T. Washington," vol. I, pp. 407–433; CARROLL C. ARNOLD, "George W. Curtis," vol. III, pp. 133–174; and MARTIN MALONEY, "Clarence Darrow," vol. III, pp. 262–312.)

———. "The Twenty-Eight Foremost American Orators." *Quarterly Journal of Speech*, 24:376–380 (October, 1938).

DONALD C. BRYANT. "After Goodrich: New Responses in British Public Address— A Symposium." *Quarterly Journal of Speech*, 48:1 (February, 1962).

ROBERT D. CLARK. "Lesson from the Literary Critics." *Western Speech Journal*, 21: 83–89 (Spring, 1957).

ALBERT J. CROFT. "The Functions of Rhetorical Criticism." *Quarterly Journal of Speech*, 42:283–291 (October, 1956).

Demosthenes on the Crown. Edited by JAMES J. MURPHY. New York, Random House, 1967.

WALTER R. FISHER. "Method in Rhetorical Criticism." *Southern Speech Journal*, 35:101–109 (Winter, 1969).

J. FREDERICK DOERING. "David Hume on Oratory." *Quarterly Journal of Speech*, 25:409–416 (October, 1939).

RALPH T. EUBANKS and VIRGIL L. BAKER. "Toward an Axiology of Rhetoric." *Quarterly Journal of Speech*, 48:157–168 (April, 1962).

DANIEL FOGARTY. *Roots for a New Rhetoric*. New York, Teachers College, 1959.

WILBUR E. GILMAN. *Milton's Rhetoric: Studies in His Defense of Liberty*. *University of Missouri Studies*, 14:5–173 (July 1, 1939). "Areopagitica," pp. 9–44.

CHAUNCEY ALLEN GOODRICH. *Essays from Select British Eloquence*. Edited by A. CRAIG BAIRD. Carbondale, Illinois, Southern Illinois University Press, 1963. (See Introduction, pp. xv–xlviii).

———. *Select British Eloquence*. New York, Harper & Bros., 1852. (Examine the memoir of Lord Chatham, the historical introduction to the speech on the "Right of Taxing America," and the text of the speech.)

LAURENCE B. GOODRICH. "Chrysostom, 'King of Preachers.'" *Quarterly Journal of Speech*, 24:27–35 (February, 1938).

LELAND M. GRIFFIN. "The Rhetoric of Historical Movements." *Quarterly Journal of Speech*, 38:184–188 (April, 1952).

———. "The Rhetorical Structure of the 'New Left' Movement: Part I." *Quarterly Journal of Speech*, 50:113–135 (April, 1964).

WARREN GUTHRIE. "The Development of Rhetorical Theory in America." *Speech Monographs*, 13:14–22 (1946).

———. "The Development of Rhetorical Theory in America, 1635–1850." *Speech Monographs*, 14:38–54 (1947).

———. "Rhetorical Theory in Colonial America." In *A History of Speech Education in America: Background Studies*. Edited by KARL R. WALLACE. New York, Appleton-Century-Crofts, Inc., 1954. Pp. 48–59.

FREDERICK W. HABERMAN. "General MacArthur's Speech: A Symposium of Critical Comment." *Quarterly Journal of Speech*, 37:321–331 (October, 1951).

KENNETH G. HANCE. "The Elements of the Rhetorical Theory of Phillips Brooks." *Speech Monographs*, 5:16–39 (1938).

ANTHONY HILLBRUNER. "Creativity and Contemporary Criticism." *Western Speech Journal*, 24:5–11 (Winter, 1960).

MARIE HOCHMUTH. "Burkeian Criticism." *Western Speech Journal*, 21:89–95 (Spring, 1957).

———. "I. A. Richards and the 'New Rhetoric'." *Quarterly Journal of Speech*, 44: 1–16 (February, 1958).

———. "Kenneth Burke and the 'New Rhetoric'." *Quarterly Journal of Speech*, 38:133–144 (April, 1952).

L. VIRGINIA HOLLAND. "Kenneth Burke's Dramatistic Approach in Speech Criticism." *Quarterly Journal of Speech*, 41:352–358 (December, 1955).

———. "Rhetorical Criticism: A Burkeian Method." *Quarterly Journal of Speech*, 39:444–450 (December, 1953).

JOHN P. HOSHOR. "American Contributions to Rhetorical Theory and Homiletics." In *A History of Speech Education In America: Background Studies*. Edited by KARL R. WALLACE. New York, Appleton-Century-Crofts, Inc., 1954. Pp. 129–152.

———. "Lectures on Rhetoric and Public Speaking by Chauncey Allen Goodrich." *Speech Monographs*, 14:1–37 (1947).

EVERETT LEE HUNT. "Matthew Arnold: The Critic as Rhetorician." *Quarterly Journal of Speech*, 20:483–507 (November, 1934).

JOHN ILLO. "The Rhetoric of Malcolm X." *Columbia University Forum*, 9:5–12 (Spring, 1966).

RICHARD L. JOHANNESEN. "Richard Weaver's View of Rhetoric and Criticism." *Southern Speech Journal*, 32:133–145 (Winter, 1966).

C. HAROLD KING. "God's Dramatist." In *Studies in Speech and Drama in Honor of Alexander M. Drummond*. Ithaca, New York, Cornell University Press, 1944. Pp. 369–392. (An appraisal of George Whitefield's speaking.)

WILLIAM C. LANG. "Public Address As a Force in History." *Quarterly Journal of Speech*, 37:31–34 (February, 1951).

WILLIAM F. MITCHELL. *English Pulpit Oratory from Andrewes to Tillotson*. London, Society for the Promotion of Christian Knowledge, 1932.

RICHARD MURPHY. "Adlai Stevenson: Part I. Stevenson as Spokesman." *Today's Speech*, 8:3–5 (February, 1960).

———. "Adlai Stevenson: Part II. Stevenson and His Audience." *Today's Speech*, 8:12–14 (April, 1960).

THEODORE F. NELSON. "Charles Haddon Spurgeon's Theory and Practice of Preaching." *Quarterly Journal of Speech*, 32:173–181 (April, 1946).

MARIE HOCHMUTH NICHOLS. "George Bernard Shaw: Rhetorician and Public Speaker." In *Rhetoric and Criticism*. Baton Rouge, Louisiana State University Press, Pp. 109–129.

THOMAS R. NILSEN. "Criticism and Social Consequences." *Quarterly Journal of Speech*, 42:173–178 (April, 1956).

HELEN F. NORTH. "Rhetoric and Historiography." *Quarterly Journal of Speech*, 42: 234–242 (October, 1956).

HORACE G. RAHSKOPF. "The Oratory of James Wilson of Pennsylvania." *Speech Monographs*, 5:40–61 (1938).

W. CHARLES REDDING. "Extrinsic and Intrinsic Criticism." *Western Speech*, 21: 96–102 (Spring, 1957).

LOREN REID, ed. *American Public Address*. Columbia, Missouri, University of Missouri Press, 1961.

ROBERT L. SCOTT and DONALD K. SMITH. "The Rhetoric of Confrontation." *Quarterly Journal of Speech*, 55:1–8 (February, 1969).

MALCOLM O. SILLARS. "Rhetoric as Act." *Quarterly Journal of Speech*, 50:277–284 (October, 1964).

HERMANN G. STELZNER. "Speech Criticism by Journalists." *Southern Speech Journal*, 28:17–26 (Fall, 1962).

WAYNE N. THOMPSON. "Contemporary Public Address: A Problem in Criticism." *Quarterly Journal of Speech*, 40:24–30 (February, 1954).

KARL R. WALLACE. "On the Criticism of the MacArthur Speech." *Quarterly Journal of Speech*, 39:69–74 (February, 1953).

RICHARD M. WEAVER. "Language Is Sermonic." In *Dimensions of Rhetorical Scholarship*. ROGER E. NEBERGALL, ed. Norman, Oklahoma, Department of Speech, University of Oklahoma, 1963. Pp. 49–64.

EUGENE E. WHITE. "Solomon Stoddard's Theories of Persuasion." *Speech Monographs*, 29:235–259 (November, 1962).

JOHN F. WILSON. "Fifty Years of Rhetorical Criticism by Laymen." In *Re-establishing the Speech Profession*. Edited by ROBERT T. OLIVER and MARVIN G. BAUER. Speech Association of the Eastern States, 1959. Pp. 8–11.

ERNEST J. WRAGE. "E. L. Godkin and the Nation: Critics of Public Address." *Southern Speech Journal*, 15:100–111 (December, 1949).

IV

PRELIMINARY ASPECTS
OF RHETORICAL CRITICISM

8

Determining the Areas
of Investigation

DEFINING THE LIMITS

On first thought, any attempt to prescribe the legitimate areas within which critical functions shall operate may seem arbitrary, if not patently presumptuous. It seems to smatter of an attempt to reduce the critic's intellectual quest to rule, to fixed system. It reminds us of a remark by Thomas Carlyle:

> The Orator persuades and carries all with him, he knows not how; the Rhetorician can prove that he ought to have persuaded and carried all with him! the one is in a state of healthy unconsciousness, as if he 'had no system'; the other in virtue of regimen and dietetic punctuality, feels at best that 'his system is in high order.' [1]

Oftentimes it is so with the critic and the academician. The former does his work, achieves his end—perhaps without direct recourse to the rules governing the province of his expression; the other, mindful of the facts which academically control the field, appeals to system, to a pattern —which the critic may have followed, whether he willed it so or not. Accordingly, just claim can no doubt be made that criticism, like other products of the intellect, achieves rightness through a "certain spontaneity" or "unconsciousness," as Carlyle puts it. "The healthy know not of their health, but only the sick."

But it is possible, as well as useful, to consider the areas within which critical inquiries in rhetoric are peculiarly active and fruitful, without restricting the critics' efforts or circumscribing unduly the province with-

[1] Thomas Carlyle. *Critical and Miscellaneous Essays.* New York, 1876. III, 11.

305

in which their work will be most rewarding. Indicating the boundaries within which speech criticism has flourished in the past, and is now operating, can in no way be regarded as a curb upon free intellectual inquiry. Its only purpose is to outline the field—to find out where the critic may direct his investigations with expectation of success and with likelihood of increasing our understanding of speakers and speechmaking.

THE THREE PRINCIPAL AREAS

There are three main areas of inquiry in speech criticism. The first embraces the actual study of oratory and orators, all those studies that fall within the system of rhetorical art and practice. The second relates to descriptive, comparative, and critical investigations of rhetorical theory and criticism. The third involves quantitative studies of the elements of the rhetorical process, attempting to check under experimental conditions rhetorical concepts.

Study of Oratory and Orators

An examination of the literature on rhetorical criticism discloses that most scholars have confined their efforts to the first division. They have operated within the frameworks of the subject, seeking answers to problems closely associated with the theory and practice of speaking. Systematically considered, they have usually evaluated orators with reference to one or more, or a combination of all, the following concepts: (1) the nature of oratory; (2) the constituents of the speaking situation; (3) the offices or duties of the orator; (4) the types of oratory; (5) the traditional parts of the art of rhetoric; and (6) the effect of the oratory.

Criticism may thus be confined, as it unquestionably was in certain of Plato's works, to a philosophical determination of the role of speechcraft in a well organized society. Individual appraisals of the orators, in Plato's case, were virtual enforcements of the thesis that speech, without full knowledge and moral virtue in the speaker, may exercise a deleterious influence on society.

Other critical investigations have approached the evaluative function through a formal recognition and analysis of one or more of the constituents of the speech situation. Assuming the elements to be the speaker, the subject, the audience, and the occasion, critics have found it consistent with their creative intention to examine the orator as a man, the audiences he faced, the topics he developed, and the circumstances under which he appeared. Many investigators have used this pattern as the over-all plan for making their critical estimates.

Oratory and orators have also been viewed in the light of the objectives in audience response sought by the speaker. Thus an estimate of a speaker's merit might derive from his ability to teach, to conciliate, and to arouse.

The base for critical effort has sometimes been the type of oratory in which the speaker interested himself. Cicero, for instance, applied a certain yardstick of measurement to a forensic speaker's effectiveness, and another to the deliberative orator. Accordingly, the classification of oratory into deliberative, forensic, ceremonial, and possibly pulpit types serves as an end in criticism as well as in theory.

Much of the critical literature has developed from the use of the traditional five canons of rhetoric, i.e., invention, disposition, elocution, memory, and delivery. For example, a speaker's merit is investigated in the light of his skill at inventing arguments, or of clothing his ideas in appropriate language, or in a combination of all the elements.

Finally, critics seek to answer the questions—if they prepare comprehensive appraisals—"What was the immediate effect of this speech upon the audience? What was the long-range effect upon the flow of historical events?"

The foregoing subdivisions are, of course, interrelated, and the ideal criticism probably affords a balanced treatment of them all. But whether a critic evaluates only a speaker's invention in a selected group of speeches, or makes a penetrating analysis only of the audiences he faced, the studies are alike directed toward a common objective. Each one seeks the revelation of an orator as an effective agent in the presence of hearers.

This brief survey is not intended to oversimplify the problems of criticism. It serves only to point out how critical studies in oratory can, and in most cases do, operate within the framework of the art with which the critic is concerned. That is to say, the classifications and subdivisions of rhetoric furnish the patterns for many of the dissertations and essays in which the merits of orators are appraised.

Cicero was the first critic to make full use of these categories for critical purposes. A substantial part of his treatment of the Greek and Roman speakers is criticism by formula. He estimates orators' merits with reference to their accomplishments as men; their use of the kinds or types of oratory; their skill in invention, style, and the other parts of rhetoric; their relative talents for the ends of oratory (to teach, to please, and to arouse); and their conformity to the cultural patterns established for the ideal speaker. It is doubtful whether any critic of antiquity confined his efforts as severely within the framework of the art of speaking as did Cicero in the *Brutus,* in the *Orator,* and, to a lesser extent, in *De Oratore.*

An Outline of Studies in This Area. In order to illustrate the implications and ramifications of this broad area of critical inquiry, consider the following tabular analysis which indicates the various types of studies suggested by the divisions and classifications of the art of rhetoric and public address.

  I. The Nature of Public Address
    A. Oratory and politics
    B. The speaker's role in the social process
    C. Political and social conditions favoring the development of public address
    D. Values of public address
      1. Social
      2. Political
      3. Aesthetic
      4. Moral and ethical
      5. Intellectual
      6. Utilitarian
    E. Characteristics of public address of a group or section

 II. Constituents of the Speaking Situation
    A. The speaker
      1. Qualifications and experience
      2. Factors accounting for his skill
        a. Native ability
        b. Home influence
        c. Training
        d. General reading
        e. Early speaking experience
      3. Rhetorical philosophy
      4. Theory in relation to his practice in discourse
    B. The occasion
      1. Social setting of the speech: its place in the historical continuum
      2. Contributing events
      3. Its immediate nature
        a. Place
        b. Time
        c. Prevailing customs
    C. The audience
      1. Nature of the audience; its composition
        a. Immediate
        b. Greater: reading, radio, television
      2. Its relation to the subject
      3. Its relation to the speaker

    D. The subject
       1. Its relation to the audience
       2. Its relation to the occasion
       3. Its relation to the speaker

III. The Services of the Speaker
    A. The ends of discourse
       1. To instruct
       2. To stimulate or inspire
       3. To persuade
    B. The speaker's skill in each of the duties

IV. The Types of Speaking
    A. Classical divisions
       1. Deliberative
       2. Forensic
       3. Ceremonial or epideictic
       4. Pulpit
    B. Current types
       1. Legislative
       2. Judicial
       3. Business or professional
       4. Academic or educational
       5. Labor
       6. Dedicatory and commencement
       7. Pulpit
       8. Radio and television
       9. Dinner speaking
       10. Campaign

V. The Parts of Rhetoric and Public Address
    A. Invention
       1. Philosophical point of view
       2. The speaker's stock of ideas
       3. The basic premises of his thinking
       4. The "status" of his discourses
       5. His lines of arguments
       6. Form of inference and evidence
       7. Exposition
       8. Amplification
       9. Adaptation of his arguments to hearers and the occasion
    B. Speech structure (*disposition*)
       1. Conception of speech plan in general
       2. Specific parts of speech
          a. Introduction
          b. Proposition

      c. Discussion proper
      d. Conclusion
   3. Factor of organization
      a. Relevancy
      b. Selection
      c. Order
      d. Proportion
   4. Consistency with subject and purpose
   5. Adaptation to demands of listeners
      a. Logical
      b. Psychological

C. Style and language (*elocution*)
   1. Types of style
      a. Grand
      b. Middle
      c. Plain
   2. Qualities of style
      a. Correctness
      b. Clearness
      c. Appropriateness
      d. Embellishment
   3. Adaptation to demand of the audience and occasion
   4. Adaptation of canons of rhetoric

D. Memory
   1. Speaker's control of his materials
   2. Adaptation to type of speech
   3. Relation of memory to preparation
   4. Relation of memory to presentation
      a. Impromptu
      b. Extemporaneous
      c. Manuscript

E. Delivery
   1. Mode of presentation
      a. Extempore
      b. Reading
      c. Memorized
   2. Elements
      a. Bodily control
         (1) Gestures
         (2) Posture
         (3) Movement
      b. Voice
      c. Articulation and pronunciation

3. Type
   a. Conversational
   b. Oratorical

VI. Effect of Speech
   A. Immediate response
   B. Delayed response
   C. Long range or ultimate
   D. Special consequences

Speaker-Centered Investigation. Representative research in rhetorical criticism in the twentieth century has centered on the career of a given speaker, on some aspect of his communicative methods, on a comparison between his theories and practice or on his speaking methods and effectiveness as compared with those of other speakers.

Traditional criticism that concentrates on individual speakers in turn is amply illustrated in the three volumes of *A History and Criticism of American Public Address.* In the main the essays in this collection adhere to classical tradition of analyses and evaluation. They follow the five traditional canons of rhetoric, although the writers do not always use these ancient labels, and evaluate the speaking on the bases of immediate and long range effects. William Norwood Brigance, editor of volumes I and II, wisely explained:

> In the critical studies, as in the historical studies, the reader will find a wide diversity in patterns of treatment. To those who would prefer that one standardized pattern of rhetorical criticism be followed, we answer that it would have been neither possible nor, in our opinion, desirable. It would not have been possible because the best scholars are not all adherents of the same philosophy of criticism. Some prefer the pure Aristotelian pattern. Some prefer their Aristotelianism diluted. Others abjure it altogether. Among such vigorous dissenters no collation would have been possible.
>
> Nor do we think it would have been desirable. Uniformity in so large a number of studies would inevitably have led to sterility. The speakers to be appraised lived in different periods and labored in different fields, moved against different backgrounds of history, aimed at different goals, and were influenced by different currents. . . . The student of critical techniques will find as much interest perhaps, and possibly as much value, in the variety of techniques here used as in the subjects to which they are applied.[2]

A survey of recent publications indicates that imaginative critics have felt no restraint in attempting variations in point of view, types of speakers considered, organizations, and standards applied. This tendency toward diversity is evident in volume III of *A History and Criticism of American Public Address* (Longmans Green & Co., 1955) that appeared

[2] William Norwood Brigance, ed. *A History and Criticism of American Public Address.* New York, 1943. I, p. x.

twelve years after the first two volumes of the series. Said reviewer Everett L. Hunt, "the excellence of the volume . . . lies in its variety. . . . The editors . . . are to be congratulated on achieving an admirable balance of unity in variety." [3]

Few restraints need be placed upon the rhetorical critic in his view of a speech except of course he must not forget that he is evaluating a speech—which takes as its main concern "the avenue of communication" between speaker and his listeners.

The critic may concentrate upon the speaker's entire career, attempting to determine what part speechmaking contributed to the emergence of the personality and to his influence upon the stream of history. These studies, sometimes referred to as personality-centered studies, discuss such topics as the following: education, speech training, study habits, sources of philosophy and ideas, rhetorical theory, method of speech preparation, important periods in speaking career, major lines of thought, characteristics of important speeches, delivery and platform behavior, and effectiveness. Some book-length career studies include Bower Aly's *The Rhetoric of Alexander Hamilton* (New York: Columbia University Press, 1941), Dallas C. Dickey's *Seargent S. Prentiss, Whig Orator of the Old South* (Baton Rouge, Louisiana: Louisiana State University Press, 1945), Robert D. Clark's *The Life of Matthew Simpson* (New York: The Macmillan Co., 1956), and Franklin R. Shirley's *Zebulon Vance: Tarheel Spokesman* (Charlotte, North Carolina: McNally and Loftin, 1962).

Instead of attempting to evaluate an entire speaking career covering a lifetime and hundreds of appearances, the critic may limit his investigation of a man's oratory to a period, a phase, a line of thought or even a single characteristic such as invention, persuasive appeals, or language patterns. It is evident that several such studies in depth are needed to embrace an extensive career or to understand a complex issue. Some persons mistakenly believe that the traditionally oriented critics are bound to a particular organization or formula in studying orators and oratory. Present-day rhetorical research suggests that such is certainly not the case. The perceptive critic lets the characteristics of his speaker guide him in deciding how to approach his analysis. For example, the evaluation of a demagogue is quite different from studying Adlai Stevenson. The critic may give considerable attention to amplification and emotional appeals in evaluating a ceremonial speaker; he will find a different outline and emphasis necessary when he studies the lecturer or the informative speaker. In all cases his principal concern is to learn how the speaker attempted to move his listeners.

Another approach to rhetorical criticism is to study a given speaker's theory and practice. In this comparative approach the critic analyzes a

---

[3] *Quarterly Journal of Speech*, 42:188–189 (April, 1956).

speaker's pronouncements about rhetoric and then studies whether he consistently applied his theoretical tenets in his speeches. Some examples are the following:

Roy F. Hudson. "Richard Sibbes's Theory and Practice of Persuasion." *Quarterly Journal of Speech*, 44:137–148 (April, 1958).

Theodore F. Nelson. "Charles Haddon Spurgeon's Theory and Practice of Preaching." *Quarterly Journal of Speech*, 32:173–181 (April, 1946).

Wilson B. Paul. "John Witherspoon's Theory and Practice of Public Speaking." *Speech Monographs*, 16:272–289 (September, 1949).

Horace G. Rahskopf. "John Quincy Adams: Speaker and Rhetorician." *Quarterly Journal of Speech*, 32:435–441 (December, 1946).

Preferring an intensive analysis of a given aspect, several critics have made investigations like the following:

Carroll C. Arnold. "Invention in the Parliamentary Speaking of Benjamin Disraeli, 1842–1852." *Speech Monographs*, 14:66–80 (1947).

Carroll C. Arnold. "The Speech Style of Benjamin Disraeli." *Quarterly Journal of Speech*. 33:427–436 (December, 1947).

Earnest Brandenburg and Waldo W. Braden. "Franklin D. Roosevelt's Voice and Pronunciation." *Quarterly Journal of Speech*, 38:23–30 (February, 1952).

Theodore Clevenger, Jr. "Alben W. Barkley's Use of Humor in Public Speaking." *Western Speech*, 20:15–22 (Winter, 1956).

Laura Crowell. "Word Changes Introduced *Ad Libitum* in Five Speeches by Franklin Delano Roosevelt." *Speech Monographs*, 25:229–242 (November, 1958).

G. Jack Gravlee. "Franklin D. Roosevelt's Speech Preparation During His First National Campaign." *Speech Monographs*, 31:437–460 (November, 1964).

Robert N. Hall. "Lyndon Johnson's Speech Preparation." *Quarterly Journal of Speech*, 51:168–176 (April, 1965).

Robert D. Kully. "Rabbi Isaac Mayer Wise: His Language of Anti Anti-Semitism." *Quarterly Journal of Speech*, 50:166–178 (April, 1964).

Rollin W. Quimby. "How D. L. Moody Held Attention." *Quarterly Journal of Speech*, 43:278–283 (October, 1957).

George T. Tade. "The Anti-Texas Address: John Quincy Adams' Personal Filibuster." *Southern Speech Journal*, 30:185–198 (Spring, 1965).

The critic may choose to concentrate upon a single speech. Some typical examples follow:

Jerald L. Banninga. "John Quincy Adams' Address of July 4, 1821." *Quarterly Journal of Speech*, 53:44–49 (February, 1967).

Arthur A. Eisenstadt. "Daniel Webster and the Seventh of March."
Southern Speech Journal, 20:136–147 (Winter, 1954).

Wayne C. Eubank. "Benjamin Morgan Palmer's Lottery Speech, New
Orleans, 1891." *Southern Speech Journal,* 24:2–15 (Fall, 1958).

Walter R. Fisher. "Gladstone's Speech at Newcastle-on-Tyne."
Speech Monographs, 26:255–262 (November, 1959).

James H. Jackson, "Clarence Darrow's 'Plea in Defense of Himself'."
Western Speech, 20:185–195 (Fall, 1956).

Ronald F. Reid. "Edward Everett's 'The Character of Washington'."
Southern Speech Journal, 22:144–156 (Spring, 1957).

Ralph E. Richardson. "Adlai E. Stevenson, Hollywood Bowl, October 9, 1954." *Western Speech,* 19:137–174 (May, 1955).

Gordon L. Thomas. "John Brown's Courtroom Speech." *Quarterly
Journal of Speech,* 48:291–296 (October, 1962).

The critic may find it to his advantage to pursue a comparative study
of two speakers who have faced the same situation, dealt with a common
topic, or opposed each other in a single debate or a campaign. For
example, Robert Ray has discussed the Thomas Dewey–Harold Stassen
campaign in the Oregon presidential primary of 1948.[4] The Kennedy-
Nixon television debates in the 1960 presidential campaign resulted in
many such studies. Perhaps the best is a book-length symposium entitled *The Great Debates, Background, Perspective and Effect,* edited by
Sidney Kraus (Bloomington, Indiana: Indiana University Press, 1962).
Other studies of this type are the following:

J. Vernon Jensen. "The Rhetorical Strategy of Thomas H. Huxley and
Robert G. Ingersoll: Agnostics and Roadblock Removers." *Speech
Monographs,* 32:59–68 (March, 1965).

Charles J. Stewart. "The Pulpit in Time of Crisis: 1865 and 1963,"
Speech Monographs. 32:427–434 (November, 1965).

Larry A. Samovar. "Ambiguity and Unequivocation in the Kennedy-
Nixon Television Debates: A Rhetorical Analysis." *Western Speech*
29:211–218 (Fall, 1965).

The case study approach is exemplified in the twenty-three essays in
the volume *Antislavery and Disunion, Studies in Rhetoric of Compromise and Conflict,* edited by J. Jeffery Auer (Harper and Row, 1963).
In these studies the critics attempt "an intensive, even microscopic investigation made . . . *in situ,* of an individual case." [5] A *case* embraces
a single speech situation, considering the historical setting, the specific
issues, causes for discussion, the occasion, the physical circumstances, the
audience, the speaker, the speech, the immediate and long-range effects.

---

[4] Loren Reid, ed. *American Public Address, Studies in Honor of Albert Craig
Baird.* Columbia, Missouri, 1961, pp. 245–267.

[5] J. Jeffery Auer. *Introduction to Research in Speech.* New York, 1959, p. 120

Obviously this view of criticism overlaps with other orientations. Its advantage is of course that the investigator focuses intently upon a carefully defined speech or episode, striving to pull all of the elements into focus without fragmenting or over-classifying his finds.

The rhetorical critic is interested in all types of speakers and speeches. It is true that the earlier critics of the present century dealt with the famous personalities in politics, education, and religion. But in recent years speech critics have considered all types of speakers and speech situations. The quick and the dead, demagogue and statesman, campaigner and lecturer, deserve critical appraisals. Each one reflects upon his time, and each gives us further insight into public address. The following list is suggestive of the scope of present critical efforts:

> Benne B. Alder. "Sinclair Lewis: The Novelist Who 'Hated' Lecturing." *Quarterly Journal of Speech*, 51:276–285 (October, 1965).
>
> Ernest G. Bormann. "A Rhetorical Analysis of the National Radio Broadcasts of Senator Huey Pierce Long." *Speech Monographs*, 24:244–257 (November, 1957).
>
> Harold A. Brack. "Ernest Fremont Tittle: A Pulpit Critic of the American Social Order." *Quarterly Journal of Speech*, 52:364–370 (December, 1966).
>
> Bruce Markgraf. "John Cage: Ideas and Practices of a Contemporary Speaker." *Quarterly Journal of Speech*, 48:128–135 (April, 1962).
>
> Marie Hochmuth Nichols. "George Bernard Shaw: Rhetorician and Public Speaker." *Rhetoric and Criticism* (Baton Rouge, Louisiana: Louisiana State University Press, 1963), 109–129.
>
> Owen M. Peterson. "Aesthetic Apostle: The Southern Lecture Tour of Oscar Wilde." *Southern Speech Journal*, 26:100–108 (Winter, 1960).
>
> Ota Thomas Reynolds and Lester Thonssen. "The Reporter as Orator: Edward R. Murrow." *American Public Address* (Columbia, Missouri: University of Missouri Press, 1961), 313–331.
>
> Hermann G. Stelzner and Danio Bazo. "Oracle of the Tobacco Bench." *Southern Speech Journal*, 31:124–131 (Winter, 1965).
>
> Ernest C. Thompson, Jr. "A Case Study in Demagoguery: Henry Harmon Spalding." *Western Speech*, 30:225–232 (Fall, 1966).

Investigation of Rhetorical Theory and Criticism

The second area of study, drawing substantially upon the same scholarly resources, deals chiefly with research that is related to rhetorical theory and criticism, rather than with that which evaluates oratory and orators. Equally important to the total critical enterprise, it often serves as the substructure for criticism proper. Among the common contributions in this area are the commentaries, translations and editions, and bibliographies.

Investigation of the rhetorical writings and teachings of philosophers, theorists, educators, and practitioners provides valuable insight into rhetorical theory. In accomplishing this type of assignment, the critic examines his subject's occasional writings, letters, lecture notes, as well as his more formal presentations. Excellent examples of this type of contribution are Karl R. Wallace's *Francis Bacon on Communication and Rhetoric* (Chapel Hill: University of North Carolina Press, 1943), Walter J. Ong's *Ramus: Method, and the Decay of Dialogue* (Cambridge, Harvard University Press, 1958), Wilbur Samuel Howell's *Logic and Rhetoric in England, 1500–1700* (Princeton, New Jersey: Princeton University Press, 1956), L. Virginia Holland's *Counterpoint: Kenneth Burke and Aristotle's Theories of Rhetoric* (New York: Philosophical Library, 1959), and the *History of Speech Education in America, Background Studies,* edited by Karl R. Wallace (New York: Appleton-Century-Crofts, 1954).

Another type of study that falls under this heading is the translation of a rare text or the preparation for reproduction of a critical edition. The critic adds to his contribution by preparing a critical introduction providing context for future readers. Wilbur S. Howell translated from the French *Fénelon's Dialogues on Eloquence* (Princeton, New Jersey: Princeton University Press, 1951). Ray Nadeau prepared a translation of Hermogenes' *On Stases* [6] and Prentice A. Meador, Jr., made available "Minucian, *On Epicheiremes.*" [7]

Recently a number of significant rhetorical classics of the past has been made available through the offset process. Among these books are Chauncey Allen Goodrich's *Select British Eloquence* with a critical introduction by Bower Aly (Indianapolis: Bobbs-Merrill Co., Inc.), John Quincy Adams' *Lectures on Rhetoric and Oratory,* prepared by J. Jeffery Auer and Jerald L. Banninga (New York: Russell and Russell, 1962), and Thomas Wilson's *The Art of Rhetorique* (Gainesville, Florida: Scholars' Facsimiles & Reprints, 1962). The series *Landmarks in Rhetoric and Public Address,* published by Southern Illinois University Press under the editorship of David Potter, is at present undertaking a most extensive project in reissuing the classics. Already published are rhetorical works of Hugh Blair,[8] George Campbell,[9] Richard Whately,[10]

---

[6] Ray Nadeau. "Hermogenes' *On Stases:* A Translation with an Introduction and a Translation." *Speech Monographs,* 31:361–424 (November, 1964).

[7] Prentice A. Meador, Jr. "Minucian, *On Epicheiremes:* An Introduction and a Translation." *Speech Monographs,* 31:54–63 (March, 1964).

[8] *Lectures on Rhetoric and Belles Letters.* Edited by Harold F. Harding. Carbondale, Illinois, 1965. Two volumes.

[9] *The Philosophy of Rhetoric.* Edited by Lloyd F. Bitzer. Carbondale, Illinois, 1963.

[10] *Elements of Rhetoric.* Edited with a Critical Introduction by Douglas Ehninger. Carbondale, Illinois, 1963.

Chauncey Allen Goodrich,[11] Joseph Priestley,[12] and Gilbert Austin.[13] Many more are promised.

The student of rhetoric can contribute much through collecting, editing, and annotating fugitive materials, particularly speeches. The editor adds to understanding through a critical introduction, headnotes, and notations on the authenticity, literary and textual allusions, and explanatory notes. Two excellent examples are Bower Aly's *Alexander Hamilton: Selections Representing His Life, His Thought and His Style* (New York: The Liberal Arts Press, 1957), and Thomas A. Hopkins, *Rights for Americans: The Speeches of Robert F. Kennedy* (Indianapolis: Bobbs-Merrill Co., Inc., 1964).

Bibliography opens a challenging field of research in rhetoric. Carefully conducted investigations into some of the areas now inadequately covered would undoubtedly lighten the task of the critics, and eventually add luster and distinction to their criticisms.

Studies in bibliography might follow any one of several lines: (1) compilation of exhaustive listings of printed matter on a particular orator, or movement, or concept in rhetoric; [14] (2) preparation of annotated guides to the genuinely significant literature on a person or concept; (3) determination of textual authenticity of extant speeches; (4) the making of comparative analyses and collations of available texts; (5) preparation of wholly satisfactory editions of the work of the orators; and (6) investigations into the publication and sale of variant editions of great speeches and debates.

Quantitative Studies

The rhetorical critic, historically oriented, and the experimentalist in speech share many goals in common and have much to gain through cooperative effort. Each one is interested in rigidly testing the basic principles of the rhetoric. Our present rhetorical literature, starting with the

[11] *Essays from Select British Eloquence.* Edited with a Critical Introduction by A. Craig Baird. Carbondale, Illinois, 1963.

[12] *A Course of Lectures on Oratory and Criticism.* Edited by Vincent M. Bevilacqua and Richard Murphy. Carbondale, Illinois, 1965.

[13] *Chironomia or a Treatise on Rhetorical Delivery.* Edited with a Critical Introduction by Mary Margaret Robb and Lester Thonssen. Carbondale, Illinois, 1966.

[14] See Harry Caplan and Henry H. King. "Pulpit Eloquence: A List of Doctrinal and Historical Studies in English." *Speech Monographs,* 22:1–159 (Special Issue, 1955); "Pulpit Eloquence: A List of Doctrinal and Historical Studies in German. *Speech Monographs,* 23:1–106 (Special Issue, 1956); "French Tractates on Preaching: A Book List," *Quarterly Journal of Speech,* 36:296–325 (October, 1955); "Spanish Treatises on Preaching: A Book-List," *Speech Monographs,* 17:161–171 (June, 1950); "Scandinavian Treatises on Preaching: A Book-List." *Speech Monographs,* 21:1–9 (March, 1954); "Dutch Treatises on Preaching: A List of Books and Articles." *Speech Monographs,* 21:235–247 (November, 1954).

Greeks, has evolved through several centuries of practice, observation, analysis, selection, and critical reappraisal. Critics have continued to reexamine the expanding theory, commending what was sound and discarding what failed to meet the tests of newer critics and the findings in related fields. Important in this never ending process of updating is utilizing new methods and enriching the subject from other fields. For example, the influence of the faculty psychology of the eighteenth century on rhetorical concepts has given way to modern psychological concepts. The striving to develop a new rhetoric is another evidence of the continuing effort to update rhetorical concepts. In summary, the student of rhetoric, like the person in any art, continually faces a threefold task: to keep what is sound from the past, to feed into the subject newly acquired pertinent data coming from research and from related fields, and to synthesize the new with the old into a meaningful whole.

The experimentalist who has mastered the scientific approach, statistical concepts, and the manipulation of computers and other modern tools can test hypotheses and generalizations that have come down through centuries of successful practice. Previously the sifting and reevaluating have been through introspective and empirical methods; but now testing can be conducted under rigidly controlled conditions, and computations can be turned over to machines. Raymond G. Smith summarizes the partnership between critic and scientist as follows:

Thus the *corpus* or classical rhetoric combines a description of speechmaking with a body of hypotheses and generalizations induced from the evidence of some twenty-five centuries of successful practice. Familiarization with this accumulation of knowledge is a condition of sound experimental scholarship. The task of the experimentalist begins with a precise statement of one of the historical hypotheses, generalizations, or implications, and, in a carefully contrived and controlled situation, a rigorous testing of its validity by application of the scientific knowledge that experimental methodology provides.[15]

Experimental studies have considered such topics as the form of proof, types of organization, difference between oral and written style, the influence of the media upon the listeners, and types of delivery. Social scientists have shown considerable interest in communication and persuasion. Some examples of quantitative studies are the following:

David K. Berlo and Halbert E. Gulley. "Some Determinants of the Effect of Oral Communication in Producing Attitude Change and Learning." *Speech Monographs*, 24:10–20 (March, 1957).
Herbert W. Hildebrandt and Walter W. Stevens. "Manuscript and

---

[15] "Rhetoric, Experimental Research, and Men of Good Will." *Southern Speech Journal*, 30:10 (Fall, 1964).

Extemporaneous Delivery in Communicating Information." *Speech Monographs*, 30:369–372 (November, 1963).

Thomas R. King. "An Experimental Study of the Effect of *Ethos* Upon the Immediate and Delayed Recall of Information." *Central States Speech Journal*, 17:22–28 (February, 1966).

Thomas S. Ludlum. "Effect of Certain Techniques of Credibility Upon Audience Attitudes." *Speech Monographs*, 25:278–284 (November, 1958).

Stanley F. Paulson. "The Effects of the Prestige of the Speaker and Acknowledgment of Opposing Argument on Audience Retention and Shift of Opinion." *Speech Monographs*, 21:267–271 (November, 1954).

Randall C. Ruechelle. "An Experimental Study of Audience Recognition of Emotional and Intellectual Appeal in Persuasion." *Speech Monographs*, 25:49–58 (March, 1958).

Gordon L. Thomas and David C. Ralph. "A Study of the Effect of Audience Proximity on Persuasion." *Speech Monographs*, 26:300–307 (November, 1959).

Ernest Thompson. "An Experimental Investigation of the Relative Effectiveness of Organizational Structure in Oral Communication." *Southern Speech Journal*, 26:59–69 (Fall, 1960).

Phillip K. Tompkins and Larry R. Samovar. "An Experimental Study of the Effects of Credibility on the Comprehension of Content." *Speech Monographs*, 31:120–123 (June, 1964).

SUMMARY

Critical inquiry into rhetoric does not differ fundamentally from similar intellectual quests in other fields. It flourishes in the atmosphere of free, spontaneous effort; and, while not defiant of rule, it does not necessarily function by formula. However, the very nature of a specific investigation—as into the qualities of a public address—requires that the critic conceive his undertaking within a certain frame of reference. A speech is always a *speech*, and never a chemical formula. Hence, it can be evaluated only through proper recognition of the field within which speeches, rather than chemical formulae, function. To this extent, if no more, areas of investigation into rhetorical criticism can be delimited. These areas are chiefly the ones which fall within the framework of rhetorical theory and practice, *per se*, and the ones which lie within the province of intellectual aims related to, or forming the substructure of, the field of rhetoric.

We have described some of the areas within which critical analysis of rhetoric is particularly fruitful. These are surely not the only ones, and we have no desire to leave that impression. The ingenuity and vision of discerning critics will carry the projects far beyond the lines indicated by this chapter. The nature of speechcraft, however, makes the areas to which we refer useful points of orientation.

EXERCISES

1. Analyze in some detail the subtopics to be treated in the investigation of one of the following constituents of the speaking situation: (*a*) the speaker's theory of discourse; (*b*) factors accounting for the skill of the speaker; (*c*) nature of the audience; (*d*) the deliberative type of speaking; (*e*) the speaker's ideas.
2. Draft a list of rhetorical studies, completed since 1930, on Winston Churchill, Franklin D. Roosevelt, and Adlai Stevenson. Classify your bibliographical items according to the apparent areas of rhetorical inquiry covered by the studies; suggest further fields of investigation of any of these speakers.
3. Make a careful investigation of the available resources for the study of public address of your section. Look into the holdings of the local, city, and state libraries. Is there a depository of manuscripts available? Does it possess private papers containing speech manuscripts?
4. What speakers of your state, past and present, have been studied? Find out whether the studies were historical or rhetorical. Consult the bibliographies listed under Readings.
5. Prepare a list of the outstanding contemporary speakers. Organize your list under six headings: political, religious, cultural, educational, business, and labor. What evidence can you find to support your choices? (For example, see "Great Preachers," *Life*, April 6, 1953, pp. 127–153. See back issues of *Speaker and Gavel*, May issue for "Speaker-of-the-Year" awards. Also see annual volume of *Representative American Speeches*.)

CLASS PROJECT IN RHETORICAL CRITICISM

The present assignment is an introduction to a series which will continue throughout the remainder of the term. An additional one will be included at the end of each chapter. Each member of the class is to select a different contemporary (living) speaker for concentrated study. Since you are going to complete ten or more different projects involving this figure, you should exercise care to find someone who is challenging and worthy of concentrated study. In making your selection consider the following aspects:

(1) The significance of the man: you may choose a local, state, regional or national figure, provided he has demonstrated his influence as a speaker.
(2) The availability of background information about the speaker, his speeches, and the occasions. Consult several periodical indexes as well as *Current Biography* and the *Biography Index*.
(3) A speaker known to have prepared his own speeches.
(4) *The availability of speech texts:* you should have a minimum of five or six complete speeches, and more if possible. Your task will be easier if you can find speeches concentrated on a common theme

within a comparatively limited period. Consult *Vital Speeches, Congressional Record, The New York Times,* and *Representative American Speeches.*

Your First Class Assignment

Prepare a seven- to ten-minute oral report, justifying your choice. Be sure to include a summary of available materials.

READINGS

BOWER ALY. "The History of American Public Address as a Research Field." *Quarterly Journal of Speech,* 29:308–314 (October, 1943).

"Articles in American Studies." *American Quarterly,* 1959 to date (Summer Issue). (This interdisciplinary bibliography has section on public address which lists articles on American speakers found in historical journals as well as speech journals.)

J. JEFFERY AUER. "American Public Address and American Studies: A Bibliography." *American Quarterly,* 9:217–222 (Summer, 1957).

————. *An Introduction to Research in Speech.* New York, Harper & Bros., 1959.

A. CRAIG BAIRD. "Opportunities for Research in State and Sectional Public Speaking." *Quarterly Journal of Speech,* 29:304–308 (October, 1943).

WALDO W. BRADEN. "The Concept of Southern Oratory: A Selected Bibliography." *Southern Speech Journal,* 29:141–145 (Winter, 1963).

————. "Research: Methods, Trends, Ideas." In *The Communicative Arts and Sciences of Speech,* KEITH BROOKS, ed. Columbus, Ohio, Charles E. Merrill Books, Inc., 1967. Pp. 66–95.

JAMES W. CLEARY and FREDERICK W. HABERMAN. *Rhetoric and Public Address, A Bibliography 1947–1961.* Madison, University of Wisconsin Press, 1964.

DALLAS C. DICKEY. "Southern Oratory: A Field for Research." *Quarterly Journal of Speech,* 33:458–463 (December, 1947).

————. "What Directions Should Future Research in American Public Address Take?" *Quarterly Journal of Speech,* 29:300–304 (October, 1943).

"The Historical Backgrounds of American Public Address." In *History and Criticism of American Public Address.* Edited by W. NORWOOD BRIGANCE. New York, Russell & Russell, 1943. GEORGE V. BOHMAN, "The Colonial Period," pp. 3–54; BOWER ALY and GRAFTON P. TANQUARY, "The Early National Period," pp. 55–110; KENNETH G. HANCE, HOMER O. HENDRICKSON, and EDWIN W. SCHOENBERGER, "The Later National Period," pp. 111–152; DORIS G. YOAKAM, "Women's Introduction to the American Platform," pp. 153–192; OTA THOMAS, "The Teaching of Rhetoric in the United States During the Classical Period of Education," pp. 193–210.

HOYT H. HUDSON. "The Field of Rhetoric." *Quarterly Journal of Speech Education,* 9:167–180 (April, 1923).

FRANKLIN H. KNOWER. "Graduate Theses—An Index to Graduate Work in the Field of Speech." *Speech Monographs,* 1935 to date. (Excellent source from which to get an over-all view of the research undertaken in the larger graduate departments of Speech.)

ARTHUR N. KRUGER. *A Classified Bibliography of Argumentation and Debate.* New York, The Scarecrow Press, Inc., 1964.

JOSEPH F. O'BRIEN. "A Re-examination of State and Local Oratory as a Field for Study." *Quarterly Journal of Speech,* 37:71–76 (February, 1951).

DOROTHY B. PORTER. "Early American Negro Writings: A Bibliographical Study." *Papers of the Bibliographical Society of America,* 31:192–268 (Third Quarter, 1945). (Observe how prominently oratory and sermonizing figure in the study.

Further research on the nature of the speechmaking in early Negro expression should be rewarding.)

JOSEPH SCHWARTZ and JOHN A. RYCENGA, eds. *The Province of Rhetoric.* New York, The Ronald Press Company, 1965.

WAYNE N. THOMPSON. "Contemporary Public Address as a Research Area." *Quarterly Journal of Speech,* 33:274–283 (October, 1947).

LESTER THONSSEN, ELIZABETH FATHERSON, and DOROTHEA THONSSEN. *Bibliography of Speech Education.* New York, The H. W. Wilson Co., 1939.

LESTER THONSSEN, MARY MARGARET ROBB, and DOROTHEA THONSSEN. *Bibliography of Speech Education. Supplement 1939–1948.* New York, The H. W. Wilson Co., 1950.

EARL W. WILEY. "State History and Rhetorical Research." *Quarterly Journal of Speech,* 36:514–519 (December, 1950).

ERNEST J. WRAGE. "Public Address: A Study in Social and Intellectual History." *Quarterly Journal of Speech,* 33:451–457 (December, 1947).

WARREN E. WRIGHT. "Judicial Rhetoric: A Field for Research." *Speech Monographs,* 31:64–72 (March, 1964).

9

Establishing the
Authenticity of Texts

THE DIFFICULTY IN GETTING RELIABLE SPEECH TEXTS

In the fifth century B.C., Thucydides introduced a new spirit into historical scholarship. Thoroughly opposed to myth-making and stylistic flourishes, the Greek historian sought to make his presentation both accurate and interesting; consequently into his *History of the Peloponnesian War* he incorporated forty-one speeches. He let the important men reveal "their characters and personalities . . . by their actions and speeches." But in the interest of objectivity, he disarmingly reports:

As to the speeches which were made either before or during the war, it was hard for me, and for others who reported them to me, to recollect the exact words. I have therefore put into the mouth of each speaker the sentiments proper to the occasion, expressed as I thought he would be likely to express them, while at the same time I endeavored, as nearly as I could, to give the general purport of what was actually said.[1]

By putting words "into the mouth of each speaker," the historian found an exciting device to reveal thoughts and feelings. But from the point of view of the rhetorical critic, what he has left is an enigma. Of course, the critic may evaluate the historian as a speech writer, but he can never make judgments about those speakers who at dramatic moments stood before the populace to offer advice. Such is the fate of many speakers whose actual words have come down through the reports of others.

From antiquity to the present day, critics have concerned themselves with establishing the accuracy of the texts upon which their analyses

[1] Benjamin Jowett, ed. *Thucydides.* Two volumes. Oxford, 1881. I, p. 15 (Bb. I:22).

323

rest. Always a difficult problem, textual criticism becomes, in some instances, as challenging an aspect of the critic's work as the making of the final estimate of the speaker's merit. The distinction between purely literary and rhetorical criticism may be traced in part to the variable nature of speech texts. Thus, in his analysis of Daniel Webster, Henry Cabot Lodge observes that the nature of the oral material, *per se*, renders difficult the establishment of any man's claim to literary fame upon speeches alone. C. W. Previté-Orton points to the advantages which the pamphlet, for instance, holds over the speech, since evaluation of the latter requires reconstruction of social settings and the use of texts which are often incomplete, if not actually unlike the original.

It would be folly to contest the force of these arguments. Unquestionably, it is difficult to get completely satisfactory texts of speeches. While true today when our facilities for getting authentic records are fairly good, this indictment has even greater cogency and pertinence when we turn to the speech texts of a century or more ago.

Alan E. Herr's comments on the problem of getting texts of Elizabethan sermons illustrate the nature of the difficulty faced by critics of later speakers. Observing that the sermons were not written in full, Herr shows how widely the final texts often departed from the original. Oftentimes the preacher composed the finished sermon after its original delivery; and the printer revised the copy to make it a more fit piece for publication. Referring to a certain John Manningham, whose penchant for taking sermon notes was evidently noteworthy, Herr reports:

> When Dr. King, afterwards Bishop of London, preached at Paul's Cross, Manningham took notes that fill nine printed pages. He begins by analysing the structure of the sermon and then notes concisely every point that Dr. King made. Any person with any imagination could expand these nine pages to twenty, which was the average length of a sermon, and publish Dr. King's sermon; with no notice to the contrary, one would accept it as a true copy.[2]

We may infer from this statement that the possibility of our being deceived on textual matters approaches the realm of the probable.

The speeches of Chatham, Burke, Fox, Sheridan, Pitt the Younger, Erskine, and others have been pieced together from imperfect newspaper reports, often greatly condensed, and pamphlets, often prepared after the fact. When reporters had an opportunity to attempt verbatim reporting they worked under difficult conditions, and of course the shorthand they attempted was clumsy and inaccurate. They did not hesitate to brighten a passage with their own words. David V. Erdman concludes:

> The simple rules of textual analysis, applied to the collation of newspaper reports of parliamentary debates, can sift out a small but sometimes significant

[2] Quoted from Alan F. Herr. *The Elizabethan Sermon*. Philadelphia, 1940, p. 78.

sprinkling of the more salient expressions of the original speakers, separating these from the common matrix of reportorial clichés on the one hand and the occasional creative substitutions of a literary reporter on the other. . . .

The student of living oratory, however, must despair of recovering in anything like high fidelity the authentic texture and structure of the curious high finish of Pitt, let alone the true eloquence of Fox. Certainly in the newspaper compendiums—and therefore in most of the texts that fill the volumes of collected parliamentary speeches—the authentic voice that survives is not that of the speaker but that of one or many ventriloquist reporters, Debrett's choice not always being of the soundest.[3]

Says Chauncey Goodrich of the texts of Chatham's speeches:

The style and language of Lord Chatham are not to be judged of by the early speeches in this volume, down to 1743. Reporters at that day made little or no attempt to give the exact words of a speaker. They sought only to convey his sentiments, though they might occasionally be led, in writing out his speeches, to catch some of his marked peculiarities of thought or expression. In 1766, his speech against the American Stamp Act was reported, with a considerable degree of verbal accuracy, by Sir Robert Dean, aided by Lord Charlemont. Much, however, was obviously omitted; and passages having an admirable felicity of expression were strangely intermingled with tame and broken sentences showing how imperfectly they had succeeded in giving the precise language of the speaker. Five speeches . . . were written out, from notes taken on the spot by Sir Philip Francis and Mr. Hugh Boyd. One of them is said to have been revised by Lord Chatham himself.[4]

So we must deal with these texts in the full knowledge that they leave something to be desired in authenticity.

In deliberative assemblies, we would expect the recording of speech texts to be fairly accurate. But this is not necessarily true. Reporters of speeches were not provided space in the House of Commons until 1834. Commenting on the inaccuracy of reporting during Chatham's time, and also upon the fact that orators were freer "to let themselves go" when there were no reporters in the House to set down what they said, Lord Curzon concludes that the contemporary speaker's reluctance to "frisk and frolic in the flowery meads of rhetoric" results from the current omnipresence of reporters. As Lord Rosebery once remarked epigrammatically, "eloquence and stenography are not of congenial growth."

The experience of the early reporters of English eloquence emphasizes the foregoing remarks. And it must be remembered that the role of the reporter is of considerable consequence in the history of oratory. Frederic Hudson called the reporter "the amanuensis of the public. Through him statesmen speak to the people; through him Congress [or Parliament] is heard; through him orators become celebrated." [5] In 1731, Edward Cave

[3] David V. Erdman. "Coleridge in Lilliput: The Quality of Parliamentary Reporting in 1800." *Speech Monographs*, 27:61–62 (March, 1960).

[4] *Select British Eloquence.* New York, 1853, p. 75.

[5] *Journalism in the United States, from 1690 to 1872.* New York, 1872, p. 720.

hit upon the idea of distributing reports of the parliamentary debates. Accordingly, he established the *Gentleman's Magazine* as the medium through which to publicize the talks of the members. The practice of giving circulation to the speakers' remarks met with strong opposition, however, and in 1738 the House resolved it an indignity to publish reports of the debates. It affirmed that it would "proceed with the utmost severity against such offenders." Cave got around these provisions, however, by giving the speakers fictitious names, or by referring to the proceedings as the "Debates in the Senate of Magna Lilliputia." He managed to get into the House secretly, took such notes as he could without being apprehended, and then retired to a tavern, there to compare copies with his accomplices and friends. Eventually William Guthrie or Samuel Johnson prepared the draft for *Gentleman's Magazine*. Guthrie did many of the parliamentary debates for Cave's publication between 1735 and 1740; and Samuel Johnson continued the work between 1740 and 1743.

Clearly, these reports were not historically accurate, despite their literary graces. Cave himself admitted their shortcomings. Alluding to the danger of publishing parliamentary debates, he hoped the reader would conceive "that it is impossible to do it in the very words of the Speakers. With regard to the major part, we pretend only to represent the sense, as near as may be expected in a summary way. . . ." [6]

That Samuel Johnson wrote speeches of high quality, no one will deny. Arthur Murphy reports a meeting in 1741 attended by several distinguished men, including Dr. Francis and Johnson, at which Francis spoke glowingly of Pitt's rhetorical skill as evidenced in the reply to Walpole. Whereupon Johnson remarked: "I wrote it in Exeter Street." Much surprised by this remark Francis said: "You have exceeded Demosthenes himself. . . ." [7] Another biographer says Johnson "had the art to give different colours to the several speeches, so that some appear to be declamatory and energetic, resembling the orations of Demosthenes; others like those of Cicero, calm, persuasive; others, more particularly those attributed to such country-gentlemen, merchants, and seamen as had seats in parliament, bear the characteristic of plainness, bluntness, and an affected honesty, as opposed to the plausibility of such as were understood or suspected to be courtiers: the artifice had its effect; Voltaire was betrayed by it into a declaration, that the eloquence of ancient Greece and Rome was revived in the British senate . . . and we are further told of a person in a high office under the government, who being at breakfast at a gentleman's chambers in Gray's Inn, Johnson being also there, declared, that by the style alone of the speeches in the debates, he could severally assign them to the persons by whom they were delivered." [8]

[6] *Gentleman's Magazine*, 1737.
[7] *Essay on the Life and Genius of Dr. Johnson*.
[8] Sir John Hawkins. *Life of Samuel Johnson*. London, 1878, pp. 112–116.

Such remarks indicate only too clearly that the speeches prepared by Johnson constitute a serious problem for the rhetorical critic. Manifestly, the debates are not genuine. In fact, Johnson knew little about debate, and seldom, if ever, attended the meetings. If, as he asserted, he always "took care not to let the Whig dogs have the best of it" in the debates, there may even be a question as to whether these texts are better than none.

How many of the public speeches delivered from the platform or published in the papers bear the marks of hands and minds other than those of the speakers to whom they are attributed, is hard to find out. The number is large.

Other reporters undoubtedly complicated the critics' problems in substantially the same way Johnson did. The story is told [9] of a parliamentary reporter named Tyas who, while covering one of Brougham's speeches, decided that a certain quotation from Cicero would strengthen an argument then being developed by the speaker. So he put it in. Subsequently, Brougham adopted the insertion and approved it for publication in his collected speeches. Coleridge reported some of Pitt's speeches in 1800. With pride in his own work and petulance toward the speaker, he asserted that Pitt had never talked that eloquently in his lifetime. Charles Dickens, a renowned reporter in the 1830's, admitted that certain pathetic appeals in Daniel O'Connell's speech on the Coercion Bill affected him so deeply that he put his pen down, forgetting to record the words. Indeed, a reporter without pen in hand is not likely to prepare a faithful copy of the proceedings of the day.

John Lord Campbell reports an incident which shows how easily a casual reader might be deceived in matters of textual accuracy.[10] On November 29, 1759, Bishop Johnson of Worcester preached a sermon at Westminster Abbey. Evidently he was given but a short time to make preparation. So Lord Mansfield, an unquestioned master of classical expression, wrote the sermon for his friend and protégé. Church officials and others pronounced the sermon unusually good, and requested that it be published. In print, it appeared as the composition of "James, by Divine Providence Lord Bishop of Worcester."

The researcher who chooses to study the deliberative speeches made in the Congress of the United States also has difficulty with the authenticity of speech texts. The volumes of printed speeches of men like Webster, Clay, and Calhoun may mislead him to think that better texts are available for the American scene. Unfortunately such is not the case. Verbatim reporting was not attempted in the Senate until 1848 and in the House of Representatives until 1850. Prior to that time reporting of the proceedings of Congress was most haphazard and irregu-

[9] Michael Macdonagh. *The Reporters' Gallery*. London, 1913, p. 31.
[10] *The Lives of the Chief Justices of England*. London, 1849. II, 566–567.

lar. Prior to 1802 Congress often met behind closed doors, keeping no more than a journal. When they could overcome the obstacles to their admission, reporters had difficulty in finding a location where they could hear and take notes. Sometimes newspapers carried running accounts of what happened in Congress, but they did not hesitate to color their reporting according to their political preferences.

Thirty-five years after the assembling of the First Congress, Gales and Seaton started publication of the proceedings from 1789 to 1824 in the *Annals of Congress*. Not completing the task until 1856, the publisher wove together a compilation from fragmentary sources: journals, newspapers, other contemporary sources.[11] Elizabeth Gregory McPherson reveals:". . . From a bundle of those bygone relics, the publishers wrote out and published, after an interval of forty years, a speech of John Randolph of Roanoke which had been delivered in the House, January 12, 1813."

The reports in the *Register of Debates* from 1824 to 1837 in thirty-nine volumes were little better. Although the publisher issued the proceedings of Congress at the end of each session, the editors admitted that the debates were "not in all cases literally reported," but were substantially accurate. They invited congressmen to revise their remarks before publication. The story of the publication of Webster's famous reply to Hayne reveals something of the practices of the day. McPherson reports: "Almost a month intervened between the delivery of Webster's reply to Hayne, January 26 and 27, 1830, and its publication in the *National Intelligencer*."

In 1833 the *Congressional Globe* became a competitor of the *Register*. It continued from 1833 to 1873, filling one hundred and eleven volumes, and was the first publication of its kind to attempt a step-by-step record of every measure coming before both Houses. Both the *Globe* and the *Register* were often accused of misrepresenting the remarks of the speakers, particularly those in the opposition party.

The Senate in 1848 and the House of Representatives in 1850 authorized verbatim reporting and made the *Globe* a semi-official publication of Congress. But not until 1873 did the United States Congress authorize the publication of the official *Congressional Record*. Both Zon Robinson [12] and Loren Reid [13] bear out the conclusion that Congress permits its members to edit, revise, and extend their remarks before

[11] The material on congressional reporting is largely based upon the article by Elizabeth Gregory McPherson, "Reporting the Debates of Congress." *Quarterly Journal of Speech*, 28:141–148 (April, 1942).

[12] Zon Robinson. "Are Speeches in Congress Reported Accurately?" *Quarterly Journal of Speech*, 28:8–12 (February, 1942).

[13] Loren D. Reid. "Factors Contributing to Inaccuracy in the Texts of Speeches." In *Papers in Rhetoric*. Edited by Donald C. Bryant. St. Louis, 1940, pp. 39–45.

they are printed in the *Record.* The reason for the earlier disregard of authentic reporting is complex. In his enlightening study of the "Factors Contributing to Inaccuracy in the Texts of Speeches," Loren D. Reid clarifies certain aspects of the problem. His analysis is threefold:

(1) Inaccuracy has resulted from the lack of "official insistence upon verbatim reporting of the speeches made by the legislative branch of the government."

(2) The second factor which, according to Reid, accounts for inaccuracy of speech texts "is the strong, almost instinctive desire of speakers to make their speeches read as well as possible." It is obvious that corrections, deletions, and revisions designed by the speaker to improve the readability of the text divorce the finished product more and more from the original utterance.

(3) Finally, Reid points to "the mechanical possibilities for error" which result from shorthand reporting, dictation, editorial revision, and printing. He concludes by observing:

> . . . the very awareness of these factors of inaccuracy should suggest the need for and the possibility of a new type of speech reporting which will be more accurate than that of the *Congressional Record* and at the same time more vivid and useful than that of the present-day metropolitan press.

What do we know about the masterpieces of some of the great speakers of the nineteenth century? In his study of Henry Clay, Ernest J. Wrage [14] observes that most of the copies of Clay's addresses are reporters' accounts—faithful to the general ideas but unsatisfactory on the side of stylistic expression. A careful study of the sources of Wendell Phillips' speech texts suggests that they evidently do not mirror with complete fidelity the form in which they were originally delivered. Ralph Korngold reports that after a speech was set in type from a stenographic transcript, Phillips did "endless revision." William Lloyd Garrison, who published many of Phillips' speeches in *The Liberator,* wrote: "Such revision, correction, alteration and addition you never say, in the way of emendating. I proposed to Phillips to send the altered 'slips' to Barnum as a remarkable curiosity." [15]

Much of the eloquence which remains of Webster does not come down to us in the form in which it was delivered. Upon the prospect of publishing his papers, Webster wrote to his editor Edward Everett: "I propose certainly to write over everything which has not been revised by myself." [16] Wilbur S. Howell and Hoyt H. Hudson discuss

[14] William N. Brigance, ed. *History and Criticism of American Public Address.* New York, 1943. II, 631.
[15] Ralph Korngold. *Two Friends of Man.* Boston: 1950, p. 180.
[16] Fletcher Webster, ed. *Private Correspondence of Daniel Webster.* Boston: 1857. II, 413.

at some length the differences between a reporter's summary and Webster's official text of a speech delivered in New York in 1837; [17] and they conclude that while both versions are fairly persuasive they express noticeably different purposes and methods. The textual accuracy of Webster's "Reply to Hayne" is also in doubt. The full record of the speech in the Boston Public Library suggests that at least three people had a hand in the preparation of the copy that was eventually published. Joseph Gales, an editor of the *National Intelligencer* and one of the first reporters in Congress, submitted a fourteen-page shorthand report; his wife's transcription of it ran to about one hundred pages; and Webster's copy, which was finally given to the press, was eighty-five pages in length. There were evidently many revisions so that the final draft differs sharply from Gales' report.[18] About the revision of the Bunker Hill Monument speech, George Tichnor, who arranged for its publication, tells a revealing tale:

. . . He [Webster] came to see me at my house about a passage he wanted to alter; he took the proof-sheet, and went to work, but did not satisfy himself with what he wrote. He grew very impatient; he thought he could do better by dictating; and walked about the room uneasily, reading the proof-sheet and his changes over and over again, dictating new matter, which satisfied him no better. At last I suggested something as a substitute, and he desired me to put it in writing, throwing himself upon the sofa in a sort of despair. I did as he desired. It took perhaps five minutes, and when I turned around to read what I had written, I found him fast asleep. . . . When I waked him, he seemed much relieved to find the matter arranged. . . .[19]

The critic who chooses to study a campaign speech or one delivered upon the lecture platform faces a more difficult problem in finding good speech texts. Oftentimes the orator speaks extemporaneously. Even if proficient at shorthand, reporters may have difficulty in hearing and recording what was said. After studying the available sources concerning Andrew Johnson's popular swing around the circle in 1866, Phifer concludes:

It is true that 1866 reporters faced serious handicaps in covering the President's speaking tour. Crowd noise and interruptions interfered with hearing; lack of space or desks made writing difficult. Reporters had to meet deadlines, even though speech texts suffered. Only large papers could afford capable (though seldom unbiased) shorthand reporters. Synopses are

17 William N. Brigance, ed. *History and Criticism of American Public Address*, II, 721–726.
18 Cf. "The Stenographic Report of Webster's Reply to Hayne." *The Phonographic Magazine*, 8:22–24 (January 15, 1894).
19 Quoted by George Tichnor Curtis. *Life of Daniel Webster*. Fourth Edition. New York, 1872. I, p. 250.

especially suspect, but even verbatim reports showed differences over questions like these: Should the President's grammar be reported exactly? Should his pronunciation and articulation eccentricities be reproduced? [20]

Doris Yoakam Twichell tells of the difficulty of studying the speaking of Susan B. Anthony:

Reports of these speeches are given in résumé or abridged synopsis, and frequently in third person. Probably the complete speeches have lost much of their flavor for they are, at least in part, the result of attempts by Miss Anthony or a confederate to write out the addresses from memory after their delivery.[21]

Pulpit speech, by comparison, is more abundantly recorded, partly because many sermons are carefully prepared and read from the pulpit. The need for continual adjustment at the moment, typical of the demands imposed upon a speaker in Congressional debate or courtroom argument, is largely absent. As we have noted, however, the preachers habitually practicing the purely extempore style have not been so accurately or frequently recorded. Theodore F. Nelson, investigating Charles Haddon Spurgeon's *Theory and Practice of Preaching*, cites this British clergyman as practicing extempore speaking. "There is no evidence that the Metropolitan Tabernacle preacher ever read his sermons at the time of presentation, nor that he engaged in writing as a step in preparation." Of the recording and printing of these sermons Nelson observed, "Beginning in 1855, Spurgeon published weekly sermons. These were the sermons he preached either on Sunday morning or evening of that week. These sermons were taken down in shorthand by recorders, transcribed by them, and submitted to Mr. Spurgeon for editing. Monday morning was devoted every week to this task. These revisions brought the speaker benefits which are ascribed to writing in preparation for speaking." [22]

Jerry Hendrix recently investigated the speaking of John Sharp Williams, Senator from Mississippi, in the Senate debate over the League of Nations. On the whole he found the versions appearing in the *New York Times* and *Congressional Record* substantially the same. The differences he found are, however, worth noting:

A first minor difference appears in the paragraph structure, punctuation and grammatical tenses. A second difference is the substitution of words in the *Times* excerpts that are similar in meaning but phonetically different. This discrepancy in transcription could have been caused by the position

[20] Gregg Phifer. "Andrew Johnson at Cleveland and St. Louis, 1866: A Study in Textual Authenticity." *Quarterly Journal of Speech*, 37:462 (December, 1951).

[21] Marie H. Nichols, ed. *History and Criticism of American Public Address*, III, 114.

[22] Ph.D. thesis, State University of Iowa, 1944, pp. 255 ff.

of the reporter in the press gallery *behind* the speaker who customarily addressed the Chair, thereby keeping his back to the press gallery reporters. These seemingly phonetic substitutions include 'exploit' for 'exhibition,' 'heresy' for 'idiocy,' 'constitutional-oiled arrangements' for 'constitutional toilet arrangements,' and 'cosmetics upon the base' for 'cosmetics upon the face.' Finally, there are omissions of words in the *Times* excerpts, as compared with the same excerpts from the *Record,* which indicate that the reporters were either unable or unwilling to quote Williams entirely *verbatim.*[23]

But Hendrix reports that on one occasion Williams materially altered what appeared in the *Record.* He admitted that he struck out remarks that he "ought not to have said." In a letter the Mississippi senator wrote, "I kept my speech out of the *Record* with a view of revising it, and shall revise out of it what I think could be offensive to anybody personally or racially." [24]

THE GHOST WRITER: A POINT OF VIEW

The uninformed may labor under the misconception that the professional speech writer, or ghost writer, as he is known in popular parlance, is a development of present-day Madison Avenue and the hidden persuaders. But, to the contrary, such persons date back to at least the days of ancient Greece. Antiphon, Isocrates, Lysias, and Isaeus prepared speeches for their less articulate neighbors. As famous a speech as George Washington's "Farewell Address" was probably written by James Madison and Alexander Hamilton. Many presidents have sought assistance with their public pronouncements. But perhaps Robert T. Oliver is correct in suggesting that "the new age of the ghost writer" has developed since the administration of Woodrow Wilson.[25] Richard L. Strout, astute columnist, puts the matter this way: "Today speeches prepared in part by other hands are taken for granted. With the complexity of modern affairs one man cannot hope to be familiar with every detail of every subject." [26]

No president since Woodrow Wilson has attempted to prepare his speeches without considerable assistance. Perhaps the most successful in enlisting superior talent was Franklin D. Roosevelt, who gained the help of Samuel I. Rosenman, Robert Sherwood, Harry Hopkins, Archibald MacLeish, Raymond Moley, Stanley High, and Charles Michelson. Harry Truman turned for help to Charles Murphy, Clark Clifford,

[23] Jerry A. Hendrix. *The Speaking of John Sharp Williams in The League of Nations Debates, 1918–1920.* Ph.D. thesis, Louisiana State University, 1964, pp. 11–12.

[24] Letter to James D. Phelon, October 17, 1919. Quoted by Hendrix, p. 15.

[25] Robert T. Oliver. *History of Public Speaking in America.* Boston, 1965, p. 515.

[26] *Christian Science Monitor,* September 22, 1960.

Charles Ross, and Matt Connelly. In discussing the 1948 campaign, John Franklin Carter (pseudonym of Jay Franklin) relates, "The 300-odd speeches were the creations of a composite human brain composed of eight or ten individuals, including the President and his family. We could not afford the time for pride of authorship or personal prestige." [27] Dwight D. Eisenhower used Emmet Hughes, Gabriel Hauge, Malcolm Moos, and Sherman Adams. John F. Kennedy called into service Theodore Sorensen, Pierre Salinger, Arthur Schlesinger, Jr., and his own brother Robert. President Lyndon B. Johnson relied heavily upon William Moyers, Jack Valenti, and Horace Busby.

In recent years political organizations at all levels from the ward to national campaign have turned over many of the tiresome aspects of campaigning to public relations firms. These agencies write speeches, prepare press releases, distribute campaign literature, edit films and film strips, and stage television spectaculars.[28]

Governors,[29] business executives, college presidents, and other prominent persons call for help on their speeches. The practice is in such demand that agencies now advertise their services [30] and one university has given a course for ghost writers.[31]

The term "ghost writing" is in popular but indiscriminate use to refer to anyone who assists another with a speech or literary production. Ernest Bormann defines the practice as that "of using collaborators to deceive the audience and make the speaker appear better than he is (or at least different)." [32] But in the field of speech writing, the critic needs to look behind the derogatory label to discover the actual relationship between speech writer and speaker; he needs a much more precise view of the practice. The help required in the preparing of a speech manuscript varies considerably from speaker to speaker.

The speech writer presents to the critic a problem that he cannot ignore. As a first essential of any kind of criticism the critic must know what he is evaluating. Therefore, he must ask searching questions about genuineness and completeness. In determining the worth of the speaker he operates upon the assumption that an intimate relation exists between thought and language or as Eric Sevareid has said, "a man's own words

[27] "Inside Strategy of the Campaign." *Life*, 25:48 (November 15, 1948).

[28] Stanley Kelley, Jr. *Professional Public Relations and Political Power*. Baltimore, 1956, *passim*.

[29] Dwight L. Freshley. "Gubernatorial Ghost Writers." *Southern Speech Journal*, 31:95–105 (Winter, 1965). Also Donald K. Smith. "The Speech-writing Team in a State Political Campaign." *Today's Speech*, 4:16–19 (September, 1956).

[30] Ernest G. Bormann. "Ghostwriting Agencies." *Today's Speech*, 4:20–23 (September, 1956).

[31] *Ibid.*, p. 23.

[32] "Ghostwritten Speeches—A Reply." *Quarterly Journal of Speech*, 47:420–421 (December, 1961).

are a man's own self." [33] The critic will attempt to determine how the speaker reveals himself through the choices he makes with reference to subject, expressed ideas, selection of argument and evidence, patterns of organization, word choice, sentence structure, resourcefulness in meeting the demands of the speaking situation and expressed attitudes. Many of these matters may appear nearly subliminal, but these almost imperceptible stimuli provide significant cues about the speaker as a person, a thinker, and a leader. However, the ghost upsets the relationship between thought and language. Not knowing whose language he is reading, he cannot draw conclusions about the speaker. Marie Hochmuth Nichols puts the point nicely:

> Ghost writing, I think, has grave implications for the person who wants to approach the study of public address as humane study. We have long turned to the individual in what we thought to be his great moments of decision, in order to discover in him the marks of humanity. We have looked, at times, to the individual as a guide for our own behavior. But individuality, it appears, is rapidly disappearing. . . . What we have thought to be that most individual thing of all—a man's thought—is giving way to the group mind. . . . The student of public address is not putting his eye to the thing that he once was, in the hope of identifying the uniqueness of the creative spirit in public discourse.[34]

In attempting to untangle the real from the synthetic, the critic cannot avoid judging the morality of the speaker. He must answer whether the speaker has deceived his listeners in using a speech writer. The speaker who takes the eloquent words of another as his own may well misrepresent himself. In reading the "canned" words of a ghost the speaker may be little more than an interpreter or an actor. Behind microphone or TV camera, the performer is shielded from direct confrontation with listeners. Makeup, lighting, teleprompters, camera lens, and canned applause heighten the deception.

The critic must of course dig into what part the speaker plays in the creative process. Evidence suggests, for example, that Franklin D. Roosevelt and Adlai Stevenson carefully directed the efforts of their collaborators. They followed procedures that are far different from those of the speaker who is a puppet for some unseen source.

But moral judgments are not simple. They must be made with reference to the context in which the speaker operates. This means that the critic must weigh carefully the demands of the speaker's office. Is it fair to demand of the President that he prepare all of his speeches? How much responsibility rests on the speaker? Does he represent himself or an organization? When the President or Secretary of State gives

[33] *Newsweek,* 39 (No. 5):71 (February 4, 1952).

[34] Marie Hochmuth Nichols. *Rhetoric and Criticism.* Baton Rouge, Louisiana, 1963, p. 46.

a policy statement that will be read carefully around the world, the critic should expect to discover that what is said is a group effort, representing the best talent available. Donald Smith's point with reference to presidential speech writers is well taken:

> The increased candor with which the work of presidential speech writers is treated seems to me both sensible and ethical, and to set a pattern which ought to be followed by executives in less prominent positions. In short, it seems to me that the public needs to understand the way in which executives or administrators conduct the work of their offices, to comprehend the significance and complexity of managerial action in our complicated age, and to get rid of some of its illusions about the way decisions are made and communicated in the modern world.[35]

The evaluation of team effort is certainly different from judging the work of a single individual. The critic has a right to expect that a team of researchers and writers, under the guidance of a perceptive leader, should produce something far different from that of a single speaker. Factors to be considered should include methods of cooperating, the assignment of responsibility, the thoroughness of research, the ability to put the composite in an attractive form, and success with which the group problem is met.

WORKING WITH SPEECHES OF THE PAST

The speech in manuscript or printed form provides the critic with a challenging task. Initially he must answer the question, "Did the orator actually deliver the speech as it is preserved?" Answering this question may be difficult, for what is reputed to be the speaker's words may be no more than the creation of a historian, biographer, or even a journalist. In 430 B.C. Pericles inspired Athenians with his famous "Funeral Oration," but the text, quoted so widely through the centuries, came from the pen of the historian Thucydides, who admitted having speakers say what he believed the occasion demanded of them.[36] Patrick Henry stands high on almost any list of great American speakers, but his reputation is largely based upon a speech fragment, what others remembered of his orations, and his most renowned speech, "Give Me Liberty or Give Me Death," a declamatory favorite. But the immortal words of that masterpiece came from William Wirt, Henry's biographer, who admitted he knew "nothing of Henry personally." He pieced together twelve hundred words from scattered fragments that ear witnesses remembered from twenty years before.[37] The genuineness of

---

[35] *Quarterly Journal of Speech*, 47:419 (December, 1961).

[36] Houston Peterson, ed. *A Treasury of the World's Great Speeches.* New York, 1954, pp. 7–14.

[37] William Wirt. *Sketches of the Life and Character of Patrick Henry.* Revised edition. Hartford, 1817, p. v.

Robert Emmet's dramatic final address to the special court, September 19, 1803, is open to serious question. A recent biographer reports:

> There are many versions of Emmet's speech. Those issued by the Government immediately after the trial contain references to the French; but persons who were present . . . were certain that these were not made by Emmet. Those issued by his friends contain other matter which it is believed was inserted by them. No one version, even those taken in the shorthand of the time, agrees exactly with another, except for the unforgettable last paragraph.[38]

The text that the critic has may be a synopsis, a press copy (released before delivery), a reading copy, an edited copy, a composite copy put together from several sources, an invented speech, or an actual stenographic transcription. The last-named is of course superior to the others provided that the reporter was competent and had an opportunity to hear. These are matters into which the critic must inquire.

A second question for the critic is, "Is the speech text complete? Does it record all that was said?" Too often the anthologist finds space too precious to print the entire speech; consequently, he deletes what he considers unimportant or uninteresting. For the average reader this practice is desirable, but for the critic it provides a real problem. If he is a careful scholar, the anthologist will attempt to indicate omitted portions by marking the ellipses. But even at best what may appear to be a complete copy may not include informal introductory sentences, platform editing, asides, and concluding remarks. If the text is a press copy or an edited version, it will probably omit ad libbed remarks that tell much about the speaker's adjustment. For example, Laura Crowell found in one speech that Franklin D. Roosevelt made 172 spontaneous alterations.[39] In reading the *Congressional Record*, the casual observer may be impressed with how grammatical and literate the members are; a little more thought perhaps will suggest that a secretary or clerk has polished his employer's remarks before they were printed.

Sometimes the critic may have several manuscripts for the same speech. Dating the manuscript and selecting the original one may prove somewhat of a task, particularly when the speech has been delivered several times. Some of Lincoln's speeches provided an interesting sample of this problem.

A study by Paul M. Angle of the available texts of four of Lincoln's speeches (Subtreasury Speech of December 26, 1839; the House-Divided Speech, the Cooper Union Address, and the Gettysburg Address) reveals

---

[38] Helen Landreth. *The Pursuit of Robert Emmet.* Dublin, 1949, p. 352. Also see, R. W. Postgate. *Dear Robert Emmet.* New York, 1943, II, 631.

[39] Laura Crowell. "Word Changes Introduced *Ad Libitum* in Five Speeches by Franklin Delano Roosevelt." *Speech Monographs*, 25:230 (November, 1958).

some of the difficulties and barriers with which the scholar is confronted in his attempt to establish accurate texts. In considering the Cooper Union Address, Angle reports that the New York *Tribune* published the speech in pamphlet form eight days after its delivery, and many other publishers also brought out editions. Referring to the accuracy of the texts, Angle concludes:

According to Lincoln's own statement, Tribune Tract No. 4 was published without supervision on his part, but Journal Campaign Document No. 1—the Springfield publication—had the benefit of his own 'hasty supervising.' The text of the latter, however, is identical with the former; the only differences are in spelling and capitalization. However, the Nott-Brainerd edition, published by The Young Men's Republican Union of New York, differs from all earlier editions in one important respect—the correction of a factual statement—and in several minor matters of phraseology. Because Lincoln read the proofs of this edition, and carried on a correspondence with one of its editors, this is the authoritative text.[40]

Similarly, in the case of the Gettysburg Address, Angle points to the difficulty of determining the best text. He observes that collectors have been largely of one opinion, "that the Gettysburg Address was first put into print, aside from the newspapers, in a 48-page booklet entitled *An Oration Delivered on the Battlefield of Gettysburg . . . ,* by Edward Everett. . . ." However, a recent discovery in the Lincoln collection, entitled *The Gettysburg Solemnities,* reveals this item to have been printed before the previously mentioned booklet. But, Angle goes on to say, "the text to be found in *The Gettysburg Solemnities* is a faulty one." It is as follows:

Four score and seven years ago our fathers brought forth on this continent a new nation, conceived in liberty, and dedicated to the proposition that all men are equal. Now we are engaged in a great civil war, testing whether that nation, or any nation so conceived and so dedicated, can long endure. We are now on a great battle-field of that war. We are met to dedicate a portion of that field as the final resting-place of those who have given their last life-blood that that nation might live. But in a larger sense we cannot dedicate, we cannot consecrate, we cannot hallow this ground. The brave men living and dead who struggled here have consecrated it far above our poor power to add to or detract. [Applause.] The world will little know nor long remember what we say; but it can never forget what they did here. [Applause.] And it is for us living to be dedicated here to the unfinished work that they have thus far so nobly carried forward. [Applause.] It is rather for us here to be dedicated to the great task remaining before us, that from this honored day we take increased devotion to that cause for which they here gave the last full measure of devotion. That we here highly resolve that these dead shall not have died in vain; that the nation shall, under God, have a new birth of freedom. [Applause.] And that government of

[40] "Four Lincoln Firsts." *Papers of the Bibliographical Society of America,* 36: 1–17 (1942).

the people, by the people, and for the people, shall not perish from the earth. [Applause.] [41]

Angle observes that among the differences between this and the accepted text is the omission of the sentence "It is altogether fitting and proper that we should do this."

Difficult as the task of finding the correct text is, Angle believes the answer is known.

> Actually, I think we do know exactly how Lincoln wanted his speech preserved. In February, 1864, George Bancroft asked for a copy of the address in order that it might be included in a volume of facsimiles entitled, *Autograph Leaves of our Country's Authors*. Lincoln complied, but because he wrote on both sides of the paper, his manuscript was not suitable for reproduction. At Bancroft's request he sent a second copy on March 11, 1864, this time writing only on one side of the sheets. This copy was duly reproduced in the book for which it was intended, which was published by Cushings & Bailey, Baltimore, 1864. As far as is known, this was Lincoln's final revision.[42]

But Lincoln's final revision was not the speech he delivered at Gettysburg. What is now believed to be the original reading copy (known as the Nicolay copy) did not come to light for thirty years and the second copy (Hay copy) was not published for forty-five years. The book *Long Remembered* (1963) gives fascimiles of the first five versions, all in Lincoln's own hand. Actually there are sixty-five differences in wording between the first two versions.[43]

We have considered at some length this reference to the Lincoln texts because it brings two matters clearly into focus. In the first place, it throws light upon the exacting assignments of determining textual authenticity—even for revised rather than for original copy; secondly, it suggests the important service that bibliographical research can perform for the rhetorical critic. In their search for possible editions of written materials, and in their solicitous regard for textual accuracy, bibliographers contribute to the enrichment of our subject by verifying and establishing some of the copy from which our speech criticisms derive. In a sense, each critic of oratory is also a bibliographer; he must find the most authentic texts before he proceeds to an evaluation of the speaker's merit.

In his study of William Pitt's last speech, which was only two sentences long, Loren D. Reid illustrates the care necessary in checking

---

41 *Ibid.*, p. 15.

42 *Ibid.*, p. 16.

43 David C. Mearns and Lloyd A. Dunlap. "Notes and Comments on the Preparation of the Address." In *Long Remembered, The Gettysburg Address in Facsimile.* Washington, D.C., 1963. Also see, Louis A. Warren. *Lincoln's Gettysburg Declaration, "A New Birth of Freedom."* Fort Wayne, Indiana, 1964, pp. 150–170.

the text of a speech.[44] This "memorable and immortal" response, given at the Lord Mayor's dinner, London, November 9, 1805, just after Trafalgar is usually remembered as follows:

I return you many thanks for the honour you have done me; but Europe is not to be saved by any single man. England has saved herself by her exertions, and will, as I trust, save Europe by her example.

But questioning the authenticity of these forty words, Reid set about to collocate this version with others he could find. Digging into earlier sources, he discovered six other versions. On November 11, 1805, two days after the event, the London *Daily Advertizer* reported:

Mr. PITT, thanked his Lordship for the honor which he had done him; but remarked, that Europe must owe its safety to various causes. England, he trusted, had gained hers by her firmness; and he hoped that the rest of Europe would follow her example!!!—(Very long and loud plaudits.)

In addition, Reid found three other newspaper reports. He continues:

The Morning Post reporter provided still another variant:
"Mr. PITT returned thanks, and in his usual strong and energetic language, said, 'England has saved itself by its firmness, and let us therefore hope that the example set will be followed by all the rest of Europe.'"
The *Morning Herald* text avoids the responsibility of a direct quotation:
"He returned his thanks in a short speech, in which he said, that Great Britain had done her duty, and that he trusted the Continental Powers would do the same."
The *Times*, with a briefer report of the festivities than many papers, is equally indecisive about Pitt's words:
"His observations were principally directed to the late brilliant victory, and to the unanimity manifested by the whole nation to resist and humble the common enemy."

In its issue of November 12, 1805, the London *Sun* attempted a "more authentic" text:

"My Lord Mayor:
I beg to return your Lordship my sincere thanks for the great, but unmerited, honour you have done me. The security of Europe will be owing to very different causes.—*England* has saved itself by its firmness; I trust it will save *Europe* by its example."

This fourth version reappeared shortly in the St. James *Chronicle, Daily Advertizer,* and the *Morning Herald.* Reid finds that fifty years later Macaulay mentioned Pitt's eloquent words in an essay published in the *Encyclopaedia Britannica* in 1859:

Several of those who heard him laid up his last words in their hearts; for they were the last words that he ever uttered in public: "Let us hope that

[44] Loren Reid. "The Last Speech of William Pitt." *Quarterly Journal of Speech,* 49:133–137 (April, 1963).

England, having saved herself by her energy, may save Europe by her example."

Through his detective work, Reid has demonstrated convincingly that Pitt's "indisputable masterpiece," recently reprinted in Houston Peterson's *A Treasury of the World's Great Speeches*,[45] does not collate with newspaper reports nor Macaulay's rendition. Good detective that he is, Reid discovered that "memorable and immortal" words, a phrase generally quoted today, first saw print in a biography by Stanhope, who wrote as a preface that Pitt spoke "nearly as follows." The biographer based his version upon a conversation which he had with the Duke of Wellington in 1838, thirty-three years after the words were uttered. Reid's conclusion is apt at this time:

> The Guildhall speech illuminates the difficulty of securing a verbatim report of any speech. It also paradoxically illustrates another point: the revised speech proved to be a more acceptable representation of the impact of Pitt's spoken words on Guildhall listeners than what was actually uttered.[46]

PREPARING AN ACCURATE SPEECH TEXT FOR STUDY

The rhetorical critic who chooses to study contemporary speaking often can obtain an actual recording of his speaker's remarks. The extensive use of sensitive audio-visual equipment as well as radio, television, and film makes available great quantities of recorded speeches. Growing numbers of public figures, sensitive about what history may say about them, are preserving recordings of their utterances. Deposited at the Franklin D. Roosevelt Library, at Hyde Park, New York, are numerous recordings of Roosevelt's speeches from the presidential years. Much of the speaking of Winston Churchill has been collected on records. Radio and television stations have preserved many of the past broadcasts in their archives. Some universities are now actively engaged in taping of the speech of important state figures. The resourceful student can turn up great quantities of recorded material.

Portable high-quality transistorized tape recorders, battery operated, provide an efficient way to capture verbatim speeches on the spot; the extemporaneous remarks that were once lost now can be captured. In addition to having the exact words, the critic may consider vocal elements which enrich words with additional meaning and cues.

With a recording in hand, the critic of course must work carefully in making a typescript for study and publication. Theodore Clevenger and his colleagues took unusual care to reproduce the Kennedy debates

---

[45] Houston Peterson. *Op. cit.*, p. 318.

[46] Earl Stanhope. *Life of the Right Honourable William Pitt*, 3d ed. London, 1867. IV, p. 437. Quoted by Reid, "The Last Speech of William Pitt," p. 137.

of 1960. They give insight into what is involved in preparing an almost exact copy.

Between the two extremes, in the years ahead, research workers in politics, history, speech, mass communication, psychology, linguistics, and a variety of other fields will apply the analytical methods of their disciplines to these debates. If their analyses are to be meaningful, they should be made from accurate texts, and our purpose has been to supply them. Specifically, it has been our effort to produce texts in standard English orthography, which reflect accurately the verbal productions of the two speakers as these were preserved on magnetic sound tapes of professional broadcast quality.

Although we have used standard orthography, we have tried to avoid the 'error of fluency' where false starts, vocalized pauses, and non-vocalized hesitations are omitted from the text of a speaker's remarks, where words or sounds not uttered by the speaker are added for the sake of grammatical form, and where unintelligible sounds are either rendered into proper words or omitted from the text. We have included transcriptions of all false starts and repetitions, all vocalized pauses (such as 'uh,' 'eh,' and 'er'), and all unusually long vocalized hesitations (indicated by . . .). Occasionally, the speaker uttered clearly recognizable phonemes which constituted no recognizable word. These sounds are recorded as phonemic transcriptions and are set off from the remainder of the text by slash marks (/−/). The phonemic system is that in current use by most American linguists, not the 'International Phonetic Alphabet.'

Our punctuation of the texts, through the study of pause length, vocal inflection, and context, reflects our considered judgment of the punctuation necessary to reflect faithfully the meaning of what was said. Because paragraph indentations in the text of an extemporaneous speech represent certain judgments about the interrelationships among a speaker's ideas, we have not attempted to divide the speeches into paragraphs. While this procedure would undoubtedly have produced a more attractive page format, it would have introduced an unwarranted bias into possible future analyses by predisposing certain judgments concerning the relationships among ideas and sentences which are best left to the independent judgment of future analysts.

The reader may better judge the usefulness of the texts for various types of analysis if we describe briefly the techniques employed and the conventions which we followed in producing them.

Raw materials for each debate included a published newspaper transcript of the debates and a sound tape recording made by a local radio station from the live broadcast. Working from these two sources, a single auditor produced what appeared to be an accurate transcript of the debate. This was typed on a mimeograph stencil, proofread, and copies were run for further analysis. In all debates, our drifts differed in a substantial number of details from the texts published in the newspaper, and were considerably more accurate.

In the second stage of production, the three transcribers listened to the tape of the debate while reading from the mimeographed texts. When one of the three thought he detected a discrepancy between the text and the tape, the recorder was stopped and the passage was played back repeatedly until a consensus could be reached. Each auditor then recorded the correct version of the passage on his copy of the text. Because it was necessary to avoid auditory fatigue and lapse of attention, each session consumed several hours. When a debate had been proofread in this manner, one transcriber typed a ditto master of the revised draft, checking it against the three proofs.

In the third stage, a single auditor proofread the ditto master against the tape recording again. He noted typographical errors, suspected discrepancies between the tape and the text, and questionable punctuation. These passages were then checked by the three transcribers until a consensus could be reached. Indicated changes were made in the ditto masters and copies of a third draft were reproduced.

This third draft was then used as the basis for the fourth and last stage of production, in which the group proofread the third draft against the tape. When questions concerning this draft arose, the same procedure was employed for arriving at agreement as in previous sessions. Indicated corrections were made on the ditto masters and copies of the fourth and final draft were produced.

We believe the texts which follow represent highly accurate accounts of what was said in the Kennedy-Nixon debates. We hope the texts will be of value to those who are interested—for whatever reason—in accurate accounts of these notable speeches.[47]

SUMMARY

Finding a fairly accurate speech text from the past is difficult. Reliable reporting was cumbersome and rare. For many years the British Parliament and United States Congress made no attempt to insure the keeping of anything like near-complete accounts of proceedings. Speakers and their advisers commonly edited and at times materially altered speeches before they were printed. Historians and biographers sought dramatic effect through invented or reconstructed speeches based upon recollections and hearsay.

To the historian, journalist, and general reader the authenticity of a speech text may be of minor concern or little consequence, but to the speech critic it is a vital matter. Basic to speech criticism is the assumption that a man's public utterance is a reliable index to his attitudes, thought processes, ability to reach rational decisions, as well as oratorical skill. Careful textual examination and thorough historical analysis therefore become an important step in the critical process. With an incomplete or imperfect copy, the critic must seriously qualify his judgments. When he does not have available a verbatim text, he can make inferences about elements of invention: argument, evidence, analysis, and adaptation. He may also study organization, but he must hold tenuous judgments about style or use of language.

---

[47] Theodore Clevenger, Jr., Donald W. Parson, and Jerome B. Polisky. "The Problem of Textual Accuracy." In *The Great Debates: Background, Perspective, Effects.* Edited by Sidney Kraus. Bloomington, Indiana University Press, 1962, pp. 345–346.

The presence of the ghost writer further complicates rhetorical criticism. To separate what originated with the ghost and what came from the speaker becomes a most difficult task. In addition to stylistic influence the ghost writer may supply ideas and determine strategy. If he relies on a ghost writer, the speaker may of course misrepresent himself. Under these conditions the critic must ask questions about the speaker's intellectual capacity, his ability to generate ideas and to draw rational conclusions, as well as about his morality.

EXERCISES

1. Investigate the authorship of the following speeches: Patrick Henry's "Give Me Liberty or Give Me Death"; George Washington's "Farewell Address," and "Chief Logan's Speech" (1774).
2. In case the critic must rely upon a speech text which is not verbatim, what limitations are placed upon his analysis? What elements of the speech can he not study?
3. Your investigation of the authorship of Patrick Henry's "Give Me Liberty or Give Me Death" speech, mentioned in the first exercise, has doubtless brought you to the conclusion that the original text is not extant. Does this fact in any way change your opinion of the speech? Why? Does the fact in any way dull the speech's luster in the American tradition? Why?
4. Make or secure an electrical recording of a speech delivered over the radio or television by the President of the United States or some other prominent national leader. Secure also an official version of the speech as released by the White House or other authorized source. Check the official version with the recording and note the differences.
5. Examine the text of Webster's argument in the Dartmouth College case (*World's Best Orations*, D. J. Brewer, ed., Chicago, F. P. Kaiser Co., 1923, X, 198–203). Read John W. Black's "Webster's Peroration in the Dartmouth College Case" (*Quarterly Journal of Speech*, 23:636–42, December, 1937). What is your conclusion concerning the authenticity of this peroration?
6. Examine the text of Charles Sumner's address on "The True Grandeur of Nations," July 4, 1845, as printed in (*a*) Charles Sumner, *The True Grandeur of Nations* (Boston, J. H. Eastburn, 1845); (*b*) Charles Sumner, *Orations and Speeches* (Boston, Ticknor, 1850), I, 1–130; (*c*) Charles Sumner, *Works* (Boston, Lee, 1870–1883), I, 1–132; (*d*) Charles Sumner, *Addresses on War* (Boston, Ginn and Co., 1902), pp. 1–132. Then study the conclusions of Carl Dallinger and Elaine Pagel concerning the extensive inconsistencies in the various texts (*History and Criticism of American Public Address*, II, 751–76).
7. Compare and contrast the various versions of Franklin D. Roosevelt's "Yalta Conference Address," March 1, 1945, as given in (*a*) *Representative American Speeches: 1944–1945* (New York, H. W. Wilson Co., 1945, pp. 40–52); (*b*) *The New York Times* (March 2, 1945); (*c*) *The Congressional Record* (March 1, 1945).
8. Select a speech or group of speeches of a contemporary orator. As one

of the preliminary steps to the full study, secure as accurate texts as possible. Explain the procedure in establishing the authenticity of these texts.

9. Investigate one of the following problems: (a) textual authenticity of the addresses of William Cullen Bryant; (b) the textual accuracy of the occasional speeches of Mark Twain; (c) the textual authenticity of representative speeches of James A. Bryce, delivered in the United States.

10. Without doubt, many speeches in public and private life are ghostwritten. Apart from any possible ethical consideration, what special problems does the ghosted speech pose for the critic?

11. Raymond Moley ("The Academic Man in Politics," *Columbia University Forum*, Fall, 1963, p. 6) says that a competent collaborator writes *with* the speaker, not *for* him. "Real collaboration is an art in itself." Comment.

12. Appraise the worth of this observation by Raymond Clapper: "Every politician's speech, like his income tax return, ought to be required to bear a sworn affidavit stating whether or not the speaker has had the assistance of others in preparation of his text. Under such a system, we probably [would] get worse speeches but more genuine ones."

CLASS PROJECT (Continued)

Prepare a 500-to-1,000-word written report, establishing the authenticity of the speech texts which you intend to study. What reasons do you have to believe that your texts are reliable and worthy of study?

READINGS

PAUL M. ANGLE. "Four Lincoln Firsts." *Papers of the Bibliographical Society of America,* 36:1–17 (First Quarter, 1942). (A careful study dealing with textual accuracy.)

DANIEL J. BOORSTIN, ed. *An American Primer.* Chicago, University of Chicago Press, 1966. Two volumes. (Scattered details of interest in studies of authenticity.)

ERNEST G. BORMANN. "Ethics of Ghostwritten Speeches." *Quarterly Journal of Speech,* 47:262–267 (October, 1961).

———. "Ghostwriting Agencies." *Today's Speech,* 4:20–23 (September, 1956).

———. "Ghostwriting and the Rhetorical Critic." *Quarterly Journal of Speech,* 46: 284–288 (October, 1960).

JULIAN BOYD. *The Declaration of Independence.* Princeton, Princeton University Press, 1945. (Assembles reproductions of the known drafts and copies of the Declaration.)

WALDO W. BRADEN and MARY LOUISE GEHRING. *Speech Practices.* New York, Harper and Row, 1958. Ch. II, "How Speakers Prepare Their Speeches," pp. 14–24; and "The Speaker's Notes," pp. 35–48.

W. NORWOOD BRIGANCE. "Ghostwriting Before Franklin D. Roosevelt and the Radio." *Today's Speech,* 4:10–12 (September, 1956).

EARL CAIN. "Obstacles to Early Congressional Reporting." *Southern Speech Journal,* 27:239–247 (Spring, 1962).

THEODORE CLEVENGER *et al.* "The Problem of Textual Accuracy." In *The Great Debates: Background, Perspective, Effects.* Edited by SIDNEY KRAUS. Bloomington, Indiana University Press. Pp. 241–347.

LAURA CROWELL. "Word Changes Introduced *Ad Libitum* in Five Speeches by Franklin Delano Roosevelt." *Speech Monographs*, 25:229–242 (November, 1958).

HENRY L. DAWES. "Has Oratory Declined?" *Forum*, 18:146–160 (October, 1894). (Notes on Seaton's reporting of Webster's "Reply to Hayne.")

DAVID V. ERDMAN. "Coleridge in Lilliput: The Quality of Parliamentary Reporting in 1800." *Speech Monographs*, 27:33–62 (March, 1960).

WILLIAM L. FINKEL. "Sources of Walt Whitman's Manuscript Notes on Physique." *American Literature*, 22:308–329 (November, 1950).

DWIGHT L. FRESHLEY. "Gubernatorial Ghost Writers." *Southern Speech Journal*, 31:95–105 (Winter, 1965).

DANIEL J. GOULDING. "Parliamentary Reporting in Great Britain During the 17th and 18th Centuries." *Central States Speech Journal*, 16:275–277 (November, 1965).

ROBERT G. GUNDERSON. "Political Phrasemakers in Perspective." *Southern Speech Journal*, 26:22–26 (Fall, 1960).

WILLIAM E. HALL. "How to Report Speeches." In his *Reporting News*. Boston, D. C. Heath & Co., 1936. Pp. 328–334.

RAY W. HEINEN. "Ghostwriting in Departments of the Federal Government." *Central States Speech Journal*, 7:10–12 (Spring, 1956).

J. A. HENDRIX. "A New Look at Textual Authenticity of Speeches in the *Congressional Record*." *Southern Speech Journal*, 31:153–159 (Winter, 1965). See comparison of speech as it appeared in *Congressional Record* and *The New York Times*.

ANTHONY HILLBRUNER. "Word and Deed: Jefferson's Address to the Indians." *Speech Monographs*, 30:328–334 (November, 1963).

ROBERT D. KING. "Franklin D. Roosevelt's Second Inaugural Address: A Study in Text Authenticity." *Quarterly Journal of Speech*, 23:439–444 (October, 1937).

ALFRED KINNEAR. "Parliamentary Reporting." *Contemporary Review*, 87:369–375 (April, 1905).

Long Remembered: Facsimiles of the five versions of the Gettysburg Address in the handwriting of Abraham Lincoln. Washington, D.C., Library of Congress, 1963. (See notes and comments on the preparation.)

ELIZABETH GREGORY MCPHERSON. "Reporting the Debates of Congress." *Quarterly Journal of Speech*, 28:141–148 (April, 1942).

———. "Reports of the Debates of the House of Representatives during the First Congress, 1789–1791." *Quarterly Journal of Speech*, 30:64–71 (February, 1944).

MICHAEL MACDONAGH. *The Reporters' Gallery*. London, Hodder and Stoughton, 1913.

ERNEST R. MAY. "Ghost Writing and History." *The American Scholar*, 22:459–61 (Autumn, 1953).

CHARLES MICHELSON. *The Ghost Talks*. New York, G. P. Putnam's Sons, 1944.

RICHARD MURPHY. "Problems in Speech Texts." In *Papers in Rhetoric and Poetic*, DONALD C. BRYANT, ed. Iowa City, University of Iowa Press, 1965. Pp. 70–86.

MARIE HOCHMUTH NICHOLS. "Ghost Writing: Implications For Public Address." In *Rhetoric and Criticism*. Baton Rouge, Louisiana State University, 1963. Pp. 35–48.

WALDO PHELPS and ANDREA BECK. "Lyndon Johnson's Address at the UCLA Charter Day Ceremony." *Western Speech*, 29:162–171 (Summer, 1965). (See text of speech indicatory of platform alteration.)

GREGG PHIFER. "Andrew Johnson at Cleveland and St. Louis, 1866: A Study in Textual Authenticity." *Quarterly Journal of Speech*, 37:455–462 (December, 1951).

R. W. POSTGATE. *Dear Robert Emmet*. New York, Vanguard Press, Inc., 1932. Pp. 224–241. (On his last speech.)

ROBERT F. RAY. "Ghostwriting in Presidential Campaigns." *Central States Speech Journal*, 8:8–11 (Fall, 1956).

LOREN D. REID. "Factors Contributing to Inaccuracy in the Texts of Speeches."

In *Papers in Rhetoric*. Edited by DONALD C. BRYANT. St. Louis, privately printed, 1940. Pp. 39–45.

———. "The Perils of Rhetorical Criticism." *Quarterly Journal of Speech*, 30: 416–422 (December, 1944).

———. "The Last Speech of William Pitt." *Quarterly Journal of Speech*, 49:133–137 (April, 1963).

RALPH RICHARDSON. "Adlai E. Stevenson, Hollywood Bowl, October 9, 1954: His Preparation and His Speaking Manuscript." *Western Speech*, 19:137–174. (May, 1955).

ZON ROBINSON. "Are Speeches in Congress Accurately Reported?" *Quarterly Journal of Speech*, 28:8–12 (February, 1942).

RAY H. SANDEFUR. "Logan's Oration—How Authentic?" *Quarterly Journal of Speech*, 46:289–296 (October, 1960).

DONALD K. SMITH. "The Speech-writing Team in a State Political Campaign." *Today's Speech*, 4:16–19 (September, 1956).

———. "Ghost Written Speeches." *Quarterly Journal of Speech*, 47:416–420 (December, 1961). Also see Ernest G. Bormann. "Ghost Written Speeches—A Reply." *Quarterly Journal of Speech*, 47:420–421 (December, 1961).

ROBERT W. SMITH. "The 'Second' Inaugural Address of Lyndon Baines Johnson: A Definitive Text." *Speech Monographs*, 34:102–108 (March, 1967).

EDITH M. STERN. "The Cash-and-No-Credit Business." *Saturday Review of Literature*, 23:11–12 (October 26, 1940).

LOUIS A. WARREN. *Lincoln's Gettysburg Declaration: "A New Birth of Freedom."* Fort Wayne, Indiana, Lincoln National Life Foundation, 1964.

ERNEST J. WESSEN. "Debates of Lincoln and Douglas." *Papers of the Bibliographical Society of America*, 40:91–106 (Second Quarter, 1946). (A bibliographical study. Contains an annotated list of variant editions of the debates.)

10

Reconstructing
the Social Settings

THE HISTORICAL SETTING

Athenian speakers of the fourth and fifth centuries excelled at eloquence and consequently exercised unusual influence in the life of their city-state. Cicero selected one of their number, Demosthenes, as the perfect orator. In accounting for Atticism, R. C. Jebb has wisely observed:

> The glory of Attic oratory, as such, consists not solely in its intrinsic excellence, but also in its revelation of the corporate political intelligence to which it appealed: for it spoke sometimes to an Assembly debating an issue of peace or war, sometimes to a law-court occupied with a private plaint, sometimes to Athenians mingled with strangers at a festival, but everywhere and always to the Athenian Demos, everywhere and always to a paramount People, taught by life itself to reason and to judge.[1]

Jebb emphasizes that "intrinsic excellence" is not sufficient to explain the power of Attic oratory; more properly this eloquence partook of and gained stature from the causes, customs, values, and issues of its day. To understand its power necessitates seeing it in the full context as it was used in the forum, the law courts, and the festivals. Jebb's point about this inseparable relation between oratory and the Athenian Demos is true of all significant speaking. The setting in which the orator speaks reveals much about what he can and does achieve.

Since every judgment of a public speech contains a historical constituent, the critic is peculiarly concerned with determining the nature of the setting in which the speaker performed. Although almost a tru-

[1] R. C. Jebb. *The Attic Orators.* Two volumes. London: 1893. I, Cxxxiii.

ism, it cannot be overemphasized that speeches are events occurring in highly complex situations, that responsiblity of critical appraisal depends heavily upon the critic's ability to understand the historical trends, the motivating forces, the immediate occasion, and most of all the composition and demands of the audience. No task is more challenging, none more essential to its successful prosecution. In a restricted sense, it may be possible to evaluate a speaker's written style through a simple examination of the text, without regard to the events which gave rise to the delivery of the speech. But even if possible, such an appraisal would be superficial; the evidence derived from the literature of speech education and criticism attests to the sterility of rhetoric when divorced from the urgency of matter and the imperatives of the particular historical moment.

The circumstances under which great speechmaking flourishes will alone affirm the importance of comprehending the total context of the speech in the process of criticism. Distinguished oratory and social crisis are closely interrelated. Ralph Waldo Emerson once remarked: "Times of eloquence are times of terror." The stress of events associated with man's quest for freedom in civil and political life, the upsurges of patriotic fervor occasioned by man's desire to preserve his rights or to extend the influence of his power—these and other manifestations of the human will have always dominated the scene during those periods most productive in public address. Accordingly, we associate Pericles with the ardent, patriotic defence of Athenian life and freedom during the crucial period of the Peloponnesian War; Demosthenes, with the epochal struggle between the Athenians and Philip of Macedon, involving again the question of freedom and personal liberty; Cicero, with the attempt to crush the conspiratorial designs of a Catiline, and thus sustain the integrity of the commonwealth; Chatham, Burke, Fox, and Pitt, with the stirring times and issues of the late eighteenth century; Clay, Webster, Calhoun, and Lincoln, with the inflammatory subjects of slavery, States' rights, and national expansion; Roosevelt and Churchill, with the global problems relating to the affirmation and establishment of the Four Freedoms; and Martin Luther King, Jr., with the civil rights struggle, giving his dramatic speech "I Have a Dream" to 200,000 followers standing in front of Lincoln Monument in Washington, D.C. These are but a few speakers whose services stemmed from great issues—men whose oratory was prompted by the ebb and flow of major events which have determined the destiny of nations. Whether these men are remembered as orators only because their speeches dealt with matters of great human concern is an academic question. It is enough to recognize that the man and the issue met, and that the issue gave free rein to the man's vision and his skill in the use of the spoken word.

With the tremendous improvements in communication facilities, especially in radio and television, able speakers exercise an influence, or at least a potential influence, over audiences the size and complexity of which would have seemed fantastically absurd fifty or a hundred years ago. The Kennedy-Nixon debates of 1960 proved that political debates can pull seventy to eighty million viewers to their television sets. The communication satellites provide the speaker with the opportunity of being seen and heard around the world—even in the territory of the enemy. The crises in public life continue to reveal the mettle of speakers; tend to link anew, and on a wider scale, the men of the hour and the issues which periodically threaten nations.

One of the characters in Tacitus' *Dialogue Concerning Oratory* puts this matter pointedly relative to ancient speechmaking. Observing that the splendor and magnitude of the subjects which engaged the talents of Crassus and Pompey accounted in large part for their claim on the public memory, Tacitus says the subject "lifts the mind above itself; it gives vigour to sentiment, and energy to expression." If the subject be a "paltry theft," the orator will be chilled by the meanness of the question. But if it deals with "a charge for plundering the allies of Rome," the speaker will rise to the dignity and proportions of his inquiry. Thus the speaker's effect "springs from the disasters of society." The "mind of the orator grows and expands with his subject. Without ample materials no splendid oration was ever yet produced." [2] In short, eloquence must have its theatre.

THE RELATION OF RHETORIC TO HISTORY

The foregoing section reminds us that public address functions within the framework of a social and political milieu, and that the criticism of it must be soundly based upon a full and penetrating understanding of the meaning of the events from which it issues and of the listeners who pause to consider what is said. Rhetoric and politics, age-old partners, cannot be divorced. The critic of speeches knows that their union is indissoluble.

The relationship of rhetoric and history has not always been wholly congenial. This circumstance arises from the conviction that when the historian employs the tools of the rhetorician—i.e., the instruments of effective expression—he may be tempted to depart from the strict presentation of recorded fact, and may venture into the inviting, but often inaccurate, field of narrative embellishment. Thus historians might make history largely an instrument of rhetoric. In the *Brutus*, we ob-

[2] *The Works of Cornelius Tacitus.* Translated by Arthur Murphy. London, 1813. II, 439.

serve that Cicero holds Atticus to task for describing the death of Cori-
olanus in such a manner as to raise questions concerning the justness of
the representation. Whereupon Atticus replies: ". . . it is the privilege
of rhetoricians to exceed the truth of history, that they may have an
opportunity of embellishing the fate of their heroes. . . ."[3] In Cicero's
works, as a whole, we find evidence that he believed the historian
should be a master of rhetoric. This is precisely the issue which develops when we comment on the relation of rhetoric to historical scholarship.

The ancient historians were unquestioned masters of an *art* of history
writing. They invented many speeches, undoubtedly elaborated upon
others, and wove them into the fabric of their historical narratives.
James T. Shotwell believes that the invention of speeches in history had
its origin in primitive storytelling. Thucydides then took over this form
of expression, and soon it became "a definite part of the historian's
trade."[4] Whether or not the speeches of Thucydides had substantial
bases in fact, their inclusion in the narrative added artistic lustre to the
history. Even if, as Shotwell remarks, these speeches seem somewhat
futile and unreal, they "gave to the antique mind the very reflection of reality." Other historians who introduced speeches into their presentations are Ephorus who probably made up the orations himself; and Livy,
in whose extant works can be found scores of speeches, many of them
of considerable length.

The historian's suspicion of the art of rhetoric in its relation to the
writing of history does not stem from any reluctance to make historical
narratives artistically pleasing. Rather, it grows out of the fear that in
attempting to achieve stylistic excellence, facts may be distorted. Thus,
J. B. Bury, who disliked the "rhetorical view" of history, registered his
opposition because such history failed to remain fully within the area
of facts. Evidently historians would borrow a description of a battle
or of a speech event from another writer—just because the account happened to be picturesque. So Bury concluded that as long as history
was considered an art, "the sanctions of truth and accuracy could not
be severe."[5]

Shotwell's observation reveals a similar point of view. Admittting
that history is at best "a poor enough mirror of reality," he says that it

> . . . is readily warped by art; and rhetoric is art of the most formal kind.
> It distorts into ordered arrangement the haphazard, unformed materials
> which chance produces or preserves. It sets its pieces like an impressario

---

[3] *Brutus.* Translated by J. S. Watson. New York, 1890. XI.
[4] James T. Shotwell. *The History of History.* New York, 1939. I, 219.
[5] *Selected Essays of J. B. Bury.* Edited by Harold Temperley. London, 1930,
p. 6.

and completes with convincing elegance the abrupt and incomplete dramas of reality. All history writing does this to some degree, since it is art. But rhetoric passes easily over into the sphere of conscious distortion.[6]

Rhetoric and history, however, are not irreconcilable, if, as Shotwell remarks, "by rhetoric we mean the use of language appropriate to the occasion." This brings us to the conception which the rhetorical critic keeps in mind when he speaks of the interrelation of the two subjects. In common with the historian, the critic is not interested in historiography written primarily with an eye to artistic effect. The accuracy and wisdom of rhetorical judgments depend largely upon the historian's making available authenticated records from which social situations can be reconstructed.

With due respect to the historians whose researches into the past make possible our present inquiries into speech criticism, the fact remains, unfortunate though patent, that the available record of past events is fragmentary. This is not the fault of the historian; it is, instead, the necessary circumstance of life that not everything is recorded, and hence, much that has happened is unknown, even to the most astute scholars. As Frederick J. Teggart remarked: "The subject matter of history consists of occurrences, which are unusual and out of the common, of events which for one reason or another compel the attention of men, and which are held worthy of being kept in remembrance." But it follows that every age "has its own criteria for distinguishing between the usual and the unusual, and the conception of what is remarkable and worthy of record is a function of the whole body of ideas current in any generation." [7]

TOTALITY OF HISTORICAL DATA: AN IMPOSSIBILITY

As indicated in Chapter 1, neither the critic nor the historian can acquire a totality of information which would satisfy completely the demands of present-day thought. Both must deal with statements and testimony which occasionally fall short of the strictest trustworthiness. Whether the historian likes it or not, he must still fill in open spots in the historical record. Since historians continue to select the data which are presumably most important in revealing the occurrence of events, their work remains, as Teggart puts it, a "personal presentation."

Frequently the historian delves into the motives of men to explain events. And motives are hard to determine. "The ascription of motives, based on the psychology of daily life, is a dubious venture for one who

[6] *Op. cit.*, I, 220.

[7] Frederick J. Teggart. *Theory and Processes of History.* Berkeley, California, 1941, pp. 18–19.

professes to limit his statements to known and documented facts." [8] If, as William Roscoe Thayer once remarked, man has a strong instinct for "certitude," he will unquestionably try to find out, if at all possible, the motives that gave rise to certain actions. The interpretations resulting from such quests make up a part of the available "facts" with which we reconstruct events of the past. In the absence of total and absolute data, we have to do the best we can with what is available. We cannot expect the historian to furnish materials which are beyond the range of the knowable.[9]

Because the historian has had to work with incomplete data, and because he has frequently been unable to set down available facts without traces of bias and passion, the claim has been made that history cannot be a science. Complete impartiality and detachment, complete freedom from emotional and aesthetic predispositions are undoubtedly difficult to achieve. What is true of the historian is no less, and possibly more, true of the literary and rhetorical critic. But whether or not these branches of research are scientific, in the usual sense of the term, is relatively unimportant. The only thing that really matters is that the method and techniques employed be severely critical. If we proceed along what F. M. Salter calls the "slow and laborious path of Scientific Method," by making painstakingly careful observations of the available facts; by drawing upon sound and workable hypotheses for our inquiries; by drawing logically valid inferences from the findings; and by making such verifications of our conclusions as the conditions will permit—if these things are done, and with appropriate objectivity, our investigations will have "scientific" integrity, whether the Scientific Method, *per se,* applies to them or is, instead, the "exclusive property of the physical sciences." [10]

The rhetorical critic therefore accepts as one of the limitations of his task the conclusion that he cannot get all facts necessary for complete reconstruction of the social setting in which a speech occurred. Despite that concession, the critic can still get a workable conception of the whole pattern of a social event. In order to appreciate the design of a fabric, it is not necessary to examine every thread.

One of the functions of historical investigation, wrote Dionysius in a letter to Pompeius, "is to determine where to begin and how far to proceed." Difficult as is the determination of the boundaries of original research, the objective sought for is clear and attainable. Like the historian, the rhetorical critic seeks some sort of unity in the pattern of

[8] *Ibid.,* p. 69.
[9] "Vagaries of Historians." Presidential Address to American Historical Association, December 28, 1918.
[10] "Scientific Method in Literary Research." *University Review,* 8, 1942.

social forces operating at a given moment in history. He seeks to secure a sufficiently large body of reliable data to enable him intelligently to understand a specific event—a speech, for example—in its relation to the larger whole of which it is a part. In keeping with the logical postulates of the organismic and Gestalt schools of thought, this doctrine asserts that the *whole* is primary, and that it governs the operation of the parts. Consequently, the specific occurrence must be explained in terms of the conditions under which it took place. Fox's speech on the Overtures to Napoleon, according to this view, is meaningful only when related to the complex historical continuum of which it is a part; criticism of it in isolation, and without regard for the social forces which prompted it, would be a venture in artistic futility.

SEEING THE WHOLE PICTURE

We recognize, as J. B. Bury remarks, that past events are relative to their "historical conditions; that they cannot be wrenched out of their chronological context and endowed with an absolute significance." He goes on to show what we have already referred to, that these events "are parts of a whole, and have no meaning except in relation to that whole." [11]

The implications of this thesis are manifold, but three dominant considerations plainly relate to the work of the historian and the rhetorical critic.

First, the historian and the rhetorician alike ground their procedures in evidence, in the collection, collation, and assessment of original sources, documents, of every kind, as established by reliable testimony. Long ago the Greek historian Thucydides reflected this spirit when he explained:

Of the events of the war I have not ventured to speak from any chance information, nor according to any notion of my own; I have described nothing but what I either saw myself, or learned from others of whom I made the most careful and particular enquiry. The task was a laborious one, because eye-witnesses of the same occurrences gave different accounts of them, as they remembered or were interested in the actions of one side or the other.[12]

The spirit of the old Greek represents a goal of the speech critic: avoid the openly subjective and analyze the data impersonally.

Second, both apply the concept of causality. Facts of history must be put into some sort of pattern; they must be articulated so as to sug-

[11] J. B. Bury. *The Ancient Greek Historians*. New York, 1909, p. 250.
[12] Benjamin Jowett, trans. *Thucydides*. Two volumes. Oxford, 1881. I, 15. Bk. I:22).

gest continuity, relationship. Both the critic and the historian may have that "supreme virtue" of truthfulness, to which Lecky refers, and yet fail to mould the facts of history into proper form. Both must be able to distinguish between proximate and ultimate causes; both must be able accurately to generalize from available data. In short, they must be mature logicians.

Putting the matter pointedly, Preserved Smith says that by "explaining" the phenomena of history,

> . . . we mean putting the observed facts in their proper relationships, especially in that causal relationship which . . . has usually been accepted by the human mind as the most illuminating means of grasping reality. . . . For, masses of fact can be grasped only when gathered into bundles under the collective action of some generalization. To describe facts promiscuously, without arrangement or order, is merely to produce the effect of a buzzing strident confusion in the most pluralistic of worlds.[13]

The causal relationships to which Smith refers are "those which lead us to see beneath the surface events of politics and the accidental action of personality and great cosmic forces governing and shaping the development of social forms."

The third conception which derives from the postulate that specific events are meaningful only in relation to the whole of which they are parts, is that of *historical development* and interpretation. Fundamentally, this suggests the truism that history does not exactly repeat itself. More importantly, it points to the necessity of studying the "slow processes of growth" in social forms, and of refraining from judging the actions of the past by the standards of our own times. Hence the critic must view the events of the past, as well as the judgments of men in the past, with an eye to a certain "historical relativity," believing, with Bury, that these judgments are not final. Rather, "their permanent interest lies in the fact that they are judgments pronounced at a given epoch and are characteristic of the tendencies and ideas of that epoch." [14] This observation accounts in part for the circumstances to which Teggart refers:

> In any age the activity of the historian arises from the perception that, judged by his standards, the histories previously written are unreliable and misinformed. The background of historical inquiry is, therefore, the existence of these earlier accounts, and, with implied reference to this background, the historian defines his purpose as being to set forth what it was that actually occurred.[15]

---

[13] Preserved Smith. "The Place of History Among the Sciences." In *Essays in Intellectual History*. New York, 1929, p. 212.

[14] *Ancient Greek Historians*, p. 252.

[15] *Op. cit.*, p. 15.

It should be said that some critics of antiquity paid considerable heed to the concept of historical continuity. In unmistakable terms, Quintilian announced his acceptance of the principle when he asked: "What art . . . came to perfection at once?" Impressed with the process of development, he remarked that "a thing is most natural, when nature has allowed it to be brought into the best condition." [16] Cicero contended that no art was invented and carried to perfection at a single stroke. He expressed his faith in a growing, enlarging principle of improvement, or at least change, through time. He carried his doctrine directly into practice when he evaluated the orators of Greece and Rome. Clearly, he regarded men as moulded by their age. Accordingly, speeches were to be appraised by the criteria applicable to their time.

THE CRITIC'S SOCIO-HISTORICAL INVESTIGATION [17]

The question may arise whether the reconstruction of a social and political setting for rhetorical criticism involves substantially the same materials and traces the same events as for straight historical narrative. In the main, the two inquiries draw upon common data. Since the rhetorical critic is concerned, however, with the effect of certain speeches upon certain people, and upon the flow of public events generally, it follows that he will be interested in some data which the historian might ordinarily overlook, or exclude as unnecessary to his assignment. Basically, the rhetorical critic takes all the historical narrative as the beginning of his investigation; discards some as not contributing directly to his project; and searches out other data having "rhetorical" significance. The differences relate, therefore, to details, not to fundamental method or facts. Undoubtedly, the rhetorical critic will seek further data than the historical record usually provides concerning audiences and speech situations generally. Likewise, he may make different judgments as to what the important elements in a particular occurrence are. Whereas the historian might decide that the price of cotton was important to an understanding of a given moment in history, the rhetorician, keeping a somewhat different objective in view, might conclude that the attitude of the planters toward slavery was of greater concern. These remarks simply confirm the previous observations that there cannot be a totality of information on a given subject; researchers are consequently obliged to work with the data they have, selecting and inter-

---

[16] *Institutes of Oratory.* Translated by J. S. Watson. London, 1856. IX, iv, 5.

[17] Allen Johnson. *The Historian and Historical Evidence.* New York, 1926. Allan Nevins. *The Gateway to History.* Chicago, 1963. Jacques Barzun and H. F. Graff. *Modern Researcher,* 1957. Anthony Hillbruner. *Critical Dimensions: The Art of Public Address Criticism.* New York, 1966.

preting those which, in their judgment, most demonstrably establish causal continua. Perhaps all investigators seek truth as the *ultimate* objective. Since they are not all seeking the same *immediate* ends, however, differences in their selection of facts will inevitably develop.

Study of the Occasion

Sometimes the question is asked: Why should not the critic let the speech stand on its own merits? Why is it necessary to give attention to historical trends, the immediate occasion, and the audience? Why should not the critic approach the speech as a literary form similar to a poem or an essay? Of course, a Gettysburg Address, Lincoln's Second Inaugural Address, and some of Churchill's war messages on occasion achieve a degree of eloquence to be considered as a literary genre. Frequently speeches of this type fall in the epideictic category and permit the speaker to make universal appeals and to achieve perfection of form; a speech of this type may result from careful writing, polishing, and even further editing before it finds its way into a memorial volume. The well-trained rhetorical critic of course must evaluate this type on its merits and assess its lasting influence. It is as much his concern as any other speech.

But the speech as a literary genre is an exception. Speeches find their cause for being in the heat of the forum, the drama of the court room, or the solemnity of the church. Under these conditions a speech is primarily a message, means of communication between speaker and listener; it is an instrument to impart information, to stir enthusiasm, or to gain social or political objectives. Not operating in a vacuum, the speaker and listeners interact within the social and political context of the moment. Not striving for permanence and perfection of form, speakers set for themselves attainable goals through what they put into their speeches. As we have stressed earlier, the critic must search out those causal factors that shaped the speech as it was delivered by the speaker to a particular audience at a particular time. As Wichelns argued many years ago, to measure most speeches as a literary genre is to miss the whole point of public address as a dynamic force.

Today a reader of William Jennings Bryan's speech "Prince of Peace" is likely to puzzle over why it was popular with lecture audiences across America early in this century. Only when the critic sees this address as Bryan delivered it to small-town middle-western listeners steeped in Fundamentalism can he sense why the Nebraskan was attractive to millions of little Americans. The Fireside Chats of Franklin D. Roosevelt today appear commonplace on the printed page, and certainly they can claim little literary merit; but these speeches take on significance when the critic views Roosevelt in the midst of a great depression or a great war, aspiring to calm fears, bolster courage, stir determination. The critic must appreciate Roosevelt's attempt to project himself into millions of homes via radio.

In summary, what type of questions should the critic ask in studying the historical trends and the occasion? He should consider such questions as the following:

1. What were the broad historical antecedents of the speech?
2. Was the speech a part of a larger movement or campaign?
3. What specific episodes and events gave rise to the speech?
4. Was the speaker's decision to speak a part of some carefully conceived strategy?
5. What elements in the occasion influenced the speaker in his choice of subject and approach to the occasion?
6. Did the speaker, the sponsoring organization, or the listeners determine the time and place of the speech?
7. What were the peculiar demands of the time and the place of the speech?
8. Under what conditions did the speaker address the listeners?

Study of the Audience

The speech critic must also make a careful study of the listeners of the speech. Of course, it has been argued that a speech to be a speech need not have an audience, that the intention of the speaker is what determines the genre of the piece. But, again, the undelivered speech is the exception. Speech criticism must determine its dimensions by the usual practice—not the exception. The purposeful speaker selects his speech goals—to inform, to stimulate, or to persuade—in terms of the predispositions of his listeners. Many successful speeches go through platform revision in meeting the unexpected or new demands of the moment. The critic must draw these factors into view in his attempt to decide what they mean and how they influence the speaker.

The same causal historical forces that shape the occasion also influence the listeners. To paraphrase Tennyson's Ulysses, the listeners are part of all that they have met. The historian, sociologist, and rhetorical critic must join in comprehending and interpreting significant causal forces at work.

Today the rhetorical critic finds substantial allies in the social psychologist, the sociologist, and even the geographer. The social scientist now operating with rigidly controlled methods helped by computers and refined statistical techniques provides the rhetorical critic with insights into attitudes, motivations, aspirations, and sentiments. Studies of population trends, group behavior, and attitudes provide detailed data that are valuable in understanding a given audience. Public opinion polls, consumer research, and the census reports offer additional insights into people's behavior in geographical units as small as the township or ward. Such sources provide detailed breakdowns relative to age, sex, education, occupation, racial background, religious affiliation, literacy, school attendance, and many other aspects of life. The fact that the modern speaker utilizes the social scientist and the public relations man and turns to these sources for information make it more imperative that the critic consider such materials.

The critic needs to consider questions like the following:

1. What was the composition of the audience?
2. In what ways were the listeners homogeneous?
3. What did the listeners know about the speaker? (What was the speaker's reputation?)
4. What did the listeners know about the speaker's subject?
5. How did the listeners stand on the speaker's proposition? Hostile? Neutral? Uninterested? Partisan?
6. Did a significant portion of the listeners hold attitudes favorable to the speaker's point of view?
7. What attitudes stood in the way of the speaker's achieving his objectives?

The questions suggested in this section and the previous one are of course not mutually exclusive nor are they exhaustive. Each speech situation puts its unique demands on the critic. He must pursue his research along the lines that give him insight into the total context of the speech.

Examples of the Use of Historical Data

A study of Stephen A. Douglas' speeches in the 1858 senatorial campaign, prepared by F. L. Whan,[18] reveals both the extent to which settings can be reconstructed and the use to which the facts can be put in the subsequent criticism. The first two sections of Whan's investigation, dealing respectively with the "Audience" and the "Occasion," trace in minute detail the principal factors which influenced the beliefs and attitudes of the people before whom Douglas appeared. This is chiefly a study of trends, including population changes; new attitudes toward agriculture and economics (according to Whan, the "Honor of extravagance, the new attitude towards tariff, the belief in the dignity of labor, and the experience with unemployment during the panic, all had a vital

---

[18] Ph.D. thesis. State University of Iowa, 1938. Also see William N. Brigance, ed., *A History and Criticism of American Public Address.* New York, 1943. II, 777–829.

influence on the 1858 campaign issues"); the educational movements of the period (the diffusion of learning and the advancement of training and schools "symbolized their [the people's] sincere belief in the manifest destiny of the State, the Union, and democracy"); the influence of religious movements; the trend of beliefs on slavery; and political alignments, especially the shifting of party affiliation and control "from the hands of the long dominant Democrats to the new Republican party." As for the immediate occasions, Whan considers more than the simple fact that Douglas was seeking re-election. He shows how the influence of the newspapers, splits in the Democratic party, local political conditions, and issues involved in the contest helped to give the speech situations distinctive character. All in all, Whan's study shows the complexity and interrelation of the many historical facts which affect importantly the outcome of speaking efforts.

In his study of Alexander Hamilton, Bower Aly deals with what he calls "the rhetorical atmospheres." Aly is eager to dispel false notions about the American Revolution and to present the problems that Hamilton faced in his speaking.

A popular conception, shared to a degree even by some persons who should know better, is that the American Revolution was generated by a mass of patriots who united to cast off the yoke of a foreign tyrant and immediately instituted by public acclaim the government under which the American people have lived ever since. Insofar as public discussion was required, it proceeded in a gentle spirit of sweetness and light permeated by the love that brothers bear each other. This conception could hardly be more mistaken.

The sources disclose that the American Revolution was begun by a small band of men who believed themselves to be struggling for the rights of Englishmen. Only by degrees did they come to assert the right to independence and then only over the objections of a highly influential and vocal group of their fellow citizens. During the Revolution the leaders were constantly beset by opposition to the movement, by apathy in the populace, and by disagreements among their supporters. After the defeat of the British forces, controversy continued. Such allegiance to a national state as had developed during the war of independence tended to disintegrate. Commonwealths disagreed with each other. A new national constitution and government were proposed and formed only against the strong opposition of such outstanding leaders as Willie Jones of North Carolina, Patrick Henry of Virginia, and George Clinton of New York. When, in spite of protest, the new government was finally erected, disagreements immediately arose; and differences of opinion, far from being expressed uniformly in the sedate language appropriate to the forum, were often couched in violent terms both in speeches and in the press.

Perhaps fortunately, the good that men said in those days lived after them; their evil words were often interred with their bones. But anyone who needs to understand the public discussion of Hamilton's generation should face the facts: it was frequently coarse, crude, and violent. Only in a highly charged atmosphere could George Washington have been called a patron of fraud, a hypocrite, and an impostor. Only at the lowest level of scurrilous doggerel could Thomas Jefferson have been accused of cohabiting with his own slaves to produce children for sale in the markets. Only in a time of unrestrained language could a newspaper have published the statement that '. . . as far as his maternal descent can be traced [Alexander Hamilton] was the son of an Irish Camp Girl.' Yet the statements were made; and they describe a level at which some public discussion took place in Hamilton's time. When the adoption of the Constitution was under debate, charges and counter-charges of lying and of bearing false witness were made and printed in the public press. The proposed Constitution was referred to by its opponents as a trap baited with illustrious names to catch the liberties of the people. Those who favored the new Constitution declared that their opponents were circu-lating handbills fraught with sophistry and falsehood. In an account not remarkable for its felicity, one controversialist reported a dream in which he observed his opponent's venerable shape changed 'into a bladder of wind, which laid before the fire of criticisms, instantly burst, and left nothing but small stink and garbage behind!'

An understanding of the rhetorical atmosphere of Hamilton's time ac-counts for some of the anomalies in the history of his reputation and suggests some of the values of his contribution to public discussion in his generation.[19]

John F. Wilson provides further insight into the way historical data can be used. He interprets for his reader why Warren G. Harding found eager listeners in his plea for normalcy. Wilson demonstrates how his-torical data can help interpret audience attitudes and predispositions.

On May 14, 1920, Warren Gamaliel Harding provided the Republicans with a campaign battle cry, and the vocabulary of the twenties with a new word—"normalcy." . . .

The quest for normalcy, in retrospect a futile one, was a desire for a re-turn to the conditions of Pre-World War I days, for a return to a kind of conservatism. The national audience to which it appealed was, for the most part, ready to applaud a philosophy of normalcy and all that such a philoso-phy meant. The quoted paragraph reflects not only the state of the audience to which it was directed; it also reveals Harding's personality, and in many ways exemplifies his public pronouncements from 1920 until his death in 1923. The Harding oratory of this three-year period is characterized by a fortuitous interaction between a confident personality and an audience at odds with itself. Scrutiny of Harding's speeches reveals the result of such an accidental interaction to be a rhetoric of conciliation and harmony, and these adjectives are chosen carefully, for it was not, by intent, a rhetoric of hypocrisy or compromise. Harding had spoken his soothing platitudes for so long that he actually believed them and believed that he stood for what he said.

Although no national audience during any particular era is entirely ho-mogeneous, Harding's audience was, for the most part, ready for soothing platitudes. It was spiritually tired, tired of the horrors and strains of war, tired of sacrifice, tired of Wilson's impersonal austerity and political idealism,

[19] Marie H. Nichols, ed. *A History and Criticism of American Public Address.* New York, Russell and Russell, 1955. III, 25–27.

and tired of the nervous tensions accompanying a recent Communist witch-hunt. It was nostalgic for what Harding called 'normalcy.' A sense of serenity, a state in which it could feel trust and in which it was possible to rely upon permanence, was what it sought. In effect, what it wanted most was quietude, a period of healing, a chance to pursue private affairs without governmental interference, and a chance to forget public affairs. Yet, this was a restless audience chiefly interested in practical matters and escape, and one whose consequent recoil from tension readied it to overlook lawlessness and immorality. It was an audience whose dominant mood accidentally and fatefully matched Harding's own.

The reasons why this audience yearned for a respite from tension were many. They faced complications rising out of war. They were burdened with: the largest debt of all time; overproduction in industry and agriculture; increased taxation; prices too high for their pocketbooks; unenforceable Prohibition; and rising immigration. All these things combined to push them to a breaking point. In addition to these domestic problems, there were added causes for concern beyond the nation's borders: touchy relations with Mexico; unrest in Cuba; tension in the Orient leading to rumors of war with Japan; tariff adjustment; the mechanics of establishing the League of Nations; and the problem of disarmament.

Nor need the list of grievances stop here. Though the automobile industry was on the upsurge, and developments in aviation, radio, and the motion picture were encouraging, the signs of progress were not strong enough to dispel a kind of restlessness reflected in protesters parading in overalls, Ku Klux Klan raids, and strikes in industry.

The audience, understandably, wanted to be rid of turmoil, to go back rather than forward. Its elected representatives rejected the League, preferring nationalism to federation. It gestured at its problems by restricting immigration, adopting a budget system, raising tariffs, and sponsoring a disarmament conference. These interests, however, were all but subsumed by its effort to create prosperity. Happiness, contentment, and spiritual good, it thought, lay in higher wages, stock market profits and big dividends, not in new schemes necessitating agitation. And it wanted a leader who felt and believed and said what it stood for, someone who would not 'rock the boat.' It found its man in Harding. He happened to bear the correct image, the image they happened to need.

But before we can come to a clear understanding of that image today, we must wipe away an after-image. We must remember that up until his death Harding was respected and popular. The audience which heard Harding speak during the twenties had never heard of the Teapot Dome and Elk Hills oil scandals, of corruption in the Veterans' Bureau and in the office of the Alien Property Custodian, of malfeasance in the Department of Justice. We must remember, too, that the audience had never heard of Nan Britton's charge that Harding had fathered the illegitimate child she bore in 1919. It is still a question whether during his lifetime Harding was ever fully aware of all the scandals which plagued his name posthumously. But we must remember to forget these unsavory matters if we are to discover Harding's true ethos during the twenties.[20]

[20] John F. Wilson. "Harding's Rhetoric of Normalcy, 1920–1923." *Quarterly Journal of Speech*, 48:406–407 (December, 1962).

Synthesis of Details Necessary

The rhetorical critic must, then, be able to put together many historical elements and facts; he must search out the relationships among data, making of them all a meaningful pattern which is faithful to the original occurrence in time. He must have what Edwin P. Whipple ascribed to Macaulay: an eye that "is both microscopic and telescopic," conversant at once with the smaller matters as well as "the larger objects of human concern."

Before concluding this discussion, it should be noted that, whereas we have been stressing the necessity of criticizing speeches in their relation to the *whole* social and political continuum of which they are but *parts*, practical as well as aesthetic considerations preclude the possibility of our avoiding all traces of analytical dissection. It is undoubtedly true that analysis—i.e., the abstracting of selected features, such as organization or delivery, from the total speech pattern—tends to a certain extent to falsify the appraisal. But it is possible to analyze the parts, then resynthesize them, and finally produce a composite evaluation which is faithful to the organic whole. This is precisely the critic's assignment.

It is often alleged that an atomistic approach to speech criticism militates against competent workmanship. Assuming that the critic does not resort solely to statistical analysis, and that he does not lose sight of the total speech situation in his solicitude over arguments from authority or the nature of special figures of rhetoric, he can conduct a certain amount of analytical inquiry with profit. A driver need not know all about the pistons, cam shaft, and ignition system to run an automobile, but he does have to know about the field of operation encompassed in driving—i.e., the use of the foot pedal, accelerator, and so on. To this extent he is making an atomistic approach to his assignment. Furthermore, a complete knowledge of the technical aspects may enable him the more fully to appreciate the total operation of the vehicle. It is the same with the critic. In order to secure a judgment of the *whole* speech, the critic will have to examine certain parts of it, and be fully conversant with other parts which he does not abstract from the total setting. It is important, however, that he appreciate the parts in their relation to the whole, not in their right as entities having importance out of context.

REWRITING THE CRITICISM OF ORATORY

The critical estimates of the orators will have to be reexamined and rewritten periodically. This circumstance arises, not from an alleged defect in current scholarship, but from the nature of the data with which the critic works. At no time will he have, as we have just seen, that totality of information, let alone consummate wisdom in interpretation, which will permit the preparation of definitive criticism. At best, he works with fragmentary data, and prepares his evaluations for an audience whose interests may differ sharply from those of a later generation. Just as historians find it necessary to rewrite history because of the extension of knowledge about past events, so the rhetorical critic, relying heavily upon historical data, must reshape and reinterpret his findings in the light of the newly discovered facts. Like the historian, the critic of public address must follow the "ever-ascending spiral" of research. However resourceful and competent his present probings into the activities of the great speakers, his work must inevitably bear the mark of preliminary inquiry. His labors will spare equally accomplished critics of tomorrow many false starts, but in no sense will he have given the final word on the complex problems of oratorical effectiveness. Were it otherwise, the light that guides the intellectually curious to original inquiry would burn dimly, indeed.

SUMMARY

In this chapter we have reaffirmed the dictum that the historical constituent is of major importance in rhetorical criticism. Speeches take place in social settings. Hence their full understanding requires such reconstruction of past events as will help to reveal the meaning of the words used by the speaker.

Much as he might desire it, the critic is unable to accumulate the totality of data which would result in complete and wholly faithful reproduction of a past event. However, he does the best he can with the available evidence, emphasizing those facts which are peculiarly significant to a study of the effect of the spoken word on public life.

In his attempt to re-create a situation sometimes long since dissolved by time, the critic acts both as an analyst and a synthesist. He assembles discrete data, establishes their interrelations, and thus rebuilds, under the limitations imposed by the nature of his investigation, the pattern in which the speechmaking occurred. He does this with full recognition of the need for comprehensiveness in research, impartiality and objectivity in the selection of details, reliability in the establishment of causal relations among the many facts, and a proper sense of historical development and interpretation. He can do no more; he should do no less.

EXERCISES

1. Criticize the ideas, audience appeals, structure, language, and other rhetorical elements of John F. Kennedy's "Address to the Nation," delivered October 22, 1962. (For copy, see *Representative American Speeches: 1962–1963*, New York, 1963, pp. 7–16.) Supply the necessary historical materials to give validity to your criticism.
2. Select an important political speech of the day. Secure abundant historical data and such other economic, political, religious, and social details as may be relevant to the address. Write an appraisal of the address in the light of this historical background. Supply footnotes that conform to the acceptable methods of citation.
3. Study the historical methods and techniques used by the critics of certain orators in American history. Examine especially a few of the studies in the *History and Criticism of American Public Address*.
4. Analyze carefully the influence of the occasion on Martin Luther King, Jr.'s "I Have A Dream . . ." (For copy, see *Representative American Speeches, 1963–1964*, New York, 1964, pp. 43–48.)
5. Wendell Phillips' lecture "Toussaint L'Ouverture" is sometimes called a eulogy, and at other times a persuasive speech. After carefully reading this speech, investigate how historical events altered the speech goal.
6. In what ways can the behavioral scientist help the speech critic in his study of the audience? For example see *The Great Debates*, edited by Sidney Kraus (Bloomington, Indiana, 1962).
7. Prepare a report on what information the Gallup Poll or *United States Census Reports* can provide the critic who studies a contemporary figure.
8. In no more than 1,000 words write an analysis of the historical trends and events which influenced one of the following speeches: Lincoln's Cooper Union Address; William Jennings Bryan's "Cross of Gold" speech; Booker T. Washington's Atlanta Exposition Speech of 1895; Douglas MacArthur's Speech to Joint Session of Congress, 1951.
9. To what extent is the following statement by Hans Kohn applicable to the rhetorical critic: "The historian is a man who tries to find out what has happened in the course of time and to correlate the events, within the limits of the available material on the one hand and of his intelligence, imagination, and ethical understanding on the other, into a meaningful sequence."
10. To what extent can historical reconstruction make use of imagination? For preliminary insight into the inquiry, see Hugh Ross Williamson's "History and the Writer" (in *Essays by Divers Hands*, London, 1955, ch. 27).
11. Examine the critical notes to selected speeches in *An Historical Anthology of Select British Speeches*, edited by Donald C. Bryant and others (New York, The Ronald Press Company, 1967).

CLASS PROJECT (Continued)

(1) Prepare a 500-word analysis of the general trends which gave rise to one of the speeches you selected for study.

(2) Prepare a 500-word analysis of the immediate occasion of the same speech. Include pertinent details about the time and the place of the speech.

READINGS

DEAN ACHESON. "History as Literature." An address delivered before the Society of American Historians, March 31, 1966, reprinted in *Congressional Record,* April 6, 1966, pp. A2015–18.

J. JEFFERY AUER. "The Historical Method." In *Introduction to Research in Speech.* New York, Harper and Row, 1959. Pp. 118–146.

DANIEL J. BOORSTIN, ed. *An American Primer.* Chicago, University of Chicago Press, 1966. Two volumes.

C. G. CRUMP. *History and Historical Research.* London, George Routledge & Sons, 1928.

BARBARA DEMING. "The Library of Congress Film Project: Exposition of a Method." *The Library of Congress Quarterly Journal of Current Acquisitions,* 2:3–36 (July–August–September, 1944). (Offers suggestive hints on selection of the events and facts necessary for subsequent study of historical happenings.)

ANTHONY HILLBRUNER. *Critical Dimensions: The Art of Public Address Criticism.* New York, Random House, 1966. Part One: Extrinsic Factors in Criticism of Public Address.

HOMER C. HOCKETT. *The Critical Method in Historical Research and Writing.* New York, The Macmillan Co., 1955.

A. JOHNSON. *The Historian and Historical Evidence.* New York, Chas. Scribner's Sons, 1926.

ELIHU KATZ and JACOB J. FELDMAN. "The Debates in the Light of Research: A Survey of Surveys." In *The Great Debates: Background, Perspective, Effects,* SIDNEY KRAUS, ed. Bloomington, Indiana University Press, 1962. Pp. 173–223.

MARIE HOCHMUTH NICHOLS. "Rhetoric, Public Address and History." In *Rhetoric and Criticism.* Baton Rouge, Louisiana State University Press, 1967. Pp. 19–33.

ROBERT T. OLIVER. *History of Public Speaking in America.* Boston, Allyn and Bacon, Inc., 1965.

———. "A Rhetorician's Criticism of Historiography." In *Eastern Public Speaking Conference: 1940.* Edited by HAROLD F. HARDING. New York, H. W. Wilson Co., 1940. Pp. 161–172.

TORSTEN PETERSSON. *Cicero: A Biography.* Berkeley, University of California Publications, 1919. "The Prosecution of Verres," pp. 123–170. (A critical estimate of oratory; throws light upon the social milieu in which oratory functioned.)

A Portion of That Field: The Centennial of the Burial of Lincoln. Urbana, Illinois, University of Illinois Press, 1967.

GREGG PHIFER. "The Historical Approach." In *An Introduction to Graduate Study in Speech and Theatre.* Edited by CLYDE W. DOW. East Lansing, Michigan, Michigan State University Press, 1961. Pp. 52–80.

J. T. SHOTWELL. *Introduction to the Study of History.* New York, Columbia University Press, 1922.

RAYMOND G. SMITH. "Rhetoric, Experimental Research and Men of Good Will." *Southern Speech Journal,* 30:8–14 (Fall, 1964).

WALLACE STEGNER. "On the Writing of History." *The American West,* 2:6–13 (Fall, 1965).

FOREST L. WHAN. "Stephen A. Douglas." In *A History and Criticism of American Public Address.* Edited by W. NORWOOD BRIGANCE. Vol. II. New York, Russell & Russell, 1943. Pp. 777–824.

11

Understanding a Speaker
and His Background

In a previous chapter we stressed the importance of viewing the speech in its fullest social, cultural, economic, and political context and understanding its relationships to historical trends and movements. Out of the total socio-political environment come many nuances which a man expresses in his public address. We agree with Marie Hochmuth Nichols' comments that "The criticism of speeches, like the criticism of all art, involves both analysis and synthesis. It is concerned with naming and identifying its object, locating its connections with the culture of which it is a part, and seeing it in relation to other similar phenomena. It is 'discriminating among values.'" [1]

But to see a speech in its fullest context the critic must also follow a second line of inquiry; he must seek to understand the utterance as an expression of the speaker's personality, as the culmination of his training, practical experience, reading, prior conditioning, aspirations, and goals. Whether the critic views the speaker as under the influence of powerful determinants or as a causal force in himself able to direct or alter the flow of events, makes no difference. What is important is not to view a speech apart from the speaker, for it is a personal expression, his vehicle to stir or move listeners. Unlike a poem or great play which may seek to enunciate a universal message, the speech is its creator speaking—his attempt to alter or control his environment, to lead his fellows toward what he desires or considers advantageous.

[1] Marie Hochmuth Nichols. "The Criticism of Rhetoric." In *A History and Criticism of American Public Address.* Edited by Marie H. Nichols. New York, 1955. III, 6.

In attempting to interpret and analyze a speaking career, the critic should direct his attention to the following: (1) speech training, (2) speaking experience, (3) general reading and study habits, (4) rhetorical philosophy, (5) methods of speech preparation, (6) background with reference to specific subject, and (7) forces motivating a speaker to speak on a given occasion.

At the outset, let us underscore one point. As elsewhere in rhetorical criticism, we are not necessarily concerned with the development of straight biography. A full knowledge of a speaker's life is important, and it is assumed that the critic is familiar with its details. But it is not his obligation to write biography in order to appraise oratory. In fact, to do so usually distorts the focus of critical effort, resulting in a concentration upon the events in the speaker's life rather than upon the influential elements which peculiarly mould him *as a speaker.* It may be alleged that if a man is preeminently an orator, everything associated with his biography relates pertinently to his oratory. This may be granted. The point to be observed, however, is that the biography must be articulated with the study of the man as a *speaker.* To produce a penetrating criticism, the critic must severely test the relevance of biographical facts, searching for causal links between the speaker's past and his oratorical effectiveness. If such focus is attained and consistently held, the unfolding story will contribute to an understanding of the man's speechmaking.

SPEECH TRAINING

As a starting point in a rhetorical study, the critic will do well to investigate his speaker's speech education, looking for early factors which steered the man toward eloquence or the lack of it. Interestingly, Quintilian argues that speech training starts at birth; he advises parents to take care in selecting the right nurse and argues that great advantage accrues to the child whose parents are well educated. The critic should ask himself: What was the influence of a speaker's early environment? Does the man's communicativeness result from training or accident? Is he a natural or a trained speaker? Can his appeal on a given occasion be accounted for as a surge of sudden inspiration or as the product of long training and a carefully conceived strategy? How does his training compare to that of great speakers? Has he studied the efforts of other speakers and great speeches? Answering these and similar questions requires a keen sense of what is pertinent and an intelligent sifting of data which a good biographer may provide. The critic may organize his inquiry around such questions as these: (1) What were the influences of parents and early home life upon the speaker's views, skills, and motivation? (2) Did the speaker have formal training in public speaking and rhetoric? Who were his teachers? What textbook did he study? What kind of models did he observe? (3) Did he participate in literary societies, debating, oratorical contests, and mock legislatures? (4) Did he observe and consult speakers and challenging intellectual companions? (5) Did he have an opportunity to study rhetorical theory?

In making analyses and seeking for what is germane to his investigation, the critic keeps his attention upon rhetorical training and influences; consequently he may ignore such vital facts as birth, marriage, parenthood, hobbies, recreation, and death because they tell comparatively little about the development of an orator's art. When published sources fail to provide the information which the investigator seeks—and they seldom do—he must turn to primary sources: diaries, journals, correspondence, and, when possible, direct interviews. The critic will be indeed fortunate to find a speaker who, moved by a particular historical sense or an interest in public address, has filed away textbooks, school mementoes, early speeches, literary society programs, and lecture notes from a favorite professor. School catalogues, college annuals, collegiate newspapers and magazines, official records, preserved lecture notes, and local histories are often quite revealing. When direct evidence is not available, the searcher may extend his query to neighboring institutions and the papers and memoirs of fellow students or acquaintances. A rural academy which existed in North Carolina in 1800 may have dropped from sight, but an analogous neighboring academy, a few miles away or sponsored by the same denomination, may open up additional avenues of inquiry. When a speaker leaves a little information about his own development, perhaps a teacher, a classmate, or an acquaintance may have jotted down reflections in a diary or journal. Or a school newspaper may report significant happenings when the orator was in school. Such materials permit inference about the speaker. The resourceful investigator, with persistence, may uncover data in strange and dusty places. Long-forgotten trunks or rusty file cabinets in attics or basements may bulge with diaries, letters, and documents. Sometimes rare finds—long passed over—are even found in archives, awaiting an alert person to recognize their significance.

Let us repeat a word of warning. Enamored with his subject, the novice may indeed deceive himself by amassing a stack of notes from old letters and musty documents and by preparing a catalogue of books in a personal library. But the presence of six books by John Dewey in the speaker's library may not explain why the speaker argued from a pragmatic position, particularly if the speaker never read beyond the title page of any of his collection.

SPEAKING EXPERIENCE

The influence of formal training and practical experience is most difficult to untangle. The critic need not worry about this overlapping because he may discuss the two in the same section. After finishing his formal schooling, a speaker may mature, gain confidence, perfect his oral presentations, or even start out in a new direction. Many American orators have learned or at least perfected their art at hustings, in court houses, and before church gatherings. The investigator should note the orator's participation in debating societies, local political campaigns, at fairs and conventions, in the activities of church, lodges, and social organizations. Men like Albert J. Beveridge, Robert LaFollette, Jonathan Dolliver, and William E. Borah, in starting their careers, availed themselves of every opportunity possible to appear before the public. Local newspapers indicate that these young men seldom missed a month of appearing before the public. It was not long before they were looked to as ceremonial speakers, and aspiring politicians sought their help on the stump.

After having an extensive influence in one locality or with one type of speaking, some orators actually have second careers, developing new subjects, winning new support, and occasionally changing their approach to public address. After serving as a United States Representative from New Hampshire, Daniel Webster moved to Massachusetts where he soon won a seat in the Senate. S. S. Prentiss established himself as a prominent attorney in Natchez, Mississippi, before he moved to New Orleans. Henry S. Foote, after serving as United States Senator from 1848 to 1852 and governor of Mississippi from 1852 to 1854, resettled in California where he became a political power. But, upon the approach of the Civil War, Foote returned to Mississippi to take the platform in behalf of Stephen A. Douglas. Robert Kennedy found it expedient to change his residence from Massachusetts to New York in order to have the opportunity of representing the Empire State in the United States Senate. James Pike, after an extensive legal career, moved into the ministry to become one of the outstanding spokesmen for a new theology. These changes in themselves are of course only biographical details, but each transition broadens the perspective of the speaker, changes his relationship to audiences and perhaps materially alters the course of his oratorical career. Horace G. Rahskopf, as a critic, throws considerable light on the development of Clarence Darrow, brilliant attorney, in the following paragraphs:

Into this maelstrom of activity came the young man from Kinsman via Ashtabula and rented desk room in an office for the practice of law. The city ignored him, but he did two things which broke the barriers and set him on his way: he sought out judge, later governor, John P. Altgeld; and he began to make speeches. The friendship with Altgeld became strong and abiding and motivated the younger man deeply. The opportunities for speaking were numerous, and Darrow took them as they came—at study clubs, before civic organizations, and in political rallies. He joined the select Sunset Club as well as the Henry George Single Tax Club, and campaigned for the Democratic party. As a result he was invited to speak at a Democratic free trade convention in February, 1889. His address, 'The Workingmen and the Tariff,' captivated the assembly. In that event a career was born. The newcomer was appointed to civic office and advanced rapidly. When Eugene Debs was arrested for leading his American Railway Union to strike in sympathy with employees of the Pullman Palace Car Company in 1894, Darrow felt obliged to resign his position as railroad attorney to defend the despised radical. The criminal trial was dismissed, but Debs was sentenced to prison for contempt of court. The event sealed the destiny of Clarence Darrow. He returned to private practice and found that 'more and more of the distressed and harassed and pursued came fleeing to my office door.'

During the years that followed the Pullman strike Darrow became known primarily as a labor attorney. By the time World War I broke out, however, labor had won substantial improvements in wages and conditions of work and the vengeful attitude of the public towards unions had declined. The war period and years immediately following, moreover, brought forward new problems to which Darrow turned his attention. Temporarily and with misgivings he abandoned his pacifism and his belief in non-resistance to support the struggle against German militarism. During this time there was a wave of 'anti-red' hysteria, national prohibition was enacted, racial tensions increased, a new criminology was developed, and the nineteenth century conflict between naturalism in science and fundamentalism in religion continued. In the courtroom and on the public platform Darrow fought for civil and constitutional rights, racial tolerance, humane attitudes toward crime and criminals, and freedom of thought and education.

The total number of his public speeches is impossible to count. A contemporary estimated that he appeared in 2000 trials. The number of lectures, debates, and platform speeches must be estimated in even larger thousands. In cities where he tried cases he was usually invited to lecture on some of the literary or social topics in which he was interested. As early as 1908 he was speaking against prohibition. In 1912 he made a tour of the Pacific Northwest. In 1928 and in 1930–1931 after returning from Europe he made extended tours under management of George G. Whitehead of the Redpath Lyceum Bureau. Many of the engagements of these tours were symposia on religion which pitted the great agnostic against representatives of Protestant, Catholic, and Jewish faiths from the local communities. Darrow once remarked that there was scarcely a city of any size in the United States in which he had not spoken at least once and in all the larger cities many times, and that "probably few men in America have ever spoken to so many people or over so long a stretch of time." [2]

---

[2] Horace G. Rahskopf. "The Speaking of Clarence Darrow." In *American Public Address*. Edited by Loren Reid. Columbia, Missouri, 1961, pp. 30–31.

GENERAL READING AND STUDY HABITS

Cicero once said, ". . . no man could ever excel and reach eminence in eloquence, without learning, not only the art of oratory, but every branch of useful knowledge." The old Roman pronounced a most severe test for anyone who aspired to eloquence, but in doing so he set forth an important yardstick for measuring the depth and substance of a speaker. And it is true that many speakers are omnivorous readers and profound students of their art.

In doing a rhetorical study, the researcher considers how well informed his speaker is, how he acquired and digested general information. If he is to get a full view of the speaker, he must look into reading tastes and habits and into efforts to collect materials for future reference. It is not unusual for a speaker to develop elaborate notetaking procedures and to assemble voluminous files.

The examples of two recent Presidents, Dwight Eisenhower and John F. Kennedy, will illustrate interesting work habits and suggest what cues a biographer may provide the rhetorical scholar. Eisenhower, the man of action, not long from the battlefields of World War II, thought of general preparation in terms of the staff command system of the Army, through which he had advanced. Sherman Adams reports that the General rebelled at "endless paper work," sought briefings upon daily events, insisted upon "keeping the conversation brief and to the point," and "listened intently." Adams records:

. . . Eisenhower was usually already in his office unless he had a breakfast appointment with a member of Congress or another government official, which would keep him a little later. Ready for him when he arrived were the latest State Department, CIA and military intelligence reports and the staff secretary, at first General Carroll and later General Goodpaster, would be on hand to give him the essentials in all the various intelligence information. Once a week the White House staff was briefed by the CIA and at the weekly National Security Council meetings the President listened to another summary of top-secret world developments by Allen Dulles, the CIA head. Eisenhower glanced at several newspapers every morning but the one more often at the top of the pile was the New York *Herald Tribune.* He paid little attention to the newspapers that continually belabored him, such as the St. Louis *Post-Dispatch,* and seldom read the Washington papers. He once said to me, 'If you want to find out how the people feel about things, read the papers, but not the New York or Washington papers.' Although he was interested in histories of the Civil War and occasionally relaxed in the evening with a paperbound Western story, Eisenhower was not much of a reader. He was impatient with the endless paperwork of the presidency and always tried to get his staff to digest long documents into one-page summaries, which was sometimes next to impossible to do. He seldom exchanged written memoranda with me or with the Cabinet members or his staff. He preferred to get his information from talking with people who knew the issues involved in the matter he was considering. He listened intently, keeping the conversation brief and to the point with no wandering digressions, and he interrupted now and then with a quick and penetrating question that brought the whole discussion into clearer focus.[3]

Now contrast John F. Kennedy with Eisenhower. How differently Kennedy approached the Presidency! The younger man, who was more the scholar and reader, provides a much different picture of work attitudes and procedures, as the account of Arthur M. Schlesinger, Jr., shows:

Dressing in the morning, he would prop open a book on his bureau and read while he put on his shirt and tied his necktie. He read mostly history and biography, American and English. The first book he ever gave Jacqueline was the life of a Texan, Marquis James's biography of Sam Houston, *The Raven*. In addition to *Pilgrim's Way*, *Marlborough* and *Melbourne*, he particularly liked Herbert Agar's *The Price of Union*, Samuel Flagg Bemis's *John Quincy Adams*, Allan Nevins's *The Emergence of Lincoln*, Margaret Coit's *Calhoun* and Duff Cooper's *Talleyrand*. He read poetry only occasionally—Shakespeare and Byron are quoted in the looseleaf notebook he kept in 1945–1946—and by this time fiction hardly at all. . . . Kennedy seldom read for distraction. He did not want to waste a single second.

He read partly for information, partly for comparison, partly for insight, partly for the sheer joy of felicitous statement. He delighted particularly in quotations which distilled the essence of an argument. He is, so far as I know, the only politician who ever quoted Madame de Staël on Meet the Press. Some quotations he carried verbatim in his mind. Others he noted down. The looseleaf notebook of 1945–1946 contained propositions from Aeschylus ('In war, truth is the first casualty'), Isocrates ('Where there are a number of laws drawn up with great exactitude, it is a proof that the city is badly administered; for the inhabitants are compelled to frame laws in great numbers as a barrier against offenses'), Dante ('The hottest places in Hell are reserved for those who, in a period of moral crisis, maintain their neutrality'), Falkland ('When it is not necessary to change it is necessary not to change'), Burke ('Our patience will achieve more than our force'), Jefferson ('Widespread poverty and concentrated wealth cannot long endure side by side in a democracy'), de Maistre ('In all political systems there are relationships which it is wiser to leave undefined'), Jackson ('Individuals must give up a share of liberty to preserve the rest'), Webster ('A general equality of condition is the true basis, most certainly, of democracy'), Mill ('One person with a belief is a social power equal to ninety-nine who have only interest'), Lincoln ('Public opinion is everything. With it nothing can fail, without it nothing can succeed'). . . . There emerges from such quotations the impression of a moderate and dispassionate mind, committed to the arts of government, persuaded of the inevitability of change but distrustful of comprehensive plans and grandiose abstractions, skeptical of excess but admiring of purpose, determined above all to be effective.[4]

[3] Sherman Adams. *First Hand Report*. New York, Harper and Row, 1961, pp. 72–73.
[4] Arthur M. Schlesinger, Jr. *A Thousand Days: John F. Kennedy in the White House*. Boston, Houghton Mifflin Co., 1965, pp. 105–106.

But let us stress that it is the task of the rhetorical critic to interpret such materials as those from Adams and Schlesinger. Remember that the goal is not biographical; it is to see the person as a speaker in his total dimension; to understand his speeches, to account for his influence upon the rostrum. Therefore, the researcher must reflect upon and weigh how work habits influenced a man's communicativeness, whether the speaker integrated his reading and thinking meaningfully into his speeches. Perhaps a third example will show how, through the use of such materials, a critic can place an orator in perspective. Concerning Lord Macaulay, Margaret Wood writes as follows:

He [Macaulay] continued his habits of omnivorous reading established early in life. Even in 1836, when he was besieged by activities in India, he studied Greek and Latin and read French, Italian, and a little Spanish. From Calcutta he wrote, 'I have read Demosthenes twice, I need not say with what delight and admiration. I am now deep in Isocrates; and from him I shall pass to Lysias.' He considered Cicero's treatises on oratory the best ever written on that subject, but he thought that next to Demosthenes, Dante should be studied by those desiring oratorical eminence.

Macaulay applied himself to writing as industriously as he did to reading. While contributing to *Knight's Quarterly Magazine* and to the *Edinburgh Review*, he was formulating many of his concepts of government. He made repeated revisions when he was writing his history, and then submitted his writing to the test of being read aloud to his family or to his friends.

His phenomenal memory enabled him to use a quantity of historical precedent and a variety of literary allusion that were astounding. His speeches, however, were more Attic than Asian in style. Greville recorded that Macaulay could repeat all Demosthenes by heart, and all Milton, a great part of the Bible, and the New Testament in Greek—that he managed to transfer contents of books to his own mind where they were always accessible. Macaulay wrote, 'I have no pleasure from books so great as that of reading over for the hundredth time great productions, which I almost know by heart.'

For the first thirty years of his life Macaulay was actually preparing to speak in Parliament. The fact that he had a photographic mind may, however, have had a negative influence on his delivery, for he was accused of memorizing his speeches. Because he said that he revised speeches in his head and that he had to force himself to forget some quotations, it may be assumed that his speeches were carefully thought out but not necessarily written and memorized. At no time when he rose in the House did he have a note in his hand or a manuscript in his pocket. The similarity of phrasing and of ideas between some of his essays and some of his speeches indicates that he consciously or unconsciously transferred material from one form of discourse to another.[5]

In comparing the two excellent accounts of Adams and Schlesinger with that of Wood, certain points of difference are evident. Wood points to evidences of Macaulay's making preparation "to speak in Par-

[5] Margaret Wood. "Lord Macaulay, Parliamentary Speaker: His Leading Ideas." *Quarterly Journal of Speech*, 44:376 (December, 1958).

liament." Does this emphasis mean that Wood lost her objectivity or perhaps slanted her presentation in the direction of isolating elements to support her position? Certainly this was not the case. She was well aware of the total biography of her man, but as a speech critic she sought, as objectively as she could, to show briefly how general reading and study influenced Macaulay's oratory.

RHETORICAL PHILOSOPHY

In their quest for eloquence, speakers may become philosophical about the nature of public address and its great principles. Public figures sometimes reflect upon their oratorical experiences or about dramatic moments in their speaking. From time to time in their busy lives they pause to comment on speakers and speaking, on instances when well chosen words made a difference, on their own triumphs during the heat of debate. With an eye to what the biographer may later say, they preserve their rhetorical recollections for later study.

Cicero, Saint Augustine, Thomas Wilson, Francis Bacon, John Quincy Adams, Albert J. Beveridge, John P. Altgeld, Theodore R. McKeldin, Norman Thomas, and others have written upon public speaking. William Jennings Bryan edited *The World's Famous Orations*, a ten-volume set. Private papers sometimes divulge letters and even unpublished essays on a speaker's rhetorical views. For example, Loren Reid uncovered a sixteen-page closely written manuscript, "Public Speaking," dated 1838, among the papers of William Ewart Gladstone.[6] In his journals Ralph Waldo Emerson made "a hundred and forty-two references to Webster, sixty-one to Everett, fifty-two to Channing, forty-six to Burke, nineteen to Choate, sixteen to Phillips, fifteen to Demosthenes, six to Chatham." Emerson gave two lectures on "Eloquence" (1847, 1867) and scattered tidbits about speechmaking through his other papers and letters.[7]

Glen E. Mills has drawn together Daniel Webster's principles of rhetoric which he found "widely scattered throughout Webster's letters, 'Autobiography,' 'Diary,' published interviews and speeches." Organizing his analysis around the five classical canons, Mills has written a splendid essay which shows how Webster attempted to analyze "the causes of effects" of speaking and writing.[8] It also shows what a critic may contribute through painstaking research.

[6] Loren Reid. "Gladstone's Essay on Public Speaking." *Quarterly Journal of Speech*, 39:365–372 (October, 1953).

[7] Theodore T. Stenberg. "Emerson and Oral Discourse." In *Studies in Rhetoric and Public Speaking*. New York, 1962, pp. 153–180.

[8] Glen E. Mills. "Daniel Webster's Principles of Rhetoric." *Speech Monographs*, 9:124–140 (1942).

METHODS OF IMMEDIATE SPEECH PREPARATION

In his attempt to penetrate the power of a speaker, the critic should investigate specific methods of preparation, pursuing such queries as the following: (1) How does the speaker collect materials for a given speech? (2) What steps does he follow in digesting and analyzing the problem? (3) What steps does he take in preparing a speech manuscript? (4) Does the speaker seek assistance from others in his speech preparation? (5) Does the speaker weaken or destroy his integrity through the use of speech writers and research assistants? (6) What effort does he make to check the accuracy of the facts and the soundness of the analysis? (7) Through the process of invention, does the speaker reveal himself to be a creative artist worthy of emulation?

Some of the difficulties accompanying research into the orator's method of preparing his speeches are revealed in Forest L. Whan's study of Stephen A. Douglas:

A second question of importance concerns the method used by Douglas in preparing his speeches. Little positive evidence remains on this point. But it seems certain that he spoke extemporaneously in every instance during the campaign of 1858. Stevens tells us that Douglas frequently admitted that he could not write a speech for delivery. The conclusion is further borne out by the lack of speech notes found in the Douglas manuscripts. Although the manuscripts contain many personal items, such as receipts for hotel bills, not a single speech outline or page of notes taken during the debates is to be found for the year 1858. One thing is certain; like all local campaigns in which Douglas participated for 25 years, that of 1858 was far too strenuous to allow either contestant to write out his speeches in full, even had he been so inclined. Lincoln claimed that he trusted to the inspiration of the moment; the more experienced Douglas may have done likewise.

More positive evidence that the speeches were not written lies within reported speeches themselves. Douglas was often interrupted by members of his audience or by an opponent on the platform. In every instance he replied to his questioner, and after his reply, worked back smoothly into the stream of thought that had been interrupted. We must conclude that Douglas carried the outline of his speech in mind and delivered that speech extemporaneously.[9]

Fuller appreciation of a speaker and his speeches results from acquiring insight into the way he went about preparing his talks. This is not a simple matter. The problem has its roots in the orator's early training, his home life, possible influence of church and school and various clubs, his reading habits and favorite methods of study, and a host of other factors. For instance, consider John Bright, the nineteenth-

[9] W. Norwood Brigance, ed. *A History and Criticism of American Public Address.* New York, 1943. II, 796–797.

century English reformer, whose early training moulded his method of writing speeches. We find that Bright's training in a home of strict Quaker observance, his early associations with English mill hands (especially with Nicholas Nuttall, whom he engaged in political discussions), his lifelong interest in such publications as the *Manchester Guardian*, his participation in the activities of the Rochdale Literary and Philosophical Society—we find that these and other influences helped to determine his way of preparing speeches.

Furthermore, the critic searches out the facts concerning the orator's sources of material. Do they stem directly from his reading, the nature of which is ascertainable? From his public and private experiences? From his consultations and conferences with others? Something has already been said about this point in the chapter on textual authenticity. It is enough to add here that speculations on the sources of speech materials might tend to modify judgments as to the relative merit of speeches. Everyone is agreed that Franklin D. Roosevelt was a speaker of consummate skill. But many have inquired: Did he prepare the talks, and, if so, how? He had, for example, much early training in French, German, and other languages. At Groton Academy the program was essentially classical—Latin, Greek, English literature, mathematics, with daily required religious services. The question arises whether such a curriculum contributed more to his speaking skills than would have wider studies in economics, later history, English composition, and speechmaking. (Groton required debating.) Roosevelt's educational experiences at Harvard also may have contributed directly to his later ideas, to his methods of speech composition, to wielding his language usages. He had a course in public address under George P. Baker, prominent teacher of argumentation. These learning experiences presumably affected favorably Franklin D. Roosevelt's later methods as a speaker.[10]

Let us turn to some illustrations of how speech critics have treated this phase of their investigations. In recent years researchers have demonstrated unusual resourcefulness in considering the speech preparation of a given orator. Through painstaking analysis of speech manuscripts at the Franklin D. Roosevelt Library, careful reading of Roosevelt's biographies and memoirs of associates, and interviews with persons such as Grace Tully, Robert Sherwood, and Samuel Rosenman, Earnest Brandenburg constructed a detailed account of Roosevelt at work on his speeches. With a deep appreciation for public address and a sense of historical significance, Franklin D. Roosevelt had preserved an unusual amount of source materials, including files and numerous versions of

[10] Marie H. Nichols, ed. *A History and Criticism of American Public Address.* New York, Russell and Russell, 1955. III, 458–530.

many of his important speeches. Brandenburg made a detailed study of seventeen addresses on international affairs, delivered by Roosevelt between September 3, 1939, and December 7, 1941.

Miss Grace Tully, who personally typed most of the drafts for the seventeen addresses analyzed, provided much general information about the procedure and the persons involved in helping Roosevelt prepare those speeches. For each of his addresses, Roosevelt called upon the tremendous resources available to him. Drafts of suggested speeches, or of portions of a possible speech, typically came from some dozen different people, members of the Cabinet, or those in position to be of special assistance.

During the period between September 3, 1939 and December 7, 1941, the President himself normally dictated to Miss Tully the first draft of a speech from his general knowledge or from materials which he had had submitted concerning certain issues. Frequently, some of his close advisers, such as Judge Samuel I. Rosenman, Harry L. Hopkins, Cordell Hull, or Robert Sherwood, were present and would intersperse comments or make suggestions.

After a first draft had been completed, copies of it were circulated to those designated by Roosevelt. For example, Secretary Hull read the speeches having to do with foreign policy. After Henry L. Stimson became a member of the Cabinet, June 20, 1940, he was called upon for suggestions concerning foreign policy. If an issue involving the military was to be included, General Marshall and Admirals Leahy and King were asked for opinions. The various comments and suggestions were then reviewed by Roosevelt or his immediate speech assistants—Rosenman, Hopkins, and Sherwood—and the President would dictate another draft. Or, a new draft might be prepared by one or more of the President's advisers working from marginal notes written into the previous draft by Mr. Roosevelt. The next draft would again be circulated.

Most Cabinet members saw some draft of the speech before it was finally delivered. Cordell Hull, or the Acting Secretary of State, usually saw one or more of the drafts of every one of the speeches of this period. With the receipt of comments and suggestions, and usually in the presence of one or more of his close advisers, Roosevelt dictated a new version of the address. He dictated (holding before him the previous draft which he had marked up in considerable detail) by striking out and substituting words, sentences, or entire sections. Each speech had some three to ten complete revisions. Available at the Roosevelt Library at Hyde Park, New York, are drafts which have been numbered for each of the addresses as follows:

Sept. 3, 1939: Drafts 1, 2, and the Original Reading Copy.
Sept. 21, 1939: Draft 2 and the Original Reading Copy.
Jan. 3, 1940: Drafts 1, 2, and the Original Reading Copy.
April 15, 1940: One draft, unnumbered, and the Original Reading Copy.
May 10, 1940: No available drafts.
May 16, 1940: Drafts 1, 2, and the Original Reading Copy.
May 26, 1940: Drafts 1, 2, and the Original Reading Copy.
June 10, 1940: No available drafts.
July 19, 1940: Drafts 1, 2, 3, and the Original Reading Copy.
Sept. 2, 1940: Drafts 1, 2, and the Original Reading Copy.
Dec. 29, 1940: Drafts 1, 4, 5, 6, 7, and the Original Reading Copy.

Jan. 6, 1941: Drafts 1, 2, 3, 4, 5, 6, 7, and the Original Reading Copy.
Jan. 20 1941: Drafts 1, 2, 3, 4, 5, 6, and the Original Reading Copy.
March 15, 1941: Drafts 1, 2, 4, 5, and the Original Reading Copy.
May 27, 1941: Drafts 1, 2, 3, 4, 5, 6, 8, 9, and the Original Reading Copy.
Sept. 11 1941: Drafts 1, 2, 3, and the Original Reading Copy.
Oct. 27, 1941: Drafts 1, 2, 3, 6, and the Original Reading Copy. . . .

Roosevelt's former personal stenographer (Miss Tully) had aided in the preparation of all the addresses analyzed, and she attempted to recall exactly which of the advisers around Roosevelt during those years had been most active in helping with each address. She had only her memory to rely upon, but she was reasonably certain that the persons whose names appear below assisted with the addresses given on the dates indicated:

Sept. 3, 1939: Messrs. Hull, Welles, Norman Davis.
Sept. 21, 1939: Judge Rosenman, Messrs. Hopkins, Hull, Welles, Senator Barkley.
Jan. 3, 1940: All Cabinet members, Judge Rosenman, Mr. Hopkins.
April 15, 1940: Messrs. Welles, Hull.
May 10, 1940: Messrs. Welles, Hull.
May 16, 1940: General Marshall, Admiral Leahy, Admiral King, Judge Rosenman, Mr. Hopkins.
May 26, 1940: Judge Rosenman, Mr. Hopkins.
June 10, 1940: Messrs. Hull, Welles.
July 19, 1940: Messrs. Thomas G. Corcoran, Benjamin Cohen, Judge Rosenman.
Sept. 2, 1940: Judge Rosenman (at Hyde Park), Mr. Ickes (on train to Tennessee).
Dec. 29, 1940: Messrs. Robert Sherwood, Hopkins, Hull, and Judge Rosenman.
Jan. 6, 1941: All Cabinet members, Judge Rosenman, Messrs. Hopkins, William Knudsen, Sherwood.
Jan. 20, 1941: Judge Rosenman, Messrs. Hopkins, Sherwood.
March 15, 1941: Messrs. Hopkins, Sherwood, Edward R. Stettinius, Jr., General James H. Burns.
May 27, 1941: Messrs. Welles, Hull, Sherwood.
Sept. 11, 1941: Judge Rosenman, Messrs. Hopkins, Hull, Stimson, Knox.
Oct. 27, 1941: Messrs. Sherwood, Knox, Hull, Stimson, Welles.

She emphasized the fact that Roosevelt's State of the Union addresses (delivered January 3, 1940 and January 6, 1941) were the product of at least ten days' careful work, and had received comment and suggestions from all Cabinet members. . . .

Robert Sherwood, who joined Roosevelt's inner circle of speech advisers and collaborators during the campaign of 1940, has explained that he is able to identify a few 'specific passages or ideas that were suggested by Hopkins, Rosenman or me or by others outside the White House, but the collaboration between the three of us and the President was so close and so constant that we generally ended up unable to say specifically who had been primarily responsible for any given sentence or phrase.' [11]

[11] Earnest Brandenburg. "The Preparation of Franklin D. Roosevelt's Speeches." *Quarterly Journal of Speech*, 35:214–221 (April, 1949).

Two other researchers have provided additional insight into how Roosevelt developed his speeches. G. Jack Gravlee, who studied F.D.R.'s campaign for the Vice-Presidency in 1920,[12] relates how Roosevelt employed Stephen T. Early as an advance man to prepare "reports concerning approaching speaking engagements." Traveling ahead of Roosevelt, Early "always tried to keep 'the Boss' well informed on any current facts or rumors pertaining to a specific locale. In addition to identifying a problem, he frequently attempted to suggest the solution that seemed to be the most feasible." Consequently, when Roosevelt appeared on the rear platform of his special train he was well informed about his listeners and their community.

Looking at another aspect of Roosevelt's *inventio*, Laura Crowell subjected several versions of the same speech to rigid inspection and carefully determined what platform alterations Roosevelt made.[13]

In a similar project, Russel Windes, Jr., has made an equally penetrating analysis of how Adlai E. Stevenson organized his speech staff in the 1956 campaign. Windes related how members were selected, how they worked together, and what they contributed to Stevenson. Windes perceptively describes how Stevenson edited his speeches:

That Stevenson spends vast amounts of time in editing his speeches is common knowledge. An examination of fifteen of his reading manuscripts used during the 1956 campaign reveals the amount and type of changes that he made in his speeches from the time the final draft was turned over to him until he delivered the speech. In the fifteen speeches Stevenson made 976 corrections in his 'beavering away' process (as some staff members called it) on his manuscripts, for an average of sixty-five changes per speech. In three of these speeches (Portland, October 11; Cincinnati, October 19; Minneapolis, September 29) he made about 125 changes each. Of the changes, 723 were additions and 246 were deletions of words, phrases, sentences, or whole paragraphs. Seven changes in position or development of paragraphs were made. Of the 723 additions, fourteen qualified or limited an assertion; 135 amplified a point or statement; 158 simplified or clarified; 216 gave more directness, force, or emphasis; 53 identified the speaker more strongly with the audience or occasion: 130 increased the energy, color, or suggestiveness of language; 17 of them were changes in transitions. Of the 246 deletions, a majority were made to bring the speech within a time limit. About one-third of the deletions concerned redundant words, phrases, and sentences. The other deletions were made to make space for qualifications to statements and simplifying and clarifying thoughts.

Stevenson's editorial work on a speech continued until the moment he stepped to the platform to deliver it. Even during the final few minutes before a speech, according to associates, he would worry about the wording of his speech. One associate reported that Stevenson would say, 'I think

[12] G. Jack Gravlee. "Stephen T. Early: The 'Advance Man'." *Speech Monographs*, 30:41–49 (March, 1963).

[13] Laura Crowell. "Word Changes Introduced *Ad Libitum* in Five Speeches by Franklin Delano Roosevelt." *Speech Monographs*, 25:229–242 (November, 1958).

this word makes the meaning much clearer, don't you?' The associate indicated that he usually agreed, although 'sometimes it didn't.' At this stage of speech preparation nobody found it profitable to argue with the Governor.

Even while delivering the speech Stevenson made extensive changes in his manuscript. In a sample of ten of his major campaign speeches he made 990 alterations in the manuscript during delivery, including additions, deletions, and spontaneous variations. In one speech, at Newton, Iowa, he made 174 alterations during a forty-five minute speech.

The finished product that reached the ears of Stevenson's listeners, therefore, was something all Stevenson's own, regardless of who had worked on it. Said one writer, 'He would tear the thing apart and put it back together until he had it the way he wanted it.' What may be most important is not the description of the preparation of a Stevenson campaign speech, but rather the impact of the process on the candidate. More bluntly, did Stevenson's speech staff run the campaign or did Stevenson? Whatever may be the case with other candidates, one may well conclude that a speech by Stevenson was a speech of Stevenson. Through the seminars and his own experience he knew the issues of the campaign; through his selection of speech writers, the program papers, and the issue book his writers knew his position on the issues; and through his extensive revision and editing his speeches expressed almost always what he himself believed. In answer to the question, naive as it may be, 'Did Stevenson write his own speeches?' one would almost have to reply, 'Yes, he did.' [14]

KNOWLEDGE OF A SPECIFIC SUBJECT

What we have discussed in the early sections of this chapter all contribute to and shape a speaker's specific knowledge on a given subject. Brain specialists now tell us that almost everything which we encounter during our lives is stored away, has made its little creases somewhere in the intricate cell complexes of our brains. Find the right stimulation, and the brain will release such experiences from the long dim past. When the orator meets an audience he expresses a message which covertly and overtly represents a synthesis of his training, experience, habits, drives, attitudes—in fact all that constituted what is referred to as personality.

Recognizing at the outset the complexity of attitudes and personality and the difficulty of ever completely understanding anyone—even himself —the critic must attempt to do what he can to estimate the speaker's grasp of his subject, to judge the depth of his thinking, to estimate whether his judgment is based upon rational means. The speech researcher must not be misled into thinking that the speech proper will provide all the clues necessary to understand the speaker's sources or his major premises. What the speaker expresses in his brief moment be-

[14] Russel Windes, Jr. "Adlai E. Stevenson's Speech Staff in the 1956 Campaign." *Quarterly Journal of Speech*, 46:32–43 (February, 1960).

fore his audience may constitute a small sample, a sign, a beginning, but little more, to uncovering the man's resources.

The critic need ask himself such questions as the following: (1) Are the basic premises of the speaker traceable to his home and his early schooling? (2) What general ideas or themes expressed in the speech come from his general reading? (3) Do the speaker's general attitudes toward the world around him suggest a source of ideas? (4) How long has the speaker thought about the subject? (5) What direct experience has he had with his subject? (6) Do the books which he has recently read provide an insight into the speaker's arguments? (7) Has he written articles or books on the subject? Has he been interviewed about his thoughts? (8) Has he made other speeches on the topic? (9) Has he developed his opinion on the topic from investigations conducted on related subjects? (10) With whom has he discussed the subject through letters or direct conversation? (11) Has his constituency influenced his position? (12) Has a pressure group exerted influence upon him?

The answers to these and similar questions demand extensive and difficult research. Of course the critic will gain much help from biographers, historians, and other critics who had their turn at attempting to understand the orator. But what have they missed? Have they looked at the man in his entire context? Again we suggest that there is no short cut; the rhetorical critic must turn to primary sources for concentrated research. On many issues the scholar must take an intellectual leap in the dark in his guesses about why his speaker argued the way he did.

MOTIVATING FORCES

Throughout this textbook we have emphasized that a speech must be evaluated in terms of the response which it receives. Interested in social control, the speaker selects a goal and plans a strategy to gain his end. It is the critic's task to measure promise by results. Herein he must concern himself with the forces that motivated the speaker on a given occasion. The way a speaker uses his materials, that is, selecting or rejecting on the basis of his over-all strategy, is determined by his motivation.

The critic therefore must ponder such questions as the following: (1) Why did the speaker choose to speak on a given occasion? (2) What did he hope to accomplish? (3) Were his goals determined on the basis of personal interests or social objectives? (4) Were the speaker's goals ethically commendable? (5) How was the goal presented in the speech? Was it concealed? (6) Was the immediate goal different from the ultimate goal?

Determining a speaker's goals may be extremely difficult because the speaker's success (persuasion) may depend upon concealing his plan and ultimate objectives. In fact he may announce to his listeners one goal which he thinks will be acceptable, but he may work toward another end. In the 1956 campaign Adlai E. Stevenson said in many of his speeches that his wish was to inform the voters. But as a presidential candidate vigorously seeking office his goal was not to inform but to persuade. The strategy of Wendell Phillips in his famous lecture on Toussaint L'Ouverture also illustrates this point. This lecture, which Phillips first gave sometime before 1860, appeared to be just another lyceum presentation. In his introduction Phillips says that "his sketch" was "at once a biography and an argument." So it is! Lecture audiences enjoyed hearing the story of the heroic Negro general who succeeded in defeating the French, the English, and the Spanish. However, when Phillips delivered this lecture in 1863 his goal changed. At that moment the orator was attempting to convince Northern audiences that Negroes should be used in the Union armies. Therefore, what appeared to be the exciting *biography* became a powerful *argument* to persuade. If the critic tries to evaluate this lecture without taking into consideration Phillips' goals, he seriously misses the point.

In his study of Robert Barnwell Rhett's speech, delivered at Grahamville, South Carolina, H. Hardy Perritt exposes the speaker's strategy in these words:

> Doubtless Grahamville was chosen as the site for the speech because it was hoped that the favorable cheers would reverberate throughout the South, reaching the ears of numbers of potential secessionists. Although he was speaking to a highly partisan audience at Grahamville, Rhett expected his words, through the public press, to reach citizens all over South Carolina and other slaveholding states who were much less sympathetic toward his views. This not uncommon dual audience of the political speaker resulted in a speech which undertook to arouse the partisans, and to convince the doubters and disbelievers of the soundness of disunion. Perhaps, therefore, the omission of any mention of separate state secession was as important as anything Rhett did say. He did not disavow separate secession by South Carolina, but he called for united action by all the South. He did not feel compelled, however, to say what he would recommend if Southern unity should prove impossible again. Furthermore, Rhett's avoidance of specific statement of his proposition until the conclusion seems to indicate a conscious arrangement of the speech to appeal to the neutral or opposed audience.[15]

As we have said earlier, the critic must make a careful analysis of the orator's strategy, that is, the plan by which he hopes to keep the speech marching toward its goal. In pursuing this part of his study, the critic must give careful attention to the speaker's motivation.

---

[15] J. Jeffery Auer, ed. *Antislavery and Disunion, 1858–1861, Studies in the Rhetoric of Compromise and Conflict.* New York, 1963, p. 104.

SUMMARY

A speech is not impersonal; it cannot be understood apart from the person who conceives, develops, and then uses it as a means to reach, stir, excite, and direct listeners. It becomes the culmination of the speaker's learning, experience, prior conditioning, aspirations, and goals. In order to see the speech in full context, the critic must become thoroughly familiar with the background and personality of the speaker. After gaining full knowledge of his subject's life, the critic must consider only those elements that peculiarly influenced the man as a speaker. The critic, of course, makes use of biographies and secondary sources whenever possible, but often he must turn to primary sources to ferret out what he seeks. He does not attempt biography; instead he concentrates upon speech training, speaking experience, general reading, study habits, rhetorical philosophy, approaches to speech preparation, background information, and the speaker's motives.

EXERCISES

1. Investigate the rhetorical training of one of the following speakers: Edward Everett, Wendell Phillips, Abraham Lincoln, Theodore Roosevelt, or Woodrow Wilson.
2. In light of their speech training and backgrounds, how do you account for the oratorical accomplishments of the following: Patrick Henry, Henry Clay, Susan B. Anthony, and Booker T. Washington? See the three volumes of *A History and Criticism of American Public Address.*
3. Prepare an analysis of the speech training of a contemporary figure such as Winston Churchill, Norman Thomas, Lyndon B. Johnson, Richard M. Nixon, or Martin Luther King, Jr.
4. Interview a prominent local speaker on how he prepares his speeches. If possible, record your interview.
5. Write a detailed report on how a famous speech was prepared. Consult the memoirs or biographies on one of the recent Presidents of the United States.
6. Through the centuries thinkers have argued that a speaker should be a man of good character. The old Roman Marcus Cato defined the ideal as "a good man, skilled in speaking." (See Quintilian's discussion in William M. Smail's *Quintilian on Education.* New York, 1938, pp. 108–119). What justification do you find for this position?
7. Study carefully the biographical sketches of speakers whose speeches are listed in *Representative American Speeches* (see Appendix of each volume). What generalizations can you make about the backgrounds of these persons?
8. Compare the speech backgrounds of prominent British speakers with equally prominent American speakers. Consult Owen Peterson, "The Role of Public Speaking in the Early Years of the British Labour Party," *Quarterly Journal of Speech,* 48:254–260 (October, 1962) and *Dod's Parliamentary Companion,* issued annually.

9. If a reader can appreciate a novel without knowing anything about the author, why should it be necessary to know about an orator in order to appreciate a speech?
10. Read Sidney Hyman's "When Washington Reads" (*The New York Times Book Review*, August 14, 1966, p. 1) for possible hints on how reading habits affect the formulation of political thought.
11. Examine a full-length biography of a man who had a certain measure of renown as a speaker (for example, *Disraeli* by Robert Blake, New York, 1967) to find out how the author—not acting in the role of a speech critic—dealt with early training as a possible determinant of later conduct.
12. For insight into the way in which Lincoln's reading affected his style and thinking, read Arthur Lehman Goodhart's "Lincoln and the Law" in *Lincoln and the Gettysburg Address*, edited by Allan Nevins (Urbana, University of Illinois Press, 1964, pp. 38–71).

CLASS PROJECT (Continued)

Prepare a 500-to-1,000-word analysis of the speech training of your speaker.

READINGS

WALDO W. BRADEN. "The Bases of William E. Borah's Speech Preparation." *Quarterly Journal of Speech*, 33:28–30 (February, 1947).

EARNEST BRANDENBURG. "The Preparation of Franklin D. Roosevelt's Speeches." *Quarterly Journal of Speech*, 35:214–221 (April, 1949).

LAURA CROWELL. "Building the 'Four Freedoms' Speech." *Speech Monographs*, 22: 266–283 (November, 1955).

G. JACK GRAVLEE. "Stephen T. Early: The 'Advance Man'." *Speech Monographs*, 30:41–49 (March, 1963).

——. "Franklin D. Roosevelt's Speech Preparation During His First National Campaign." *Speech Monographs*, 31:437–460 (November, 1964).

BEN PADROW and BRUCE RICHARDS. "Richard Nixon . . . His Speech Preparation." *Today's Speech*, 7:11–12 (November, 1959).

LOREN D. REID. "Did Charles Fox Prepare His Speeches?" *Quarterly Journal of Speech*, 24:17–26 (February, 1938).

——. "Gladstone's Essay on Public Speaking." *Quarterly Journal of Speech*, 39: 265–272 (October, 1953).

——. "The Education of Charles Fox." *Quarterly Journal of Speech*, 43:357–364 (December, 1957).

——. "Gladstone's Training as a Speaker." *Quarterly Journal of Speech*, 40:373–380 (December, 1954).

RALPH RICHARDSON. "Adlai E. Stevenson, Hollywood Bowl, October 9, 1954." *Western Speech Journal*, 19:137–174 (May, 1955).

THEODORE T. STENBERG. "Emerson and Oral Discourse." In *Studies in Rhetoric and Public Speaking in Honor of James Albert Winans*. New York, Russell & Russell, 1962. Pp. 153–180.

EUGENE E. WHITE and CLAIR R. HENDERLIDER. "What Harry S. Truman Told Us About His Speaking." *Quarterly Journal of Speech*, 40:37–42 (February, 1954).

——. "What Norman Vincent Peale Told Us About His Speaking." *Quarterly Journal of Speech*, 40: 407–416 (December, 1954).

RUSSEL WINDES. "Adlai E. Stevenson's Speech Staff in the 1956 Campaign." *Quarterly Journal of Speech*, 46:32–43 (February, 1960).

RUSSEL WINDES, JR. and JAMES A. ROBINSON. "Public Address in the Career of Adlai E. Stevenson." *Quarterly Journal of Speech*, 42:225–233 (October, 1956).

V

THE STANDARDS
OF JUDGMENT

12

The Integrity of Ideas

The organization of this part of the book approximates the conventional framework of rhetorical study. Rhetoricians since Aristotle have generally accepted his concept that the modes of persuasion, depending upon the effect they produce in hearers, "are of three kinds, consisting either in the moral character of the speaker or in the production of a certain disposition in the audience or in the speech itself by means of real or apparent demonstration." These, in the order mentioned by Aristotle, are usually called the ethical, the pathetic or emotional, and the logical. Most rhetorical estimates are based in some degree upon this classification, many being so firmly founded upon it as to become noticeably stereotyped. The next three chapters will deal respectively with the logical, the pathetic, and the ethical modes of persuasion. In the conventional rhetorical scheme, these three chapters should be grouped under the general head of Invention; Chapter 15, dealing with "The Structure of Oral Discourse," embraces the idea of Disposition; Chapter 16, on "The Style of Public Address," covers the conceptions originally included under Elocution; and Chapter 17 embodies the data on Delivery. The only part of the conventional scheme not covered by this analysis is Memory, a canon no longer given individual status but usually considered (when its treatment seems relevant) under delivery.

INTELLECTUAL MATERIALS IN DISCOURSE

Students of speechmaking, whether critic or practitioner, are still divided on the question as to what degree of emphasis the so-called rational appeal should be given in the process of their art. Aristotle was impelled to write his *Rhetoric* because he felt that his predecessors had neglected to give logical materials their deserved place in speechcraft.

While the *Rhetoric* surely gives emotional and ethical proof due consideration, Aristotle held to his conviction that the most important ingredient of a speech is rational demonstration through severe argumentation.

Although language, emotional appeals, and delivery complete the process, intellectual substance (knowledge, meaning, thought) has been and continues to be the core of communication.

The initial question for the critic is, "What did the speaker say?" [1]

We agree that the concept of man as intellectual revelation only partly describes him as a human being. Man, as the philosophers, psychologists, and scientists have repeatedly made clear, is primarily a creature not so much of reason and thought as of complicated sensory and other autonomic reactions. His biological and physiological systems register elemental organic responses, but also reflect higher-center stimuli that give him a degree of uniqueness in his environment. These upper cortical responses breed the materials of knowledge and of systematic thinking. As Pascal described the concept of man, "Man is but a reed, the weakest in nature, but he is a thinking reed." His intelligence is never more "than a frail bark afloat on a sea of brute nature." [2] He is governed by instincts, tensions, emotions of fear, pride, anger, anxiety, timidity, intermittent confidence, bravado, hope, affection, pity, gregariousness, and a long list of similar drives, motives, sentiments. Despite these patterns of feeling and impulsivenes the reflectiveness, the stirring of *What?* and *Why?* account for man's survival and progress.

In this recognition of the total man, his finiteness and his essence, we by no means discount the inevitability of his emotionality. But we address ourselves here to man's stature as a seeker after knowledge, as a thinker, as a communicator of meaning. The essence of his message, we assume, is defined by these thought processes.

The importance of reason emerges in the Greece of Plato and the philosopher-rheoricians of 600–350 B.C. [3] Greek influence, especially that of Plato and Aristotle, Heraclitus, Parmenides, differentiated reason from the prevailing poetic, mythic, religious impulses.

In his allegory of the cave in the *Republic*, Plato illustrates his view of the world as universal rather than particular and as reasonable rather than irrational. Men are chained in the darkness of the cave, backs to the light, and see only shadows of objects reflected on the walls. One

---

[1] "Intellectual activity," "reason," "logic," and "thought" are used interchangeably in this and other chapters. Here and there we attempt to explain the terms in their special interpretations.

[2] Harold Larrabee. *Reliable Knowledge.* Boston, 1964, p. 33.

[3] William Barrett. *Irrational Men.* Garden City, 1958, p. 70. Cf. George Kennedy. *The Art of Persuasion in Greece.* Princeton, New Jersey, 1963. Ch. 2.

prisoner frees himself and progresses toward the mouth of the cave and toward the sunlight. This experience, as Plato views it, is man's evolution from darkness to light, from ignorance and superstition to reason. Aristotle wrote his *Rhetoric* as a protest against predecessors and contemporaries who exalted emotion and the technical aspects of the subject and who failed to give value and place to logic and reason in communication.[4] Although Aristotle gave prominence to ethical and pathetic proofs, he expounded rational communication as basic.[5] Said Aristotle, "It would seem, too, that this [reason] is the true self of every man, since it is the supreme and better part. What is naturally proper to every creature is the highest and pleasantest for him. And so, to man, this will be the life of Reason, since Reason is, in the highest sense, a man's self." [6]

The importance of reason and logic in demonstrative, deliberative, and forensic discourse has prevailed in classical, medieval, and modern rhetorical theory and speech criticism. George Campbell, in his lectures before the students at Aberdeen, Scotland, stressed the need for logic and substance in discourse. In line with his faculty psychology, he stated that every speech was designed to enlighten the understanding, please the imagination, move the passions, and influence the will. Nevertheless he recognized the central role of reason. Said he, "As logic therefore forges the arms which eloquence teacheth us to wield, we must first have recourse to the former, that being made acquainted with the materials of which her weapons and armor are severally made, we may know their respective strength and temper, and when and how each is to be used." [7]

To Richard Whately, British rhetorician of the first quarter of the nineteenth century, rhetoric was an "offshoot of logic." [8] To Hugh Blair, eighteenth century Scottish rhetorician and preacher, reason and argument were foundations of eloquence. Said he, "In order to persuade a man of sense, you must first convince him, which is only to be done by satisfying his understanding of the reasonableness of what you propose to him." [9] Chauncey Allen Goodrich, first professor of rhetoric at Yale College in the first and second quarters of the nineteenth century, also stressed reason as central in communication. He stated that "A powerful understanding appealing to the sense of truth is the chief instrument to

---

[4] George Kennedy. *Op. cit.,* pp. 82 ff.

[5] *Rhetoric.* 1354a, 14 ff.; 1354b, 9 ff.

[6] *Nicomachean Ethics.* X, vii. Translated by H. Rackam. London, 1926.

[7] *Philosophy of Rhetoric.* Edited by Lloyd Bitzer. Carbondale, Illinois, 1963, p. 34.

[8] *Elements of Rhetoric.* Edited by Douglas Ehninger. Carbondale, Illinois, 1963, p. 12.

[9] *Lectures on Rhetoric and Belles Lettres.* Edited by Harold Harding. Carbondale, Illinois, 1965. II, 3.

be relied on. The rest should be subsidiary to this. It is then to the understanding of men that eloquence should be chiefly addressed." [10] Goodrich commends Edmund Burke as superior in communication because of his "intellectual independence" and because Burke had "remarkable comprehensiveness," amplitude of mind, and "sublety of intellect."

The late W. Norwood Brigance, an acknowledged authority on public speaking in the twentieth century, used to remind his students that "Reason's basic use, then, is to show men how to fulfill their needs and how to solve tough problems. If Reason be man's newest and weakest intellectual achievement it is also the extremely important one by which he climbed slowly, painfully and with many backslidings, from slavery to civilization. Let there be no misunderstanding of its importance. Without the effective use of Reason, at least by a creative and dominant minority, no free society can maintain itself." [11]

LOGICAL PROOF IN RHETORIC

Today writers differ in their views on the emphasis which logical proof should receive in classroom instruction. While all are convinced of the importance of rational demonstration, there are differences of opinion concerning the chronological order in which analyses of materials, audiences, and personal situations should be undertaken by student speakers. In his essay "Logic and Public Speaking," Wilbur E. Gilman [12] remarks that the teachers of today fall into three groups "according to which one of the three kinds of Aristotelian modes of persuasion they emphasize." He goes on to say that one group, of which Elwood Murray is a representative, emphasizes the adjustment of the speaker to his own speaking situation; another, of which Alan Monroe is a representative, emphasizes the adaptation of material to listeners; and the last group, of which James A. Winans is an exponent, stresses the speaker's search for the ideas necessary to the effective development of subject matter. Gilman then expresses his view, that the exacting analysis of subject matter should come first and hence facilitate the making of subsequent adjustments to the audience and the speaking situation.

Interrelation of Theory and Criticism

The foregoing is another reminder that the theory and criticism of public address are inseparable. The processes of original conception and

---

[10] John Hoshor. "Rhetorical Theory of Chauncey Goodrich." *Speech Monographs*, 14:1–37 (1947). Cf. *Goodrich's Essays in Select British Eloquence.* Edited by A. Craig Baird. Carbondale, Illinois, 1963, p. xxxvi.

[11] *Speech: Its Techniques and Disciplines in a Free Society.* New York, 1952, Appleton-Century-Crofts, p. 147.

[12] *Quarterly Journal of Speech*, 26:667 (December, 1940).

of critical evaluation of the creations of others are fundamentally alike, and interrelated. Each of us is both an originator and a critic, but more often the latter. As Albert E. Avey says:

Most of us spend more time listening to arguments presented to us than in originating them from our own minds. And even when we have occasion to originate and construct them our own products at once stand before us for review and judgment as to their soundness and perfection.[13]

W. T. G. Shedd once remarked that every complete speech is "the evolution of an idea." Each speaker serves as a middleman between a reasonable concept and the world of reality in which that idea can appropriately take root. It follows that a great speech must be more than, as Samuel Johnson said about a good conversation, "that of which nothing is distinctly remembered, but a general effect of pleasing impression." In short, oratory to be great must deal with ideas which make a difference in the affairs of men and states.[14] Consequently, a seriousness of design characterizes the overwhelming majority of speeches which students and critics pronounce significant.

Most orators share John Bright's opinion that only a sense of duty should prompt a speaker to take the platform. He said he would not deliver a speech simply to rejoice with men in their own good fortune. Evidently, like most great speakers, Bright agreed with Emerson that the eloquent man is he who "is inwardly drunk with a certain belief. . . ."

This implies that important speechmaking must deal largely with the determination of points of fact, and the determination of expediency in proposed courses of action. In other words, forensic and deliberative speaking have always been the two favored branches of oratory since they presumably deal with the urgencies of the times and hence draw most freely upon the capacities and ingenuities of speakers. Furthermore, excepting the celebrated forensic speeches of antiquity, the greater share of remembered oratory is of the deliberative variety.

Why great forensic speeches fail to command the interest of succeeding generations is not completely clear, but that the forensic speaker is forgotten sooner remains a fact. Edward A. Parry has remarked that the great lawyer is like the accomplished actor; both occupy the stage for a brief moment, win applause, and then make their last bow before the curtain falls. "Nothing is so elusive," Parry continued, "as the art of acting, unless indeed it be the sister art of advocacy." [15] That the forensic speaker is as fully a dealer in ideas as the deliberative is acknowledged. Severity in logical development characterizes the one as clearly as the other; and, in many cases, no doubt, the courtroom orator is the superior.

[13] *The Function and Forms of Thought.* New York, 1927, p. 359.
[14] Compare the view of Cicero on this theme.
[15] *The Seven Lamps of Advocacy.* London, 1923, p. 111.

The prominence of deliberative speaking in oratorical literature probably results from the nature of the subject matter. While the case at law is important, it usually is of more temporary interest and has a more limited field of reference and application than the matter of public expediency with which the orator deals in a deliberative assembly. Consequently, most of the great forensic speeches remembered today contain broad principles of public conduct which transcend the immediate cause to which the speeches are devoted. Thus Lord Erskine's address in the case of Lord George Gordon, his defense of John Stockdale in a libel suit, his speech in the case of the Dean of Asaph involving the rights of juries, and the speech in behalf of Thomas Hardy on a treason charge are all appeals to high principles of personal and civil liberty, going well beyond the confines of the particular individual's cases. In other words, Erskine is remembered not only as a speaker of sound ideas and cogent reasoning, but as a mouthpiece of liberty and fair play for the common man.

Obviously, this explanation does not alone account for the relative eclipse of courtroom as contrasted with deliberative oratory. Daniel Webster's speech in the White murder trial has no important bearing upon any profound governmental or personal doctrine, yet it remains a classic to which students return for the study of seasoned rhetoric and brilliant argument. But, in the main, the ideas which live within the memories of succeeding generations, and the ideas whose integrity is tested and appraised more often in later history, are the ones which deliberative speakers have developed in addresses on the burning issues of their time. Hence, they are ideas directed to expediency of certain conduct or action.

The great demonstrative orations, such as Lincoln's Gettysburg Address, proclaim broad principles of human conduct which are often closely associated with purely deliberative affairs. They deal, at least in their finest representations, with noble themes, universal doctrines, expressions of man's higher aspirations. Despite this tendency toward what the classical writers would have called sublimity in expression, the truly fine demonstrative speeches grow out of and derive their substance from the practical, matter-of-fact doings of men and women. They are more closely related to deliberative talk than many people suppose.

Our assumption, then, is that speaking and writing involve a logical movement; that this method of development tends to minimize haphazard trial and error, and utilizes deliberation; that speakers with such cognitive perceptions apply sufficient skill to move toward consistent and dependable judgments; and that a given society "progresses" most satisfactorily when their decisions and behavior express deliberative rather than demagogic concepts and appeals.

DETERMINING INTEGRITY OF IDEAS

With our primary interest now focussed upon the evaluation of logical content, our objective will be to determine how fully a given speech enforces an idea; how closely that enforcement conforms to the general rules of argumentative development; and how nearly the totality of the reasoning approaches a measure of truth adequate for purposes of action. As Avey says of argumentative analysis:

> Critical estimation consists in judging the value of a discussion as an instance of proof, the determination of how far it succeeds in showing the necessity of the truth of the contention offered, on the basis of accepted logical principles.[16]

How does the critic determine the relative integrity of ideas in a speech? The evaluation cannot be made by formula; it is a complex problem and does not yield to mechanical, rule of thumb treatment. However, the critic proceeds by method. And he finds that the integrity of ideas can be judged through three principal means: determination (1) of the intellectual resources of the speaker, (2) of the severity and strictness of the argumentative development, and (3) of the "truth" of the idea in functional existence.

DETERMINING THE SPEAKER'S INTELLECTUAL STOCK

While it is not true that great ideas flow only from the minds of men of corresponding intellectual stature, the relationship between cogency of thought and personal resources is sufficiently close to interest the critic. The preparation and background that the speaker brings to the process of logical invention figures strongly in the determination of argumentative soundness and integrity. Cicero believed that genius, method or art, and diligence were the three basic requisites for finding arguments; and of the three, he assigned to genius the chief place.[17]

To find the factors which contribute to individual skill in logical development is admittedly difficult. In fact, John F. Genung believed that the "original discovery of the thought" was too individual to be within the scope of ordinary instruction. We can, however, point to some of the outward manifestations of inventive skill which influence the arguments men compose and deliver. These considerations will indicate, in part at least, the speaker's supply of thought and the adequacy of its support.

[16] *Op. cit.*, p. 359.
[17] *De Oratore.* J. S. Watson edition, 1897. 11, 35.

Both as critics and as creators of arguments, we look first to the capacity for formulation of ideas. This will contain, to use Genung's words, "a natural ability to grasp facts and ideas not as isolated or vagabond but in combination, as helpers or as goals to other facts or ideas." [18] This implies sound judgment on the part of the speaker; judgment to make fine discriminations between the essential and the nonessential; facility in making analyses of questions, to the end that significant items are held constantly in view; capacity to sense that which lies at the center of issues, rather than to develop what is tangential to them. In short, we are appraising the speaker's powers of observation, alertness, and ability in independent analysis. To the extent to which this matter concerns the preliminary formulation of argument, it may be referred to as the prospective aspect of logical invention.

THE SOCIAL-POLITICAL BACKGROUND OF THE IDEAS

A closely related consideration in appraisal of the relative integrity of ideas in the light of personal resources is the speaker's recognition of the pressing problems of his time. After all, the reflective undertakings in which orators engage are essentially ventures in problem solving. Such distinguished orators as Demosthenes, Burke, Webster, and Calhoun are associated with great movements in history. There were undoubtedly many other competent speakers whose names might now be indelibly inscribed upon the memory, had they been equally skilled in sensing the nature of the problems of their day, and in placing them in the context of a larger social system. One of the marks of the great orator is the facility to direct intellectual energy to the manifestly urgent necessities of the moment. And, as Brand Blanshard states, "the more precisely thought can locate its objective, the less groping, the more quick and neat and effortless will be the manner of reaching for it." [19] Clearly, then, nobility of conception stamps the intellectual effort of the praiseworthy speaker. The grand themes derive from momentous events, actual or impending; great speeches translate those themes into catalogs of proposed action.

THE IDEAS AND REFLECTIVE THINKING

In a more formal sense, the orator is appraised as a man thinking reflectively. Hence the pattern of thought set forth by John Dewey and others serves as a framework for critical analysis. The presentation of a

18 J. F. Genung. *The Working Principles of Rhetoric.* Boston, 1900. Pp. 388, 390.
19 Brand Blanshard, *The Nature of Thought.* London, 1940. II, 66.

speech is a good example of a reflective experience. And so, according to the Dewey formula, the speaker's logical capacities are estimated in the light of (1) his recognition of the problem which, at the moment, is disturbing or is about to disturb the status quo; (2) his analysis of the nature and bearing of the problem upon the social setting; (3) his fertility of mind in suggesting ideas relevant to the solution of the difficulty; (4) his acuteness in examining, through reasoning, the implications of his suggestions; and (5) the verification of his judgment following the acceptance of the most feasible solution.[20]

This reflective process, underlying the Dewey formula and assumptions, is a thought movement controlled not by chance, whim, daydreaming, or artificial structuring of ideas, but rather by conscious inspections of facts and related assumptions, and by systematic inference. A deliberate examination is made of whatever alleged facts and principles may be clearly or dimly seen. Inference is the ability "to see and describe the connection between facts and related phenomena whose close association may be immediately apparent." From this immediate connection, based on the observer's previous experiences, relationships may be established. Experience must obviously continue to govern the speaker's view and reason. "This inferential experience is not random guessing, but judicial, even theoretically scientific survey of the probabilities and hazards accompanying a fresh-novel-position." Speech critics agree, with Creighton, that "it is essential in inference that there be a real transition from one fact to another—that the conclusion reached shall be different from the starting point."[21]

Inference in every case has the element of speculation, a gap between observation and verification of facts and the implied judgment or conclusion. Although absolute certainty is impossible, the mental direction, we believe, is orderly and precise. Whether this reflective activity attempts generalizations from data, close association between individual cases or groups, as in analogy, or causative connections, the process of relating the known to the unknown is the same.

What is the explanation that justifies proceeding from simple facts and the more complicated data to the wider logical horizon with its hypothetical and speculative elements?

The answer is that inference is a description of relationships among various facts and groups of facts and principles. The reasoner and speech critic stress the principle of assumed and implied relationships. Experimentally and otherwise, events and trends are causally connected; certain phenomena apparently occur in harmony and association with other phenomena. Hence there is justification for the whole underlying

[20] John Dewey. *How We Think.* Boston, 1910. Ch. 6.
[21] *An Introductory Logic,* 4th ed. New York, 1920, p. 325.

method of inference with its specific details and constituents at one end and its philosophical penetrations at the other. This principle is that of the "implicative system." [22]

Underlying all logic is that hypothesis or assumption, repeatedly verified, that orderliness is the basis of overt thinking. We discover in the minutiae, the materials, elements, objects of any kind their orderly character. By classification of these small units (nuclei) or "little systems" we note their practical identifications and connections. As Josiah Royce stated it, "Order belongs to individuals, to collections, to arrays of things, to persons, deeds, or events." [23]

Why do we have faith in these patterns of order that grow out of our repeated testings? Despite the exceptions and the undependable theory that sequences invariably repeat themselves, we proceed on our conviction that the universe with its myriads of mysterious details is still orderly and that its processes will continue to function as they have. "The uniformity of nature, the conviction that things will continue to occur as they have is undoubtedly the best founded generalization in the whole range of human experience. . . . For knowledge to be possible, our universe must, to that extent, be an ordered cosmos; which is but another way of saying that the existence of scientific prediction and control depends on the intelligibility of our universe and the possibility of framing universal laws." [24]

THE SPEAKER'S PREMISES

The prospective aspect of logical analysis is furthered by determining the premises from which the speaker argued. Did the speaker exercise wisdom in selecting the basic postulates upon which his reasoned case rests? The critic who searches out these premises will, of course, find that their isolaton can be effected only through a thoughtful study of the historical pattern in which the speeches are set. Not only that, but the accuracy with which the fundamental tenets of a man's reasoning are uncovered will depend upon penetrating insight into the orator himself, his training, social conditioning, and relation to and attitude toward the complex problems of his time. And in all of this inquiry, the critic must act dispassionately and with detachment. He must survey the thought

[22] Cf. D. S. Robinson. *The Principles of Reasoning*, 3d ed. New York, 1947; Joseph Ratner, *Intelligence in the Modern World*; John Dewey, *Philosophy*. New York, 1947, pp. 8, 15, 108, 111 ff.

[23] "Order." In Hastings' *Encyclopedia of Religion and Ethics*. New York, 1960. IX, 533 ff.

[24] Columbia Associates in Problems in Philosophy. *Philosophy: An Introduction to Reflective Thinking*. New York, 1923, p. 93.

of others in the light of conditions operative at the time.[25] Only through such a measure of impartiality can we get at the roots of a speaker's ideas.

A cursory examination of recent studies of public speakers will show the extent to which this phase of critical inquiry can be taken.

In his careful analysis of Burke's principal speeches, H. Clay Harshbarger [26] reveals the basic assumptions from which Burke argued and which he so clearly enunciated and used in the development of his arguments. Harshbarger shows how Burke fortified his reasoning on the American crisis by articulating his contentions with these major premises. Burke, it is shown, postulated happiness as the end of government. To this claim he linked three other assumptions which served as the substructure of much of his reasoning: (1) The means of attaining the end of happiness was expediency; "not the narrow furthering of selfish interest, but rather the much broader adaptation of government to the present circumstances of the people in the attainment of which the necessity exists for large and liberal ideas." (2) The most useful criterion for judging the validity of the means was an appeal to the wisdom of the ancestors. And (3) the medium in which the means was to be rendered efficacious was the Constitution of the British Empire, or the Empire itself, with the Parliament serving as the residuum of the common authority, together with other and lesser legislatures under it.

In her study of Charles Evans Hughes, Mary Margaret Roberts found that the main premises from which Hughes argued were deeply rooted in his conservative Christian home. Hoping to make a minister of their son, the elder Hughes trained his son "for Christian Scholarship, provided a strong moral basis for his thinking and conduct and stressed development of character-personality traits essential in religious leadership." Although young Charles failed to follow parental wishes about the ministry, he did exercise strong moral and progressive leadership as a crusading investigator and reform governor of New York. Later these traits were brought to bear when he was a justice of the Supreme Court (Mary Margaret Roberts, "The New York Legislative Campaign Speaking of Governor Charles Evans Hughes, 1907–1910," unpublished Ph.D. dissertation, Louisiana State University, 1959).

Carroll Arnold's study of "The Parliamentary Oratory of Benjamin Disraeli: 1842–1852" probes with some completeness into the inventive process of the orator. Arnold concludes that

[25] Cf. Benedetto Croce. *History.* Translated by Sylvia Sprigge. New York, 1954, p. 27.

[26] *Burke's Chief American Works: An Edition with Notes and an Introduction.* Ph.D. dissertation. Cornell University, 1929.

Experience generally and national experience particularly were the sources from which Disraeli drew the theories of statecraft which he advocated in the House. Political reforms . . . must result from the painstaking selection of the best practices of the past; hence, a State was never the product of mere abstract principles, but it was instead the evolved result of national experience.

Arnold shows how these principles applied and what they meant to the issues before the House of Commons between 1842 and 1852.

Applied to the issues which came before the House of Commons during the decade, these principles meant in practical politics, (1) that the forms and responsibilities of the legislative and administrative sections of government must be maintained; (2) that Irish administration must be suited to the taste of social evolution prevailing there, and to the legal unity of Ireland and England; (3) that even uneconomic practices should be retained if they contributed to the strength of the imperial fabric; (4) that legislation must be based on a broad and inclusive appreciation of all social and political motives, for which the economic interpretation alone was inadequate; and (5) that reforms could not be legislated but must evolve, hence legislation to create a status for the new industrial interests was unwise, for these interests should find their privileges and responsibilities within existing social and political institutions.[27]

The importance of such discoveries to the critics is evident. With them, he is able the more accurately and deeply to probe the thinking of an orator—to push back beyond the commonplace and superficial manifestations of the orator's thought to the basic ideas which not only permeated, but determined, the line of argument used in a given case.

This section, then, simply indicates that the ideas with which a speaker deals make a difference in the run of human affairs. His ideas affect other ideas, and eventually large segments of the social situation react in one way or another to the impact of the concepts. The critic, searching always for the source of the speaker's reasonings as well as for the reasons themselves, tries to appraise the personal resources of the orator and to get at the root of the man's thinking. In that way he may begin the difficult job of determining the integrity of the logical proof. But it should be borne in mind that this step is merely preliminary to the second investigative aspect of logical analysis, judging the severity and strictness of the arguments advanced by the speaker.

TESTING THE EVIDENTIAL AND INFERENTIAL DEVELOPMENT

In passing judgment upon the logical aspect of a persuasive address, we ask the question: "Did the speaker enforce his point?" As previously indicated, proof may be of several kinds; but at this moment we are

[27] "Invention in the Parliamentary Speaking of Benjamin Disraeli." *Speech Monographs*, 14:66–80 (1947).

primarily concerned with the establishment of that measure of assent which indicates a reasonable degree of truth. Fundamentally, the constituents of logical proof are evidence and argument or reasoning. Each conforms to general rules and admits of rigorous testing.

We have stated above that the origin in every case lies in observation, personal experiences, data, having to do with the existence of things, occurrence of events, the specific character of phenomena. These materials are thus particulars, instances, figures, testimony of witnesses or authorities, incidents (evidence).

The inferential activity of the speaker-writer is his interpretation of and reaction to such materials. His mental activity may lead (1) to generalizations based upon the array of cases or examples; (2) or to comparison between specific objects or relationships; (3) or to the causal connection that apparently exists between events or particulars; (4) or to the statements of others who speak with surety and experience concerning events or theories; (5) or by deduction of relatively specific conclusions derived from general statements which in turn have been framed from preceding generalizations or hypotheses.

The logical modes are the practical substance of discourse. They are not academic forms to be viewed as accessories. Rather, they compose the texture of the unfolding discourse. They are not forms rigidly following each other, but are flexibly utilized in ways and at points that invite their application.

Examining the Evidence

Evidence is the raw material used to establish proof. It may include the testimony of individuals, personal experiences, tables of statistics, illustrative examples, or any so-called "factual" items which induce in the mind of the hearer or reader a state of belief—a tendency to affirm the existence of the fact or proposition to which the evidence attaches and in support of which it is introduced. Thus, in his attempt to establish ground for conciliation with the Colonies, Burke introduced comparative data as to the export trade of England to the Colonies in 1704 and in 1772; and he remarked: "The trade with America alone is now within less than £500,000 of being equal to what this great commerical nation, England, carried on at the beginning of this century with the whole world." Previously, he had presented figures to reveal the accuracy of this claim. Then he turned to his conclusion: "This is the relative proportion of the importance of the colonies at these two periods; and all reasoning concerning our mode of treating them must have this proportion as its basis, or it is a reasoning weak, rotten, and sophistical." [28]

[28] "Conciliation with America." In *The Works and Correspondence of Edmund Burke.* London, 1852. III, 247–253.

Roosevelt, asking for a declaration of war against Japan, cited the evidence for Japan's unprovoked attack on the United States: on December 7th, the United States was suddenly and deliberately attacked in Hawaii by Japanese naval and air forces. He also cited the other facts of previous immediate hours: Japanese forces attacked Hong Kong, Guam, Philippine Islands, Wake Island, etc., etc. Concluded the President: "I ask that the Congress declare that a state of war has existed between the United States and the Japanese Empire." [29]

Here are typical displays of evidence, and upon the relevance and merit of these and allied materials will depend much of the argument's claims to integrity. The critic's chief function at this point is to test the speaker's evidence to determine whether it serves as an adequate and valid substructure of reasoning. Since the principal types of evidence used by the speaker, apart from the reference to his own authority, are statistics and testimony, we shall refer briefly to the criteria governing their reliability.

Edwin A. Burtt tells us that the problem of statistics, on the critical side, must be approached through two cardinal principles.[30] The statistician must discover, and subsequently the critic must examine, "some qualitative unit in terms of which he can translate the phenomenon he is studying into a magnitude whose variations are mathematical." That is, the task deals with counting: finding out "how much of the phenomenon is present in the locality or under the conditions which determine (the investigation)." The second principle of statistical inquiry "is that the limits of the field within which the measurements hold should be carefully determined and clearly stated." Thus, if an investigator finds that a certain group of men gives 10 per cent of its time to political interests, he should not point to general conclusions regarding the public as a whole, unless he has made the necessary checks on the limitations of his study. This brings up the whole problem of sampling, of finding out whether the instances chosen represent a systematically typical segment of the group as a whole. Burtt concludes "Wherever it is possible, each single case within the field to which the conclusion is to apply should be examined. . . ." This is not always feasible or possible. In recent years, the public opinion polls have done much to refine such statistical inquiries, so that we no longer regard accuracy of judgment in generalization as an immediate function of numbers. Through systematic sampling, remarkably accurate estimates of the public's thoughts and actions are made weekly, to the end that prediction of political developments is materially facilitated.

[29] A. Craig Baird, ed. *Representative American Speeches: 1941–1942.* New York, 1942, pp. 15 ff.

[30] *Principles and Problems of Right Thinking.* New York, 1928, pp. 315–319.

It follows, then, that the evaluation of statistical units requires investigation into the methods employed by the statisticians in collecting, classifying, and interpreting the data. The critic of speeches, however, makes two judgments; one, of the speaker's wisdom in choosing a certain body of figures; another, of the statistician's severity and accuracy in setting forth the facts from which the inferences are drawn. The tests applied to the statistics will accordingly fall into the following categories: (1) Are the instances from which the inference is developed sufficiently numerous to be significant? (2) Are the units included in the investigation properly and carefully defined? (3) Is there comparability between the things compared? (4) Are the instance of such a character as to provide a systematically typical sample of the field as a whole? (5) Are the facts reported and classified accurately? (6) Do the statistics furnish an index to the information desired, *i.e.*, is the relationship clear between the conclusion derived from the figures and the conclusion sought in the subject of the discourse? These tests, it should be noted, relate closely to the ones used in checking arguments from specific cases or generalizations. We shall refer to them later.

Much of the evidence used by speakers in support of their ideas is of a testimonial nature. In other words, outside authorities often furnish testimony which the speaker incorporates into his speech, hoping thereby to give credibility to his cause and plausibility to his claims. Or he may rely mainly on his own reputation for expertness to enforce his propositions. What is the value of such evidence? How is its validity determined? Several tests serve to orient the critic in his appraisal.

Although consistency may occasionally be a hobgoblin it is, nevertheless, the guiding consideration for the critic when he appraises speech compositions. Addresses must present unified, internally consistent ideas. The parts must be consonant with one another, producing, in the end, a composite that is logically harmonious. This means simply that the evidence used by a speaker must be at peace with itself; what is affirmed at one point must not be denied at another. Nor does this allow any tampering with data to fit them to the demands of the speaker's thesis. It is assumed that if the evidence does not sustain an argument, the speaker will refrain from developing the contention. The appeal must clearly be to the truth of the case, not to the whim of the speaker.

Since inconsistencies of statement or of combined facts even though not palpably obvious, cast suspicions upon the integrity of argument, critics will turn to some, if not all, of the following tests of evidence:

1. Is the testimony or evidence consistent with itself and with the known laws of logical argument?
2. Is the particular authority whose testimony is used to support a contention reliable?

3. Has the authority had an opportunity to examine and observe the data from which he speaks?
4. Does he entertain any prejudices which might influence his judgment on the matter at issue?
5. Is he generally recognized as able and competent in the given field?
6. Are the facts in the testimony causally related one to the other?
7. Is the source citation or the authority specific? That is, does it indicate exactly where the testimony comes from, and whether it is first- or second-hand?
8. Does other evidence corroborate what is introduced?
9. Is the evidence recent?
10. Does the evidence satisfy the listeners?

The last test, while very important, must be considered in a specific light. It does not suggest that the speaker should use evidence, even though inadequate and faulty, provided it satisfies the hearers' demands and prejudices. On the contrary, it reminds us that evidence, however good, must be so adapted to the hearers that they will remain sensibly aware of its essential merit. The speaker alone can provide for such adaptation; he must prepare the minds of the audience for the ready acceptance of the evidence used to support the arguments. A more complete discussion of this aspect of the process of conviction will be reserved for the next two chapters.

TESTING THE INDUCTIVE AND DEDUCTIVE DEVELOPMENT

Aristotle recognized two general modes of inference—from the specific to the general, and from the general to the more concrete conclusions. The varied use of these terms has led to much difference in the discussion of their application. Aristotle seemed to emphasize logic by example rather than by syllogism (deduction). It was not until Francis Bacon and his contemporaries condemned Scholastic reasoning and substituted the chief emphasis and more experimental concept of the term that induction took on its modern meaning.[31]

Induction begins with specific materials, facts, events, "data." Although the "realities" behind these things cannot be scientifically verified, the philosophers, rhetoricians, and experimentalists in general assume those evidences of the "referents." From these concrete elements more general conclusions may be arrived at.

Deduction, on the contrary, frames a conclusion which in turn relates to premises. It sets up assumptions or hypotheses that either prove them-

[31] *Advancement of Learning and Novum Organum.* Aphorism XIX. Rev. ed. New York, 1944. Bk. 1.

selves as the outcomes of the inductive method or tentatively furnish the guideposts in the framing and solution of the problem.

These two methods, long treated as disparate, are complementary. All inductive inferences have a deductive element. "Every thought process is really both deductive and inductive and can be exhibited as either a deduction or an induction according to the point of view used in interpreting it.[32]

Inference from Specific Instances. What are the specific procedures of induction? What of their validity? The generalization may be based on specific instances, upon statistics, or circumstantial details. The several tests are applied by logicians, rhetoricians, and scientists.

(1) Are the instances examined "true" or what they appear to be?

Generalizations obviously begin with a close examination of the underlying facts (evidence, phenomena, data). The reliability of such details must be tests of their sensory verification, including memory, and the support from other witnesses. The question to be answered is: Are the facts to be relied upon?

(2) Are the instances examined sufficient in number to warrant the generalization? Important though this method of induction is, it is only a starting point. Bacon and later logicians condemned it because it ignored negative examples. To Bacon, it was "puerile, precarious, and exposed to the danger from contradictory instances." It may lead to "special pleading" and, as J. S. Mill would say, to ignoring the full question.

(3) Are the instances representative?

The obligation is to examine each specimen as well as the number or range of cases. This is the method of sampling. Here we assume the use of a considerable number of items, chosen at random from an extensive group, to represent the entire field under survey. Random sampling, however, is subject to the prejudices or whims of the sampler (a current criticism of the method in poll-taking). Often the samples need to be sampled. To protect the procedure, the validity of the samples is to be determined by checking the character of the selections. This character of the sample may be more important than its size. Reliable statisticians *e.g.*, George Gallup and his poll takers, constantly aim to increase the validity of their sampling techniques.

(4) Are negative instances discoverable?

Logic and science alike demand the inclusion of "contradictory experience." Propositions are established neither by favorable citations, nor by the multiplication of unfavorable instances. "The dovetailing of positive and negative data and the addition of any other details with respect

[32] D. S. Robinson. *Op. cit.,* p. 206.

to the units under consideration constitute the only sound inferential methods."

(5) Does the method of eliminating alternative hypotheses validate the conclusion?

Another test establishing a conclusion from instances is the application of the method of residues (the eliminative theory of induction). Here we examine alternative hypotheses and reject those that are logically unsatisfactory. By the method of residues the remaining proposition or conclusion is preferred.

The difficulty with this method is that it overemphasizes the negative factors in induction. Failure to eliminate a hypothesis, for example, seems to justify its validity. Also the number of alternatives to be eliminated may be far too numerous for adequate analysis.

Thus the eliminative theory, like that of the simple enumeration, either by counting positive cases only, or by also including negative cases, is hardly a satisfactory basis for logical judgment.

(6) Does the generalization conform to the laws of probability and causation (scientific analysis)?

In addition to observation and experience, what shall be our final and indispensable venture from the known to the unknown? The laws of causation, implied in every generalization, are basic to our sound conclusions.

Inference by Analogy. As we suggested above, inference characteristically relates from one particular instance to another. The logical method is that of comparison, resemblance, or analogy. Here the critic matches two allegedly related objects or events. If they are alike in observable and verifiable details, then we conclude that they probably resemble each other in certain other respects accepted for one but not clearly verified for the other. Note that analogy assumes the general principle or proposition that makes possible the reasoning. The method starts with the placing of the concrete items for comparison in a general field (order system). The reasoner then postulates that the items in the field are related. Thus such reasoning involves both induction and hypothesis applying to the field represented by these cases.

Analogy may deal with objects or relationships. As John Stuart Mill stated it, "Two things resemble each other in one or more respects; a certain proposition is true of one; therefore it is true of the other." This type, we usually label as "logical analogy." [33]

Richard Whately, on the other hand, conceived analogy as dealing with a "resemblance of ratios," or relationships (mathematical analogy). The relation here viewed is that between the captain of a ship and the

[33] *System of Logic.* New York, 1872. Bk. 3, ch. 20.

commander in chief and the President of the United States in his direction of "the ship of state." ($a : b :: c : d$, where a is the captain, b the ship, c the President, and d the affairs of the United States.)

The effort to compare ratios sometimes leads to the distinction between objects in the same field (literal analogy) and those in a different class (figurative analogy).

These comparisons, simple or complex, follow the law of continuous variation and of continuous similarity. As in all other applications of continuous variation and similarity, we stop where our logical judgment dictates. The more immediate resemblances are literal; the more remote ones are those of metaphors, similes, or other figures.

Karl Wallace suggests that the validity of the comparison can be more dependable if each resemblance can be reduced to a proportion. The process of proof then might be made more workable if the rhetorician were to treat the analogy more exactly and at greater length, thus suggesting knowledge it seems to deny if limited to a comparison of the objects or events themselves.[34]

The analogy, even though widely used in communication and professional investigation, is often looked upon as insufficient for satisfactory reasoning. Many logicians and speech critics regard inferential analogy as explanation rather than as genuine inference.

Consider the following criteria for validity:

1. Are the facts under observation reliable?
2. Are the two objectives or relationships alike in significant details? The problem is to decide what is "representative" or "important."
3. A related inquiry deals with the number of resemblances. The mere accumulation of details of resemblance may not justify a conclusion.
4. A further question has to do with significant differences. Highly important, as in generalization, is the need for objective survey to face any crucial differences.
5. Does review of similar instances confirm the validity of the comparison under examination? The investigation in this case is not so much a scrutiny of the two cases as it is an examination of related ones.
6. Another question implied above is, Does examination of the underlying generalization confirm or deny the validity of the analogy? Inherent in each analogy is a general principle or connection. Every comparison is in reality an inference from a particular case to the character of the general field, and in turn the focusing on the related concrete cases.

[34] Karl Wallace. "On Analogies: Redefinition and Some Implications." In *Studies in Speech and Drama in Honor of Alexander M. Drummond*. Ithaca, New York, 1944, pp. 412–426.

7. Finally, we ask, does inference from causal relation confirm or deny the validity of the analogy?

It is not enough to define, explain, and conclude that certain factors are present in example B because the similarities seem to resemble those of example A. The ultimate question is, why should this unknown solution be supported with respect to factors not directly discernible?

Inference from Causal Relations. As we have suggested, causal reasoning is more basic than any other type—in fact, it is the method to which the other tests refer. Arguments from causal relation establish links between particulars—by noting the impact or influence of one event upon another, or by tracing the cause of an observed event.

Inference by causation is usually classified as from cause to effect (*a priori*), from effect to cause (*a posteriori*), and from effect to effect. Reasoning from cause to effect points to a known situation or group of circumstances and looks to alleged results. Causation from effect to cause concentrates on a fact or set of facts and attempts to explain possible causes. In addition, causal reasoning is sometimes described as that from "effect to effect." Two or more "effects" emerge from the same cause. The separate "effects" are not mutually influential on each other, but each is presumably the result of a common cause. Combined induction and deduction are involved. Induction occurs in the examination of the instances or details. In every case a general condition or proposition is implied. Under such generalization as expressed or assumed, a specific conclusion is derived.

Basically, the concept of causation presupposes an interaction of phenomena. A given event is part of an unbroken series—cause and effect operate within a system, with certain forces impinging more directly upon the event than others, but all occurring within a series of happenings. "Action and reaction are equal and opposite" would more obviously describe what takes place in many instances. "Causation, then, is interaction; cause and effect are simultaneous; the effect is not contained in the cause; there is a passive factor." [35]

In addition to the concept of interaction, the modern view of time and space renders obsolete the notion of causation as chronological. The theory of relativity abolishes one cosmic time and one specific space. Space-time is substituted. Everything is relative. Theory proceeds "from next to next." There are no direct relations between "distant" events, such as distance in time or space. As Bertrand Russell concludes, ". . . and of course there are no forces acting at a distance; in fact, except as a convenient fiction, there are no forces at all." [36]

[35] Cf. F. R. Tennant. "Cause." In Hastings' *Encyclopedia of Religion and Ethics.* New York, 1911. III.
[36] *Outlines of Philosophy.* London, 1927, p. 117.

In this newer universe, time and space are united in a four-dimensional world of "events." For illustrative purposes, of course, the speaker and the critic of speeches view "cause" and "effect" in our earthbound perspective.

Moreover, the problem of affixing causes and results must deal with the reciprocity of phenomena. Causes and effects are so closely identified, items are so coexistent, that causes and results are sometimes hard to distinguish. Is the flame the cause of the melting wax of the candle? Or is the melting wax the cause of the flame?

This reciprocity of phenomena suggests also the complexity of the items under examination. The factors at work as causes or results are seldom single and obvious. Any close examination will quickly note the many strands at work to make up the total activity.

The general rules for testing causal arguments may be summed up in these questions: (1) Is there a causal connection between the two events? (2) Is a particular cause adequate to produce an alleged effect? (3) Is the alleged cause adequate to produce the known result? (4) Are there any other causes operating in such a way as to preclude the likelihood of the known cause producing the alleged effect? (5) Does the application of other methods of scientific induction confirm or reject the inference from causal relations? (6) Have the alleged facts been verified?

The causal connection, assumed, often vanishes upon close examination. This failure to identify items or phenomena associated only by chance is the fallacy of *post hoc ergo propter hoc* (after this fact, therefore because of it).

The discussion of causation suggests a re-examination of John Stuart Mill's canons of causality: (1) phenomena are causally related when they occur in a sequence; (2) they are not so related when an antecedent is invariably absent; (3) they are causally related when any variation in one phenomenon has a corresponding variation in the other.[37]

Inference from Deductive Patterns. Much communication is developed deductively. General ideas are expounded or claimed, followed by detailed supports. The method is thus clear—even if not always persuasive. For situations in which the reader or listener would be opposed to the conclusions advanced, the inductive approach would sometimes be preferable. This is a practical matter of persuasive approach more than one of logical order.

The deductive pattern is rhetorically justified as a series of assumptions and hypotheses rather than as one of syllogistic severity. The as-

[37] Cf. *Logic.* Bk. III, ch. 9; D. S. Robinson. *The Principles of Reasoning.* Chs. 20, 21; Bertrand Russell. *Op. cit.,* pp. 280–286; Joseph Ratner. *John Dewey's Philosophy.* New York, 1939, pp. 147–151.

sumptions stem from the preliminary analysis of the problem and consist of tentative answers derived from the tentative issues. These assumptions may or may not be expressed. In any case, they underlie the evaluation of the thinking.

What is a hypothesis? It is a preliminary framing of conclusions or propositions to be verified or rejected by the appropriate evidence and reasoning. The methods are usually applied to scientific investigation.

Only hypotheses capable of "proof" should be applied. Expert judges should pass judgment. Tentative development of the problem will test the relevancy and practicability of such propositions. Every hypothesis should harmonize with the known findings of previous research and should square with what is understod by the "laws of experiences." Every hypothesis should also obviously lend itself to modification as penetration into the subject suggests adjustment to fit the direction of the analysis and preliminary conclusions.

Evaluating Deductive Patterns. Traditional logic has organized its concepts and treatment of deduction under the syllogistic forms of major premises, minor premises, and conclusions. The framing of the major premise of the typical forms may be categorical (assertion without qualification), disjunctive (the major premise lists alternative possibilities), and the hypothetical (the major premise expresses a condition).

The categorical syllogism defines, classifies, and asserts without qualification. Its form is represented in this example:

> All rhetoricians rely upon the classics.
> Thomas Wilson is a rhetorician.
> Therefore, Thomas Wilson relies upon the classics.

Schematically, this syllogism, with its three propositions and three terms, looks as follows:

	MIDDLE TERM	MAJOR TERM
MAJOR PREMISE:	All rhetoricians	rely upon the classics.
	MINOR TERM	MIDDLE TERM
MINOR PREMISE:	Thomas Wilson	is a rhetorician.
	MINOR TERM	MAJOR TERM
CONCLUSION:	Thomas Wilson	relies upon the classics.

The validity of these syllogisms can be determined through certain tests or rules which specifically relate to the categorical pattern:

1. The syllogism must contain a major premise, a minor premise, and a conclusion.
2. It must contain three terms: major, middle, and minor. The arrangement of these terms in the propositions conforms to the scheme previously outlined.

3. The middle term of the syllogism must be distributed—*i.e.*, used in a universal sense, meaning "all" or "every"—in at least one of the premises.
4. To be distributed in the conclusion, the term must be distributed in one of the premises.
5. Two negative premises make impossible the drawing of a valid conclusion.
6. If one premise is negative, the conclusion must likewise be negative.
7. Negative conclusions cannot be drawn unless one premise is negative.
8. The facts alleged in the premises should be true.

In a disjunctive syllogism the major premise is a disjunctive proposition, listing alternative possibilities. Its form is as follows:

Either overproduction or underconsumption was responsible for the postwar depression.
Overproduction was not responsible.
Therefore, underconsumption was responsible for the postwar depression.

When testing such an argument, we usually refer to these criteria:

1. The alternative possibilities mentioned in the major premise should be as exhaustive as the case will permit.
2. The enumerated possibilities should not overlap.
3. If the minor premise affirms one of the alternatives, the conclusion must deny the other.
4. If the minor premise denies one of the alternatives, the conclusion must affirm the other.

The last basic type of syllogism is the hypothetical, in which the principal assertion is conditioned. Complex in structure, the sentence setting forth the major premise contains an antecedent (the conditional clause) and a consequent (the main clause). This illustration brings out its structure and also suggests its relation to causal patterns of reasoning:

If world peace is to be achieved, the United Nations must be supported.
World peace must be achieved.
Therefore, the United Nations must be supported.

In order to test such a syllogism, care must be taken to insure compliance with these rules: (1) If the minor premise affirms the antecedent, the conclusion must affirm the consequent. (2) If the minor premise denies the consequent, the conclusion must deny the antecedent. (3) A denial of the antecedent or an affirmation of the consequent does not make possible the realization of a reliable conclusion. In general, these rules aim to examine the consistency and structure of the reasoning rather than its validity as measured by evidential and inductive test.[38]

The rhetorical critic finds a knowledge of deductive forms extremely useful in comprehending, analyzing, and testing the development of a speech. Of course, the speaker does not cast his presentation in a syllogistic form for the convenience of the critic. Bare syllogisms are not usually evident. The speaker would not ordinarily gain his objective by arranging his arguments into chains of syllogisms, for the listeners would lose interest and in most cases could not follow such a tight progression of interrelated ideas. The speaker puts his speech into a looser, logical construction without stressing or emphasizing logical techniques.

It is the critic's task to analyze the speech minutely and reveal its logic. In this process, he may find it necessary to state implied or unstated premises, to restate some thoughts in concise form and find others that are buried in stylistic devices. The premises of a given syllogism may be located several paragraphs apart. But when the critic views the speech as a whole, relates it to basic ideas of the speaker and listeners, and notes the progression of points, he is able to see its premises and their relationships. He can then frame a syllogism and apply the various tests. Thus he makes full use of the critical process. He observes how the speaker bases his speech on major premises that are acceptable to both himself and the listener. As Bitzer believes, it is at this point that the speaker and the auditor are united.[39]

Since Bacon, many logicians have looked askance at the practical value of syllogistic reasoning. George Campbell, in the late eighteenth century, said that "It is long since I was convinced, by what Mr. Locke hath said on the subject, that the syllogistic art, with its figures and moods, serves more to display the ingenuity of the investor, and to exercise the address and fluency of the learner, than to assist the diligent inquirer in his researches after truth." [40]

According to F. C. S. Schiller, the syllogistic form may be impotent to a disputant. He cannot be coerced because he can refuse to admit the truth of its premises and can demand proof of them. Thus if the truth of a premise is disputed, it has to be proved; but proved it can be only by further syllogism. Hence, to Schiller, "the demand for true premises is doubled at every step backward the inquiry takes." [41]

---

[38] See representative texts on logic for full treatment of syllogistic reasoning and the violations of rules.

[39] For further discussion on interpreting the syllogism, see Lloyd Bitzer. "Aristotle's Enthymeme Revisited." *Quarterly Journal of Speech*, 45:399–408 (December, 1959); Charles Mudd. "The Enthymeme and Logical Validity." *Ibid.*, 45:409–414 (December, 1959); George Kennedy. *Op. cit.*, pp. 96–99.

[40] *Op. cit.*, Bk. I, ch. 6.

[41] *Logic for Use.* London, 1929, p. 271.

Syllogistic formalism puts down conditions under which the conclusions inevitably follow. Given these rigid assumptions, "absolute" certainty and "truth" operate. "Logic in use" in communication, however, is based on the principle of logical probability. Propositions that constitute human knowledge cannot be assumed as "absolutely true." All conclusions, no matter how plausible, are to be accompanied by qualification. Probability depends on the amount and character of the supporting evidence. Russell states that "At the very best, induction and analogy only give probability. Every inference worthy of the name is inductive, therefore all inferred knowledge is at best probable." [42] This principle applies to all investigations, experimental, scientific, and otherwise. Even the law relating to the uniformity of nature, as we suggested above, is largely assumption. "The most we can hope is that the oftener things are found together, the more probable it becomes that they will be found together another time . . . It can never reach certainty. Thus probability is all that we ought to seek." [43]

The network of surrounding circumstances, the complexity of phenomena, of causal functioning in the "implicative whole," will govern the judgments of speaker and his critic. The fallacies of "allness" statements will be avoided.

The critic, then, will ascertain the *relative,* the *probable* status of major deductive claims by checking them against determinable criteria of causation, definition, factual verification, attendant circumstances, and related inductive technique.

To sum up the whole matter, the thinking of the orator must be characterized by features which, according to Avey,[44] can best be suggested by this alliteration: clearness in language usage; consistency, in the sense of being free from contradiction; completeness, to the extent of providing conclusions only when adequate facts have been surveyed; consecutiveness in its order of thought presentation; and cogency, in the sense that all of the parts are held together and articulated with the main proposition.

FUNCTIONAL APPRAISAL OF IDEAS

So far we have dealt with two of the means by which we assess the integrity of ideas in a speech: an examination of the intellectual resources of the speaker and the testing of the arguments developed in the speech. We now turn to a third means of appraising logical proof.

In the long run, integrity of ideas depends upon the accuracy and

[42] Bertrand Russell. *Op. cit.,* p. 285.
[43] Bertrand Russell. *Problems of Philosophy.* London, 1946, pp. 101 ff.
[44] Avey. *Op. cit.,* p. 285.

power of the intellectual conceptions in real experience. Did the speaker's ideas take root in society and result in good for the group as a whole? Was the speaker right, as determined by an appeal to historical reality? Obviously, such a test cannot be applied to contemporary address since we do not know the turn of future events. But where time has afforded the critic perspective, where it has given him an opportunity to survey the ebb and flow of human events subsequent to the presentation of a certain speech or speeches, he is in a position to observe the impact of an idea upon the course of history.

Surely, the accuracy of an orator's vision should figure in the critic's final evaluation of the speeches. Acuity of intellect, as revealed through the orator's ability to foresee the consequence of political action, is a laudable possession. If history confirms an orator's judgment; if future events prove the accuracy of the speaker's ideas, then the critic must be impressed by the weight of such public address. The integrity of an idea can hardly be subjected to a more severe test than the practical fact that it worked, and in conformity with the speaker's predictions. This does not rule out the speech on a currently "unpopular" or minority cause as faulty rhetoric. Such an address can still be evaluated in the light of other criteria. And, possibly, in the even longer run of history, it may be found to be right and true. But critics cannot find the answers to such questions by looking into a crystal ball; they cannot be expected to fold back the years still unrevealed to man.

It would seem highly significant, therefore, in the appraisal of Burke's ideas, to observe the unusual scope of political wisdom which enabled the speaker to foresee the consequences of the American crisis—consequences originally conceived in prophecy and subsequently confirmed in fact. Likewise, the vision of John Bright in anticipating and pleading the causes to which he devoted his life is remarkable in its conformity to later historical occurrence. Not alone, obviously, but to an important degree, Bright developed ideas which resulted in the repeal of the Corn Laws in 1846; the support of the North during the Civil War; the passage of the Reform Bill of 1867, and the disestablishment of the Church of England in Ireland. These are, indeed, practical measures of the worth of ideas.

APPRAISAL OF REFUTATIVE SKILL

Many great speeches depend for their excellence upon the speakers' skill at adapting arguments to the claim of their opponents. Thus evaluations of certain of Lincoln's speeches in the Illinois campaign or of Fox's addresses before the House of Commons result in large part from an assessment of the speaker's ability in refutation and rebuttal.

The critic is concerned, therefore, with determining how effectively an orator meets objections and defends his own case. Among the factors accounting for competency in this department of argumentative development—and hence serving the critic as general standards for analysis—are the speaker's ability (1) to pick out the relevant and significant points of clash; (2) to resolve the contested issues to their lowest logical denominators; (3) to reveal clearly the relation of the opponent's claims to his own; (4) to meet and overcome the salient contentions with adequate argument and evidence; and (5) through it all, to preserve the structural wholeness of the speech as a constructive enforcement of an idea.

PRACTICAL VALUE OF BRIEFING

The practical task of analyzing a complete argument is often simplified by reducing the logical continuity to an outline, or brief. Whereas a sequence in reasoning may be deeply imbedded in elaborate detail or in excessively involved language, recasting of the fundamental thought in this form permits more careful examination of its validity and consecutiveness. Briefing has the effect of revealing the framework of arguments; it brings into sharp focus the underlying analysis upon which the logical case rests.

If we turn to one of Burke's arguments in the "Conciliation" speech, we find its basic pattern to be substantially as follows:

I. Force is an unsatisfactory method of coping with the American problem, for
   A. It is a temporary expedient.
   B. It is uncertain.
   C. It impairs the very object you seek, for
      1. The things you fight for are depreciated by the strife.
      2. It breaks the spirit of a country—and spirit made the American colonies what they are today.
   D. It is out of harmony with English colonial practice.

Such schematic representation helps the critic by laying bare the skeleton of the contention. It returns the argument to the analytical form which it originally assumed in the speaker's thinking. And when an entire speech is so briefed, the critic is in a fair position to judge the consecutiveness of the reasoning. This type of briefing has been used widely as an exercise in rhetorical training. Theodore Parker stated that a study and analysis of the arguments in the English State Trials helped him materially to get clearness of arrangement in his own speeches.

As the example from Burke's speech shows, the system of briefing rests upon a few well established rules of outline construction. If the scheme is to serve the analyst well, it should (1) include only complete sentences expressing the speaker's judgments; (2) isolate the major points and show the relation of subordinate material to them; (3) develop sequences according to a causal or "for" relationship; (4) employ a uniform system of symbols to make clear the order of ideas in the case; and (5) express one, and only one, point under each head. Constructed thus, a brief becomes a balance sheet of the speaker's thought, and accordingly facilitates a scrutiny of the total argumentative plan of a discourse.

A SPECIMEN LOGICAL ANALYSIS

Bower Aly's analysis and evaluation of Alexander Hamilton's debate before the New York State Convention for ratification of the Federal Constitution, at Poughkeepsie, New York, on June 24, 1788, illustrates the method of applying logical principles and proofs in rhetorical criticism:

Hamilton's typical development of logical proof in his speech on the Powers of the Senate is that of causal relation. While he may resort, in refutation, to the device of turning the tables, or to a defense of a supposed inconsistency, his chief reliance is on bringing evidence to bear in support of the relation of cause and effect. In the process, he depends more frequently on what he calls "common sense" or "experience" as a court of last resort than on other authority. His characteristic method appears to be that of starting from an accepted fact, a truism on which all agree, to build a bridge by logical sequence over a stream of doubt to reach an acceptable conclusion. The bridge between the truism and the conclusion is buttressed firmly in the basic assumptions of his hearers.

In one instance he rests his whole case on an appeal to common sense.

"Whenever, therefore, Congress shall mediate any infringement of the state constitutions, the great body of the people will naturally take part with their domestic representatives. Can the general government withstand such a united opposition? Will the people suffer themselves to be stripped of their privileges? Will they suffer their legislatures to be reduced to a shadow and name? The idea is shocking to common sense."

In another case he appeals to the history of ancient and modern republics; and in another he depends upon the fact, known to his hearers, that such "considerations as these induced the Convention which formed your state Constitution to institute a Senate upon the present plan." Rhode Island, in still another case, is set up as an example of bad government, having been betrayed by the multitude.

Hamilton's enthymemes are thus typically developed out of the immediate experience of his hearers; and his maxims are commonly those which they are willing to accept. "There are two objects," he says, "in forming systems of government—safety for the people, and energy in the administration." From this principle he goes on to develop a conclusion. Again he supposes "it is a truth sufficiently illustrated by experience, that when the people act by their representatives, they are commonly irresistible." And again he goes on to his conclusion. He does not hesitate to deal with any point, whether it be weighty or obscure, so long as it helps him to establish his thesis. He calls into account the duty of sixpence per pound on salt in the State of New York, the compromises effected between counties, and the nature of legislatures. Finally, he reasons to the conclusion: If the members of Congress are too dependent on the state legislature, they will be eternally forming secret combinations from local views. This is reasoning from the plainest principles. Their interest is interwoven with their dependence, and they will necessarily yield to the impression of their situation. Those who have been in Congress have seen these operations. The first question has been, How will such a measure affect my constituents, and, consequently, how will the part I take affect my reelection? This consideration may be in some degree proper; but to be dependent from day to day, and to have the idea perpetually present, would be the source of numerous evils.

In general, it may be concluded, Hamilton's speech on the Powers of the Senate exhibits characteristics of ethical, emotional, and logical proof quite similar to those shown in his speech on the Principles of Union. The speech is remarkable for its directness of appeal to the audience, for the sustained quality of its logical proof, and for its persuasive exposition. How effective it was in the immediate situation is another question.[45]

FINAL DETERMINANT OF LOGICAL CRITICISM

Our discussion suggests that logical proof should ideally achieve Truth as the final desideratum. As John Lawson said, "Rhetoric must be the Handmaid of Truth." The Emersonian dictate of making the orator "the vehicle of truth" is, however, a state to which we can hopefully aspire, rather than one we can easily attain. The orator, who deals with social problems and hence with matters involving value judgments and variant interpretations, can do no more than earnestly strive for a logical coherence which in the long run may approximate truth.

Although in testing the arguments for validity we may find them acceptable, we are ever mindful that their validity is no necessary guarantee of their truth. What the public speaker strives to achieve in reasoning on social and political matters is a high degree of certainty, or at least of probability. The nature of the orator's art and the materials with which he deals require reliance upon the probable. He cannot hope to get all of the evidence, and so his judgments are constantly subject to revision.

Since the public speaker himself operates under limitations imposed by his subject and his data, the critic must prepare his analysis with full

---

[45] *The Rhetoric of Alexander Hamilton.* New York, Columbia University Press, 1941, pp. 159 ff.

recognition of the limitations. As Avey remarks in *The Function and Forms of Thought*, good judgment demands "no greater certainty of proof in a given case than the data available and the nature of the field of discussion warrant. To be satisfied with little rigor in mathematics would be inferiority in intellectual standards. But equally to demand dogmatic certainty in practical realms bespeaks a bigotry which is reprehensible. A sense of fitness must operate here as elsewhere." [46]

On last analysis, the quality of criticism resulting from an examination of logical proof is proportionate to the critic's understanding and knowledge of the subject under discussion. Arguments require scrutiny that goes beyond the determination of validity. Judgment must operate in the critical function; this implies the necessity of appraising not only the validity of the line of reasoning, but also of the material content— the facts—upon which the speech is based. In the words of Avey:

> The best equipment for significant criticism must be thorough knowledge of the principles of logic and methodology together with an extensive acquaintance with the facts of the field under discussion. And that discussion will rank highest under criticism which realizes most fully the requirements of formal validity and uses most significantly the facts which are relevant to the issue and objectively true.[47]

EXERCISES

1. What does it mean to "prove a point"? What constitutes proof?
2. How does explaining a point differ from proving a point?
3. Investigate the differences between argumentation and exposition. Consult several textbooks on logic and argumentation and debate.
4. Usually a speaker bases a speech upon generally accepted but unstated premises. For the speaker to succeed, the listeners must accept these premises without question. Analyze the unstated premises upon which the following were based: William Jennings Bryan's "Cross of Gold" speech or J. W. Fulbright's "The Two Americas," found in *Representative American Speeches, 1965–1966*, pp. 115–141, or the Inaugural Address of John F. Kennedy, *Representative American Speeches, 1960–1961*, pp. 35–40.
5. Brief the arguments found in a persuasive speech. If you are not familiar with rules of briefing, consult the short explanation in this chapter, or a longer treatment in a textbook on argumentation and debate. You may need to recast some of the points and to supply unstated points in order to make your brief logical and complete and to make it conform to good briefing practice. Why is briefing a valuable step in preparing a rhetorical criticism?
6. Investigate the interrelationship of logical and emotional appeal. What experimental findings can you find on the subject?

[46] *Op. cit.*, pp. 368–369.
[47] *Ibid.*, pp. 369–370.

7. Evaluate the major arguments and their supporting evidence in a speech found in the annual editions of *Representative American Speeches* (New York: The H. W. Wilson Company) or *Vital Speeches of the Day*.

8. What did the classical rhetoricians mean by invention? Discuss why invention and arrangement are sometimes analyzed together. Why are the two closely linked?

9. Reduce to a brief the argument presented in any recent debate in the United States Senate. Comment on the methods of logical development.

10. Cast the arguments of a single deliberative speech into syllogistic form, supplying missing premises when necessary. Apply the various tests of syllogistic reasoning to each syllogism.

11. Analyze the logical elements in a presidential radio or television speech which you personally heard. What factors permit the President to make categorical statements without supporting evidence?

12. A speaker may (*a*) clarify, (*b*) amplify, or (*c*) prove a proposition. How do these three processes differ? If possible, find examples of each one from the same speech.

13. Make a careful study of Webster's speech on the White murder case. Appraise the method of using evidence and of framing arguments.

14. Summarize the political and other premises that dominated the thinking of Albert J. Beveridge, Henry Clay, Daniel Webster, or Stephen A. Douglas.

15. For a detailed analysis and critique of one of America's celebrated court-room speeches, read Howard Bradley and James A. Winans' *Daniel Webster and the Salem Murder* (Columbia, Missouri; Artcraft Press, 1956). The study reveals the anatomy of an argument, and also sheds incidental light on textual authenticity and the reconstruction of a speech setting.

16. Assess this remark by Joseph Wood Krutch (*American Scholar*, Winter, 1958–59, pp. 93 f.): "Bad logic and pretended facts are more dangerous than imagination and opinion. Even the simple-minded do not believe a thing just because a poet says so. But they seldom doubt what they are told that 'science proves.'"

17. Present a critique of the analogical development in Stringfellow Barr's sustained argument *Consulting the Romans: An Analogy Between Ancient Rome and Present-Day America* (An Occasional Paper of the Center for the Study of Democratic Institutions, 1967). Apply the conventional tests to the analogy. Are they helpful in assessing the case?

CLASS PROJECT (Continued)

Prepare a 500-to-1000-word analysis of the integrity of the ideas found in a single speech of your selected speaker. You may find it necessary to limit yourself to a single major argument. You may wish to trace the development of this line of thought through several speeches.

READINGS

A. CRAIG BAIRD. *Argumentation, Discussion and Debate.* New York, McGraw-Hill Book Co., Inc., 1950.

———. *Rhetoric: A Philosophical Inquiry.* New York, The Ronald Press Co., 1965. Ch. 3, "Analysis, Definition, Fact"; ch. 4, "Logic and Reason in Discourse."

MONROE C. BEARDSLEY. *Thinking Straight: Principles of Reasoning for Readers and Writers,* 3d ed. Englewood Cliffs, New Jersey, Prentice-Hall, Inc., 1966.

SAMUEL L. BECKER. "Research on Emotional and Logical Proofs." *Southern Speech Journal,* 28:198–207 (Spring, 1963).

LLOYD BITZER. "Aristotle's Enthymeme Revisited." *Quarterly Journal of Speech,* 45:399–408 (December, 1959).

MAX BLACK. *Critical Thinking,* 2d ed. Englewood Cliffs, New Jersey, Prentice-Hall, Inc., 1952.

WALDO W. BRADEN and EARNEST BRANDENBURG. *Oral Decision Making.* New York, Harper and Row, 1955.

W. NORWOOD BRIGANCE. "A Genetic Approach to Persuasion." *Quarterly Journal of Speech,* 17:329–339 (June, 1931).

———. "Can We Re-Define the James-Winans Theory of Persuasion?" *Quarterly Journal of Speech,* 21:19–26 (February, 1935).

STUART CHASE. *Guides to Straight Thinking.* New York, Harper and Row, 1956.

LAURA CROWELL. *Discussion: Method of Democracy.* Chicago, Scott, Foresman, 1963.

JOHN DEWEY. *How We Think.* Boston and New York, D. C. Heath & Co., 1933.

RODNEY B. DOUGLASS and CARROLL C. ARNOLD. "On Analysis of Logos: A Methodological Inquiry." *Quarterly Journal of Speech,* 56:22–32 (February, 1970).

DOUGLAS EHNINGER and WAYNE BROCKRIEDE. *Decision by Debate.* New York, Dodd Mead & Co., Inc., 1963.

WILBUR E. GILMAN. "Logic and Public Speaking." *Quarterly Journal of Speech,* 26:667–672 (December, 1940).

WALTER R. FISHER. "John Bright: 'Hawker of Holy Things.'" *Quarterly Journal of Speech,* 51:157–163 (April, 1965).

WILBUR S. HOWELL. "The Positions of Argument: An Historical Examination." In *Papers in Rhetoric.* Edited by DONALD C. BRYANT. St. Louis, privately printed, 1940. Pp. 8–17.

EUGENE KNEPPRATH and THEODORE CLEVENGER, JR. "Reasoned Discourse and Motive Appeals in Selected Political Speeches." *Quarterly Journal of Speech,* 51:152–156 (April, 1965).

HAROLD A. LARRABEE. *Reliable Knowledge.* Boston, Houghton Mifflin Co., 1964.

JAMES H. McBURNEY and KENNETH HANCE. *Discussion in Human Affairs.* New York, Harper and Row, 1950.

JOHN STUART MILL. *System of Logic.* New York, Longmans, Green, 1872. Book III, ch. 20.

MAURICE NATANSON and HENRY W. JOHNSTONE, JR., eds. *Philosophy, Rhetoric, and Argumentation.* University Park, Penn., Pennsylvania State University Press, 1965.

CHARLES S. MUDD. "The Enthymeme and Logical Validity." *Quarterly Journal of Speech,* 45:409–414 (December, 1959).

JAMES H. ROBINSON. *The Mind in the Making.* New York, Harper & Bros., 1921.

DANIEL S. ROBINSON. *The Principles of Reasoning,* 3d ed. New York, Appleton-Century-Crofts, Inc., 1947.

EDWARD Z. ROWELL. "Prolegomena to Argumentation." *Quarterly Journal of Speech,* 18:1–13 (February, 1932); 18:224–248 (April, 1932); 18:381–405 (June, 1932); 18:585–606 (November, 1932).

STEPHEN TOULMIN. *The Uses of Argument.* New York, Cambridge University Press, 1958.

KARL R. WALLACE. "The Substance of Rhetoric: Good Reasons." *Quarterly Journal of Speech,* 49:239–249 (October, 1963).

CHARLES H. WOOLBERT. "The Place of Logic in a System of Persuasion." *Quarterly Journal of Speech Education,* 4:19–39 (January, 1918).

13

The Emotional Mode
of Speech Development

THE PROBLEM OF EMOTION IN DISCOURSE

Commenting on the purpose of council meetings, a character in Austin Tappan Wright's *Islandia* observes that it is not proper to force decisions through the stultifying influence of emotional appeals. Action so achieved, according to this claim, is won by falsity and trickery. Such observations are both important and provocative, for they suggest another of the persistent problems in rhetoric: the place of emotional appeal in the process of persuasion. Much has been written about it; schools of thought have debated the question; and pedagogical technique since antiquity has been partially moulded by the relative emphases accorded the concept from period to period. To this day, the matter has not been resolved to the satisfaction of all students, although all realize the significance of emotional appeal in speechmaking.

The problem with which we are concerned is clear. It assumes that at least two forms of expression operate in rhetoric: the one appeals to the intellect while the other addresses the emotions. As John Ward put it: ". . . bare conviction is not sufficient for many persons, to excite them to action. They will acquiesce in the truth of a thing, which they cannot contradict, or will not give themselves the trouble to examine; and at the same time remain unconcerned to prosecute it."[1] Joseph Priestley looked upon emotional proof as an energizer and expediter of

[1] *A System of Oratory.* London, 1759. II, 299–300.

conduct: "The genuine and proper use of the passions undoubtedly is to rouse men to just and vigorous action upon every emergency, without the slow intervention of reason." [2]

When we come to analyze the differences between the two types of appeal, we run into difficulties—difficulties both of definition and interpretation. Common sense tells us, of course, that both thought and feeling function in public address; that is, the notion of communication presupposes both an ideational and an emotional state in the speaker. Demonstration of an idea to others has its root in feelings and attitudes which result from the speaker's having, either directly or vicariously, experienced the thought. As John H. Gardiner says: "When you undertake to explain, you must put into your words the warmth of your personal interest . . . If you are arguing, you must be not only clear but moving . . ." [3]

The problem affects the listeners no less than the speaker. They are the respondents in the rhetorical process; to the speaker, their reaction is, an all-important consideration. To affect them as human beings requires more than error-free demonstration; there must also be judicious appeal to the feelings. The achievement of the goal of effective response therefore draws upon the two offices of rhetoric which, though blended, may yet be regarded separately. The first of them, says Thomas De Quincey, is "the literature of *knowledge;* the other, the literature of *power.* The function of the first is—to teach; the function of the second is—to move: the first is the rudder; the second, an oar or a sail." [4] The metaphor is well chosen; for, indeed, the emotional counterparts of rhetoric may with propriety be said to furnish the dynamic or the energizing force which moves speech and writing toward the goal of readier acceptance.

George Campbell, the Scotch rhetorician of the late eighteenth century, concluded in his *Philosophy of Rhetoric* that "when persuasion is the end, passion must also be engaged. If it is fancy which bestows brilliancy to our ideas, if it is memory which gives them stability, passion doth more: it animates them. Hence they derive spirit and energy. To say that it is possible to persuade without speaking to the passions is but, at best, a kind of specious nonsense. The coolest reasoner always, in persuading, addresseth himself to the passions some way or other. This he cannot avoid if he speaks to the purpose. To make me believe

[2] *A Course of Lectures on Oratory and Criticism.* Edited by Vincent Bevilacqua and Richard Murphy. Carbondale, Illinois, 1965, p. 80.

[3] *The Forms of Prose Literature.* New York, 1900, pp. 176–177.

[4] "The Literature of Knowledge and the Literature of Power." *North British Review.* (August, 1848). Cf. Masson ed., XI, 51.

it is enough to show me that things are so; to make me act, it is necessary to show me that the action will answer some end." [5]

Campbell adds that when a speaker attains a rational end without the emotional, he is often

> . . . as far from his purpose as before. You have proved beyond contradiction that acting thus is the sure way to procure such an object. I perceive that your reasoning is conclusive, but I am not affected by it. Why? I have no passion for the object. I am indifferent whether I procure it or not. You have demonstrated that such a step will mortify my enemy. I believe it: but I have no resentment, and will not trouble myself to give pain to another. Your arguments evince that it would gratify my vanity. But I prefer my ease. Thus passion is the mover to action, reason is the guide. [6]

Gary Cronkhite suggests the avoidance of confusion in the use of "reason or logic" and "emotion" by substituting "recognition" and "activation." [7]

The foregoing warns us that the process of persuasion is complex, and that the materials and methods employed to achieve the end of influencing listeners are varied. One of the modes of persuasion, the logical, has already been discussed. But as this discussion indicates it is not enough, by itself, to complete the task of inducing belief or action. So we turn to another mode, traditionally called the pathetic or the emotional. Concerning this, Aristotle reminds us that "proofs may be conveyed through the audience, when it is worked up by the speech to an emotional state." Then follows the essential point, that there is "a wide difference in our manner of pronouncing decisions, according as we feel pleasure or pain, affection or hatred. . . ." [8] Briefly, then, pathetic proof includes all those materials and devices calculated to put the audience in a frame of mind suitable for the reception of the speaker's ideas.

It is of interest to recall that Aristotle acknowledged the value of pathetic proof, while at the same time expressing suspicious concern over its injudicious use; and he was disturbed by the stress placed upon it by his predecessors. Thus he says, at the beginning of his treatise, that the only "true constituents" of the rhetorical art are the *logical* proofs; all others are merely accessory.

Much of the adverse criticism of public speaking as an art, from before Aristotle's time up to the present, has grown out of people's

[5] *The Philosophy of Rhetoric.* Edited by Lloyd F. Bitzer. Carbondale, Illinois, 1963, p. 77.

[6] *Ibid.*

[7] Gary L. Cronkhite. "Logic, Emotion, and the Paradigm of Persuasion." *Quarterly Journal of Speech,* 50:13–18 (February, 1964).

[8] *The Rhetoric of Aristotle.* Translated by Lane Cooper. New York, 1932, p. 9.

fears of the orator's exercising demagogic influence. Critics have viewed apprehensively the control which an orator can exercise over audiences by appealing to their feelings. It has been held, and with justification, that an irresponsible orator can, through emotional manipulation, induce belief or action—all without the support of factual data or with the data distorted and warped to suit his sinister design. As Plato once charged, orators can deal in words without knowledge. But these strictures do not reject the necessity and ethical wisdom of using emotional proof; rather, they illustrate the need for honest, high-principled reliance upon it as a means of making truth the more palatable, and, accordingly, the more decisive in the social process. Recognizing with A. K. Rogers [9] that the "normal human mind is not content merely to be logical and realistic," and that "it craves food for its emotions also," we shall now turn to a more direct analysis of the constituents of emotional proof as they function in the process of speechmaking.

ROLE AND CONCEPTS OF EMOTION IN COMMUNICATION

What is the emotional (or, in Greek terms, the pathetic) mode of communication? To Aristotle the pathetic was one of the three elements of establishing ideas. "Secondly, persuasion is effected through the audience, when they are brought by the speech into a state of emotion; for we give very different decisions under the sway of pain or joy, and liking or hatred." [10]

Psychologists agree that emotion is a consciousness or awareness of bodily changes. According to Robert Oliver, it is "a state of bodily tension accompanied by an intellectual concept of what the tension means." [11] The physiological reactions from the stimulus communicated to the higher centers of the nervous system—"this fused complex of sensory experience"—is what we call an emotion.

Emotions are thus a complex reaction to a specific situation. "Since emotion is a word or name, there is always a tendency to think that emotion is some thing, some discrete, distinct definable unity. Experiments have uniformly shown that emotion, like perception, cognition, and attention, does not exist *as a unique entity,* but that there is a variety of perceptive experiences, attendant reactions, and cognitive experiences. It is also true that such emotions as anger, fear, pity, disgust do not exist in unique independence, but in relation to concrete situa-

[9] "Prolegomena to a Political Ethics." In *Essays in Honor of John Dewey.* New York, 1929, p. 334.

[10] *Rhetoric,* p. 9.

[11] *The Psychology of Persuasive Speech,* 2d ed. New York, 1957, p. 251.

tions—in such phenomena as fighting reactions or fearfulness, in the experience of pity or of withdrawal from noxious objects." [12]

The modern concept of persuasion gives it wider connotation than that which limits it to emotion. Brembeck and Howell define persuasion as the conscious attempt to modify thought and action by manipulating motives of men toward predetermined ends.[13]

The dominant basis of belief and action, according to them, is desire expressed through a system of motives. William James wrote of attention in communication. James Winans, like James, explained that "what holds attention determines action." To him persuasion was "the process of inducing others to give fair, favorable, or undivided attention to propositions." [14] Ideas which "arouse emotion" held attention. The best way to fix attention was to awaken desire for the end sought. Desire was a motive.

W. Norwood Brigance took exception to this assumption of Winans' that described persuasion as a mental process. Brigance contended that "the generally accepted view today is that persuasion takes place, not on an intellectual, but rather on a motor level." [15] Even though psychologists are divided on many aspects of emotional processes, they are agreed that the basis for belief and action is need or desire. According to Brigance, persuasion is the process of "vitalizing old desires, purposes, or ideals, of substituting new desires, purposes, or ideals, for old ones." [16]

More specifically, behavior in communication is to be analyzed with relation to stimulus, tendencies, and responses. Stimulus, the source of behavior, is a form of energy which affects the sensory receptors of the organism. These stimuli may be largely limited to biological reactions. Man is a biological organism; the primary sources of motivation to *him* are in common with those of animals—hunger, sleep, sex, eliminative functions, and self-preservation. These primary reactions—drives—are related both to internal stimuli (*e.g.*, hunger) and to external or environmental stimuli (avoidance of injury). Such elemental drives stimulate primary emotions, which observers describe as rage, affection, and fear.

Since the developing individual moves into social adjustments and faces pressures, the satisfaction of his drives automatically leads to social motives such as *conformity*, subsistence motives, and social approval

12 Edwin Garrigues Boring, Herbert S. Langfeld, and Harry Porter Weld. *Introduction to Psychology*. New York, 1944, p. 183.
13 *Persuasion*. New York, 1952, p. 24.
14 *Public Speaking*. Rev. ed. New York, 1917, pp. 194 ff.
15 "Can We Re-define the James-Lange Theory of Persuasion?" *Quarterly Journal of Speech*, 21:19–26 (February, 1935).
16 *Speech Composition*. New York, 1939, pp. 19–26.

status. Some of these are described as ego drives or motives, those for example of respect, assertiveness, pride, dignity. Other motives, sublimated, serve the virtues of trust, integrity, loyalty, fair play, good sportsmanship, justice, and intellectual and aesthetic satisfaction.[17] These reactions become stereotypes, attitudes, sentiments. They are "the chief foundation stones of human behavior." [18]

Is emotional to be set off sharply from logical expression? A frequent error is to assume that they are exclusive. The old "faculty psychology" with its departmentalized intellect, feelings, and will has long been abandoned. All reaction is the common product of complicated nervous, muscular, and glandular activity. Some of the tendencies we label as predominantly "intellectual" and "logical"; others are largely "emotional." These tendencies are not to be placed upon a single continuum with their extremes at opposite ends. Rather a more realistic view would be to "place them in two continua which cross at some point between the two extremes." Viewed in this fashion, some communications would be highly illogical or highly motivated—with excess emotional content. Others would be put down as neither logical nor emotional motivation. Still others would employ the devices of motivation in balanced conjunction.

John Dewey has explained the place of emotion in human behavior:

> The conclusion is not that the emotional, passionate phase of action can be or should be eliminated in behalf of a bloodless reason. To check the influence of hate, there must be sympathy, while to rationalize sympathy, there are needed emotions of curiosity, caution, respect for the freedom of others—dispositions which evoke objects which balance those called up by sympathy, and prevent its degeneration into maudlin sentiment and meddling interference. Rationality, once more, is not a force to evoke against impulse and habit. It is the attainment of a working harmony among diverse desires.[19]

Some scholars have suggested that logic strongly permeates all communication. The late Charles H. Woolbert stated that logic becomes the basis of all persuasive speaking and writing. He expounded such logic as occurring at the "subconscious" level, or at a "partly concealed" level. His "logic" differs from the usual concept in which the listener or reader develops an intellectual reaction as contrasted with the more excessive emotional responses.[20] To him, "logic" is pretty close to "persuasion."

Though some experimenters have suggested that non-logical com-

---

[17] Cf. A. Craig Baird and Franklin H. Knower. *General Speech*, 3d ed. New York, 1963, pp. 281 ff.

[18] Brembeck and Howell. *Op. cit.*, pp. 118–119.

[19] *Human Nature and Conduct*. New York, 1922, pp. 195–196.

[20] "The Place of Logic in a System of Persuasion." *Quarterly Journal of Speech Education*, 4:19–39 (January, 1918).

munication has influenced audiences more effectively than the logical type, the evidence has not been conclusive. Franklin H. Knower, for example, dealt with the question, "Is an attitude more markedly changed by an argument which is predominantly factual and logical or one which is predominantly emotional?" He concluded that "Although these college students would no doubt have denied that they could be swayed by an emotional appeal, the data show that on the whole approximately as many were swayed by one type of argument as by the other." [21]

Concerning the intellectual quality of mankind, W. Norwood Brigance observed that man "has lived on this planet for untold thousands of years. To survive during these years he has been forced to adapt himself to biological conditions and to the physical universe. Out of this survival he has acquired wants and culture patterns. These wants and culture patterns are old. Through them man has survived. Reason and logic, on the other hand, are new." [22]

The Persuasion-Conviction Dualism

In the first comprehensive analysis of rhetorical processes, Aristotle inquired into the psychological reactions of listeners. He made the term "persuasion" embrace not only the appeals to the emotions of the hearers, but made persuasion nearly synonymous with the goal or end of speaking. As previously indicated, he regarded logical proof as the "true constituent" of oratory; but his extensive and penetrating treatment of the emotions demonstrated his recognition of the place of emotional appeal in the attempt to influence hearers. Link these matters with Aristotle's expressed opposition to the schools of thought that placed the primary emphasis upon the ways of disposing hearers in the speaker's behalf, and we observe that the dualism reaches deep into antiquity.

Theoretically, of course, there is no clear-cut dichotomy in the Aristotelian system, such as we find in the persuasion-conviction scheme of later times. And the three modes of proof which he mentions are not treated as sharply separated entities; all apparently unite in greater or lesser measure to induce the end-product of persuasion. These distinctions are, however, purely verbal; the Aristotelian analysis takes into account the differences between the materials that *demonstrate* and those that *predispose* listeners to receive the logical demonstration.

Cicero's rhetorical theory involves a recognition of the different offices of logical and emotional appeal. This is evident from his remark that the proper concern of an orator "is language of power and elegance ac-

[21] Franklin H. Knower. "Experimental Studies in Changes of Attitudes." *Journal of Social Psychology*, 6:315–345 (August, 1935).

[22] W. Norwood Brigance. *Speech*. New York, Appleton-Century-Crofts, 1952, pp. 102 ff.

commodated to the feelings and understandings of mankind." Like Aristotle, he indicates that persuasion is the objective of the orator's art, asserting that three things contribute to its achievement: "that we prove what we maintain to be true; that we conciliate those who hear; that we produce in their minds whatever feeling our cause may require." [23] Because of possible difficulties in translation, it is hard to tell whether he held consistently to that view. In a later section, he speaks of the necessity of arranging material so as to prove, to inform, and to persuade. Hence there may be some justification for the belief that Cicero compartmentalized the types of appeals more severely than did Aristotle. Be that as it may, he sustained the tradition of separating the appeals according to the basic nature of hearers.

The *Institutes* of Quintilian furnish no new data on the dualism. It is apparent that Quintilian looked upon logic and emotional appeal as playing supporting roles in the rhetorical process. Without declaring either the one or the other to be primary, he proceeded on the assumption that both contributed to the handling of audiences.

The later writers furnish data to support the belief that tradition has fixed the dichotomy securely in the literature of the subject. It is quite probable, of course, that the more recent investigators—especially those who were not philosophers themselves—took their notions not only from empirical observation, but from the classics and from the thoughts relative to the dualism of mind and matter, and of the division of the mind into separable faculties.

Thomas Wilson was a disciple of the classical school which elevated logical proof to the position of primacy. The tongue was ordained to express the mind so that others might grasp the speaker's meaning, he remarked. But he did not ignore the other phase of man's makeup, for he assured the readers of his *Arte of Rhetorique* that people are persuaded through appeals to the affections. By linking amplification with the moving of the affections, he made the figure of speech a virtual key to persuasion.

The empirical philosophy of Thomas Hobbes, with its reliance upon an epistemological dualism, brings forth a clear distinction between persuasion and conviction. Hobbes differentiates between speech that expresses emotional content and speech that expresses thought content. He observes that the "forms of speech by which the passions are expressed, are partly the same, and partly different from those, by which we express our thoughts." It is to be recognized, however, that there is a "feeling" attached to mere thought inasmuch as thought involves motion. This division of speech forms for passion and for thought is,

---

[23] *De Oratore.* Watson translation. II, 27.

indeed, suggestive of the dichotomous treatment still prevalent in current speech theory.

Because of his familiarity with the psychology of his time, Campbell gave a new turn to the dualistic concept. He approached the problem through the medium of speech objectives, observing that every speech is intended "to enlighten the understanding, to please the imagination, to move the passions, or to influence the will." Making the analysis much more atomistic than in the classical tradition, Campbell restricts the field of operation for any one of the ends. While he allows for the interaction of the appeals, he sets up one, and only one, as the *principal* motivator:

> . . . a discourse addressed to the understanding, and calculated to illustrate or evince some point purely speculative, may borrow aid from the imagination, and amid metaphor and comparison, but not the bolder and more striking figures. . . . Still less will it admit an address to the passions, which, as it never fails to disturb the operation of the intellectual faculty, must be regarded by every intelligent hearer as foreign at least, if not insidious.[24]

Using the term "conviction" and the term "persuasion" in their more modern sense, Campbell states that the former is characterized by the predominant quality of argument. Persuasion, on the other hand, has its "marvellous efficacy in rousing the passions, and by some secret, sudden, and inexplicable association, awakening all the tenderest emotions of the heart." Here we have, indeed, the modern statements of the controversial dualism. Groupings of the powers of the mind according to its faculties are evident in these separations of the basic psychological appeals. We also see evidence of this division in Blair's and Whately's work.

Perhaps the most cogent objections to the uncritical acceptance of persuasion and conviction as the basic constituents of the rhetorical process came from Mary Yost. In 1917, she published an article entitled "Argument from the Point of View of Sociology" in which she vigorously opposed the standard treatment of argumentation.[25]

Stimulated by the Yost pronouncements, Woolbert [26] (of the behavioristic school of psychology) promptly entered his indictment of the traditional classification. Urging a study of the reactions of hearers rather than disproportionately elaborate analyses of subject matter, Woolbert asserted that behavioral manifestations to stimuli were essentially unitary—that they defied the artificial divisibility into rational and

---

[24] *Op. cit.*, pp. 1–2.

[25] *Quarterly Journal of Public Speaking*, 3:109–124 (April, 1917).

[26] "Conviction and Persuasion." *Quarterly Journal of Public Speaking*, 3:249–264 (July, 1917).

emotional responses. In general, he branded the conventional dualism as useless at best, and pernicious at its worst. Modern psychology—and especially behaviorism—did not sanction the distinction between perceived and nonperceived action which the dualism presupposed.

Edward Rowell, former professor of philosophy at the University of California, restated the controversy and resolved it by his own findings and philosophical judgment. "Psychological monism," he said, "is invalid, for at some points in human behavior such distinctions (pluralism and dualism, *i.e.*, reasoning and feeling) become not only legitimate but scientifically inescapable." Taken negatively, psychological monism is no more than:

> . . . a repudiation of the old faculty psychology which talked of reasoning as the work of a reason, of willing as the work of a will, and so forth. Taken positively, it is a recognition of the functional approach to psychological processes . . . views men as unified reaction-systems which can exert . . . reasoning, feeling, willing, and so forth. Psychological monism makes no denial of the reality . . . between reasoning, feeling, and willing. All it denies is the idea that these forms of behavior are expressions of individual faculties. This monism is as pluralistic as it is monistic.[27]

Winston Brembeck and William Howell in their *Persuasion* found no difficulty in focussing on motives and analyzing emotional appeals, and on "a maximum of fact and logical reasoning, or in varying combinations of these employments." [28]

Robert Oliver in his *Psychology of Persuasive Speech* treated the motivative approach similarly and indicated how the emotional and logical aspects of the persuasive process have a common basis. Without our return to a naïve concept of faculty psychology, the dichotomy is significant to the extent that it emphasizes the role of hearers in determining the object of speeches. Whether we call these constituents by one name or another is of little moment; but that we take them into account when creating or criticizing oratory is important. That such a division is inconsistent even with modern schools of psychology is open to doubt when we consider the duality from the point of view of audience response.

Emotional Mode of Persuasion

Emotional proof, as we have just indicated, is designed to put the listener in a frame of mind to react favorably and conformably to the speaker's purpose. Assuming the purpose to be scrupulously honorable,

[27] "The Conviction-Persuasion Duality." *Quarterly Journal of Speech,* 20:470 (November, 1934).
[28] *Op. cit.,* p. 24.

to the speaker's best knowledge, we may ask: What is the broad meaning of this concept of emotional proof as a mode of persuasion? The discussion of three related inquiries should throw some light upon the whole matter: (1) the principle of audience adaptation, (2) the practical applications of the principle, and (3) the assumptions underlying the total concept.

PRINCIPLES OF AUDIENCE ADAPTATION AND ADJUSTMENT

Aristotle observed that a speech was composed, or grew out of the interaction, of three elements: the speaker, the subject, and the persons addressed. He added that of the three elements, it was the last, the audience, that determined a speech's end or object. Never seriously questioned, this pronouncement has almost become a rhetorical axiom. It announces that, for the speaker, the audience is the most important element in the situation and that, if he is to be effective, the speaker must adjust both himself and his ideas to it. The basic consideration, then, is *adaptation,* or adjustment to the variables of human behavior as found in a specific group of hearers. Even though he wished and were able to present the Truth as he saw it in purely logical form, he could not do so, owing, perhaps, to what John Lawson calls "the Imperfection of Mankind." "If our Hearers were always serious, attentive, knowing, and unprejudiced," Lawson went on, "we should have nothing to do but to lay Truth before them in its own genuine Shape; But as Men actually are, we find it necessary, not only to shew them what is right, but to make Use of all the Skill we have, to induce them stedfastly to behold it." [29] Therefore speakers adapt what they have to say to the peculiar audience conditions facing them.

Such adaptation does not imply mechanical or arbitrary orientation simply for the sake of rhetorical expediency. Speakers can make adjustments to hearers without distorting, suppressing, or in any way vitiating the integrity of their ideas; but practical wisdom decrees that they expound their views with forethought of the emotional makeup of the audience, with full recognition of the possible reactions of the group to the presentation. A critic of oratory, writing in the *Edinburgh Review,* once declared there is never a speech "which does not somehow give to its hearers the feeling that the arguments are used not because they are sound but because they fit the understandings of those to whom they are addressed, that the sentiments are not those of the speaker but simply what best suit the emergency. . . ." [30] The imputation here is manifestly false, as the record of distinguished British and American

[29] *Lectures Concerning Oratory.* Dublin, 1760, p. 165.
[30] 139:287 (January, 1874).

oratory attests, but that speakers attempt to adapt their ideas to hearers is unquestionably true, and thoroughly wholesome. Were it otherwise, critics would find even more to censure in the annals of public address. Whether we like it or not, some truth inheres in Cicero's dictum that "mankind makes far more determinations through hatred, or love, or desire, or anger, or grief, or joy, or hope, or fear, or error, or some other affection of mind, than from regard to truth, or any settled maxim, or principle of right, or judicial form, or adherence to the laws." [31] It is the orator's task to link the truth to man's emotional nature so as to insure the most responsible beliefs and actions consistent with human limitations. This implies, as Alexander Bain remarks, that the course of action "shall be so described, or expressed, as to coincide, or be identified, with the active impulses of the individuals addressed, and thereby command their adoption of it by the force of their own natural dispositions." [32] It is the critic's job to appraise the orator's success in effecting that union.

So far, our discussion has dealt largely with the more general aspects of pathetic proof. But the critic, like the speaker himself, must approach this problem in a practical way. The question that arises, therefore, is: How does the speaker make necessary adjustments to his hearers in order to dispose them favorably toward his ideas and purposes? The answer necessarily deals with the factors of audience analysis.

Speech is plainly an instrument of social control whose function is to bring about adjustment and coordination of the social body. In its serious operation in the practical world, it should not be a medium for the realization of personal achievement, exhibition, or development. The range of its effective use is limited to situations in which there are people whose conduct can be controlled or influenced by words and actions.

The critic is interested in determining the extent of the speaker's control over his audience. Recognizing that no one is able to gain complete mastery over listeners, the critic looks to the speaker's facility and competence in handling the two aspects of audience analysis: analysis of the group prior to the delivery of the speech and audience adjustment during the presentation of the address.

The preanalysis of an audience is designed to furnish the speaker with information that will enable him to adapt his material to the hearers. This is a purely investigative undertaking which the speaker conducts prior to his talk, and upon the data of which he relies for guidance in composing the speech. So far as the critic is concerned, the question requiring resolution is: To what extent, and with what measure of suc-

[31] *De Oratore.* II, 42.
[32] *The Senses and the Intellect,* 3d ed. New York, 1888, p. 528.

cess, did the speaker adapt himself and his message to the ascertainable facts relating to the composition of the audience? In other words, did the speaker evince an intelligent understanding of the nature of the problem, and did he apply that insight to the practical task of disposing his hearers in his behalf?

The lines of study bearing relevantly upon this inquiry are manifold. Each speech situation has unique features that demand individual analysis. But, by and large, the critic will try to determine how fully the speaker took the following audience characteristics into account in the preparation and presentation of his speech: (1) age level; (2) sex; (3) intellectual and informational status with regard to the subject; (4) the political, social, religious, and other affiliations; (5) the economic status; (6) known or anticipated attitude toward the subject; (7) known or anticipated prejudices and predispositions; (8) occupational status; (9) known interest in the subject; (10) considerations of self-interest in the subject; and (11) temper and tone of the occasion. The general objective, it will be seen, is to find out how completely the speaker adapts his remarks within the limitations imposed by the particular audience situation.

Another phase of this matter is the adjustment that the speaker makes to his hearers *during* the speech. Here we are dealing either with the response he makes to such overt behavior as applause or heckling, or to the intangibly tacit reactions indicating degrees of satisfaction or dissatisfaction with the proceedings. Since the critic frequently deals with speeches which he did not hear, he must necessarily rely upon texts which, at their best, serve as unsatisfactory if not wholly unreliable indicators of these subtle reactions. In this particular, therefore, he operates under several restrictive conditions.

PRACTICAL APPLICATIONS OF THE FOREGOING PRINCIPLES

The foregoing observations have their roots in common soil. They posit the thesis that the speaker must have penetrating insight into the human emotions; that he must be conversant with the motivating elements that energize behavior, be it belief or action. Since antiquity, rhetoricians have regarded a knowledge of the emotions, or of the soul, as an indispensable condition to competency in speaking. As Plato remarks in the *Phaedrus:* "Since the power of speech is that of leading the soul, it is necessary that he who means to be an orator should know how many kinds of soul there are. . . ." [33] Aristotle, whose remarks on the emotions still make eminently good sense after these many years,

[33] Translated by Henry Cary. London, 1854. I, 350–351.

believed that the only effective way of considering pathetic proof was through an analysis of emotional behavior. So he analyzed the several emotions in the light of (1) the conditions under which people assume the particular emotion; (2) the objects of it; and (3) the causes which induce the state.

As to the practical wisdom that should guide the speaker in his attempts to induce emotional states, the rhetoricians have been generous in their counsel. Cicero was explicit in urging the speaker not to hasten into pathetic portions of the speech before making all points luminously clear. Men are desirous, he remarked, first to learn

> . . . the very point that is to come under their judgment; nor, when you have entered upon that track, are you suddenly to diverge from it; for you are not to suppose that as an argument is understood as soon as it is stated, and a second and a third are then desired, so you can with the same ease move compassion, or envy, or anger, as soon as you make the attempt. Reason itself confirms an argument which fixes itself in the mind as soon as it is delivered; but that sort of eloquence does not aim at instructing the judge, but rather at agitating his mind by excessive emotion, which no one can produce unless by fulness and variety and even copiousness of language, and a proportionate energy of delivery. Those, therefore, who speak either with brevity, or in a low submissive strain, may indeed inform the judge, but can never move him, an effect on which success altogether depends.[34]

John Lawson urged speakers not to attempt pathetic excursions on subjects undeserving of such efforts; to use emotional appeals, not as substitutes for reason, but as adjuncts to it; to make emotional appeals short. "Seek not to keep long in Motion a Spring formed for quick, but short Action." The speaker should conceal the attempt to play upon the feelings, for emotion should be perceived only by its effects; and he should avoid the excessive use of pathetic proof before an audience which is clearly unmoved.[35]

Hugh Blair laid down rules similar to Lawson's. Said Blair:

> The first is to consider carefully, whether the subject admit the Pathetic, and render it proper; and if it does, what part of the Discourse is the most proper for attempting it. To determine these points belongs to good sense; for it is evident, that there are many subjects which admit not the Pathetic at all, and that even in those that are susceptible of it, an attempt to excite the passions in the wrong place, may expose an Orator to ridicule. All that can be said in general is, that if we expect any emotion which we raise to have a lasting effect, we must be careful to bring over to our side, in the first place, the understanding and judgment. The hearers must be convinced that there are good and sufficient grounds for their entering with warmth into the cause. They must be able to justify to themselves the passion which they feel; and remain satisfied that they are not carried away by mere delusion.

---

[34] *De Oratore*, II, 53.
[35] *Op. cit.*, 178 ff.

Unless their minds be brought into this state, although they may have been heated by the Orator's discourse, yet, as soon as he ceases to speak, they will resume their ordinary tone of thought; and the emotion which he has raised will die entirely away.[36]

Identification

The basic principle of speaker-audience relations is that of identification. Kenneth Burke, among the most original thinkers in recent rhetoric, makes identification the key to persuasion. In contrasting the "old" rhetoric with the "new," he remarked that "the key term for the 'new' rhetoric would be identification, which can include a partially 'unconscious' factor in appeals." [37]

To Burke, identification is identical with consubstantiality. "A doctrine of consubstantiality, either explicit or implicit, may be necessary to any way of life. For substance in the old philosophies was an act; and a way of life is acting—together; and in acting together, men have common sensations, concepts, images, ideas, attitudes that make them consubstantial." [38]

Burke's concept of identification turns out to be the classical procedure of close audience adjustment and interpersonal activities in communication. His new insight is in the interpretation of the term persuasion as linked with identification, and this in turn with "substance" (an act or activity) and with social intercourse as "acting together."

Identification, it should be noted, if it fulfills the concept of close correspondence and fairly complete communication, calls for the speaker's self-analysis with respect to his own intellectual, social and moral equipment. He must both understand himself and his audience. He is to ensure himself and others of his intellectual control over his theme and its details; of his selection and interpretation of the logical framework and order of his discourse; of his direction of the emotional-imaginative appeals and proofs so as to enforce and not distort the basic propositions; of his insight into social results, the implications of and direct reactions to his speech that contribute to the "good" society. He is thus a qualified "agent."

The audience, too, if genuine identification occurs, is to be analyzed in detail with respect to its educational capacities and understanding; its emotional reaction; its prevailing motives as related to the economic, social, and other desires and needs and programs; its beliefs, imbedded habits, attitudes, and outlooks.

---

[36] *Lectures on Rhetoric and Belles Lettres.* New ed. London: William Tegg, n.d., pp. 383 ff.

[37] "Rhetoric—Old and New." *Journal of General Education,* 5:203 (April, 1951).

[38] Kenneth Burke. A *Rhetoric of Motives.* Englewood Cliffs, New Jersey, 1953, p. 21.

On such factors associated with the speaker and the audience does the experience of adjustment and identification occur.

Arrangement

Emotional appeal has frequently been linked with the concept of arrangement. Thus it was deemed more appropriate and effective to concentrate the pathetic elements in certain parts of the speech, preferably in the introduction and conclusion. Not that emotional details were to be excluded elsewhere; but the tacit assumption remained that their influence would be greater if used at appropriate times and in strategic places. Cicero remarks that while "solicitation and excitement" produce significant effects in other parts of the speech, "their proper place is chiefly in the exordium and the peroration"; but, he adds, even "to make a digression from what you have proposed and are discussing, for the sake of exciting the passions, is often advantageous." [39] Admitting that pathetic appeals are peculiarly effective in the peroration, Quintilian states that they "are admissible also in other parts." [40] And Blair urges speakers to determine carefully "what part of the Discourse is the most proper" for attempting emotional persuasion. We see, then, that pathetic proof, though properly a division of rhetorical invention, is also considered an aspect of disposition. This reminds us of the indivisibility of the elements of rhetoric; and of the necessity for the critic to look upon a speech in its entirety, a Gestalt, which, though reducible to parts for reasons of practical convenience, is nevertheless to be appraised as a totality.

The Speaker's Personality

What traits of the speaker strongly influence the outcome of a given communicative situation?

One factor is the speaker's purpose or motive. Is he merely attempting to attract attention to himself? To satisfy his inner pride? To defend himself from hostile criticism? To deliver a genuine appeal for some cause in which he strongly believes?

The speaker is usually considered an interpreter of the mood or emotional state which he proposes to induce in the hearers. "Be yourself possessed with the Passion you would excite," wrote John Lawson. In the main, the observation is plausible. The point nevertheless is highly controversial, as the varying opinions of great actors indicate. But that the speaker must competently simulate the emotional state—even though

---

[39] *De Oratore*, II, 77.
[40] *Institutes of Oratory*, Watson edition. VI, 1, 51.

it does not take complete possession of him—is admitted by many writers. Cicero remarks:

> Nor is it possible that the judge should feel concern, or hate, or envy, or fear in any degree, or that he should be moved to compassion and tears, unless all those sensations which the orator would awaken in the judge shall appear to be deeply felt and experienced by the orator himself.[41]

Simulated or feigned emotion is by definition synthetic; only the most accomplished actor can give it a plausibility that induces confidence. But great orators, speaking on significant issues, are not on display as performers. Their histrionics are accessories. Exhibitionism in speech is not a congenial ally of responsibility of statement.

A personality trait important in communication is general intelligence. A high IQ is not essential. Some speakers with such superior mental traits have had serious speaking problems. We assume, however, that the speaker should know his subject; should avoid quagmires of confused thinking. Audiences will no doubt detect such lapses in platform common sense. The speaker will function better if he has knowledge of his subject. Thus far all rhetoricians, from Cicero on have expounded the necessity of the speaker's broad education; his familiarity not only with his immediate subject, but with knowledge in general.

Another trait is the speaker's social intelligence. More effective speakers have presumably had more experience than others in talking to audiences and in understanding the ways of human nature. Their social sensitivity guides them in the selection of the proper ideas for the occasion, the "right" appeals, and the other factors that make for maximum attention and satisfactory response. He who secures relatively better reactions from all kinds of audiences is presumably one who studies people, knows them in detail, and uses his social adaptiveness to good account.

In addition to intelligence, knowledge of audiences, and tact, the good speaker will have self confidence. If he is not sure of his preparation, his ideas and his right to speak, he may be easily disconcerted or irresolute as audiences react negatively. Confidence without egotism and ability to forget the self in committal to the speaking purpose, are more likely to ensure desirable behavior toward the speaker.

One other personality trait concerns emotional control. Personality includes both the intellectual and emotional behavior. Rational thinking reflects the well-organized personality. Uncontrolled, disorganized thinking indicates a lack of emotional balance. Such emotionality is marked by extravagant imagery and by exaggerated conclusions. The

[41] *De Oratore*, II, 45.

production is an expression of belief and desire more than careful thinking.

Language and Emotion

Note the basic postulate that language is capable of performing a dual function of appealing both to the rational and to the emotional nature of man. This is a fundamental distinction, upon the validity of which must inevitably rest much of the traditional theory concerning pathetic proof.

Although rhetoricians have always considered the varying uses of language in different contexts, they have not given the matter as full attention as have the semanticists and their disciples during the past few decades. The development of the so-called science of meaning has placed increasing emphasis upon words as multiedged instruments. The effect of words in a particular place varies with the conditions of the moment. Accordingly, words have both *referential* and *emotive* value. While this distinction is not completely adequate, it helps to illustrate the functional bearing of certain words in certain places. I. A. Richards indicates that words may be used for "the sake of the references they promote" or for "the sake of the attitudes and emotions which ensue." [42] He then remarks that in the case of the former (the referential) there is need for precision and clearly established relations—in short, for what we would call logical development. On the other hand, the emotive words may not make up a wholly logical sequence and yet be peculiarly effective.[43] Poetic or emotional language uses words in such relationships as will help to objectify fresh meanings.

Many speeches illustrate how referential and emotive materials overlap. One example will illustrate the point. In a dramatic radio-television address on October 22, 1962, John F. Kennedy informed his fellow citizens of the Soviet missile build-up on the island of Cuba. In the speech he analyzed the available evidence, made a powerful emotive appeal to fear and material well-being, and announced a quarantine of all shipments of military offensive materials to the troubled island.

This Government, as promised, has maintained the closest surveillance of the Soviet military build-up on the island of Cuba. Within the past week, unmistakable evidence has established the fact that a series of offensive missile sites is now in preparation on that imprisoned island. The purpose of these bases can be none other than to provide a nuclear capability against the Western Hemisphere.

Upon receiving the first preliminary hard information of this nature last

[42] *Principles of Literary Criticism*, 5th ed. New York, 1934, p. 126.

[43] Cf. James Burnham and Philip Wheelwright. *Introduction to Philosophical Analysis*. New York, 1932, pp. 71–72.

Tuesday morning [October 16] at 9:00 A.M., I directed that our surveillance be stepped up. And having now confirmed and completed our evaluation of the evidence and our decision on a course of action, this Government feels obliged to report this new crisis to you in fullest detail.

The characteristics of these new missile sites indicate two distinct types of installations. Several of them include medium-range ballistic missiles, capable of carrying a nuclear warhead for a distance of more than one thousand nautical miles. Each of these missiles, in short, is capable of striking Washington, D.C., the Panama Canal, Cape Canaveral, Mexico City, or any other city in the Southeastern part of the United States, in Central America, or in the Caribbean area.

Additional sites not yet completed appear to be designed for intermediate range ballistic missiles—capable of traveling more than twice as far—and thus capable of striking most of the major cities in the Western Hemisphere, ranging as far north as Hudson's Bay, Canada, and as far south as Lima, Peru. In addition, jet bombers, capable of carrying nuclear weapons, are now being uncrated and assembled in Cuba, while the necessary air bases are being prepared.

This urgent transformation of Cuba into an important strategic base—by the presence of large, long-range and clearly offensive weapons of sudden mass destruction—constitutes an explicit threat to the peace and security of all the Americas, in flagrant and deliberate defiance of the Rio Pact of 1947, the traditions of this nation and hemisphere, the joint resolution of the 87th Congress, the Charter of the United Nations, and my own public warnings to the Soviets on September 4 and 13. This action also contradicts the repeated assurances of Soviet spokesmen, both publicly and privately delivered, that the arms buildup in Cuba would retain its original defensive character, and that the Soviet Union had no need or desire to station strategic missiles on the territory of any other nation.

The size of this undertaking makes clear that it has been planned for some months. Yet only last month, after I had made clear the distinction between any introduction of ground-to-ground missiles and the existence of defensive antiaircraft missiles, the Soviet government publicly stated on September 11, that, and I quote, 'the armaments and military equipment sent to Cuba are designed exclusively for defensive purposes,' and, I quote the Soviet government, 'there is no need for the Soviet government to shift its weapons for a retaliatory blow to any other country, for instance Cuba,' and that, and I quote the government, 'the Soviet Union has so powerful rockets to carry these nuclear warheads that there is no need to search for sites for them beyond the boundaries of the Soviet Union.' That statement was false.

Only last Thursday, as evidence of this rapid offensive build-up was already in my hand, Soviet Foreign Minister Gromyko told me in my office that he was instructed to make it clear once again, as he said his government had already done, that Soviet assistance to Cuba, and I quote, 'pursued solely the purpose of contributing to the defense capabilities of Cuba,' that, and I quote him, 'training by Soviet specialists of Cuban nationals in handling defensive armaments was by no means offensive,' and that 'if it were otherwise,' Mr. Gromyko went on, 'the Soviet government would never become involved in rendering such assistance.' That statement also was false.

Neither the United States of America nor the world community of nations can tolerate deliberate deception and offensive threats on the part of any nation, large or small. We no longer live in a world where only the actual firing of weapons represents a sufficient challenge to a nation's security to constitute maximum peril. Nuclear weapons are so destructive and ballistic missiles are so swift, that any substantially increased possibility of their use or any sudden change in their deployment may well be regarded as a definite threat to peace.

For many years, both the Soviet Union and the United States, recognizing this fact, have deployed strategic nuclear weapons with great care, never upsetting the precarious status quo which insured that these weapons would not be used in the absence of some vital challenge. Our own strategic missiles have never been transferred to the territory of any other nation, under a cloak of secrecy and deception; and our history, unlike that of the Soviets since the end of World War II, demonstrates that we have no desire to dominate or conquer any other nation or impose our system upon its people. Nevertheless, American citizens have become adjusted to living daily in the bull's-eye of Soviet missiles located inside the U.S.S.R. or in submarines.

In that sense, missiles in Cuba add to an already clear and present danger —although it should be noted the nations of Latin America have never previously been subjected to a potential nuclear threat.

But this secret, swift, and extraordinary build-up of Communist missiles— in an area well known to have a special and historical relationship to the United States and the nations of the Western Hemisphere, in violation of Soviet assurances, and in defiance of American and hemispheric policy—this sudden, clandestine decision to station strategic weapons for the first time outside of Soviet soil—is a deliberately provocative and unjustified change in the status quo which cannot be accepted by this country, if our courage and our commitments are ever to be trusted again by either friend or foe.

The 1930's taught us a clear lesson: Aggressive conduct, if allowed to grow unchecked and unchallenged, ultimately leads to war. This nation is opposed to war. We are also true to our word. Our unswerving objective, therefore, must be to prevent the use of these missiles against this or any other country and to secure their withdrawal or elimination from the Western Hemisphere.[44]

Traditionally, emotional appeal has been associated with the ceremonial address, those which commemorate great events and eulogize great personalities. Ambassador Adlai Stevenson, late United States Representative to the United Nations, delivered his tribute to John F. Kennedy at a Plenary Meeting of the General Assembly, on November 26, 1963. In this eulogy Mr. Stevenson demonstrated how restrained, simple language can stir deep emotional response.

President Kennedy was so contemporary a man—so involved in our world —so immersed in our times—so responsive to its challenges—so intense a participant in the great events and great decisions of our day, that he seemed the very symbol of the vitality and the exuberance that is the essence of life itself.

Never once did he lose his way in the maze; never once did he falter in

[44] Lester Thonssen, ed. *Representative American Speeches: 1962–1963*. New York, 1963, pp. 9–12.

the storm of spears; never once was he intimidated. Like the ancient prophets he loved the people enough to warn them of their errors. And the man who loves his country best will hold it to its highest standards. He made us proud to be Americans.

And so it is that after four sorrowful days we still can hardly grasp the macabre reality that the world has been robbed of this vibrant presence by an isolated act conceived in the strange recesses of the human mind.

We shall not soon forget the late President's driving ambition for his own country—his concept of a permanently dynamic society spreading abundance to the last corner of this land, and extending justice, tolerance and dignity to all of its citizens alike.

We shall not soon forget that as the leader of a great nation he met and mastered his responsibility to wield great power with great restraint. 'Our national strength matters,' he said just a few weeks ago, 'but the spirit which informs, and controls, our strength matters just as much.'

We shall not soon forget that he held fast to the vision of a world in which the peace is secure; in which inevitable conflicts are reconciled by pacific means; in which nations devote their energies to the welfare of all their citizens; and in which the vast and colorful diversity of human society can flourish in a restless, competitive search for a better society.

We shall not soon forget that by word and by deed he gave proof of profound confidence in the present value and the future promise of this great organization, the United Nations.

And we shall never forget these ambitions, these visions, these convictions that so inspired this remarkable young man and so quickened the quality and the tempo of our times in these fleeting past three years. And our grief is compounded by the bitter irony that he who gave all to contain violence, lost his all—to violence.

Finally, let me say, as several speakers have reminded us here this afternoon, that John Kennedy never believed that he or any man was indispensable; of Dag Hammarskjold's death he said: 'The problem is not the death of one man—the problem is the life of this organization.' But he did believe passionately that peace and justice are indispensable. And he believed—as he told this Assembly in 1961—that 'in the development of this organization lives the only true alternative to war. . . .'

So, my friends, we shall honor him in the best way that lies open to us—and the way he would want it to be—by getting on with the everlasting search for peace and justice for which all mankind is praying.[45]

Essentially little or no difference exists between the motivative appeals in persuasion and the personal-moral-ethical appeals in the same discourse. Only a shadowy line of demarcation exists between these factors. Sincerity, intelligence, good will, and similar patterns fall into either category—according to the results aimed at. If "good will," for example, aims mainly at limited economic or political outcomes, the motivative effect is "emotional." If the manipulation of these materials attempts to suggest social betterment of the immediate and larger con-

[45] Lester Thonssen, ed. *Representative American Speeches: 1963–1964.* New York, 1964, pp. 31–32.

stituency, then the technique may properly be described as "ethical" (in the broad meaning of the word).

Those approaches and details that involve value judgments become moral-ethical motives. Intangible though it may be for speech critics to decide whether personal motives of speakers and communicative results are "moral" in their tendencies, the differentiations of material and method are to be understood by the speakers and their critics. The appraisal of the logical and emotional materials and of the overcasting of moral factor raises the basic question affecting the good or bad society. On the surface all motivative drives may be grouped together. Under more deliberate analysis, however, the personality of the speaker and his individual attitudes may so dominate his discourse, or parts of it, as to suggest for the critic ethical appeals.

A POINT OF VIEW

Admittedly, emotion plays a significant role in speech. If, as Rogers declares, the normal mind "is not content merely to be logical and realistic," the critic's first obligation is to equate emotional coloration in oratory with his conception of thorough, objective analysis. This is not easy, but it is an imperative of the obligation which critical inquiry imposes. There can be no doubt that allegiance to "large principles of truth and reason" is the desideratum of oratory, be it political, forensic, or ceremonial speaking. But all men are not completely prepared, intellectually and emotionally, to receive the truth in its boldest and least adorned guise; it must often be articulated or identified with feelings that will conduce to the good of the people themselves, of their party, or of their country. Any critic who fails to recognize this patent fact cannot possibly hope to evaluate the oratory of any period with the acuity and insight that the task requires.

But the recognition of emotional proof—made necessary by a defect in human nature, if you will—places a further and no less challenging obligation upon critics. They are now charged with the responsibility of assaying the relative merits of the appeals, not only in the light of their immediate effect upon hearers, but also as to their long-range impact upon the social organization. Emotional excitation is an instrument of indeterminate power, and when used unscrupulously it may move men to foolish or evil deeds; it may even obscure, if not covertly frustrate, human reason. Without becoming the moral guardian of the spoken word, the critic nevertheles stands between oratory as an art—capable of both good and evil use—and the verdict of a responsible, intelligent interpretation as to its influence upon the society to which persuasion ministers as a coordinating agency.

Finally, we may say that emotional appeals—pathetic proof generally —should be regarded as facts or data of rhetoric, but not as the basic principles of the art. With Aristotle, we would say that the proof of cases —the enforcement of ideas through logical means—is the true desideratum of discourse. As human beings, however, we are probably neither prepared for nor desirous of acting solely upon rational demonstration, assuming it to be possible. So we extend the range of the rhetorical process to include what the Greeks called the "accessories" of the art. As H. L. Hollingworth remarks: "the instincts do not always lead men aright, and . . . the emotions are by no means infallible guides to truth." [46]

This is not intended to minimize the importance of emotion in oratory; nor is it designed as an indirect way to hold pathetic proof in contempt. Rather, it is a way of saying that great public speaking should, first of all, be a demonstration of significant ideas. That is a principle of the art. If, however, the ideas require emotional coloration—and they probably will—in order to insure their successful reception by hearers, then that is an auxiliary fact supplementing our conception of the art of oratory. The first, let us repeat, is a *principle;* the other is a *datum* of rhetoric.

EXERCISES

1. Evaluate the ethical proof in one of the following:
   (*a*) Henry Ward Beecher's "Address at Liverpool," in S. B. Harding, *Select Orations Illustrating American Political History* (New York, The Macmillan Co., 1924, pp. 392–413).
   (*b*) The Lincoln-Douglas debate at Ottawa, Illinois (*ibid.*, pp. 309–341).
   (*c*) The Kennedy-Nixon debates of 1960.
2. Evaluate the emotional appeals in one of the following:
   (*a*) Wendell Phillips' "The Murder of Lovejoy."
   (*b*) Richard M. Nixon's "The Expense Fund Speech." See Goodwin F. Berquist, Jr., *Speeches for Illustration and Example* (Chicago, Scott, Foresman & Co., 1965, pp. 196–206), or *U.S. News and World Report*, October 3, 1952, pp. 60–70.
   (*c*) Adlai E. Stevenson's "Eulogy of Eleanor Roosevelt." See *Representative American Speeches, 1962–1963*, pp. 179–183.
3. Evaluate the ethical appeal in a representative debate of a recent session of Congress.
4. Evaluate the ethical appeal in a typical courtroom plea in a criminal trial. (Suggested sources are: J. M. O'Neill, *Classified Models of Speech Composition* [New York, Century Co., 1922]; Frederick C. Hicks, *Famous American Jury Speeches* [St. Paul, West Publishing Co., 1925].)
5. Compare and contrast the emotional appeals used by John F. Kennedy and Richard Nixon in one of their debates of 1960. (For texts, see *The Great Debates: Background, Perspective, Effect,* edited by Sidney Kraus [Bloomington, Indiana University, 1962].)

[46] *The Psychology of the Audience.* New York, 1935, p. 110.

6. Is it possible to stir principally an emotional response with a factual speech? Give an example.
7. Is it possible to stir an emotional response with an expository speech? Give an example.
8. Investigate the relationships of emotional appeals to stereotypes, motives, and sentiments.
9. What are the characteristics of "emotionally loaded" language?
10. Compare the lists of motives found in several textbooks on public speaking.
11. Find examples from speeches of the following appeals: (a) patriotism, (b) the profit motive, (c) fair play, (d) social approval, (e) adventure, and (f) physical well-being.
12. Is a speaker unethical when he uses emotional appeals? Attempt to formulate a guiding principle for the speaker in using emotional appeals.
13. Do you believe that the major appeal in the Gettysburg Address is emotional or logical?
14. Are there any circumstances under which emotional discourse can have moral and ethical value? Specify.
15. For an enlightening account of the role of irrational impulse in public actions, read Gunnar Myrdal's "'With What Little Wisdom the World Is Ruled,'" in *The New York Times Magazine,* July 18, 1965, pp. 20–26.
16. Comment on this observation by Irwin Edman in his *Human Traits and Their Social Significance* ([Boston, Houghton Mifflin Co., 1920], p. 438): "The greatest ethical reformers have not been those who have convinced men through the impeccability of their logic. They have been rather the supreme seers, the Hebrew prophets, Christ, Saint Francis, who have won followers not so much by the conclusiveness of their demonstration as through the persuasive fervor and splendor of their vision."
17. Do you agree with Walter Lippmann that "when there is panic in the air, with one crisis tripping over the heels of another, actual dangers mixed with imaginary scares, there is no chance at all for the constructive use of reason . . . "? Why?

CLASS PROJECT (Continued)

Prepare a 500-to-1000-word written analysis of the motivational devices which your speaker used in one speech. Why did he use this type of material?

READINGS

HERBERT I. ABELSON. *Persuasion.* New York, Springer Publishing Co., 1959.
WILLIAM ALBIG. *Modern Public Opinion.* New York, McGraw-Hill Book Co., Inc., 1956. Ch. V, "Psychological Processes and Opinion," pp. 73–95.
A. CRAIG BAIRD. *Rhetoric: A Philosophical Inquiry.* New York, The Ronald Press Company, 1965. Ch. 7, "Emotional Response."
SAMUEL L. BECKER. "Research on Emotional and Logical Proofs." *Southern Speech Journal,* 28:198–207 (Spring, 1963).
DAVID I. BERLO. *The Process of Communication.* New York, Holt, Rinehart and Winston, 1960.
CHARLES BIRD. *Social Psychology.* New York, D. Appleton-Century Co., Inc., 1940. "Motivation," pp. 29–58; "Propaganda," pp. 305–341; "The Behavior of Crowds," pp. 345–368; "Suggestion, Suggestibility, and Stereotypes," pp. 258–300.

EDWIN GARRIGUES BORING, HERBERT SIDNEY LANGFELD, and HARRY PORTER WELD. *Introduction to Psychology*. New York, Wiley, 1944.

ROBERT N. BOSTROM. "Motivation and Argument." In *Perspectives on Argumentation*, GERALD R. MILLER and THOMAS R. NILSEN, eds. Chicago, Illinois, Scott, Foresman & Co., 1966. Pp. 110–128.

WINSTON L. BREMBECK and WILLIAM S. HOWELL. *Persuasion: A Means of Social Control*. New York, Prentice-Hall, Inc., 1952.

WILLIAM NORWOOD BRIGANCE. *Speech: Its Techniques and Disciplines in a Free Society*, 2d ed. New York, Appleton-Century-Crofts, Inc., 1961.

J. A. C. BROWN. *Techniques of Persuasion*. Baltimore, Penguin Books, 1963.

KENNETH BURKE. *A Grammar of Motives*. Englewood, New Jersey, Prentice-Hall, Inc., 1945.

THEODORE CLEVENGER, JR. *Audience Analysis*. Indianapolis, Bobbs-Merrill Co., 1966.

ARTHUR R. COHEN. *Attitude Change and Social Influence*. New York, Basic Books Press, 1964.

GARY LYNN CRONKHITE. "Logic, Emotion and the Paradigm of Persuasion." *Quarterly Journal of Speech*, 50:13–18 (February, 1964).

DENNIS G. DAY. "Persuasion and the Concept of Identification." *Quarterly Journal of Speech*, 46:270–273 (October, 1960).

JOHN DEWEY. *Human Nature and Conduct*. New York, Holt, Rinehart, and Winston, 1922.

JON J. EISENSON, J. JEFFERY AUER, and JOHN V. IRWIN. *The Psychology of Communication*. New York, Appleton-Century-Crofts, Inc., 1963.

WALLACE C. FOTHERINGHAM. *Perspectives on Persuasion*. Boston, Allyn and Bacon, Inc., 1966.

R. BARRY FULTON. "Motivation: Foundation of Persuasion." *Quarterly Journal of Speech*, 49:295–307 (October, 1963).

MURRAY A. HEWGILL and GERALD R. MILLER. "Source Credibility and Response to Fear-arousing Communications." *Speech Monographs*, 32:95–101 (June, 1965).

ADOLF HITLER. *Mein Kampf*, RALPH MANHEIM, trans. New York, Houghton Mifflin Co., 1943. Pp. 468–77.

H. L. HOLLINGWORTH. *The Psychology of the Audience*. New York, American Book Co., 1935. "Types of Audience," pp. 19–32; "Impressing the Audience," pp. 63–108; "The Psychology of Persuasion," pp. 109–139; "Directing Action," pp. 141–159; "Experimental Studies of Audience Effects," pp. 185–203.

CARL I. HOVLAND, IRVING L. JANIS, and HAROLD H. KELLY. *Communication and Persuasion: Psychological Studies of Opinion Change*. New Haven, Yale University Press, 1953.

EVERETT HUNT. "Ancient Rhetoric and Modern Propaganda." *Quarterly Journal of Speech*, 37:157–160 (April, 1951).

———. "The Rhetorical Mood of World War II." *Quarterly Journal of Speech*, 29:1–5 (February, 1943).

RICHARD L. JOHANNESEN, ed. *Ethics and Persuasion*. New York, Random House, 1967.

FRANKLIN H. KNOWER. "The Psychology of Communication." In *Communicative Arts and Sciences of Speech*. Edited by KEITH BROOKS. Columbus, Ohio, Charles E. Merrill Books, 1967. Pp. 129–148.

CLYDE W. MILLER. *The Process of Persuasion*. New York, Crown Publishers, 1946. Pp. 148–222.

GERALD R. MILLER. *Speech Communication*. Indianapolis, Bobbs-Merrill Co., 1966.

———. "Studies on the Use of Fear Appeals: A Summary and Analysis." *Central States Speech Journal*, 14:117–124 (May, 1963).

WAYNE C. MINNICK. *The Art of Persuasion*. Boston, Houghton Mifflin Co., 1957.

ALAN H. MONROE and DOUGLAS EHNINGER. *Principles and Types of Speech*, 6th ed. Chicago, Scott, Foresman, 1967.

EDWARD J. MURRAY. *Motivation and Emotion*. Englewood Cliffs, New Jersey, Prentice-Hall, Inc., 1964.

ROBERT T. OLIVER. *The Psychology of Persuasive Speech*, 2d ed. New York, David McKay Co., 1957.

RANDALL C. RUECHELLE. "An Experimental Study of Emotional and Intellectual Appeals in Persuasion." *Speech Monographs*, 25:49–58 (March, 1958).

ROSS SCANLAN. "Adolf Hitler and the Technique of Brainwashing." In *The Rhetorical Idiom*. Edited by DONALD C. BRYANT. Ithaca, New York, Cornell University Press, 1958. Pp. 201–220.

————. "The Nazi Party Speaker System, I." *Speech Monographs*, 16:82–97 (August, 1949); II, *ibid.*, 17:134–148 (June, 1950).

DONALD K. SMITH and ROBERT L. SCOTT. "Motivation Theory in Teaching Persuasion: Statement and Schema." *Quarterly Journal of Speech*, 47:378–383 (December, 1961).

L. SUSAN STEBBING. *Thinking to Some Purpose*. London, Penguin Books, 1959.

OTIS M. WALTER. "Toward an Analysis of Motivation." *Quarterly Journal of Speech*, 41:271–278 (October, 1955).

JAMES WINANS. *Public Speaking*, rev. ed. New York, Century Co., 1917. Pp. 197 ff.

CHARLES H. WOOLBERT. "A Behavioristic Account of Intellect and Emotions." *Psychological Review*, 31:265–272 (July, 1924).

————. "Persuasion: Principles and Method." *Quarterly Journal of Speech Education*, 5:12–25 (January, 1919); 5:110–119 (March, 1919); 5:211–238 (May, 1919).

14

The Character
of the Speaker

ETHICAL APPEAL IN DISCOURSE

Ralph Waldo Emerson defined eloquence as "the art of speaking what you mean and are." [1] On another occasion he supplemented this reflection by saying: "The reason why anyone refuses his assent to your opinion, or his aid to your benevolent design, is in you. He refuses to accept you as a bringer of truth, because, though you think you have it, he feels that you have it not. You have not given him the authentic sign." [2]

Much has been written under various captions about what Emerson calls the "authentic sign." Writers are virtually of one mind, however, in declaring that the force of the speaker's personality or character is instrumental in facilitating the acceptance of belief. Macaulay tells us that a comparison of Pitt the Younger with Charles James Fox reveals how the former inspired respect and confidence because of the correctness of his private life. Conversely, a personal touch which is neither pleasing nor inspiring may, and often does, militate against the speaker's likelihood of achieving the desired response. As John Lawson said in his *Lectures:* "You cannot be much affected by what he [the speaker] says, if you do not look upon him to be a Man of Probity, who is in earnest, and doth himself believe what he endeavoreth to make out as credible to you.[3]

Like many of the concepts with which the modern students of rhetoric deals, this one received its first fairly specific statement at the hand

[1] *Journals of Ralph Waldo Emerson.* Boston, 1909–14. IX, 342.
[2] *Works of Ralph Waldo Emerson,* p. 143.
[3] *Lectures Concerning Oratory.* Dublin, 1760, p. 172.

of Aristotle. It will be recalled that Aristotle believed success in persuasion depended upon three things; or, to put it differently, the proofs provided "through the instrumentality of the speech" were of three kinds: "in the moral character of the speaker or in the production of a certain disposition in the audience or in the speech itself by means of real or apparent demonstration."[4] We have already discussed the last two, namely, emotional or pathetic proof and logical proof. Let us now turn to what is usually called *ethical* proof.

Classical and Later Points of View

Although Aristotle devotes little space to the concept of ethical proof, he says enough to enable us to perceive its essential role in the process of persuasion. "The instrument of proof is the moral character," he says,

. . . when the delivery of the speech is such as to produce an impression of the speaker's credibility; for we yield a more complete and ready credence to persons of high character not only ordinarily and in a general way, but in such matters as do not admit of absolute certainty but necessarily leave room for difference of opinion, without any qualification whatever.[5]

That Aristotle looked upon this mode of persuasion as important and effective is plain. Censuring his predecessors for not regarding high character in the speaker as contributing to effectiveness, Aristotle sets up the general rule "that there is no proof so effective as that of the character." It may be observed, however, that his respect for the efficacy of ethical proof did not argue against the primacy of the logical materials. While recognizing the speaker as a major factor in persuasion, Aristotle still looked upon logical argument as the most important element in the speech.

The foregoing remarks establish Aristotle's concern for the personal character of speakers. But what are the constituents of ethical appeal? What are its signs in the speech proper?

Aristotle answers these queries directly. He holds that there are three sources of personal credibility in orators; "or in other words there are three things, apart from demonstrative proofs, which inspire belief, viz., sagacity, high character, and good will." He then remarks:

It is *the want* of all these qualities or of one of them that occasions great errors in matters of discussion or deliberation; for either people are so foolish that they entertain erroneous opinions, or, although their opinions are right, they are so corrupt that they do not express their true sentiments,

4 *Rhetoric.* Welldon ed., p. 10.
5 *Ibid.,* pp. 10–11.

or, although they are persons of sagacity and high character, they are not well-disposed to their audience, and perhaps in consequence do not recommend the best policy, although they understand it.[6]

The inference is that "if a person is supposed to command them all, he will be deserving of credit in the eyes of his audience."

Similar "ethical" requisites are evident in Cicero's remark that character contributes to success in speaking if "the morals, principles, conduct, and lives of those who plead causes, and of those for whom they plead, [are] such as to merit esteem . . ." Furthermore, the "feelings of the hearers are conciliated by a person's dignity, by his actions, by the character of his life. . . ."[7]

All these sources of credibility resolve to the essentials set forth by John Ward in his *System of Oratory:* wisdom, integrity, benevolence, and modesty.

Aristotle hoped to include in his *Rhetoric* the data which would help the speaker get credit for the three sources of personal credibility. In line with that intention, he stated that sagacity and high character "must be ascertained from our analysis of the virtues, as it is by the same means that we shall succeed in establishing our own character and the character of others. . . ."[8] That is to say, the speaker is to get his cues from Book I of the *Rhetoric,* and especially from those sections dealing with moral nobility and the human virtues. As for good will, or a "friendly disposition," it can best be considered in the light of the speaker's knowledge of human emotions.

Speaking from the point of view of the orator himself, Cicero recognized the importance of ethical qualities in discourse. In *De Oratore,* he concluded:

It contributes much to the success in speaking, that the morals, principles, conduct, and lives of those for whom they plead, should be such as to merit esteem; and that those of their adversaries should be such as to deserve censure and also that the minds of those before whom the cause is pleaded should be moved as well toward the speaker and toward him for whom he speaks.[9]

Cicero discussed good nature, liberality, gentleness, piety, grateful feelings, freedom from selfishness and avarice. One's ability in speaking, he said, lay in his capacity to induce these effects through the character of the speaker. Said he, ". . . everything that characterizes men of probity, and humility, not acrimonious, not pertinacious, not litigious, nor

[6] *Ibid.,* pp. 113–114.
[7] *De Oratore,* Watson edition. II, 43.
[8] *Rhetoric.* Welldon ed., p. 114.
[9] *De Oratore.* II, 43.

harsh, very much conciliates benevolence, and alienates the affections from those in whom such qualities are not apparent." [10]

Quintilian was more positive in stressing ethical standards than were the previous rhetoricians. The perfect orator, in his words, "cannot exist unless he is a good man."

Quintilian directly connects excellence in presentation with nobility of character. "Can a bad and unjust man speak on such themes as the dignity of subject demands?" He answers negatively. "Shall we then dignify the traitor, the deserter, the turncoat with the sacred name of orator? The bad man and the perfect orator can never be identical. For nothing is perfect if there exists something else that is better." Continuing, he remarks, "Bad men, in their speaking, drop their mask unawares. Even when they tell the truth they fail to win belief. Audiences can detect the truth or falsity of their character." Quintilian refers to the character of Cicero. The latter possessed moral courage and loyalty to conviction, as illustrated by the manner of his death. "In meeting it he displayed singular fortitude. Therefore let those that are young, or rather let all of us, whatever our age, since it is not too late to resolve to follow what is right, strive with all our hearts and devote all our efforts to the pursuit of virtue and eloquence . . ." [11]

Christian education and morality reflected the Greek and Roman ethical philosophy. St. Augustine's *On Christian Doctrine*, similar in teaching aims to Quintilian's *Institutes*, assumes a moral quality and end in all oral discourse. "Insistence upon Truth as the over-all objective is a cardinal tenet of his treatise." [12]

George Campbell, Hugh Blair, and Richard Whately, leaders in Christian thought as well as rhetoric in Britain (c. 1770–1830) adopted the classical position.

Campbell gives "reputation" a "considerable power" in *ethos,* an ethical role denied by Aristotle but strongly upheld by Quintilian. Like Aristotle, Campbell stresses the personal qualifications of character and intelligence. He strongly affirms Quintilian's "good man" theory.

> The reputation of the attestor hath a considerable power. Now the speaker's apparent conviction of the truth of what he advanceth adds to all his other arguments and evidence . . . Sympathy in the hearers to the speaker may be lessened in several ways, chiefly by these two: by a low opinion of his morals. The latter is the more prejudicial of the two . . . Hence it hath become a common topic with rhetoricians, that in order to be a successful orator, one must be a good man; for to be good is the only

10 *Ibid.*

11 *Institutes of Oratory.* Translated by H. E. Butler. London, 1922. XII, i, 16–34.

12 See above, Chapter 4.

sure way of being long esteemed good, and to be esteemed good is previously necessary to one's being heard with due attention and regard.[13]

Hugh Blair, in his *Lectures on Rhetoric and Belles Lettres,* expounds his view of ethos and suggests the importance of the concept in rhetorical theory. According to this Scotch preacher-rhetorician, "What stands highest in the order of means [of improving in eloquence] is personal character and disposition. In order to be a truly eloquent or persuasive speaker, nothing is more necessary than to be a virtuous man. This was a favorite position among ancient rhetoricians." [14]

Blair mentions all nine of the virtues which Aristotle recommends, and concludes that the speaker equipped with ethical firmness has that which "bespeaks a consciousness of his being thoroughly persuaded of the truth, or justice of what he delivers." [15]

In contrast to Campbell and Blair, Bishop Richard Whately makes clear that he is discussing the "impression produced in the minds of hearers" rather than "the real character of the speaker." [16] Since he is primarily concerned with argumentative discourse, he gives comparatively little space to ethics. He cites Aristotle's distinction between "real" character and that by which the audience is persuaded. Like Aristotle, Whately divides character into intelligence, virtue, and good will, but unlike Aristotle, the nineteenth century English rhetorician blends ethical expression with the pathetic. Thus the ethical becomes subsidiary to the pathetic appeal.

Among early American rhetoricians, John Quincy Adams, first professor of rhetoric at Harvard (1806–1808), gave a full chapter to the "intellectual and moral qualities of an orator" in his *Lectures on Rhetoric and Oratory.* Said this United States Senator and Harvard professor, "The first and most precious quality then which contributes to the success of a public speaker is an honest heart; a sentiment which I wish above all others may be impressed with indelible force on your minds." Such integrity of heart is founded upon an enlarged and enlightened morality. He is to be a person alert to this duty; correct in his estimate of good and evil; of strong moral sense, in all applications in judicial, deliberative, and pulpit discourse. In the speech itself, according to Adams, no uniform rule may be prescribed. "The only advice I can give you for all such emergencies is, before you enter upon that profession,

[13] *The Philosophy of Rhetoric.* Edited by Lloyd Bitzer. Carbondale, Illinois, 1965, p. 97.
[14] Hugh Blair. *Lectures on Rhetoric and Belles Lettres.* Edited by Harold F. Harding. Carbondale, Illinois, 1965. Lecture XXXIV, p. 228.
[15] *Ibid.,* p. 232.
[16] *Elements of Rhetoric.* Edited by Douglas Ehninger. Carbondale, Illinois, 1963, p. 188.

to lay the foundation of your conduct in a well digested system of ethics . . ." [17]

Chauncey Goodrich was the first professor of rhetoric at Yale. In his lectures he gave only qualified endorsement of Quintilian's insistence upon ethical qualities. "Virtue," Goodrich stated, "is certainly not necessary to eloquence though it is favorable to its most perfect exercise." [18] In the essays on British eloquence, however, Goodrich reflects his New England Congregational background by discounting Sheridan and others for their apparent lack of strong moral qualities in their character and utterances.

American theorists and teachers of rhetoric and public address of the later twentieth century have sustained the Aristotelian-classical tradition in stressing the importance of high moral character in the speaker and his ethical appeals. W. Norwood Brigance, Richard Murphy, Karl Wallace, Robert Oliver, Donald Bryant, William D. Howell, Winston Brembeck, Lionel Crocker, and Franklyn Haiman, to mention but a few, have expounded or implied the principles and methods of ethics in communication.

W. Norwood Brigance, for example, cited Aristotle and Quintilian, and adopted the classical principles of excellence in communication through character and personal integrity. His analysis of the problem, however, was oriented toward the audience. "We believe men of good will more fully and readily than others." He framed a "Hippocratic Oath for Public Speakers," that would call for a state licensing examination for competence, and would require an "oath of responsibility" of every speaker. [19]

Karl Wallace urged the (1) duty of search and inquiry, (2) allegiance to accuracy and fairness, (3) expression of individual motive, and (4) toleration of dissent. [20]

Donald Bryant and Karl Wallace, in their *Fundamentals of Public Speaking*, discussed "persuasion and the ethics of the speaker." They insisted on respect for ends—"social ideals are inherent in public speaking"; honoring the opinion of others; honoring the speaker's own opinion; playing fair with the hearers; respect for information; proper speaker motivation; and sound character and trustworthiness. [21]

Richard Murphy met effectively the criticism that (1) all rhetoric is immoral, or (2) that it is amoral. He agreed that "rhetoric lags in a concern for value," that members of the speech profession lacked professional standards; that there was no enforcing agency. He pleaded for

---

[17] *Lectures on Rhetoric and Oratory.* New York, 1810, pp. 344, 351.

[18] John P. Hoshor. "Lectures on Rhetoric and Public Speaking." *Speech Monographs*, 14:11 (1947).

[19] *Speech Composition.* New York, 1947, pp. 7–8.

[20] "An Ethical Basis of Communication." *Speech Teacher*, 4:9 (January, 1955).

[21] *Fundamentals of Public Speaking*, 3d ed. New York, 1960, pp. 287 ff.

speech organizations to set up standards of ethics and attempt to enforce them.[22]

Giles W. Gray and Waldo Braden, in their text on public speaking, adopt the proposition that good speaking requires realization of social responsibility. Citing the Oath of Hippocrates for the physician, these authors maintain that the speaker, like the physician, has a social responsibility. The authors echo Quintilian's *Institutes*, Book XII, chapter 1, and Paul's letter to the Corinthians—to indicate the common Roman and Christian foundations of ethics.[23]

In a chapter on the "ethics of persuasion" in his *Psychology of Persuasive Speech*,[24] Robert Oliver also accepts the utilitarian principle of social effects. In the long run, according to him, what is good for society as a whole is ethical and what is detrimental to society is unethical.

Franklyn S. Haiman raises the question of whether persuasive discourse adheres to the democratic ethic.[25] Is persuasive technique inherently unethical by democratic standards? Persuasion is analogous to the use of the atomic bomb which, like persuasion, is unethical. Haiman is pessimistic about the present use of persuasion and would label most of it "unethical" and revert to a Platonic condemnation of the entire practice.

Winston L. Brembeck and William S. Howell, in their text, *Persuasion: A Means of Social Control*,[26] give a detailed endorsement of the social context theory, with suggestions for applying ethical standards to persuasion. The popular approaches, such as "the end justifies the means," they reject. They regard the social context theory as the most practicable. Their position is to a considerable degree an adaptation of Vilfredo Pareto, in his *The Mind and Society*.[27]

RELATIONSHIPS OF ETHICS IN COMMUNICATION

The Speaker's Personality

What of the role and character of personality as ethical factors in communication? What of the speechmaker's image as an individual, as well as his ideas, language, organization, and delivery? His personality is

[22] "Preface to an Ethic of Rhetoric." In *The Rhetorical Idiom*. Edited by Donald C. Bryant. Ithaca, New York, 1958, pp. 125–143.

[23] *Public Speaking: Principles and Practice*. 2nd ed. New York, 1963, pp. 56–60.

[24] *The Psychology of Persuasive Speech*, 2d ed. New York, 1957, pp. 20–36.

[25] "A Re-examination of the Ethics of Persuasion." *Central States Speech Journal*, 3:4–9 (March, 1952).

[26] *Persuasion: A Means of Social Control*. Englewood Cliffs, New Jersey, 1952. Pp. 443–466.

[27] *The Mind and Society*. Edited by Arthur Livingston. Translated by Borgiamo and Livingston. New York, 1935.

perhaps more influential in the determination of results than that of any of his other speaking abilities.[28] "The whole man speaking" accurately describes his speech as the product of his entire physiological and psychological processes—the totality of his "aptitudes, abilities, experiences, feelings, loyalties, emotions, interests, ambitions, adjustments, and traits." [29]

When a speaker addresses persons or groups and establishes interpersonal relations with them, his personality becomes a social force. This trait is both individual and social. Gardner Murphy refers to personality as "the social force of the individual." [30] The speaker's voice, diction, gestures and other visual and auditory elements are highly revealing, apart from the message itself. The audience sizes up the speaker's total impression as tactful, sincere, friendly, pleasant, honest, or at the other end, as pugnacious, indifferent, ignorant, insincere. These traits describe not only the speaker's character as he impresses his listeners and observers, but in the long run, the genuineness of the man or woman. The platform role, we believe, should faithfully reflect the real speaker, "the inner man."

This factor of social influence in turn links up with the critic's concern for the social goals of all communication. How do the platform qualities of assertiveness, arrogance, sincerity, fidelity to truth, and all the rest affect the behavior of immediate and later audiences? Here the critic does more than check the tangible outcomes of a specific speaking situation; he also tries to probe the speaker's intent (difficult though this may be). The critic raises a question about the social worth of the speaker's contribution in relation to resultant behavior patterns in the audience.

The problem becomes a moral one: Are the consequences socially justifiable? Speech is justified only if it betters society. According to the critic, the speaker must face responsibility for his choice of aims, insofar as he can determine what goals are socially and morally preferable. Ethics, as John Dewey stated, "is the science of conduct" that is, of "Man's activity in its whole reach." Other branches of knowledge of man's conduct (anthropology, psychology) "simply describe, while the business of ethics is to judge." He relates moral action to conduct viewed from the point of values. Action is examined by the end which it realizes. "Conduct," as Dewey defines it, "implies more than something taking place; it implies purpose, motives, contention, that the agent knows what he is about, and that he has something which he is aiming at." What is this speaker's intent and goal? The main ethical-moral

[28] Dayton Heckman, Franklin Knower, and Paul Wagner, in *The Man and the Message*, report that 200 professional speakers viewed personal attributes among the most important determinants of success. Cf. Franklin H. Knower, "The Speaker's Personality." In Baird and Knower, *General Speech*. New York, 1957. Ch. 13.

[29] Baird and Knower. *Op. cit.*, p. 207.

[30] *Personality*. New York, 1947, p. 999.

problem, according to Dewey, is "What is the conduct that really deserves the name of conduct? What is the true end and summum bonum of man? The end or good decides what *ought to be*. Any act necessary to fulfill that end is a duty." [31]

Rhetoric's alliance with social amelioration and morality means a dedication to the enforcement of values in the social structure. As has been repeatedly said, the function of rhetoric is that of committal to the improvement of the human condition.

In his study of Plato's *Phaedrus*, Richard M. Weaver states that "It is impossible to talk about rhetoric as effective expression without having as a term giving intelligibility to the whole discourse, the Good." [32]

Ethos and Emotional Appeals

The distinction between these terms is not always clear; and in some instances it may be virtually nonexistent. Ethos and pathos have, indeed, much in common. The speaker who establishes his own moral integrity and imposes strictures upon that of his opponent is unquestionably using both ethical and pathetic proof. He is establishing credence in his own probity and character, and, at the same time, is predisposing the minds of the hearers toward the readier acceptance of his cause. Despite the apparent indivisibility of appeal, this difference seems to stand out: ethos refers chiefly to what the speaker chooses to do; pathos, to what the listeners' reaction is.

In the Aristotelian sense, the difference between ethos and pathos, as interpreted by Irving J. Lee, seems to be "the moral states evidenced in the speech and the emotional states aroused in the audience." [33]

The rhetorical critic views the emotional-ethical process as a unit. The modes of development are regarded as a continuum. The relative emphasis varies from speech to speech and from speaker to speaker. The real judges of the appeals as "emotional" or "ethical" are the members of the audience. If their needs and desires are closely met by physical, economic, political and similar motivational elements, the effect is primarily "emotional." If the motivational development of the discourse evokes audience reactions suggestive of personal happiness and of an ideal state or world, the techniques are chiefly "ethical." The distinctions cannot be sharply drawn. There is some point in the semantic suggestion to classify the extra-cognitive elements of the speech as "activative," to cover the varied drives, motives, sentiments, habits, beliefs.

---

[31] *Outlines of a Critical Theory of Ethics*. New York, 1957, pp. 1 ff.
[32] *The Ethics of Rhetoric*. Chicago, 1953, p. 23.
[33] "Some Conceptions of Emotional Appeal in Rhetorical Theory." *Speech Monographs*, 6:67 (1939).

Ethical and Logical Elements

As we stated in Chapter 12, logical elements are compounded of tentative propositions; of analysis of issues and of definitions; of generalizations, causal inferences, analogies and general premises, to be framed and tested by probability and relativity; of semantic qualities of verbal clearness, correctness, audience adaptation; and of other marks of intellectual insight and method.

The social direction of these emerging ideas in communication is of basic concern to speakers and critics. What of the direction and strength of intellectual discourse? Here the speaker and speech critic resort to standards and goals that incorporate not only emotional (pathetic) elements, but value judgments. Insights into such propositions and their inferences have to do with the questions affecting the good or bad society. What are the affecting elements of the discourse that relate to justice and injustice?

These questions are ethical. It is no accident that Aristotle identified reasoning with ethics. Intellectual appeals and excellence are not to be separated from emotional proofs, and these in turn (or simultaneously) become ethical proofs. Intellectual quality is inevitably identified with social, psychological, and ethical components that together comprise a given communication.

Ethical Appeals and Organized Society

Rhetoric and politics have much in common in their concern about organized society, its problems and conduct. As Aristotle stated: "Ethical studies may fairly be called political, and for this reason rhetoric masquerades as political science, and the professors of it as political experts."[34]

To Aristotle and his age, politics described the total community in its political, social, economic, intellectual and moral relations. Communication (rhetoric) appropriated these political principles and detailed community problems to aim at a social, ethical society.

Aristotle's ethics, no doubt, is social; and his politics is ethical. He does not forget that in the *ethics* "the individual man is a member of society, nor in the *politics* that the good life of the state exists only in the good lives of is citizens."[35] Said he, "If there is some end to the things we do, which we desire for its own sake, clearly this must be the good and chief end. . . . It would seem to belong to the most authoritative art and that which is truly the master art. And politics appears to be of

[34] Aristotle. *Nichomachean Ethics.* X, ix, 1180–81.
[35] W. D. Ross. *Aristotle.* New York, 1959, p. 183.

this nature. For it is this which ordains which of the sciences should be studied in a state . . . The end of this science should include the others, so that *this end must be* the good for man." [36]

Although Aristotle, as Ernest Barker suggests, made ethics a branch of politics, in the end he conceded that ethics was dominant. "Ethics and politics are still closely connected; but there is a shifting of values which seems to result in an enthroning of ethics or moral philosophy, with 'nomothetics' or political philosophy serving as its chief minister." [37]

Ethics and Scientific Tests

In consonance with the spirit of our scientific age, teachers of public speaking increasingly suggest experimental methods for testing ethical behavior and results. "A rigid and unrealistic interpretation of a non-experimental belief for purposes of persuasion is unethical . . . Ethical standards for persuasion can be formulated through a context analysis using both experimental and non-experimental bases of behavior and the concept of social utility." [38] Kenneth Anderson and Theodore Clevenger, Jr., have summarized the extensive experimental research in ethos.[39] They reviewed the studies dealing with the influence of ethos upon the intended effect of the communication; the studies assuming that ethos is fixed; and those assuming that ethics is variable. Among other studies included in their review were those dealing with extrinsic ethos (techniques employed before the message itself began) and the intrinsic ethos (those produced by the speaker during the presentation). These investigators reported that "findings are not yet sufficiently numerous and sophisticated to permit definite conclusions about the operation of ethical proof." They concluded that "The utilization of improved designs and measuring devices can create experimental conditions that may lead to more meaningful results than those obtained in the past." The later Judeo-Christian morality with its varied and often inconsistent guides for conduct has strongly modified the Greek-Roman interpretations and applications of ethical proofs.

Contemporary science has inevitably led to the rejection of *ex cathedra* propositions and has insisted on evidence and experimentation as tests of moral validity and direction. Contemporary logic, psychology, politics, anthropology, semantics, and other sciences have all affected heavily the

[36] *Ethica Nichomachea.* Edited by W. D. Ross. In *Works of Aristotle.* Oxford, 1925, pp. 1094a ff.

[37] *The Politics of Aristotle.* Oxford, 1946, p. 356.

[38] Brembeck and Howell. *Op. cit.*, p. 458.

[39] Kenneth Anderson and Theodore Clevenger, Jr. "A Summary of Experimental Research in Ethics." *Speech Monographs*, 30:59–78 (June, 1963).

interpretations and applications of the Greek-Roman-medieval precepts for "good" conduct.

Ethics and Value Judgments

The purpose and method of ethics, however, as we have said, is not simply to describe but to judge "goodness or badness," "right or wrong," of behavior. The critics are thus confronted with values. Action is to be interpreted by the end which it tries to realize. Conduct, then, as John Dewey states, "implies purpose, motive, intention."

Experimentation can never quite furnish final pronouncements concerning these values. Only the judgment of those who have significant intellectual and cultural experience and understanding can do so. The formulations that relate to the character and "progress" of civilization should progressively provide dependable guides. We who attempt to move within these values, conscious of the limitations, may nevertheless do so with some assurance. At least we are committed to "democracy of purpose that weaves together the strands of private and public morality"; to loyalty to the intellectual integrity of speakers; to their good will; to Aristotle's nine virtues and other qualities that our civilization rates highly.

Although no yardstick can be applied indiscriminately to all communication, the principles of social behavior and the analysis of specific appeals in relation to their audiences will more and more yield patterns of genuine moral improvement. Our speakers must still be "good men" skilled in speaking and writing.

Ethical Appeals and Utilitarianism

Another view of the highest good derives from an emphasis on social consquences. This was the doctrine of utilitarianism, the wellbeing of the community rather than merely that of the individual. Jeremy Bentham (1748–1832) and John Stuart Mill (1806–1873) were prominent expositors of such social ethics. To these philosophers, whether a given action was right or wrong was to be determined by social behavior. A right action is one that produces the greatest happiness to the greatest number. Here was hedonism, but the pleasure or well-being concentrated on the group alone. Any action that produced benefits would be "right." The consequences of the act, not the motives of the agents, would be the determinant. The process of aims and methods would thus be semiscientific, semi-experimental. Bentham, for example, insisted that the pleasurable results were to be measured solely by "the intensity, duration, certainty, propinquity, fecundity, purity, and extent." He would obviously examine in detail whatever later conditions were to be assigned to these "causes."

The critics of such theory and its applications ask, What constitutes "effect"? If ethical values are to be weighed by such later conditions, what is to be said of "results" of today that become different tomorrow? Shall we limit our horizon to immediate after-conditions, or shall we attempt to survey the long-range "consequences"?

Furthermore, what degree of probability is sufficient to justify the alleged consequences? Is it not also necessary to appraise the motives with which the action is done? Do evil purposes justify an act that apparently produces beneficial results? Critics of utilitarianism quickly pointed out that means were not to be separated from ends. The moral worth of the transaction must take account of motives, but the process must be exemplified in its totality—with no distinction between means and ends. Such in general have been the logical and speculative qualifications attached to the utilitarian treatment and validation of ethics.

Ethical Appeals and Duty

The disposition of some utilitarian theorists to minimize motives has been countered by those who have conceived duty as the supreme good. This was the Kantian philosophy of describing right conduct as a reflection of the sense of duty accompanying all behavior.

What, according to Kant, distinguished the moral man from the nonmoral one? A sense of duty. Every man has a moral pulse, a sense of obligation—that which he ought to do, despite his opposing inclinations. The moral man suppresses his random impulses and follows the line his moral nature indicates. Such is Kant's good man.

What, then, is the test of moral action in a specific situation? To Kant every action is weighed in the light of its contribution to a universal code of behavior. "Nothing in the world is good except good will. There is therefore, one categorical imperative, which may be thus stated: in conformity with that maxim only which you can at the same time will to be a universal law." [40]

How far should the speech critics go in applying the Kantian ethical concepts? Do such concepts account sufficiently for the results? Furthermore, what is to be done about a conflict of motives or duties? Sentiments and other complicated reactions confuse the "duties" to be obeyed. Moreover, many critics believe that duty and moral sensitivity are a correlative of learning. Adherents of Kantian "duty" have sometimes defended intuitionism; every person has inherited the impulse toward the right and needs only to develop it.

[40] Immanuel Kant. *The Philosophy of Kant.* New York, 1888, p. 241.

These are but a few of the implications growing out of attempts to link ethical proofs with ultimate ends in the furtherance of the "good society." All have relevance for the speech critic. They embrace Aristotelian conceptions of virtue; the goals of individual behavior, stoic or hedonistic; right conduct as gauged by both individual and social living; utilitarianism in its various forms as the test of such values; and duty and similar motives as suggestive of the moral consequences that are assumed as the outcomes.

THE CONSTITUENTS OF ETHICAL APPEALS

The possibilities for the use of ethos in the subject matter of a speech are manifold. Assuming, as Aristotle suggested, that the three constituents of ethical proof are character, sagacity, and good will, a speaker may give credibility to his message in a variety of ways. Any attempt to present an inclusive catalog of ethical attributes or manifestations would be futile. Our summary is therefore purely exploratory.

Character

How does the audience gauge the character of the speaker? To Aristotle these character traits are evidenced by an analysis of what is "virtuous." The audience must be convinced that the speaker is virtuous. He can create such quality either for himself or for those who are associated with him.

The noble is that which is desirable in and for itself, and also wins praise; or is that which is good, and also pleasant because good. If this definition is right, then it must follow that virtue is noble, since virtue is good, and is worthy of praise. Now virtue, in the popular conception, is a faculty tending to confer many great benefits—indeed, 'all manner of benefits on all occasions.'

The elements of virtue are:

Justice	Magnificence	Gentleness
Courage	Magnanimity	Prudence
Temperance	Liberality	Wisdom [41]

In general, a speaker focuses attention upon the probity of his character if he (1) associates either himself or his message with what is virtuous and elevated; (2) bestows, with propriety, tempered praise upon himself, his client, and his cause; (3) links the opponent or the opponents' cause with what is not virtuous; (4) removes or minimizes unfavorable impressions of himself or his cause previously established by his opponent;

[41] *The Rhetoric of Aristotle.* Translated by Lane Cooper. New York, 1932, pp. 46–47.

(5) relies upon authority derived from his personal experience; and (6) creates the impression of being completely sincere in his undertaking.

Sagacity

According to Aristotle, the speaker establishes sagacity in the discourse if he handles his materials in such a way as to demonstrate intellectual integrity and wisdom. He is consistent and logical in his inferences from causal reasoning, specific instances, analogies, and deductive propositions, and handling of evidence.

As certain qualifications vary with the circumstances, it may be said that a speaker helps to establish the impression of sagacity if he (1) uses what is popularly called common sense; (2) acts with tact and moderation; (3) displays a sense of good taste; (4) reveals a broad familiarity with the interests of the day; and (5) shows through the way in which he handles speech materials that he is possessed of intellectual integrity and wisdom.

Good Will

Finally, to impress the good will of the speaker upon an audience, he must understand what kinds of people others love and admire, what kinds of people many hate and despise, and the causes of these feelings.

Good will can be best understood through the emotions. The emotions are those states which are attended by pain and pleasure, and which, as they change, make a difference in our judgments; for example: anger, pity, fear, and the like, and also their opposites.

To create good will in his listeners the speaker must know his audience so that he can present himself as a friend to what they consider good, an enemy to what they consider evil. He must present himself as one who has done some good service to them or to their friends.

The speaker must establish close rapport with his audience and destroy any feelings of animosity they may have toward him. To create this impression of good will, the speaker must prove

that men are enemies or friends; if they are not enemies or friends, to make them appear to be either; if their friendship or enmity is pretended, to refute them; if there be a dispute whether an act was done through hatred, to refer the act to either emotion as the speaker may choose.[42]

This good will is revealed by the speaker through his ability to (1) capture the proper balance between too much and too little praise of his audience; (2) identify himself properly with the hearers and their problems; (3) proceed with candor and straightforwardness; (4) offer neces-

[42] *Ibid.*, p. 107.

sary rebukes with tact and consideration; (5) offset any personal reasons he may have for giving the speech; and (6) reveal, without guile or exhibitionism, his personable qualities as a messenger of the truth.

Aristotle assumed that truth, right, and justice would prevail if properly advocated; and that proper communication would prevent the triumph of fraud and injustice.

Effective ethical appeals thus require the speaker to reflect personal qualities of intelligence, good will, and character. One or the other of these traits he may concentrate on, or his discourse may be a blending of intellectual, social and moral virtues. To emulate these favorable qualities will lead him to exalt also those similar personalities of his associates. He may also denigrate the virtues of his opponents (and thus may violate his own axiological principles).

Image of the Speaker

Like all other human beings, every speaker embodies a certain image, the composite of his personality. As the speaker reacts to his world, the image represents the reflection of his total experience: spatial (the concept of his location in space); temporal (the identification with his experiences through an uninterrupted continuum from days gone by to the present hour); mental (the exercise of his intellectual powers in the successive conditions that call for choices); emotional (the behavior patterns as affected by his reactions to external and internal stimuli); ethical and axiological (the value judgments by which he estimates patterns of experience as "good or bad," "better or worse").

The description of him as viewed and assessed by others—be they few or many—is his public image or reputation. This public delineation of the speaker may or may not be accurate. It may be an assessment based upon partial judgments, inaccurate data, biases, distortions of his motives and actions, or the calculated creations by friends or public relations experts.

The messages to him from members of the audience may tend to strengthen his image; from others, to weaken it. As the messages reach him, he may show that his personal character has only been rendered more plausible and trustworthy; or, according to his honesty and understanding in self-evaluation, he may recognize changes that justify the impression of him; or he may examine the images of the individuals or the "public image" that would destroy his integrity and other facets of his being.

With this play of silent and audible messages to and from him, he may the better understand his own image and the hierarchy of images that possess his audiences. He establishes integration (identification) with his observer-listeners. They may or may not have a prior impression of his reputation. In any case, they react to his personality as he continues speaking. And he may try to correct their possible distortions of him and substitute an image of his valid leadership.

This personal image, always changing, may represent, through his own interpretation or those of others, a fairly authentic description of the real person. Or he may be utterly unable to understand himself, lost as he may be in an inner turmoil of competing impulses and decisions. Or his self-evaluation may result in acute insight into his over-all personality.

His problem as a speaker calls for the presentation and concentration on those traits favorable to acceptance of himself and his message. His method is similar to all speakers who would establish ethical proofs.

The speaker, the critic hopes, will be governed by an image or images favorable to the "good society" and that he will reflect close correspondence between his utterances and his inner self—the truth of his message and of his own reality.[43]

INSTANCES OF ETHICAL PROOF

The history of public address contains striking examples of effective ethical defense. Typical instances would include speeches by Robespierre as he faced the guillotine on July 26, 1794; Robert Emmet on the eve of being sentenced to death, September 19, 1803; Edward VIII on his resignation of the Crown, December 11, 1936; and David Lilienthal as he defined democracy, February 3, 1947.

The effectiveness of the attributes of character, intelligence, and good will in the speaker will obviously be maintained and strengthened only if undergirded by the rationale of ethical discourse. Rhetorical excellence requires alertness and understanding of values and exercise of "value judgments." This is axiological discourse—the rhetoric of commitment.[44]

Note how Dorothy Bishop summarized William Jennings Bryan's use of ethos in his "Cross of Gold" speech at the Democratic National Convention in Chicago on July 8, 1896.

Bryan's emotional conclusion is fraught with implied ethical appeal. By the close of the speech he had assumed complete accord with his audience; therefore, he assumed that what he first outlined as true of a wing of the party was true of the whole. He reminded his audience that he had behind

---

[43] Cf. Waldo Braden. "Southern Oratory Reconsidered: A Search for an Image." *Southern Speech Journal,* 29:303–315 (Summer, 1964).

[44] Cf. Ralph T. Eubanks and Virgil L. Baker. "Toward an Axiology of Rhetoric." *Quarterly Journal of Speech,* 48:157–178 (April, 1962); Thomas R. Nilsen. *Ethics of Speech Communication.* Indianapolis, 1966; Maurice Natanson. "The Limits of Rhetoric." *Quarterly Journal of Speech,* 41:133–139 (April, 1955); Charles L. Stevenson. *Facts and Values: Studies in Ethical Analysis.* New Haven, 1963. Chs. 1–5.

him and the silver Democrats the "producing masses of this nation and the world," supported by the commercial and laboring interests. In his final sentence, he aligned himself—as he did in his opening paragraph—with the cause of humanity by announcing (this time to the Republicans, not to the gold Democrats), "You shall not press down upon the brow of labor this crown of thorns, you will not crucify mankind upon a cross of gold."

Bryan's use of ethical appeal in the "Cross of Gold" speech is a masterpiece of subtlety. His choice of nonlogical appeals was apt for the occasion and purpose.

Bryan focused attention upon the probity of his character by several means. He associated himself completely with his message, and his message with what is virtuous and elevated—with the cause of humanity. He tempered praise of himself by keeping it entirely indirect. He gave high praise to his clients and cause, but not to the direct derogation of those who opposed his clients. He linked his opponents and their cause with that which is not virtuous—self interest, special privilege to the few, destruction of the possibility of Democratic success, foreign domination, and, finally, the crucifixion of mankind. He sought to minimize the charges leveled against himself— that is, of being a destroyer of business interests, of the nation's economy, of party harmony. He referred to experience—his own experience with and support from the masses, as well as to the experience of distinguished Americans and Democrats of the past. His humility and devotion to a principle above the interest of the individual established his sincerity.

Bryan proved his sagacity by the use of common sense—what was best not only for the people as a whole but for the Democratic party. He gave evidence of tact and moderation, he pointed out that his outright defiance of the gold interests came only after all other methods of gaining a hearing had failed. He displayed good taste in his criticism—by declaring not a note of bitterness and retaliation but his determination to see right prevail. He displayed broad familiarity with the issues of the day and proceeded to justify his concentration on the currency issue. He created the impression that, if time allowed and the occasion demanded, he could give an exclusive treatment of the subject. He knew that his audience was familiar enough with his decisions on the tariff and money question in the House of Representatives to accept his conclusions without complete proofs.

Finally, Bryan established his good will toward his audience. He demonstrated that he held no personal rancor. He chastised the gold advocates; yet he was principally concerned with the success of the party as a whole. He identified himself thoroughly not only with the masses—the rank and file of the party—but with the party as an organization. He was straightforward in his criticism and in the advocacy of his cause. He knew that the expression of humility and the almost complete elimination of personal reference would offset personal reasons for giving the speech. He displayed his personal qualities as a messenger of the truth of the cause of the bimetallism platform.[45]

John H. Sloan noted how William Jennings Bryan used ethos in a speech before the Democratic National Convention in 1904. Bryan based

[45] Waldo W. Braden and Mary Louise Gehring. *Speech Practices.* New York, Harper and Row, 1958, pp. 159–160. Copyright © 1958 by Waldo W. Braden and Mary Louise Gehring.

the speech firmly on his own character and reputation. In his words, this is how he had kept the faith:

> Eight years ago, a Democratic Convention placed in my hands the standard of the party and commissioned me as its candidate. Four years later that commission was renewed. I come tonight to the Democratic Convention to return the commission, and to say that you may dispute whether I have fought a good fight, you may dispute whether I have finished my course, but you cannot deny that I have kept the faith.

He claimed loyalty to his party: "I am here to discharge a duty that I owe to the party. . . ." He claimed loyalty to his country: "I have always believed . . . that a man's duty to his country is higher than his duty to his party." He claimed humility: "I failed, you say? Yes, I did. I received more than a million more votes than a Democrat has received before, and yet I failed." He claimed the right to make sincere suggestions: "Some of you have called me a dictator. It was false. You know it was false. . . . Why have I not a right to make suggestions?" He claimed loyalty to his followers: "I came . . . because I owed a duty to the six million brave loyal men who sacrificed for me."

These examples demonstrate that Bryan was able to discuss his own leadership, his power over millions of voters, his earnest belief in the Democratic party, and his moral courage without appearing to brag or to be maudlin. Furthermore, he could object to Parker as a possible nominee and never mention his name or appear to have this objection as his dominant purpose in the speech. Bryan's ethical appeals served him well.[46]

Orville A. Hitchcock and Ota Thomas Reynolds made a careful analysis of how the Negro orator Ford Douglass made use of personal and emotional appeals in a speech delivered on July 4, 1860, to an antislave gathering near Framingham, Massachusetts.

In keeping with his argument that the Negro was not inferior, Douglass did not come before his audience in an apologetic attitude. He spoke in straightforward and dignified fashion about a problem that concerned him deeply and intimately. He talked frankly about the fact that he was colored and showed pride in his race, even going to the extreme of disparaging the heritage of many of those in his audience. He did not seek to qualify himself as a political expert, except through remarking that he knew Lincoln and by recounting his experience with the Testimony Law petition. In this carefully developed personal example he offered his strongest ethical argument. Later he made brief personal

---

[46] John H. Sloan. " 'I Have Kept the Faith,' William Jennings Bryan and the Democratic National Convention of 1904." *Southern Speech Journal*, 31:119–120 (Winter, 1965).

references, such as "What can I say then as a black man," but he did not labor his relation to the subject.

Our first reaction today would be that Douglas was too critical of his country and too tactless in dealing with his opponents to win good will. We would wonder about the extremeness of his views, the positiveness of his opinions, his occasional sarcastic manner, and his tendency to "protest too much." It must be remembered, however, that he spoke to a partisan group, dedicated to abolitionist views.

The speech had strong emotional motivations, but these appeals did not predominate over the more logical aspects. Only occasionally did Douglass "pull the stops." Logic and emotion usually were closely interwoven. The basic appeal was to love of freedom, and its opposite, hatred of oppression. The orator sought to arouse indignation and anger that would lead ultimately to justice and fair play. Shame was used to this same end. The softer appeal to pity, although present, was subdued. The appeal to pride was not that of pride in country, but rather to pride in the noble cause of antislavery. Through biblical quotations and direct references, religious feelings were tied in. Humor, sometimes cutting, was employed with effect.

The emotional impact of the speech cannot be ignored. Even after a lapse of a century, one is caught up in the determination and enthusiasm of those who fought to liberate the slaves.[47]

THE NEED FOR SYNTHESIS TO RESULT FROM ANALYSIS

With this chapter on ethical proof we close that section of the book dealing largely with rhetorical invention. We have concerned ourselves with the search for and the analysis and development of arguments suitable to the enforcement of ideas and the establishment of belief in hearers. Our attention has centered chiefly about kinds of proof. Occasionally we found it necessary to consider details relating to disposition or arrangement, to style, and to delivery. In other words, speeches are totalities made up of several interrelated aspects, and the study of one aspect automatically directs attention to all the others.

The critic's inquiry thus becomes more complex as the number of specific points of investigation increases. It is the critic's job, however, to maintain a conception of rhetorical unity in the midst of his analytical examination of the discrete elements.

[47] Orville A. Hitchcock and Ota Thomas Reynolds. "Ford Douglass' Fourth of July Oration, 1860." In *Antislavery and Disunion, 1858–1861*. Edited by J. J. Auer. New York, Harper and Row, 1963, pp. 147–148.

EXERCISES

1. In order to establish his ethos, a speaker must demonstrate that he possesses the virtues which his listeners admire. Prepare a list of virtues that American speakers must conform to, to win respect from their listeners. In other nations, are these same virtues respected?
2. Does the speech goal alter the need for ethical appeal? Compare the informative, ceremonial, and persuasive speeches in this regard.
3. Consider carefully the importance of reputation on a speaker's success.
4. By what means do speakers attempt to avoid seeming immodest when they mention their qualifications? In formulating your answer consult several issues of Vital Speeches of the Day.
5. Aristotle says "Truth and justice are by nature more powerful than their opposites." Under what circumstances is this true?
6. Is it necessary for an ethical person to include ethos in a speech?
7. Read Daniel Webster's introduction to his speech in the Knapp-White murder trial. In what ways, specifically, does he try to establish his probity and his good will toward all the parties in the case? Compare this opening with one in a comparable case in recent times.
8. Investigate the problems that these speakers had with ethos: Charles James Fox, Benjamin Disraeli, Andrew Johnson, Harry Truman, and Richard M. Nixon. Determine how each speaker tried to overcome his problem.
9. Investigate how Adlai Stevenson established his ethos.
10. Make a careful analysis of how Douglas MacArthur used ethical appeal in his Address to Congress (sometimes called "Old Soldiers Never Die"), delivered April 19, 1951. See Representative American Speeches, 1951–1952, pp. 21–30. If possible, listen to a recording before you prepare your analysis.
11. Analyze how Richard Nixon defended himself in "The Expense Fund Speech" (sometimes called "The Checkers Speech"), delivered October 3, 1952. (Found in Goodwin F. Berquist, Jr., Speeches for Illustration and Example [Chicago, Scott, Foresman & Co., 1965, pp. 196–206].)
12. Investigate the problems women orators face in establishing their ethical appeal. (See Lillian O'Connor's Pioneer Women Orators [New York, 1954, pp. 134–157].)
13. Can you conceive of instances or mention specific ones in which the appeal to personality was decisively proper in advancing a public cause?
14. With the advent of television, and its extensive use in political campaigns, the power of personality has been enlarged. Do you see any dangers in this tendency? Will the less attractive man—for example, a Lincoln with warts—be at a disadvantage?
15. How reliable an index do you believe the marks of ethical proof in a speech are in revealing the true man? Specify instances which confirm or negate the conventional assumption.
16. Examine the following for insights into the role of ethical factors in persuasion: Charles W. Lomas, The Agitator in American Society (Englewood Cliffs, New Jersey, 1968); and Parke W. Burgess, "The Rhetoric of Black Power: A Moral Demand?" (Quarterly Journal of Speech, 54:122–133, April, 1968).

CLASS PROJECT (Continued)

In less than 1,000 words, analyze how your speaker sought to demonstrate his common sense, his good moral character, and his good will.

READINGS

KENNETH ANDERSEN and THEODORE CLEVENGER, JR. "A Summary of Experimental Research in Ethos." *Speech Monographs*, 30:59–78 (June, 1963).

STEPHEN K. BAILEY. *Ethics and the Politician.* An Occasional Paper of the Center for the Study of Democratic Institutions. Santa Barbara, California, 1960.

A. CRAIG BAIRD. *Rhetoric: A Philosophical Inquiry.* New York, The Ronald Press Company, 1965. Ch. 6, "Ethical Responsibilities."

DAVID K. BERLO and HALBERT E. GULLEY. "Some Determinants of the Effect of Oral Communication in Producing Attitude Changes and Learning." *Speech Monographs*, 24:10–20 (March, 1957).

DOROTHY ANN CRESAP BISHOP. "Bryan's Use of Ethical Proof in the 'Cross of Gold' Speech." In WALDO W. BRADEN and MARY LOUISE GEHRING, *Speech Practices.* New York, Harper and Row, 1958. Pp. 157–160.

WINSTON L. BREMBECK and WILLIAM S. HOWELL. *Persuasion: A Means of Social Control.* Englewood Cliffs, New Jersey, Prentice-Hall, 1952. Pp. 443–466.

W. NORWOOD BRIGANCE, ed. *History and Criticism of American Public Address.* New York, Russell & Russell, 1943. (Examine representative appraisals of ethical proof. See vol. I, pp. 419–423; vol. II, pp. 609–614; vol. II, pp. 813–818.)

DONALD BRYANT and KARL WALLACE. *Fundamentals of Public Speaking,* 3d ed. New York, Appleton-Century-Crofts, Inc., 1960. Pp. 287 ff.

JOHN DEWEY. *Reconstruction in Philosophy.* Boston, Beacon Press, 1957. Pp. 193 ff.

RALPH T. EUBANKS and VIRGIL L. BAKER. "Toward an Axiology of Rhetoric." *Quarterly Journal of Speech*, 48:157–168 (April, 1962).

BRADLEY S. GREENBERG and GERALD R. MILLER. "The Effect of Low-Credible Sources on Message Acceptance." *Speech Monographs*, 33:127–136 (June, 1966).

FRANKLYN S. HAIMAN. "An Experimental Study of the Effect of Ethos in Public Speaking." *Speech Monographs*, 16:190–202 (September, 1949).

———. "A Re-examination of the Ethics of Persuasion." *Central States Speech Journal*, 3:4–9 (March, 1952).

ANTHONY HILLBRUNER. "Invention and Ethos: The Metamorphosis of Alexander Hamilton." *Central States Speech Journal*, 11:41–48 (Autumn, 1959).

THOMAS R. KING. "An Experiment Study of the Effect of Ethos upon the Immediate and Delayed Recall of Information." *Central States Speech Journal*, 17:22–28 (February, 1966).

NORMAN W. MATTIS. "Phillips Brooks and the Problem of Personality in Rhetorical Criticism." In *Eastern Public Speaking Conference: 1940*, edited by HAROLD F. HARDING. New York, The H. W. Wilson Co., 1940. Pp. 301–305.

WAYNE C. MINNICK. *The Art of Persuasion.* Boston, Houghton Mifflin, 1957.

RICHARD MURPHY. "Preface to an Ethic of Rhetoric." In *Rhetorical Idiom*, DONALD C. BRYANT, ed. Ithaca, New York, Cornell University Press, 1958. Pp. 125–143.

MAURICE NATANSON. "The Limits of Rhetoric." *Quarterly Journal of Speech*, 41:133–139 (April, 1955).

THOMAS R. NILSEN. *Ethics of Speech Communication.* Indianapolis, Bobbs Merrill, 1966.

ROBERT T. OLIVER. *The Psychology of Persuasive Speech,* 2d ed. New York, Longmans Green & Co., 1957, pp. 20–36.

STANLEY F. PAULSON. "The Effect of the Prestige of the Speaker and Acknowledgement of Opposing Arguments on Audience Retention and Shift of Opinion." *Speech Monographs*, 21:267–271 (November, 1954).

EDWARD L. PROSS. "Practical Implications of the Aristotelian Concept of Ethos." *Southern Speech Journal,* 27:257–264 (May, 1952).

EDWARD ROGGE. "Evaluating the Ethics of a Speaker in a Democracy." *Quarterly Journal of Speech,* 45:419–425 (December, 1959).

PAUL L. ROSENTHAL. "The Concept of Ethos and the Structure of Persuasion." *Speech Monographs,* 33:114–126 (June, 1966).

WILLIAM M. SATTLER. "Conceptions of *Ethos* in Ancient Rhetoric." *Speech Monographs,* 14:55–65 (1947).

CHARLES L. STEVENSON. *Facts and Values: A Study in Ethical Analysis.* New Haven, Yale University Press, 1963. Chapters 1–5.

PHILLIP K. TOMPKINS and LARRY A. SAMOVAR. "An Experimental Study of the Effect of Credibility on the Comprehension of Content." *Speech Monographs,* 31:120–123 (June, 1964).

OTIS M. WALTER. "What You Are, Speaks So Loud. . . ." *Today's Speech,* 3:3–6 (April, 1955).

KARL R. WALLACE. "An Ethical Basis of Communication." *Speech Teacher,* 4:1–9 (January, 1955).

RICHARD WEAVER. *The Ethics of Rhetoric.* Chicago, Henry Regnery Co., 1953. Pp. 23 ff.

15

The Structure of
Oral Discourse

INTERRELATED CHARACTER OF DISPOSITION

Theophrastus is reported as saying that an "unbridled horse ought to be trusted sooner than a badly arranged discourse." Believing that good organization is essential in a speech, the ancient rhetoricians designated it the second part of rhetoric. They called it *dispositio*, and in the broad sense it dealt with the selection, orderly arrangement, and proportioning of the parts of an address.

Disposition is almost inextricably interwoven with invention. This is even more patent to the critic than to the creator of the speech. The critic seeks to understand an event during or, in a large number of cases, after the occurrence of the speech. And why a speaker arranged his material in a certain way cannot be fully determined until it is known why he chose certain arguments, or why he developed them as he did. Consequently, any distinctions that we may draw between finding and organizing arguments must candidly be accepted as semiarbitrary, as serving the ends of academic convenience almost as much as of theoretical accuracy.

Invention and disposition have often been linked in the manner previously suggested. John F. Genung looked upon the original aspects of discovery in invention as too individual to fall within the scope of ordinary textbook treatment. So he asserted that real invention did not begin

. . . .until to the original conception there is applied a process of organization, that is, of verifying, sifting, and selecting for ulterior disposal. It is in the various stages of organization, of working up thought to a completed form and effect, that invention centres.[1]

[1] *The Working Principles of Rhetoric.* Boston, 1900, p. 388.

The mutual dependence of finding and arranging material is thus clearly indicated. And the distinction between *originative and organizing* invention is accordingly specified.

Two additional opinions from homileticians corroborate Genung's view. John A. Broadus held that arrangement reacted directly upon invention. "One has not really studied a subject when he has simply thought it over in a desultory fashion," Broadus remarked. "The attempt to arrange his thoughts upon it suggests other thoughts, and can alone give him just views of the subject as a whole." [2] And George W. Hervey made disposition a part of invention—"first because the proper exercise of invention either proceeds from or results in thinking according to some method, good or bad; secondly, because in searching for the best method the most pertinent and useful thoughts are not infrequently suggested to us." [3]

Dispositio has frequently been unduly limited in translation as "arrangement." It apparently confines itself to the order of listing the main propositions and the divisions of given speeches.

English rhetorical theory continued to interpret the term as *order.* Wilson, in his *The Arte of Rhetorique* (1555), gave a few pages to the subject; he included the divisions of the speech under invention. Leonard Cox's *The Arte or Crafte of Rhetoryke*, appearing in 1524, placed emphasis on invention and disposition and hence departed from the medieval rhetoric of adornment, amplification and rigid patterns. Cox's successors, however, produced rhetorics of style and delivery. The influence of Peter Ramus was to limit rhetoric to those two aspects. John Ward's *System of Oratory* (1759), adheres closely to the classical sources of Cicero and Quintilian, though including much of the discussion of *dispositio* under invention. He adopts, for example, Cicero's six parts of a speech.[4]

George Campbell, in his *Philosophy of Rhetoric* (1776), almost completely ignored speech structure. Hugh Blair's *Lectures on Rhetoric and Belles Lettres* (1783) called *dispositio* the "conduct of a discourse" and merely named and described the parts.[5] Whately, in his *Elements of Rhetoric* (1828), focussed on arrangement as a means of giving order to logical arguments.[6] William Sandford in his *English Theories of Public*

---

[2] *A Treatise on the Preparation and Delivery of Sermons.* New edition. New York, 1898, p. 260.

[3] *A System of Christian Rhetoric.* New York, 1873, p. 332.

[4] "John Ward's Concept of Dispositio." *Speech Monographs*, 24:258–263 (November, 1957).

[5] *Lectures on Rhetoric and Belles Lettres.* Edited by Harold Harding. Carbondale, Illinois, 1965. II, 179–202.

[6] *Elements of Rhetoric.* Edited by Douglas W. Ehninger. Carbondale, Illinois, 1963. Ch. 3.

Address, 1530–1828, similarly noted that *dispositio* was treated as arrangement of material.[7] John Genung, in his *Practical Elements of Rhetoric,* discussed under invention the general process in the ordering of materials, including the determination of the theme, and the construction of the plan.[8] Charles Baldwin's *Ancient Rhetoric and Poetic,* concluded that arrangement as the proper concept of *dispositio* was inadequate and suggested rather that disposition should refer to the plan of the whole composition.[9]

Note the classical nature of the term. Aristotle conceived it as chiefly planned adaptation to the audience and speech. The thesis and proof were the essential "parts." He treated briefly the introduction, statement, proof, and epilogue, but stressed the principles of adaptation. He offered advice on selecting, ordering, and adapting the materials according to the audience, the subject, and the speaker.[10]

Cicero's *dispositio* stressed adaptation of the product of *inventio* to the particular situation. He viewed the process as the grouping of ideas invented in the natural order (exordium, narration, proof, and peroration). In *De Inventione,* he treats six parts: exordium, narration, division, evidence, contradiction, and peroration. The main object of disposition, however, was the exercise of prudence and judgment. The construction of each speech was determined by the specific problems which each audience presented.[11]

Quintilian considered disposition as arrangement, but refused to draw up or prescribe many formal rules for the parts of the speech.[12] Like Cicero, he said that *dispositio* included selection, elimination, ordering, massing or proportioning, and coloring. The time, place, speaker, purpose, and audience would determine the proper handling of structure. In general, the classical rhetoricians conceived of *taxis* or *dispositio* as planned adaptation.

What, then, is the preferred designation for this major division of rhetoric? According to Russell Wagner, "arrangement" and "planning" hardly cover the case. "Composition" and "speech construction" are also objectionable. "Organization" comes closest to a satisfactory term, but implies commitment to plan or outline. "Structure" also implies much

---

[7] *English Theories of Public Address.* Columbus, Ohio, 1931, pp. 16–19.

[8] *Practical Elements of Rhetoric.* Boston, New York, 1886, pp. 217–282.

[9] *Ancient Rhetoric and Poetic.* New York, 1924, p. 67.

[10] *The Rhetoric of Aristotle.* Translated by Lane Cooper. New York, 1932. Book III, chs. 13–19. Cf. George Kennedy. *The Art of Persuasion in Greece.* Princeton, New Jersey, 1963, pp. 113–114.

[11] *De Oratore.* London. Translated by E. W. Sutton and H. Rachman. 1942, pp. 436 ff. Two volumes. *De Partitione Oratoria.* In *The Orations of Marcus Tullius Cicero.* London, 1913. Translated by C. D. Yonge. IV, pp. 486–527.

[12] Donald Lemen Clark. *Rhetoric in Greco-Roman Education.* New York, 1957, pp. 79–83.

more than "outline" but is often confused with syntax. Wagner prefers the term "disposition," in view of the full meaning as contained in the older works. He defined the concept as "the functional selection and use of materials for a particular purpose." [13]

Objectives of Inquiry in This Field

The critic who evaluates a speaker's finished discourse proceeds with two objectives in view: First, he examines the speech as an instance of rhetorical craftsmanship, *per se*. That is, he considers the speech from the point of view of its basic construction, as an assembly of many parts bound together in an orderly and balanced whole. Secondly, he appraises the total plan of organization with reference to the peculiar audience conditions to which it was presumably accommodated. In other words, the critic recognizes the possibility that a speech may be a masterful combination of discrete elements, a model of unitary cohesion, considered *in vacuo*, and yet be ineffective in its adaptation to the audience for which it is intended. These two distinct problems are connected. Let us consider them in order.

ANALYZING A SPEECH FOR CRAFTSMANSHIP

In its broadest sense, disposition embraces the following matters: the emergence of a central theme or proposition, the general method of arrangement adopted for the speech, the order in which the parts of the discourse are developed, and the proportioning of materials.

Thematic Emergence

Selection of the materials of a given discourse is centered in the proposition or thesis, whether it is framed mentally or recorded. The purpose of the speaker or writer is to reduce his thesis to a clearcut statement that embodies both his over-all idea and his rhetorical aim of informing, entertaining, persuading, convincing, inspiring, or combining some of these ends. This proposition, the working idea or plan of the discourse, is sufficiently definite for the writer or speaker to refer to at every step in his preparation. It is a nucleus-thought, expressed or implicit, which must be in his mind as a central point of reference, a constant determiner and suggester of the scope and limits of his subject. It is the germ of the whole work and the essence both of the speaker or writer's thought and his specific audience purpose.

---

[13] "The Meaning of Dispositio," in *Studies in Speech and Drama in Honor of Alexander Drummond*. Edited by Herbert A. Wichelns. Ithaca, New York, 1944, pp. 285–294.

The thesis or proposition and its analysis are of course dependent upon the subject itself. Since the choice of purpose and topic is made, the whole vista of materials is open. The reading, thinking, interaction with people and events, including the speaker's previous experiences, all openly or subtly play for inclusion and primacy in what is to be uttered.

Obviously, the proposition as phrased is not the subject. The latter is the class-idea on which the more specific topic is based. The principle is both that of appropriating to the full the materials comprising the subject and simultaneously limiting the scope of treatment to avoid undue comprehensiveness. The aspects to be selected will be partly affected by the writer or speaker's view of what is best said; and the extent of the audience's familiarity with the subject.

The comprehensive statement is exact, suggestive, and brief. It incorporates the speaker's approach to the problem and perhaps reveals his speaking motives.

This development is also shaped by the speaker's approach to his audience. Aristotle assumed and explained that each speaker should become a judge of people. He advised the most suitable means of influencing others. In communication it is axiomatic that the speaker or writer must adapt his theme and analysis to the peculiar needs of each audience.

In addition to the subject itself, the personality of the speaker and the adjustment of the speaker with his audience and the occasion itself become major determinants of what is included, excluded, and expanded.

The occasion may call for ceremonial or epideictic discourse, the eulogy of some important figure, a historic event enshrouded in a century of previous tributes; a political appeal over the radio or television or before a cheering face-to-face audience. The scene may be that of a courtroom, with plea to jury or judge, or that of a religious service with an appropriate sermon. Each occasion strongly affects the thesis or proposition and selection of material. The critic is interested in finding out whether the speaker's conception of his task—be it to explain, to entertain, to convince, or to persuade—is clear, and whether the selection and arrangement of the ideas conduce to their effectiveness.

Methods of Division and Arrangement

In general, method here implies the choice of a principle by means of which the materials of a speech are divided; that is, the way the speaker selects the points to support his proposition. This is the search for a basis of division (analysis), or the determination of the most suitable major units of the subject. Whether the speaker consciously considers this point or not, he is obliged to effect such divisions of data as will provide ready manageability of details.

Actually two steps are involved in this phase of *dispositio*. The first is referred to as analysis, which we have just discussed. Once a speaker partitions his proposition, he still must order his points. Generally the method of analysis dictates the sequence of presentation. But on occasion after the speaker has determined what the points are, he must arrange them in another order to fit the requirements of the occasion or the audience.

How are the suitable units of the subject arrived at? The various methods of grouping materials into basic divisions include the (1) historical, (2) distributive, (3) logical and (4) psychological.

Historical Method. According to the historical basis of division, material is arranged in chronological order. The order may be, and often is, from past to present to future, or from a prophecy of the future to the past to the present. Instances of the use of the historical order in public speeches are numerous. In the last part of Burke's speech on "American Taxation," we find that he traces the chronology of the American problem through four distinct periods: The Navigation Acts, the efforts to get revenue from America, the Rockingham Ministry and the Stamp Act repeal, and, finally, the taxation imposed by Townshend. Charles James Fox also relied heavily upon this method in his speech on the rejection of Bonaparte's overtures. And Webster's address in the White murder trial illustrates the scheme of using a time order to determine the major divisions of the speech.

Distributive Method. According to the distributive method of arrangement, matters having a common thought center and an obvious connection among themselves are grouped in certain sections. If a certain body of subject matter deals with the political implications of a World Union, and another body of data deals with the economic implications of the plan, an effort may be made to distribute the materials according to the relation they bear to the specified ideas. In Burke's speech to the Bristol electors in 1780, he made use of this method, although the historical order also figures in the development. Asserting that "bad laws are the worst sort of tyranny," Burke set forth his reasons for taking a part in the repeal of certain cruel enactments against the Catholics. "To prove this—to prove that the measure was both clearly and materially proper, I will next lay before . . . the political grounds and reasons for the repeal of that penal statute, and the motives to its repeal at that particular time." He then broke down the "political" unit of his speech and discusses such distributed considerations as (1) the loyalty of the Roman Catholics, (2) the claims of humanity, (3) the beneficial effects of the repeal on the British Empire, and (4) the beneficial example set for foreign countries.

Logical Method. In the logical order the arrangement of materials is determined by the continuity of the reasoning process; materials are placed at those points where they serve as links in the uninterrupted sequences or chains of thought. Practically all speeches which are developed around a proposition of policy (recommending a new course of action) rely in greater or lesser measure upon this method. Its use is, of course, not limited to deliberative speaking, as a casual examination of specimen forensic and ceremonial talks will reveal.

Psychological Method. The psychological order is determined by the predisposition or inclination of the listeners. The first three approaches are definitely subject-centered, that is, the nature of the subject and the speaker's purpose determine the basis of division to be used. However, sometimes the speaker must arrange his points in terms of (1) importance, (2) interestingness, (3) complexity, or (4) acceptability. It is obvious that the three schemes of arrangement may be a method of analysis as well as order of the points. Psychological order is primarily a means of arranging the points in sequence for oral presentation.

In line with the psychological order of organization is the motivated sequence pattern advocated by Alan Monroe, and widely used. It is one of the few later contributions to the treatment of *dispositio.*

Monroe's formula asks: (1) What materials shall be used to gain attention? (2) What factors in the situation create a need (or lack of it) for this proposal? (3) What program or ways may provide (benefits) called for by this need? (4) What application of the proposal can be visualized by the speaker and audience? (5) What action should be taken to insure the application of the proposal (or to block such application)?

These questions are not far different from Dewey's analysis of the thinking process. The questions are also somewhat like instructions for use in sales talks. As Monroe states, the motivated sequence consists of five steps which correspond to the natural processes of people's minds. The formula is that of psychological appeals and reactions.[14]

Outline of Bases of Division

Since the foregoing methods of arrangement admit of elaboration, the following tabular analysis presents the common bases of division:

I. Historical Order
   A. Material can be divided as to time units.
   B. It can be from past to present to future, or from present to past to future; or any other derivative of this pattern.

[14] *Principles and Types of Speech.* Chicago, 1939. Ch. 12.

II. Distributive Order

    A. Material can be divided according to the parties involved in the problem: for example, capital and labor; or the Northerners and the Southerners; etc.

    B. The division can be made according to legal and ethical implications.

    C. The nature of the subject matter can determine the division:
        1. The material may be specific and general.
        2. The material may be familiar and novel.
        3. The material may be debatable and undebatable.
        4. The material may be admitted and contested.

    D. The division can be made according to the fields of inquiry involved in the subject. These fields may, for example, be the economic, political, social, etc.

    E. The division can be made according to the definitional requirements of the case.

III. Logical Order

    A. Material can be divided according to proof requirements implicit in the problem-solving technique:
        1. Statement dealing with the immediate cause of the controversy.
        2. The origin and history of the question.
        3. The definition of ambiguous words or terms.
        4. The exclusion of granted material.
        5. The listing of main heads or issues.
        6. The logical development of those issues.

    B. The material can be divided according to the framework of a logical pattern for discussion of policy:
        1. The definition of terms.
        2. The statement of goals in accordance with which the problem is analyzed and solved.
        3. The statement of factors involved in the problematic situation (the "felt difficulty," including causes and results).
        4. The weighing of representative solutions for tentative adoption.
        5. The analysis of a solution representing the consensus of those engaged in the analysis.
        6. The program to implement any formulated judgment.

    C. The material can be divided according to issues developed by the *proponents* of a proposed course of action:
        1. Present conditions are bad; the proposed plan will correct the difficulties; the proposed plan is practicable.
        2. The present system is good; the proposed plan is better.

D. The materials can be divided according to issues developed by the *opponents* of a proposed course of action:
1. There are instances of irregularities in the present system, but they are not numerous or serious.
2. There are some evils in the present system, but they are not inherent in the system.
3. There are evils in the present system, but the proposed plan is not a remedy.
4. Abuses exist; the proposed plan may have some advantages; but it introduces new evils.
5. Abuses exist; the proposed plan has some merit; but a better plan is available.
6. Abuses exist; the proposed plan is just; but it is inexpedient.
7. Abuses exist; the proposed plan is expedient; but it is not just.

E. Material can be divided according to refutative requirements inherent in the subject:
1. A speaker may first discuss objections to his plan and then give arguments in its favor.
2. It is sometimes possible to show that all methods, save one, of correcting present evils will fail.

F. The materials can be divided according to proof requirements for developing a proposition of fact (to determine the truth or falsity of a proposition or an alleged fact):
1. The subdivisions may consist of a listing of types of evidence, including statistics, testimony of witnesses, authorities, circumstantial details.
2. The subdivisions may include the classification of types of arguments—causation, analogy, deduction, etc.

IV. Psychological Order
A. Relative importance of the main and subpropositions.
B. Complexity of the main and subpropositions.
C. Interestingness.
D. Acceptability.

These schematic representations are not intended to suggest that a *single* basis of division necessarily prevails throughout an orator's speech. The principles often work in combination, so that the historical, distributive, logical, and psychological methods may all be in operation in a given discourse. Assuming that the principles are not in conflict and that structural consistency is maintained, we may on occasion find such an interlacing of methods quite satisfactory. Witness, for instance, the multiple principles of division in Burke's speech "On Conciliation" or on "American Taxation." Fundamentally, however, the subjects of discourse usually yield to a single principle of division; and, other things being equal, analyses resulting from the application of one basis of partition are more likely to be characterized by clarity, relevancy, and economy of style and effort.

RHETORICAL ORDER IN DISPOSITION

Thus far we have discussed the speech as an instance of craftsmanship in relation to two concepts: the emergence of a central thesis or proposition and the method of arranging the subject matter. We turn next to the *order* in which the parts of a speech are developed.

Plato remarked that "every speech ought to be put together like a living creature, with a body of its own, so as to be neither without head, nor without feet, but to have both a middle and extremities, described proportionately to each other and to the whole." [15] In other words, a speech should have a beginning, a middle, and an end. To realize this expectation, rhetoricians have devised certain parts that contribute to the formation of a whole artistic piece, and have given general instructions as to the order in which these parts shall appear.

The parts of a speech were conceived in terms of function, of utility. Consequently, their names are unimportant, so long as the task assigned to the units is adequately fulfilled. Because simplicity is a virtue in this instance, many rhetorical critics use the Aristotelian plan of organization as the criterion for evaluating *disposition*. This would seem to be a defensible standard since the critic is not interested in form for its own sake, but rather for the contribution it makes in eliciting a desired response from hearers.

Aristotle believed that "the only indispensable parts *of a speech* are the statement of the case and the proof." [16] He added, however, that if other parts were necessary, the total number should not exceed four: the exordium, exposition or statement of the case, proof, and the peroration. These are the four parts whose functions many critics examine when evaluating the structure of selected orations.

The functions of the parts are almost set forth by their descriptive titles. The *introduction*, which Aristotle said conformed to the prologue in poetry, is intended to enlist the attention and interest of the listeners, to render the audience well disposed toward the speaker, and to prepare the way for the ideas to come. The *statement* of the case sets forth clearly and concisely the nature of the subject presently to be devel-

[15] *Phaedrus.* In *The Works of Plato.* Translated by Henry Cary. London, 1854. I, 342–343.
[16] *Rhetoric.* Welldon ed., p. 275.

oped. The *proof* contains the elaboration of subject matter through which the idea or ideas are enforced. And the *peroration* or conclusion, to quote Aristotle, proposes "to inspire the audience with a favorable opinion of yourself and an unfavorable one of your adversary, to amplify or depreciate the subject, to excite the emotions of the audience and to recall the facts to their memory."

Rhetorica ad Herennium (c. 86 B.C.) provided a pattern of rhetorical instruction in Rome during the days of Cicero. According to this treatise, invention was developed in six divisions of the address: *exordium, narratio, divisio, confirmatio, confutatio,* and *conclusio.*[17] The *exordium* rendered the audience attentive and friendly; the *narratio* stated the facts; the *divisio* or *partitio* outlined the main points to be developed; the *confirmatio* developed the constructive argument; the *confutatio* consisted of rebuttal; and the *conclusio* or *peroratio* gave the conclusion. This division influenced later rhetoricians importantly in their treatment of *dispositio.*

Cicero in *De partitione oratoria* listed four parts, including *partitio* with *narratio,* and combining *confirmatio* and *refutatio.* Quintilian discussed the parts of *dispositio* as relating to forensic speaking, but warned that "Excessive subdivision is a fault into which many rhetoricians have fallen." [18]

In the preface to Book VII, Quintilian explained that any rules concerning arrangement must be general:

> The whole of this book, therefore; will be devoted to arrangement, an art the acquisition of which would never have been such a rarity, had it been possible to lay down general rules which would suit all subjects. But since cases in the courts have always presented an infinite variety, and will continue to do so, and since through all the centuries there has never been found one single case which was exactly like any other, the pleader must rely upon his sagacity, keep his eyes open, exercise his powers of invention and judgment, and look to himself for advice. On the other hand, do not deny that there are some points which are capable of demonstration and which accordingly I shall be careful not to pass by.[19]

These "points" he defines as "the distribution of things and their parts in advantageous places."

Later rhetoricians were inclined to elaborate on four, five, six, or even more parts, especially for forensic speaking and writing. John

---

[17] A. S. Wilkins. *M. Tulli Ciceronis "De Oratore,"* 3d ed. Oxford, 1890–93. I, 56–64. George Kennedy, *The Art of Persuasion in Greece.* Princeton, New Jersey, 1963, p. 266.

[18] *The Institutio Oratoria of Quintilian.* Translated by H. E. Butler. London, New York, 1921–22. Four volumes. Bks. II, VII, XI, p. 223.

[19] *Ibid.,* VII, preface.

Quincy Adams, for example, in his *Lectures on Rhetoric and Oratory,* developed successive lectures on the proposition and partition (Lecture XIX), Confirmation, Ratiocination (XX), Induction (XXI), Confutation (XXII), Digression and Transition (XXIII), and Conclusion (XXIV).[20]

Textbook authors on public address in the first quarter of the twentieth century taught that forensic discourse, specifically argumentation and debate, should be formally developed. The introduction of such forensic types should contain (1) immediate cause for discussion, (2) definition of terms, (3) brief history of the case, (4) statement of admitted or waived matter, (5) conflicting arguments, (6) statement of issues and or statement of what a speaker proposes to prove.[21]

CLASSIFICATION OF PARTS OF A SPEECH: VARIATIONS

Other rhetoricians, of course, have set up their own classifications of the parts of a speech. But all are in virtual agreement, the only essential differences being in the number of parts admitted and the labels attached to them. Thus Cicero and Quintilian include *narration* as a part, and suggest that it come after the exordium, especially in forensic speeches. In it, the speaker tells of the events that lead to the question at issue. Other parts mentioned by classical rhetoricians include *division,* in which the parts of the case are outlined; *refutation,* in which counter-arguments are introduced; *amplification,* in which the key issue of a case is given heightened effect through stylistic embellishment and emotional coloration. A fairly faithful reproduction of the more complex classical division is found in the late nineteenth century speech plan discussed by Charles Coppens. He says the following parts may appear in an oration: introduction or exordium, narration or explanation, proposition, division, proofs or argumentation, pathetic (or emotional excitement), and conclusion or peroration.[22]

It is apparent from an examination of any typical speech that all, or virtually all, of these parts are still with us. True, we have dropped some units and have subsumed others under the headings of the remaining ones. But, fundamentally, we still retain the divisions announced by the ancient theorists.

---

[20] *Lectures on Rhetoric and Oratory.* Two volumes. Cambridge, 1810.

[21] *Principles of Argumentation.* Boston, 1898. William T. Foster, *Argumentation and Debating,* new edition. Boston, 1932. James M. O'Neill and James Howard McBurney, *The Working Principles of Argument.* New York, 1932. James M. O'Neill, Craven Laycock, and Albert L. Scales, *Argumentation and Debate.* New York, 1928.

[22] *The Art of Oratorical Composition.* New York, 1855, pp. 106–107.

FUNCTIONS OF THE PARTS

How do the principles of selection of materials, order, and proportion apply?

The structure of a given discourse depends on the speaking situation and speaking type. Deliberative, epideictic, and forensic speaking have distinctive organizations, according to their specific aims. The forensic speech before the courtroom and judges and juries, for example, usually has a larger number and more extensive development of each part. The legal practices and tradition require a statement of facts and other elements not always so precisely treated in deliberative or epideictic speaking.

Introduction

What of the introduction? Its purpose is normally to gain attention; state the subject; in some cases define it; and announce the main issues or points to be developed. Definitions or explanations may or may not be necessary, depending upon what is to be talked about and the speaker's needs to use expositional details in the speech.

The main points may or may not be listed at the outset. To withhold such listing of the propositions often adds to suspense and heightens interest. A specialized audience, listening to a scientist, may want only clearcut and direct presentation. Attention and interest in the subject are automatic and need no rhetorical aids. (See, for example, Thomas Huxley's well-known lecture "A Piece of Chalk.")

The introduction, whatever the occasion, audience, and theme, should stimulate attention and interest. References to the author himself, to the immediate occasion, the audience, the sponsors of the program, and early identification of the subject with the needs of the audience, all help to set the proper atmosphere. These approaches are psychological as well as logical.

Body

The main body of any discourse, whether long or short, should meet the expectations suggested by the introduction.

If the address is argumentative and refutative, the constructive and refutatory content may be presented in the Ciceronian order with the constructive arguments first. Or the refutation, if a formidable case has preceded, may come immediately, especially if a speaker has extempore skill in rebuttal. Or construction and refutation may be closely blended.

Israel's Foreign Minister Abba Eban, before the United Nations Assembly in New York on June 20, 1967, gave direct reply to Russia's Premier Aleksei Kosygin, the preceding speaker. Kosygin argued that Israel should be condemned as the aggressor in the United Arab Republic–Israeli six-day war of June 3–9 and that the territory captured on the Sinai Peninsula along the Suez Canal, in Jerusalem and Jordan, should be returned. In his speech which was previously prepared but adjusted to the Russian Prime Minister's argument, Eban argued that Israeli's only demand was for living in peace; that direct peace talks with Egypt, Jordan, and Syria should be made; that the right of passage through the Suez Canal and Gulf of Aqaba be granted. He indicted Russia, which "for fourteen years has afflicted the Middle East with a headlong armaments race." "Five times," he reminded Kosygin, "Russia has vetoed the Security Council vote to condemn Arab aggression."

The Eban debate was a thorough blending of constructive and rebuttal materials.

In the amplification of chronological or logical development, it becomes again a matter of selecting those details that best enforce the preferred pattern. History may proceed chronologically forward or backward. Logic may treat testimony, statistics, analogies in any order. Causal materials may deal reason forward or backward. And so with the other methods. Details may combine procedures—historical, logical, and other. Each mode, however, must justify itself and be clearly integrated with these aspects of division.

The main body of a discourse will carry with it both logical and motivational materials, in some cases almost indistinguishable. Emotional material, as we have said previously, will be included at whatever points the speaker regards as appropriate. The entire process is thus without rigid rules, except the aims of effective communication.

Conclusion

Order in the conclusion again depends on the occasion, the type of speech, the audience, and the aims of the topic. Conclusions often contain such devices as summaries, series of questions, prophecies, quotations, brief anecdotes, and striking statements. The function of the conclusion, if it involves more than "just stopping," is to recapitulate and thus to help the audience recall.

Moreover, speakers may strengthen the "action step," or the speaker may pay farewell compliment to the auditors. Who is to say what logical, expositional, motivative elements are to be included or excluded in this final action? The style and content should at least strengthen what has gone before and should give final effect to the speech's contribution of information, persuasion, or appeal for action. The one principle here is economy of materials, and of the time, attention, and interest of the audience.

PROPORTION IN DISPOSITION

Proportion, another principle of disposition (structure), deals with the position and space of the content.

Its aim is to set forth the most important ideas and parts so that a listener or reader can properly understand them, and react favorably to them. The aim is to secure vividness, as George Campbell would suggest.

Such proportion is partly a matter of position. What is presented at the beginning or at the end may be more easily remembered than what intervenes.

The trained speaker will place at the beginning ideas or information of genuine importance to the success of his theme. These preliminary materials, as we have already suggested, may comprise a somewhat formal explanation of the plan of treatment, or a fairly complete statement of the purpose of the speech or article. Proportion calls for a significant beginning. The end should similarly be impressive. Summaries and restatement of the major points also contribute to satisfactory proportioning.

A second proportioning device is space. We may be more impressed by what a speaker talks most about, provided the development or restatement does not create boredom. What is chiefly before the attention should penetrate more deeply than that which is revealed briefly.

Thus repetition of ideas—in one or more places through explanation, illustration, logical detail, comparison and contrast with other ideas or information—all help ordinarily to make the more important concepts impressive.

The principle of proportion can be illustrated through a well-known speech. In contrast with similar addresses, John F. Kennedy talked directly to peoples abroad in his inaugural speech on January 20, 1961. In turn, he addressed the allies, the Latin American states, the emerging new nations, the United Nations, and the "adversaries" (the Soviets and their fellow states)—to "begin anew" the quest for survival, peace, and worldwide progress. He balanced well his proportions in recognizing each group of the world citizens. He devoted the last half of his speech to an exhortation for unity in the "struggle against the common enemies of man: tyranny, poverty, disease, and war itself."

The golden mean in style applies equally well to the structure of a discourse. Selection, order, and proportion call for discrimination between the important and the trivial; between excess and paucity of materials; between ideas and data; between economy of space and the number of points to be treated. Moreover, it concerns the avoidance of superficial and scanty material, and the obvious necessity of securing audience cooperation and response.

SYNTHESIS AND OUTLINING

To facilitate the task of assessing the plan of a speech, the critic will find it helpful to prepare an outline or brief of the entire address. This will enable him to appreciate more fully the basic divisions of the discourse, the functions they serve, the space allotments accorded them, and the relation of details to the larger rhetorical pattern. The brief is no less useful here than it is in tracing the logical continuities in an argument. There is no better way of viewing the internal makeup of a speech; nor of checking the coherency of the total sequence.[23]

ANALYSIS OF TOTAL SPEECH AND THE AUDIENCE

Previously we said that the critic considers rhetorical *disposition* from two related points of view: he examines the speech as an instance of craftsmanship, and he evaluates the total plan of organization with reference to existing audience conditions. We are now ready to discuss briefly the second item.

A speech conforming to the principles of good organization may be ill-adapted to the specific audience for which it is intended. In other words, so-called natural or logical structure may not coincide with the most effective sequence of presentation. It may be necessary to alter the natural order sharply to accommodate the speech to certain people. Coppens calls this the "oratorical" method of arrangement; and he defines it as "that which departs designedly from the natural order to avoid some special difficulty or to gain some special advantage, sacrificing regularity to usefulness."

Accordingly, certain speeches may not contain all the parts previously mentioned. Or they may contain the conventional parts but present them in different order. Perhaps no two speeches will be introduced in the same way; yet the introductions may serve substantially the same functions. These are but a few of the many variables. No one can anticipate them in the abstract. They are the direct consequences of real speech situations.

[23] Donald C. Bryant and Karl R. Wallace. *Fundamentals of Public Speaking*, 3d ed. New York, 1953–60. Pp. 145 ff. William Norwood Brigance, *op. cit.*, 210 ff. Alan H. Monroe, *Speech*, 3d ed. Chicago, 1949, pp. 261 ff.

The critic may find here, as elsewhere, that attempts to reduce rhetoric to a set of rules, either on the creative or the critical side, is a venture in futility. Many effective speeches stand as refutation of the claim that a particular way of organizing materials must be followed.

The position which arguments should occupy in the proof is also subject to variation with changes in audience conditions. Whereas we may favor the order of climax, circumstances may militate against its effective use in certain cases. H. L. Hollingworth points out that there is evidence to show that the reverse order of climax may produce more permanent results, at least in printed appeals.[24] What is true of the uncertainties of appeal regarding the number of points and the order of climax also concerns the position of repeated materials and other devices calculated to impress hearers.

The foregoing remarks stress the importance of the critic's being thoroughly familiar with the audience conditions under which the orator performed. It seems certain that in no other way will he gain the insight necessary to full understanding of why a speaker disposed his materials as he did. Essential as it is for the critic to know the *craft* of rhetorical disposition, and to be able to appreciate the plan which the speaker chooses, it is even more important that he determine the degree and success of the speaker's accommodation to the variabilities of audience behavior. If there are alleged irregularities in the organization and arrangement of a speech, it is the critic's job, indeed, to point them out, but only after he has examined the social milieu and has found no compelling reason for the speaker's departure from conventional plans. This is not an invitation to rhetorical chaos under the protective guise of artistic deviation of audience requirements. Most speeches will doubtless follow the traditional scheme, for experience has fixed it as fundamentally good. But where there is deviation, it must not be arbitrarily and automatically assigned to the speaker's perversity or ineptitude. Responsibility of judgment requires that the critic's pronouncements issue from the facts of the situation, rather than from the rules of the savants.

SPEECH STRUCTURE RELATED TO PERSISTENT THEME

Our discussion of disposition has suggested the age-old controversy of matter vs. form. We need not labor the question with further remarks. It is enough simply to point out that the most impressive and truthful matter conceivable can lose lustre and attractiveness through faulty organization, and conversely that perfect organization can never

[24] *The Psychology of the Audience.* New York, 1935. Ch. VII, "Impressing the Audience"; ch. XII, "Experimental Studies in Audience Effects."

transform drivel into shining truth. Form is not a sterile concept. It makes a difference whether material combines into a unified whole or remains an inchoate mass of disjointed particulars; under no circumstances, however, should we regard form as an independent virtue.

William Shedd once remarked that mere form is a ghost, "and a ghost possesses neither being nor reality." Disposition, as the rhetorical counterpart of form in its broader sense, must be viewed as a means; through it the potency of subject matter asserts itself and makes its purposes evident to the perceiving mind. But it remains a means—not a terminal value.

EXERCISES

1. Should the speech goal influence the speech organization? Does the organization of the informative speech differ from that of a persuasive speech?
2. What is psychological organization as contrasted with logical organization?
3. Through the centuries there has been considerable controversy over whether invention and organization belong in rhetoric or logic. What justification is there for placing these two canons in logic?
4. Critics have difficulty separating invention and organization into discrete classes. In what ways do these two canons overlap?
5. Distinguish among the following terms: rhetorical outline, analysis, and briefing.
6. Check schemes of speech organization found in several public speaking textbooks. Compare what you find with the classical conceptions.
7. Does Monroe's "motivated sequence" constitute a new approach to organization? Compare it to John Dewey's steps in *How We Think*.
8. In your critical evaluation of a speech, what criterion determines your judgment that a speech is well- or ill-organized? Some speeches that we regard as praiseworthy follow a conventional structural design; others do not. Examine, for instance, Loren Eiseley's "Man: The Lethal Factor" (*Representative American Speeches: 1962–1963*, pp. 39–55); and George Champion's "The Consensus Complex vs. The Free Market" (*Representative American Speeches: 1965–1966*, pp. 187–199). The first address is free-flowing and expansive in range; the second is organized tightly about three points. How will you judge organizational excellence in these or comparable cases?

CLASS PROJECT (Continued)

In 1,000 words or less, analyze how your speaker adapted his speech organization to his audience.

READINGS

A. Craig Baird. *Rhetoric: A Philosophical Inquiry.* New York, The Ronald Press Company, 1965. Ch. 9, "Structure."
Bert E. Bradley. "John Ward's Concept of *Dispositio.*" *Speech Monographs*, 24: 258–263 (November, 1957).

WILLIAM T. FOSTER. *Argumentation and Debating*, 2d ed. Boston, Houghton Mifflin Co., 1932.

History and Criticism of American Public Address. W. NORWOOD BRIGANCE, ed. New York, Russell & Russell, 1943. I, 251–255; I, 315–318; I, 425–428; II, 545–548.

EDMUND H. LINN. *Preaching as Counseling: The Unique Method of Harry E. Fosdick*. Valley Forge, Judson Press, 1966. Ch. 4, "Organizing the Ideas."

EDD MILLER. "Speech Introductions and Conclusion." *Quarterly Journal of Speech*, 32:181–183 (April, 1946).

ALAN H. MONROE and DOUGLAS EHNINGER. *Principles and Types of Speech*. 6th ed. Chicago, Scott, Foresman & Co., 1966. Ch. XVI, "Adapting the Speech Organization to the Audience: The Motivated Sequence."

RUSSELL H. WAGNER. "The Meaning of *Dispositio*." In *Studies in Speech and Drama in Honor of Alexander Drummond*. Edited by HERBERT A. WICHELNS. Ithaca, New York, Cornell University Press, 1944. Pp. 285–294.

16

The Style of
Public Address

THE COMPLEXITY OF STYLE

In Xenophon's accounts of an evening festivity following the Pan-athenaic games, a man appears at the door leading to the hall where the banquet is about to begin, and announces: "You all know that I am a jester; and so I have come here with a will, thinking it more of a joke to come to your dinner uninvited than to come by invitation." [1] Like the jester, style usually comes uninvited. Warp and woof of a speaker's expressive endowment, it is not likely to reflect faithfully either the man or the message if it must be summoned from arcane quarters for special duty.

Style is a puzzling concept. It embraces a broad panoply of mean-ings, from compositional grace to a man's personal attributes to the temper and tone of an entire society. Adlai E. Stevenson says "com-munism is the corruption of a dream of justice" and his admirers reply, "Here is felicity of statement. The man has style." But the style—as determined from a study of his major speeches, not from a single sen-tence—is many things: grace of expression, of course, but also an urbane culture, an acute intelligence, civilized wit, a finely honed sense of values, a very considerable vocal eloquence.

Of John F. Kennedy, it was said he had style. The reference was not alone to his command of language, which was admittedly good, although like all mortals here below he often worked his way into grammatical and syntactical quagmires from which there was no means of graceful

[1] *Anabasis, Books IV–VII and Symposium and Apology.* Translated by O. J. Todd. New York, 1932, p. 385.

escape. Style meant more than artistry in language. It was a certain sophistication of manner and wit, a youthful yet mature outlook, a fresh conception of political leadership. He was one of those uncommon men who, as Emmet John Hughes said, "detested cant but delighted in eloquence. He could appeal for conciliation without forswearing power. He could respect ideas without confusing them with deeds, exhort action without unharnessing it from reason, and esteem words without becoming infatuated with his own." [2] All of these attributes, and more, are expressions of a man's style, whether the scholarly definitions embrace them or not.

It is perhaps cheap philosophy to say that man must live within the framework of limitations. Cliché or not, it is a viable truth. The boundaries of style are indeterminate. No one is going to come up with a definition and analysis of it that will please all, or for that matter, even a few. This chapter is intended neither as a disclaimer of others' views nor as a statement of an original thesis. Rather, it sets forth a common sense point of view which, we hope, will help to orient the critic in assessing the style of public address. This we propose with full knowledge of the hazards. For in the history of man's restless search for statements on style that make sense, there have been distressingly few finds that one would label bonanzas.

> Rules for good verse they first with pain indite,
> Then show us what is bad, by what they write.

Style, said Hugh Blair, is "the peculiar manner in which a man expresses his conceptions, by means of Language." This definition affords a useful point of departure because it stresses the relation between thought and language. As Blair observes, "Style has always some reference to an author's manner of thinking. It is a picture of the ideas which rise in his mind, and of the manner in which they rise there; . . ." So "style is nothing else than that sort of expression which our thoughts most readily assume." All of which is an indorsement of Quintilian's dictum that we should bestow great care on expression,

provided we bear in mind that nothing is to be done for the sake of words, as words themselves were invented for the sake of things, and as those words are the most to be commended which express our thoughts best, and produce the impression which we desire on the minds of the judges.[3]

The functional idea introduced by Quintilian is significant. It postulates style as an indivisible element of the process of persuasion, and focuses attention upon what language *does*, rather than exclusively upon what it *is*. John F. Genung emphasizes this thesis by saying that style

[2] *Newsweek*, December 2, 1963, p. 52.
[3] *Institutes of Oratory*, VIII, Introduction, p. 32.

is "the skillful adaptation of expression to thought." [4] And the nature of subject matter determines the extent to which style becomes an influence. Certain facts such as statistics do not, as Genung indicates, admit of stylistic enhancement; but, when they are expressively translated, they may yield to felicitous statement. Thus, through the concept of style is thought "made to stand out as adapted to act upon men." The writer's or speaker's effort is directed, "not so much to the qualities of style in themselves, as to the demands of his subject, in order to bring out in its fullness what is essentially there." Style is an instrument of communication, inextricably interwoven with the other parts of rhetoric.

Under its older title *elocutio*, style was the third part of rhetoric. It referred chiefly to the way in which the speaker clothed his ideas with language. But, like the other parts of rhetoric, it is closely interrelated with its correlative members. Thus style and invention play interacting roles, since the conception of thought and its expression are virtually inseparable. Likewise, the arrangement accorded ideas is in itself a stylistic consideration, for the position an idea occupies in the total discourse may influence materially the way in which language is employed to express it.

Style and Personality

The relationship between style and ethical proof has given rise to a considerable body of literary comment. It has been alleged, and with reason, that personal character is clearly revealed by the speaker's style of expression. While this concept has been considered chiefly in relation to written, rather than oral, expression, the thesis seems equally applicable to the latter. In other words, a man may be said to speak as he does because of what he is. As a speaker, in a face-to-face situation, he is the style. His words reveal his inner character.

Like the writer, the speaker reveals more than technical craftsmanship through his expression. "If a writer's [or speaker's] personality repels, it will not avail him to eschew split infinitives . . ." or other syntactical irregularities, wrote F. L. Lucas. "Soul is more than syntax. If your readers [or listeners] dislike you, they will dislike what you say." [5]

That this revelation will always be complete and unalterably exact, in speech or writing, cannot be claimed. As John A. Symonds [6] once remarked, the secret of a man's personality is not always revealed by his actions and words. However, it may be said that the qualities of style are closely identified with the qualities and limitations of the man,

---

[4] *The Practical Elements of Rhetoric.* Boston, 1886, p. 15.

[5] *Style.* New York, 1962, p. 48.

[6] "Personal Style." In *A Book of English Essays, 1600–1900.* Edited by S. V. Makower and B. H. Blackwell. Oxford, 1927, pp. 389–390.

and accordingly tell us a good deal about him. The analyst of a speaker's style will undoubtedly be able, as Symonds suggests, to detect broad distinctions of temperament, both moral and emotional, in the productions. He will be able to find evidence linking the speaker with his inborn traits, his training, habits, and general outlook on life. But he cannot expect a man's expression to be an open revelation of his character. The epigrams "style is the man" and "the man is the style" are only conditionally acceptable.

Much has been written about the relation of sincerity to a speaker's effectiveness. Here again the speaker's manner and expression may not be true reflectors of his character. It is possible to feign sincerity. And if a man is a dunderhead, speaking nonsense, it scarcely makes a cosmic difference whether he is sincere or not. But our inclination is to believe that a man's faith in his cause and devotion to it are generally revealed through his style. Such revelation of character may result less from the deliberate use of art in composition than from spontaneous outpouring of personal convictions. "Indignation does not require artifice," said Demetrius; ". . . the style should be natural in such denunciations, and the words should be simple." [7]

Even such a comment postulates art as a necessary condition, for it tells the speaker what he *should* do. In reality, however, what he does will probably not be dictated by rule. His expression will be governed only by the nature of his subject, and by his natural promptings to say what his thoughts and feelings demand.

Shifting Emphases

With the possible exception of invention, no part of rhetoric is more complex than style. Its ramifications are elaborate, extending, as has just been suggested, deeply into the fundamentals of invention and disposition and losing themselves in them, so that what we arbitrarily call style becomes indistinguishable from the other elements.

The concept of style has enjoyed varying measures of emphasis ever since Aristotle wrote his *Rhetoric*. The classical works generally accorded it a balanced treatment. But in later years, when the doctrine of exornation began to take root, there was a tendency to make style the *sine qua non* of rhetoric. Paraphrasing Alexander Pope, a time came when

> Others for *language* all their care express,
> And value speech, as women men, for dress.

[7] *Aristotle's Poetics: Demetrius on Style*. Translated by T. A. Moxon. Everyman's Library. New York, p. 207.

When schools of declamation held sway in Greece and Rome, style was practically everything. Style and delivery, linked indissolubly, marked the speaker of skill. The essential relation of manner to matter was lost sight of, with the result that cogency of ideas figured for nought. Display was the keynote. Divorced from what Charles S. Baldwin called the "urgencies of subject," style moved toward decoration, exhibitionism, "virtuosity." During the eighteenth century in England, there was a resurgence of interest in the conception of rhetoric as style. Thomas Gibbons' *Rhetoric*, devoted exclusively to tropes and figures, illustrates an extreme in the stylistic approach. During recent years, rhetoricians have given less emphasis to style; instead, they have regarded language as a functional element, important chiefly for what it *does* rather than for what it *is* in its own right.

Plan of This Treatment

The purpose of this chapter is twofold: to present a short survey of some ideas persistently associated with the problem of style; and, secondly, to develop a point of view on stylistic matters. This conception should afford the critic a convenient yardstick for measuring an orator's skill in expression, by making style a function of the broader consideration of rhetorical adaptation and adjustment to the audience.

CLASSIFICATIONS

Fruitless and even pernicious as is the effort to classify the types of style, the impulse to do so has the authority of the ages to support it. Sensibly conscious of certain distinguishing marks in the style of selected speakers, rhetoricians have found it convenient to group modes of expression into classes. We have already shown how the three-way classification of style got its first development in Latin in the *ad Herennium*. It was believed that there was a Grand, a Middle, and a Plain style, each with distinctive characteristics. Cicero continued this tradition by describing the three complexions, as he put it, of eloquence. There is one sort, he said, "which has a fulness but is free from tumor; one which is plain, but not without nerve and vigor; and one which, participating of both these kinds, is commended for a certain middle quality." [8] While recognizing the shortcomings of classificatory schemes, Quintilian accepted the standard division: the plain, the grand, and the middle. "Of these," he remarked, "the nature is such that the *first* seems adapted to the duty of *stating facts,* the second to that of *moving the feelings,* and the third, by whichsoever name it be designated, to that

[8] *De Oratore,* III, 52.

of *pleasing,* or *conciliating,* . . ." [9] By linking the types of style to their function, such classifications become less suspect. Here Quintilian makes the styles conform fairly closely to the so-called "offices" of the orator in explaining, conciliating, and moving. And for the first, he postulates the necessary condition of perspicuity; for the second, gentleness of manner; and for the third, energy.

Quintilian also subdivided styles on another basis. He turned to the distinction between the speaking of the *Attic* and the *Asiatic* orators, observing that the former were "compressed and energetic" in their style while the Asiatics were "inflated and deficient in force." And the Attics were distinguished by their freedom from redundancy; the Asiatics, by their lack of judgment and restraint. Quintilian went on to report that some critics had added a third kind of eloquence, the Rhodian, which had a character intermediate between the other two. It derived its quality from the country itself and from its founder, Aeschines, who, exiled in Rhodes, "carried thither the accomplishments then studied at Athens, which, like certain plants that degenerate when they are removed to a foreign climate and soil, formed a union of the Attic flavour with that of the country to which they were transplanted." The orators of this school were "accounted somewhat deficient in vigour and spirit, though nevertheless not without force, resembling, not pure springs, nor turbid torrents, but calm floods."

It is interesting to note how the doctrine of classes has pervaded the conception of style. During the second half of the nineteenth century, such a widely used textbook as G. F. Quackenbos' *Composition and Rhetoric* [10] used an elaborate division of the types. There is the *dry* style, said Quackenbos, which excludes ornament of all kinds and aims only at intelligibility, eschewing everything manifestly intended to "please either the fancy or the ear." A *plain* style is one degree above the dry; it strives for perspicuity, first of all, but also considers precision, purity, and propriety. "Such figures as are naturally suggested and tend to elucidate [the] meaning, . . . [the writer] does not reject, while such as merely embellish he avoids as beneath his notice." The *neat* style employs ornaments, but not the most elevated or sparkling kinds. "Beauty of composition is sought to be attained rather by a judicious selection and arrangement of words than by striking efforts of imagination." The sentences are of moderate length, and free from superfluities. *Elegant* style "possesses all the beauty that ornament can add, without any of the drawbacks arising from its improper or excesive use." This was regarded as the perfection of style. A *florid* style employs ornaments everywhere. These may spring

[9] *Institutes,* XII, 10, 59.
[10] New York, 1862, pp. 263–264.

from a luxuriant imagination and have a solid basis of thought to rest upon: or, as is too often the case, the luxuriance may be in words alone and not in fancy; the brilliancy may be merely superficial, a glittering tinsel, which, however much it may please the shallow-minded, cannot fail to disgust the judicious.

It is observed that only those of "transcendent genius" can continuously engage in ornament with any expectation of success. Quackenbos believes, however, that time usually corrects excess in the use of this style; and he quotes as supporting testimony Quintilian's dictum that "luxuriance can easily be cured; but for barrenness there is no remedy."

The *simple* style is characterized by sentence structure that "bears no marks of art; it seems to be the very language of nature." It aims always to be consistent with nature. *Labored* style—the exact opposite of the simple—is stamped by "affectation, misplaced ornament, a preponderance of swelling words, long and involved sentences, and a constrained tone, neither easy, graceful, nor natural." The *concise* style, aiming at brevity, "rejects as redundant every thing not material to the sense." It relies upon strong, compact sentences which suggest more than they express directly. The *diffuse* style employs repetitions freely; indulges in long sentences "making up by copiousness what . . . [it] lacks in strength"; and draws often upon amplification. And, finally, the *nervous* style produces a strong, and the *feeble* style a slight, impression upon the hearer. They are often considered synonymous with the diffuse and concise styles, though Quackenbos doubts the wisdom of such an identification.

As illustrations of the various styles, Quackenbos mentions Aristotle for the dry; Locke and Swift for the plain; Addison for the elegant; Ossian for the florid; Homer and Goldsmith for the simple; Markham for the labored; Bacon for the concise; Cicero for the diffuse; and Burke for the nervous style.

These classifications suggest the pervasiveness of the effort to compartmentalize kinds of expression according to features or qualities. Classifications persist in recent rhetorical criticism. When Chauncey Goodrich, for instance, calls Thomas Erskine's style "chaste, forcible, and harmonious"; and when, in his appraisal of Curran's oratory, he contrasts it with Erskine's "Attic taste," he is obviously holding close to the line established by the classifiers.[11]

QUALITIES

For many years rhetoricians have analyzed style in terms of the qualities that contribute to its excellence. Cicero speaks of Theophrastus'

[11] *Select British Eloquence.* New York, 1853, pp. 636, 789.

attempt to establish four such features: correctness, clearness, ornateness, and propriety. The classical tradition accepted, generally, such or a variant classification. Any attempt to analyze expression according to its distinguishing qualities reveals traces of arbitrary subdivision, but it is nevertheless helpful in highlighting the elements which manifestly contribute to stylistic excellence. We shall, accordingly, discuss briefly the qualities of correctness, clearness, appropriateness, and embellishment.

Correctness

Correctness refers chiefly to word choice or usage. Fundamentally, it deals with the selection of the best word for the particular task. It is a highly individual matter, the eventual choices varying with many circumstances, including the speaker's knowledge, his language facility, his understanding of the audience, and the character of the response sought through the speech.

In its more complex form, it embraces the whole doctrine of purity and excellence in diction. Aristotle believed correctness of language to be the foundation of all good style. He listed as its constituent elements: (1) proper use of connecting words; (2) use of specific rather than general words for things; (3) avoidance of ambiguity; (4) accurate classification of nouns as to gender; and (5) correct expression of plurality, fewness, and unity.[12]

Approaching the problem from approximately the same point of view, but with a different emphasis, Cicero remarked that all speech was a matter of words, and that the words had to be studied both as individual units and as parts of a compositional whole.[13] Each of these aspects had a peculiar merit. As for word choice, he suggested that the orator use metaphorical words often, new ones sometimes, and very old ones rarely.

One of the most detailed treatments of word choice and usage is found in George Campbell's *Philosophy of Rhetoric*. His analysis has been used widely; it still serves, as a matter of fact, as a standard for many studies in the field. Campbell [14] puts words to a threefold test: (1) Are they reputable? That is, do they enjoy good standing among men of taste? As he puts it, the words must be authorized by the practice of a great number, if not the majority, of distinguished writers or speakers. (2) Are they in national use? In other words, they should be divorced from provincial or foreign attachments. And (3) are they

---

[12] *Rhetorica.* Translated by W. Rhys Roberts. p. 1407a.
[13] *De Oratore,* III, 37.
[14] New edition. New York, 1851. 164 ff.

in present use? This simply suggests that time and period affect usage, but it does not imply that words are necessarily the worse for being old or the better for being new.

Recognizing purity of diction as the foundation of excellence in other aspects of style, Campbell sets forth his canons of usage. These canons are intended to show how purity, or "grammatical truth," may be realized. In their briefest form, the canons state:

The first canon, then, shall be, When use is divided as to any particular word or phrase, and the expression used by one part hath been preoccupied, or is in any instance susceptible of a different signification, and the expression employed by the other part never admits a different sense, both perspicuity and variety require that the form of expression which is in every instance univocal be preferred. . . .

The second canon is, In doubtful cases regard ought to be had in our decisions to the analogy of the language. . . .

The third canon is, When the terms of expression are in other respects equal, that ought to be preferred which is most agreeable to the ear. . . .

The fourth canon is, In cases wherein none of the foregoing rules gives either side a ground of preference, a regard to simplicity (in which I include etymology when manifest) ought to determine our choice. . . .

The fifth and only other canon that occurs to me on the subject of divided use is, In the few cases wherein neither perspicuity nor analogy, neither sound nor simplicity, assists us in fixing our choice, it is safest to prefer that manner which is most comfortable to ancient usage.

Note should also be made of these subcanons:

All words and phrases which are remarkably harsh, and unharmonious, and not absolutely necessary, may justly be judged worthy of this fate [that is, merit degradation]. . . .

When etymology plainly points to a signification different from that which the word commonly bears, propriety and simplicity both require its dismission. . . .

When any words become obsolete, or, at least, are never used, except as constituting part of particular phrases, it is better to dispense with their service entirely, and give up the phrases. . . .

All those phrases which, when analyzed grammatically, include a solecism, and all those to which use hath affixed a particular sense, but which, when explained by the general and established rules of the language, are susceptible either of a different sense or of no sense, ought to be discarded altogether.

Needless to say, word choices, however discriminating, can be appreciated only when they appear in an orderly arrangement—in composition. Regarded as the medium through which beauty and sense are imparted to language, it includes an extensive range—from the careless, primitive moulding of words into united forms, to the artificially conceived elaborations which aim primarily at nicety, however puerile. For our purpose, composition is regarded as a tool with which the speaker works. Nicety of effect for its own sake is not enough. There-fore, we may confine our remarks to two aspects of composition: struc-ture and rhythm.

Structure has to do with the way in which words are assembled and related so as to convey thought with economy of effort and effectiveness of purpose. Obviously, this suggests that the laws of grammar must serve as the basis of operation. However, it also implies a further and, for the orator, a very important fact: that the purpose he entertains will mould the materials in a particular way adapted to the require-ments of the audience situation. Thus both grammatical and rhetorical principles operate in the finished composition of public address.

Composition is a complex process. It begins with the syntactical principles governing number, mood, case, and tense, and it extends to the construction of the finished paragraph. All these arrangements cannot be considered here; the proper province of their discussion lies in a standard textbook on grammar. Suffice it, however, that critical inquiry looks to these aspects of composition and appraises their usage in the light of the practical requirements of the audience situation in which they are employed. Hence the inquiry deals with matters of syntax; the collocation of qualifying elements in sentences, since force and emphasis may depend upon the position certain parts occupy in the construction; the accuracy and specificity of the antecedents, or, as John F. Genung expresses it, the "retrospective" and the "prospective" references; the precision with which relations are indicated in sentence structure through the use of conjunctions and other correlating devices; the effectiveness with which thoughts are emphasized and expanded consistent with the demands of the speaker's purpose; the presence of comparable facility in securing effectiveness through brevity; the use of repetition, and the employment of devices for securing emphasis.

Extending the discussion of structure, we acknowledge the impor-tance of variety in the finished patterns of sentences. Thus interspersing long with short sentences tends to enhance style, breaking, as it does, the sameness of thought patterns. Conversely, an unbroken sequence of long sentences tends to become monotonous, while a succession of short ones may produce a staccato, choppy effect.

The subject matter, it is true, will determine in some measure the type of sentence to be employed. But, in the main, good style is the result of the judicious use and interaction of three kinds of sentences: the periodic, the loose, and the balanced. A periodic sentence is one in which neither idea nor grammatical structure is completed until the final words; adaptable to the building of a climax, it contains some pri-mary feature that is more effectively carried across to the listener through delay in revelation. A loose sentence, on the other hand, does not fol-low this principle of suspense. It is so constructed, both in grammar and in the presentation of the idea, that it could be terminated, possibly at several points, before the end is reached without violating grammatical sense. Finally, the balanced sentence is a compound sentence in which the different elements, through similarity of form, answer each other or set each other off.

Naturally, an orator's style is not judged by rule as to the statistical proportion of one sentence type to another. The speaker has certain thoughts to communicate. The language in which he clothes those thoughts is not determined by law; it is suggested by the requirements of himself and of his hearers. He must fulfill more than a simple grammatical function. Accordingly, it would be folly to require that certain thoughts be expressed in certain ways. The variables of rhetorical effectiveness militate unalterably against such a procedure.

The final stage is the assembly of related sentences into paragraphs which should be specific units of the thought structure. Here we have occasion to observe the interweaving of materials which make up single topics. The prime consideration is unity, for the series of sentences in each paragraph must represent an unbroken continuity. On the whole, however, the construction of paragraphs follows the same general lines as the development of a complete discourse.

Rhythm has long been considered a pleasing attribute of prose style. Through it, speech seems to take on added beauty, and to become a more effective instrument for conveying the emotional fervor of the speaker. As it relates to prose, however, rhythm has a special significance. Aristotle believed that prose should be rhythmical to a certain extent, but not metrical. Cicero agreed, but added that an oration should not be inharmonious, "like the conversation of the common people."

The sources of rhythmical prose are manifold. They rest in the structure of the sentences; in their arrangement in the paragraph; in the combination of metrical feet; in the delivery accorded the material by the speaker, and, according to Cicero, in the figures of speech. No doubt what the speaker should strive for, however, is what Genung calls an "unmeasured rhythm, ever varied, yet never neglected. . . ." To achieve an effect pleasing to the ear, the speaker relies chiefly upon "the easy flow of accented and unaccented syllables"; upon the "musical regularity, yet variety, of the natural pauses"; upon the distribution of accented syllables, "in order that the stress may not fall on too many words in succession"; upon variety in the "time" of the speech; upon the gradual suspension of sense, rather than the abrupt termination, at the end of sentences, and upon the measures of volume proportionate to the importance and emphasis of the ideas.[15] Whereas the poet holds

15 Genung, *op. cit.,* pp. 169–170.

to more fixed metrical schemes, the speaker conforms to no such patterns. He uses metre only to serve the larger purpose of achieving oratorical effectiveness.

The virtue of correctness thus embraces a variety of concepts, including those of words and of their union. But, by and large, it deals with word choice that insures accuracy in developing the speaker's thought—an accuracy that is unimpaired by modish colloquialisms, archaisms, and word coinages. Correctness facilitates the use of language as an effective vehicle for conveying thought.

Clearness

Closely related to correctness, and no less important in the total process of language usage, is clearness. ". . . let excellence of style be defined," said Aristotle, "to consist in its being clear; (a sign of this is that the diction, unless it make the sentiment clear, will not effect its purpose. . . .") [16] Like the other qualities of good style, this one concerns both the choice of words and their arrangement. It arises from a certain simplicity and perspicuity which Quintilian considered the first virtue of composition. "Let there be proper words, and a clear order," he observed; "let not the conclusion of the sense be too long protracted; and let there be nothing either deficient or superfluous." [17] The true end of style, Quintilian remarked later, is that the judge not only understand us, "but that he may not be able not to understand us." In the words of Philo Buck, the "highest ends can be reached by the simplest means; and this is one very great secret in style." [18]

Perspicuity is an essential in all types of discourse, regardless of the purpose the speaker tries to realize. A speaker must be understood, or he labors to no avail. And the clearness of the speech must be, as it were, an unrecognized element of its merit. As John Broadus once said: "Style is excellent when, like the atmosphere, it shows the thought, but itself is not seen." [19]

Barriers to Clearness. What, then, are the possible violations against perspicuity which may mar the clarity of discourse? Again we may turn to Campbell for helpful guidance. The first general cause grows out of an obscurity which may take various forms. (1) It may result from a defect in the expression, as when a fairly well established elliptical expression fails to convey meaning to the hearers. Or, this defect

---

[16] *Rhetoric.* Buckley edition, p. 207.
[17] *Institutes.* VIII, 2, 22.
[18] *Literary Criticism.* New York, 1930, p. 92.
[19] *A Treatise on the Preparation and Delivery of Sermons.* New edition. New York, 1898, p. 361.

may result from an overconciseness which carries the thought to a point just short of intelligibility. (2) There may be a faulty arrangement of words, resulting in unclear constructions. As Campbell remarks:

A discourse . . . excels in perspicuity when the subject engrosses the attention of the hearer, and the diction is so little minded by him that he can scarcely be said to be conscious that it is through this medium he sees into the speaker's thoughts. On the contrary, the least obscurity, ambiguity, or confusion in the style, instantly removes the attention from the sentiment to the expression, and the hearer endeavours, by the aid of reflection, to correct the imperfections of the speaker's language.[20]

(3) Obscurity may arise from using the same word in different senses. (4) Uncertain references in pronouns and relatives may be the cause. (5) Too artificial or complicated sentence structure may militate against perspicuity. This is particularly true where the sense of the statement is too long suspended. (6) The injudicious use of technical words and phrases may prove another "source of darkness" in composition. And (7) extremely long sentences are likely to admit of excesses against the dictates of clearness.

The second violation of perspicuity often arises from double meaning. Here, as Campbell remarks, the "fault is not that the sentence conveys darkly or imperfectly the author's meaning, but that it conveys also some other meaning which is not the author's." There is, then, the possibility of varied and various interpretation of the meaning. When such misinterpretation develops from an expression having more meanings than originally intended, it is known as equivocation; when it results from an arrangement of words that renders the whole construction equivocal, it is called ambiguity.

The last general offense against perspicuity is that which results from a speaker's failure to convey his meaning at all. In other words, this is the offence of unintelligibility. It may arise, first, from a confusion of thought on the part of the speaker. And it is evident that no language medium, however perfect, "will suffice for exhibiting a distinct and unvarying image of a confused and unsteady object." Furthermore, unintelligibility may arise from an "affectation of excellence," as when a speaker tampers with an otherwise perspicuous statement by inserting a clause of doubtful meaning, simply for purposes of exhibition. Finally, unintelligibility may arise from a want of meaning. Campbell distinguishes "want of meaning" from that of confusion of thought, by saying:

When this is the cause of difficulty, the reader will not fail, if he be attentive, to hesitate at certain intervals, and to retrace his progress, finding himself bewildered in the terms, and at a loss for the meaning. Then he

[20] Op. cit., p. 244.

will try to construe the sentence, and to ascertain the significations of the words. By these means, and by the help of the context, he will possibly come at last at what the author would have said; whereas, in that species of the unintelligible which proceeds from a vacuity of thought, the reverse commonly happens. The sentence is generally simple in its structure, and the construction easy. When this is the case, provided words glaringly unsuitable are not combined, the reader proceeds without hesitation or doubt. He never suspects that he does not understand a sentence, the terms of which are familiar to him, and of which he perceives distinctly the grammatical order. But if he be by any means induced to think more closely on the subject, and peruse the words a second time more attentively, it is probable that he will then begin to suspect them, and will at length discover that they contain nothing but either an identical proposition, which conveys no knowledge, or a proposition of that kind of which one cannot so much as affirm that it is either true or false.[21]

Granted that all thoughts do not admit of equally clear expression, it is generally agreed that good style preserves the integrity of thoughts while at the same time achieving intelligibility. The fusion of those two elements requires, as John F. Genung observes, that the speaker or writer subdue "language to perfect flexibility and obedience." Thus clearness really becomes "the intellectual quality of style." [22]

Appropriateness

The quality of appropriateness embraces much of what has been said relative to correctness and clearness. This is true because the latter elements derive much of their character from the fact that they are adapted to the circumstances in which the expression is used. What may be correct or clear before a certain group may be decidedly not so to another. These virtues reside partly in their propriety, in their being fitted to the special conditions of the moment. Thus we must look to appropriateness as an important stylistic quality. It is, indeed, the most functional aspect of the whole problem of style; through it we are best able to study language as a tool of adaptive behavior used by the orator to adjust himself to his audience situation.

It is generally recognized that the style of expression should be appropriate to the subject; that is, the mode of expression should be consistent with the nature of the address. Aristotle holds unmistakably to this doctrine. He affirms that when weighty matters are being discussed, the casual manner of expression should not be used; when trivial topics are being considered, there should not be a manner of solemnity. Cicero accepts substantially the same point of view. Indicating that propriety, or the *becoming* in oratory, is essential, he says

. . . no single kind of style can be adapted to every cause, . . . For capital causes require one kind of oratory, panegyric another, judicial pro-

[21] *Ibid.*, p. 270.
[22] *Op. cit.*, p. 21.

ceedings another, common conversation another, consolation another, reproof another, disputation another, historical narrative another.[23]

Cicero's conception of copious language springs directly from the doctrine of propriety, his conviction being that 'copiousness of matter produces copiousness of language; and, if there be an inherent dignity in the subjects on which he [the orator] speaks, there must be . . . a certain splendor in his expression."

It should be observed that Quintilian formalized this concept by saying that the style should be adapted not only to the cause, but to particular parts of the cause. Thus the orator will rely upon different arts and modes of expression in the exordium, narration, and so on, as his intention is to conciliate, or to inform, or to induce to action. The speaker accommodates himself to the purpose in view; and his style changes with the accommodations.

The doctrine of propriety also governs the use of figurative language. Hugh Blair, for instance, insists that we suit the tropes and figures to the subject; that we avoid forcing subjects into a state of elevation through the use of figures that are not congruous with the content.

The concept of appropriateness goes beyond this point, however. Style must also be appropriate to the type of oratory used and to the particular audience addressed. The style of deliberative oratory, said Aristotle, "is exactly like sketching; for in proportion as the crowd is larger, the view is taken from a greater distance. . . ." [24] He says that the forensic style is highly finished, as is that addressed to a single judge since there is little room for rhetorical artifice. Ceremonial speaking is the most literary of all, chiefly because it is intended to be read. Cicero agreed in general with this belief. He indicated that it was of consequence to consider "who forms the audience, whether the senate, or the people, or the judges; whether it is a large or a small assembly, or a single person, and of what character. . . ." All these considerations he relates closely to subject matter, remarking that "it is the part of art and nature to be able to do what is becoming on every occasion. . . ." [25]

The concept of adapting style to the audience and to the type of oratory has remained essentially unchanged since antiquity. It is still considered important, even though treated less formally. For instance, we believe that ceremonial oratory, because of its very nature, yields to somewhat different stylistic development than expositional analysis, which is intended simply to enlighten the understanding. In short, we still believe, as Aristotle did centuries ago, that "to each kind of rhetoric is adapted a peculiar style."

Finally, in considering appropriateness, it is assumed that the style

[23] *De Oratore.* III, 55.
[24] *Rhetoric.* Buckley edition, p. 248.
[25] *De Oratore.* III, 55.

should be consistent with the speaker himself. In other words, it should help to reveal the character of the speaker; it should not seem to clash with his personality. Thus it is generally agreed that the style should be congruent with the speaker's age. Aristotle regarded this matter as important; Cicero deemed it significant to inquire who the speakers were, of what age, rank, and authority, in order that the *becoming* qualities in oratory might be evaluated. So far as this matter concerns the critic of oratory, it centers largely about one inquiry: Does the speaker's style represent the person employing it; or, does it, instead, seem to cloak the thoughts in language unsuited to him as an individual?

Embellishment

The primary function of embellishment is to adorn or elevate through the judicious use of tropes and figures. Both Cicero and Quintilian devote considerable space to an analysis of the devices which add lustre to ordinary expression. It was the rhetoricians of Tudor England and of the late eighteenth century, however, who were most systematic and comprehensive in treating this apect of style. So it is that we turn to one of the latter for most of our classifications. Thomas Gibbons' *Rhetoric* provides a usable list of the tropes and figures upon which speakers continue to rely. While it is true that the figures no longer receive the attention they used to, we are perhaps in a better position to assess their value now than were the men of the periods during which figurative forms enjoyed fuller status. We no longer make *elocutio* the primary point of concern in rhetoric; instead, we appraise it in its relation to the larger function of getting responses. But we use tropes and figures regularly, even though we may not assign fancy names to them, as our predecessors did. Figurative language represents a part of the total process of rhetoric and therefore cannot be overlooked.

Tropes and Figures. There is a distinction between tropes and figures. While this distinction is not discussed frequently in the contemporary literature of speechcraft, it seems to be valid. A trope, says Thomas Gibbons, *"is the changing a word or sentence with advantage, from its proper signification to another meaning. Thus, for example, God is a Rock."* A figure, on the other hand, *"is the fashioning or Dress of a Composition, or an emphatical manner of speaking different from what is plain and common."* The distinction, then, is that the trope

   . . . is a change of a word or sentence from one sense into another, which its very etymology imports; whereas it is the nature of a Figure not to change the sense of words, but to illustrate, enliven, ennoble, or in some manner or another embellish our discourses. . . .[26]

[26] Thomas Gibbons. *Rhetoric.* London, 1767, pp. 1–3.

The following definitions and examples, taken from Gibbons, cover certain of the tropes most frequently used in public address:

A *Metaphor* is a Trope, by which a word is removed from its proper signification into another meaning upon account of Comparison. . . . Thus our blessed Lord is called *a vine, a lamb, a lion,* &c.

An *Allegory* is a change or continuation of Tropes, and more generally of Metaphors; and differs from a single Trope in the same manner as a cluster on the vine does from only one or two grapes.

> Did I but purpose to embark with thee
> On the smooth surface of a summer's sea,
> While gentle zephyrs play in prosp'rous gales,
> And fortune's favour fills the swelling sails;
> But would forsake the ship, and make the shore,
> When the winds whistle, and the tempests roar. . . .

A *Metonymy* is a Trope, in which one name is put for another, for which it may be allowed to stand by reason of some relation or coherence between them. . . . Thus Mars among the Heathens is used for *war,* Cere for *corn.* . . . 'He has a good heart'. . . .

A *Synecdoche* is a Trope, which puts the name of the whole for a part, or the name of a part for the whole; a general name for a particular under that general, or a particular for the general. . . . Put up your *weapon,* that is, your sword.

Under the Synecdoche we may also range the *Autonomasia,* which is a Trope by which we put a proper for a common name, or a common name for a proper. . . . Thus, that man is an Hercules. . . . he is gone to the City, . . . meaning *London.*

An *Irony* is a Trope, in which one contrary is signified by another; or, in which we speak one thing, and design another, in order to give the greater force and vehemence to our meaning. . . . Under the *Irony* we may include the *Sarcasm,* which may be defined to be an *Irony* in its superlative keenness and asperity.

An *Hyperbole* is a Trope, that in its representation of things either magnifies or diminishes beyond or below the line of strict truth, or to a degree which is disproportioned to the real nature of the subject. . . . *whiter than snow, blacker than a raven.* . . . *deaf as a rock, blind as a mole.* . . .

A *Catachresis* is the most licentious as to language of all the Tropes, as it borrows the name of one thing to express another, which has either no proper name of its own; or if it has, the borrowed name is used either for surprising by novelty, or for the sake of a bold and daring energy. . . . Thus Quintilian allows us to say, that we *dart* a ball or a stake, though darting belongs only to a javelin. . . . Thus Virgil says, 'The goat himself, man of the flock, had stray'd,' by man, evidently intending the father and leader of the flock.

Among the most common figures, the following should be noted:

An *Ecphonesis* is a Figure, that by an exclamation shews some strong and vehement passion.

Aporia, or doubting, is a Figure whereby we express an hesitation where to begin our discourse, or a difficulty what to do in some arduous affair, or what to resolve upon in some critical emergency.

The *Epanorthosis* is a Figure whereby we retract or recall what we have spoken or resolved.

Aposiopesis is a Figure whereby a person often through the power of some passion, as anger, sorrow, fear, &c. breaks off his speech without finishing the sense.

Apophasis, or denial, is a Figure by which an Orator pretends to conceal or omit what he really and in fact declares.

Anacoenosis is a Figure by which the speaker applies to his hearers or opponents for their opinion upon the point in debate; or when a person excuses his conduct, gives reasons for it, and appeals to those about him whether they are not satisfactory.

Anastrophe, or inversion, is a Figure by which we suspend our sense, and the hearer's expectation; or a Figure by which we place last, and perhaps at a great remove from the beginning of the sentence, what, according to common order, should have been mentioned first.

Erotesis is a Figure by which we express the emotion of our minds, and infuse an ardor and energy into our discourses, by proposing questions.

Prolepsis is a Figure by which a speaker suggests an objection against what he is advancing, and returns an answer to it: or it is a Figure by which a speaker, more especially at the entrance upon his discourse, removes any sort of obstruction that he foresees may be likely to prevent the success of his cause.

Epanaphora is a Figure, in which the same word is gracefully and emphatically repeated; or in which distinct sentences, or the several members of the same sentence, are begun with the same word.

Apostrophe is a Figure in which we interrupt the current of our discourse, and turn to another person, or to some other object, different from that to which our address was first directed.

Periphrasis is a Figure in which we use more words than what are absolutely necessary, and sometimes less plain words, either to avoid some inconvenience and ill-effect which might proceed from expressing ourselves in fewer or clearer words, or in order to give a variety and eloquence to our discourses, and multiply the graces of our composition.

Synchoresis is a Figure whereby we grant or yield up something, in order to gain a point, which we could not so well secure without it.

Asyndeton is a Figure, occasioned by the omission of conjunctive particles, which are dropped either to express vehemence or speed; or sometimes it may be from a noble negligence or nice accuracy, arising from an attention to our ideas. . . . 'There was . . . an horrible spectacle in the open plains, pursuit, flight, slaughter, captivity.'

The very opposite to this Figure is the *Polysyndeton;* for as the *Asyndeton* drops, so the *Polysyndeton* on the contrary abounds with conjunctive particles.

Oxymoron is a Figure, in which the parts of a period or sentence disagree in sound, but perfectly accord with one another in meaning; or . . . it is sense in the masquerade of folly. . . . *A coward dies often, a brave man but once.*

Enantiosis is a Figure, by which things very different or contrary are compared or placed together, and by which they mutually set off and enhance each other.

Climax, according to Mr. Blackwell's definition, is, 'when the word or expression, which needs the first member of a period, begins the second, and so on; so that every member will make a distinct sentence, taking its rise from the next foregoing, till the argument and period be beautifully finished: or . . . , it is when a word or expression, which was predicate in the first member of a period, is subject in the second, and so on, till the argument and period be brought to a noble conclusion.'

The *Hypotyposis* is a Figure, by which we give such a distinct and lively representation of what we have occasion to describe, as furnishes our hearers with a particular, satisfactory, and complete knowledge of our subject.

The *Prosopopoeia* is a Figure which consists in describing good and bad qualities of the mind, or the passions or appetites of human nature as real and distinct persons; in clothing with corporeal forms, or endowing with speech and action imaginary beings, or general notions and abstracted ideas; in introducing persons silent as speaking, or persons deceased as living; and in making rocks, woods, rivers, temples, and other inanimate beings, assume the powers and properties, and express the emotions of living, and even reasonable creatures.

Parabole is a Figure that compares one thing with another, to which it bears a resemblance.

An *Epiphonema* is a pertinent and instructive remark at the end of a discourse or narration.

Additionally, let us list the following figures which we all use, whether or not we give them fancy labels.

Anaphora—the repetition of a word or words at the beginning of successive clauses in a sentence. ("Now the trumpet summons us again—not as a call to bear arms, though arms we need, not as a call to battle, though embattled we are. . . .")

Antiphrasis—the use of a word to express a meaning that is directly opposite to its true one.

Antistrophe—the repetition of an expression in inverse order. ("The leader of the moment and the moment of the leader")

Antithesis—a contrasting of ideas, either by positioning at the beginning and end of a sentence or clause, or in similar positions in successive clauses or sentences. ("If a free society cannot help the many who are poor, it cannot save the few who are rich.")

Ellipsis—omission of words ordinarily needed for the full expression of meaning.

Epanalepsis—an echo; opening and closing a clause or sentence with the same word.

Epistrophe—the ending of successive clauses or sentences with the same word or words. ("Are they fearful of the mounting crisis? I am too. Are they suspicious of their leaders? I am too.")

Euphemism—the use of agreeable words for indelicate ones. ("Waste disposal" for "garbage collection.")

Hyperbaton—inversion of word order for dramatic effect. ("Sounded the alarm" for "the alarm sounded.")

Litotes—a kind of understatement which affirms a state or condition through denial of the contrary. ("A speaker of no small competence.")

Metabasis—a movement from one point to another through connecting summary; a transition.

Paradox—an affirmation of a truth that appears contradictory.

Paralepsis—giving emphasis to a point by appearing to pass over it practically unnoticed. ("I will mention but one instance from his catalog of misdeeds.")

Paronomasia—punning.

Personification—ascription of personal qualities to inanimate things or abstract ideas. ("The hand of mankind's final war.")

Simile—a comparison of conditions or objects in certain particulars. ("Words, like people, should live at peace with one another.")

Synonymy—the repeated use of different words of similar meaning to heighten emphasis.

Use of Ornamentation. The practical question with which the critic must deal in appraising the embellishment of a speech is: Do the tropes and figures contribute to the realization of the speaker's aim and object? If, as Emerson believed, "nothing so works on the human mind . . . as a trope," it is necessary to inquire into the sources of its effectiveness.

Rhetoricians agree that figurative forms should not be used as substitutes for reason. Even Gibbons—a disciple of the school of exornation —declared that discourses should first "enlighten the understanding, and inform the judgment" before figures were introduced "to affect and engage the passions. . . ." The figures must help to reinforce thought, but should not be regarded as the thought, *per se*. Accordingly, illustrative value is their chief virtue. By themselves they may conceivably have decorative value, but that is significant only if the more important service of support to thought is initially rendered.

Figurative forms must, therefore, be used sparingly. "Nothing so quickly tireth," says John Lawson, as the excessive use of figures. By their nature they are likely to attract notice; as illustrators and supporters of thought, they lose their functional significance as soon as they do nothing more than focus attention upon themselves. Under such circumstances, they tend to "*strangle* our meaning," as Gibbons put it.

It is perhaps true that modern rhetoric avoids the generous use of ornamental material and so-called eloquent expression. "I will never aspire to be a preacher of pretty sermons," said theologian Reinhold Niebuhr in 1929. "I'll keep them rough just to escape the temptation of degenerating into an elocutionist." He went on to say that the temptation to engage in extravagance of statement and feeling "increases with the size of the crowd." [27] Classroom teachers know that their students are, by and large, suspicious of extended figures of speech and are reluctant to use them. They nurture a self-consciousness in such communication born no doubt of searing experience: audience responses running from bored smiles to uncivil guffaws. Yet the day of "expansive oratory" is not over. Winston Churchill—surely one of the greatest,

[27] *Leaves from the Notebook of a Tamed Cynic.* Meridian Books, 1957, p. 27.

if not the supreme, orator of the twentieth century—gave speeches that were elegantly impassioned, in the best sense, and suffused with literary embellishments of richest hue. Whether in the crowded intimacy of the House of Commons—and he believed that a measure of inconvenience in seating all the Members contributed to oratorical effectiveness, as well as to a sense of parliamentary urgency—whether, we repeat, before the House or on the public platform, Churchill appreciated the value of the right word with the right sound in the right place. He gave testimony to the claim that "the true test of an art is its highest possibility."

But the notion is current that the studied composition of speeches in language of power and elegance is somehow suspect, that it results in a contrived rhetoric. "If you are to persuade an audience," said former Australian Prime Minister Sir Robert Menzies, "you must metaphorically be down off the platform and among your listeners." The object of a persuasive address "is to have your audience not leave saying 'He can speak,' but saying 'He was right.' " [28] One might counter that there is no inherent conflict between speaking with power—even rhetorical elegance—and speaking what is right, provided the speaker makes the appropriate adjustment to his listeners. "Grace in speech," said the late Lord Justice Birkett, "makes speech memorable; lucidity makes it enjoyable to the hearer; and grace and lucidity come only from a knowledge of words and their quality, and a sense, innate or acquired, of the appropriate word in its appropriate place." [29]

Perhaps there are not many Monets left in the world whose disciplined artistry will goad them to paint eighty-three different haystacks in order to get the right one; or Platos who allegedly—but probably apocryphally—will write seventy versions of the first paragraph of a dialogue. But it is our good fortune to have lived in an age when at least a few speakers have achieved measurable greatness through the development of sublime themes and the studied mastery of felicity and grace in the composition and delivery of their addresses.

Finally, figures and tropes require a development that is economical of detail and of the time necessary for presentation. Failing this standard, they may easily become show-pieces, interesting perhaps, but ineffective in revealing swiftly the point under development. Remembering Herbert Spencer's observation that figures should be used with economy of attention, we may say with him: "To bring the mind more

[28] Albert E. Norman. "Australia Writes." *Christian Science Monitor*, June 19, 1963.
[29] *The Magic of Words.* London, 1953, p. 14.

easily to the desired conception, is in many cases solely, and in all cases mainly, their [figures'] object." [30]

ECONOMY

Spencer's popular thesis that good style and economy of effort are indissolubly linked applies not only to figures of speech; indeed, it embraces the whole concept of expression in language. Spencer believed that style, to be good, had to make minimum demands upon the hearer's mechanism of reception—upon interpreting the symbols—in order that it might enlist maximum energy to appreciate the full meaning of the thought. As he put it:

To so present ideas that they may be apprehended with the least possible mental effort, is the desideratum towards which most of the rules . . . point. When we condemn writing that is wordy, or confused, or intricate—when we praise this style as easy, and blame that as fatiguing, we consciously or unconsciously assume this desideratum as our standard of judgment. Regarding language as an apparatus of symbols for the conveyance of thought, we may say that, as in a mechanical apparatus, the more simple and the better arranged its parts, the greater will be the effect produced. In either case, whatever force is absorbed by the machine is deducted from the result. A reader or listener has at each moment but a limited amount of mental power available. To recognise and interpret the symbols presented to him requires part of this power; to arrange and combine the images suggested requires a further part; and only that part which remains can be used for the realization of the thought conveyed. Hence, the more time and attention it takes to receive and understand each sentence, the less time and attention can be given to the contained idea; and the less vividly will that idea be conceived. How truly language must be regarded as a hindrance to thought, though the necessary instrument of it, we shall clearly perceive on remembering the comparative force with which simple ideas are communicated by mimetic signs. . . . No phrase can convey the idea of surprise so vividly as opening the eyes and raising the eyebrows. A shrug of the shoulders would lose much by translation into words. Again, it may be remarked that when oral language is employed, the strongest effects are produced by interjections, which condense entire sentences into syllables. And in other cases, where custom allows us to express thoughts by single words, as in *Beware, Heigho, Fudge*, much force would be lost by expanding them into specific verbal propositions. Hence, carrying out the metaphor that language is the vehicle of thought, there seems reason to think that in all cases the friction and inertia of the vehicle deduct from its efficiency; and that in composition the chief if not the sole thing to be done is, to reduce this friction and inertia to the smallest possible amount. Let us then inquire whether economy of the recipient's attention is not the secret of effect, alike in the right choice and collocation of words, in the best arrangement of clauses in a sentence, in the proper order of its principal and subordinate propositions, in the judicious use

[30] "The Philosophy of Style." *Westminster Review* (new series), 58:446. October, 1852.

of simile, metaphor, and other figures of speech, and even in the rhythmical sequences of syllables.[31]

This doctrine draws upon the qualities of correctness of word choice, perspicuity of statement and arrangement, and wisdom in the selection of illustrative details and ornamental features. The validity of Spencer's philosophy is freely accepted, especially in its relation to speechmaking, where the hearer has no opportunity to back up for a review of material previously presented. Instant and exact intelligibility is a prime requisite of the speaker's style. So the less attention the style attracts to the mechanics of word composition, the more energy will be available to appreciate the ideas in the discourse.

ORAL VERSUS WRITTEN STYLE

Since antiquity, the rhetoricians and critics have recognized a difference between oral and written style. Aristotle spoke of the written style as being "more finished" and of the oral style as admitting of "dramatic delivery."[32] Although asserting in one place that *"to speak well* and *to write well* are but the same thing," Quintilian[33] nevertheless saw that the two were not identical, and that good writing would have to be altered some if it were translated into the oral medium. He recognized the necessity of suiting materials to the capacities of judges, adding, however, that the speech would probably be "edited" later "lest it be thought to be the offspring of his judgment, and not a concession to circumstances."

Quintilian observed further that the language of ordinary discourse and that of a "truly eloquent man" are of a different nature. Were this not true, and were it sufficient for an orator

. . . to express his thoughts plainly, he would have nothing to study beyond mere suitableness of words; but since he has to please, to move, and to rouse the minds of his audience to various states of feeling, he must have recourse, for those purposes, to the means which are afforded us by the same nature that supplies us with ordinary speech; just as we are led by nature to invigorate our muscles with exercise, to increase our general strength, and to acquire a healthy complexion.[34]

In his essay "On Familiar Style," William Hazlitt suggested that a familiar style in writing was the approximate equivalent of the expression used in common conversation. It was like the expression of one "who had a thorough command and choice of words, or who could dis-

[31] *Ibid.*, pp. 436–437.
[32] *Rhetorica.* Roberts edition, 1413b, 9.
[33] *Institutes.* XII, 10, 55–56.
[34] *Ibid.*, XII, 10, 43.

course with ease, force, and perspicuity, setting aside all pedantic and oratorical flourishes." This point of view does not set up artificial distinctions between types of discourse having communication of ideas as the common goal.

Many of the things we say about oral vs. written style are embarrassingly obvious. Yet they are relevant. The living presence of the speaker is a language by itself, at once personal, subjective, intimate. Listeners care who is before them. And if the speaker is at all sensitive and responsive, he tries to give something of himself through words and expressive actions. On the other hand, an essayist, for example, may write with such detachment that the reader never gives him a thought. All the attention focuses on what is said. This is, of course, open to exception, for skilled writers of the familiar essay often reveal more of their personality and the warmth of their human concern than scores of less talented speakers do in their medium.

In general, oral expression is a swift, merciless revealer. You can talk to an acquaintance for a half hour without discovering whether he is at home in integral calculus; but if he is a linguistic cripple, you will learn much about his language habits in one minute. Similarly, an argument heard and an argument read may seem to be quite different pieces. The one may *suggest* the nature of the man; the other *exposes* it. At the bar, said Lloyd P. Stryker, the lawyer "stands intellectually naked and alone. Habits of thought and speech cannot be borrowed like garments for the event. What an advocate gives to a case is himself; he can bring to the bar only what is within him. A part written for him will never be convincing." [35]

To use an expression favored by people in the theatre, spoken discourse grows out of "a sense of occasion." There is an audience, often in close contact; there is a feeling of communion, for all have ostensibly come to hear and see, at one time, and with minimal distraction, the same words. Unlike a television movie or a microphone speech which will be attended at large by an assortment of people—some of whom will listen, or drink beer, or quarrel with the family—a face-to-face situation makes personal, specific demands upon the speaker. The writer faces about the same problem as the television actor in the movie, or the speaker who faces the solitary microphone: he is not a participant in an occasion. Consequently, what he says cannot conceivably be responsive to what goes on out front. Regrettably, what went on out front cannot be recaptured either, once the occasion is over. "Most speeches, when recalled," wrote Lord Justice Birkett, "are without the fire and the glow with which they were invested by the speaker's presence; the dramatic setting has gone; and the emotions of the moment

35 *The Art of Advocacy.* New York, 1954, p. 234.

have vanished irrevocably."[36] Understandably, some authors try out their lectures before living audiences before putting them in print. This helps to preserve a trace of the original glow and insures a more sensitive recognition of what is clear, precise, and appropriate.

More specifically, however, in what ways do the two styles differ? If, as the Most Reverend A. M. Ramsey once said, an orator "must have something of the eye's appreciation of words as well as the ear's response to them when spoken,"[37] what differences in the two media must the speaker take into account? In a discerning essay on the theme, Stanley Burnshaw[38] examined three fundamental dissimilarities: (1) The word order differs and this produces "its own linguistic logic." The speaker arranges ideas subjectively, with a view to meeting hearers' expectations and enlisting their response. Juxtaposition of words is common in speaking; sentence continuities are often broken in order to capture spontaneity of expression. (2) Oral style cannot give as much intellectual content as written discourse, largely because a speaker has to deal with many distractions and inattentions in an audience setting. A listener lets someone else work, namely, the speaker, and he in turn does not dare lose his audience. Moreover, he must be ready to recapture attention if it wanes. (3) Writing permits greater intellectual refinement, subtlety, and delicacy than does speaking.

While the standards of good language appear to be essentially the same for writing and speaking, the nature of the media produces differences in word choice, composition, and usage. Words that might be acceptable in an essay might be too "hard" or dissonant in a speech. Limitations of time ordinarily force speakers to a greater economy of words. The fact that a listener cannot pause for reflection and cannot back up in time and development, often results in a speaker's making generous use of repetition and restatement. Additionally, oral style is characterized by the liberal use of contractions, personal pronouns, elliptical phrases, simplicity in sentence structure, digressions, interjections, idiomatic expressions, and connotative words.

These are, however, superficial manifestations of difference. Basically, the mode of expression is a function of the end which the speaker hopes to realize. The needs and capacities of the hearers and the nature of the occasion will govern the speaker's choice of language.

PERSISTENCE OF CONVENTIONAL ANALYSIS

The conception of style deriving from a study of its qualities and constituents, such as we have considered, is time honored. It has been

[36] *Op. cit.*, p. 12.
[37] *Oratory and Literature.* London, 1960, p. 6.
[38] "Speaking Versus Writing." *Today's Speech,* September, 1958, pp. 16–19.

widely accepted, and even today serves as a basis for much investigation in the field. Before we turn to a somewhat broader view of style, we should observe how the critics of the past dealt with stylistic matters in their studies of the orators. One of the illustrative analyses to which we shall turn is Chauncey Goodrich's study of Burke.

After discussing Burke's skill in debate, intellectual independence, subtlety and comprehensiveness of intellect, and power of generalization, Goodrich says:

His *method* was admirable, in respect at least to his published speeches. No man ever bestowed more care on the arrangement of his thoughts. The exceptions to this remark are apparent, not real. There is now and then a slight irregularity in his mode of transition, which seems purposely thrown in to avoid an air of sameness; and the subordinate heads sometimes spread out so widely, that their connection with the main topic is not always obvious. But there is reigning throughout the whole a massive unity of design like that of a great cathedral, whatever may be the intricacy of its details.

In his *reasonings* . . . Mr. Burke did not usually adopt the outward forms of logic. He has left us, indeed, some beautiful specimens of dialectical ability, but his arguments, in most instances, consisted of the amplest enumeration and the clearest display of all the facts and principles, the analogies, relations, or tendencies which were applicable to the case, and were adapted to settle it on the immutable basis of the nature and constitution of things. Here again he appeared, of necessity, more as a teacher than a logician, and hence many were led to underrate his argumentative powers. The exuberance of his fancy was likewise prejudicial to him in this respect. Men are apt to doubt the solidity of a structure which is covered all over with flowers. . . .

In respect to Mr. Burke's *imagery,* however, it may be proper to remark, that a large part of it is not liable to any censure of this kind; many of his figures are so finely wrought into the texture of his style, that we hardly think of them as figures at all. His great fault in other cases is that of giving them too bold a relief, or dwelling on them too long, so that the primary idea is lost sight of in the image. Sometimes the prurience of his fancy makes him low and even filthy. He is like a man depicting the scenes of nature, who is not content to give us those features of the landscape that delight the eye, but fills out his canvas with objects which are coarse, disgusting, or noisome. Hence no writer in any language has such extremes of imagery as Mr. Burke. . . .

His *language,* though copious, was not verbose. Every word had its peculiar force and application. His chief fault was that of overloading his sentences with secondary thoughts, which weakened the blow by dividing it. His style is, at times, more careless and inaccurate than might be expected in so great a writer. But his mind was on higher things. His idea of a truly fine sentence, as once stated to a friend, is worthy of being remembered. It consists, said he, in a union of thought, feeling, and imagery—of a striking truth and a corresponding sentiment, rendered doubly striking by the force and beauty of figurative language.[39]

[39] *Op. cit.,* pp. 239–240.

It will be remembered that Goodrich presents the full texts of the orator's important speeches. His conclusions can, therefore, be checked directly as to fact, and indirectly as to interpretation, by referring to the texts. This is important. Critics who appraise the talks of others are expected to quote sufficiently liberal portions of the speeches to give meaning and literary wholeness to their investigations. Failing to do so, they court the hazard of making their judgments and analyses seem perfunctory, dissociated from the living remarks which made the criticism necessary and significant. While this does not mean that critical estimates should be largely reviews of speeches, supported by extensive quotation, it suggests the advisability of quoting enough to give the reader a fair understanding of what was said and an appreciation of the relation between the critical comments and the text.

GOLDEN MEAN

The critic will recognize, of course, that a speaker may regard style as a means of opening the minds of hearers to his ideas, and yet run afoul of good practice in the wording of the speech. This may occur when the speaker, intent upon enforcing his point and convinced that certain devices or elements are properly adapted to that end, uses those elements in excess of the requirements for clear understanding. Thus a speaker may use more examples than are necessary or desirable; he may use more epigrammatic statements than can properly be understood by the hearers in a limited time; he may make more appeals to visual imagery than can have any appreciable effect upon the ability of the hearers to comprehend a given thought.

The Golden Mean has special relevancy to speech length. For time has something to do with oral style, as it has with taste—to which style is closely related. We recall reading somewhere (possibly in a book by Saint Exupéry) about some Moorish chieftains who were taken to see a giant waterfall. After they had gazed upon the wonder for what the guide thought was an interminable period, he asked them what they were waiting for. "To see it stop," they said. Untold listeners in voluntary or captive audiences often feel the same way about torrents of words. Restraint is a mark of good style, for it is boorish, as F. L. Lucas reminded us, to waste a reader's or listener's time. Temper this reflection, however, with the countering advice that "if brevity becomes an end in itself, it becomes an irrelevance." [40]

Consequently, the critic will look for proportion in the use of language. There is a point—difficult to determine because of the variable nature of

[40] Charles W. Ferguson, "A Sane Approach to Style." *Saturday Review*, September 26, 1959, p. 34.

speaking situations—at which the speaker can strike the balance between excess and deficiency; a point at which there is neither too much nor too little, be it of illustrations, long sentences, parables, or any other element of clearness or impressiveness. This is nothing more than a restatement of Aristotle's Golden Mean, applied to the speaker's style of expression. It simply means that in the light of a given set of conditions a speaker must know how much of any material *can* be used without loss of interest and comprehension by the audience, and how much *must* be used to insure the likelihood of getting the intended response. This is a personal matter, varying from speaker to speaker and from situation to situation. That is what makes stylistic analysis a difficult aspect of speech criticism.

A RHETORICAL VIEW OF STYLE

Let us look at another conception of the role of style in public speaking. It is not new, but it provides a different focus. It takes us back to the basic principle of communication. Richard Steele put it well in his essay on "Conversational Talent." He remarked that many people attempt to be eloquent before they can speak; they "affect the flowers of rhetoric before they understand the parts of speech" and hence many talk well, but few are understood. "The matter is not to make themselves understood, but admired." Steele's observation reminds us that we speak to communicate ideas, not to display artifices which may hinder the expressive function.

Throughout the series of operations involved in the preparation of a speech, the speaker uses and works with words. He relies upon a process of symbolic formulation—a process which imposes severe demands of accuracy, specificity, and clarity upon language. The extent to which a speaker's control of meanings through words is successful will be revealed when he finally delivers his speech. The expression which he then gives to his ideas, together with whatever rhetorical devices he uses to enhance effectiveness, may be called his style.

To the critic of public speaking, style should not be regarded as a mysterious quality. It is not a combination of esoteric elements which are added to a speech, or superimposed upon it, in order to give it literary acceptability. According to the broad conception, style or language is important only to the extent that it helps prepare and subsequently open the minds of the hearers to the ideas developed in the speech. Far from regarding style as a static consideration, this view makes it functional, variable, and personal. Whether the speech contains beauty in the formal sense of meeting the requirements of traditional standards of aesthetics; whether the speech is a model of purity in language usage as determined by abstract criteria—these are auxiliary considerations. If these highly desirable qualities can be achieved without the loss of the more important and immediate consideration—the acquisition of the response for which the speaker is striving—then, surely, the speaker is interested in them. But they are ancillary matters, except as they contribute to the basic purpose of style, which is to prepare the minds of the hearers for the speaker's purpose and ideas.

We may look upon style, therefore, as a medium through which a speaker tries to secure a response. Like all other aspects of a speech, this one takes us back to the concept of rhetorical adaptation. There is no such thing as *a* style for a particular speaker. True, the speaker may have certain characteristics which stamp his language pattern from others. But in many cases those marks are related to delivery or speaking mannerisms. Style becomes a function of the elements in the speech situation; thus the language employed in a speech is variable. It will be subject to the influences of the speaker's background, his experience, the end he wishes to achieve, the ability and willingness of the audience to comprehend the ideas, and the peculiar conditions surrounding the occasion.

According to this conception, style is neither a mysterious embellishment added to a speech nor a literary veneer superimposed upon it. Instead, it represents the way in which a language pattern is used, under a given set of conditions, (1) to make ideas acceptable and (2) to get the response sought by the speaker. Style becomes the instrumentality through which ideas are made meaningful; it clothes the reason and emotion of the speaker in words that will have influence.

Components

The essential components of a speaker's style are aspects of the communicative act. An effective style—that is, one capable of preparing and opening the minds of the listeners for a particular subject—depends upon a speaker's having (1) an idea worth presenting, (2) an unmistakably clear conception of the idea, (3) a desire to communicate it, (4) a willingness to adapt it to a particular set of circumstances, and (5) a mastery of language adequate to express the idea in words.

We must keep in mind, of course, that an analytical breakdown of the "components" of style will never reveal completely the unique essence of a speaker's language. In the synthesis, new attributes—intangible and personal—ultimately give the style its distinctive character. Like humor and frogs, style can be dissected, but as E. B. White once said of humor, "the thing dies in the process and the innards are discouraging. . . ."[41] Nonetheless, certain rhetorical instruments or devices do, under proper conditions and use, contribute to the effectiveness of discourse.

[41] *The Second Tree from the Corner.* New York, p. 173.

Let us conclude with three questions: Does the speaker's style serve as an instrument of adjustment—as the cohesive element which adapts language to the end he seeks? Does it reveal him as a man of integrity who seriously cares about what he says? Does his expression contribute fully to the communication of ideas and the acquisition of the intended response? A speaker's words are appraised for their function. Stella Benson once remarked that words "are like citizens in cities; as long as they live in accord with their neighbours, they are beyond outside challenge." Their "neighbors" in this case are the conditions of the speech situation: the speaker himself, his purpose, his subject matter, the audience, the time, and the place. In a sense, this is a return to the doctrine of decorum, or propriety, as an essential quality of style.

EXERCISES

1. Summarize and comment on Georges-Louis LeClerc de Buffon's "Discourse on Style" (in Rollo W. Brown, *The Writer's Art* [Cambridge, Harvard University Press, 1921, pp. 277–288]).
2. Study Thomas De Quincey's "Style as Organic and Mechanic," from his *Essay on Style* (Cf. Brown, pp. 295–301).
3. Evaluate the style in one of the following:
   (*a*) John F. Kennedy's "Inaugural Address" (*Representative American Speeches, 1960–1961*, pp. 36–39).
   (*b*) Douglas MacArthur's "Duty, Honor and Country."
   (*c*) Adlai Stevenson's "Eulogy of Eleanor Roosevelt" (*Representative American Speeches, 1962–1963*, pp. 178–183).
   (*d*) Martin Luther King, Jr.'s "I Have a Dream" (*Representative American Speeches, 1963–1964*, pp. 43–48).
4. Compare and contrast one of Woodrow Wilson's essays with one of his representative speeches on a similar theme with respect to qualities of style. Suggested examples: Woodrow Wilson's "First Inaugural Address," March 5, 1913 (in James M. O'Neill, *Models of Speech Composition*, New York, Century Co., 1922, pp. 488–491); and Woodrow Wilson's "The New Freedom" (in Willard Thorp, Merle Curti, and Harold Baker, *American Issues*, Vol. I, *The Social Record*. Chicago, J. B. Lippincott Co., 1941, pp. 873–878).
5. Study and evaluate the figures of speech in a representative address by Robert G. Ingersoll ("Eulogy at His Brother's Grave," in W. Norwood Brigance's *Classified Speech Models* [New York, F. S. Crofts & Co., 1928, pp. 400–402]; or Wendell Phillips' "Eulogy on Daniel O'Connell" [*ibid.*, pp. 373–400]).
6. Compare a speech from the Bible with a contemporary orator's address on a similar theme (*e.g.*, a dedicatory speech of today with Solomon's consecration of the temple, *Chronicles* II, 6).
7. Read "On Metaphor" by Howard Nemerov in the Autumn, 1969, issue of *The Virginia Quarterly Review* (pages 621–636). Assess the use of metaphorical expressions in a well-known speech, for example, Franklin D. Roosevelt's "Quarantine Speech" in Chicago on October 5, 1937.
8. In his essay "Economists and the History of Ideas" (*American Economic*

Review, 52:6, March, 1962), Paul A. Samuelson refers to Yale's Tjalling Koopmans, a good writer himself, as holding an austere stylistic conviction: "Exceptionally fine writing is a biasing factor which might bring to an argument more attention and credence than it really deserved." Appraise this view, citing examples from speechmaking to confirm your answer.

9. Many addresses have been given on the theme of the "American scholar." Make an extensive comparative analysis of selected orations on the subject, beginning with Edward Tyrrel Channing's "Literary Independence" of August 27, 1818, and including Ralph Waldo Emerson's "The American Scholar" of August 31, 1837; Gerald W. Johnson's "The Provincial Scholar" of April 26, 1955; Howard Mumford Jones' "The Scholar as American" of October 3, 1960; and James B. Conant's "Man Thinking About Man" of June 9, 1964.

CLASS PROJECT (Continued)

In 1,000 words or less, evaluate the language of your speaker. Consider the factors of clarity and meaningfulness.

READINGS

CARROLL C. ARNOLD. "The Speech Style of Benjamin Disraeli." *Quarterly Journal of Speech,* 33:427–436 (December, 1947).

GLADYS BORCHERS. "An Approach to the Problem of Oral Style." *Quarterly Journal of Speech,* 22:114–117 (February, 1936).

A. CRAIG BAIRD. *Rhetoric: A Philosophical Inquiry.* New York, The Ronald Press Company, 1965. Ch. 8, "Language and Style."

STANLEY BURNSHAW. "Speaking Versus Writing." *Today's Speech,* 6:16–19 (September, 1958).

DONALD C. BRYANT. "Of Style." *Western Speech,* 21:103–110 (Spring, 1957).

——. "Aspects of Rhetorical Tradition: Emotion, Style, and Literary Association." *Quarterly Journal of Speech,* 36:326–332 (October, 1950).

MONROE C. BEARDSLEY. "Style and Good Style." In *New Rhetorics,* MARTIN STEINMANN, JR., ed. New York, Charles Scribner's Sons, 1967. Pp. 191–213.

JOHN CIARDI. "The Act of Language." In *Adventures of the Mind.* Edited by RICHARD THRUELSEN and JOHN KOBLER. Second series. New York, Random House, 1962. Pp. 311–323.

DALLAS C. DICKEY. "Were They Ephemeral and Florid?" *Quarterly Journal of Speech,* 32:16–20 (February, 1946).

HENRY LEE EWBANK. "Four Approaches to the Problem of Speech Style." *Quarterly Journal of Speech,* 17:458–465 (November, 1931).

RAY EHRENSBERGER. "An Experimental Study of the Relative Effectiveness of Certain Forms of Emphasis in Public Speaking." *Speech Monographs,* 12:94–111 (1945).

CHARLES W. FERGUSON. "A Sane Approach to Style." *Saturday Review,* 42:12–14 (September 26, 1959).

WALTER R. FISHER. "The Importance of Style in Systems of Rhetoric." *Southern Speech Journal,* 27:173–182 (Spring, 1962).

EDMUND GOSSE. "Style." *Encyclopaedia Britannica,* Chicago, Encyclopaedia Britannica, Inc., 1959. Vol. 21, p. 488.

GILES W. GRAY and WALDO W. BRADEN. *Public Speaking: Principles and Practice,* 2d ed. New York, Harper and Row, 1963. Chs. XXV, XXVI, and XXVII.

ROBERT GRAY GUNDERSON. "Lincoln's Rhetorical Style." *Vital Speeches of the Day*, 27:273–275 (February 15, 1961).

NANCY HALE. "The Two-Way Imagination." In *Adventures of the Mind*. Edited by RICHARD THRUELSEN and JOHN KOBLER. New York, Vintage Books, 1963. Pp. 65–77.

S. I. HAYAKAWA. *Language in Thought and Action*, 2d ed. London, George Allen and Unwin, 1965.

MOSES HADAS. "Style the Repository." *The American Scholar*, 34:213–219 (Spring, 1965).

GILBERT HIGHET. "The Gettysburg Address." In *Readings in Speech*, HAIG A. BOSMAJIAN, ed. New York, Harper and Row, 1965. Pp. 240–247.

MARIE HOCHMUTH, ed. *A History and Criticism of American Public Address*, Vol. III. New York, Russell & Russell, 1955. (Examine appraisals of style, pp. 34–36, 89–93, 121–122, 169–171, 187, 239–240, 402–403, 447–449, 505–515.)

HOYT H. HUDSON. "The Field of Rhetoric." *Quarterly Journal of Speech Education*, 9:167–180 (April, 1923).

WENDELL JOHNSON. "The Spoken Word and the Great Unsaid." *Quarterly Journal of Speech*, 37:419–429 (December, 1951).

F. L. LUCAS. *Style*. New York, Collier Books, 1962.

MARTIN MALONEY. "Language and Semantics." In *Introduction to the Field of Speech*, edited by RONALD F. REID. Chicago, Scott, Foresman & Co., 1965. Pp. 14–27.

HOWARD H. MARTIN. "'Style' in the Golden Age." *Quarterly Journal of Speech*, 43:374–382 (December, 1957).

RICHARD MURPHY. "The Speech as Literary Genre." *Quarterly Journal of Speech*, 44:117–127 (April, 1958).

ROGER NEBERGALL. "An Experimental Investigation of Rhetorical Clarity." *Speech Monographs*, 25:243–254 (November, 1958).

C. K. OGDEN and I. A. RICHARDS. *The Meaning of Meaning*. London, Routledge and Kegan Paul, 1923.

WAYLAND M. PARRISH. "The Rhythm of Oratorical Prose." In *Studies in Rhetoric and Public Speaking in Honor of James A. Winans*. New York, Century Co., 1925. Pp. 217–231.

———. "The Style of Robert B. Ingersoll." In *Studies in Speech and Drama in Honor of Alexander M. Drummond*. Ithaca, New York, Cornell University Press, 1944. Pp. 393–411.

ELAINE PAGEL. "Concepts of Perspicuity as a Factor in Public Speaking." *Quarterly Journal of Speech*, 26:38–44 (February, 1940).

RALPH POMEROY. "Aristotle and Cicero: Rhetorical Style." *Western Speech*, 25:25–35 (Winter, 1961).

A. QUILLER-COUCH. *A Lecture on Lectures*. London, Hogarth Press, 1927. Pp. 18–21.

I. A. RICHARDS. *The Philosophy of Rhetoric*. New York, Oxford University Press, 1936.

DAVID RIESMAN. *The Oral Tradition, The Written Word, and the Screen Image*. Antioch, Ohio, Antioch Press, 1956.

DONALD E. SIKKINK. "An Experimental Study of the Effects on the Listener of Anti-climax Order and Authority in an Argumentative Speech." *Southern Speech Journal*, 22:73–78 (Winter, 1956).

STEPHEN SPENDER. "The Connecting Imagination." In *Adventures of the Mind*. Edited by RICHARD THRUELSEN and JOHN KOBLER. Second Series. New York, Random House, 1962. Pp. 21–33.

HERMANN G. STELZNER. "'War Message,' December 8, 1941: An Approach to Language." *Speech Monographs*, 33:419–437 (November, 1966).

RICHARD M. WEAVER. "The Spaciousness of Old Rhetoric." In *The Ethics of Rhetoric*. Chicago, Henry Regnery Co., 1953. Pp. 164–185.

JOSHUA WHATMOUGH. *Language*. New York, New American Library, 1957.

17

The Delivery
of the Speech

IMPORTANCE IN RHETORIC

Losing favor in Athens, Aeschines, the great adversary of Demosthenes, moved on to the island of Rhodes. To entertain the Rhodians he read the famous speech that he had spoken against Ctesiphon at the time when Demosthenes was on the defense. Upon entreaty he read the following day his rival's reply "in a very attractive and loud voice." When his listeners expressed enthusiasm for his interpretation, Aeschines, supposedly replied, "How much more you would have admired it if you had heard Demosthenes himself!" Remembering well the power of his opponent, Aeschines knew the importance of delivery.[1]

Some years ago, after he had delivered a speech at Columbia University, Heywood Broun wrote in his daily column that he had learned one thing about public speaking, even though it had not been of great use to him. "People respond less to ideas," he remarked, "than to particular vocal tones." He added that he was informed a certain note played on a violin could bring down a bridge. On this observation he reflected: "That may not be true, but it is sure that there can be such a thing as a sound within the throat which will bring down a house."[2]

In Broun's comments we find the modern facsimile of an ancient conviction. From the beginning of the art of speaking, there has been a full recognition of the need for effective delivery; but coupled with this acknowledgement has been the suspicion, if not open distrust, of the use

[1] *Cicero's De Oratore.* Translated by H. Rackham. Cambridge, Harvard University Press, 1948, pp. 169–170 (III, lv).
[2] *New York World-Telegram,* 1932.

of vocal manipulation to induce responses from listeners. Aristotle commented very briefly on delivery, and that only because he believed the imperfections of hearers made it essential. He did not regard delivery as an elevated topic of inquiry; and he would have preferred that ideas be received upon their own demonstrable merit, rather than upon the auxiliary support of vocal management. It is reported that Demosthenes, on an occasion when his voice failed him, and the audience hissed, cried out: "Ye are to judge of players, indeed, by their voice, but of orators by the gravity of their sentences." [3] Admirable as such a condition might be, it has never existed, and probably never will; so we must equate delivery with the total rhetorical process, assessing its value in the light of the support it gives to an orator's effort to elicit responses from an audience.

FINDING INFORMATION ABOUT DELIVERY

The critic may experience great difficulty in locating *eye* and *ear* witnesses for the speeches he wishes to study. When observers do notice voice and visible action, they may squeeze in a sentence or two on the subject among other matters, and most often what is said is subjective, inexact, and confusing. But it is upon such scraps and pieces that a biographer must rely for whatever he reports on delivery, and that the rhetorical critic must depend in assessing the worth of a man's speaking.

The problems of studying delivery became evident to one of the authors of this book when he attempted to find information on Lincoln's voice.[4] A search of Lincolniana turned up few direct comments on Lincoln's voice and action, but it revealed that almost everything else, from Lincoln's romances to his reading preferences, had received book-length treatments. What does remain on the subject of voice is flavored with political bias and the journalistic excesses of the day. More or less typical is an 1848 remark in the *Bristol County Democrat* of Taunton, Massachusetts, describing Lincoln's voice: "His awkward gesticulation, the ludicrous management of his voice and the comical expression of his countenance, all conspired to make his hearers laugh at the mere anticipation of the joke before it appeared." [5]

Recently the Lincoln scholar Louis A. Warren devoted an entire book to the Gettysburg Address, meticulously examining the event. But of some two hundred pages, he included one paragraph of less than 200

[3] *Lives of the Ten Orators.* In *Plutarch's Essays and Miscellanies.* New York, 1905, V, 52.

[4] Waldo W. Braden. "Lincoln's Voice." *Lincoln Herald*, 67:111–116 (Fall, 1965).

[5] Ray P. Basler, ed. *The Collected Works of Abraham Lincoln.* New Brunswick, New Jersey, Rutgers University Press, 1953. II, 7.

words and five scattered references to Lincoln's "vibrant voice." He cites sentence-or-less descriptions of three ear witnesses, two of whom are not identified, and four reminiscences, made long after the occasion.[6]

Biographers tell us that Lincoln had a high-pitched voice. What does this phrase mean? Ear witnesses described the vocal quality as follows: "His voice is not heavy, but it has a clear trumpet tone"; "his voice, though sharp and powerful at times, has a frequent tendency to dwindle into a shrill and unpleasant sound"; "soft and sympathetic as a girl's"; "excited in its shrill tones, sometimes almost disagreeable." These fragments, open to a variety of interpretations, tell the reader almost nothing about what is meant by "high-pitched."[7]

What information is available about Lincoln's bodily action? The posed pictures, the only ones available, verify that he was tall, awkward, and ill clothed, but they suggest nothing about how he behaved on the platform. Statements from *eye* witnesses are no easier to locate than those of *ear* witnesses.

Biographers and historians have written of the dramatic and impelling delivery of Patrick Henry, Daniel Webster, Stephen A. Douglas, William L. Yancey, Robert G. Ingersoll, and Wendell Phillips. But the concrete evidence upon which these opinions were based is tenuous because it comes from untrained casual observers who happened to record their reactions when writing about other matters.

To evaluate a speaker who was prominent before 1920, before extensive collections of newsreels and recordings, the critic can do little more than report what others have said; consequently, to determine what delivery contributed to a speaker's power is most difficult. At the outset, therefore, we suggest that whatever the critic says on the subject should be carefully qualified.

Study of Recent Orators

Since 1920 more primary source material, including recordings and newsreels, has become available for analysis. Radio necessitates extensive recording; television adds the video dimension. But generally speaking critics have been timid about attempting to assess the influence of delivery upon effectiveness. Growing interest in rhetorical criticism occasionally has stirred the study of this aspect of a contemporary figure. Ernest Bormann, for example, based a dissertation on Huey P. Long upon recordings supplied from the archives of radio networks.[8] James Stansell

[6] *Lincoln's Gettysburg Declaration: A New Birth of Freedom.* Fort Wayne, Indiana, Lincoln National Life, 1964.

[7] Braden, *op. cit., passim.*

[8] Ernest G. Bormann. *A Rhetorical Analysis of the National Radio Broadcasts of Senator Huey P. Long.* Ph.D. thesis. State University of Iowa, 1953.

made a careful analysis of the delivery of Eric Johnston by viewing news-reels and by direct observation.[9] Under the direction of C. M. Wise, one of the best phoneticians of the period, Joseph Mele prepared a detailed analysis of the dialectal characteristics of Harry S. Truman.[10] Brandenburg and Braden did a phonetic analysis of the diction of Franklin D. Roosevelt.[11] Perhaps the increased interest in linguistics as well as the coming of the speech scientist should open up new techniques and quantitative research. At present primary source materials are being accumulated to challenge the critic who is imaginative and resourceful.

THE CRITIC'S VIEW

Eager to see the speaker in full dimension, the critic must consider at least four elements: (1) the mode of delivery, (2) general appearance, (3) bodily action, and (4) voice, including articulation and pronunciation. The key concern of the critic must center around what these four attributes added to the meaning and acceptability of the message, how they served as causal factors in gaining attention, holding interest, and in stirring the speaker's desired response, and what part they played in the emerging image of the speaker.

ANALYZING THE ORATOR'S MODE OF DELIVERY

There are probably as many methods of delivery as there are public speakers. Each orator has his own way of going about the business of delivering a talk. Whatever the method, the critic will want to discover it. In general, the critic should find out whether the speech is delivered impromptu, from memory, from manuscript, or extempore; and, if the latter, whether the man spoke with or without notes. The orator's own reflections on his method, when obtainable, are of real service.

Delivery is of course closely related to speech preparation. The impromptu speaker may not have the control over his voice and body that comes with having a manuscript in hand. A memory slip may upset a presentation. A well prepared manuscript may stimulate a forceful presentation, while a pile of cumbersome notes may bring defeat. What the speaker takes to the platform may provide the critic with suggestive clues as to effectiveness. For example, Mary Louise Gehring found that over

[9] James J. Stansell. *A Rhetorical Study of the Public Speaking of Eric A. Johnston During His Presidency of the United States Chamber of Commerce.* Ph.D. thesis, Louisiana State University, 1951.

[10] Joseph C. Mele. *Harry S. Truman's Pronunciation During His Presidency.* M.A. thesis. Louisiana State University, 1956.

[11] Earnest Brandenburg and Waldo W. Braden. "Franklin D. Roosevelt's Voice and Pronunciation." *Quarterly Journal of Speech,* 38:23–30 (February, 1952).

a period of fifty years Russell Conwell presented his famous lecture "Acres of Diamonds" from a loose topical outline haphazardly scribbled on a single sheet of paper.[12] Into this loose structure he could insert recent incidents and local color.

The inability of Herbert Hoover to read from a manuscript explains why he was overshadowed by Franklin D. Roosevelt in 1932 in reaching the radio audience. His impromptu speaking ability and the common man touch had much to do with Harry S. Truman's success on rear-platform appearances that helped win the 1948 election. The constant editing of his speech manuscripts right up until the moment of delivery suggests why Adlai Stevenson had difficulty fitting his speeches into a tight radio schedule.

The public address system, television, and the teleprompter are significantly influencing public address. How should the speech utilizing these mechanical and electronic devices be classified? Although they are read, they are presented in a manner to suggest directness and close proximity. Chet Huntley, N.B.C. news commentator, has said: "The microphone has tuned the ear of the audience to subtleties. . . . The camera can suit the action to the word. It can reveal, unerringly and indelibly, the twinkle of expression about the eyes, the trace of a smile, the foregathering of a frown." [13] The Nixon-Kennedy television debates of 1960 demonstrated influences of the mass media. The temperature of the studio, the color of a shirt, the make-up, the lens opening and angle became important elements in this confrontation. Many persons believe that the television camera had much to do with the outcome of the election. One authority thinks that "political television" has become "a giant supermarket for the projection of personality." [14]

In this same vein Harvey Wheeler, professor of political science at Washington and Lee University, has made some shrewd observations about the impact of television upon delivery.

Television also has a built-in situational bias regarding style of delivery. The orator haranguing a partisan rally develops a special technique for that situation. It is one that responds to exaggeration and caricature. Exaggeration of dress, of physique, of mannerism, of gesture, of diction, and of content was characteristic of the traditional orator. The major arguments had to be developed with a special cadence of thrust and pause until an organic revivalist response could be elicited from the aroused partisans. In the

[12] Mary Louise Gehring. *The Invention of Russell H. Conwell in His Lecture "Acres of Diamonds."* M.A. thesis, Louisiana State University, 1951. For copy of Conwell's notes see Waldo W. Braden and Mary Louise Gehring. *Speech Practices.* New York, Harper and Row, 1958, p. 1.

[13] Chet Huntley. "What's Happened to the Spellbinder?" *TV Guide,* Vol. 4, No. 42:10–11 (October 20, 1956).

[14] Malcolm Moos. *The Great Debates.* An Occasional Paper published by the Center for the Study of Democratic Institutions, 1962, p. 8.

hands of a master like Alben Barkley it was possible in this way to develop a powerful emotional dialectic between speaker and audience. Partisans viewing such an event on television figuratively transport themselves to the scene and become emotionally involved with the actual audience. . . .

But when a television debate like that between Kennedy and Nixon is stated, it is television's intrinsic bias that obtains. Both candidates are present together. . . . There is no direct or immediate mass response to the speakers to provide the home viewers with vicarious emotional involvement in the proceedings. The viewer is isolated, atomized, and relaxed. He is in intimate contact with each speaker by turns. It is the setting of a living-room conversation, not a mass rally. In such a setting all of the exaggerations that have a positive effect on a mass rally have a negative effect on the living-room viewer.[15]

PHYSICAL FACTORS

A second inquiry which may yield interesting information on the ways of a speaker is: Do the speaker's appearance and physical characteristics contribute to his effectiveness? There has been some disposition to build up a stereotype of the orator as a large, imposing-looking person. Presumably it is felt that a man of majestic mien has a better chance of success with the fluctuating behavior of audiences than a man of less attractive bearing. Thus we read that certain orators "looked their part"; prominently mentioned among them are Bryan, Chatham, Bright, La Follette, Webster, and Phillips. Chauncey Goodrich attributes some of Lord Chatham's success to "his extraordinary personal advantages." "In his best days . . . his figure was tall and erect; his attitude imposing." Indeed, Goodrich observes, few men "have ever received from the hand of Nature so many of the outward qualifications of an orator." [16]

The uncritical acceptance of striking physical appearance as an index of oratorical excellence is not recommended. The way an orator looks—the way he impresses his hearers as a physical specimen—is an accessory. Stephen Douglas was a short man, but his oratory was not correspondingly diminutive. And Edmund Burke "derived little or no advantage from his personal qualifications. He was tall, but not robust; his gait and gesture were awkward; his countenance, though intellectual, was destitute of softness, and rarely relaxed into a smile; and as he always wore spectacles, his eye gave him no command over an audience.[17]

Gregg Phifer carefully researched available publications to learn about the appearance of Andrew Johnson at the time he made his famous "swing around the circle" in 1866. Phifer suggests how Johnson's physical characteristics contributed to the speaker's effectiveness.

[15] Harvey Wheeler. *The Great Debates*, p. 16.
[16] *Select British Eloquence*. New York, 1853, p. 71.
[17] *Ibid.*, p. 237.

Photographs, drawings, and word pictures of Johnson reveal, if not a handsome man, at least an impressive one, whose physical appearance must have enhanced rather than detracted from his effectiveness as a speaker. He stood five feet ten, was "square built, broad-chested . . . compact . . . manly . . ." His was a build for strength and endurance.

The President's face and head were imposing. One reporter described Johnson's body as "merely a suitable pedestal for his massive head." Even Charles Dickens, whose recollections of things American were seldom complimentary, thought he could have picked out Johnson from any crowd as "a character of mark." In an age of profuse whiskers the President was smooth-shaven, swarthy of countenance. But the dominant feature of his face, all agree, was his eyes, dark, sparkling, penetrating. Even the passionately Radical Chicago *Republican* (September 3) paid him this left-handed compliment: "Nearly all, in speaking of the President, agree that he is not as ugly as they had expected to find him." The President's full head of hair had originally been black, but since at the time of the swing around the circle Johnson was fifty-seven years old, his hair was sprinkled with white in an iron gray. . . .

Johnson's dress matched his appearance. He was a tailor, and a good one. His dress reflected his occupation. Ben Truman, who as one of the White House secretaries had wide opportunity to observe, called him "one of the neatest men in his dress and person I have ever known," adding that "he was so scrupulous about his linen that he invariably changed all of it daily, and sometimes oftener." Colonel E. C. Reeves, for many years his secretary after he left the White House, called him "always neat in person and attire," testifying that "his well-fitting apparel was as appropriate as a lady well-dressed, fresh from her boudoir." The *World*, in the same report cited earlier, pictured him at the opening of the swing around the circle as "decently clad in a sober and somewhat worn black frock-coat. . . ."

Johnson radiated strength and power, not conciliation or good humor. His massive head, swarthy skin, iron-gray hair, and penetrating black eyes combined to impress the observer or listener with a feeling that here was a man to remember.[18]

However, the critic who would give his readers a picture of a speaker should consider even the "nonessentials." Oftentimes these "nonessentials" figure prominently in the judgments of men; and it is the critic's job to analyze the reason speeches do or do not take root in the hearers' lives. In all probability, rhetorical effectiveness can be enhanced by the impress of a striking personality.

BODILY ACTION IN SPEAKING

How does the speaker manage himself while he is on the platform? What of his bodily action, his movement on the stage, and his gestures? Does he supplement his words with appropriate action? These and other

[18] Gregg Phifer. "Andrew Johnson Delivers His Argument." *Tennessee Historical Quarterly*, 11:225–227 (September, 1952).

questions have been asked by critics since antiquity. Cicero found Publius Antistius' delivery blameworthy because of "a few ridiculous gestures, of which he could not entirely break himself." And Curio's action was such as to provoke ridicule: the swaying and reeling of his body from side to side prompted Julius to inquire *who it was that was speaking from a boat?*" On another occasion when Curio and Octavius, then consuls, had been summoned to the forum, and Curio had given a tiresome harangue, "while Octavius sat silently by him, wrapped up in flannels, and besmeared with ointments, to ease the pain of the gout," Cnaeus Sicinius said: "*Octavius, you are infinitely obliged to your colleague; for if he had not tossed and flung himself about today in the manner he did, you would certainly have been devoured by the flies.*" [19]

For an object of praise Cicero looked to the gestures of Antonius. His actions were such as "to correspond to the meaning of every sentence, without beating time to the words." In a singular manner, his "hands, his shoulders, the turn of his body, the stamp of his foot, his posture, his air, and, in short, all his motions, were adapted to his language and sentiments." [20]

In our search for data relating to the bodily action of the orators of the past we turn to the testimony of their contemporaries, or of those who knew contemporaries. Thus N. W. Wraxall comments on Richard Sheridan's manner of speaking:

His countenance and features had in them something peculiarly pleasing, indicative at once of intellect, humor, and gayety. All these characteristics played about his lips when speaking and operated with inconceivable attraction; for they anticipated, as it were, to the eye the effect produced by his oratory on the ear. . . .[21]

This is properly a part of delivery in the stricter sense. Goodrich refers to the Younger Pitt's harsh features, but observed that they were "lighted up with intelligence by the flashes of eye," and his "gesture was animated, but devoid of grace. . . ." To Thomas Erskine, Goodrich also attributes an "animated gesture." And John P. Curran, the Irish orator, had, Goodrich says, "an eye that glowed like a live coal." Sir James Mackintosh says that Charles Fox gave an initial impression of being awkward, but after a time no one thought of anything except his ideas and the lucid simplicity with which he developed them.

Observers and critics of oratory look, then, to such physical manifestations as grace of movement on the platform, facility in gesticulation,

---

[19] *Brutus.* LX.
[20] *Ibid.,* XXXVIII.
[21] *Select British Eloquence,* p. 404.

meaningful use of facial expression, and the effective use of the eyes as instruments of audience control. Relative to the latter, it may be observed that the rhetoricians have long considered the action of the eyes important in oratory. Cicero mentioned the eyes, "by whose intense or languid gaze, as well as by their quick glances and gaiety" orators were able to reveal the workings of their mind. Quintilian was of the same opinion, believing that the mind manifested itself through the eyes. Gilbert Austin, emphasizing delivery above all other parts of rhetoric, regarded the eyes as the most expressive part of the countenance:

> As the principal object of every public speaker must be to obtain the attention of his audience; so every circumstance which can contribute to this end must be considered important. In the external demeanour nothing will be found so effectually to attract attention, and detain it, as the direction of the eyes. It is well known the eyes can influence persons at a distance; and that they can select from a multitude a single individual, and turn their looks on him alone, though many lie in the same direction. The whole person seems to be in some measure affected by this influence of another's eyes, but the eyes themselves feel it with the most lively sensibility.[22]

Additional insight into a speaker's ways is afforded through a study of his mannerisms and distinguishing habits of dress. For instance, the picture of John Bright is sharpened when we visualize his manner of taking a position before popular audiences. William Robertson comments on Bright's mild eccentricities as follows:

> . . . he is welcomed with deafening cheers, and waving of hats and handkerchiefs. He walks quietly toward the table, apparently unaffected by the excited reception, but a close observer might detect that it is with difficulty he suppresses his emotion. So anxious are they to hear him speak that the preliminaries of the meeting are hurried through, and at length the orator stands up. He is received with rapturous and sustained applause, and while they are enthusiastically greeting him he quietly arranges his position, places his hat on the table before him, and on the rim of it lays his scanty notes, and then surveys the vast assembly with subdued emotion.[23]

Goldwin Smith [24] tells us that when Bright finished with a note-sheet, he dropped it into the hat, and moved on to the next sheet.

Each orator provides the critic with new and different focuses of investigation. But the foregoing material suggests some of the leads the investigator should pursue. Since visual appeals operate to influence hearers, the critic will want to effect as complete a reconstruction of the original scene as possible.

[22] *Chironomia.* Edited by Mary Margaret Robb and Lester Thonssen. Carbondale, Illinois, 1966, p. 101.
[23] *Life and Times of the Right Hon. John Bright,* London, 1880, p. 558.
[24] *Reminiscences.* New York, 1910, p. 238.

VOICE AS A DETERMINANT

Finally, the critic must assess the vocal skill of the speaker. And here, as we have already indicated, the task takes a difficult turn. If the critic has not himself heard the speaker, as is more than likely, he must depend upon testimony which, even if trustworthy, is subject to verbal confusion. While one observer may pronounce an orator's speech "flat," another may call it "harsh"; and neither may be too exact in his definition of the terms. Judgments of voice require skill to an extent not ordinarily found in the untrained commentator. The lack of uniformity in nomenclature today attests to the difficulty inherent in the formulation of such opinions.

The nature of the problem is revealed by reference to a few observations by Goodrich in *Select British Eloquence*. Goodrich quotes Wraxall as saying the tones of Sheridan's voice were "singularly mellifluous" and unaccompanied by an "unpleasant Irish accent" such as Burke had. Apropos of Pitt's voice, Goodrich remarks that it was "full and clear, filling the largest room with the volume of sound." Erskine's voice was "somewhat shrill but beautifully modulated." Curran's speech "was uncommonly distinct and deliberate; the modulations of his voice were varied in a high degree, and perfectly suited to the widest range of his eloquence."

A comparison of ancient and modern criticism reveals that Goodrich, for instance, treated the subject of delivery (as far as it concerns vocal attributes) with no more comprehensiveness or acuity than did Cicero. In the *Brutus*, Cicero speaks of Cnaeus Pompeius' "sonorous and manly" voice; Publius Autronius had a "very clear and strong voice"; Caius Memmius' voice was "sweet and sonorous"; Antonius had a voice that was "strong and firm, though naturally hoarse." Here, as in much of contemporary criticism, loose terminology is a barrier to full understanding.

We do not infer that such observations are irresponsible; indeed, they are the composite judgments derived from careful research into the testimony of men who presumably knew what they were saying. But because the observations are couched in equivocal language, it is seldom easy to determine just what the distinguishing marks of the orator's vocal delivery were. Thanks to the present-day recording equipment, critics of the future will be able to deal more accurately with all phases of vocal delivery.

Testimony relative to articulation and pronunciation is also subject to a variety of vagaries. Omission of details seems to be one of the most conspicuous faults. The writers of memoirs and personal reflections on orators rarely discuss at any length the habits of diction cultivated by the speakers. In consequence, the full account of many orators' speaking accomplishments will remain permanently incomplete.

But some evidence concerning these matters is usually available and the discerning critic will assess its value in relation to the speaker's proper place in the history of public address. Phifer gives the reader an excellent view of the voice control and vocal problems of Andrew Johnson. He shows how these audio elements were important in the President's speaking in 1866.

In most speaking situations one of Johnson's most valuable assets was his voice. He spoke with a reserve of power that made listening easy. His voice was singularly penetrating, carrying to the edge of the largest gathering without effort. Yet it was always pleasant, 'low and sympathetic.' Senator McCreery of Kentucky remembered the charm of Johnson's speaking as 'due in a measure to the modulations of a clear, mellow voice, the tones of which rose and fell as passion, interest, or indifference predominated at the moment.'

At least two of the reporters who covered Johnson's tour were of the same opinion. The New York *World* thought that Johnson's voice had 'a quietness and ease not expected from the square-built, hard-visaged, cold-eyed statesman.' And the Cincinnati *Commercial* described the President's voice as 'resonant and far-reaching . . .'

Though the President was from eastern Tennessee, only one of the many reporters who heard him speak during his western excursion called special attention to his regional dialect. This was L. L. Walbridge, who, on the evening of September 8, reported for the *Missouri Democrat* Johnson's speech from the balcony of the Southern Hotel in St. Louis. During Walbridge's testimony at the impeachment trial House Manager Ben Butler asked whether or not the witness could 'give inaccuracies of pronunciation.' The reporter answered with a positive 'Yes, sir.' He thought, for example, that 'ware' rather than 'were' accurately represented the President's speech. . . .

Born in North Carolina and raised there, and later a resident of South Carolina and Tennessee, Johnson probably reflected in his speech many of the characteristics of his region. Since Radical papers used his southern origins as a point of attack, some of his defenders, probably including Henry F. Zider, thought it necessary to answer these charges along with many others.

Johnson's southern dialect was not the only factor in his voice to receive attention from the reporters. Toward the end of the first week and the beginning of the second week of his western tour newspaper reports began to tell of his hoarseness. On September 3 the *Daily Morning Chronicle* of Washington reported that 'the President is suffering from hoarseness owing to frequent and loud speaking, but in other respects is in good bodily condition.' The next day it continued: 'The voice of the President seems to be constantly failing and to-day he has seemed very much fatigued, but he bears up bravely and astonishes the reporters.' On September 4 the Chicago *Republican* said that Johnson's 'voice grows hoarser and hoarser,' adding on the following day that 'the President has become so hoarse that it is with difficulty he can speak; it is not likely that he will improve, as towards night he generally grows worse. . . .'

For seventeen days Johnson subjected himself and especially his voice to enormous strain. Neither radio nor public-address system aided his vigorous campaigning, and he could not even count on the newspapers to convey his message impartially to the people. He had to reach with un-aided voice the crowds, a few hundred to many thousand, that came to hear him. Should the President's hoarseness be attributed to strain? Then, how explain the fact that his voice got better rather than worse during the last two weeks of campaigning? After newspaper complaints from Albany, Cleveland, and Oberlin, and Johnson's own testimony during his Cleveland speech, how could he even keep going? Possibly he had a cold, though neither Welles nor the papers give any hint of this. Perhaps the two-night lay-over in Chicago helped him recover, though rainy weather dogged his footsteps through Illinois and Indiana. But, instead of quitting altogether, Johnson's voice seemed to get better with additional campaigning.[25]

PROBLEM IN ASSESSING DELIVERY

The critic's task is, then, peculiarly taxing. And the more remote the period in which an orator lived, perhaps the greater the difficulties. Hard as the assignment may be, however, it should not preclude the use of such reliable information as may be available. Recalling a remark attributed to St. Jerome, we may say: "Remote as we are from perfect knowledge, we deem it less blameworthy to say too little rather than nothing at all." Surely there are some facts with which the critic can deal, despite the limitations of testimony.

Fundamentally, the critic is desirous of getting data which shed light upon the speaker's skill in eliciting the intended response from his hearers. This means an interest in such matters as distinctness and loudness of utterance, the rate of speaking, and the pleasantness or unpleasantness of the vocal quality. In short, the critic asks, Was the delivery clear, intelligible, and pleasing?

While it is claimed—how responsibly no one can tell—that George Whitefield could be understood by a crowd of 20,000 in the open fields, it is known that other speakers could not reach the last row of an audience less than one-hundredth that size. In one of his early speeches at Castle Garden in 1850, William Maxwell Evarts is known to have "broken down" so that he was forced to withdraw, and chiefly because a large part of the audience could not hear and, in consequence, whistled and shouted.

Here, as elsewhere, however, the critic is concerned with the delivery of the *particular speech,* not the over-all estimate of the orator's delivery. Important and illuminating as the general estimate of a speaker's vocal skill is, it is subordinate to a penetrating understanding of its effectiveness on a *specific* occasion. After all, delivery is another *means* of achieving a response; it is not a terminal value. An important public speech is not

[25] Phifer, *op. cit.,* 227–31.

a satisfactory laboratory for testing a speaker's orotund qualities and pleasing cadences. Once the speaker takes the floor to develop an idea, we have a right to expect a lively enforcement of his thoughts. He is there to communicate something worth passing on. Delivery serves as a tool by which to enhance the impressiveness of the communication; it is not the focus of attention. If it were, it would be a distraction. There are places where men assemble to appreciate vocal artistry *in its own right*, but the platform of the public speaker is not one of them.

So the critic attempts to appraise a speaker's delivery in a given speech, to the end that he may the better understand why the audience responded as it did. He determines its congruency with the nature of the speech; its unobtrusiveness as a vehicle of communication; its intelligibility to the respondents; its agreeableness to the ear, generally. All these facts are not easy to find, but they still are relevant to the critical function. It is not a case of matter *vs.* manner; it is not a question of whether *what* is said is more important than *how* it is said. It is both *what* and *how* it is said that make for effectiveness in public address.

EXAMPLE OF THE ANALYSIS OF DELIVERY

The Kennedy-Nixon debates of 1960 stirred the interest of millions of Americans and led to considerable discussion about what factors contributed to the effectiveness of the speakers.

Harvey Wheeler, who was quoted earlier, provides us with an excellent criticism of delivery. In considering the Kennedy-Nixon debates, he had to assess how the two speakers adapted themselves to the medium of television.

The debates had only begun when it became apparent that the styles of delivery of the two candidates were not equally well adapted to the exploitation of television's built-in situational bias. Vice-President Nixon had long ago developed an effective oratorical technique for addressing mass partisan rallies. It held close to the traditional model and aimed at the emphasis and exaggeration of a few themes with large emotional potential. Mr. Nixon was fond of saying that he had studiously patterned his style after that of Harry Truman. Nixon's great success with the 'Checkers' speech probably deceived him into assuming that the same style was well adapted to a television debate. But the 'Checkers' speech was over a moral issue, not policy questions. And in that speech he was by himself on television—unchallenged by opponent or reporters. His audience was pre-structured on the basis of individual reactions to him as a person. As a result, in the first debate the Vice-President's style of delivery conspired to give him the appearance of ineptness. The gestures necessary in a mass rally appeared stagey and artificial in the conversational atmosphere of the living-room. Emotional issues which can be drummed into an organic audience of partisans seemed thin in an empty studio face to face with a pleasant Ivy-Leaguer with a hair-trigger mind. This unexpected failure of previously invincible methods probably accounts for the bewilderment and shock that Nixon and his supporters displayed after the first round. In the three following rounds, Nixon progressively adjusted his style to the specific situational bias created by the debates. But even at the end he was far from master of the situation.

Kennedy, on the other hand, was the fortuitous beneficiary of his oratorical defects. He is not an orator. He seems temperamentally unable to develop an emotional theme. He addresses a rally gestureless, inflectionless, and at a rate of speech so rapid as to render his arguments almost unintelligible. A Kennedy speech, especially at the beginning of the campaign, was the auditory counterpart of a page from the Appendix of the Congressional Record. Reporters who followed him were unanimous in their opinion that the masses who gathered to hear him were at their highest pitch of enthusiasm before he started to speak, with enthusiasm ebbing steadily to the end. Though he improved, Kennedy remained a woefully inept orator. However, the very characteristics that told against him on the hustings worked to his advantage in his debates with Nixon. His unadorned style of delivery fitted well into the viewer's living-room. And although his rapid rate of speech prevented much of his content from being assimilated, what did come through was the picture of a bright, knowledgeable young man of great earnestness, energy, and integrity.[26]

SUMMARY

It is clear that an investigation into the character of a speaker's delivery includes the two standard constituents of critical inquiry. First, it requires exacting research. Facts on a speaker's delivery are, at best, scattered, if not downright elusive. Only on rare occasions does the biographer or the commentator assemble such observations in one chapter or section. Instead, he weaves them into the fabric of his story. Furthermore, the sources from which such data stem are numerous—so numerous that the investigator cannot rest in his search until he has examined large portions of contemporary and near-contemporary literature. In his attempt to reveal the portrait of his chosen orator, he must first scrutinize the portraits of the men with whom the orator lived and worked. He who would know a particular man who participated in the important doings of society must be conversant with the social milieu in all its ramifications.

Secondly, the critical analysis of an orator's delivery requires severe testing of authorities. If the critic has not heard the orator, he must depend upon the word of those who did or of those who knew someone who did. The possibility of error is considerable, especially in view of the varying judgments as to whether an orator's rate was fast or slow, his articulation sharp or dull, his quality pleasing or unpleasing—and any number of other differences and disparities in definition. Accordingly, the critic must continue his role of logician, testing the evidence according

[26] Wheeler, *op. cit.*, p. 18.

to criteria discussed in Chapter 12. Only after he has culled the untenable observations and has accumulated the concurrent evidence is he in a position to estimate the speaker's skill in the management of voice and action.

EXERCISES

1. To what extent do experimental data on delivery assist the critic in evaluating modern oratory?
2. What tests must the critic apply to testimony concerning the delivery of an orator?
3. From the point of view of the critic, what is the relative importance of delivery in the final assessment of an oration's merit? How does it compare with the other parts of rhetoric, *i.e.*, invention, disposition, style, and memory?
4. Do you believe, as is often alleged, that audiences today are impatient of oratorical flourishes in both style and delivery?
5. Of reporter Edward R. Murrow, some felt that his "doom-edged, oracular" style and delivery were better adapted to telling about war and disaster than about the ordinary happenings in political life. For effectiveness, must the delivery fit the subject, as it were? Cite examples to confirm or refute this view.
6. Have styles of delivery changed? If possible, find descriptions of the delivery of such speakers as Stephen A. Douglas, Robert G. Ingersoll, Wendell Phillips, Woodrow Wilson, and John F. Kennedy.
7. Discuss the standard of naturalness as a criterion for judging delivery.
8. How have radio and television influenced the canon of delivery?
9. Does the teleprompter provide the critic with a problem in judging delivery?
10. Investigate the standards of delivery imposed upon the speaker by tradition in the House of Commons. Are there similar standards in the United States Senate?
11. What did Winston Churchill mean when he said: "We shape our buildings and afterwards our buildings shape us." (See Waldo W. Braden. "Speaking in the House of Commons," *Southern Speech Journal*, 34:67–74 [Winter, 1958].)
12. Compare Quintilian's discussion of delivery (found in the *Institutes of Oratory*, XI, III) with that found in modern textbooks on public speaking. What similarities do you find in the two treatments?

CLASS PROJECT (Continued)

In 1,000 words or less, summarize what *eye*witnesses tell you about the delivery of your speaker. If possible, include your direct observations of his platform technique.

READINGS

DAVID W. ADDINGTON. "The Effect of Mispronunciation on General Speaking Effectiveness." *Speech Monographs*, 32:159–163 (June, 1965).

WILLIAM A. BEHL. "Theodore Roosevelt's Principles of Speech Preparation and Delivery." *Speech Monographs,* 12:112–122 (1945).

JOHN WAITE BOWERS. "The Influence of Delivery on Attitudes toward Concepts and Speakers." *Speech Monographs,* 32:154–158 (June, 1965).

WALDO W. BRADEN. "Lincoln's Voice." *Lincoln Herald,* 67:111–116 (Fall, 1965).

EARNEST BRANDENBURG and WALDO W. BRADEN. "Franklin D. Roosevelt." In *History and Criticism of American Public Address.* Edited by MARIE HOCHMUTH. New York, Russell & Russell, 1955. III, 458–530.

———. "Franklin D. Roosevelt's Voice and Pronunciation." *Quarterly Journal of Speech,* 38:23–30 (February, 1952).

KEITH BROOKS, ed. *The Communicative Arts and Sciences of Speech.* Columbus, Ohio, Charles E. Merrill Books, 1967. Chs. 12–16.

OTTO A. DIETER. "Arbor Picta: The Medieval Tree of Preaching," *Quarterly Journal of Speech,* 41:123–144 (April, 1965).

GILES W. GRAY and WALDO W. BRADEN. *Public Speaking,* 2d ed. New York, Harper and Row, 1963.

FREDERICK W. HABERMAN. "English Sources of American Elocution." In *A History of Speech Education in America.* Edited by KARL WALLACE. New York, Appleton-Century-Crofts, Inc., 1954. Pp. 105–126.

DONALD E. HARGIS. "Memory in Rhetoric." *Southern Speech Journal,* 17:114–124 (December, 1951).

PAUL HEINBERG. "Relationships of Content and Delivery to General Effectiveness." *Speech Monographs,* 30:105–107 (June, 1963).

HERBERT W. HILDEBRANDT and WALTER W. STEVENS. "Manuscript and Extemporaneous Delivery in Communicating Information." *Speech Monographs,* 30:369–372 (November, 1963).

History and Criticism of American Public Address. W. N. BRIGANCE, ed. New York, Russell & Russell, 1943. See for Criticism of Delivery: Vol. I, 279–280, 473–474, 358–360; vol. II, 646–648, 675–676, 959–963.

WAYNE E. HOOGESTRAAT. "Memory: The Lost Canon?" *Quarterly Journal of Speech,* 46:141–147 (April, 1960).

ORVIN LARSON. *When It's Your Turn To Speak.* New York, Harper and Row, 1962. Ch. 8.

CHARLES MUDD and MALCOLM O. SILLARS. *Speech: Content and Communication.* San Francisco, Chandler Publishing Co., 1962. Ch. 15.

RICHARD MURPHY. "Theodore Roosevelt." In *History and Criticism of American Public Address.* Edited by MARIE HOCHMUTH. Vol. III. New York, Longmans, Green & Co., 1955. Pp. 355–358.

RAY NADEAU. "Delivery in Ancient Times: Homer to Quintilian." *Quarterly Journal of Speech,* 50:53–60 (February, 1964).

WAYLAND M. PARRISH. "The Concept of 'Naturalness.'" *Quarterly Journal of Speech,* 37:448–454 (December, 1951).

———. "Whately on Elocution." In *The Rhetorical Idiom.* Edited by DONALD C. BRYANT. Ithaca, New York, Cornell University Press, 1958. Pp. 43–52.

18

The Standards
of Effectiveness

SPEAKING AND AUDIENCE RESPONSE

Many years ago, an author published a book containing no punctuation marks. He was roundly criticized for it. So in the second edition he put a full page of marks at the end of the book, and invited the readers to "pepper and salt" the text with them as they saw fit. Perhaps the simplest way to deal with the subject of this chapter would be to list alphabetically the various standards by which speeches can be evaluated for effectiveness, and then ask the critic, creatively and imaginatively, to use the one or more which pleased his fancy and conviction. In a sense, that is what we do. We shall try to avoid arbitrary judgment, for this is a sensitive and uncertain area and only the crassest of presumption would prompt anyone to speak with a sense of finality on it. On the other hand, we have a point of view, as the foregoing chapters show. But we are fully mindful that no single measure of effectiveness—the one we favor generally, or any other—is likely to be satisfactory if used singly and routinely.

We believe that response is a major determinant of rhetorical effectiveness. Daniel O'Connell reportedly remarked that a "good speech is a good thing, but the verdict is *the* thing." A speech is intended to do something. It is a specific engagement of listeners on a specific occasion for an ostensibly specific purpose. The measures of effectiveness will vary with a host of conditions. Thus a ceremonial speech may not exercise a profound influence upon the life of a community, as far as observable changes in belief or action are concerned, and yet it may be a commendable piece of rhetoric. The judgment of such a speech will be made with the type of oratory constantly in mind. While the acquisition of a response will still be the end of the speaking activity, other factors will also figure prominently in its analysis—factors which might command less attention in the analysis of a deliberative speech on an occasion of great social urgency.

The effectiveness of oratory is a function of audience adaptation. The speech is viewed in the light of what people *do* as a result of hearing it. Some have held that great and extensive changes in audience behavior can be expected from hearing a speech; others are almost apologetically modest in their claims for the efficacy of the spoken word. Emerson believed that the secret of eloquence—be it in a half-hour's discourse or in a few sentences only—was "to persuade a multitude of persons to renounce their opinions, and change the course of life." [1] Through the influence of eloquence, he said, an audience can be made to go forth "not the men they came in, but shriven, convicted, and converted." Plutarch conceived of discourse exercising a purgative function. After listening to a speech, the hearer should "inspect diligently and try faithfully the state and temper of his mind" to see whether or not

. . . his affections are more moderate, if any afflictions grow lighter, if his constancy and greatness of spirit are confirmed, if he feels any divine emotions or inward workings of virtue and goodness upon his soul. For it becomes us but ill, when we rise from the barber's chair, to be so long in consulting the mirror, or to stroke our heads and examine so curiously the style in which our hair is trimmed and dressed, and then, at our return from hearing in the schools, to think it needless to look into ourselves, or examine whether our own mind has discharged any turbulent or unprofitable affections and is grown more sedate and serene. For, as Ariston was wont to say, the bath and a discourse are of no use unless they are purgative.[2]

While acknowledging the impact of wise words upon society, W. E. H. Lecky nevertheless believed that the influence is slow to make itself known. Saying that the wisdom of a teaching or of a policy is determined by its results, he remarks that "these results are in most cases very gradually disclosed." [3]

By its inherent nature, we believe, speech seeks response. If this is not true, then many textbooks preach a dubious doctrine, for they rest upon the durable assumption that speaking is purposive, and they provide an armory of instructions on how to achieve demonstrable results in informing, persuading, or entertaining hearers. Moreover, the theory usually underscores the fact that a speech situation embraces a complex cluster of variables; that there are different ways of doing the same thing under different conditions, and that the catalog of variabilities is so long

[1] *The Complete Writings of Ralph Waldo Emerson.* New York, 1929. II, 1030.
[2] *Plutarch's Miscellanies and Essays,* 6th ed. Boston, 1898, pp. 450–451.
[3] *Historical and Political Essays.* London, 1908, p. 9.

that pat, magical formulas of procedure have not yet been devised. If, indeed, this is a fair note on the practical application of rhetorical theory, then it would seem reasonable that the critical evaluation of speeches would have to be consonant with the theory. Otherwise we are assessing an art in a context alien to its natural setting, in fact one in which it does not actually flourish.

Admittedly, it is a difficult task to trace the effect of a speaker's words upon the public mind. Influences at work in an audience at a given moment are many and intricately interrelated. To establish causal relations between spoken words and subsequent actions or trends requires more than patience, more than a full understanding of the processes of history, more than a penetrating insight into the rhetorical art. It also requires a certain insensitivity to frustration, even failure, for there will be times when it seems next to impossible to check the results of a speech. But that is no cause for despair; other contributory standards of effectiveness will also be used in making the critical analysis. From them all should come a reasonably etched portrait of an orator, even though some important lines cannot be confidently incised because of the indecisiveness or unavailability of certain information. But the ease or difficulty with which criticism can be conducted is irrelevant. Nor is the concession that we cannot always find the answers to our questions germane. The nature of the imprecise disciplines makes that obvious. It is one of the limitations with which we must live. For that matter, it also applies to the sciences. If all experiments were successful the first time they were carried out, the shape of our society would be unrecognizably different. The failure of a scientific experiment is an invitation to further inquiry, information, and refinement of technique. It is no less so in rhetorical criticism, even though our soundest conclusions will partake of the *probable,* the unfinished. In our area, it could scarcely be otherwise. If we were *sure* of every judgment, faithfully arrived at, we would not be workers in the field of criticism.

THE RANGE OF EFFECTIVENESS

Effectiveness is not a fixed point. Rather, it is a spectrum, a continuum. Different speakers can be effective for different reasons, and even for contradictory reasons. Some are effective—in the pure, raw sense of eliciting responses—because what they say is packed with superlative ideas and argument. On the other hand, however, it is possible—again in the pure, raw sense—for a speaker to be effective without doing much thinking. A demagogue may give a talk which we consider irrational, contradictory, and nonsensical; but thousands of listeners may find it to their liking and do what they are told. The speech indulges their prejudices and tells them what they want to hear. Some will say, this is a reflection on the intelligence and sophistication of the audience, which is partially true. But the world is not made up of audiences in which all are solons and logicians and critics. So we have to assess the oratory realistically, namely, in the context in which it occurred. And for many people, this was effective oratory, even though we may be shocked by much that went on, and will in our evaluation question its morality.

In some instances, effectiveness may even derive from a speaker's inability—or reluctance—to perform well, *in terms of the textbooks*. One of the authors of this book heard Jimmy Walker, one-time mayor of New York City, on various occasions. Unmistakably, he did not speak by the book, if you please, but he was utterly charming and his audiences usually responded enthusiastically. Fiorello La Guardia, another former mayor of New York City, did things the unconventional way, and his delivery and bodily deportment were far from exemplary. But at his best, he captivated audiences. And, in general, it is a bit cavalier of us to dismiss orators to whom intelligent people listen intently.

Speakers are often effective despite—conceivably even because—they violated the principles of artistic craftsmanship. Gilbert Highet refers to the teacher-composer Theodor Leschetnizky who trained such immortals as Artur Schnabel, Ignace Paderewski, and Alexander Brailowsky; and quotes Leschetnizky as saying: "I have no method and I *will have* no method." [4] And testimony has it that "a verbatim description of one of his lessons leaves no clear impression on us except charm, metaphors, cigar-smoke, and enthusiasm." Of William James, someone said: "In his classroom he was precisely what he was everywhere else—just as unorganized, just as stimulating and irresistibly charming." [5] It is not unusual to come upon speakers whose broken English represents much that is unacceptable in approved diction, yet they are effective. In fact, their accents seem almost to contribute to their effectiveness.

These random reflections are not intended as endorsements of wayward practices in speechmaking. Instead, they are mentioned only to point up three earlier observations: (1) that effectiveness is not a fixed point on a scale; (2) different speakers can be effective for different, even contradictory, reasons; and (3) we must be mindful of the social setting in which the speech is given if we are to appraise it meaningfully.

TWO BASIC APPROACHES TO EFFECTIVENESS

Measures of effectiveness can be examined from two points of view: individual and societal. According to the former, a speech is regarded as successful if it enables the speaker to realize his fullest potentialities

[4] *The Art of Teaching.* New York, 1950, p. 233.
[5] *Ibid.*

as an individual, or to reveal fully his intellectual and moral qualities. If it brings out his character, or reveals him as a person endowed with a fine delivery, it is presumably a good speech. This position is untenable. It violates the entire doctrine of speech as communication, and places the emphasis upon speech as exhibition, as a form of display. As far as the audience is concerned—and the hearers are the most important part of the equation since it is for them that the speech is designed and given— it is of little importance whether a speaker achieves his *personal* ambition to speak agreeably to his own preconceived notion of individual better- ment.   Even though he should hit upon materials that enable him to practice his vocal skills successfully, it is of little concern to the listeners. They did not assemble for the purpose of giving the speaker *practice* in his art; they came to hear his ideas—to be informed, or convinced, or whatever the purpose is. Hence we may dismiss *individual* measures of effectiveness as being incidental to a serious consideration of the stand- ards by which a speech is to be appraised.

The societal point of view provides, on the other hand, a reasonable approach to the study of effectiveness. According to this conception, the success of oratory must be evaluated in terms, not of the speaker alone, but of the larger social sphere within which he functions. Thus the speech is studied in its possible relation to social change. This is a com- plex conception embracing a recognition of such factors as attitudes to- ward change—conservatism, liberalism, and the like—the influence of tradition, and the power of the coercive authorities in the state. Social changes involve people in *association*, rather than individual actions, *per se*. In any dynamic social situation, therefore, a particular speech is seldom, if ever, the sole force operating to produce a certain effect. In- stead, it is one of many agencies acting as determinants of change. It functions along with natural forces and other social instruments in a complex interrelation.

STANDARDS IN CURRENT USE

What, then, are the standards by which the effectivenes of a speech is measured? There are many, for each critic brings to his job certain personal guides and hunches. Whether we like it or not, complete ob- jectivity is impossible; even if it were attainable, it might be, as someone suggested, a mark of insanity. A critic's preferences and biases will show when he assesses a speech. Though we may wish that his caprices were removed from the evaluation, a residual factor of "I like this be- cause I like it" will doubtless remain. This is not an invitation to the greater cultivation of that attitude; it is but a candid acknowledgment of its existence.

Excluding the many subjective criteria—most of which defy classifi-cation and analysis—we may point to the following measures of effective-ness. They are among the more common ones in current use.

(1) Charles James Fox once observed: "Did the speech read well when reported? If so, it was a bad one." This test of readability has been widely discussed, and it has come to be considered a possible stan-dard for measuring the effectiveness of a speech. In essence, it declares that there is a sharp difference between oral and written style and that if a speech reads well after it is translated into print, it must not have been agreeable to the ear of the listener. If accepted in its entirety, this would mean, and a good many people would accept it as true, that Burke's speech "On Conciliation" is not an effective oration, despite the fact that according to other standards it is considered a masterpiece of oratorical prose. It reads well today: in fact, it is a virtual preface to political economy. The speech is quotable; its maxims have become the common stock of school boys and of statesmen.

George M. Trevelyan probably had Fox's dictum in mind when he contrasted the oratory of Gladstone and Bright: "Of the two, it is Bright whose speeches can be read with greatest pleasure, though that, perhaps, is no test of oratory." [6] But people do make it a test. The test of read-ability—be it on the morning following the delivery of the speech, or fifty years later—has a popular appeal. But the standard is inadequate by itself, for it abstracts one quality—the simple appeal to a reader—from the complicated social pattern in which speech functions. Thus it neg-lects the essential goal of speech—the acquisition of a response from the audience, not from the critic alone.

(2) A widely accepted measure of the merit of a speech is its techni-cal or artistic excellence. If it is praiseworthy as a model of craftsman-ship—that is, if it is superior in its inventive conception, structure, and stylistic composition and grace—it may be viewed as an effective speech. Effective, that is, as a specimen of artistic superiority. This criterion sets up the speech as something to be viewed largely from the outside, with-out major regard for the immediate conditions which prompted it. The speech is seen as a finished product having certain rhetorical features which conform agreeably to fixed principles or rules. The critic's judg-ment is thus based upon the speaker's ability to master technique, to construct a speech which has the essential qualities of good rhetoric, as viewed from the printed page. Admittedly, a speech may sound notes which have both beauty and universality of appeal. And it may, as the Most Reverend A. M. Ramsey once remarked, become great literature if "it voices worthily, in the midst of a particular situation, either the inner

---

[6] *The Life of John Bright.* Boston, 1913, p. 383.

meaning of a long tradition or some timeless fact of experience or conscience." [7]

But artistic mastery of rhetorical craftsmanship cannot, alone and apart from other criteria, be regarded as a wholly satisfactory measure of speech effectiveness for the great bulk of public oratory. That would ignore the inescapable fact that departures from accepted norms of composition, structure, and style may be necessitated by *peculiar* audience conditions. Technical accuracy, however desirable, is no virtue if it militates against the speaker's likelihood of communicating his ideas.

Important speeches are not ordinarily composed with an eye to their artistic acceptability in future years. A statesman who has to rouse or mould the mind of a nation, as John Morley remarked, "has something else to think about than the production of literary masterpieces. The great political speech, which for that matter is a sort of drama, is not made by passages for elegant extract or anthologies, but by personality, movement, climax, spectacle, and the action of the time." [8]

(3) Speech may be judged by the honesty and integrity of the orator and the social utility of his message. Does the talk reflect high moral intent? Does it express ideas and feelings that are ethically praiseworthy? Is it a noble search for the truth? Is a good man, in short, using his art to do good things?

That this standard should be included in the critic's lexicon is indisputable. But that it can be used as the major measuring stick is doubtful. It calls for a kind of psychological probing into an orator's motives which is not likely to come off satisfactorily. Even if a message were judged to be true and good, it might still come from the mouth of a scoundrel, for bad men have been known to espouse good causes; and good men have been known, perhaps unwittingly, to espouse bad causes.

(4) The effectiveness of a speech may be judged by the character of the *immediate*, surface response. If a speaker succeeds in holding the audience's unbroken attention; if he receives a favorable response in the form of applause or cheering; if he does these or other things which relate straightway to the response of the moment, he is presumed to have carried through his communicative attempt competently. This is an incomplete, though sometimes accurate, indicator of rhetorical merit. The nature of many speech occasions—a political rally, for instance—is such as to provoke applause and enthusiastic reception, even though what is said may be conspicuously faulty both in validity and expression. Such cursory judgments are seldom adequate; they need supplement from other standards. They need such collateral support as will insure *interpretation*

[7] *Oratory and Literature.* London, 1960, p. 6.
[8] *The Life of William Ewart Gladstone.* New edition in one volume. New York, 1932. II, 590.

of the response, rather than the uncritical announcement that people applauded or hissed or just remained silent. And silence may mean either attention or inattention, for as Alice B. Greene remarks, "Applause is lightly given, but not silence." [9] Simple adherence to the afore-mentioned standard would throw little light upon the *why* of speech effectiveness. Indeed, if a speaker holds the attention of the audience throughout a speech, that is an important fact. But it is a transient criterion of effectiveness in the world of statesmanship.

(5) Another standard embraces the appraisal of an orator's wisdom in anticipating future trends. This is essentially a test of the speaker's vision, of his capacity to understand the meaning of current happenings, of his foresight in appreciating their probable effect upon the course of history. It is a test such as might be used in evaluating the merit of a Burke, or of any other orator who was not immediately successful, but who foresaw the shape of things to come with more than ordinary per-spicacity. The criterion would apply in part, surely, to the labors of a John Bright. During the later years of his life, says Trevelyan, "men be-gan to reflect that John Bright had been right about Free Trade, right about the Crimea, right about the American Civil War, and right about the Franchise. . . ." [10] With such a test, we link the concepts of states-manship and oratory; we measure a man's greatness as a speaker in terms of his competence in gauging the effects of a contemporary action upon the destinies of men.

(6) More significant is the test which measures effectiveness by the substantial responses associated with possible changes in belief, attitude, or action. Unlike the immediate responses, previously discussed, these may come hours, days, or months after the delivery of the speech. Thus, in an extended debate in the House of Commons or in the American Con-gress, a vote may not be taken for days after the delivery of certain sig-nificant speeches. But the fundamental test will be: Did these speeches have an effect upon the subsequent disposition of the question? Did they help to produce the delayed response? Did they create a readiness in listeners to act in a certain way when the right stimulus came along? (This is a legitimate end of persuasive discourse.)

Of course, some critics of the social scene, as we have previously indi-cated, question that oratory in the modern assemblies—perhaps even else-where—has any influence at all. A staff member of the United States Senate remarked recently that Senator Russell Long was "one of the very few members left who can make a speech that will change some minds right on the floor." [11]

[9] *The Religious Uses of Silence.* Ph.D. thesis. Columbia University, 1938, p. 11.
[10] *Op. cit.,* p. 387
[11] *Time,* February 8, 1963.

The unqualified use of this test would, of course, render a manifest disservice to many great speakers. Burke's speech "On Conciliation" failed to carry the question; the resolution with which he closed his celebrated address was lost; on the vote on the previous question Burke's case was rejected by a count of 270 to 78. Similarly, his motion deriving from the speech on "American Taxation" was rejected, 182 to 49. Despite the fact that Fox was regarded by Loren Reid and others as "the most effective orator of the opposition," he failed to get the vote of the House on most of his important speeches. It must be remembered that, with a large segment of the House under the direct control of the king, Fox faced only a small minority of men who were willing—the case being sufficiently cogent—to alter their beliefs. Accordingly, we cannot say that a speech is necessarily unsuccessful if it fails to get the vote. Facing an insuperable task, the orator may still be a great interpreter of truth or justice within the restricted field of effective action.

On the other hand, there are surely some speeches which have a profound effect upon hearers, and upon the votes that subsequently decide the question at issue. Lord Curzon declares that he has often seen votes affected by speeches in the House of Commons. He mentions specifically the addresses of Mr. Fowler in a debate in the House in 1895; and he refers to the unmistakable influence of Gladstone's speech in moving a vote of credit in the Russo-Afghan crisis of 1885. Furthermore, Curzon points to the celebrated instances of divisions turned by the speech of Wilberforce in the Melville case of 1806, by Plunket's speech on Catholic Emancipation in 1807, and by Macaulay's speeches on the Copyright Bill in 1842 and on the proposal of 1853 to make the Master of Rolls incapable of sitting in the House.[12]

By extension, this criterion or measure tries to assay the long-range effects of oratory upon society. Over a period of years, did a speech or series of speeches exercise a discernible influence upon the course of events? Lecky, it will be recalled, believed that the wisdom of a policy was usually disclosed "very gradually." He held that the "final consequences" determine the sagacity of a proposal. However, he urged the historian not to overlook the part that "chance and the unexpected" play in human affairs, saying that "success is not always a decisive proof of sagacity." [13]

Unquestionably, many speeches over the years have exercised long-range effects. Apropos of Ebenezer Porter's pulpit speaking, Clyde Yarbrough holds that the sermon on "The Fatal Effects of Ardent Spirits" resulted in the formation of a committee which started the nineteenth-

[12] *Modern Parliamentary Eloquence.* London, 1913, p. 22.
[13] *Op. cit.,* pp. 9–14, *passim.*

century temperance reformation in America.[14] J. E. Thorold Rogers asserted that there was not a homestead in England in which there was not an added comfort as a result of John Bright's oratory on social reform. He said higher wages, steadier employment, and "more solid independence" were Bright's enduring monument.[15] Trevelyan bears out this testimony by asserting that seldom "has any public man, after labouring long years in the wilderness, seen so many of the reforms which he has urged placed upon the Statute Book." He goes even further, saying that, not by his arguing in the Cabinet or by his sharing in the affairs of a party, "but by his public orations as a private citizen he [Bright] profoundly modified English politics and the relations and balance of English politics and the relations and balance of English classes." [16] The evidence is specific. Not alone, of course, but nevertheless very effectively, he labored for and realized his aims in the repeal of the Corn Laws in 1846; in his efforts to keep England from turning to a Southern sympathy during the Civil War; in bringing about the Reform Bill in 1867, and in disestablishing the Church of England in Ireland.

The case for Charles James Fox is similar. Edward Lascelles believes that Fox's "greatness rests on the vindication after his death of those principles and causes for which he lived." Continuing, Lascelles says:

> On that day in 1832 when without revolution or bloodshed the Reform Bill became law; on that day two years later when eight hundred thousand slaves became free; and when, more than a century after his death, Parliament in the greatest of wars met discontent by projects for an extension of the franchise, posterity added its tribute to the immortal memory of Mr. Fox.[17]

A critic may, indeed, turn to such tangible results when appraising an orator and his speeches. The testimony of service to society is no servile guide to oratorical merit. As John Morley put it:

> Is not the highest object of our search in a study of the career of a conspicuous man an estimate of his contributions to the cause of the collective progress of mankind? We have to ask first, what general advance was made by this cause, while he was still a witness of it; and next, what place and part he took as an actor in it.[18]

In recent times, many speeches have had a pervasive influence. Senator J. W. Fulbright's address "Old Myths and New Realities," delivered on March 25, 1964, elicited a letter response from 10,000 persons within the first three weeks. His theme has stimulated scores of other speakers

---

[14] Quoted from doctoral dissertation.
[15] *Public Addresses of John Bright, M.P.* Edited by J. E. T. Rogers. London, 1879, p. 366.
[16] *Op. cit.*, p. 4.
[17] *The Life of Charles James Fox.* London, 1936, p. 329.
[18] *Edmund Burke.* New York, 1924, p. 45.

to assess our policy in Europe and Asia. The "vast wasteland" has been a household term, with application to the mass media, since Newton Minow gave it eloquent expression in "Television and the Public Interest" on May 9, 1961. Roscoe Pound allegedly inspired the founding of the American Judicature Society with his talk in 1906 on "The Causes of Popular Dissatisfaction with the Administration of Justice." George Marshall's speech at Harvard University on June 5, 1947, created something less than a sensation at the time of its delivery, but the subject has influenced profoundly the course of world history. Dean Acheson remarked that perhaps few people realized at the time "that they had heard the greatest peacetime offer in history. . . . But the proposal was clear and the whole world was stirred when it realized the full magnitude of the Marshall Plan." [19]

UNITY THROUGH DIVERSITY OF STANDARDS

The search for a simple standard of effectiveness is certain to end in failure. We cannot turn to a quantitative guide such as the National Rooster Crowing Contest uses to determine its winners. It seals the judgment by the number of times the rooster crows. For some years, the champion was a bantam named Beetlebaum that crowed 109 times in thirty minutes. Indeed, this is not a richly imaginative criterion, but it is decisive, irrefutable, and fair! All the judge need do is count.

But the judgment of excellence in a speech is a complex matter. Conceivably, a single measure may be neither possible nor desirable. We must find a certain unity in a diversity of measures. Accordingly, the critic may wish on occasion to use such combinations of the standards as will give promise of strengthening the rhetorical evaluation. For there are many objectives, critically, upon which agreement is substantial: An effective address brings out the moral and intellectual character of the speaker; it elicits some sort of immediate response; it bears the stamp of artistic craftsmanship within the limitations set by the speech situation; it conduces to the common good; hopefully, it exercises an influence upon subsequent events, provided its concern is man and his manifest destiny.

It is unlikely that any two speeches will do all or part of these things in the same way or in equal measure. That is not important. What matters preeminently in our view, however, is that, in adjusting the critical focus, we never lose sight of the underlying postulate: *A speech is a venture in the communication of ideas and feelings to a specific audience.* And what happens because of the speech is, among other things, of concern to the critic.

[19] *The Reporter,* November 26, 1959, p. 25.

We believe that *response* is a key determinant in any study of oratorical effectiveness. This presupposes the speaker's recognition of the need to adapt his materials to listeners; to keep his audience, rather than formal rules, constantly in mind. Unlike the writer who may deliberately prepare his copy for the ages, the orator must direct his remarks to the immediacy of the occasion. This does not close the door to statesmanlike conduct. But it does require that the speaker adapt himself to conditions as he finds them, and that he communicate his ideas with a view to their taking root in the lives of the hearers, and, either immediately or subsequently, influencing their belief or action.

Clearly, the response to a speech need not be immediate. Speeches may be inadequate to produce a certain effect at once and still be none the less great. But a good idea, initiated by a speaker, may in turn be supplemented by other addresses and writings, and eventually result in wholesome action. This may be referred to as the theory of cumulative effects in oratory. The concept is consistent with the democratic process. Individual pronouncements are important; they contribute to the unfolding of a case as a whole; they stimulate the wholesome exchange of additional views and opinions; they encourage that collision of error with truth to which John Stuart Mill refers in his "Essay on Liberty of Expression." But the final result may derive from many causes, rather than a single one. Great speeches are often important links in a long chain of circumstances.

It is conceivable, therefore, that society profits from the slow-tempo response to public address. If changes of opinion or action could be induced immediately, and without the necessary reflection, the effect upon society might be unwholesome, if not pernicious. Rabble-rousers and demagogues hope for instantaneous responses, and often get them. Yet the critic of such oratory will not regard the acquisition of the response as the total measure of speech effectiveness. This is true whether the demagogue happens at the moment to be telling the truth or not, for the critic will, as best he can, also search out the motive for the remarks. Recalling William Blake's line, the critic will note that

> A truth that's told with bad intent
> Beats all the lies you can invent.

EXERCISES

1. How seriously should a critic consider the approval or disapproval of a speech as reported in the newspapers and by the commentators? As a backdrop for preliminary study, examine some of the reactions in the American and British papers to the Gettysburg Address.
2. Russell Conwell evidently delivered "Acres of Diamonds" some 6,000 times. Is that necessarily a measure of its effectiveness?

3. Appraise this statement by Thomas Nilsen ("Criticism and Social Consequences," *The Quarterly Journal of Speech*, 42:173–178 [April, 1956]): "The evaluation of effect should be a judgment about the contribution the speech makes to, or the influence it exerts in furthering, the purposes of the society upon which it has its impact."

4. One school of thought in this discipline holds that while rhetoric deals in probabilities, criticism of rhetoric must not; that if we cannot be sure what the effects of a speech were, we should not try to evaluate them. Comment on this position.

5. What differences do you perceive between a successful novel or poem and a successful speech?

6. Comment on the virtues and limitations of the classical treatises as yardsticks for the measurement of excellence in public address.

7. There has long been controversy over whether the great public figure must be an eloquent person. Some observers have pointed out that intellectual and moral greatness are not necessarily conjoined with skill in speaking, and indeed should not be so regarded in the public mind. On the other hand, we come upon reflections like that from André Maurois, that "the worth of a statesman's character is often equivalent to the excellence of his prose." What is your opinion?

8. To what extent are the principles set forth in this book applicable to the criticism of classroom speeches?

9. In his *Science and Human Values* (p. 35), J. Bronowski says "the act of appreciation re-enacts the act of creation, and we are . . . actors, we are interpreters of it." Do you believe this applies as well to the art and criticism of speaking?

10. Do you believe that the study of "bad" models of public address helps in appreciating and assessing "good" ones? Is the gospel of perfection reinforced by studying some speeches that did not come off well? As a teaching device, this practice is not uncommon. For example, Edgar Whitney, distinguished watercolorist, has his students study some paintings that fall short of his standards of excellence; and through them he underscores techniques and practices that are "right."

11. Assume that you are the regular speech critic for the daily newspaper serving your area. Write an evaluation of the next important speech delivered by the President of the United States. Keep the paper's readership in mind, as well as your own obligation as a critic. How does the evaluation differ from the sort of critique you might prepare as a classroom project?

12. Do you believe that the criteria for the selection of speeches intended for publication in a compilation or anthology would ordinarily be different from these to which we have directed your attention in this book? Why? Compare the standards in Part V with those discussed in the Preface of *Representative American Speeches: 1966–1967*.

CLASS PROJECT (Continued)

(1) As a final assignment for the speaker whom you have studied in depth during this course, prepare a statement on overall effectiveness. Before preparing this paper, read carefully the papers that you have previously pre-

pared. This final paper is more than a summary of what you have previously stated. It is an overview of your entire study.

(2) Prepare an appraisal of one of your classmates as a rhetorical critic. If possible, consult the papers which he has prepared.

READINGS

W. NORWOOD BRIGANCE. "Effectiveness of the Public Platform." *Annals,* 250:70–75 (March, 1947).

———. "What Is a Successful Speech?" *Quarterly Journal of Speech Education,* 11:372–377 (November, 1925).

ROBERT CATHCART. *Post Communication: Criticism and Evaluation.* Indianapolis, Bobbs-Merrill Co., 1966. Pp. 89–111.

PAUL H. DOUGLAS. "Is Campaign Oratory a Waste of Time?" *The New York Times Magazine,* October 19, 1958. Pp. 26+.

FREDERICK W. HABERMAN. "General MacArthur's Speech: A Symposium of Critical Comment." *Quarterly Journal of Speech,* 37:321–331 (October, 1951).

ANTHONY HILLBRUNER. *Critical Dimensions: The Art of Public Address Criticism.* New York, Random House, 1966.

MARIE HOCHMUTH. "The Criticism of Rhetoric." In *History and Criticism of American Public Address.* Edited by MARIE HOCHMUTH. Vol. III. New York, Russell & Russell, 1955. Pp. 1–23.

JOSEPH WOOD KRUTCH. "If You Don't Mind My Saying So. . . ." *The American Scholar,* 36:14–17 (Winter, 1966–67).

JAMES H. MCBURNEY and ERNEST J. WRAGE. *The Art of Good Speech.* New York, Prentice-Hall, 1953. Pp. 21–32.

THOMAS R. NILSEN. "Criticism and Social Consequences." *Quarterly Journal of Speech,* 42:173–178 (April, 1956).

WAYLAND MAXFIELD PARRISH and MARIE HOCHMUTH. "The Study of Speeches." In *American Speeches.* Edited by WAYLAND MAXFIELD PARRISH and MARIE HOCHMUTH. New York, Longmans, Green & Co., 1954. Pp. 1–20.

JOHN M. VORYS. "How a Member of Congress Measures the Response of His Constituents." *Quarterly Journal of Speech,* 32:170–172 (April, 1946).

HERBERT A. WICHELNS. "Some Differences Between Literary Criticism and Rhetorical Criticism." In *Historical Studies of Rhetoric.* Edited by RAYMOND HOWES. Ithaca, New York, Cornell University Press, 1961. Pp. 217–224.

JOHN F. WILSON and CARROLL C. ARNOLD. "Judging the Speech." In their *Public Speaking as a Liberal Art.* Boston, Allyn and Bacon, 1964. Pp. 323–343.

RUSSEL R. WINDES, JR. "A Study in Effective and Ineffective Presidential Campaign Speaking." *Speech Monographs,* 28:39–49 (March, 1961).

VI

REFLECTIONS ON
CRITICISM AND
PUBLIC ADDRESS

19

Postscript
to an Inquiry

THE RHETORICAL ENTERPRISE

Like college catalogs and academic curricula, textbooks are largely acts of faith. They set forth a point of view, offer suggestions on a methodology, and provide, hopefully, a mild trace of persuasive inspiration. If the authors are honest, they make no extravagant claims and promises, knowing full well that what they believe in may not impress the reader as sparkling wisdom; and knowing that a methodology, even if good, can be used and abused in a variety of ways. So a textbook is an act of faith expressed in a hope: the hope that it says something worth saying in language sufficiently precise to permit ready application of its precepts, yet sufficiently flexible to encourage variation and imaginative freedom in its use.

The enterprise of learning is a house of many rooms, and there is no need for people of sharply divergent views to occupy the same quarters. But it is necessary and wholesome for the widest possible range of opinion to be expressed by those who live under the common roof.

There are, fortunately, many conceptions of the nature of rhetorical criticism, and of the best way to practice it. To call one right and another wrong is of course to betray the liberal tradition. Irrespective of the philosophic assumptions and methodology, all schools of thought in this discipline must deal with imprecise data. The eternal verities are not likely to be found in this imperfect world, and least of all in an area where predisposition, opinion, interpretation, and judgment are, if not sovereign, at least dominant. There are no absolutes; there are no finalities in rhetorical criticism. Only ways of looking at man and the world, and of projecting the means that will ensure intellectual rigor and emotional sensitivity in the portrayal of man in the role of speaker.

Everyone with a point of view is automatically biased. But even bias can have a certain objectivity, provided it comes from honest inquiry and reflection. Readers of this book need no tabular analysis to classify the authors' predispositions and sympathies. They are doubtless quite evident. The existence of a credo on the rhetorical art is, however, immaterial. What matters is its integrity, which of course can be determined and judged only by those who test it for themselves.

COMPONENTS OF A POINT OF VIEW

The rationale of an art is invariably complex. But it is proper, in summary, to bring together, however briefly, certain elements which shape the conception of a subject, and give it a semblance of unity. Perhaps this will help us to get what Bernard Bosanquet called a "connected vision of the totality of things."

The Critical Apparatus—Use and Abuse

With Burke, we believe the "past is the best source for the reenforcement of opinion." The emphasis in this book has revealed an abiding faith in the classical treatises as yardsticks of excellence in oratory. This is not accidental; nor is it disrespectful to the moderns. It requires no apology since it gives added lustre to contemporary efforts.

We can, it seems to us, appropriate the wisdom and counsel of the ancients and use it as a guide to an intelligent understanding of our subject. The older contributions are not error-free, nor are the moderns. Fully mindful of the fact that "in no sense can antiquity *privilege an error* or novelty *prejudice a truth*," [1] we yet believe that the ancient treatises give a balanced account of the speaking art and articulate it closely with the related fields of politics, ethics, and law. This does not argue for the servile acceptance of ancient doctrines. It simply suggests that "the greatest compliment we can pay to the greatness of the past is to surpass it, but in common courtesy we should doff our hats as we pass." [2]

These remarks should not be construed as an embossed invitation to use the traditional patterns of criticism slavishly. That would make for a Procrustean scheme, devoid of ingenuity and sensitivity, and certain to result in a deadening uniformity. There is no conceivable reason why

[1] Adapted by Holbrook Jackson. *The Anatomy of Bibliomania*. New York, 1932, p. 128.
[2] "A Yardstick for Civilization." In *Essays in Intellectual History*. New York, 1929, p. 359.

the critical apparatus need produce such a result, if the critic uses his resources skillfully and imaginatively. Hosts of speakers rely upon a much more uniform set of rules in the composition and delivery of their talks, and yet manage, if they are perceptive, to achieve amazingly varied results. The fact that Cicero and a novice speaker use a similar set of rhetorical principles, with outcomes at polar extremes, argues neither for nor against the adequacy of the rules or the viability of their application.

Inevitably, over a period of years, some problems will arise in the use of a critical method, regardless of its nature. The faults may derive from the method, or from its application, or as is often the case, from a combination of both.

Two such difficulties deserve notice.

(1) An analytic method of evaluation, based upon a suggested critical standard, can easily produce a form of segmented criticism. For analysis alone is not enough. The accompanying synthesis can alone integrate the many parts and make of the seemingly discrete components a whole piece. It is so in poetry; it is no less so in the appraisal of oratory. A public address exists for a purpose quite beyond that of affording a researcher, complete with note cards and an attaché case, a convenient subject of analytical inquiry. Like a poem, an oration is capable of enlarging the intellectual store, of disciplining imagination, and of providing new insights into the world of thought and feeling. The likelihood of its doing so if the evaluation stops short of meaningful synthesis is remote. Speaking of poetic analysis, Douglas, Lamson, and Smith remarked some years ago, following an examination of the parts of a creative act, that "we should finally return to it as an experience itself, unified, complete, and unique." Rhetorical critics have the same obligation.

Unaccompanied by insightful synthesis, analysis can produce uninspired rhetorical estimates. Conceivably, in our solicitude for objectivity and intellectual rigor, we lose sight of the value of imaginative thrust in criticism. In our eagerness to find and stick to the "facts"—and no one would downgrade responsible research—we may come by the notion (mistakenly, we believe) that, if the data are used in a sprightly, interesting manner, our craft has somehow been prostituted to an evil mission. But neither the message of the angels above nor of man below proclaims that critical writing should be an exercise in desiccation. Moreover, the lively portrayal, both in analysis and particularly in synthesis, of the facts and interpretations of an orator's performance does not render the report fictional. We might even argue that slightly fictionalized detail could add luster and color and human interest appeal, without violating historical or critical integrity. In a recent essay "On the Writing of History," Wallace Stegner remarks that "it is not the presence of dramatic narrative that makes false history false. Falseness derives from inadequate or in-accurate information, faulty research, neglected resources, bias, bad judgment, misleading implication, and these afflict the expository among us about as often as they afflict the narrative." Continuing, Stegner says:

> It is true that the excitment of story-telling, like the excitement of phrase-making, often tempts a writer into misrepresentation. But the excitement of analysis, the excitement of generalization, can do the same; and the laudable lust for absolute accuracy can lead to dullness, can cause a man to proffer a set of notes instead of a finished book, as if one did not write history, but collected it.[3]

Perhaps some of our rhetorical estimates stand in need of an injection of sprightliness, which judicious synthesis can provide.

The difficulty to which we have alluded may stem in part from a position of defensiveness, a self-conscious attitude toward our art. A decade or so ago we felt obliged, in our estimates of speakers, to set up the criteria or standards, often at wearisome length, before turning to our subject. Our efforts reminded us of the old Navajo preacher who, at the end of the first hour of his talk, said: "Now that you know who I am, I'll preach my sermon next week." In years gone by, when graduate administrators viewed speech criticism through the glass darkly, over-solicitude in establishing our right to walk in the same halls with physi-cists and historians was perhaps explainable. We were under searching scrutiny, and while our efforts were not considered any worse than those of palm readers and tattoo artists, neither were they regarded as much better. Little wonder that some of the criticisms of the time were labored, not a little stilted, and embarrassingly self-conscious. That was nearly a generation ago. While traces of the malaise persist, surely there is less hesitation to speak out boldly, write confidently, and assert in-tellectual independence.

(2) A servile adherence to analytic investigation, untempered by imaginative synthesis, can obscure the "living presence," or a reasonable approximation, of the orator. Do we underscore clearly the distinctive features of the orators we study? Do we point up the characteristics that actually *distinguish* one orator from another? This is a sensitive area in speech criticism. But if our judgments are to be readable and discrimi-nating, we must deal with speakers as individuals, rather than as carbon copies. Because our experience convinces us that Franklin D. Roosevelt was a different sort of speaker than Harry S. Truman, we are not going to be delighted to read, successively, two evaluations that make them appear substantially alike. This is not a wayward comment. For ex-ample, in our evaluation of oratorical style, we sometimes move little

[3] *The American West,* 2:7 (Fall, 1965).

beyond simple identification of a speaker's use of antithesis, irony, or metaphor. An an item of general information, that has some value but not much. As a critical note, it means little unless it sheds light upon the *distinctive* way in which the orator used it.

The Union of Oratory, Practical Affairs, and Ethics

Rhetoric has long been the handmaid of politics. While it is not necessary to regard politics as a branch of rhetoric, we must recognize fully the importance of speechcraft as a means of realizing desirable ends in political action. Nowhere are the relations of men to their constituencies more fraught with social consequence than in the area of political representation. And the politician, seeking to provide programs for the social body, need not, as George Catlin alleges the reformer used to do, play the role of an evangelist. He can become the social guide provided he recognizes his obligation as a speaker to embrace knowledge of the facts, high ethical resolve, and a sense of public good.

Admittedly, rhetoric is a practical art. And the political figure is a practical man. He seeks to realize his ends by bringing people into line with his own or his constituency's will. In so doing, he relies upon the techniques of persuasion. As a practical man, he will frequently gauge the wisdom of proposed actions in the light of expediency. But here the full importance of rhetoric must assert itself. The mere possession of the tools of persuasive manipulation—without a stabilizing ethic to control their usage—is not enough. If politics—and, in its turn, rhetoric—is associated with the means of getting things done, it is imperative that ethics, which deals with ends and the relative values of what is achieved, be reunited with the political art. Rhetoric, as the intermediary between the will to action and the achievement of the result, must accordingly be conceived as both a political and an ethical instrument. This is another way of saying, perhaps, that there must be a *moral principle* supporting and guiding the liberal tradition. While there has been some disposition to resist the inclusion of such a principle in the scheme of learning—a circumstance resulting from our virtual deification of the so-called scientific spirit and method—its return as an active force in the field of knowledge is necessary. A sustained faith in democracy itself depends upon it.

One of the logical implications of an appeal to a closer union between politics and rhetoric is the wisdom of extending training in oratory to every citizen. The practical uses of rhetoric to which Aristotle referred are even more applicable to society today than they were to the Greece of his time. True, the complexity of modern society makes it more difficult for every man to participate directly in the deliberations of assemblies and in the administration of justice. Many of these duties have been delegated to men of professional rank. But every citizen still needs —in fact, needs more imperatively today—a familiarity with rhetoric, to the end that he may avail himself of its advantages in the true Aristotelian sense: (1) of perceiving the difference between truth and error; (2) of understanding how people are moved to action, despite the absence of compelling argument; (3) of arguing both sides of a question in order to determine the truth; and (4) of being able to defend himself with speech.

Democratic society rests upon a premise that the collective body of the common people is competent to exercise supreme authority in the state. In such a scheme, the power of public address must be a force of no mean proportion. If each citizen is to be—or is *naturally,* as Aristotle put it in his *Politics*—a "political animal," and if speech is to be the instrument by which advantage and disadvantage, truth and justice, are to be sustained, it follows that each man must be something of a statesman and of an advocate in his own right. Each citizen must serve as a balance wheel in an exceedingly complex political mechanism. Only then will Aristotle's remarks regarding the collective wisdom of the masses be correct:

> For it is possible that the Many, of whom each individual is not a virtuous man, are still collectively superior to the few best persons, *i.e.* superior not as individuals but as a body, as picnics are superior to feasts supplied at the expense of a single person. For as the total number is large, it is possible that each has a fractional share of virtue and prudence and that, as the multitude collectively may be compared to an individual with many feet, hands and senses, so the same is true of their character and intelligence. It is thus that the Many are better judges *than the Few* even of musical and poetical compositions; for some judge one part, some another, and all of them collectively the whole.[4]

Democracy lives by talk. It functions through speech. Indeed, "Language is democracy," as Henry N. Wieman observes, "when language carries the full load of a people's most cherished meanings from each to all and back again from all to each." [5] When men have something on their minds, freedom to speak it constitutes the natural outlet for their will to action. But it presupposes literacy on their part, a knowledge of what they express, and a recognition of the responsibility inherent in free expression. Quite properly, the inculcation of such principles of conduct is the task of those who train the citizenry in speechcraft. An enlightened conception of rhetoric as an aid to politics is one of the surest protectors of democratic society. Tyranny cannot flourish where responsible men

---

[4] *The Politics of Aristotle.* Translated by J. E. C. Welldon. London, 1897, pp. 128–129.

[5] "Democracy and Language." *Ethics,* 52:221 (January, 1942).

have the right to say responsible things. But men have that right only if they impose upon themselves certain restraints dictated by their control of facts and by their consideration of the welfare of others. Without that restraint some men will be free, as L. T. Hobhouse remarks, "but others will be unfree." Some will exercise their full will, while the rest will have only such freedom as the powerful allow them.[6] This is not an appeal for silence. It is, instead, an appeal for the free expression of statements for which the speaker is answerable.

The foregoing remarks suggest that intelligent men will always deal with noble themes in their discourses. It is evident that this is not wholly true. But it is within the province of the rhetorician to insist upon nobility of conception in the expression of topics. Hundreds of years ago, Isocrates developed a theory of culture, based on such a premise, which urged precisely this. The revival of certain features of the Isocratic doctrine is overdue. While holding to a defense of practical knowledge, Isocrates insisted that the individual strive for good conduct—that he be a citizen whose ethical principles shone through his actions. The citizen was to be a cultivated speaker, "for the power to speak well is taken as the surest index of a sound understanding, and discourse which is true and lawful and just is the outward image of a good and faithful soul."[7]

In Isocrates' theory of culture, there was no room for discourses on petty and unjust causes. Instead, the themes were to be grand in their scope and nature, honorable in their motives, and "devoted to the welfare of man and our common good. . . ." The speakers were to embrace subjects of broad, almost universal character. Thus oratory and disciplined statesmanship were linked in common bond.

The closer union of politics and rhetoric will insure for speeches a more permanent place in historical records. Surely this would be desirable. It is regrettable that the great speeches of history today find such inadequate representation in our textbooks. The speech is a document; faithfully reproduced, it presents a trustworthy record of what was said. If a message of moment, it speaks not only for the present, but for the future; and it speaks in terms which defy the hazards of trickery imposed by those who would seek to misinterpret it.

With the attachment of increasing importance to speeches as documents will come a fuller realization of the relation between oratory and practical action. There is a logic of discourse, the goal of which is the attainment and protection of personal liberty. This is its design: to achieve and hold fast to the rights for which men have fought and died since the beginning of history. Rabble-rousers and tyrants use speech,

[6] L. T. Hobhouse. *Liberalism.* New York, n.d., p. 23.
[7] *Isocrates.* Translated by George Norlin. Cambridge, Massachusetts, 1928. II, 327.

indeed, to make secure their own self-contained ambitions. But in making expression their exclusive monopoly; in assuming that audiences were made for public address, rather than the reverse, and that only the rulers can exercise speech as an instrument of control, tyrants misread the history of mankind. There is adequate testimony to disprove their thesis. Ever since Corax devised an art of speech to meet the practical demands of people who sought restitution of their property, the line has been unbroken. It is a continuous, never-yielding search for liberty as the goal of political utterance. That there are frequent setbacks, no one will deny. But that there is an inexorable logic of speechcraft which postulates the freedom of man as the object of its efforts, history proves and man's conscience confirms.

So closely connected with the concept of a union of politics and rhetoric that it would be folly to dissociate them, is the wisdom of linking rhetoric with ethics. This is no new idea. The ancients recognized the necessity of doing precisely this. If man is a political animal; if he uses speech to achieve his ends in deliberative situations, he also needs a guiding ethic, a set of principles which will enable him to judge the right from the wrong and to govern his conduct by appeal to moral standards.

This is simply another way of saying that rhetoric is to be used to give effectiveness to truth. It is not intended to give effectiveness to the speakers, *per se*, or to techniques, *per se*. It is not an instrument, to adapt a remark from Macaulay, by which people are to be maddened by sophistry, calumny, and stimulants, so that in the fulness of bread, they rave as if famine were in the land. Rhetoric must take truth, or a reasonable approximation, as its substance.

The cultivation of a sense of responsibility for the uttered statement is a crying imperative for public speakers today—just as it was yesterday and will be tomorrow. We can but hold in contempt those "whose talent consists in language, and who by . . . superior eloquence . . . decorate error with the garb of truth." To deceive through words is no less reprehensible than to cheat through more overt and demonstrable ways. It is still deception. To use rhetoric as an instrument for making promises which he has no intention of keeping, or which involve so many conditions that they cannot possibly be consummated, even though he were willing, is as culpable in a speaker today as it was in ancient Greece centuries ago.

The issue is one involving the reconciliation of the instrumental means of acquiring responses from hearers with the ethical considerations relative to the character of the desired ends. It has been said that "the consciousness of end must be more than merely intellectual." This is an important truth, although there has been some tendency to veer away from moral or ethical concepts in rhetorical theory. It has been assumed that the techniques of rhetoric are amoral, capable of both enlightened and evil use, depending upon the character of the speaker. If a slicker uses persuasive guile to sell a yokel the Grand Canyon, there is nothing in the art of rhetoric to correct the misrepresentation. The evil must be traced to the user of the language. While this is unquestionably true, it does not absolve critics of the responsibility of considering the ethical implications of public statements. Nor does it release teachers from the obligation of inculcating moral principles in speakers, and of advising future citizens of the necessary duty of holding themselves strictly accountable for what they say.

There is a need for the establishment of a more binding relationship between the instrumental and the ethical components of the speaking art. Overemphasis of *technique* in speaking; the disposition to regard rhetoric as an instrument of power, by which a speaker may improve himself, make more money, control people—these are the snares which beset a sound point of view in contemporary public speaking. Disproportionate emphasis upon the purely instrumental means of controlling people through persuasion is likely to nuture a perfunctory regard for truth in statement and honesty in purpose. If not held in check by some other instruction, it develops into a doctrine of self-realization through the crafty use of tested techniques. The speaker who serves his state with scrupulous regard for trustworthiness of statement and with solicitous concern for the possible good his remarks may do the common cause need not be an instrument of cold calculation, devoid of vehemence and force. Quite the contrary. Society needs orators who, working with facts, are also poets and philosophers, men who can costume truth effectively. Society needs speakers who possess the intellectual and emotional resources ascribed by Hoyt Hudson [8] to the liberally educated person: a full body of information, a severe operative logic, and a sensitive, disciplined imagination. In an age which is often impatient of deep feeling in public address, there is a deserved place for speakers who embrace sound ideas with passionate zeal. Society stands to gain if these conceptions are expressed—not necessarily elegantly—but, surely, carefully, accurately, and with a show of beauty. The tradition of a free America is richer because Webster took pains to prepare the "Plymouth Oration"; because Lincoln conceived the "Gettysburg Address"; and because Phillips confirmed the rights of man in his speech on the "Murder of Lovejoy." It may be doubted whether any considerable number of men is willing today to spend the time necessary for the development of great themes, in dignified and distinctive expression. The need for it is as urgent now as at any time in history. The opportunities for it are multi-

[8] *Educating Liberally.* Stanford University, California, 1945, pp. 10 ff.

plied a thousandfold by the extension of the public platform through radio-television. The audiences are ready, provided the speakers have the competence, patience, and will to meet the challenge. To paraphrase Cicero, great speakers will, even in our time, be "expected with impatience, and heard with pleasure."

Although rhetoric is a practical art, it derives from humane sources. Ralph Barton Perry and Everett Lee Hunt, among others, have written discerningly about the freedom that results from man's capacity to make intelligent choices. In Hunt's words:

> An enlightened choice is a choice based upon a wide knowledge of all the alternatives, but knowledge about the alternatives is not enough. There must be imagination to envisage all the possibilities, and sympathy to make some of the options appeal to the emotions and powers of the will. Such dignity as man may have is achieved by the exercise of free choice through the qualities of learning, imagination, and sympathy; and we should add to those qualities as a fitting accompaniment, what may be called civility. . . . The exercise of free choices through an imaginative and sympathetic learning and a dignified civility . . . is the mark of the liberally educated, humane man.[9]

Proper training in rhetoric helps to realize these attributes.

The Orator's "Long Detour"

In the Platonic dialogues, we learn of the long road or circuit that a man must follow to arrive at true philosophic wisdom. The road leads through dialectic. Werner Jaeger refers to the concept as "the long detour."

Apart from its specific Platonic context, it conjures up an idea of wide applicability and relevance to students of rhetoric, speakers, and critics alike. In effect, the image means that the art and craft of rhetoric is difficult, and the easy routes are snares. Everyone knows this. But we act from time to time on comfortable convictions, improperly arrived at, that belie our better judgment. We search for the easy route, the fast way, hoping in the process to bypass disciplines and exercises which are indispensable to the highest competence. We try, frequently on administrative request, to turn out sawdust Ciceros in fifteen simple lessons; or polish off a critical assessment of a speech, in the classroom or out, by placing a dozen near-meaningless check marks, tidily arow, on an evaluation sheet. Does this nurture and sustain the best in the tradition of our discipline? Should we try to do less, and in the process do more, by raising the sights, by raising the standards? Would not individual man and society gain by our insisting that there is no way to high accomplishment in the rhetorical art except over "the long detour?"

[9] "Rhetoric as a Humane Study." *Quarterly Journal of Speech*, 41:114 (April, 1955).

THE EXPECTATION

Despite occasional doubts about current practices in our discipline, one towering fact seems sure, and it puts the minor details in proper perspective. Great orators will arise to meet recurring crises in society. Their words will help to secure, protect, and preserve liberty. The spoken word is eternal. And it is a treasured legacy. When the future of the state is in doubt, some men will come forward to express the aspirations of the people in dignified, honest speech. Their words may yet help man to realize the genuinely good life. The able critic can assist the people to enjoy and appreciate the oratory.

Carlos Baker once remarked that it was the critic's obligation to serve "as keeper of our ancestral domain. . . ." [10] We believe that rhetorical criticism helps to preserve the rich heritage of our discipline. "There is a tradition in the courts of law," said the late Lord Justice Birkett, "that an advocate should try to laugh naturally, or at least to smile appreciatively, when the judge makes a joke or an alleged witticism, however feeble it may be. But even this was anticipated over eighteen centuries ago," when Quintilian remarked:

For it will be desirable to enlist the temperaments of the judges in the service of our cause, where they are such as are likely to be useful, or to mollify them, if they are like to be adverse, just according as they are harsh, gentle, cheerful, grave, stern or easy-going.[11]

Such reminders of the wisdom of our predecessors keep us humble.

[10] *New York Times Book Review*, July 17, 1960.
[11] *The Magic of Words.* London, 1953, p. 11.

Index